Rut on wråg.

EX·LIBRIS·SUNE·GREGERSEN

Reshaping of the Nominal Inflection
in Early Northern West Germanic

NOWELE Supplement Series (NSS)

ISSN 0900-8675

NOWELE Supplement Series is a book series associated with the journal *NOWELE: North-Western European Language Evolution.* The supplement series is devoted not only to the study of the history and prehistory of a locally determined group of languages, but also to the study of purely theoretical questions concerning historical language development. The series contains publications dealing with all aspects of the (pre-) histories of – and with intra- and extra-linguistic factors contributing to change and variation within – Icelandic, Faroese, Norwegian, Swedish, Danish, Frisian, Dutch, German, English, Gothic and the Early Runic language. The series will publish monographs and edited volumes.

For an overview of all books published in this series, please see
http://benjamins.com/catalog/nss

Editor

Stephen Laker
Kyushu University, Fukuoka

Co-editors

John Ole Askedal
University of Oslo

Hans Frede Nielsen
University of Southern Denmark

Advisory Editors

Michael Barnes
University College London

Rolf H. Bremmer, Jr.
Leiden University

Julia Fernández Cuesta
University of Seville

Volkert F. Faltings
Universität Flensburg

Kurt Gustav Goblirsch
University of South Carolina

Alexandra Holsting
University of Southern Denmark

Christer Lindqvist
Universität Greifswald

Robert Mailhammer
University of Western Sydney, Penrith NSW

Jürg R. Schwyter
University of Lausanne

Arjen P. Versloot
University of Amsterdam

Volume 31

Reshaping of the Nominal Inflection in Early Northern West Germanic
by Elżbieta Adamczyk

Reshaping of the Nominal Inflection in Early Northern West Germanic

Elżbieta Adamczyk

Adam Mickiewicz University & Bergische Universität Wuppertal

John Benjamins Publishing Company

Amsterdam / Philadelphia

™ The paper used in this publication meets the minimum requirements of
the American National Standard for Information Sciences – Permanence
of Paper for Printed Library Materials, ANSI z39.48-1984.

DOI 10.1075/nss.31
Cataloging-in-Publication Data available from Library of Congress:
LCCN 2017055190

ISBN 978 90 272 0035 8   (HB)
ISBN 978 90 272 6441 1   (E-BOOK)

John Benjamins Publishing Company · https://benjamins.com

To the memory of my parents
Anna and Michał Adamczyk

Table of contents

Acknowledgments

This book is the result of a few years of research, during which I benefited greatly from the advice, support and encouragement of many individuals whom I would like to thank. First and foremost, I would like to express my gratitude to Professor Jacek Fisiak, who sparked my interest in English historical linguistics many years ago, and on whose guidance and unfailing support I could always count. I wish to thank Professor Katarzyna Dziubalska-Kołaczyk, the Dean of the Faculty of English at Adam Mickiewicz University in Poznań and Piotr Gąsiorowski, the Head of the Department of Older Germanic Languages, who in various ways enabled and facilitated the realisation of this project. I am particularly indebted to Piotr for encouraging and motivating me throughout the years to pursue and complete this project as well as for his trust in me. I am also very grateful to my new colleagues from the Linguistics section of the English and American Studies at the University of Wuppertal for their encouragement and enthusiastic support in the final stage of completing the book.

This project was greatly facilitated by the grant from the Polish National Science Centre (NN104378940) and at an early stage by the Hertie Foundation (Gemeinnützige Hertie-Stiftung). I am very grateful to both institutions for their generous financial support.

The work has substantially benefited from advice and valuable and constructive feedback from several colleagues and experts in the field of Old Germanic linguistics. In particular, I wish to thank Professor Ann Marynissen for her feedback on the Old Low Franconian chapter, Professor Arend Quak for his comments on the Old Saxon and Old Low Franconian chapters, Piotr Gąsiorowski and Ron Kim for commenting on the Proto-Germanic part of the study. I gratefully thank Marcin Krygier for his advice and comments on some aspects of the Old English content, but also for inspiring my interest in nominal morphology. I owe a special debt to Arjen Versloot not only for his detailed, critical and insightful comments on the entire manuscript, but also for his assistance with the analysis of the Old Frisian material as well as for many inspiring discussions of various aspects of the book. Furthermore, I wish to thank Professors Jerzy Wełna, Theo Vennemann and Elżbieta Wąsik for their advice, inspiration and encouragement over the years. I would also like to thank Joanna Śmiecińska for commenting on fragments of the manuscript as well as for her continuing support and encouragement. I am indebted to Derk Drukker from the Fryske Akademy in Leeuwarden for kindly preparing the searchable database of the *Dictionary of Old English* material, which greatly facilitated the analysis of the Old English data. I am grateful to Merve Altay for her dedicated assistance with technical aspects of the manuscript at the later stage of the project, as well as to Colin Phillips for proofreading parts of the manuscript at various stages.

I wish to express my deepest gratitude to the Series Editor, Professor Hans Frede Nielsen, for accepting the book for the NOWELE Supplement Series and for his trust in this project. I am very grateful to the four anonymous reviewers of the manuscript at John Benjamins, from whose constructive and valuable feedback the text has greatly benefited. I owe a great debt of thanks to Stephen Laker, whose suggestions substantially improved the language, style and structure of the text, but also for his insightful content-related comments. I would also like to thank the editorial team at John Benjamins for editorial and technical work on the manuscript. All the remaining errors are solely mine.

Most importantly, I would like to thank my family and friends who have supported me throughout this project. In particular, I gratefully thank my sister, Magdalena, who was not only always ready to give advice on the text and read fragments of the manuscript, but who also offered me unswerving and dedicated support and on whom I could always rely. My very special thanks are due to my husband, Arjen, who apart from being lovingly supportive and understanding, inspired many ideas in this book. His expertise, insight and genuine fascination for historical linguistics, especially Old Germanic linguistics, never cease to amaze me.

E.A.
Amsterdam, August 2017

List of abbreviations

Languages and dialects

ANGL.	Anglian	OE	Old English
AVEST.	Avestan	OFRIS.	Old Frisian
DU.	Dutch	OHG	Old High German
EOE	Early Old English	OICEL.	Old Icelandic
ER	Early Runic	OIR.	Old Irish
FÖHR-AMR.	dialect of Föhr/Amrum	ON	Old Norse
GO.	Gothic	OLF	Old Low Franconian
GR.	Greek	OS	Old Saxon
IE	Indo-European	PDE	present-day English
K.	Kentish	PGMC.	Proto-Germanic
LAT.	Latin	POL.	Polish
LOE	Late Old English	PIE	Proto-Indo-European
LG	Low German	PWGMC.	Proto-West Germanic
MDU.	Middle Dutch	SE	Southeastern
ME	Middle English	SKT.	Sanskrit
MHG	Middle High German	SW	Southwestern
MLG	Middle Low German	SWM	Southwest Midlands
NEM	Northeast Midland	WANG.	Wangerooge
NORTH.	Northumbrian	WFRIS.	West Frisian
NWM	Northwest Midland	WGMC	West Germanic
NWGMC.	Northwest Germanic	WS	West Saxon

Linguistic and other terms

ABL.	ablative	MASC./M	masculine
ACC.	accusative	MON.	monosyllabic
ADJ.	adjective	N.	neuter
DAT.	dative	NEUT.	neutral
DIS.	disyllabic	NOM.	nominative
FEM./F	feminine	PL.	plural
GEN.	genitive	PTCP.	participle
H	heavy syllable	SG.	singular
IND.	indicative	SYLL.	syllable
INSTR.	instrumental	UML	*i*-umlaut/*i*-mutation
L	light syllable	V	vowel
LOC.	locative	VOC.	vocative

Sources

B₁	*First Brokmer Manuscript*
B₂	*Second Brokmer Manuscript*
C	Manuscript C of *Heliand*
CRK	*Chronicle compilation*
DOE	*Dictionary of Old English*
DOEEC	*Dictionary of Old English Electronic Corpus*
E₁	*First Emsingo Manuscript*
E₂	*Second Emsingo Manuscript*
E₃	*Third Emsingo Manuscript*
EWN	*Etymologisch Woordenboek van het Nederlands*
F	*Fivelgo Manuscript*
GEN	*Genesis*
H	*Heliand*
H₁	*First Hunsingo Manuscript*
H₂	*Second Hunsingo Manuscript*
LW	*Leiden Willeram*
M	Manuscript M of *Heliand*
OED	*Oxford English Dictionary*
OFO	*Oudfries(ch)e Oorkonden*
ONW	*Oudnederlands Woordenboek (Old Dutch Dictionary)*
R₁	*First Riustring Manuscript*
R₂	*Second Riustring Manuscript*
RB	*Rhyming Bible*
ROM	*Hoe dae Fresen Rom wonnen (Frisian Rhyme Chronicle)*
S	*Straubing Manuscript*
U	*Codex Unia*
WPS	*Wachtendonck Psalms*

List of tables

List of figures

Introduction

0.1 General remarks

Language is an inherently dynamic phenomenon, constantly evolving over time. The dynamics and the scope of this evolution are determined by a range of interacting forces and factors deriving from various domains, which are partly universal and partly idiosyncratic, i.e. language- and/or language-group-specific. This property of language manifests itself in many different ways and involves all levels of linguistic structure. One of them is the area of nominal morphology, which is the focus of the present study, and which constitutes ample and auspicious ground for the study of the dynamics of language. This book is devoted to a study of the nominal morphology in early Germanic languages, concentrating on the transformation of the system of nominal inflection and paradigms in Old English, Old Frisian, Old Saxon and Old Low Franconian.

The most prominent characteristic of the evolution of the inflectional morphology in Germanic languages is a gradual reduction of inflectional contrasts, which, depending on the language or dialect, had a different scope and dating. This has been recognised in many morphological, syntactic and typological studies on Germanic, where observations like this one can be found: "The history of inflectional morphology in the G[ermanic] languages has been largely one of loss of inflectional distinctions and even of entire inflectional categories. This process of 'deflection' (…) though evidenced in all G[ermanic] languages, has progressed unevenly across the family." (Harbert 2007: 90). With respect to the scope of deflection, the individual Germanic languages represent a continuum, ranging from systems with very limited case and number inflection (English), to those retaining a relatively complex inflectional configuration (Icelandic, Faroese, Elfdalian or German). As the original elaborate case system is only residually retained in present-day Germanic, the divergent paths of the development of nominal morphology are manifested in the typological diversity of the plural formation patterns found across present-day Germanic, which include the use of case/number allomorphs, root vowel and consonant alternations, or pure suffixation. Much as the process of deflection can be considered the most dominant diachronic trend in the development of Germanic inflectional morphology, it is not, however, of primary concern to the present work. The focus of this study is instead on the stage in which the nominal systems of Germanic languages are still fully-fledged with respect to the categories of case and gender, exhibiting only sporadic traces of the changes in these systems (e.g. in the Late Old English period). The transformation of the nominal systems at this early stage is a consequence of the gradual decline of inflectional distinctions, and involves a range of analogical developments, manifested in the change of the paradigmatic (declensional) affiliation of nouns, leading to a complete reorganisation of the nominal system inherited from Proto-Germanic.

Although often presented and described as static constructs in the traditional handbook accounts, the nominal paradigms of Old Germanic languages were in a state of constant and gradual transformation. The propensity to reorganise, resulting in a continuous state of flux, seems to have been an inherent feature of the paradigms, going back to the Proto-Indo-European parent language. Not only does this instability reflect the general shifting nature of language, but it also underlies the dynamic character of the nominal system. The attested material clearly indicates that the nominal system in Old Germanic was exposed to the pressure of two interacting forces: 'regular' phonological developments (phonological attrition) and analogical readjustments (analogical levelling). The evolution of the nominal system, occasioned by an interplay of these phonological and morphological factors, is manifested in a steady reorganisation of inflection and an ensuing reduction in the declensional class diversity inherited from the Proto-Germanic ancestor. The changes in the shape of the nominal paradigms, induced primarily by phonological developments, are evinced in the gradual infiltration of analogical inflections from the productive paradigms (*a*-stems and *ō*-stems) into the less productive paradigms inherited from Proto-Germanic.[1] The focus of the present study is on the stage where the reconfiguration of the nominal system is expressed in synchronic fluctuations between the inherited and analogical inflectional patterns. This synchronic variation is most prominently attested in the unproductive declensional types, known as minor classes, which, with the increasing amount of analogical inflection in their paradigms, tended to lose their original integrity and their status of independent declensional classes. An illustrative example of these inflectional vacillations may be the Late West-Saxon paradigm of *tōð* 'tooth', affiliated with the root nouns, where the inherited, *i*-mutated NOM. PL. form *tēð* is found alongside the analogical form *tōðas*, with the marker *-as* extended form the *a*-stems:

---

1.   The change of paradigmatic affiliation of nouns is not a Germanic-specific development; it is a more general phenomenon, and parallel developments are attested also in other Indo-European languages, e.g. in Vulgar Latin, with transfers from the *u*- and *ē*-stems to *o*- and *ā*-declensions (Gmc. *a*- and *ō*-stems), or in Slavic with shifts from the *i*-stems and *n*-stems to the *o*-/*jo*-stem declension.

1. *And heora <u>teð</u> wæron horses tuxum gelice* (...)   (LS 10 (Guth))
   'and their teeth were like horse's tusks'
2. *and heora <u>toþas</u> wæron gelice horses twuxan.*   (LS 10.1 (Guth))
   'and their teeth were like horse's tusks'

The examples above come from the related texts of the Vercelli Homily XXIII (LS 10 (Guth)) and the Vespasian (D. xxi) *Life* (LS 10.1 (Guth)), separated from one another by around one century, both being adaptations to Late West Saxon, dated to the late tenth and late eleventh centuries, respectively. The amount of novel inflection permeating the inherited paradigms varied depending on the paradigm and declensional type, and in its most advanced form resulted in a complete shift of a noun to another declensional class. The consequence of these analogical changes is a polarisation of nouns towards a few major declensional classes, and a concomitant reduction in the number of classes, i.e. the elimination of the less productive inflectional patterns to the benefit of the productive ones. This tendency can be observed in all the Germanic languages, but its scope, dating, and precise conditioning differ depending on the dialect.[2] In the long run, the process has had serious typological implications, reflecting a "crisis" in the typological structure of Germanic, as observed by Ramat (1981):

> Die Vermeidung der Zahl von Flexionsparadigmen ist also im Germ. ein allgemeines Phänomen des morphologischen Ausgleich (und ist auch anderen Sprachen des Idg. eignen) und stellt die erste Phase einer Krise des auf Flexion beruhenden Sprachtyps dar, der Krise die im English der Gegenwart am weitesten ihr fortgestrittenes Studium erreicht hat ...   (Ramat 1981: 63)

The first indications of this typological shift can be recognised already in the Common Germanic stage (Ramat 1981: 60; cf. Chapter 2).

The reshaping of the nominal inflection was a multifaceted process, embracing a range of phonological and morphological developments, conditioned by a range of factors. As a complex phenomenon, the restructuring process and the explanation of the mechanisms it involved constitute a challenge to linguistic explorations. This has been made explicit by Lahiri & Dresher (1984: 141), according to whom "[d]eclension shifts are a deceptively simple form of analogical change which nevertheless pose interesting diachronic and synchronic problems. Diachronically, we would like to be able to account for such shifts, and to predict under what conditions and in what direction they are likely to occur." (Lahiri & Dresher 1984: 141).

---

2. In the context of the Germanic language family, the term "dialect" will be used interchangeably with the term "language" to refer to the sister languages (especially in Chapter 2) (following the practice of scholars in the field, e.g. Nielsen 1989, 2000).

The explanation of the phenomenon and the conditioning of the shifts involves a recourse to a range of interacting forces deriving from different linguistic domains. Apart from the phonological processes and system-related factors, such as the functionality of the system, they involve a number of extramorphological determinants, such as the frequency of occurrence, the salience of inflectional markers, or the semantic makeup of declensional classes.

The present survey is comparative in nature and examines the material from four languages traditionally affiliated with two sub-branches of West Germanic: (1) the Ingvaeonic subgroup, known also as North Sea Germanic, a coastal language continuum, including Old English, Old Frisian and (to some extent) Old Saxon; and (2) the Istvaeonic subgroup (or Inland WGmc.), represented here by Old Low Franconian.[3] They may be subsumed under the general term "Northern West Germanic" languages, partly in compliance with their geographical distribution, but primarily to indicate the exclusion of Old High German from the study. The data from Gothic and Old Scandinavian, which retain more inflectional diversity in their nominal systems, with more declensional types attested, serve as occasional reference points. It must be emphasised that the West-Germanic branch formed a continuum of dialects and sub-dialects rather than a uniform linguistic system. It was rather an assembly of independent languages, which through their geographical closeness underwent a number of common, primarily phonological developments (e.g. Nielsen 2000: 289; Krogh 1997: 27–28). Although many details of the dialectal variation in early Continental Germanic are not attested, in view of the history of the tribal relations it must be assumed that such a dialectal differentiation existed, and therefore the dialects constituted a continuum rather than uniform, separate languages with clearly-defined boundaries. An example may be the Frankish tribes, which formed a conglomeration of peoples rather than one Frankish tribe communicating in one language. Accordingly, terms such as 'Old Saxon' or 'Old English' refer to an abstraction of reality (Seebold 2013: 56). This complies with the observation that the "identification of languages as separate units may rather be seen in terms of an accumulation of features over time in a diffuse wave model (…)" (Versloot 2014: 40, 45). These features have a diverse and multiple origin and disseminate with various intensity across the Germanic linguistic area. An example of this characteristic in West Germanic is the linguistic shape of Old Saxon, with the largely hybrid nature of its nominal inflection, combining features

---

3.   The terms *North Sea Germanic* and *Ingvaeonic* will be used here interchangeably. The former, perhaps more transparent, is geographically-oriented, while the latter refers primarily to tribal relations. Both can be used in the synchronic and diachronic meaning, i.e. to refer to a group of dialects sharing a number of linguistic features and/or to refer to a "common pre-stage between West Germanic and the attested dialects" (de Vaan 2010: 316; cf. Nielsen 1994: 104–109).

from North Sea Germanic and Franconian. Such a heterogeneous morphological profile places it in an intermediate position between these two West Germanic subgroups, which is indicative of the fact that these languages form a continuum.

The present study encompasses a large span of time, ranging from the seventh century, where the earliest attestations of Old English come from, to the fourteenth century, with the Old Frisian material. Given that in Old English the language internal time span reaches nearly 400 years, it was considered requisite to include a diachronic component in the study (corresponding approximately to the dialectal one, due to the nature of the available corpus), which enabled a comparison of inflections in Early and Late Old English. Such an approach, secured by the abundant Old English material, makes it possible to capture the dynamics of the restructuring process. For the other investigated languages, where most of the attestations span a period of less than 100 years, the quantitative analysis is more of a synchronic nature. The overall time span covered by the examined material allows us to trace the restructuring process from its earliest attested stage, where it operated sporadically, until the moment where it can be viewed in terms of a more widespread and systematic tendency, steadily disseminating throughout the lexicon. One may expect discrepancies with respect to the progression of nominal inflection restructuring in West Germanic to proceed alongside the sketched dividing line (Ingvaeonic vs. Istvaeonic), and shared developmental patterns to be found in the more closly related languages. Much as the processes that affected the nominal inflection of the examined languages can be expected to run largely in parallel, the adopted cross-linguistic perspective offers more insight into the mechanisms of the process and allows for generalisations of a more universal nature.

0.2   Aims of the study

In the most general terms, this study aims at presenting a coherent picture of the restructuring of the nominal inflections in the early Northern West Germanic languages, and framing its implications for the theory of morphological change. Assuming that language variation is to a large extent orderly and patterned, it is the purpose of the present study to identify the systematic patterns behind the restructuring process in order to uncover its mechanisms. As the study is empirical in nature, the results of the qualitative and quantitative investigation of the individual corpora form the basis for theoretical considerations, including determining the role of the factors conditioning the restructuring processes. More specifically, the main objectives of the present study involve three interrelated planes of investigation, and can be formulated as follows:

1. to identify the patterns of reorganisation of the nominal inflection in the individual Germanic languages using a complete-corpus analysis, with a view to presenting a typology of interdeclensional transfers;
2. to explore the mechanisms behind the analogical restructuring, including identifying the factors controlling the process, as well as evaluating their significance and share in the process;
3. to frame the theoretical implications of the findings for the theory of morphological change.

As regards the first objective, the study examines the inflectional diversity at a micro-level, encompassing idiosyncratic features identifiable for the individual languages, and macro-diversity, comprising the variation across the sister languages, with characteristics of a more general Germanic scope (whether pan-Germanic, West Germanic or Anglo-Frisian). The intention is to characterise the transformation of the nominal system inherited from Proto-Germanic in the individual Old West Germanic languages, where the dynamics of the process can be expected to be different and conditioned by a range of diverse factors. The comprehensive quantitative analysis of the process in the selected languages enables verifying the tendencies that are discussed in the handbooks with respect to their adequacy, making them more precise and finer. In this sense, the present research offers a refinement and occasionally a correction of the generalisations made in earlier treatments of Germanic historical morphology. Within the purview of the present study is a comparison of the tendencies present in the Anglo-Frisian sub-branch on the one hand, and the rest of West Germanic on the other. Its aim is to determine to what extent the germs of the disparate trajectories of the later inflectional developments were present in the nominal systems in the Old Germanic period. The pattern of retention of archaic inflectional features and the direction of levelling identified at the earliest attested stages can be viewed as forerunners to the tendencies found in the later stages of the development of English, Frisian, (Low) German and Dutch. While references will be made to these later stages in the discussion of the forms in the 'Old' stage where relevant, the diachronic development that led to the modern shape of inflection is beyond the scope of this study. The disparities in the evolution of the nominal inflection in the individual Germanic languages can be ascribed to a variety of interacting factors. Among the most essential contributors to this disparate state of affairs are phonological developments (especially the attrition of unaccented vowels and *i*-mutation), affecting individual dialects at a different pace and to a varying extent. Inasmuch as the morphological realignments (*inter-* and *intra*paradigmatic shifts) are a direct response to these phonological incentives, the scale and the direction of the analogical reorganisation of inflection will accordingly vary across languages. It is the intent of the present study to examine these interrelated factors and features, which were consequential for the divergent paths of development of the declensional systems in the individual languages, resulting eventually in the emergence of considerably different inflectional profiles in present-day Germanic.

Examination of the factors that guided the process of reshaping the nominal inflection in early Germanic is in fact the focal part of the research question. The systematic investigation of the variation in the inflectional patterns in the individual Northern West Germanic languages allows us to identify an array of determinants deriving from different domains, which turn out to interact often in a synergetic way. In order to characterise the process of restructuring, the share of these interacting factors in the process, and possibly their relative ranking, need to be estimated. The factors involved in the restructuring process are of a twofold nature. On the one hand, the study identifies the abovementioned language-specific factors, responsible for the divergent inflectional development of languages which had a common historical origin and were closely related. On the other hand, the study looks into the impact of non-language-specific factors, whose more universal nature enables framing the restructuring process in more general terms. The two universal factors which turn out to have most profoundly affected the dynamics of the restructuring process are the frequency of occurrence (with the conserving effect of high token frequency) and the morpho-phonological salience of inflectional exponents. Although the relevance of both for the formation of morphological patterns has been acknowledged in earlier studies, it has not been sufficiently substantiated with a systematic corpus-based analysis of the early Germanic material.

Furthermore, the findings of the study are hoped to have a wider relevance to morphological theory and the study of morphological change. The systematic investigation of the restructuring process in the individual Old Northern West Germanic languages reveals a number of patterns, which give insight into a range of theoretical issues, enabling several theoretical inferences and generalisations.

Two further objectives, which refer directly to the findings of the current research on early Germanic nominal morphology, but which are more peripheral to the interest of the present study, include (1) evaluating the validity of the traditional, diachronically-biased classification of nouns and the more recently postulated, synchronically-oriented taxonomy of nominal paradigms, and (2) placing the tendencies and patterns identified for the individual languages in the context of the debate about the nature and evolution of Germanic nominal inflection (e.g. Nielsen 1989, 1994, 2000, 2001; Krogh 1996, 2013).

The former is a theoretical issue, which has been addressed to some extent in a few recent studies (cf. 0.3). The effects of the reorganisation of the early Germanic nominal inflection have some theoretical implications for the traditional philological taxonomy of nouns. The nominal morphology of Older Germanic languages has traditionally been analysed in etymological terms, resulting in classifications which largely reflect the prehistoric situation. The inadequacy of the traditional classification of nouns in Old English has been recognised as a "consequence of an overwhelming ambition to taxonomize which carries the writers beyond the bounds of plausibility" (Hogg 1998). Although this aspect remains beyond the primary concern of the present study, problems involving the taxonomy of the nominal paradigms in Germanic will be addressed in respective chapters. This refers in particular to the Old English material, where the traditional philological taxonomy has been widely applied in the standard historical treatments. The findings from the present corpus-based study create a sound basis for a critical evaluation of both the traditional, diachronically-biased classification and the more recently attempted, synchronically-oriented taxonomy of nouns. Accordingly, the existing classifications of the declensional classes can be confronted with the findings of the current study, with a view to streamlining the description of the declensional class system.

The final objective of the study refers in particular to aspects such as the placement of Old Saxon within the West Germanic language continuum, and the estimation of the extent to which the tendencies present in the reorganisation of the nominal inflection follow the traditional division within West Germanic (North Sea Germanic vs. Continental Germanic), defined largely by phonological criteria. The nature and scope of the study will reveal and delineate certain methodological problems pertaining to Germanic comparative linguistics, especially the comparison of historical corpora incompatible with respect to their size, attestation dates, and genre composition.

It is a characteristic of diachronic studies that they mirror typology, inasmuch as language change is limited by the same constraints as those holding for descriptions of cross-linguistic variation. Accordingly, the present study, with its cross-Germanic context, has also a typological dimension. Although modest from a typological perspective – since limited only to four Germanic languages – the study attempts to offer some typological observations. In particular, it tries to detect the seeds of the typological shift which took place in Germanic nominal inflection in the later period.

This last aspect invokes also the question whether the tendencies observed in the earliest attested material find their continuation in the further development of the nominal system in the individual languages. Although the present study is a synchronic investigation of the nominal inflection in the *oldest* attested stages of Northern West Germanic, it also tries to determine to what extent the changes in this early period can be indicative of the later developments in the inflectional system of the individual languages. It must be emphasised that the present study does not intend to trace these morphological developments into the later period, not

even into the *Middle* stage, where the reduction of many final vowels to /ə/ transformed the nominal profiles entirely. In English and Frisian, this period involves
typically the dissolution of the case and gender system, while in Middle Dutch and
Middle Low German further extensive restructurings take place (cf. Marynissen
1996, Wegera 1985). Although the major developments, such as those involving
the loss of case and gender distinctions, are to be dated beyond the Old Germanic
period, the changes taking place at the early stages of attestation are the starting
point for later developments, which had more radical typological consequences.

Significantly, none of the investigated languages has a direct continuation
into present-day *standard* languages. Old Low Franconian, as attested in the
Wachtendonck Psalms, is the ancestor of the present-day Limburg dialect rather
than Modern Standard Dutch, and Old Frisian represents primarily the eastern
variety of Frisian, and thus does not reflect well-attested Modern Frisian, which
is a continuation of the early West Frisian dialect. (Admittedly, however, a reflex
of Old East Frisian can be found in the present-day Saterland dialect.) Old Saxon
continues as modern *Plattdeutsch*, which from a sociolinguistic perspective is a
variety of German and not a standard language. And finally, Old English, dominated by the West-Saxon material, can hardly be viewed as a direct predecessor
of what is nowadays known as *standard* English, irrespective of how broadly the
term is understood.

0.3   Existing research

The present work is empirical in nature: by framing the investigated phenomena
quantitatively, the study affords insight into the dynamics of the changes in the nominal inflection. A systematic and detailed quantitative examination of the textual
material from early Northern West Germanic, conducted on the complete corpora
of the four selected languages, allows an adequate and fairly exact estimation of the
scope of the reorganisation of the nominal system inherited from Proto-Germanic.
The study responds to the apparent gap in existing research on nominal morphology of early Germanic, where the reorganisation of nominal paradigms, although
recognised in a few more recent studies, has not been subjected to a systematic *comparative* investigation of a quantitative nature. In the standard grammars of Older
Germanic languages, the restructuring tendencies involving analogical reshufflings
in the declensional classes are qualitatively observed and briefly discussed; none
of them, however, provides an exhaustive description of these developments (e.g.
Prokosch 1939, Krahe & Meid 1969, Ramat 1981, Brunner 1965, Campbell 1977,
Gallée 1993, Bremmer 2009). Boutkan's study on *Auslautgesetze* (1995) may be
considered an exception, as in this work references to interdeclensional analogical

reshufflings are frequently made, and occasionally general tendencies, including the chronology of the transfers, are summarised (although with the primary objective of reconstructing the Proto-Germanic constellation of declensions).

Admittedly, an investigation of the phenomenon of interdeclensional shifts, covering the factors involved in the mechanism of restructuring, is not an entirely novel enterprise. Some observations about this phenomenon have been made in a number of individual studies on morphological developments in Old English (e.g. Hogg 1997a, Lass 1997b, Kastovsky 1997, Krygier 1998, 2002), where especially the question of a taxonomic classification of Old English nouns is addressed. An early systematic study where a fruitful endeavour was made at a quantitative framing of the changes in the nominal system was Dahl's (1938) investigation of the nominal inflection in Early Old English. The study focuses primarily on the vocalic stems, including the productive classes of the *a*-stems and *ō*-stems. Two other early publications, representing a quantitative (though not comparative) approach to the Old Germanic material, are Sjölin (1970) and Boutkan (1996); the former is an investigation of the late-classical Old Frisian manuscript F (Fivelgo), the latter provides a complete account of the grammar of the Old Frisian manuscript R_1 (though without a morphological analysis). More recent similar studies include the monographs of Marynissen (1996), Kürschner (2008), Bertacca (2009), and Thöny (2013). The focus of these monographs as well as the methodological approaches adopted therein are in various ways different from the general profile of the present study. They explore the changes in the inflectional system in the historical stages of Germanic languages outside the period investigated in the present study (Marynissen, Thöny), and/or offer no quantitative, corpus-based analysis of the analogical developments (Bertacca, Kürschner, Thöny). More specifically, in his comprehensive study of interdeclensional realignments in early Germanic, Thöny (2013) concentrates primarily on the period where the Proto-Germanic system of root-(stem suffix)-ending was largely intact, and the shifts of nouns between declensional classes were primarily due to derivational rather than inflectional interactions. Bertacca (2009), whose study is confined to English, places his analysis consistently within the framework of Natural Morphology, and is concerned primarily with the later stages in the development of nominal inflection (i.e. Late Old English/Early Middle English), where the case and gender systems were about to dissolve. Kürschner (2008) takes the story even further into present-day Germanic, where most of the languages examined in his study retain only the contrast in number (singular/plural). This advanced stage of reorganisation in case and gender systems is not yet displayed in the Old Germanic period, where the nominal system was exposed to extensive analogical remodelling, but the categories of case and gender remained intact. The present study, with its empirical anchoring, seems to come closest to the work of Marynissen (1996), in which a systematic quantitative analysis was applied to investigate the transformation of the nominal inflection in the Middle Dutch period.

A desideratum in the existing research seems to be a more systematic approach to the available early Germanic material, which would enable us to chart the evolution of the nominal inflection in quantitative terms. Still little is known about the scope and the mechanisms of the restructuring process as it operated in the earliest attested period of (West) Germanic. Particulars concerning the relative chronology of analogical developments, their exact spread across paradigms, their motivation, or systemic triggers, and the factors conditioning the dynamics and the direction of innovations, remain largely obscure, and the explanations offered are usually idiosyncratic and provisional. The present corpus-based study, with its comparative approach, seems particularly suited to fill this apparent lacuna in research on early Germanic nominal morphology, with respect to both the detail of the coverage it offers and the theoretical claims it makes. It is hoped that by providing statistical information, the present study will offer a more exact and comprehensive account of the process of restructuring of the nominal system in Northern West Germanic languages. Positioning itself within the general interest area represented by the respected and valuable studies discussed above, the book, with its cross-Germanic scope and quantitative component, aims at providing a systematic data-underpinning for the qualitative observations (including some from the previous studies) and at refining the picture of the restructuring of nominal inflection in early Germanic.

Although diachronic studies of a comparative nature were abundant in the Neogrammarian and structural traditions (e.g. Streitberg 1896, Meillet 1917, Boer 1924, Prokosch 1939, Krahe & Meid 1967–1969), they appear to be less frequent in more recent scholarly research on historical Germanic morphology (cf. Nielsen 1985, Boutkan 1995, Griepentrog 1995). In view of this, the cross-Germanic perspective adopted in the study can be viewed as another advantage of the present work. This comparative perspective seems to be particularly desirable for the study of Old Germanic languages, which, as observed by Dal (1983: 92), "(…) bilden in so hohem Grade eine Einheit, daß ihre Systeme nur durch eine vergleichende Betrachtung erforscht und verstanden werden können". Such a broader frame of reference allows one to identify and distinguish between linguistic patterns which are typically language-specific and those which have a wider scope and thus a more universal character. Especially the identification of the latter gives an opportunity to gain some more insight into the mechanisms of the restructuring process. By describing the mechanisms involved in the restructuring process and identifying the factors that controlled the changes in the inflectional system (such as frequency of occurrence and morpho-phonological salience), the present research is intended to contribute to a better understanding of the mechanisms underlying morpho-logical change.

Another feature that distinguishes this study from the traditional treatments of the nominal inflection in early Germanic is the lack of anachronism that character-ises many of these accounts. The paradigms of declensional classes, as presented in the standard historical grammars, can be easily interpreted as static entities, while their actual dynamics remain hidden in the occasional references to diachronic, dialectal or lexical variants and exceptions. These 'classical' paradigms are evidently biased by including predominantly archaic forms, representing thus a stage of lan-guage that possibly never existed in reality – a fact that has been recognised in recent studies (most notably in Hogg & Fulk 2011 with reference to Old English). This bias towards presenting normative paradigms is avoided in the present work, where a complete range of the attested inflections is studied at face value, allowing one to capture the dynamics of the inflectional paradigms, and leading to a much more diversified picture of Old Germanic inflectional classes than that presented in the standard historical handbooks. A corollary of this approach is the aforemen-tioned opportunity to look anew into the traditional systematisation of declensional classes in Northern West Germanic, where the stem suffix serves as a major clas-sificatory criterion.

0.4   Organisation of the book

The book is organised into eight chapters, four of which discuss the transformation of the nominal systems in the individual Northern West Germanic languages. The study opens with a chapter devoted to a discussion of the theoretical framework and the methodological basis for investigating the reorganisation of nominal inflec-tion (Chapter 1). It introduces the terminology relevant to the study and presents the textual material as well as the details of the method applied in the analysis. It outlines also the essential theoretical assumptions of the study, and discusses concepts relevant for the investigation of the restructuring process, such as anal-ogy, syncretism, markedness, morphological productivity, or paradigm stability. As the declensional systems of the individual Germanic languages are anchored in the Proto-Germanic constellation of declensions, the discussion of the origin and the early development of the nominal inflection in Proto-Germanic is the focus of Chapter 2. It serves as a background for the examination of the inflec-tional systems in the individual Germanic languages, presenting a comprehensive overview of the declensional configuration reconstructed for Proto-Germanic. The presentation follows the traditional classification of nouns based on etymological criteria, and therefore takes the traditional paradigmatic configuration as a point of departure. Such an approach was found legitimate in view of the comparative nature of the present study. The grounding of the phenomenon under scrutiny in the Proto-Germanic context was indispensable, as this earliest stage constitutes a direct starting point for reorganisation of inflection in early Germanic. This chapter also gives an opportunity to broaden the perspective of the research by occasional references to the shape of the nominal inflection in Gothic and Early Runic, which align closest to the original Proto-Germanic inflectional configuration, preserving many archaic inflectional characteristics, as well as Old Norse and Old High German, which follow quite different pathways of inflectional development from the rest of Germanic, retaining more inflectional diversity. The empirical part of the study consists of two stages, including (1) the investigation of the process of restructuring in the individual languages, and (2) the comparison of the findings, with a view to identifying formal and distributional similarities and discrepancies. The first stage is presented in four consecutive chapters (3 to 6) and is aimed at presenting a coherent picture of the early Northern West Germanic declensional system as attested in the surviving records. The order in which the languages are presented is determined by their dialectal affiliation; accordingly, the Old English material is presented first (Chapter 3), followed by its closest relative Old Frisian (Chapter 4), and the other two sister languages on the Continent, Old Saxon (Chapter 5) and Old Low Franconian (Chapter 6). Presenting the Old English material first has an independent advantage: of all the investigated languages, Old English offers the most extensive material and can thus serve as a reference point inasmuch as the range of the potential morphological developments is expected to be best attested here. Given the discrepancies between the examined languages, the possibility that some tendencies can be absent from Old English while present in the Continental sister languages, cannot be excluded. Yet, the most likely scenario is that Old English will evince the widest scope of developments in the inflectional system.

Despite the expected inadequacy of a classification based on the stem-type criterion for a synchronic description of the declensional systems attested in Old Germanic, the presentation and discussion of the individual class profiles follows the traditional classification. In view of the comparative nature of the present study, such an approach turns out to be an expedient method of presentation, enabling a transparent and systematic cross-Germanic comparison. The pivotal part of the book is contained in Chapters 7 and 8. The former is devoted to a contrastive analysis of the material, involving a detailed comparison of the quantitative findings from the investigation of the individual corpora, as well as a synopsis of the tendencies and patterns underlying the restructuring process in the individual languages, focusing on the cross-linguistic parallelisms and disparities. The observations from this contrastive treatment form the basis for the theoretical considerations presented in Chapter 8, which is an attempt at a formulation of the major principles underpinning the mechanisms of the restructuring process, including the factors conditioning it. Also, the theoretical implications for the mechanisms of morphological change and language variation are addressed. Conclusions of a more general nature are presented in the final section of the book, followed by an Appendix, which includes a complete inventory of lemmas used in the quantitative analysis of the respective corpora.

CHAPTER 1

Theory and methodology of the research

1.1   Nominal system in Old Germanic languages

Deriving from the common ancestor, Old Germanic languages share a range of characteristics in the area of nominal morphology, showing numerous formal similarities and parallel developments. This common profile of the morphological system is largely true of the earliest stages of attestation of Germanic, but not so much of modern Germanic, where the departure from the original shape of nominal morphology is substantial, and varies in the individual sister languages. One of the prominent shared features of the nominal system is related to its formal organisation. The nominal systems of all Old Germanic languages were organised into a range of declensional classes, which were originally (in Proto-Germanic) characterised by distinct inflectional profiles, depending on the type of stem.[4] This means that the assignment of nouns to a given class was originally determined by the structure of the stem, in particular the phonological component of the stem. Accordingly, in most general terms, the nominal classes can be subdivided into vocalic and consonantal, with a further division depending on the exact stem vowel (-a-, -ō-, -i-, -u-) or consonant (-n-, -s-, -r-, -t-). Such an overt declension class marking guaranteed both coherence and transparency. In the earliest attested stage of Germanic, as a result of the fusion of class exponents with grammatical markers (number and case), the old stem elements are no longer transparent, and accordingly the affiliation with a given declensional class is no longer identifiable through the phonological component of the stem, but determined lexically (see Section 2.2 for details). This declensional architecture, based entirely on the diachronic criteria, varies to some extent across the West Germanic dialect continuum, but the discrepancies between the individual languages are very limited at

---

4.   The declensional classes reconstructable for Proto-Indo-European have a different nature than those known from Proto-Germanic (Eichner 1974; Beekes 1995: 174–195; Ringe 2006: 41–50; Clackson 2007: 90–100; Fortson 2010: 113–134; Meier–Brügger 2010: 321–353; Thöny 2013: 50 ff.). The variation in the accentuation patterns gave rise to a range of ablaut patterns in the root and stem suffixes, but the actual case-number endings were largely identical for all nouns in all genders. The declension classes and genders in the Indo-European languages are believed to "have their respective origins in earlier and later semantic classifications, both "desemanticised" extensively in prehistoric times (…)" (Carstairs-McCarthy 2000: 636).

this early stage of attestation of Germanic. The situation looks different when the declensional configuration is approached from a synchronic perspective, i.e. when the affiliation of nouns is to be determined on the basis of synchronic criteria, such as the inflectional ending. The picture becomes much more blurred and a range of problems emerge, largely related to the fact that the nouns do not consistently show affiliation with one declensional type. The ambiguity with respect to declensional affiliation is a consequence of continuous interdeclensional interactions, whereby the paradigms of individual nouns become increasingly unstable, showing more and more analogical inflectional features.[5] On a more theoretical plane, this complication brings the question of delimiting the exact boundaries of declensional (inflectional) classes and establishing precise criteria for defining them. Formally, inflectional class (here declensional class) can be defined as "a set of lexemes whose members each select the same set of inflectional realizations", where the "realization" refers to an inflectional form (Aronoff 1994: 64). Alternatively (and more generally) it has been defined as: "a set of words (lexemes) displaying the same paradigm in a given language" (Carstairs-McCarthy 1994: 739; cf. Blevins 2004: 42), or "the set of paradigms that exhibit the same inflectional pattern" (Haspelmath & Sims 2010: 159).[6] In other words, an inflectional class is considered to be a "flag" that a lexical item bears "to assure that it will manifest the appropriate set of inflections" (Aronoff 1994: 65). In the Natural Morphology framework, the basis for defining an inflectional class is "the uniformity and distinctiveness of paradigms" (Wurzel 1989: 63). Inflectional classes have no "universal basis" in this approach, but are language-specific.[7] The question of the exact theoretical definition of declensional/inflectional class is of secondary importance to the present study. This is due to the nature of the present investigation, the focal point of which are the declensional classes as defined by purely etymological criteria, i.e. as inherited from Proto-Germanic. While the synchronic assignment of nouns to a given class in the individual Older Germanic languages can still be problematic, their etymological affiliation, based on the cross-linguistic material, is relatively certain and will serve as the primary index and the point of departure for the present quantitative analysis.

---

5.   The term *paradigm* (of a given lexeme) is understood here as a set of morphosyntactic properties or property combinations for a given lexeme (Carstairs-McCarthy 1998: 322).

6.   In Aronoff's approach (1994), inflectional classes represent "morphology by itself" categories, i.e. they are "purely morphological", or in other words, "neither mediate between morphology and another linguistic level nor have any substantial properties characteristic of another" (Aronoff 1994: 71).

7.   In the framework of Natural Morphology, a clear distinction is made between macro-classes, classes, (sub)sub-classes, micro-classes (mini-micro-classes), which form a hierarchical structure based on the principle of default inheritance (Corbett & Fraser 1993; cf. Bertacca 2009).

Admittedly, the question of a precise definition of declensional class becomes very much relevant when a synchronic approach to the classification of nouns is applied. As the present study in a way combines the diachronic and synchronic approaches to the changes in the nominal system, the findings will allow us to verify to what extent the declensional system based on the diachronic criteria corresponds to the state of affairs actually attested in the available material (Chapter 8).

On a purely theoretical plane, there is no synchronic functional motivation for the existence of inflectional (declensional) classes in the linguistic system. They are considered to increase the complexity of the system and to constitute a formal ballast (Wurzel 1986: 76; Kürschner 2008: 366–368), which implies their gratuity in the system. Assuming that the existence of inflectional classes is not functionally justified, their reduction and eventual loss in morphological change can be considered a natural consequence (Mayerthaler 1980). The reduction of inflectional classes takes place through the extension of one inflectional type at the expense of other types.

Another shared characteristic of the early Germanic languages with respect to nominal inflection involves case, number and gender assignment. In all of them, case marking interacts with the category of number, i.e. case and number are realised jointly and expressed by a single exponent, varying depending on a given class and/or grammatical gender. This fused marking system displays some symptoms of disintegration already at this early stage, in particular in Late Old English, where the case system begins to collapse, and consequently the contrast in marking the category of number emerges as the primary inflectional distinction. Although certain paradigms reflect a correlation between declension (stem) class and gender (e.g. all *s*-stems are neuter, all *ō*-stems are feminine and all *nd*-stems are masculine), there is no absolute one-to-one correspondence between them.[8] In other words, there is no direct correlation between gender and inflectional class, although both are inherent properties of the noun and an interaction between them does exist.[9]

---

8. A different opinion was expressed by Schwink (2004), who argues that nouns in Old Germanic languages were assigned gender based on their declensional class affiliation: "The membership of a noun in a declensional class almost universally implies its gender" (Schwink 2004: 23, 99; cf. Waxenberger 1996: 30).

9. On the interaction between these two categories in modern Germanic languages, see e.g. Carstairs (1987), Kürschner & Nübling (2011), Enger (2004), Schwink (2004). It has been postulated that the level of interdependence between gender and declension class varies across Germanic language varieties, and depends on the complexity of these two categorisation systems (Kürschner & Nübling 2011: 379). The link between gender and declension serves the purpose of enhancing the memorability of a high number of classes (allomorphs) and eventually safeguards their complementary function in marking the category of number (p. 382).

The gender system attested in the Older Germanic languages involved three genders.[10] The assignment of gender to nouns was based predominantly on morphological criteria, "with semantic core rules" (Schwink 2004: 69). The semantic component is most prominent in the class of nouns of relationship where gender assignment is entirely semantic. It is only in the later stage of the development of West Germanic that the gender systems follow divergent developmental paths, leading to a considerable variation across present-day Germanic.[11]

From the perspective of the present study, an essential shared characteristic of the nominal inflection in the early Germanic languages is the multifunctionality of inflectional endings (across classes), manifested in a considerable number of overlapping forms and syncretisms. This property of the nominal inflection is a consequence of a wide range of regular phonological developments that affected the shape of inflectional syllables, rendering the once distinct exponents of class affiliation identical and thus indistinguishable across different classes. The significance of this feature for the analogical restructuring of paradigms lies in the fact that it constituted one of the factors triggering interparadigmatic reshufflings of nouns (for details see Section 2.2.2). For instance, the formal syncretism of the NOM./ACC. SG. of the heavy syllable *i*-stems (OE *wyrm* < **wurmi-z*) and *a*-stems (OE *dæg* < **daga-z*) in Old English, emerging because of the reduction of vowels and consonants in unstressed syllables, was clearly a factor facilitating the analogical transfer of the *i*-stems to the *a*-stem declension (cf. Section 3.5.2).

1.2   Nominal paradigms in Old Germanic languages

Morphosyntactic relations in Old Germanic paradigms were expressed through both suffixation (with a range of inflectional endings partly overlapping across declensional types), and/or stem alternation, which could occasionally accompany suffixation or serve as a category marker on its own. Some morphosyntactic categories across various declensional classes could also be expressed by zero

---

10. Cf. the gender system reconstructed for Proto-Indo-European, with a main subdivision into common (or animate) and neuter (inanimate) gender (Szemerényi 1999: 155–156), with feminine being the new third gender on account of, among others, the derivational nature of feminine nouns.

11. The system of declensional classes which exists in modern Germanic languages is only partly etymologically conditioned, but largely dependent on phonological criteria, which are language-specific. Gender seems to play a significant role here as well, although the opinions of linguists as to the precise interaction between these two categories vary. It has commonly been considered to be decisive for declensional class affiliation in Modern German (e.g. Köpcke 1993).

marking (especially the NOM./ACC. SG. and also the NOM./ACC. PL., e.g. in the neuter heavy-syllable *a*-stems). While in the productive declensions, i.e. *a*-stems, *ō*-stems and *n*-stems, suffixation was the prevailing mechanism of expressing morpho-syntactic relations (including zero inflection), the minor paradigms show a more diversified paradigmatic structure, with root vowel alternation (*i*-mutation, as in OE, OFris. *fōt – fēt*), or consonantal alternation (*r*-formative in the *s*-stems, e.g. OE *lamb – lambor*, or *þ*-formative in dental stems, e.g. OE *hæle – hæleð*) serving as alternative and/or additional inflectional mechanisms. This refers in particular to minor *consonantal* declensions, i.e. root nouns, *s*-stems, *r*-stems, *nd*-stems and dental stems. The alternation involving an *i*-mutated vowel is most consistently attested in the root nouns (OE, OFris.), *nd*-stems (OE) and partly *r*-stems (OE). The alternation involving stem consonants is found in the *s*-stems, where the inherited forms containing the *r*-element alternate with *r*-less forms (OE, OFris., OS), as well as in the dental stems in Old English, where the dental element -*þ*- is residually preserved in the paradigm. In contrast, minor vocalic declensions, i.e. *i*-stems and *u*-stems, show only suffixation, and the presence of the *i*-mutated vowel in the root of the *i*-stems is a relic feature, which in the synchronic grammars of Old North Sea Germanic languages does not serve any distinctive function.

The inherited stem alternations tended to be gradually eliminated in Germanic languages and the early stage of this elimination can be captured in the Old Germanic material (but cf. Modern Icelandic and Modern High German, where stem-vowel alternation is still a productive mechanism of forming the plural). The tendency towards ousting allomorphic variation from paradigms under the analogical pressure of more common affixation (here suffixation) patterns is considered to have a more universal scope. As stem changes are in general rare in language, they can be expected to be more susceptible to analogical pressures of patterns which employ suffixation (or affixation) (Haspelmath 2006: 59). They also tend to be less productive, at least in Germanic languages. At the same time, it has been argued that the learnability and processability of stem alternations is as easy as that of affixation patterns (Bybee & Newman 1995: 635ff). In other words, allophonic alternation is not less learnable and not necessarily a complication in the system, but constitutes an equally efficient way of marking case and number relations as suffixation. However, it must be observed that in Germanic languages stem change is clearly rarer than affixation as a way of marking morphosyntactic categories. This clear preference for affixation can be accounted for diachronically, namely by recourse to grammaticalization of lexical items, which is an essential process in the emergence of morphological patterns and which "forms affixes more readily than stem changes" (Bybee & Newman 1995: 637). The resulting low (type) frequency of stem alternations renders them more prone to analogical levelling from the more productive affixation patterns, hindering their own potential productivity. Consequently, in contrast to affixes found in the productive declensions, stem alternations are retained only residually in highly frequent (in terms of token frequency) lexical items (Bybee & Newman 1995: 635, 638). The distribution of suffixation and internal alternation patterns in the nominal paradigms in Older Germanic languages complies with these assumptions.[12] The productive classes, i.e. the *a*-stems and *ō*-stems as well as the *n*-stems (the latter productive at a later stage), characterised by high type frequency, used suffixation as the basic inflectional mechanism, while internal vocalic or consonantal alternation was much more widespread in minor unproductive classes, comprising highly frequent lexical items. Also the present-day nominal morphology of West Germanic languages corroborates this interpretation: even in languages where *i*-mutation or/and consonantal alternation are not productive morphological patterns, stem (root) alternation survived in high (token) frequency lexemes (cf. PDE *children, men*) (although frequency is clearly not the sole conditioning factor here).[13]

The presence of internal (stem) alternations in the paradigms of early Germanic played a significant role in the reshaping of the nominal system. By being essentially more resistant to analogical pressures than suffixes, such stem alternations could in a way regulate the dynamics of the analogy-based restructuring process, in most cases inhibiting the operation of analogical levelling. This refers in particular to the reflexes of the process of *i*-mutation, whose function, dating and scope varied substantially in the individual Old Germanic languages (cf. Chapter 7).

---

12. This does not mean that such a preference is a universal feature of all languages. In fact, there are languages in which stem alternation is a productive morphological pattern, rendering the morphological system very stable (e.g. Semitic languages) (Haspelmath 2006: 29).

13. This tendency does not hold for Modern German, where the amount of allomorphy has increased with time (e.g. Nübling 2000). This refers in particular to the category of number, which, in contrast to case, shows more plural allomorphs in Modern German than it did in the earlier historical periods. This phenomenon in German is known as *Numerusprofilierung* and refers to the divergent development of case and number inflection, whereby the category of number gained in importance at the cost of the category of case (Wegera 1987; Wurzel 1989; Dammel & Nübling 2006: 101; cf. Section 8.5).

1.3   Morphological restructuring of the nominal system in early Germanic

1.3.1   Introduction

The nominal system of early Germanic underwent considerable changes involving a complex interplay of phonological and morphological processes. The reorganisation of nominal morphology was triggered by phonological developments that affected the system of unaccented vowels. The process of phonetic attrition of unaccented vowels induced the reduction of inflectional endings, considerably affecting the shape of the nominal paradigms inherited from Proto-Germanic. As will become evident in the subsequent chapters, the scale of this development, as well as the exact conditioning and dating varied depending on the language, leading to different dynamics in the nominal systems of the individual Older Germanic languages.

The process held directly responsible for the phonologically-induced reduction of vowels in inflectional syllables was the change in the accentuation pattern, i.e. the development of the fixed initial dynamic accent in Proto-Germanic (e.g. Meillet 1970, Bennett 1972, D'Alquen 1988) (see Chapter 2 for details). The process triggered by this major change involved the loss of "phonological material" (or "phonological clarity") (Schwink 2004: 69, 100) in inflectional syllables, which occasioned a large-scale confusion and coalescence of distinctive inflectional markers, in particular a reduction in many case and number (and possibly gender) distinctions in the nominal system. A further corollary of the reduction of unstressed vowels was the demise of etymological stem-type distinctions, i.e. the weakening of transparent formal criteria for declensional class assignment (stem formative). Another consequence of phonological changes was an increase in formal syncretisms of inflectional exponents across different declensional classes, which rendered the system of declension classes less transparent. The emergence of case syncretisms, both formal and functional, can be considered the *direct* cause of the restructuring of the nominal system, since it largely undermined the stability of the system (Coleman 1991: 208).

The loss of distinctiveness in inflectional endings and paradigms encouraged the operation of a range of analogical processes, including *intra-* and *inter*paradigmatic reshufflings, resulting in the major reorganisation of the declensional constellation inherited from Proto-Germanic. Both developments, i.e. the merger of class-specific inflectional exponents and the syncretisms, induced a steady decline of the original declensional diversity inherited from the Proto-Germanic ancestor. From a broader Germanic perspective, a further consequence of these tendencies was a gradual change in the typological status of inflection, namely its transition from stem-based towards word-based inflection, which occurred to a varying degree in the individual Germanic languages (e.g. Kastovsky 1994; Harnisch 2001).

To sum up, the reduction of inflectional contrasts and the regularisation of inflectional markers were the tendencies that led to a reduction in the range of inflectional variation *within* and *across* paradigms. While the former involved essentially *intra*paradigmatic relations, with an extension of one paradigm form at the expense of another, the latter entailed *inter*paradigmatic relations, i.e. the extension of an inflectional marker from one paradigm to another. As they represent two different levels of the operation of analogical processes and as their effects have a different share in the process of restructuring, they will be discussed separately in the next two sections.

1.3.2   Interparadigmatic transfers

The distinction between *inter-* and *intra*paradigmatic transfers is based on the contrast between *inter-* and *intra*paradigmatic analogy, which goes back to Mayerthaler (1980: 82–83) ("interparadigmatischer" and "intraparadigmatischer Ausgleich"). The *inter*paradigmatic transfer can be defined as a change of declensional class affiliation of nouns, which takes place under the analogical influence of another declensional class (e.g. Wurzel 1989; Kürschner 2008; Thöny 2013; cf. the definition of *inflection class shift* in Gardani 2013: 64–69). The symptoms of the transition to another declensional class are manifested in the vacillation of forms in the paradigm between the inflectional patterns of two or more declensions. The focus of the present study is on the vacillation that takes place between the inflectional features inherited from an earlier stage (Proto-Germanic) and the innovative features extended by analogy from another declensional class. The shift in class membership is driven by morphological productivity of individual declensional types and occurs from the unproductive (minor) to the productive (major) declensional types. In other words, the analogical pressure of inflections of the productive types, which affect the shape of minor classes, results in the emergence of competing paradigms: *archaic* – continuing the inflectional features of the original (PGmc.) paradigm, to a large extent receding, and *innovative* – showing inflectional characteristics of the productive declensions. The scope and dynamics of this vacillation varies, essentially depending on the lemma, declensional class and language. The presence of a substantial number of spontaneous overlaps of inflectional features across classes leads to more systematic transfers between inflectional classes and consequently to shrinking and gradual disintegration of the paradigms inherited from Proto-Germanic.

Reorganisation of the nominal system inherited from Proto-Indo-European is traceable to the prehistoric stage, where it emerged in the wake of the Proto-Germanic phonological innovations in unstressed syllables. The evidence from the individual Germanic languages clearly indicates that reshufflings between declensional classes took place before the time of the first written attestations. It is manifested, for instance, in the forms of the GEN. PL. (OE -*a*, OFris. -*a*, OS -*o* and OLF -*o*) and DAT. PL. (OE -*um*, OFris. -*un*, OS, -*un*, OLF -*un*), which are found across all minor classes. In formal terms (and for the practical purposes of this study), two stages in the reorganisation of the minor paradigms can be distinguished: (1) the prehistoric stage, comprising early transfers which are not attested in the synchronic grammars of the individual Germanic languages, and (2) the historical stage, comprising analogical shifts occurring at the earliest attested stages of the investigated languages. This approach, despite its obvious limitations, is functional from the perspective of the present study, as it creates a clear borderline, separating the paradigms that will and will not be of relevance to the present quantitative investigation. Obviously, what needs to be underscored is that much as this approach is expedient for the present analysis, it is principally idealistic and oversimplifies the actual linguistic reality. The process of analogical remodelling of inflection was a continuous and gradual development, and the nominal system, as part of a dynamically evolving linguistic structure, was in a state of constant change. The activity of the analogical process intensified with an increase in the dynamics of the developments in the phonological system. The fact that the nominal system was never a static entity, even in the Proto-Germanic period, needs to be allowed for when characterising the reorganisation of the nominal inflection in the early Germanic languages.

An essential feature of interdeclensional shifts is their systematic nature across Germanic; that is why, despite all the "local" discrepancies in the patterns of reorganisation of the declensional systems in the individual Older Germanic languages, the major tendencies can be expected to run parallel and to be largely universal (i.e. pan-Germanic). Lahiri and Dresher (1984) relate this characteristic closely to the presence of "important forms" in the paradigm, on which the direction of analogical processes (and thus the mechanism of declension shifts) is largely reliant. Such a category in the nominal inflection of Germanic languages, occupying the highest position in the hierarchy of morphosyntactic categories, is the NOM. SG. The assumption of systematicity of declension shifts implies that "the choice of important forms is a principled one, itself perhaps the result of the interaction of developmental factors with universal grammar." (Lahiri & Dresher 1984: 159). Taking the findings of several later studies into account, especially those exploring the significance of frequency effects in morphological processes, these "important" forms can be interpreted as forms with higher frequency of occurrence. This view can already be found in Mańczak (1980) who claims that the most frequent forms in the paradigm show the highest resistance to change and are thus likely to serve as the basis for change in other forms. Much in the same line, Bybee (2007: 10) concludes that: "within a paradigm it is the higher frequency form that serves as the basis for the reformation".

An essential prerequisite for interdeclensional transfers is the existence of formal similarities across paradigms, with a range of overlapping inflectional features. The cross-paradigmatic similarities have been considered to be the major factor triggering analogical reshufflings between paradigms (Blevins 2004: 55). The early mergers that occurred in the Proto-Germanic period, for instance, the confluence of the NOM./ACC. SG. forms of the heavy-syllable *i*-stems with those of the *a*-stems, corroborate such a claim. The formal similarity of the NOM./ACC. SG. occasioned a gradual transition of the less productive historical *i*-stems to the productive class of *a*-stems. A similar development where the form of the NOM./ACC. SG. played a significant role was the prehistoric shift of the original *s*-stems to the *i*-stem declension, which can be explained as a generalisation of the PIE *-es-* formative in the NOM./ACC. SG., whereby this form fell together with the NOM./ACC. SG. of the *i*-stems (cf. OE *sige* 'victory' < *segiz and OE *i*-stem *wine* 'friend' < *weniz) (Casaretto 2000: 218). This formal similarity of the NOM. SG. of the *i*-stems and *s*-stems furthered the *inter*paradigmatic realignments between these two classes. On top of that, the analogical transfer of the original *s*-stems to the *i*-stem declension may have been facilitated by another cross-paradigmatic formal similarity, namely, the presence of the root vowel conducive to the operation of *i*-mutation (Unwerth 1910: 2).

Although the process of restructuring involving the extension of analogical inflections across paradigms affected primarily the minor stems, some traces of this development can also be found in the productive declensional classes. This refers not only to the traces of the productive vocalic inflections, *a*-stems and *ō*-stems, in the paradigms of the relatively productive *n*-stems (Adamczyk 2007), but also the presence of the *n*-stem inflections in the paradigms of both *a*-stems and *ō*-stems (Hogg & Fulk 2011).[14] Moreover, in Continental Germanic, traces of the masculine and feminine *i*-stem inflection, which constituted a fairly widespread inflectional pattern there, are to be found in the *a*-stem and *ō*-stem paradigms (e.g. in Old Saxon and Old High German), and, in turn, an interaction between the *ja*- and *i*-stems is commonly found in Old Saxon. Likewise, the conflation of the feminine *ō*-stem and *n*-stem patterns is very widespread in Old Low Franconian and Old High German. These analogical reshufflings involving interactions between two productive declensional types stay essentially beyond the purview of the present quantitative investigation and will be referred to only occasionally where relevant.

---

14. For details of the development of the *n*-stems in Germanic see Kroonen (2011).

An important question related to the mechanism of interdeclensional transfers refers to the rate of shifts to a new class, i.e. whether they occurred abruptly or gradually. This issue encompasses two aspects and can be split into two parts, i.e. (a) whether the analogical extension of new inflections affected the entire paradigms (all paradigm cells) simultaneously, and (b) whether the change involved *all* nouns belonging to a given declensional class (cf. Enger 2010). It can be assumed that the interdeclensional shifts occurred in terms of paradigms, or individual morpho-syntactic categories rather than in terms of entire declensional classes (e.g. Wurzel 1989: 126). The scope of the present study is extensive enough to gain insight into this aspect of the process of analogical remodelling of the nominal inflection.

What remains more problematic in this context is whether prior to following the "destination" declension, as demonstrated in the earliest attested sources, the nouns went through an intermediate stage, where they declined according to one of the minor or another major pattern. The evidence provided by the sister languages can sometimes give some clue about the potential intermediate paths of transition across declensional classes, but in general the details of the intermediate shifts are very difficult to capture. An example here is the OE feminine *i*-stem *ened*, *æned* 'duck', OS *anud* (MLG *ān(e)t*, *ēnde*), OLF *ened*, ON *önd*, OHG *anut*, *enita*, which originated in PGmc. **anud-/*anad-/*anid-*. It is believed to be an original root noun which was first attracted by the *u*-stems (at a prehistoric stage), and later transferred to the *i*-stems (*EWN*, s.v. *eend*).

Another closely related problem germane to the investigation of interde-clensional shifts is that of the *default* declensional class, i.e. the new inflectional pattern that the minor stems are most likely to follow. The template for the an-alogical transition of nouns was created by the most dominant and productive declensional classes, i.e. the *a*-stems and *ō*-stems, and these two classes can be considered *default*. However, as will be evident in the analysed data, the shift to a new declensional pattern oftentimes involved a stage when a given noun showed a predilection for more than one inflectional pattern. Accordingly, the variation found in the paradigms of minor stems may potentially testify to a competition between two different productive patterns. This refers in particular to a compe-tition between *a*-stems, *ō*-stems vs. *n*-stems and (to some extent) *i*-stems (e.g. in Old Saxon and Old Low Franconian). The question of default declensional class is essential in the context of interpreting a range of inflectional forms whose classi-fication as archaic/innovative or ambiguous depends on which class is considered to be the more likely direction of analogical transition.

1.3.3   Intraparadigmatic transfers

Aside from being exposed to external analogical pressures from other declensional classes, the nominal paradigms were also subject to the activity of analogical processes operating within the paradigms. *Intra*paradigmatic analogy involves an extension of a new inflectional form at the expense of other forms within one paradigm (e.g. Trask 1993). In some cases, especially in minor consonantal stems, it entailed also the elimination of the stem-vowel or stem-consonant alternation (i.e. the levelling of the *i*-mutated vowel and the *r*- and *þ*-formative). This type of analogical pressure dates back likewise to the prehistoric stage, and results in a number of syncretisms within the paradigms. Some well-known examples include the extension of the ACC. SG. form to the NOM. SG. in the OE light-syllable feminine root nouns, or a much more widespread extension of the NOM. form to the ACC. in all minor stems in the plural, attested in all West Germanic languages (Boutkan 1995, Ringe 2006; for details, see Section 2.2.4). In the historical period, the effects of intraparadigmatic analogy are evident especially in the elimination and extension of the *i*-mutated vowels from the paradigms of stems conducive to this process (e.g. in root nouns, *nd*-stems or *s*-stems), as well as the elimination and occasional extension of the consonantal elements (such as the *r*-formative in the *s*-stems and *þ*-formative in dental stems).

By influencing the internal structure of the paradigms, the intrapardigmatic pressure plays (indirectly) a significant role in the process of inflectional restructuring, often working as a factor enhancing or triggering extraparadigmatic analogical interactions. In the context of this study, the presence of the vocalic alternation (*i*-mutation) in the paradigm has a different effect than the presence of consonantal alternations (*r*-formative). While the former affects the shape of the root vowel, the latter, as a result of regular mergers between the stem and the vowels of inflectional syllables, turned out to be crucial for the shape of the inflectional ending rather than of the root (e.g OE *lamb*, PL. *lambru*). Accordingly, in contrast to consonantal alternations, the root vowel alternation, when accompanying an inflectional ending, is not taken into account as the sole criterion in the classification of forms as inherited or analogical. For instance, the DAT. SG. forms *æce* 'oak', *byrge* 'city' will be classified as innovative on account of their inflectional endings, despite the vestige of *i*-mutation retained in the root vowel (see individual chapters for a more detailed account). An exception here is the class of light-syllable root nouns in Old English, where the lack of *i*-mutated root vowel (in combination with the presence of an inflectional ending) is interpreted as an innovative feature (cf. analogical *hnute* 'nut' vs. inherited *hnyte*) (cf. Section 3.5.4). The indirect significance of intraparadigmatic alternations (*i*-mutation) can be well illustrated by the paradigms of the OE *nd*-stems and root nouns, where the elimination of the *i*-mutated vowels from the singular of (some of) the *nd*-stems or root nouns rendered these paradigms more uniform and thus possibly more vulnerable to the analogical pressure of inflections from other declensions.

1.3.4 Syncretism in nominal inflection in Old Germanic languages

The syncretisms present in the declensional systems of the early Germanic languages had a direct bearing on the restructuring process of the nominal inflection. In fact, many of the syncretisms can be dated already to the prehistoric period, both to Proto-Germanic and Proto-Indo-European. In the paradigms of nouns, just as in other areas of inflectional morphology, syncretisms are a result of two developments: phonological convergence and analogy (Coleman 1991: 200). The former involved large-scale reductions of vowels and consonants in unstressed syllables, which are well attested in all the investigated languages, especially at the later stage. Their effect was a significant decrease in the effectiveness of marking category distinctions across inflectional classes (Allen 1995: 163). Analogical developments involved an extension of one inflectional ending at the expense of another, such as the wide-ranging spread of the GEN. SG. *a*-stem marker *-es* to minor stems. Irrespective of the original source, syncretic developments were gradual, proceeding "not by massive confusion of forms, but by the encroachment of one form into the functional territory of another" (Allen 1995: 162).

An essential distinction which needs to be made when analysing instances of syncretism is between the syncretism of forms and syncretism of functions. These two types of syncretism are closely intertwined and in many cases the presence of the formal syncretism leads to a loss of a morphosyntactic category. In the nominal system of earliest attested Germanic many of the syncretisms are instances of formal syncretism, induced by the phonological reduction affecting unaccented syllables (such as the syncretism of the nominative and accusative in the *a*-stems and many minor stem classes). Despite their wide scope, these syncretisms had no effect on the loss of a category distinction. It is only at the later stage, for example, in Late Old English and especially in Early Middle English that the loss of important category distinctions takes place as well (most notably the merger of the accusative and dative).[15] At the same time, many functional syncretisms occurred already at the

---

15. Various degrees of syncretism can be distinguished, including sporadic syncretism, partial syncretism (affecting "all morphs of a particular case morpheme in one or more, but not in all, paradigms"), full syncretism (affecting all morphemes) and total syncretism (affecting all morphemes sharing the same case function, irrespective of number or gender) (Coleman 1991: 200). Instances of partial syncretism are very common in the nominal system of Germanic languages (e.g. GEN. SG. in Old English; the *i*-mutated vowel present in both the singular (DAT.) and the plural (NOM./ACC.) of root nouns and *nd*-stems); the syncretism of the dative and instrumental, both singular and plural, instantiates total syncretism.

prehistoric stage, eliminating the distinction between, for instance, the nominative and vocative, or the dative and instrumental (the latter retained largely apart in Old Saxon and to some extent in Old English and Old Frisian) (e.g. Ramat 1981: 61).[16]

The appearance of syncretism in paradigms is strongly correlated with the frequency of individual morphosyntactic categories. Syncretisms or syncretic forms tend to appear more frequently in rarer inflectional categories (and less frequent words/word types), which can be attributed to the greater difficulty involved in remembering the distinct forms when they do not occur too often (Croft 2003: 113; Haspelmath 2006: 20; Hawkins 2004).[17] Furthermore, case syncretisms in paradigms tend to involve cases which are placed in adjacent positions on the feature (markedness) hierarchy as defined by Greenberg (1966), i.e. nominative will tend to be syncretic with accusative, accusative with dative, etc. (Hawkins 2004: 66, 70). This is largely confirmed by the early Indo-European evidence where the most common conflations involved the nominative and accusative, or the dative and instrumental or ablative (rather than nominative and dative). According to Hawkins (2004: 77–78), the collapse of distinctions in the paradigms of Germanic languages complies with "the relative rankings of their respective hierarchy positions", with more syncretisms present in the lower positions on the hierarchy. This refers not only to the case marking hierarchy, but also to the number and gender marking hierarchies.

When analysing the declensional system of the early Germanic languages, it can be observed that some of the formal syncretisms are present in the paradigms of both major and minor classes from a very early stage. An instance of such widespread and early syncretism is that of the NOM./ACC. SG. and NOM./ACC. PL. in the neuter *a*-stems, which dates back to the prehistoric stage, and is found not only in all Germanic but also in all Indo-European languages (Ringe 2006: 42).[18] Some

---

16. Two conditions are considered necessary for a functional syncretism to take place, namely (a) "the degree of partial synonymy must be high enough to call for a reduction of redundancy, and (b) functional and possible formal merging of morphemes must not engender unacceptable ambiguity" (Luraghi 1987: 356; cf. Baerman et al. 2005: 38ff.).

17. Cf. Greenberg's Universal: "(…) distinctions existing in the unmarked member are often neutralized in the marked categories" (Greenberg 1966: 27). In other words, the marked member will tend to show syncretisation of the distinctions (e.g. inflectional contrasts).

18. Some of the early syncretisms emerged as a result of redundancy of marking distinctive case morphology. This refers to the neuter declensions in Indo-European languages, which due to their semantics, consistently lack distinctive inflections for the subject and direct-object relations (as they are more likely than masculines and feminines to appear as direct objects rather than subjects) (Plank 1987: 178; Clackson 2007: 177).

further examples of formal syncretisms found across declensional classes in Old Northern West Germanic languages include:

- the lack of formal differentiation between the NOM. and ACC. SG. in all masculine declensions (except the *n*-stems);
- the syncretism of the ACC., GEN. and DAT. in the OE, OFris. ō-stems (*-e*);
- the syncretism of the GEN. SG. and GEN. PL. in the OE, OFris. masculine and feminine *u*-stems;
- the syncretism of the ACC. SG. and ACC. PL. in the heavy-syllable ō-stems (OE) and masculine and feminine *n*-stems;
- the syncretism of the DAT. SG. and NOM./ACC. PL. in the OE, OS root nouns and in the *u*-stems;
- the syncretism of the NOM./ACC. SG. and NOM./ACC. PL. in the light-syllable masculine *i*-stems, *r*-stems and dissyllabic *nd*-stems.

All these numerous syncretisms present in the declensional system of the early Germanic languages affected the transparency of the system, rendering it unstable and thus susceptible to analogical pressures (cf. Section 2.2.2; Coleman 1991).

1.4   Theoretical framework

1.4.1   Introduction

Much as theoretical frameworks can offer valuable insights into the process of language change, their application in this primarily descriptive study of a comparative nature is rather limited. The present investigation is not strictly embedded in one specific theoretical model. Instead, a number of theoretical approaches and concepts taken from morphological theory, which were considered to have explanatory power for the mechanism of the restructuring of the nominal system in early Germanic languages, were employed and will be discussed in relation to individual aspects of the restructuring process. The present section is intended to introduce some basic concepts underlying the adopted approach.

Following the tradition of diachronic linguistics, the study concentrates primarily on surface phenomena rather than underlying grammatical structures formulated in a static system of grammatical principles. As regards the most general theoretical framework underpinning the present research, the work stays in the spirit of "dynamic philology" (Zipf 1936), exploited in numerous empirically-oriented studies, where corpus data analysis serves as a principal method for gaining insight into linguistic variation and change. Accordingly, the present study is primarily oriented towards a qualitative and quantitative framing of the observed morphological patterns. It employs the evidence from corpus analysis and cross-linguistic comparison, which gives the findings and observations a more general validity. The study takes recourse to a combination of theoretical concepts such as morphological productivity, morpho-phonological salience, or system economy, employing them to discuss and explain individual aspects of the restructuring process. In terms of narration and nomenclature, the present research draws on some of the insights of two morphological theories, i.e. the Markedness Theory and Natural Morphology (Mayerthaler 1980; Wurzel 1989, 1990, 2001; Dressler 1985a). Terms such as *markedness*, *iconicity* or *transparency* will be particularly useful not so much for explaining the patterns, but for framing the discussion of the relevant phenomena. On the conceptual plane, the work is most indebted to functionalist (Greenberg 1966; Bybee 1985, 2007), usage-based (Paul 1920, Langacker 1987, 1988, 1999; Bybee 1985, 1995, 2010) and deterministic approaches (Beckner et al. 2009), where language is conceived of as a dynamic system conditioned by a complex interplay of competing factors, which strives to achieve a balance and increase its functionality.[19] The theoretical paradigm known as usage-based model postulates that linguistic structure is shaped by or emerges from language use, and as such is dynamic as it is constantly changing by cognitive processes that are involved in language use (Langacker 1987, 1988, 1999; Bybee 1985, 1995, 2001; Diessel 2007). Language is thus not a "rigid, homogeneous, self-contained, or finely-balanced" system (Croft 2000: 231), but shows considerable dynamics and thus variation. In other words, language is viewed as a "probabilistic system of emergent structures and fluid constraints that are grounded in the language user's experience with concrete words and utterances" (Diessel 2016: 209). The inflectional variation found in the minor paradigms is a reflex of these dynamics, which tend to work towards preserving the functionality of the paradigms and the system. A central notion in this approach to language and language change is frequency of use/occurrence which is correlated with entrenchment and processing of linguistic constructions or expressions in the mental grammar (see Section 1.4.6.1 below). The use of linguistic expressions or structures reinforces their mental representation, having an effect on the "representation and activation of linguistic knowledge" (Diessel 2004: 23).

---

19. One of the essential features of this approach to language is that a linguistic system involves speakers in the speech community who interact with each other, and the linguistic structure is ultimately a result of "interrelated patterns of experience, social interaction, and cognitive mechanisms" (Beckner et al. 2009: 1–2). This characteristic is fully acknowledged in the present study, even if the descriptions of the inflectional developments offered depict language in a rather abstract way.

The changing nature of language is also the central issue in the approach to language as a complex adaptive system, where the fact that language is in a state of constant flux, change and reorganisation is referred to as *perpetual dynamics*. As a complex system defined through dynamical rules, language has a "fundamentally far-from-equilibrium nature" (Beckner et al. 2009: 13). The analogical transitions of nouns between classes are a reflex of this continuing change and remodelling that goes back to the prehistoric period. The interdeclensional shifts of nouns are not confined to one specific period in the history of Germanic languages, but their intensity and scope changes over time. Another property of language, as defined in the mentioned approach, and relevant in the context of the restructuring of nominal inflection is *adaptation through competing factors*, which "interact, and feed into each other, resulting in an expanding upward spiral" (Beckner et al. 2009: 13). The complexity of the emergent patterns will in principle depend on these factors and interactions between them. The restructuring of the nominal system is determined by a range of interacting and competing factors, the most prominent of them being the frequency of occurrence and the salience of inflectional markers, the latter being determined by phonological processes operating at the prehistoric stages of the Old Germanic languages. Probably the most basic characteristic of language as a complex adaptive system is its *intrinsic diversity*, which entails heterogeneity of linguistic structures, or the existence of variation visible at all levels of linguistic structure. This is reflected also in the nominal morphology of individual languages (as they are attested in the extant written records), with the existing inflectional variation (irregular patterns) reflecting a lack of a single homogenous linguistic system. This micro-variation is only to a limited extent explored in this study, but it must have been part of the variation present in the speech communities of the past. Finally, there is also a cognitive dimension to framing language in terms of an adaptive system, which can be considered the underlying mechanism; namely, language can be said to be "fundamentally molded by the pre-existing cognitive abilities, processing idiosyncrasies and limitations, and general and specific conceptual circuitry of the human brain." (Beckner et al. 2009: 17). In other words, the linguistic structure will always emerge within the bounds of these cognitive capacities and will be shaped by cognitive processes.

The dismantling of the complexity inherent in language reveals the interrelated patterns of linguistic organisation, existing at various levels. As these patterns are pertinent to a system which is constantly changing, they can be viewed as emerging patterns. The changes in the nominal inflection and their dynamics as found in the earliest attested stages of Northern West Germanic give a perfect opportunity for capturing the transformation of the (morphological) system, involving the emergence of new patterns.

1.4.2 Analogy

According to Anttila (1977: 69), "all change mechanisms have an analogical in-gredient"; analogy[20] can be accordingly viewed as the main driving force in the evolution of linguistic structure and as "an agent of change" (Anttila 2003: 431; cf. Paul 1920).[21] In the process of reorganisation of the nominal systems in the early Germanic languages, this "great diachronic engine[…]" (Collinge 1985: 249) has played a fundamental role. The developments in the nominal inflection of the Older Germanic languages illustrate in detail the working of the process of analogy, since the change of declensional affiliation of nouns relies on the mechanisms of analogy. Nominal inflection in the Old Germanic languages constituted a robust territory for the operation of analogical processes. The existence of an elaborated system of case-and-number inflections as well as gender classes, which showed many formal similarities and syncretisms, was particularly suited for the activity of both intraparadigmatic and interparadigmatic analogy. The formal similarities existing across paradigms affiliated with different declensions (such as syncretic inflectional markers) facilitated analogical reformulation of the inflectional profiles of the inherited classes (e.g. the spread of the GEN. SG. marker from the *a*-stems to other declensions, which occurred partly prehistorically). The similarities found within a single paradigm induced analogical interactions of forms in the paradigm, which resulted, for instance, in the elimination of allomorphic variation from the singular paradigm, as in the OE *nd*-stems or OE, OFris. root nouns.[22] The para-digms of minor stems emerge as particularly well-suited targets for the working of analogical processes due to the fact that most of them were characterised by a lack of distinctive inflectional endings, which was only in some classes (in consonantal

---

20. The term has been used in a variety of ways and a number of definitions, often conflicting, exist. It is not the purpose of this study to explore the different meanings the term may have. The section discusses only those aspects of analogy which are relevant to the phenomenon under study. For more details, see Antilla (1977, 2003), Itkonen (2005), Fertig (2013).

21. This view has been shared by many linguists and a more recent opinion on the study of analogical mechanisms was formulated by Blevins & Blevins (2009): "Nearly all grammatical traditions have regarded analogy as a central determinant of the form and evolution of linguistic subsystems, though it is only with the advent of better modeling techniques that it has become possible to investigate the psycholinguistic reality of analogical patterns and to represent and even measure the analogical pressures on a system." (Blevins & Blevins 2009: 10).

22. On the criticism of explaining changes such as the elimination of *i*-mutation from the nom-inal paradigms as instances of meliorative change, see Lass (1997a). One of the major objections to such explanations is that it implies that languages (i.e. speakers) strive towards some desired configuration (p. 345).

stems) compensated by the presence of morphophonemic alternation serving as an exponent of morphosyntactic categories.

Formally, two phenomena of analogical nature seem to be involved in the process of the remodelling of the nominal inflection: analogical levelling and four-part analogy, the latter operating on the basis of a proportional model (as defined by Hock 1986 and 2003; McMahon 1994: 72; cf. Fertig 2013: 47–51).[23] The generalisation of the inflectional pattern of the productive types to minor paradigms is an instantiation of the latter. Intraparadigmatic changes, such as the elimination of consonantal or vocalic alternation from the paradigm, involved levelling, whereby morphophonological alternations are eliminated by an extension of one stem alternant to other stem forms in the paradigm.[24] The stem form which is extended across the paradigm is largely determined by frequency of use (Haspelmath & Sims 2010: 273).

One of the essential conditions which render proportional analogy successful is that the pattern that is generalised should be productive (Hock 2003: 441). In the context of the restructuring of the nominal paradigms, this productivity is closely related to type frequency: the most expansive declensional classes, the *a*-stems or *ō*-stems, were characterised by high type frequency, i.e. they comprised many nouns. Another condition for the operation of analogy is related to the overall shape of the declensional system, in particular the existence of asymmetries between declensional classes, as argued, for instance, by Coleman (1991): "At the morphological level itself analogy was the major disruptive force, but it could only operate where there was already some asymmetry between declensions (…)" (Coleman 1991: 199). The asymmetries refer to the presence of formal syncretisms across paradigms, which activated the operation of analogical processes. This complies with the assumptions made in the computational model of analogy (Skousen 1989, 1992), where it is posited that the more shared features a given paradigm or set of words has, the greater the probability that this paradigm (pattern) will be used as the basis for analogical remodelling.

In very general terms, the mechanism of analogy involved the following components: (1) the formal similarity of case forms across paradigms served as the

---

23. For a discussion of the distinction between proportional and non-proportional analogy and the controversial status of a range of changes with respect to this contrast, see Fertig (2013: 43ff).

24. In more strict terms, the levelling as defined by Hock (1986) refers essentially to the elimination of stem alternation. However, the exact definition of this term poses some difficulties, and levelling has been interpreted in many ways, with the main theoretical question being whether it can be considered to be a proportional or non-proportional mechanism (see Fertig 2013: 71–76). It has also been understood in broader terms as referring to regularisation and not strictly to elimination of alternations (e.g. Blevins & Blevins 2009: 6; Campbell 2004: 106), and this broader interpretation will be adopted in the present study.

trigger for analogical change; (2) the template for analogical modification was provided by the productive declensional classes, especially the *a*-stems, *ō*-stems and *n*-stems, and gender played an important role in that it directed the process; (3) the substance for analogical replacement was supplied by minor stems, which were susceptible to analogical innovations, either because they had idiosyncratic or rare case-and-number exponents, or were characterised by zero endings, lacking thus explicit marking. Theoretically, the extension of analogical inflection could have involved the entire declensional patterns rather than individual inflectional endings. Such a mechanism has been referred to as *structural* analogy and defined as: "the analogical extension of a valid structural model (or internal pattern of case oppositions and syncretisms) replacing an earlier model whose internal configuration violates the principles and rules of the declensional system" (Igartua 2005: 298). The application of this type of analogy will be discussed in more detail in Chapter 4, where the changes in the OFris. *i*-stems can be interpreted as an instantiation of structural analogy (cf. also Thöny 2013 who discusses such structural analogical shifts for prehistoric Germanic). However, in the majority of cases, as will become evident in the course of the investigation, the process of restructuring involved the extension of analogical inflections in individual morphosyntactic categories rather than entire paradigms (see the discussion in Chapter 8).

Analogy operating within paradigms (i.e. intraparadigmatic analogy) entailed the levelling of morphophonemic alternations, i.e. *i*-mutation and consonantal alternations (-*r*, -*ð*-formative) from the paradigms. As stated by Hock (2003: 442), "the process is most successful if the alternations do not signal important morphological distinctions". In other words, analogical changes tend to adhere to the hierarchy of morphosyntactic categories, including the case/number hierarchy. Accordingly, the elimination of the *i*-mutated vowel from the paradigm of the singular of the root nouns or *nd*-stems (i.e. from the DAT. SG. and the replacement by its unmutated equivalent, as in OE *fēt* → *fōt* 'foot') had different dynamics from the elimination of the *i*-mutated vowel from the plural paradigm, where it served to mark a significant morphosyntactic contrast, namely the singular vs. plural distinction (especially once the *i*-mutated vowel was eliminated from the singular). Therefore, the operation of analogical levelling tends to be more successful in the singular paradigm, where the contrast is less crucial.

The study of analogical mechanisms can hardly be pursued without reference to phonological developments and the intricate interaction that exists between these two linguistic mechanisms. Traditionally the interplay between phonology and analogy has been framed in terms of the so called Sturtevant's Paradox (Sturtevant 1947: 109), which states that sound change which is regular produces irregularity (e.g. by introducing allomorphic variation into the paradigm), while analogical change, being irregular, produces regularity (e.g. by eliminating allomorphic variation from paradigms). In the later studies on analogy this straightforward correlation was considered not entirely adequate and some refinements were suggested. In a somewhat amended version proposed by Hock (2003: 457), the relation between these two mechanisms of language change has been defined as follows: "Sound change typically is regular, and morphologically or semantically motivated analogy typically is irregular; but phonologically motivated analogy (such as morphophonemic and rule extension) tends to be as regular as sound change, and changes such as dissimilation and metathesis require a general phonological motivation to become regular." (cf. for a similar reformulation Fertig 2013: 97–98 who emphasises that there is nothing paradoxical about the way sound change and analogy interact). In the present study, this interaction can be well captured as many of the analogical developments occurring in and across the paradigms can be considered a direct reaction to a range of phonological processes which affected final (unaccented) vowels in inflectional syllables (*Auslautgesetze*) (cf. Section 2.2.2).

Finally, it is worth emphasising that analogy should not be viewed as a factor triggering the developments in the inflectional system of the Older Germanic languages, but it was rather the main mechanism involved in the reorganisation of the nominal inflection.

1.4.3 Markedness

One of the concepts employed across several morphological theories, which will be relevant for the present study is *markedness*. The concept has found a wide range of applications in linguistics, making its way through various theoretical frameworks (e.g. Croft 2003, Haspelmath 2006). It is one of the central notions used in the framework of Natural Morphology (e.g. Wurzel 1988), but was the focus of scholarly attention already much earlier;[25] notably, Greenberg (1966) associated the concept of markedness with frequency, arguing that the most frequent categories tend to be *unmarked*. This general, theory-independent application of the term has been explored, among others, by Haspelmath (2006: 27), who argues that "'markedness' lost its association with a particular theoretical approach and became established as an almost theory-neutral everyday term in linguistics", acquiring thus a "polysemous" nature.

Admittedly, the concept of markedness is very broad and encompasses a range of senses, not all of which will be relevant in the context of the present investigation.

---

25. The concept goes back ultimately to the Prague School linguists, i.e. the works of Trubetzkoy and Jakobson (1930s). For a detailed overview and criticism of the concept, see Haspelmath (2006).

One of the senses in which the term will be used in the present study is *formal markedness*, understood as "coding complexity" (entailing overt and covert marking). Accordingly, "marked" refers to "overtly coded" in contrast to unmarked, i.e. "uncoded" (Haspelmath 2006: 30). Another sense of markedness relevant in the context of the present study is *semantic markedness*. It is implicated in the concept of constructional iconicity, as formulated in the Natural Morphology framework, where it correlates with *formal markedness*. Morphological structures that have the property of constructional iconicity, i.e. the semantic content is expressed in them by form/construction, are generally preferred, or, in other words, natural.[26] Both formal and semantic markedness are relevant for defining the salience of inflectional exponents and their hierarchy on the salience scale.

Markedness has also been defined as "rarity in texts", which refers to systematic skewings in the text frequency of forms/constructions (Haspelmath 2006: 33). As mentioned earlier, the role of frequency in explaining markedness asymmetries has been underscored already by Greenberg (1966), who generally considered frequency to have an explanatory power in linguistic mechanisms. The significance of frequency of use in defining markedness was also postulated by Haspelmath (2006), who in his critique of the concept demonstrates that it (in its many senses) can easily be replaced by frequency (cf. Mańczak 1970). The view is shared also by Hawkins (2004), according to whom markedness hierarchies (as formulated by Greenberg 1966) can be interpreted as "conventionalizations of performance frequency rankings" (Hawkins 2004: 64). In accordance with this principle, the nominative case which is more frequent than the accusative will tend to be unmarked (expressed by zero forms), and by the same token singular in contrast to plural will tend to be unmarked. Much in a similar vein, Diessel (2007) defines the notion of (typological) markedness as referring to "crosslinguistic asymmetries in the encoding of grammatical phenomena" that are actually shaped by the frequency of use over time, i.e. frequency effects of diachronic change (Diessel 2007: 119).

With reference to nominal morphology, markedness is most commonly used to define the status of inflectional exponents and morphosyntactic categories. Nouns which are inflectionally marked are those whose "inflection class membership is relatively unpredictable on purely extramorphological (phonological, syntactic or semantic) grounds" (Carstairs-McCarthy 1991: 230). In other words, the predictability of inflection class membership based on these criteria renders the forms unmarked (or natural). The concept of markedness is involved also in

---

26. In the Natural Morphology framework, markedness is viewed as a concept which is not only descriptive but also has explanatory power, involving formulations about structural preferences in language (see also Wurzel 1989: 195ff. on the explanatory power of the concept of naturalness in general, cf. Lass 1980).

the interpretation of the hierarchy of individual grammatical categories, defined by Hawkins (2015: 218) as "markedness hierarchies" of features such as case and number. This feature hierarchy was specified by Greenberg (1966) and with regard to case marking involves the following order (Hawkins 2004: 64):

NOMINATIVE > ACCUSATIVE > DATIVE > other

According to Hawkins (2004, 2015), these feature hierarchies (both of case and number (singular > plural > dual > trial) are tightly linked to frequency of use, "correspond[ing] to performance frequency hierarchies in languages with rich morphological inventories" (Hawkins 2004: 64–68; Greenberg 1966; Croft 2003). Accordingly, the nominative as the least marked case is also the most frequent one, while genitive, used less frequently, is considered marked. Consequently, it can be expected that changes that affect individual features (cases or morphosyntactic categories) follow the frequency patterns, or in other words, are determined by frequency of use.[27] The lower positions on the feature hierarchy will tend to collapse distinctions before all higher positions. For instance, the distinctions in the plural will tend to be more readily reduced than in the singular, and the contrasts in the neuter paradigm will tend to be collapsed before those in masculine and feminine paradigms (Hawkins 2004: 78; Dahl & Koptjevskaja-Tamm 2006).

An aspect of markedness which will find its application in the present study, in that it will account for some patterns of the restructuring of inflection, is "local markedness", which results from "markedness reversal", as originally formulated by Tiersma (1982) (see also Mayerthaler 1980: 48ff.; Croft 2003: 135; Haspelmath & Sims 2010: 270–272). It refers to a context in which categories that are unmarked follow the marked patterns, and consequently the markedness patterns are reversed. The concept of local markedness is entirely dependent on frequency of use, which in turn largely relies on "real-world considerations", i.e. semantic factors (Tiersma 1982: 834). Its heavy reliance on frequency of use supports the explanation of the concept of markedness in terms of frequency. In his study devoted to English and Frisian nominal morphology, Tiersma argued that in certain contexts a category such as the singular, which is generally considered to be unmarked, can appear as marked. A crucial observation made in the study was that a plural-singular ratio higher than one favoured the retention of irregular plural forms. In other words, the more frequent (and irregular) plural tended to survive better than the less frequent singular. With such a plural-singular ratio, the plural becomes the unmarked form

---

27. A clear distinction needs to be made by mergers between these cases occurring as a result of phonological developments, which across Germanic is very often the case in the singular (e.g. NOM./ACC. SG.), and the mergers motivated by morphological factors, which appear primarily in the plural (e.g. NOM./ACC. PL.).

in contrast to the marked singular. In more general terms, the markedness reversal in this aspect of nominal morphology involves the following correlation: the nouns occurring more frequently in the plural tend to be characterised by unmarked plural and marked singular.

The concept of local markedness can be used to account for the anomalous (inflectional) behaviour of certain classes of nouns. For instance, in English certain nouns denoting animals that typically occur in pairs or groups, and are thus more frequently used in the plural, do not carry a plural marker (e.g. *fish*, *deer*, *sheep*, *moose*); consequently, it is the plural that can be considered unmarked in these nouns. The concept is defined as follows: "When the referent of a noun naturally occurs in pairs or groups, and/or when it is generally referred to collectively, such a noun is locally unmarked in the plural" (Tiersma 1982: 835). As a result, analogical change is less likely to affect the plural, which is the unmarked category, than the singular in such nouns.

In order to account for the mechanism involved in the reversal of markedness patterns, Haspelmath (2015: 204) resorts to economic motivations. Namely, the reversed pattern of markedness is interpreted as a competition between system economy and system pressure. In instances where plural is more frequent, consti-tuting thus the category of "unmarked", while the singular is overtly marked, it is the system economy that wins over system pressure, in compliance with the assumption that the shorter the form, the more economical it is. Much as this mechanism works for some non-Germanic languages (especially Welsh, adduced by the author), in the examples mentioned above (of the type *sheep*), the system pressure and econ-omy pressure are rather in balance and neither overrules the other. Haspelmath's account of the dominant economy pressure would involve a theoretical situation, where the PDE plural 'sheep' would require a new overtly marked singular form (e.g. **sheeper). In contrast, a case in which the system pressure wins over economy pressure involves the rare instances of the type *breech – breeches*, where the more frequent unmarked plural acquires a new ending. This development occurs only after the extension of the plural root (*brēc*) to the singular, at the expense of the original singular form *brōc*, complying with the economy pressure, which works in favour of the more frequent plural form.[28]

---

28. A similar case is the development of Modern Icelandic *gæs – gæsir* 'goose – geese' < Old Icelandic *gás – gæs*: first, the economy pressure pushes the less frequent singular form out, and consequently, the system pressure works towards adding a new plural ending. The first stage of this development, involving the elimination of the less frequent singular allomorph, can be found in North Frisian, with *täis – täis* 'tooth – teeth', where *täis* < OFris. *tēth* 'teeth'.

A final observation about markedness regards the fact that the concept can also be interpreted in the context of structural complexity, in line with the claim made by Croft (2003): "the marked value of a grammatical category will be expressed by at least as many morphemes as is the unmarked value of that category" (Croft 2003: 92). This implies that the marked structures or values will tend to be more complex than the corresponding unmarked ones (cf. the singular, predominantly unmarked in Germanic vs. mostly marked plural). The link between markedness and complexity is manifested also on the formal level, referring to the formal complexity. According to Greenberg (1966: 29): "An unmarked form will have at least as many allomorphs or paradigmatic irregularities as the marked form." This implies that the marked forms can be expected to be more uniform, i.e. characterised by less allomorphy (for instance, in early Germanic the GEN. and DAT. PL. tend to be more uniform across classes than the NOM. and ACC. PL., which are much more differentiated; see Section 1.4.6.2 for a discussion of complexity).

In the context of analysing the developments in the nominal system of the early Germanic languages, the use of the notion of markedness is practical, especially as the term acquired the mentioned theory-neutral status, which makes it very appealing to a study not committed to one particular morphological theory. Accordingly, this term, as well as the related terms of uniformity and transparency of paradigms, will be used in the present study, even if their actual meaning in fact amounts to pure frequency effects.

1.4.4 Iconicity, uniformity and transparency of the paradigms

In the Natural Morphology framework, constructional iconicity, uniformity and transparency are the three major properties of morphological structures, considered to be universal naturalness parameters. It is expected that morphological structures (e.g. paradigms) fulfilling these three criteria are natural and thus sustainable, i.e. resistant to modification and change. The concept of *constructional iconicity* refers to the relationship between form and meaning, which ideally should be one to one. In other words, an increase in semantic content should always correspond to an increase in formal shape, i.e. a new meaning should always be expressed by a new form (Wurzel 1989; cf. Haiman 1983, 1994). Accordingly, the presence of zero marking, allomorphy or double/redundant marking as formal exponents of morphosyntactic categories is disfavoured, as all of these inflectional markers violate to a lesser or greater extent the principle of iconicity (Dammel & Kürschner 2008: 248). For the same reason the presence of syncretic inflections is not preferred (e.g. English *deer* – PL. *deer*). The concept of *uniformity* refers broadly speaking to the shape of the paradigm, in which the stem should preferably be invariant. In other words, paradigms in which stem morphemes lack allomorphy tend to be preferred, i.e. are more natural. Accordingly, suffixation as a way of expressing morphosyntactic relations will be preferred to stem alternation (such as *i*-mutation or consonantal alternations), as it allows the stem form to remain unchanged throughout the paradigm (cf. Bybee & Newman 1995 and Section 1.2). The principle of *transparency*, as defined in the framework of Natural Morphology, is in a way a direct effect of constructional iconicity. It assumes that one category/inflectional exponent should have only one function; in other words, homonymy, whether of inflectional exponents or morphological paradigms, should be avoided (cf. Haspelmath 2006: 31). Transparency of paradigms is considered to be a vital criterion for the stability of declensional classes. The paradigms which are more transparent tend to be resistant to the pressure of analogical features from other declensions. The Proto-Germanic inflectional system cannot be considered entirely transparent, as the morphological paradigms were typically characterised by homonymy, with one morpheme serving the function of marking both case and number. With the gradual (partial) elimination of fused encoding, observable in the attested stages of Germanic, the transparency of the nominal system tended to gradually increase.

The relevance of the discussed universal naturalness parameters, however, has been questioned by linguists working within other morphological frameworks. One of the objections against the concept of constructional iconicity is that it does not comply with the principles related to the efficiency of the forms/system, and in fact, it often works against efficiency. Inspired by the principle of economy as formulated by Haiman (1983), Hawkins (2004) postulated the Minimize Forms principle, which defines the general efficiency factors, expressing a preference of human processor for minimising the formal complexity of linguistic forms (phoneme, morpheme, word). The reduction in formal complexity, according to the author, occurs "in proportion to ease of processing, including frequency (as well as the number of forms with unique conventionalized property assignments, thereby assigning more properties to fewer forms") (Hawkins 2015: 223). What is essential in the context of the present study is that the formal complexity is believed to be dependent on frequency, i.e. frequency (alongside the ease of processing) has a regulating effect in defining the shape of morphological structures or forms.

This evident link between frequency of occurrence and iconicity, uniformity and transparency has been analysed also by Haspelmath (2006: 32), who considers frequency to have enormous explanatory power in morphological mechanisms. According to Haspelmath (2006), the three universal naturalness parameters, just as the concept of markedness, can be explained by reference to frequency of occurrence, including type and token frequency, and the regular mechanisms of language change.[29] Accordingly, the concept of constructional iconicity can be to a large extent explained by recourse to the economy principle, going back to the studies of Zipf (1936), which involves frequency of occurrence and predictability. Based on the assumption that "frequency implies predictability", it can be concluded that signs or items used more frequently will tend to be more predictable and, in line with the economy of effort principle, will tend to be shorter. Likewise, the principle of transparency and its effects, according to Haspelmath (2006: 59), are dependent on frequency: the morphological categories which are not very frequent tend to be less diversified (more syncretic) than the more frequent categories, because the distinctions in these rare categories are harder to remember. The final principle, i.e. the principle of uniformity which postulates that forms without allomorphy are preferred can be interpreted in the context of frequency as well, namely the elimination of allomorphy from the paradigms seems to be largely dependent on frequency (Bybee 1985: 119–123). The forms which are irregular, i.e. characterised by some morphophonemic alternations, tend to be regularised, while allomorphic alternations present in highly frequent words tend to be resistant to regularisation and thus stable. Such an approach to these theoretical concepts gives the frequency of use the major explanatory power (see Section 1.4.6.1 below on frequency effects). The fact that all of them have an apparent link to frequency indicates that frequency may be one of the major forces behind the changes in inflectional morphology.

1.4.5 Productivity and paradigm stability

The concept of productivity, which plays an essential role in analogical change, is crucial for interpreting the developments in nominal morphology, which were largely analogy-driven. As with the concept of markedness, productivity has been defined in many ways and frameworks, and with reference to various linguistic levels (e.g. Wurzel 1989, Bybee 1995; Bauer 2004, Gardani 2013).[30] In the study of

---

29. In contrast, in the approach presented by Mayerthaler (1980), where the major factor explaining morphological patterns is *naturalness*, frequency does not have any explanatory value, but is rather viewed as an epiphenomenon of markedness (Bauer 2004: 49): the less marked forms or constructions tend to be more frequent than the marked ones (Mayerthaler 1980: 136–140).

30. Most studies and thus definitions of morphological productivity focus on the productivity of patterns and processes in derivational morphology rather than inflectional morphology. A notable exception is the comprehensive study by Gardani (2013), focusing on inflectional productivity. In the present study the focus remains on the productivity of inflectional (declensional) patterns and inflectional markers.

inflectional morphology, productivity can be analysed with reference to inflectional classes or patterns, or individual inflectional exponents. Irrespective of the exact theoretical approach, it seems that the major (although not the sole) determinant of productivity of a given inflectional class is the frequency of occurrence/use, in particular type frequency (cf. Baayen 2009).[31] According to Bybee (1995, 2010), type frequency plays a major role in the determination of both morphological productivity and regularity: "the higher the type frequency the greater the productivity or the likelihood that a construction will be extended to new items" (Bybee 2010: 66). In other words, "(…) the greater the number of types in a construction, the more bases there are for the item-based analogy that creates novel instances of the construction." (Bybee 2013: 62). According to Baayen (1992), productivity does not rely solely on type frequency, but it is rather a result of an interaction of type frequency, token frequency and phonology: "type frequency, token frequency and shared patterns of phonological similarity jointly determine the qualitative output of the model" (Baayen 1992: 142). Also in the framework of Natural Morphology productivity is derived from type frequency, and a number of other factors related to inflectional class stability (Wurzel 2001). In all the investigated Germanic languages, the most productive declensional classes were the *a*-stems, *ō*-stems and *n*-stems (and to some extent the *i*-stems), which were characterised by high type frequency. In contrast, all the remaining declensional classes, including root nouns, *u*-stems, *s*-stems, *r*-stems, *nd*-stems, and dental stems, showed much lower type frequency and were clearly unproductive.

Another important determinant of productivity in the interpretation proposed by Bybee (2010) is *schematicity* (Bybee 1995: 430; Bybee 2010: 67), which involves the degree of dissimilarity of the class members, where the *schemas* refer to generalisations created by set of words characterised by similar patterns of semantic and phonological connections. The productivity of a given schema depends on (a) the defining properties of the schema and (b) its strength, "derivable from the number of items that reinforce the schema" (Bybee 1995: 430). The more open the schema, i.e. the fewer restrictions on the items to which it can apply, the more productive it is. Highly schematic classes will comprise many class members. In contrast, classes where the defining criteria are more specific, i.e. the degree of similarity is high, will tend to be less *schematic* and thus less productive. Accordingly,

---

31. Also phonological properties can be the determinant of morphological productivity (Diessel 2004: 32). The well recognised piece of evidence against the claim that type frequency determines productivity is the German *s*-plural inflection, which is productive despite constituting a minority pattern (low type frequent), e.g. in nouns ending in an unstressed vowel other than /ə/ (e.g. Köpcke 1988; Wurzel 1989: 146–147).

in this interpretation, the productive classes are characterised by both high type frequency and high schematicity. This condition is indeed fulfilled by classes such as the *a*-stems, *ō*-stems or *n*-stems in all the investigated languages, and to some extent by the *i*-stems in Continental Germanic dialects.

The concept of productivity has often been associated with that of the *default*, equivalent to general or predominant (Zwicky 1986), and accordingly, a productive inflectional class can be considered at the same time a default inflectional class. Although in many cases such an equation is relevant (e.g. present-day English plural marker *-(e)s*), these two concepts need not necessarily overlap (Bauer 2004: 61ff). Sometimes a noun may shift to a declensional class which is not more productive but equaly productive. An example may be the shift of certain German nouns to a class characterised by the presence of the *i*-mutated vowel in the plural (as in *der General/Admiral, der Mops* 'pug', die *Generale/Admiral-e/Mops-e* > *die Generäl-e, Admiräl-e, Möps-e*) (Dressler 2003: 42). Clearly, the inflectional pattern with *i*-mutation cannot be considered the default pattern in Modern German, and yet it attracts nouns affiliated originally with other declensional types. The German material demonstrates that the default marker can be "a minority form" in contrast to English where the default marker *(e)s* is "the only productive one" (Bauer 2004: 62) (see the discussion in Chapter 7).

This implies as well that productivity of morphological patterns, here inflectional patterns, is a gradual phenomenon and changes over time. In other words, it means that certain inflectional patterns are either more or less productive than others, and that fully productive and entirely unproductive patterns mark the extreme poles of a scale. The competition between two productive classes in the Older Germanic languages is essentially better attested in Continental Germanic languages, as the present analysis will reveal. In Continental Germanic the dominant vocalic *a*-stems and *ō*-stems show some competition with the *n*-stems and *i*-stems. In English, the gradualness of morphological productivity of certain patterns is well manifested only in the Middle English period, where the plural marker *-en* (< *-an*) competes with the plural inflections of the dominant *a*-stems and *ō*-stems.

In the present study, the application of the terms 'productive' and 'unproductive' follows the definition provided by Wurzel (1987: 87–92), where type frequency is the underlying parameter. According to the author, the main criterion for the productivity of an inflectional class is its 'openness' or scope, manifested in three main properties: (a) extension of an inflectional class by borrowing and neologisms; (b) extension of an inflectional class through transferrals from other classes and (c) maintenance of the present word inventory, or in other words, resistance to losing words to other inflectional classes (cf. Wurzel 1989: 149).[32] An inflectional class which does not show any of the above-mentioned features is considered unproductive. This definition complies to a large extent with the one found in Bauer (2004: 1–2, 12, 25), where three main prerequisites for productivity are identified, i.e. frequency, semantic coherence and the ability to create new forms (Bauer 2004: 20).[33] The question of semantic coherence and its role in morphological productivity is controversial. In general, it refers to internal coherence of a pattern and can involve different levels, namely phonological, morphological and semantic (e.g. van Marle 1985: 54). With regard to inflectional morphology, it has been observed in earlier studies (e.g. Kürschner 2008: 376) that homogeneity of declensional classes, understood as semantic coherence, works against their productivity. This seems to be confirmed by the smaller and semantically uniform classes, such as the *r*-stems (denoting nouns of relationship), or *s*-stems (denoting animals), which tend to be unproductive.

Importantly, productivity of a given inflectional class, as defined here, is only *potential* and "for [it] to become effective in extending morphological phenomena to new instances, another purely factual precondition is essential, namely the existence of 'candidates' to which inflectional classes or markers can be extended" (Wurzel 1989: 157). In line with the above-defined criteria, the classes known as minor, i.e. *u*-stems, root nouns, *r*-stems, *s*-stems, *nd*-stems and dental stems, are unproductive and constitute good candidates to which analogical inflections, extended from the productive classes, i.e. the masculine and neuter *a*-stems, feminine *ō*-stems and *n*-stems, can be attached.[34] The class of *i*-stems has a fairly ambiguous status as its assignment to either of the types depends on the language: in most of the North Sea Germanic (OE and OFris.), the class can be clearly viewed as unproductive, but in Continental Germanic, including here Old Saxon, it shows considerable traces of productivity, as will become evident in the course of the investigation. That is the reason why this declensional class is interpreted differently in the respective languages, with consequences for the applied method of quantitative investigation (cf. Section 1.5.3).

---

32. The definition of productivity as formulated by Wurzel (1989) is in fact more complex, and a number of additional factors are taken into consideration. In general, productivity is defined by recourse to the concept of system congruity and class stability, and a close interaction between them (Wurzel 1989: 112ff.).

33. Bauer (2004) offers a detailed analysis of productivity and comes up with a definition that takes into account a wide range of factors that interact and determine productivity (see Bauer 2004: 60).

34. The class of *r*-stems has occasionally been considered productive in the sense that "it contained all its potential lexical stock" (Bertacca 2009: 120). The class is considered unproductive in this investigation.

The concept of morphological productivity when referring to inflectional morphology is tightly linked to the idea of stability of paradigms and morphological patterns. Paradigms and morphological patterns which are stable will tend to be more productive. When analysing morphological stability patterns, Coleman (1991) enumerates a number of morphological criteria needed to guarantee the stability of a paradigm. They include: the number of variations in paradigmatic pattern, the average percentage of distinct morphs in each paradigm, the average percentage of distinct morphs per morpheme, and the asymmetry of the system. The overall conclusion is that the fewer syncretisms in the paradigm, the more stable it tends to be. It implies that a non-diversified paradigm, i.e. one containing few distinct markers, can be viewed as an instable pattern and in such a paradigm stability will try to be resumed by attraction of distinctive markers from other declensional classes. If these criteria are applied to the nominal systems of the investigated Old Germanic languages, it can be concluded that hardly any of the attested paradigms can be considered stable. The presence of numerous formal syncretisms in the nominal paradigms, as demonstrated in Section 1.3.4, was one of the characteristic features of the nominal system of the early Germanic languages. Given the different formal make-up of individual declensional classes and paradigms, the degree of stability will vary also depending on the declensional type. The only class which seems to comply with the enumerated stability criteria is the class of *a*-stems in Old English, which will be the subject of discussion in Chapter 3.[35]

Morphological stability of paradigms and morphological patterns can be disrupted by phonological developments (especially reductions in unstressed syllables), analogical mechanisms (although these can also work as a way of restoring stability disturbed earlier by phonological changes), and potentially syntactic changes. The stability of inflectional exponents can be affected primarily by phonological developments. The destabilising effect of phonology is evident, for instance, in the development of the OE, OFris. DAT. PL. marker *-um*. The phonological reduction (*-um* > *-en*) occurred despite the fact that the ending *-um* was morphologically a very stable marker, serving as an exponent of this category across all declensional classes, both major and minor (Coleman 1991: 208).

---

35. The concept of paradigm stability is not entirely equivalent to class stability as postulated by Wurzel (1989). The latter is essentially dependent on paradigm-structure conditions as defined in the Natural Morphology framework, in that the stable inflectional classes are those whose paradigms follow the "dominant paradigm structure condition, applying to words having the relevant extramorphological properties", while unstable inflectional classes are those whose paradigms follow a pattern that "does not agree with the dominant-paradigm structure condition" (Wurzel 1989: 125–126).

The concept which is related to stability of paradigms and inflectional exponents is that of *superstable* markers (*überstabile Marker*). The term was introduced
by Wurzel (1987: 82–83; 1989) and refers to inflectional exponents which show a
remarkable degree of stability and therefore can be found across various paradigms
of a given declensional system, but they do not directly affect the stability of a given
declension or system. An example of such a marker is the aforementioned DAT. PL.
inflection *-um* (*-un*), found in all investigated languages across all declensional
types, or the GEN. PL. marker *-a* whose scope is similarly wide. These superstable
markers derive always from productive classes and their spread is described in
terms of an 'avalanche effect': the spread of a marker to a new inflectional class increases its stability and the potential to transfer further to other declensions (Wurzel
1987: 83). Although the extension of a superstable marker does not correspond
to or necessarily result in a subsequent change of noun class affiliation, it clearly
reduces the differences between individual declensional types (Dammel & Nübling
2006: 98). The appearance of superstable markers in the system has been viewed as
indicative of the early stage of morphological simplification, which potentially leads
to deflection (Dammel & Nübling 2006: 100). It also indicates that the category it
marks is weak and thus likely to be reduced or eliminated. From the perspective of
the present study, it is important to stress that the realignments between declensional types will tend to take place from the unstable inflectional paradigms to the
stable ones. To translate it into productivity relations, the declensional class shift
will occur from paradigms or classes which are unproductive or less productive to
those which are productive.

1.4.6 Factors conditioning the restructuring process

Apart from describing both the general and more fine-grained tendencies in the
restructuring of the nominal inflection in Old Northern West Germanic languages,
the present investigation aims at identifying the principles underlying the mechanisms of the restructuring process, which eventually determined the shape of
the respective declensional systems. Accordingly, the focal part of the research
question, as formulated in the *Introduction*, refers to the factors which conditioned
and guided the remodelling of the nominal paradigms in the early Germanic languages. They derive from different domains and interact often in a synergetic way,
i.e. reinforcing each other. In order to describe the mechanisms of the restructuring process, the significance of these interacting factors and their relative ranking needs to be estimated. The factors involved in the process are of a twofold
nature: (1) language-specific and thus responsible for the divergent inflectional
developments in the individual languages, and (2) non-language-specific, whose

more universal nature enables framing the process of restructuring in more general terms. An additional layer of conditioning is created by factors of extralinguistic nature, which are largely language-specific. These include, for instance, the dates of attestation of the extant sources (cf. 9th c. Old Saxon vs. 14th c. Old Frisian), the geographical conditions (e.g. the vicinity of the West Germanic dialects on the Continent) and socio-political circumstances (e.g. the socio-cultural impact of Franconian on the surrounding dialects). The inclusion of this last group of factors can be helpful in accounting for the discrepant patterns identified in the nominal systems of the sister languages.

The significance of universal factors that can potentially influence the restructuring of inflectional morphology has already been observed in a few earlier studies (e.g. Kürschner 2008). They operate on various levels of linguistic structure and, as they come into interaction with language-specific factors in one way or another, their final effects seem to have a varying scope in the individual languages. The following factors of a more universal nature were considered relevant for the analysis of morphological developments in this study:

1. frequency of occurrence (operating at various levels)
2. salience of inflectional markers
3. semantics, including semantic features of lemmas and declensional classes
4. syllable structure
5. lexical factors, which refer to lemma-specific properties[36]

The ultimate shape of the morphological structures (paradigm, declensional class) emerges from an interaction between these factors, which, as will become evident, are to a certain extent class-specific. What is important in the context of the present comparative study is that these factors had a largely language-specific impact, since each of the investigated languages had a different phonological profile, which resulted in different dynamics of analogical changes affecting the systems, including their different chronology and scope. Consequently, a more detailed discussion of these factors needs to be relegated to the respective chapters and their immediate effects as reflected in the data will be the focus of the theoretical discussion in Chapter 8. In what follows, some preliminary considerations concerning the most relevant factors entailed in the restructuring process are presented. Importantly, the influence of lexical factors, on account of their nature, is shifted to the more detailed discussions of individual classes in the individual languages.

---

36. Cf. the hierarchy of conditioning factors for the plural patterns, presented by Kürschner (2008: 17), where a subdivision is made into "signifiébasierte" and "signifiantbasierte Konditionierung".

1.4.6.1 *Frequency effects in nominal morphology*

The role of frequency of occurrence/use in linguistic change has been widely recognised. Its significance for linguistic structure and language change was made explicit by Greenberg (1966) who argued that frequency is "an ever present and powerful factor in the evolution of grammatical categories and thus helps in explaining the types of synchronic states actually found" (Greenberg 1966: 65–69). Also the more recent approaches to grammar, in particular those treating grammar as a dynamic system have defined frequency "as an important determinant of linguistic structure and language use" (Diessel 2007: 109; Hooper 1976; Bybee 1985; Bybee 1995; Haspelmath & Sims 2010). Greenberg (1960, 1966) postulated a very tight relation between the frequency of occurrence of specific items and the rate of their development, and thus proneness to modification or change. It is argued that words of higher frequency tend to preserve the inherited morphological patterns longer, whereas those used infrequently tend to submerge to the impact of new, dominant patterns. The existence of such a direct correlation between the archaism of forms and the frequency factor was observed and recognised in fact much earlier, notably by Hermann Paul (1920: 227) who argues: "Nur besondere Häufigkeit kann einigen Wörtern Kraft genug verleihen sich dem sonst übergewaltigen Einflusse auf lange Zeit zu entziehen. Diese existieren dann in ihrer Vereinzelung als Anomala weiter." Accordingly, language change tends to affect less frequent items first or more easily, while the more frequent items will tend to retain archaic features.

The exact mechanisms of the operation of frequency of occurrence have been examined in detail in numerous studies, and it has long been recognised that frequency can have an adverse effect on the phonological and morphological structure. In phonology, high frequency of occurrence leads to reduction, i.e. items used more frequently tend to be more prone to change (e.g. phonetic reduction, coalescence or assimilation), and the development of new forms. This correlation, known as Reducing Effect of frequency, refers in particular to *token* frequency, and was recognised already by Zipf (1929, 1936) (cf. Hooper 1976; Bybee & Hopper 2001). More specifically, Zipf's law defines "the correlation between frequency, length, and categorical status", and is considered to be possibly "the most powerful generalization about the relationship between language structure and language use." (Diessel 2007: 118). In contrast, in morphology, token frequency can have a distinctly conserving effect, rendering lexical items, structures or expressions resistant to the working of analogical processes.

An important distinction to be made in the context of changes in the morphological system is the one between *type* and *token* frequency. Type frequency refers to "the dictionary frequency of a particular pattern (e.g. stress, an affix, or a consonant cluster)." (Bybee & Hopper 2001: 10). It is decisive for the analogical spread of a given (inflectional) pattern (Fertig 2013: 118) (cf. Skousen's algorithm that works along the same principle of type frequency). As such, type frequency is closely related to morphological productivity (of a given pattern) in that productivity relies on type frequency (Wurzel 1989; Bybee 1995; Köpcke 1993; Bauer 2004). It is assumed that the more types a given category or pattern comprises, the greater the chance that the pattern will be extended to new contexts (Diessel 2016: 223). In this sense, type frequency plays a crucial role in the regularisation processes in morphology, including the generalisation of patterns such as inflectional paradigms (e.g. Liberman et al. 2007; Carrol et al. 2012 for verbs).[37, 38]

While type frequency results in the generalisation of patterns (or categories) or formation of new templates, (high) token frequency can lead to conservation of morphological patterns (e.g. Bybee 2007). With reference to the retention of conservative properties in high frequency words, Bybee & Hopper (2001: 17) claim that "high frequency units are resistant to reformation on the basis of productive patterns". This correlation is commonly known as the Conserving Effect of high token frequency. The effect is to be attributed to lexical strength of individual items, namely the fact that "each use of a word or construction increases the strength of its exemplar cluster, making that word or phrase more accessible lexically" (Bybee 1985: 75).

The effect of conservation of morphological features is only one of the effects that token frequency may have on language structure and change. Many findings in frequency studies postulate and prove that it is high token frequency that serves as a trigger for certain changes (e.g. Haiman 1994; Bybee & Hopper 2001; Bybee 2003; Krug 2003). It has been commonly recognised that high frequency forms tend to be shorter (as a result of the aforementioned Reducing Effect of high token frequency in phonological change), but at the same time, they also tend to be more distinct. The shortness of forms is evoked by the language users' preference for economical structures, where 'economical' is nearly equivalent to 'predictable' or 'default' (Haspelmath & Sims 2010: 272). The correlation of token frequency with the length of token-frequent forms and their formal distinction has been interpreted as a collateral effect of their higher lexical autonomy. As a result of frequent use, they become well entrenched in the mental lexicon and their retrieval is

---

37. The more frequently used verbs tend to remain irregular and the less frequently used ones tend to regularise more easily.

38. Many of these studies investigate the significance of type frequency in the context of first language acquisition, including the acquisition of inflectional morphology. Type frequency of an inflectional marker is considered to be the decisive factor in the acquisition of inflectional morphology (Bybee 1995).

more automated. From the perspective of production and perception, as argued by Werner (1987: 597), the shortness and prominence of forms that occur frequently is an efficient and desirable combination of features.

The second characteristic, i.e. the distinctiveness of forms occurring frequently, brings forward the question of salience which will be the focus of Section 1.4.6.2. It has been observed that "frequently used values tend to be more differentiated than rarely used values" (Haspelmath & Sims 2010: 268). In other words, less frequent morphological categories tend to show less differentiation (more syncretism/homonymy) than the more frequent categories, and this difference can be ascribed to the memorisation process, in which distinctions are more difficult to be remembered in the less frequent categories (Haspelmath 2006: 29).[39] This interpretation stays in line with the observations of Hawkins (2004), who, applying a performance-driven approach to morphological restructuring, argues that "progressive loss of feature combinations" in morphological systems is dependent on frequency of use. In other words, the elimination of formal differentiation is ascribed to performance pressure which "works towards retaining or eliminating certain distinctions" (Hawkins 2004: 79). Accordingly, the less frequent categories, such as the DAT. PL., will be more prone to "lose their distinctiveness and be eliminated."

When describing the relation between frequency of use and formal differentiation or distinctiveness, Haspelmath & Sims (2010: 268–270) enumerate three different aspects, which include: (a) syncretism – frequent categories or values tend to show less syncretism, (b) the differences between inflection classes – shared exponents involve primarily less frequent values; (c) the presence of more cross-cutting values in frequent categories. The data from the Older Germanic languages show these correlations: the singular paradigms tend to be more differentiated than the plural ones across most declensional classes; the shared exponents are characteristic of the less frequent categories such as the GEN. and DAT. PL., which tend to have the same markers across all minor declensional types; and there is more formal differentiation across paradigms in the category of, for instance, the more frequent DAT. SG. than the less frequent DAT. PL.

---

39. The variation (or asymmetries) in frequencies can be ascribed to a range of factors, including different frequencies of the relevant entities in the real world, the existence of "social and communicative biases when describing entities in the world", or differences in syntactic or semantic complexity between clause types in which the relevant morphemes appear (ditransitive vs. transitive vs. intransitive clauses) (Hawkins 2004: 64–65). Haspelmath (2008), referring to universal pragmatic motivation of frequency asymmetry, points to the fact that, e.g., nouns denoting people will appear more often in the nominative, whereas inanimate nouns, more often in the accusative. These aspects will need to be taken into account when interpreting the data (cf. Haspelmath 2008: 7).

Significantly, the two effects of frequency, namely the conserving effect in morphology and the reducing effect in phonology tend to interact. This becomes conspicuous especially in certain categories, such as the NOM. SG., where differentiation in terms of formal exponence could be expected on account of it being a frequent category, but for exactly the same reason it is subject to phonological reduction. This kind of interaction between the different frequency effects need to be taken into consideration when trying to explain the developments in nominal paradigms.

Another correlation related to formal marking is that between frequency and irregularity, where irregularity is understood as a deviation from a uniform paradigm, manifested in stem alternation. Irregularity, i.e. the presence of allomorphy (*i*-mutated vowel or consonantal alternations), seems to be a characteristic of categories which are more frequent (e.g. the NOM./ACC. PL.), while the less frequent categories (such as the GEN. SG. or PL.) tend to be more regular. The reason for this tendency is that irregularity is more easily remembered when a category occurs more often; in contrast, infrequent forms "must follow analogically other parts of the system (…)", becoming thus regular (Greenberg 1966: 68–69). Some more insight into the mechanism of this process is offered by Bybee (1985), who argues that the levelling of stem alternations is frequency-sensitive: "the proposal that infrequently-used forms fade [from memory] accounts for the tendency to regularize infrequent irregular forms, for an irregular form that is not sufficiently reinforced will be replaced by a regular formation" (Bybee 1985: 119–123). The implication of this correlation for the reorganisation of the nominal system in the early Germanic languages is that the analogical developments (resulting also in reductions in the number and diversity of case forms) are more likely to affect the less frequently used forms and categories, while the high frequency of irregular forms will prevent them from being eliminated (cf. Winter 1971: 55–57).

The assumption of a close correlation between frequency and the archaism of forms has its cognitive dimension too, as observed above. Namely, the irregular forms, which are usually high frequency items, must be deeply entrenched in the mental lexicon (Bybee 1985). Entrenchment refers to a process which results from repeated activation of mental representation of a given element through which the mental representation is strengthened and consequently made stable (Langacker 1987: 57–59).[40] The deep entrenchment of forms in the lexicon strengthens the representation of linguistic elements in memory (or leads to memory strength and

---

40. "Every use of a structure has a positive impact on its degree of entrenchment, whereas extended periods of disuse have a negative impact. With repeated use, a novel structure becomes progressively entrenched, to the point of becoming a unit; moreover, units are variably entrenched depending on the frequency of their occurrence" (Langacker 1987: 59).

fast lexical access). In other words, it facilitates the memorisation process, and, in consequence, these forms tend to be more resistant to external influences of any sort, in compliance with the rule "the more entrenched a form is, the less likely it is to be replaced by some frequent patterns" (Smith 2001: 364; cf. Bybee 1985, 2006; Haspelmath & Sims 2010: 276). In this sense, the process of entrenchment is a factor counteracting language change, and in this case, morphological change, i.e. analogical levelling.

Another related aspect that comes into play here is the question of autonomy of forms as defined by Bybee (1985). The forms which are more frequent and thus better entrenched are also more autonomous in the sense that they do not depend on the pressures of the dominant (type frequent) categories or patterns. This "autonomy" effect of token frequency is interpreted as "an extreme instance of the Conserving Effect" (Bybee 2007: 15). The autonomous forms are more resistant to change and may also serve as the basis for the reorganisation of the paradigm. In other words, high frequency can lead to both entrenchment and automatization. The frequent, well memorized forms, as a result of phonological processes, will tend to be short (fused) and irregular, while the less frequent and less well-memorised forms, will tend to create interparadigmatic connections and follow general templates (Paul 1920; Bybee 1985; Werner 1987).[41]

Given that the effects of frequency are evident on so many levels of linguistic structure, the restructuring of nominal inflection in the Older Germanic languages must have been frequency-sensitive as well. The significance of this factor is to be investigated in the systematic quantitative analysis, but it can be observed at this point that the changes in the nominal system illustrate the interaction between the two types of frequency, i.e. type and token frequency. The relevance of frequency is evident in the very existence of major and minor declensional classes, with their entirely different frequency profiles. The *a*- and *ō*-stems, which in the Old Germanic languages comprised the majority of nouns, were characterised by high type frequency, while classes such as root nouns, which are relics of once productive (PIE) patterns, contain only a limited number of nouns with high token frequency. In the case of the *a*-stems, the high type frequency results in the generalisation of inflectional patterns, while in the case of the root nouns, the high token frequency works as a factor reinforcing the inherited inflectional pattern. The fact that such a constellation of declensions was inherited from the Germanic parent language

---

41. This complies with the findings of research on first language acquisition (e.g. Stemberger & MacWhinney 1986; Alegre & Gordon 1999), where it is argued that high-frequency inflected forms are stored forms, while low-frequency ones are derived by rule.

indicates that the process of restructuring was frequency-sensitive from the early stages of its operation.

Another important aspect of frequency for this study is the distinction between *absolute frequency* and *relative frequency* (Corbett et al. 2001: 202–203; Haspelmath 2008: 10). The former will refer in particular to the absolute lemma frequency or the frequency of any morphosyntactic category. The relative frequency will refer to the relation between the frequencies of individual categories (which are paradigmatic alternatives), such as the singular-plural ratio. Naturally, it must be remembered that the material available in the written sources is only to a limited extent indicative of lexical frequency in ordinary usage. For some lemmas it is in fact very difficult or hardly possible to assume such a straightforward correlation between the frequency of occurrence in the text and frequency of use in everyday speech. Given the nature of the investigated corpora, it can be expected that words belonging to more elevated registers will be better represented in the material than those used in less formal everyday contexts. This factor needs to be reckoned with when interpreting the findings from the quantitative investigation. At the same time, it is an evident and serious shortcoming of the limited textual material that can hardly be remedied in any way.

1.4.6.2 *Salience of inflectional marking*
The notion of *salience* is fairly broad and its precise definition depends on the theoretical approach adopted: it is framed differently when employed in cognitive linguistics (*cognitive salience, ontological salience*) and differently when applied in phonology or morphology. In a broad, theory-neutral approach salience could be understood as equivalent to prominence or conspicuousness and thus seems to be a relative concept. Two aspects of salience are relevant in the context of the present study: phonological salience and morphological complexity. Phonological salience, known also as perceptual salience, is defined in terms of acoustic weight: a zero ending is considered to be less salient than a vowel, which in turn is less salient than a VC-ending (Goldschneider & DeKeyser 2001: 22–23). It involves perceptual salience, which depends on three factors: (a) the number of phones in the functor, i.e. morpheme (phonetic substance), (b) the presence/absence of a vowel in the surface form (syllabicity), and (c) the total relative sonority of the functor. The following assumptions are involved:

a.   the more phones in a functor, the more perceptually salient it should be
b.   functors containing a vowel in the surface form should be more perceptually salient than those without a vowel
c.   functors that are more sonorous should be more salient.

The basis for sonority hierarchy is the one provided by Laver (1994: 504), where each level of hierarchy is assigned a value, with the (low) vowels being the most sonorous and voiceless stops being the least sonorous.[42]

In the context of the present investigation, the major assumption that can be made with respect to salience is that the more salient elements (inflectional exponents) will tend to be more resistant to analogical pressures. In most general terms, overt marking can be expected to be preferred over zero marking across all declensional classes. In other words, it is the phonological shape of inflectional markers that determines their proneness (or resistance) to analogical developments. Whether this interpretation is applicable also to the patterns of morphological restructuring is to be evaluated in the course of the investigation.

The preference for the type of marking between these two extremes, i.e. zero marking and overt marking, can be expressed on a scale, which involves the concept of morphological complexity. Morphological complexity is understood here as complexity of formal marking, i.e. of inflectional exponents, but the concept in more general terms refers to "a property of the language system which is analysable with respect to its effect on language users" (Dammel & Kürschner 2008: 245). It has been defined in quantitative and qualitative terms, and can be viewed as both an absolute and relative concept, the former taking into account the language system itself (i.e. the length of the description of a given linguistic phenomenon), the latter refers to the language speaker and hearer, i.e. how difficult a given linguistic phenomenon is to process, learn or acquire (Miestamo 2008: 24–25; Dahl 2004: 40–42). With respect to the quantitative measurement of complexity, a system or a form which consists of more elements will be more complex, i.e. the number of allomorphs is decisive. As far as the qualitative aspect is concerned, morphological complexity can be presented on a scale which can be referred to as a complexity hierarchy of morphological marking (here of case/number exponency) (Wurzel 1990: 139; cf. Corbett et al. 2001: 212–214; Dammel & Kürschner 2008: 248–256). The ranking corresponds to the ranking of naturalness proposed in the Natural Morphology framework, with 'regular' or 'non-complex' being more or less equivalent to *natural* (cf. Dahl 2004: 115ff., who equals the concept of *naturalness* with "lack of complexity"). In fact, this approach incorporates the ideas of iconicity and transparency in that formal complexity is defined in terms of deviations from constructional iconicity. The aspects which were considered relevant for defining complexity include: (1) stem involvement, (2) redundant marking, (3) zero expression, (4) subtractive expression, (5) allomorphy, (6) fusion of number and case

---

42. In fact, Golschneider & DeKeyser (2001: 36) postulate a broader interpretation of the concept of salience, which includes all the structural levels (i.e. phonological, morphological, syntactic, semantic and numerical). The term is used in the context of first language acquisition, where salience emerges as an essential factor, being the "the ultimate predictor of the order of acquisition".

expression. In most general terms, the marking of categories by means of suffixation and not involving allomorphy can be considered the "canonical simple pole" of "formal complexity scale", while stem/root alternation (in the absence of instances of lexical suppletion in the analysed stage of early Germanic) would occupy the opposite end of the scale (Dammel & Kürschner 2008: 248).

The ranking is reminiscent also of the *irregularity ranking* postulated by Corbett et al. (2001), where suppletion and suffixation (inflectional irregularity) stand as opposite poles of the scale; more specifically, (1) stem irregularity ranks higher than inflectional irregularity, (2) segmental irregularity ranks above prosodic irregularity, (3) suppletion ranks higher than augment irregularity and the latter higher than simple stem alternation (Corbett et al. 2001: 212). Within the augment and stem irregularity a further ranking has been proposed by Corbett et al. (2001), which for the Germanic conditions corresponds roughly to consonantal root allomorphy (e.g. OE *hæle* ~ *hæleð*- 'hero'; OFris. *beke* (DAT. SG.) ~ *betze* (LOC. SG.) 'back') and vocalic root allomorphy (e.g. *i*-mutation). The hierarchy corresponds to Jespersen's (1922) argument that regularity and lack of complexity of morphological markers/ forms or constructions constitute the properties which guarantee a high level of functionality of a morphological system.

The present study, availing itself of the hierarchies discussed above, combines the perceptual salience and complexity of the different types of inflectional marking techniques to create a ranking which will be referred to as *salience scale*. Importantly, the scale does not refer to the complexity of the morphological system as a whole, but is confined exclusively to the complexity of inflectional exponence. The scale applied in the present study takes the ranking of Dammel & Kürschner (2008) as the starting point, but selects only these features from the scale which are relevant for the nominal systems as attested in the earliest stages of the individual Germanic languages (Figure 1).[43] Given that the shape of the nominal system of modern Germanic languages diverges considerably from that found in the earlier attested stages (Old Germanic), some of the criteria used in the original complexity scale are not relevant for the analysis, and were excluded. Two of the original criteria are, however, applicable to the present ranking, namely stem involvement and zero marking. The status of the zero marking was modified in that it was not considered to be a separate marking technique, but part of the phonological salience scale, where it occupies the lowest position (as will be confirmed by the data in the course of the analysis). Other factors, i.e. the fusion of number and case expression, and subtraction are not relevant to the present study, the former being the default

---

43. The scale in the study of Dammel & Kürschner (2008) referred to the marking of the category of the plural, but is here extended to the entire paradigm. The qualitative criteria involved in the scale included: (a) iconicity of the formal techniques used for marking, (b) assignment principles, and (c) direction of determination between stem and the marker (Dammel & Kürschner 2008: 246).

condition for nominal inflection in Older Germanic languages, the latter being not attested in the early Germanic material. Likewise, the feature *redundancy* is considered irrelevant, as there was hardly any redundant marking in the early Germanic nominal system, with *i*-mutation being not yet visible in Continental Germanic and functional *i*-mutation (Old English and Old Frisian) appearing without additional marking (except for the OE alternation of /k/ and /ʧ/ in *bōc – bēċ* and OFris. *beke* (DAT.SG.) ~ *betze*).

Figure 1. The combined salience and complexity scale of inflectional marking

For suffixation, the type of suffix is ordered according to the abovementioned sonority scale, i.e. vowels will tend to be less salient than consonants, and a nasal consonant /n/ will be less salient than a fricative /s/. As regards vocalic stem modulation, only qualitative modulation is relevant here (i.e. *i*-mutation), since distinctive contrasts in vowel quantity (length) emerge only at the later *Middle* stage of Germanic attestation, i.e. after the operation of the process of Open Syllable Lengthening. With regard to consonantal stem modulation, a distinction needs to be made between the alternations which are synchronically transparent and those which are obsolete and are recognised synchronically only as a part of the inflectional suffix. This refers to the consonantal alternation in the *s*-stems and dental stems (in the languages where it is attested), where the markers -*(e)r* and -*eþ* (as in OE *lomb – lombor* or OE *hæle – hæleþ*) are historical stem formatives, but in the *Old* stage of Germanic can be considered part of the inflectional suffix (inflectional ending). These consonantal alternations stay in contrast with the 'genuine' consonant stem modulation, as in OE *bōc – bēċ* (DAT.SG. & NOM./ACC. PL.), OFris. *beke* (DAT. SG.) ~ *betze* (LOC. SG.), which are, however, very rare in Old Germanic languages and have no distinctive (independent) function.

Although morphological complexity can be expected to induce simplification, it may also contribute to a retention of morphological irregularities on account of their perceptual salience. This effect of morphological complexity seems to be correlated with the function that a given exponent has. For instance, the elimination of *i*-mutation from the singular paradigm of root nouns can be interpreted as an instantiation of category marking simplification. However, the retention of the same exponent in the paradigm of the plural, to serve as a plurality marker, goes counter to this tendency and can be accounted for by the fact that a more distinct, salient marker was necessary to keep an important functional contrast, i.e. the singular-plural distinction.

When looking at the nominal morphology of early Germanic, the ending that seems to be a good candidate for a salient inflectional marker is the GEN. SG. ending -*es* (-*as*), as well as the OE/OS ending -*as* (-*os*), marking the NOM./ACC. PL. in the masculine *a*-stems. Both markers score fairly well on all the three criteria of perceptual salience, namely, they consist of two phones, of which one is a vowel and the other one of perceptually the most robust consonants (e.g. Laver 1994: 262–263). Given such a phonological shape, they tended to be more resistant to phonological reductions which affected inflectional syllables. In contrast, markers which score low on the salience scale, such as zero markers and vocalic endings, can be expected to be less stable and more susceptible to analogical pressures. Although this pattern is a valid generalisation, the present-day Germanic evidence indicates that the correlation need not always hold. The Modern German evidence shows that an inflectional marker which is not salient can also be productive and become dominant. The plural ending -*en* is clearly less salient than the marker -*s* and yet it is the most productive marker in German. It must be emphasised, however, that salience is not the sole factor conditioning the attested morphological (inflectional) patterns and such conflicting evidence does not undermine the significance of salience in the restructuring process. And even if the salience of the endings -*es*/-*as*/-*os* is relatively high when compared with other suffixal exponents (vowels), it is lower than the salience of internal markers such as *i*-mutation (vocalic root alternation) or consonantal stem alternation (*r*-formative, or *þ*-formative).

It can also be expected that salience of inflectional markers will interact with frequency of use in a synergetic way, i.e. that their cumulated effect on the morphological patterns or forms will be enhanced. More specifically, the more frequent items/forms will tend to be more salient than the less frequent ones. Winter (1971) combines these two factors under the term of *prominence*, postulating a distinction between quantitative and qualitative prominence. He claims that the more prominent forms are more likely to survive in a given system over time (Winter 1971: 61), which is reminiscent of the conserving effect of frequency (on its own). In the present study these two factors, i.e. frequency and salience, are considered as independent determinants in the restructuring process, and will be treated and examined separately. An important question which emerges is in what way the interaction between them occurs, and in particular whether the salience can be considered an independent factor which shows its own effects in the process of restructuring, or should it rather be viewed as an epiphenomenon of frequency. The intricate relation between these (and other) factors involved in the process of restructuring of inflection will be the focus of the discussion in Chapter 8.

Finally, salience, just like frequency, seems to be a notion which can be approached both in relative and absolute terms. It means that a given morphological feature/pattern will not always be universally salient, but rather *relatively* salient. An example may be the stem/root-vowel alternation which can be considered a salient feature in Germanic languages, where it is rather rare, but from a perspective of a language where it is a default marker of certain grammatical categories (e.g. the ablaut in pre-Proto-Indo-European), it will not be considered salient or prominent.

1.4.6.3   *Other factors: gender, semantics, syllable structure*

Gender is one of the factors involved in the reorganisation of nominal inflections, but rather than affecting the dynamics of the process, it has a clear function in guiding the direction of interdeclensional analogical transfers. According to Keyser & O'Neil (1985: 104), analogical transition of nouns from one paradigm to another tends to be accompanied by consistent preservation of the inherited gender. In other words, gender-class affiliation of nouns does not change alongside the change of the declensional class. The tendency can be tentatively referred to as a "principle of gender conservation". In compliance with this principle, the interparadigmatic realignments which occurred in the minor declensional types in the investigated languages are expected to have entailed primarily parallel shifts in the masculine, neuter and feminine inflection, whereby masculine and neuter stems followed the pattern of the largest masculine and neuter class, the *a*-stems, whereas feminine stems subdued to the impact of the most numerous feminine class – the *ō*-stem declension. Given the information found in the standard historical grammars of the individual Older Germanic languages, this principle seems to have been at work in early Germanic. At the same time, it is far from being universal, as admitted by the authors themselves, who cite Slavic languages to demonstrate that transfer of nouns across gender-classes alongside declensional class change is feasible. The essential prerequisite for gender change is an extension of the unhistorical gender forms throughout the paradigm rather than their confinement to one or two morphosyntactic categories. Accordingly, only the instances where gender change systematically (in all paradigm forms) accompanied morphological class realignments can be considered genuine instances of a shift in gender.[44] The present study verifies to what extent this principle was operative in the remodelling of the nominal inflection at the earliest attested stages of Northern West Germanic.

---

44. Importantly, the term *gender shift* as used in the present study does not refer to a transition from morphological or grammatical gender to a semantic or natural one, but it refers only to the more or less systematic acquisition of a new gender by nouns which undergo the process of analogical transference to other declensional types. It is thus used in compliance with the definition formulated by Jones (1988: 11), where *gender shift* is viewed as "the reclassification of nominal lexical items under different gender class groupings".

An important aspect related to the significance of gender is the relation between gender and class assignment. As suggested by Krygier (2002: 315) with reference to the Old English grammatical system, they should be treated as independent features, operating in a parallel way, with gender being a secondary property, marked externally, i.e. beyond the paradigm. It must be observed that gender as a grammatical category was not transparently represented in the inflectional system. The impossibility of any categorical statements about gender and declensional affiliation was made explicit by Lass (1997b: 108), who concludes that "it's never entirely safe to say that some particular noun N 'was an X-stem of gender G'" (cf. Schwink 2004). The implied gender variation, accordingly, needs to be conceived of not only as a significant property of the grammatical system, present therein presumably from a very early stage, but also as a feature which will render any rigid descriptions or classifications problematic.

A factor of an entirely different nature, which played a crucial role in the reorganisation of the nominal system in early Germanic languages is semantics, relevant on the lemma level and declension class level. One aspect where it emerges as prominent is with productivity patterns, in that they can be sometimes secured by semantic factors. For instance, the heavy-syllable neuter nouns denoting game animals, which constituted a semantically coherent group, retained the historical pattern of forming the plural until present-day English (*deer*, *sheep*, etc.). It could be expected, accordingly, that semantically cogent groups, i.e. classes or subclasses which are characterised by a specific semantic profile, for instance, nouns denoting animals or nouns of relationship, will display a distinct pattern of inflectional restructuring, being essentially more likely to retain the historical inflection.

Semantics does not necessarily affect the restructuring process directly, but most often through its manifestation in frequency of use, especially in lemma frequency. Accordingly, the patterns of restructuring found in the paradigms of nouns which on account of their semantics show very high frequency of occurrence (e.g. nouns of relationship) can be expected to differ from the patterns found in nouns with much lower frequencies (e.g. nouns referring to plant names). A further effect of semantics is reflected in morphosyntactic categories and their frequencies. For instance, the fact that agent nouns such as *nd*-stems or nouns of relationship, on account of their semantics, will tend to occur more often in the subject (nominative) than object position (oblique cases) will affect the restructuring pattern of their paradigms. Likewise, the fact that certain nouns, on account of their semantic profiles, tend to be used more often in the plural (e.g. *brothers* and *sisters* in contrast to *mother* and *father*) or in the singular (e.g. nouns referring to deity) will in many instances adequately account for the inflectional patterns found in the material examined.

Another level of the process of restructuring where semantics is involved is in grammatical categories, and in particular their semantic transparency. Inflectional markers that encode referential categories, such as number (but also tense or aspect), which are semantically transparent, will tend to be less easily affected by analogical developments than markers that encode formal categories, such as declension class or grammatical gender. Accordingly, the category of number is in a way superior to the category of case, since, being a referential semantic category, it is an inherent property of the noun, in contrast to case which is syntactically conditioned. This has been made explicit by Plank (1991), who states: "A commonly encountered hypothesis (…) is that if nouns and other nominal words inflect for both Case and Number, Case, a surface syntactic category, is less important than Number, a referential semantic category, hence will more readily admit non-distinctions." (Plank 1991: 23; cf. Booj 1996). Semantics can thus be expected to play a role in the inflectional reorganisation, affecting the patterns of restructuring on various levels, in a more or less direct manner.

Syllable structure is yet another factor likely to determine the dynamics of the nominal system. It does not have a direct influence on the analogical developments in the nominal inflection, but its relevance is manifested in the phonological profiles of individual declensional classes and their paradigms. More specifically, the chronology and scope of phonological processes affecting the light and heavy syllables differed, and consequently, the inflectional paradigms of light- and heavy syllable-stems emerged as different. This refers in particular to the early, prehistoric developments in these two types of stems, where processes such as apocope of vowels in inflectional syllables, conditioned by syllable weight of the stem, led to their different shapes by the time of the first attestations of Germanic. The resulting divergent profiles of the light- and heavy-syllable stems showed different levels of susceptibility to the effects of analogical pressures.

1.5   Methodology of the research

1.5.1   Terms and definitions

As some of the terms and definitions used in this study have a wide scope in the existing literature, in order to avoid ambiguity, they need to be clarified and their meaning precisely defined. One such term that has been applied to many different linguistic phenomena is *morphological reanalysis* or *morphological restructuring*. Generally speaking, both refer to a change of the morphological pattern (here inflectional pattern) that already exists in the system. In the present study, these terms will denote the emergence of innovation in the paradigms of minor stems, induced by analogy, i.e. by the analogical influence of any of the productive declensional patterns, whether vocalic (i.e. *a*-stems, *ō*-stems, *i*-stems) or consonantal (*n*-stems). Occasionally the term *disintegration* (of a declensional class or paradigm) will be used in a similar meaning, though on a more local scale, referring to a process whereby the original inflectional pattern, inherited from Proto-Germanic, is largely disrupted by the intrusion of analogical inflections. An inflectional paradigm that does not consistently preserve the inherited features, but to a greater or lesser extent displays analogical characteristics, will be occasionally referred to as "disintegrated". In strict terms, the process of reorganisation of the nominal paradigms, as it is found in the earliest attested stages of the examined languages, does not entail disintegration or collapse of entire nominal paradigms – insofar as disintegration is understood as a loss of inflections and the categories that they mark, i.e. case, number and gender. While the term *disintegration* could be justified when applied to the developments taking place in Late Old English, where analogical levelling of paradigm forms cannot be easily separated from the effects of the dissolution in the gender and case systems (beginning towards the end of the Old English period; e.g. Lass 1992: 107; Kastovsky 1999; Jones 1988; Curzan 2009), it clearly does not seem adequate in the case of Continental Germanic or Scandinavian. High German and Icelandic testify to a variety of levelling processes and interparadigmatic transfers, showing at the same time hardly any traces of the abandonment of gender and case system. The same holds partly true for Low German and Dutch, where there is at least a 400-year gap between the earliest attested stage, i.e. the period examined in this study, and the time of the dissolution of the gender and case systems. In fact, even within Old English there is a difference between the early period dated between the eighth and tenth centuries, in which the system is reshaped or transformed rather than disintegrated, and the later period of the eleventh – twelfth century, where symptoms of an actual dissolution of the gender and case system are detectable. Accordingly, when used in the present study the term *disintegration* will be understood only as a reduction in the declensional diversity inherited from the Proto-Germanic ancestor.

Secondly, the terms *archaic* and *innovative*, as employed in the present study with reference to paradigms or paradigm forms, deserve clarification. The former, used interchangeably with the term *conservative*, refers to the inflectional features inherited from Proto-Germanic, which show the expected phonological development from the PGmc. forms and paradigms, without any disruptions of analogical nature. In other words, the archaic nominal paradigms are those which consistently continue the PGmc. paradigms in the sense that they developed in line with the regular phonological processes. The term *innovative* is synonymous with *analogical* or *novel*, and refers to analogical inflectional features present in the inherited paradigms, extended most often from the *a-*, *ō*-stems and *n*-stems. In other words, every form which cannot have developed from the 'classical' paradigm through regular phonological change is considered innovative. Significantly, the innovativeness of the minor paradigms is confined to the effects of *inter*paradigmatic realignments, occasioned by the activity of analogical pressures from other paradigms, rather than of *intra*paradigmatic realignments, caused by the analogical pressure from within the paradigm. Admittedly, an interaction between these two analogical forces is inherent in the mechanism of the restructuring process, yet in the present study the intraparadigmatic realignments are not subjected to a quantitative examination and thus have no *direct* bearing on the findings from the quantitative analysis (cf. Section 1.3.3 above). For instance, the elimination of the *i*-mutated vowel from the DAT. SG. of OE root nouns (as in *byrg* → *burg*) or the extension of the *i*-mutated vowel to the NOM./ACC. SG. (→ *byrg*) are not considered yet (on their own) to be innovative features in the paradigm. At the same time, these intraparadigmatic changes have a profound indirect influence on the scope and the dynamics of the restructuring process, as they determine the overall profile of the paradigms or classes, and in that sense constitute an inseparable part of the internal mechanism of the process. Accordingly, the extension of the *i*-mutated vowel to the singular in *byrg* obliterates the important functional distinction between the singular and the plural. This development is consequential for the further restructuring of the paradigm in that the functional pressure of the system will work towards restoring the opposition, most likely through the adoption of a new inflectional marker in the plural (*burga, -e* or *burgas*).

The presentation of archaic and innovative features in individual declensional classes is framed as a competition between two paradigms and is depicted in a tabular form. Such a way of presenting is not to imply that the two competing paradigms actually existed simultaneously. This convention serves rather as an efficient way to present the variety of potential inflectional forms, with a transparent, unambiguous marking of their source, i.e. indicating which of them are continuations of the original PGmc. pattern and which emerged as an effect of analogical pressures of other declensional types. It must be noted that due to the insufficient attestations of various lemmas, the paradigms presented in the tables as *archaic* are "reconstructed" on the basis of the entire available inventory of a given class, and the chosen lexeme serves to represent a given declensional type. Likewise, the paradigms presented as *innovative* include the *potential* innovative inflections that may appear in the paradigms and not necessarily forms that are actually attested.[45]

Another term related to the question of competing paradigms, which deserves terminological clarification is *declensional shift/transfer*. It is essential to define the scope of this term, because many nouns show only sporadic vacillation between two competing forms, but they do not consistently follow a new inflectional pattern. Accordingly, *declensional shift/transfer* is understood here in broader terms as a tendency of nouns affiliated with minor classes towards shifting to other declensional classes, manifested in the appearance of new, analogical inflections in the paradigm; it does not necessarily involve a complete transition of a noun to another class, with consistent extension of analogical inflectional endings in the entire paradigm. As the present investigation will reveal, analogical reshufflings tended to occur clearly beyond the level of class or paradigm in that they affected individual morphosyntactic categories across various classes rather than entire paradigms (at least in the examined period).

The last terminological remark refers to the term *minor classes/declensions*. In the present study, it is employed to include all declensions which were no longer unambiguously productive by the time of the earliest attestations of the (West) Germanic languages. In the standard treatments of Old English nominal morphology (e.g. Campbell 1977), the definition of *minor declensions* is narrowed down to encompass only unproductive *consonantal* classes, i.e. excluding vocalic *i*-stems and *u*-stems. Much as the *u*-stems easily fall under the definition of an unproductive class in all the investigated languages, the status of the *i*-stems is somewhat ambiguous. While they can definitely be classified as *minor* from the perspective of Old English and Old Frisian, they show some productivity in the Continental Germanic languages, especially in Old High German, but also in Old Low Franconian and partly Old Saxon. Despite this ambiguous status of the *i*-stems with respect to

---

45. An alternative convention of presenting the paradigms would be to show only the forms which are factually attested in the material (e.g. Boutkan 1995: 264), as illustrated by the OLF root noun paradigm below (cf. Table 6.7). Such a convention was considered less transparent and therefore not followed in this study.

archaic			innovative	
SG		PL	SG	PL
NOM.	*man*	man	*man*	fuoti, tende, *-a
GEN.	*man	*manno*	mannis	*manno, -n*
DAT.	*man	*mannon, fuozen*	manni, -e	*mannon, fuozen*
ACC.	*man*	man	*man*	fuoti, fuoze, uozen

productivity, they were incorporated into the present investigation under the heading *minor*. The inclusion of these stems into the study was guided entirely by the demands of a comparative study, which needs to stay consistent also when it comes to the scope of the analysis. As this class poses a range of methodological problems, its treatments will vary depending on the language (cf. the discussions in the respective chapters, and especially in Chapter 6).

1.5.2 The corpora: Characteristics and methodological considerations

The present qualitative and quantitative examination of early Northern West Germanic nominal morphology was based on (as far as possible) complete corpora of four languages, available either in an electronic form, as corpus dictionaries, or as standard authoritative text editions. Accordingly, the investigation of the Old English material was conducted using the *Dictionary of Old English Electronic Corpus* (henceforth *DOEEC*) (Healey et al. 2009), which constitutes the most exhaustive corpus of Old English, covering over 3,000 texts. The analyses of the Old Saxon and Old Low Franconian material, where no electronic text corpora are available, were based on the respective comprehensive corpus dictionaries, i.e. Tiefenbach's *Altsächsisches Handwörterbuch* (2010) and *Oudnederlands Woordenboek* (Schoonheim et al. 2009). The Old Frisian material was examined on the basis of the most recent and authoritative editions of the texts dated before 1400 (for more details on the corpora, see the respective chapters). As the study was intended to be as far as possible exhaustive, the analysis was based on the complete corpora, with some "local" limitations, which varied depending on the language, including, for instance, the confinement of the study to the Classical Old Frisian period, or the limitation of the quantitative analysis of the *i*-stems in Old English.

The discrepant characteristics of these corpora with respect to the size, genre as well as attestation dates are commonly recognised and can theoretically pose a number of methodological difficulties in a study of a comparative nature like the present one. The direct consequence of these formal discrepancies is that the analysis will necessitate juxtaposing the diversified (with regard to genre) Old English material which spans several centuries, with the very modest corpus of Old Low Franconian (three major sources,), or the genre-wise undiversified corpus of Old Frisian, confined almost exclusively to legal texts. The question of different dates of attestation of individual languages is particularly acute in the case of Old Frisian. While the Old English material dates back to as early as the (late) seventh century, Old Saxon to the ninth century, the earliest attestations of Frisian date from the latter half of the thirteenth century (excluding the scant runic inscriptions dated between the sixth and ninth centuries), which means that they are contemporaneous with the "middle" stages of the other West Germanic languages. This late attestation date of Old Frisian becomes particularly problematic when it comes to a cross-Germanic comparison, necessitating some methodological considerations (cf. Section 4.2). Another challenging question related to the nature of the available corpora involves the reliability of the findings from the examination of small corpora, such as the Old Low Franconian corpus. The paucity of the attested material may have serious implications for the interpretation of the data. However, as the aim of the study is to examine the details of the restructuring process based on the earliest Northern West Germanic languages, it was considered legitimate to include all the extant evidence, even if scant or chronologically widely discrepant. Some of these problematic questions were addressed in Versloot & Adamczyk (2014), in which the impact of corpus composition (with respect to genre and size) on the interpretation of linguistic data was investigated, drawing on a comparison of the Old English and Old Frisian data. The findings of this quantitative study, which entailed a comparison of the Old Frisian corpus with the entire Old English corpus (*DOEEC*) and the Old English legal texts sub-corpus (extracted from the *DOEEC*), demonstrated that, despite the discrepancy in their sizes and composition, the limited corpus of Old Frisian is reliable enough to allow for inferences about genre-independent features, such as phonological and morphological patterns.[46] At the same time, the variation in text type has a substantial impact on the number of attested lemmas, which in the context of the present study is rather unfortunate. Significantly, much as the lack of specific lemmas in Old Frisian can to a large extent be ascribed to the remarkably homogenous nature of the corpus, the discrepancies between Old English and Old Frisian at the lexical level cannot be interpreted as a difference between the two language realities and their lexicons (Versloot & Adamczyk 2014: 565). These observations are assumed to be valid also for the other smaller corpora investigated in the present study, Old Saxon and Old Low Franconian. Two further implications of the study relevant for the present analysis are related to lemma frequency distributions in the corpora. Namely, (1) it can be expected that only high frequent items will be attested in the smaller corpora, and (2) no conclusions can be drawn from the fact that an item is not attested in the corpus. In other words, the evidence based on the fact that a lemma is not attested in the corpus (i.e. negative evidence) cannot be treated as conclusive; the only evidence that should count as valid is the presence of any attested word form, be it archaic or innovative (i.e. positive evidence).

---

46. The scope of the study was confined to the investigation of inflectional morphology of nouns in these two languages and the findings are based entirely on this selected sample.

Admittedly, the smaller corpora must be viewed as representing samples of larger linguistic realities that most likely could have been characterised by the same variation as the (relatively) abundantly attested Old English material. In explaining the patterns found in the most limited corpora, such as Old Saxon, Old Frisian and Old Low Franconian, recourse to the evidence from the later stages of attestation will occasionally be made. However, such an approach has many limitations and hazards, and cannot be applied uncritically. The evidence from the later stages of the development of the individual Germanic languages cannot be indiscriminately treated as a conclusive source of information about the earlier stages, but in many cases it may turn out to be adequately informative. For instance, the evidence from modern Northern Frisian dialects, which tend to preserve many archaic plural forms, can shed some light on the earlier state of affairs, confirming the probability that such forms existed in Old Frisian (cf. Chapter 4).

Another characteristic of the examined corpora is the dialectal component which they to various extents incorporate. As any other natural language, Older Germanic languages had synchronic dialectal differentiation, although this variation is not equally well attested in the extant records. The wide scope of the material examined in the present study affords insight into the diatopic variation observable in the restructuring process, which is attested primarily in Old English and to a lesser extent in Old Frisian and Old Saxon. Therefore, due attention will be paid to potential dialectal discrepancies, and an examination of the material representing particular dialects, as far as they are identifiable, will result in a more detailed description of the analogical developments in the nominal inflection. At the same time, much as the present study will attempt to formulate some generalisations about the dialectally-determined patterns (especially in the Old English material which is fairly diversified in this respect), the details of this variation stay beyond the primary focus of the study. Except for the chapter devoted to Old English, where the corpus was prepared in a way so as to enable a systematic diatopic examination, the other chapters cover the dialectal contrasts rather as supplementary information to the description of the phenomenon under study, i.e. the contrasts are explicitly referred to whenever they offer additional insight into the mechanisms of the restructuring process.

What needs to be underscored is that the dialectal contrasts which are detectable in some languages tend to correlate strongly with diachronic contrasts. Accordingly, the early Old English material is predominantly represented by Mercian, while the later sources are predominantly West-Saxon; the early Old Frisian sources come from the eastern part of the Frisian-speaking territory, while later texts are primarily western. Likewise, while the older Old Low Franconian source (*Wachtendonck Psalms*) derives from the south-east, the younger text of *Leiden Willeram* is western

(Holland). This fact constitutes one of the major complications in the interpretation of the variation attested in the available material.[47]

As regards the selection of the languages for the present study, the investigation comprises four of five West Germanic languages, which can be more precisely termed *Northern West Germanic*, as announced in the title of the book. The largest part of the medieval Continental West Germanic attestation is the Old High German material, a much smaller part Old Saxon and only a minor fragmentary part Old Low Franconian/Old Dutch (e.g. Klein 2003: 56). As Old Saxon and Old Low Franconian frequently pattern alike with respect to morphological developments, a common term reflecting this morphological similarity will be used to refer to these two languages, i.e. Inland or Continental West Germanic, as opposed to Coastal West Germanic, including Old English and Old Frisian (similarly, Hogg 1992a: 2; Findell 2009: 4). The exclusion of Old High German from the study, which had also its practical rationale, was motivated by two reasons: firstly, the selected four languages form an adjacent geographical and typological continuum, while Old High German is in a way a typological outlier among the West Germanic dialects; secondly, the contrast between North Sea Germanic (OE, OFris.) and Continental Germanic (OLF, OS) is sufficiently covered to admit of conclusions about the nature of the restructuring process across the West Germanic language continuum.[48] The practical reasons for not including the Old High German material relate to the size and nature of its corpus, which is well-known for its strong dialectal diversification. The inclusion of the Old High German material would not only greatly enlarge the scope of this already quite extensive study, but it would also result in a more fragmented picture of the investigated developments.[49]

Each of the languages investigated in this study can be viewed as unique and this term will appear with reference to individual languages on a few occasions

---

47. Such a correspondence between the diachronic and dialectal contrasts is not found in the Old Saxon material, where the dialectal picture is more fragmented. The majority of sources derive from the south-west of the Saxon-speaking region.

48. While these four languages share a range of North Sea Germanic phonological developments (e.g. in stressed syllables), with regard to nominal morphology, Old Low Franconian and Old Saxon differ fundamentally from Old English and Old Frisian, as will become clear in the course of the present investigation.

49. An independent study covering the Old High German material is without a doubt an enterprise worth pursuing. The arguments for the exclusion of this language from this study, especially the size of the corpus and its dialectal diversification, could be at the same time valid reasons for the examination of the Old High German nominal system in a separate study, bringing potentially valuable insights into the mechanisms of the restructuring.

when introducing their general profiles. The uniqueness of the individual West Germanic dialects entails a range of different features; accordingly, the uniqueness of Old Saxon and Old Low Franconian is related to their positioning in the West Germanic linguistic continuum; the uniqueness of Old Frisian lies in the nature of the available material (legal documentation); and finally the uniqueness of Old English may be sought in the abundance and diversity of the available sources. It is hoped that the scope of the material used in the present study will provide insights into the mechanisms of the remodelling of the nominal inflection in the examined languages.

1.5.3   Scope of the study and procedures

The scope of the present study was confined to the paradigms of unproductive, i.e. minor classes, including two vocalic classes: *i*-stems and *u*-stems, and five consonantal classes: root nouns, *r*-stems, *s*-stems, *nd*-stems and dental stems (as far as attested). Some of these declensions represent semantically closed classes, for example, the *r*-stems contained only nouns of relationship, *nd*-stems comprised masculine nominalised participles (original present participle formations, known as *nomina agentis*), *s*-stems were largely nouns associated with agriculture. Not all of these classes are equally well attested in the examined languages, which is a consequence of the differences in the size and text-type (genre) composition of the respective corpora. For instance, the class of dental stems is very scantily represented in the investigated languages, with a full paradigm attested only in Old English. Accordingly, with the less well-attested classes, the interpretation of the findings must be cautious and the ensuing conclusions framed in terms of tendencies rather than absolute rules.

The analytical part of the study involves a quantitative investigation of the restructuring of nominal paradigms in individual languages (discussed in the respective chapters), and a systematic comparison of the findings (summarised in Chapter 7), aimed at identifying both language-specific and more universal tendencies underlying the process. In order to account for both, namely the divergent developmental trajectories that the sister languages followed as well as the more universal patterns emerging from the investigation, a close scrutiny of the factors conditioning the restructuring process in individual languages is undertaken (Chapter 8). The organising principle of the investigation is the systematic examination of the process per language and per declensional class (as defined diachronically). In the case of the better attested classes, the investigation was conducted separately for masculine, feminine and neuter nouns, with a further subdivision based on the stem weight (where relevant). The quantitative analysis involved examining the incidence of inherited vs. analogical inflections in the paradigms of minor stems. The percentage of the analogical forms in the paradigms is taken to represent their level of morphological innovation; in other words, it reflects how far a given paradigm has departed from its original, historical inflectional shape.

The distribution of nouns across declensional classes in the present study is based on diachronic criteria and may be considered inadequate from a synchronic point of view, but for the purpose of a cross-linguistic comparison, such an approach turns out to be practical and efficient. Even if detached from the linguistic reality, which has to be acknowledged, such a diachronic presentation of the declensional system has some evident advantages, the most important being the consistency and transparency of the systematic treatment.

As observed earlier, interdeclensional shifts of nouns did not begin only at the earliest attested stages of Germanic. Rather, many of the analogical reshufflings can be traced back to the prehistoric period. The focus of the present study is on the reorganisation of the nominal system in the earliest attested period of the languages under examination rather than on the prehistoric shifts.[50] The Proto-Germanic stage and the nominal system reconstructed for this stage is taken as the point of departure for the qualitative and quantitative analysis. Accordingly, it is the affiliation of nouns with individual classes reconstructed for Proto-Germanic rather than for the earlier stages (Proto-Indo-European) that serves as the primary reference point for the investigation. For instance, the examination of changes in the paradigm of *duru* 'door' takes the Proto-Germanic form as the starting point, where *duru* is reconstructed as a *u*-stem. The fact that this noun can be traced back to the root nouns in Proto-Indo-European (e.g. Griepentrog 1995) strays beyond the scope of the present study, and *duru* is accordingly included in the inventory of the *u*-stems rather than of root nouns in all the examined languages (see Appendix).

Both qualitative and quantitative analyses of inflectional morphology in the earliest attested stages of each of the selected languages are burdened with a range of difficulties related primarily to the nature of the available corpora. The first step of the investigation was the selection of lemmas which were affiliated with minor classes in the examined Old Germanic languages. On account of the comparative nature of the study, the criteria for the classification of nouns must be consistent and the same (or parallel) for all the investigated languages. All the lemmas included in the quantitative analysis of individual languages are presented in the Appendix, alongside the nouns which transferred to other declensions at a prehistoric stage, and were thus excluded from the quantitative study. Establishing the original class

---

50. See the systematic study of Thöny (2013) who focuses primarily on the interparadigmatic transfers in prehistoric Germanic.

affiliation of some nouns turned out to be quite problematic. The study relies in this respect on the information found in the standard historical grammars and etymological dictionaries of the respective languages (see individual chapters for more details). The inventories of PGmc. stems presented in the studies of Bammesberger (1990) and Griepentrog (1995), as well as the lists of attested forms found especially in the early works of authors such as van Helten (1891, 1911) served as a valuable additional reference for the selection. However, in some cases the problem of classification became more acute, since the evidence availed by the early attested languages does not always allow us to determine the affiliation of individual nouns. In some instances, a cognate set shows divergent declensional affiliations across Germanic, which from the point of view of a comparative study has serious methodological implications. Some nouns attested as minor stems in one language can follow productive patterns in some other (investigated) language(s) (e.g. OFris. *fretho*, which shows evident traces of the *u*-stem inflection vs. OE *friþ* following the *a*-stem pattern, cf. the relic of the *u*-stem in OE *freoþo*, attested primarily in poetic texts). The source of such discrepancies is the chronology of interdeclensional transitions in the individual Old Germanic languages: the analogical transfer of nouns to productive declensions did not occur simultaneously in all the examined languages. Thus, while in one language a given shift may occur prior to the first written attestations, leaving no vestiges of the historical inflection in the paradigm, in another, the transition may be well attested in the available material. The fact that the individual Germanic languages testify to divergent declensional affiliations of individual nouns can additionally be ascribed to a number of factors other than the discrepant chronology of interdeclensional transfers. One of them can be the existence of parallel formations in Proto-Germanic (Kluge 1926, Bammesberger 1990, Thöny 2013), or the independent development of new word-formation patterns in the individual Germanic languages. The problem may be illustrated by the Go. form *lustus* and its cognates in West Germanic. Two derivations can be traced back to the root **lus-* 'to desire': a *tu*-stem derivative *lustu-* (m.) to a verbal root **lus-*, and a *ti*-stem derivative *lusti-* (f.) (from **leusan-*) 'desire, lust' (Kroonen 2013, s.v. *lustu-*, *lusti-*). The forms attested in individual languages seem to go back to the *u*-stem variant and testify to different gender-class affiliation: Go. *lustus* (m.), OE *lust* (m.), OFris. *lust* (m. f.), OS *lust* (f.) and OHG *lust* (m. f.) (cf. ON *lyst*). This particular example is still relatively transparent, as the lack of *i*-mutation in Old English and Old Saxon, and the present-day German form *Lust* point unambiguously to their origin in the *u*-stems. However, accounting for such variation can be more problematic in other instances (cf. Section 2.2.1). Accordingly, an important distinction that needs to be made in the present study is between the inflectional paradigmatic variation resulting from the processes of analogical interdeclensional reshufflings, and the variation resulting from the derivational process that occurred at the prehistoric stage, in Proto-Germanic, which strays beyond the purview of the present analysis.

Another type of variation found in the paradigms is one emerging from the vocalic alternations in Proto-Indo-European, which appear as variants in Proto-Germanic (arguably interpretable as ablaut variants, e.g. Krogh 2013: 145). It can be well illustrated by the variation in the NOM. PL. marker of the masculine and feminine *u*-stems, where the Go., ON, OHG and OS ending -*i* goes back to *-*ewez*, whereas the OE and OFris. ending -*a* derives from *-*awez* (e.g. *suni* vs. *suna* 'sons'). Some of these allomorphs cannot be traced back to Proto-Indo-European, but are later developments (cf. Boutkan's [1996] distinction between "high" and "low reflex"). These two sources of variation go beyond the scope of the present study, whose primary focus is on the developments which entailed a change in the declensional class affiliation as a consequence of analogical remodelling. The existence of several sources of inflectional variation in paradigms is one of the features of the early Germanic nominal inflection which has implications on the methodology applied in this study, at the same time demonstrating that the process of restructuring was a multifaceted and multilayered, complex development.

Some of the analogical reshufflings attested in the material may have been an idiosyncratic feature of one language only, not shared by the sister languages. An illustrative example of such a language-specific analogical transition is the class of *u*-stems in Gothic, comprising nouns which originated as root nouns (e.g. *fōtus* 'foot', *tunþus* 'tooth'). The evidence of all Germanic languages, except Gothic, indicates that these nouns were affiliated with the class of root nouns, while in Gothic they declined according to the *u*-stem pattern. The *u*-stem inflection therein can be ascribed to a Gothic-specific change rather than a common Germanic development (Bammesberger 1990: 198). The transition between these two classes was possible because of the formal similarity of the accusative in the singular and plural in the two declensional types in Proto-Germanic (Bammesberger 1990: 198; van Loon 2005: 179; Ramat 1981: 62; cf. Lass 1986: 478).

For the purpose of cross-linguistic consistency, the present study took into account all nouns which (apart from being etymologically minor stems) showed inflectional features of historical (unproductive) inflection in the paradigms in at least one of the investigated languages. Accordingly, nouns which do not show traces of historical inflection, although their etymological affiliation with minor stems in the examined languages can be confirmed by external (Germanic) evidence, were excluded from the analysis on account of their prehistoric transfer to the productive classes. This procedure was consistently applied to all nouns except OE *friþ* 'peace' and *liþ* 'member'; these two nouns were excluded from the quantitative analysis of the Old English material, where no traces of the *u*-stem inflection are attested, in contrast to the other investigated languages, where the corresponding lemmas show traces of the archaic pattern (see 3.5.3.2 for the justification of this choice).

Another aspect of the analysis which turned out to be occasionally problematic concerns the procedure of classifying the forms as *archaic* and *innovative*. Applying consistent criteria for this classification was essential as the decisions were consequential for the final results of the quantitative analysis, depending entirely on which forms were interpreted as inherited and which as analogical. A number of formal principles and criteria which were employed in the classification procedure need to be made explicit. On account of the differences in the exact phonological and morphological conditions in the individual languages (e.g. the chronology of certain phonological changes), they need to be specified separately for each language. For the sake of transparency, the treatment of individual problematic forms, provided they do not have a more general scope (like the DAT. PL. marker *-um* [*-en*, *-un*] found across West Germanic), is relegated to sections devoted to particular declensional classes in the individual languages. The principles of classification applying cross-linguistically include:

1. Paradigm forms which testify to any departure from their phonologically expected historical shape by displaying inflections pertinent to productive declensional types are considered to be analogical and classified as *innovative*.
2. Paradigm forms which on account of their inflectional shape cannot provide any reliable information about the restructuring process are classified and counted as *neutral*; this refers to forms that are homophonous with the corresponding case forms from the default (productive) paradigms; for example, the forms of the GEN. PL. (*-a, -o*) and DAT. PL. (*-um, -un*), which as a result of prehistoric analogical developments happened to be identical with the respective forms of the *a*-stems and *ō*-stems (except in the *s*-stems, where their historical inflection is reflected in the *r*-formative). The number of such uninformative forms depends on a given inflectional type, lemma and language (or dialect), although there are a number of overlapping forms that had to be excluded in nearly all classes, in all the investigated languages.
3. Unambiguous paradigm forms which were found in ambiguous syntactic contexts were counted irrespective of their syntactical application; for example, the marker *-um* is always interpreted as a DAT. PL.[51]

---

51. This means that a form such as OE *meolcum* 'milk' is counted as the DAT. PL. despite the fact that the noun is uncountable (cf. Plank 1987: 203–205; Bammesberger 2001).

4. Regular phonological reduction is not explicitly marked except in the con-
    texts where it causes confusion between archaic and innovative inflection; for
    instance, the variation in the DAT. PL. between -*um* ~ -*on* (e.g. OE *nihtum* ~
    nihton) is irrelevant for the present study, although the former marker is clearly
    more archaic (see Section 3.5.4).[52]
5. When case and number interpretation is ambiguous, other formal criteria are
    decisive, namely, the forms of the accompanying demonstrative or possessive
    pronouns, or the forms of the accompanying verbs.

The last two points are relevant for the analysis of the Old English and (partly) Old
Low Franconian material, as well as for the data from the Old Frisian manuscript
Unia, which is not lemmatised. In the case of Old Saxon and the rest of Old Frisian,
the interpretations of paradigmatic forms found in the dictionaries and glossaries
to the editions of the respective texts were consistently adhered to, except for a few
single instances in the Old Frisian corpus, where a different interpretation from
the one offered in the glossaries was considered correct and given to several forms.

In view of the fact that a substantial proportion of paradigmatic forms which
were uninformative as regards the restructuring of inflection was substantial, the
procedure of identifying and excluding *neutral* forms from the quantitative analysis
deserves some elaboration. The exclusion of forms which are overlapping in the
archaic and innovative paradigms prevents the (over)interpretation of paradigms,
such as the novel OE singular paradigm of *fōt: fōt – fōtes – fōte – fōt*, as 50 percent
archaic, based on the NOM./ACC. SG. form *fōt*, which continues the expected historical inflection. The paradigm testifies to a complete overlap with the *a*-stems, which
is overtly seen in the GEN. SG. and DAT. SG. Such an interpretation of paradigmatic
forms is, however, not entirely unproblematic. The ACC. SG. form *fōt* can still be
interpreted as archaic when contrasted with a potential ACC. SG. **fōtan*, with the
ending -*an* extended from the *n*-stems. The consequence of this interpretation is
that the overall level of archaism/innovativeness of the paradigm would change
substantially. The solution considered acceptable in such cases was to identify the
default analogy class for a given minor declension, or subclass, i.e. the pattern(s)
which was (were) most likely to attract the nouns of a given minor class or paradigm. In the majority of cases across Germanic, the *a*-stem declension fulfills
this role for masculine and neuter nouns, and the *ō*-stem declension for feminine
nouns. Although the *n*-stem inflection could potentially be an attractor as well, it
is assumed that only one inflectional pattern can function as the main attractor (cf.

52. A clear separation between the effects of phonological and morphological processes in the
nominal inflection is fundamental for the classification of forms. As this aspect differs per language, close attention is given to it in the respective chapters.

Section 1.4.5). Given this assumption (which will be substantiated in the course of the investigation), all paradigm forms that are homophonous with the corresponding forms from the default paradigm are counted as neutral. Accordingly, forms such as the DAT. SG. OE *fōt (fēt)* are counted as archaic, DAT. SG. *fōte* as innovative, and ACC. SG. *fōt* as neutral. The potential analogical ACC. SG. form **fōtan*, although formally innovative, is excluded from the calculation as the corresponding form *fōt*, which overlaps with the forms of the productive *a*-stems, cannot be unambiguously ascribed to the archaic pattern. Likewise, the GEN. PL. forms in *-a* are neutral, while GEN. PL. *-ena*, innovative, but again the latter must be counted as neutral as there is no unambiguously archaic corresponding form attested (the endings *-a, -o* can be both archaic or innovative). For the same reason the DAT. PL. form is consistently interpreted as neutral. In contrast, the OFris. *u*-stem paradigm of *frethe* 'peace': *frethe – fretha – fretha – frethe* is considered 100% archaic, despite the fact that the NOM. ACC. SG. marker *-e* is also a characteristic of the *ja*-stems, and the GEN. DAT. SG. ending *-a* of the *n*-stems. As these two declensional types are clearly non-default classes for the transfers of the *u*-stems in Old Frisian, they are not considered to have constituted a likely source for the attested inflections, and accordingly these forms do not need to be counted as neutral in the analysis. The figures for neutral forms will consistently be presented in italics and placed in the left-hand column of the tables presenting the competing paradigms and inflections, marked as *archaic*. The notation is arbitrary and is in no way meaningful for the present study.

Some of the attested lemmas, although classifiable as minor stems through external evidence (i.e. cognate forms from the sister languages), are uninformative not only in regard to paradigmatic restructuring, but also their actual synchronic affiliation with a given declension class in a given language. This refers in particular to nouns attested only, and very often singly, in the NOM SG., especially in the early glosses. In the majority of cases these forms had to be classified as neutral in the present study.

Although etymological affiliation with minor classes was an essential criterion in the selection of the inventory of nouns for the quantitative analysis, two nouns which were included in the study did not originally (in Proto-Germanic) belong to minor declensional classes, i.e. PDE *summer* (*u*-stem) and *child* (*s*-stem). Their pattern of inflection as attested in the Old Germanic languages, however, clearly testifies to the historical affiliation with minor inflectional classes. The latter, on account of its very high frequency of occurrence, is examined and discussed separately in the respective sections, and the findings are interpreted also in the context of its fairly problematic etymology.

Some of the nouns relevant to the present investigation are attested in the onomastic material, appearing as the first or second elements of place or proper names (e.g. OE *Ēadburg*, OFris. *mimigerde forda* 'Münster', OS *Almeri, Astanfelda*,

Liefburgahūsoro, OLF *Hrintsalis*). Except for cases where such forms belong to lemmas which are scantily attested in the corpora, the present investigation essentially does not take into consideration the onomastic material because of its unique nature. It is assumed that the morphological development of these forms was guided by independent rules and that the analogical changes in inflectional morphology took different paths in proper nouns and in common nouns. In general, onomastic material tends to show greater inflectional archaism (e.g. Campbell 1977: 5; Quak 2003; Clark 1992: 452ff; Mills 2011), and accordingly it will be referred to occasionally, in particular in cases when it can offer valuable information about the inflectional patterns unobtainable otherwise (i.e. based on the evidence of common nouns).

Admittedly, any diachronic investigation is largely determined and often limited by the nature of the material which forms its basis. Some of the direct problems resulting from the profiles of the corpora examined in the present study have already been signalled, but a further complication related to the nature of the available material and the ensuing limitations involves the exact dating and provenance of texts or manuscripts. This refers in particular to the Old English material, where many of the texts incorporated in the corpus pose considerable difficulties. For instance, the question of dating of the manuscript (vs. composition) of *Beowulf* (e.g. Chase 1997), or the dialectal mixture and provenance of *Vespasian Psalter* (e.g. Kuhn 1959; Ball 1970) are some of the issues on which the scholarly community is not unanimous. A closely related problem is that of the existence of (oftentimes many) copies of certain texts, which very often complicates the issue of determining the provenance and/or dating of a given text, and may have implications for the interpretation of the data. Bede's *Historia ecclesiastica* may serve as an example: the text is preserved in a number of manuscripts dated between the eighth and twelfth centuries. The edition of the text selected for the *DOEEC* is that of Miller (1890–1898) which is based primarily on manuscript T (Tanner 10, the Bodleian Library, Oxford), dated to the tenth century, and supplemented by manuscripts C (second half of the 8th c.), O (early 11th c.) and Ca (second half of the 11th c.) (Miller 1890: 25–34; cf. Rowley 2011: 16–17). Accordingly, the text is classified as *Early* in the *DOEEC*; however, the analysis of the material demonstrates that, with respect to Old English nominal morphology, the text is actually relatively innovative. As the present study consistently adheres to the labelling used in the *DOEEC*, the text is placed among other sources classified as *Early*, and the relevant attestations are counted as such. However, as it will become clear in the course of the analysis, the characterisation of the text as *Early* can be questioned and (consequently) so can be its treatment as such in the present analysis. The scope of the present study precludes tackling such problematic issues individually for each text in the Old English corpus, and accordingly, the dating and provenance of texts provided in the *DOEEC* is consistently adhered to in the analysis. The same approach was applied to the other investigated corpora which pose similar problems related to localisation or dialect mixture (e.g. OS Straubing fragment of *Heliand*, or OLF *Leiden Willeram*).

Another problematic aspect of the study, which has less serious methodological consequences, is related to the fact that the extant material cannot be taken to represent an exact reflection of the spoken language in any of the investigated languages. It is a predicament of a much more general scope, which any diachronic study of language has to face. The idiom attested in the available sources does not represent the registers of the majority of the early Germanic social classes (Nielsen 1994: 196), but rather more or less (as far as possible) "standardised" written varieties of the dialects that were actually spoken in the respective territories of north-western Europe. The standardisation involves here a more local dimension, i.e. the adjustment of the language of texts to the standards of a given scriptorium in which they were produced. In this respect the position of Old English is the most fortuitous, as the Old English corpus offers a relatively wide coverage of the written material deriving from different scriptoria. A closely related issue is that the register of the written language cannot ideally reflect the spoken idiom on account of the topics covered in the early textual material. For instance, the register of the corpus of Old Frisian composed of legal texts, or the Old English religious or poetic texts, can be expected to be too formal and refined to contain certain lexical items which must have been common in the spoken language. Accordingly, nouns denoting animals or other agricultural terms which may have been frequently used in everyday conversational language are not well represented in the corpora. This aspect will be referred to in the respective chapters when the distribution of inherited and analogical forms is interpreted as a reflex of frequency effects operating at the lemma level.

CHAPTER 2

Nominal inflection in Proto-Germanic

2.1   Introduction

The present chapter constitutes the background and starting point for further investigation into the reorganisation of the nominal inflection in Germanic. As the declensional systems of individual Germanic languages are anchored in the Proto-Germanic system of declensions, this proto-system will naturally be considered a reference point for estimating the scale of the restructuring process of nominal inflection in the daughter languages.[53] The purpose of this chapter is two-fold: firstly, it aims to sketch the original pattern of nominal inflection as far as it can be reconstructed for Proto-Germanic, with particular attention to the origin of inflectional endings and the criteria for the classification of inflectional types; and secondly, it attempts to outline the analogical realignments occurring at early stages, with a view to estimating their extent and consequences for the structure of the paradigms in the daughter languages. In accordance with the focus of the present study, the systematic presentation of the Proto-Germanic material is confined to minor declensional classes, which because of their restricted membership and lack of productivity constituted an obvious target group for the operation of analogical processes.

   Although this study is devoted to an investigation of the restructuring processes in Northern West Germanic languages, the present chapter affords an opportunity to broaden the perspective by referring to the nominal inflections in Gothic and Early Runic, which generally remained closest to the original Proto-Germanic inflectional system and retained many archaic inflectional characteristics, as well as Old Norse, which often follows quite a different path of inflectional development from the rest of Germanic. Recourse to the evidence of these sister languages, representing the

---

53. The terminology adopted in the present study follows that introduced in Prokosch (1939: 27), where *Proto-Germanic* refers to the prehistoric stage with no clear division into dialects, while *Common Germanic* denotes the stage with linguistic developments affecting independently all Germanic dialects. It stays in accordance with the more detailed chronology offered by van Coetsem (1994), where a further subdivision into Early and Late Proto-Germanic is postulated (van Coetsem 1994: 17–18; 193). For a further terminological discussion, see Ramat (1981: 8–13), Mottausch (2011: 173–174).

eastern and northern branches of Germanic, is made especially when they diverge from the developments in West Germanic and can thus shed more light on the process of restructuring in Germanic as a whole, supplementing the overall picture. Such a comprehensive approach, with a broader pan-Germanic perspective, will hopefully provide an adequate background for the qualitative and quantitative investigation of analogical reshaping in the individual West Germanic languages.

The immediate roots of the process of analogical restructuring of the Germanic system of nominal inflection are to be sought in the early stages, i.e. in Proto-Germanic. However, the propensity of the nominal paradigms to be reorganised, resulting in a continuous state of flux, seems to have been an inherent feature of nominal paradigms, with origins in the PIE parent language. The evidence from individual Indo-European languages indicates that the reorganisation of the PIE nominal system must have been a general phenomenon, taking place prior to the first attestations of the individual daughter languages. In many of them, the reconfiguration of the system entails interparadigmatic or interdeclensional transfers of nouns, determined commonly by the increasing productivity of a few dominant inflectional patterns and diachronic instability of others.[54] The evidence from early Germanic dialects likewise demonstrates that the analogical reshufflings between inflectional classes must be dated to the prehistoric period, partly to Proto-Germanic, partly to Common Germanic, and their emergence is intimately linked to the overall change of the phonological profile of Proto-Germanic and the oldest Germanic languages.

In the present study two stages of the restructuring process will be distinguished, namely (1) the early, prehistoric analogical reshufflings, entailing *intra-* and *inter*declensional transfers, and (2) extensive analogical shifts dating from the historical stage of the individual Germanic languages. In both stages, certain further chronological substages can be identified. Prehistoric change, for instance, comprises developments of differing antiquity, including those of a general pan-Germanic nature, those pertinent to specific sub-branches of Germanic (e.g. Northwest Germanic, West Germanic), as well as those dated shortly before the attestations of individual Germanic languages (e.g. pre-Old English, pre-Old Saxon). Knowledge of the prehistoric stage of the restructuring process can be

---

54. E.g. the transfer of *u*-stems to IE *o*-declension (Gmc. *a*-stems) in Slavic and Baltic languages, or the large-scale transition of *n*-stems to *a*-stems in Latin. A more general trend to be observed in many IE sister languages is the gradual replacement of the athematic declensions by the thematic ones – a process which has its parallels also in the verbal system. The attractiveness (productivity) of thematic paradigms, which are historically younger, belonging to the less ancient layer of IE derivation, could be *potentially* (though not necessarily) ascribed to their transparent structure, characterised by a lack of internal accentual shifts or alternations in ablaut grades (Fortson 2010: 84, 113).

gained primarily through extensive comparative analysis of the material provided by the daughter languages, especially the earliest attested North Germanic (Early Runic) and East Germanic (Gothic).[55] Much as such a comparison can offer a wealth of information about the prehistoric stages of the process, it is not devoid of complications, which often render the findings and observations tentative or speculative. In contrast, the second stage of the restructuring process is a directly observable phenomenon, which, at least theoretically, can be captured in the available Older Germanic material. There, the attested synchronic variation among inflectional forms reflects a competition between archaic and novel inflectional patterns which can often be quantitatively analysed.

2.2   Reorganisation of the nominal inflection in Proto-Germanic

2.2.1   The Proto-Germanic nominal system: General characteristics

In the course of the evolution from the Proto-Indo-European parent language, the Proto-Germanic nominal system experienced numerous morphological developments, triggered primarily by changes in the phonological system. The most prominent of them included the marginalisation and levelling of ablaut alternations of the root, stem or ending, which became lexicalised and morphologised in later Indo-European (Clackson 2007: 71–72); reduction in the system of cases (from eight to six, including the vocative); and erosion of unaccented (inflectional) syllables, as well as the emergence of new declensional classes with stems ending in vowels (Ringe 2006: 268). Another significant change was a substantial growth in the productivity of the *n*-stems. These innovations modified the overall shape of the nominal system, opening the way for its further transformation in Proto-Germanic and subsequently in the individual Germanic languages.

Notwithstanding all these innovations, the Proto-Germanic system remained altogether relatively close to its predecessor in at least two respects. One is a considerable archaism of inflection, discernible in the diversity of declensional classes, especially in Early Runic and Gothic (Meillet 1970: 61, 63, 90). In fact, the early Germanic evidence points to the existence of a more diversified system

---

55. In line with Nielsen's (2000) definition, Early Runic refers here to the language of the Germanic inscriptions between AD 200 and 500. Although a predecessor of Old Norse, Early Runic is still fairly distant from it in terms of phonological and morphological archaism, and this distance is clearly more substantial than to the Common West Germanic stage. To use the phrasing of Nielsen, Early Runic stays "closer to Proto-Germanic than to the later attested North and West Gmc. languages" (Nielsen 2000: 286; cf. Fortson 2010: 350).

of declensions in Proto-Germanic than in the PIE parent language, which was a combined effect of phonological developments as well as changes affecting the internal structure of the noun.[56] The nominal system in Proto-Indo-European was characterised by the variation in accentual patterns, giving rise to numerous ablaut alternations in the root and stem suffixes, whereas the actual case-and-number in-flections remained largely identical for nouns of all inflectional classes and genders. As in other Indo-European branches, the elimination of most traces of this ablaut variation in Proto-Germanic was compensated for by the emergence of a nominal system based on a division into inflectional classes.

One of the direct and profound consequences of phonological changes in Germanic was the fusion of PIE case-and-number endings (inflectional forma-tives) with the stem vowels (stem formants), which led to the emergence of the final segment of the stem as the basic classificatory criterion for PGmc. nouns (Ringe 2006: 196). This fusion resulted in a major change in the structure of the noun: the threefold division of the noun reconstructed for Proto-Indo-European was reduced to a twofold structure in Proto-Germanic.[57] Accordingly, the PIE noun structure consisting of the root + stem-forming suffix + inflection (case-number ending) (e.g. $*g^h$ ost-i-s, $*s\bar{u}n$-u-s) was replaced by one where the root was followed directly by an inflectional marker (e.g. $*gast$-iz, $*sun$-uz).[58] This development entailed a rea-nalysis of the vocalic or consonantal element which constituted originally a deri-vational suffix, attaching to the root to form the stem, into a marker of inflection (Ringe 2006: 173). As a result, the original suffix was eventually ridden of its deri-vational function in the structure. Given the evidence of Early Runic (dated ca. AD 200–500), which is commonly believed to represent the late Common Germanic stage, the process occurred relatively late, namely in the transition period between late Common Germanic and historical Germanic. The reconstructed paradigms in Early Runic demonstrate that in many inflectional classes the stem suffix was

---

56. For instance, from a Proto-Indo-European perspective, the *i*- and *u*-stems were subsumed under the consonantal stems, containing the semivowels *j* and *w*, respectively. The development of these vocalic classes in Germanic is a consequence of a regular phonological change which affected all PIE sonants, whereby *j* > *i*, *w* > *u* (Beekes 1995: 135; cf. Ringe 2006: 268).

57. The change is an indication of a more general typological shift, which started already in the PIE stage, whereby the original agglutinative morphological structures were transformed into those of a fusional nature (e.g. Ramat 1981: 60; Hogg & Fulk 2011: 7).

58. The formation of nouns in PIE was a more complex process. While in thematic nouns the inflectional ending was added to a thematic vowel, in athematic stems the inflection was attached directly to the root, without an intervening suffix or thematic vowel (root nouns); the stem could also be formed by addition of more than one suffix to the root (Clackson 2007: 73–74; Beekes 1995: 171–174, 179ff.; Szemerényi 1999: 155ff.).

still recognisable as a separate element in most of the case forms (e.g. the singular paradigm of masculine *a*-stems, with the stem suffix -*a*-: NOM. *stainaz*, GEN. *stainas*, DAT. *stainai*, -*ē*, ACC. *staina* (-*ā*?)). This is not to imply that the stem element was a productive suffix, but it indicates that the paradigm remained for some time largely transparent from a synchronic point of view and, consequently, the fusion of the suffix must have been a gradual process, taking place after the Proto-Germanic stage (pace Ringe 2006, Hogg & Fulk 2011).[59]

The morphological changes in the structure of the noun had a wider ranging consequence for the development of the Germanic nominal system in that they led to the elimination of the semantic function of the stem suffix. The original declensional system in PIE was semantically motivated, which was expressed through the stem suffix (Ramat 1981: 61). For instance, the suffix -*a*- served originally to create deverbal nomina agentis (often denoting animals or concrete concepts) and nomina actionis (verbal abstracts), the suffix -*ō*-, apart from serving to form nomina actionis and adjectival abstracts, had an inherent collective function, whereas the suffix -*i*- served, among others, to form names of tribes and peoples (Krahe & Meid 1967: 58–67). With the loss of a transparent stem suffix element, this original semantic motivation disappeared and most of the declensions were no longer semantically-defined in Proto-Germanic. Vestiges of the original state of affairs can be seen, for instance, in the *r*-stems, which constituted a semantically coherent class of nouns, comprising kinship terms, built on the agent-noun suffixes (*-*ter*-/*-*tor*-), or the subgroup of the *i*-stems denoting tribal names.

The Proto-Germanic declensional system can be subdivided into three major types of stems, which followed separate inflectional patterns (Lehmann 2005–2007: § 3.1; cf. Prokosch 1939: 226–227):

a. the vocalic stems (stems ending in a vowel, including *a*- and *ō*-stems, and the older sonorant stems, i.e. *i*- and *u*-stems)
b. consonantal stems (stems ending in a consonant, i.e. *r*-stems, *s*-stems, *nd*-stems, *þ*-stems)
c. root nouns (nouns without stem extension)

Due to the significance of stem type for the inflection of nouns, Proto-Germanic nominal morphology is formally referred to as stem-based. Depending on the amount of detail included in the classification of stem types, the number of nominal classes in Proto-Germanic may range from seven (Bammesberger 1990: 13–15) to nine or even ten (Prokosch 1939 and Ringe 2006: 269, respectively). This complex

---

59. The stage of fusion is attested in Early Runic for the DAT. SG. where two variants – the unfused -*ai* and the fused -*ē* – are found, and can be dated to the 4th and 5th century AD (Boutkan 1995: 361).

and elaborate system of declensional classes may be divided into two main sub-groups, i.e. *minor* and *major* types, with productivity serving as the main organising criterion.[60] If a further feature is added, namely the shape of the stem (whereby nouns may be classified into vocalic and consonantal stems), the classification of these classes may be illustrated as presented in Table 2.1.

Table 2.1 Classification of Proto-Germanic nominal stems

Major declensional types		Minor declensional types	
vocalic	consonantal	vocalic	consonantal
a-stems (m, n)	*n*-stems (m, f, n)	*i*-stems (m, f, n)	root nouns (m, f, n)
ō-stems (f)		*u*-stems (m, f, n)	**-es-/-os*-stems (n)*
			r-stems (m, f)
			nd-stems (m)
			þ-stems (m, f)

* For reasons of transparency, the **-es-/-os-* stems will be referred to as *s*-stems in the present study.

The status of the *i*-stems as a minor class is not entirely unambiguous. As regards the Ingvaeonic dialects, the *i*-stems are evidently a minor class, with very limited productivity; however, from the perspective of Old Norse and of Continental West Germanic, including Old Saxon, the class still shows substantial productivity, which continues into the later stages of development, especially in the feminine paradigm (cf. Section 2.2.3.1).

It must be noted that gender is not directly reflected in the classification of PGmc. declensions. Only the *a*-stems and *ō*-stems may be viewed as parallel gender classes in that the former comprised nouns of masculine and neuter gender, and the latter feminine nouns only; the *s*-stems included only neuter nouns, whereas *nd*-stems were typically masculine; the other declensional classes comprised nouns representing two (*r*-stems) or all three genders (*i*-stems, *u*-stems, root nouns). Furthermore, there are many parallelisms in inflection of nouns of different genders, in particular between the masculine and neuter stems, which share a number of inflectional features. As will be evident in the present study, gender emerges as an important factor in the analogical restructuring of declensions in West Germanic, largely determining the directions of analogical shifts between inflectional classes.

---

60. Cf. the use of the term "minor declensions" in Campbell (1977), where it applies to un-productive *consonantal* classes only. In the present study, the term will consistently refer to all unproductive (or nearly unproductive), classes, including the *i*-stems and *u*-stems.

The declensional system as presented in Table 2.1, where the stem element is taken as the basis for defining inflectional classes, has been used in the Germanic philological tradition in presentations and discussions of the declensional systems of individual older Germanic languages. Accordingly, the nominal morphology of the Older Germanic languages has been analysed in primarily phonological terms, with classifications which reflect earlier stages in the development of Germanic. The loss of the stem suffix clearly obliterated the transparency of the declensional system and the motivation for a classification based on the criterion of original stem-type. Consequently, the diachronic approach to Germanic inflection, although an expedient way of organising declensional types into a coherent system, especially from a comparative perspective, turns out to be synchronically inadequate when confronted with the attested material, even for some older Germanic languages such as Old English (cf. Section 3.7). This aspect will be explored in more detail where relevant, but at the same time, the traditional diachronic approach will be consistently used for the sake of transparency as the basis for cross-linguistic comparison.

2.2.2   Restructuring of the system: Tendencies and patterns

To a large extent the nominal system continues the PIE inflections by regular phonological change; at the same time, the origin of some of the PGmc. inflectional markers needs to be sought in a number of early non-phonological innovations. One of the significant morphological modifications in Proto-Germanic was the analogical redistribution of ablaut grades in the stem-forming suffix, which opened the way for further analogical reshufflings between declensional paradigms. This was the case, for instance, with the s-stems, where the o-grade of the suffix (*-os), characteristic of the NOM./ACC. SG., was analogically replaced by the e-grade (*-es), typical of the oblique cases (cf. Section 2.2.3.5); or the elimination of ablaut variants in the GEN. SG. of consonant stems in favour of a uniform marker *-iz (< PIE *-és; Ringe 2006: 201). Another early development that influenced the restructuring process in Germanic was the functional merger of morphosyntactic categories, i.e. of the ablative, locative and instrumental with the dative, as a result of which the Old Germanic case system emerged with a reduced number of cases (Ringe 2006: 199; Ramat 1981: 60). Two further processes with far-reaching consequences are the phonological fusion of stem vowels and endings (see above, Section 2.2.1), and a number of very early analogical transformations which can be dated to Proto-Germanic.

Given the evidence from individual Old Germanic languages, the process of reorganisation of the nominal system, involving analogical restructuring of inflection, must be dated prior to the first attestations of Germanic. The wide-ranging impact of analogical processes entailed a twofold development whereby the Proto-Germanic nominal system was subject to the pressure of two major analogical forces: the *intra*paradigmatic pressure of case forms in the paradigm, leading to syncretism of inflectional contrasts within the paradigm, and *inter*paradigmatic pressure which, aiming at regularisation of inflectional endings, resulted in shifts of nouns across declensions.[61] The reorganisation of the Proto-Germanic nominal system was a cumulative effect of the interaction of these two tendencies, which seem to have complemented each other in that the presence of syncretisms rendered the system susceptible to further changes involving analogical transfers across classes. This complies with the rule that the existence of cross-paradigmatic similarities is an essential condition for the activation of analogical reshufflings between classes (Blevins 2004: 55). These purely morphological processes interacted with and, in fact, were largely instigated by a number of phonological changes, originating at the Proto-Germanic stage. The two most prominent developments were the changes affecting unaccented vowels and consonants, including those appearing in inflectional syllables, as well as the operation of *i*-mutation, taking place at a later stage (ca. 6th–10th c.) and to different extents across Northwest Germanic languages. Both exerted a direct influence on the morphological structure of the nominal paradigms.

The extensive reduction of vowels (and consonants) in unaccented syllables is one of the major phonological features distinguishing Old Germanic from its Proto-Indo-European ancestor. This large-scale development, commonly known as *Auslautgesetze*, was a corollary of a major change in the accentual conditions, i.e. the fixation of a prominent dynamic (stress-timed) accent on the root (initial) syllable in place of the PIE pitch (musical) accent, which entailed the loss of short vowels and consonants, and shortening of long vowels and diphthongs in word-final syllables (Boutkan 1995: 29; cf. D'Alquen 1988; Liberman 2001). As the process is assumed to have occurred largely at the dialectal stage of Germanic, its consequences for the morphological system varied in the individual Germanic languages (cf. the NOM. SG. of the *i*-stems: ER -*gastiz*, Go. *gasts*, ON *gestr*, OE *giest*, OS, OHG *gast* < PGmc. *-iz*).[62] Of particular value here is the Early Runic evidence, which attests to a limited application of the processes of apocope and syncope, and thus preserves many inflections unaffected by phonetic reduction.

---

61. The term "syncretism" is used here to denote a condition when identical inflectional markers serve to express different syntactic features (e.g. the ending -*a* in the OE *u*-stems used as a marker of the GEN. SG., DAT. SG., NOM. and ACC. PL.) (cf. Prokosch 1939: 230; Ringe 2006: 41).

62. For a detailed discussion of *Auslautgesetze*, see Boutkan (1995); for a general overview of the developments, see especially pp. 39–42 *idem*.

The phonological innovations which turned out to be most consequential for the shape of inflectional paradigms were the reductions in short unaccented syllables, i.e. the loss of PGmc. protected *-a-, *-i- and *-u-.[63] The loss of *-a- was a generally applied reduction in all Germanic languages, which for West Germanic has traditionally been dated early, i.e. to ca. the fourth century (Prokosch 1939: 133; Boutkan 1995: 40). New runic findings and the Runic Frisian evidence (*ko(m)bu* < *-a-, 7th/8th c.), however, point to a later dating of this process (Versloot 2016b: 22–27) (cf. Early Runic, where the vowel is still attested after a stressed heavy syllable). Likewise, the loss of unaccented *-e and *-o can be dated relatively early. The reduction of the unaccented vowels *-i and *-u, which appear to have been more resistant to loss, is conventionally dated to the sixth/seventh century and varied depending on the dialect and the length (weight) of the stem vowel. Accordingly, in West Germanic languages, these vowels disappeared from final and medial syllables after a heavy stem, but were preserved after a light stem (Boutkan 1995: 64–66, 68–72; Campbell 1977: 144). In Gothic, final *-i was consistently lost, whereas final *-u was consistently retained, irrespective of the length of the preceding syllable.[64] In North Germanic, the earliest Runic evidence points to consistent retention of -u and -i, whereas in Old Norse neither -i nor -u are preserved.

The consequences of these vocalic reductions, coupled with the loss of final consonants (especially the loss of *-n and *-t/*-d, vs. the retention of *-s and *-r; Boutkan 1995: 43–59) were far-reaching for the shape of the nominal inflection. The reduction of vowels in unaccented syllables led to the loss of the original thematic element, which rendered declensional classes no longer identifiable through the phonological component of the stem (e.g. *dag-a-z* > Go. *dags*; *gast-i-z* > Go. *gasts*).[65] Specifically, it resulted in the loss of an explicit NOM./ACC. SG. marking in masculine and neuter paradigms in all inflectional classes.[66] This development

---

63. The unprotected vowels *-a, *-i and *-u were lost already in the Proto-Germanic period (Campbell 1977: 137).

64. A number of Gothic light-syllable *i*-stems, such as *agis* 'terror', *hatis* 'hate' or *riqis* 'darkness' (cf. *gasts*), has been adduced to prove that the distinction with respect to weight of the syllable applied originally to all Germanic languages, including Gothic, but was obliterated there by analogical levelling (Prokosch 1939: 134).

65. The use of the terms 'thematic' and 'athematic' follows the traditional (older) terminology, which is not entirely adequate from the perspective of Indo-European linguistics (see Hogg & Fulk 2011: 8–9). When referring to the Germanic situation the term 'thematic' will be eqivalent to 'vocalic' and will refer to the stem formatives -a-, -ō-, -i- and -u- in the four vocalic classes.

66. The paradigms of feminine stems, in contrast, escaped this early loss of the ending at least in some declensional classes (e.g. light-syllable *i*-stems and *u*-stems), which rendered them more resistant to the spread of analogical inflections.

turned out to be particularly significant for the structure of the *i*-stem and *u*-stem declensions in North and West Germanic, where the apocope of **-i* and **-u* rendered the NOM. and ACC. SG. forms indistinguishable from those of the productive *a*- and *ja*-stems (heavy-syllable). Such formal merger of case endings created conditions conducive to the operation of analogical levelling. In particular, the lack of explicit marking in the NOM. SG. resulted in a situation where class affiliation could no longer be unambiguously determined from the shape of the NOM. SG. and, consequently, the identical phonological profile of this category across multiple declensional classes triggered further inflectional confusion and eventually reanalysis.

The other phonological development crucial for the unfolding of the restructuring process in the later stages of individual Germanic dialects was *i*-mutation. The significance of *i*-mutation for the restructuring of the Germanic inflectional system varies depending on language and inflectional class. While entirely absent from Gothic, the effects of its operation are abundantly attested in the nominal paradigms of the other early Germanic languages, although with differing scope and chronology in North Germanic and in the West-Germanic dialect continuum. Accordingly, Old Norse testifies to a general application of phonological *i*-mutation (as well as *a*- and *u*-mutation), without extensive morphologisation or levelling of the resulting alternations. The West Germanic languages, in contrast, display diverse effects of *i*-mutation. Old English and Old Frisian witness an early implementation of the process and traces of its morphologisation, but they predominantly evince levelling of paradigmatic vowel alternations that arose through *i*-mutation, while the Continental West Germanic languages (OHG, OLF, OS) attest to a late implementation of *i*-mutation and subsequent growth in productivity in nominal morphology. The gradual morphologisation of *i*-mutation, which was occasioned by the reduction of vowels in inflectional syllables, reinforced the distinctiveness of some of the inflectional paradigms by introducing allomorphic variation. The role of *i*-mutation was particularly significant in those classes in which morpho-phonological alternation served a specific morphological function, such as distinguishing singular and plural. The effects of *i*-mutation can be more clearly observed in later stages of the restructuring process, i.e. in the individual Germanic languages, when its conserving effect emerges as a prominent feature, rendering certain paradigms more resistant to the workings of interparadigmatic analogy.

Two examples illustrating the role of *i*-mutation in the nominal inflection restructuring involve the paradigms of root nouns in Old English and the heavy syllable masculine *i*-stems in Old High German and Old Saxon. In Old English, the mutated vowel of the root nouns developed as a marker of case and number, which has survived vestigially into present-day English in the fossilised plurals *men*, *women*, *feet*, *geese*, *teeth*, *mice*, *lice*. In comparison, the relatively late operation of *i*-mutation in Old High German and Old Saxon (preceded by the loss of /i/ in the NOM. SG.) resulted in the emergence of a contrast between singular and plural in masculine stems (e.g. *gast – gesti*), which survives into present-day German (cf. *Gast – Gäste*) and has even enjoyed some productivity (cf. *General – Generäle*).[67] In contrast, in classes where the mutated vowel was consistently present throughout the paradigm (e.g. in the OE and ON *i*-stems), the process seems to have had no special bearing on the analogical restructuring of inflection.[68]

Aside from its role as a salient exponent of morphological categories, the presence of *i*-mutated vowels can function as a diagnostic feature for the (relative) chronology of the restructuring process (just as it does for phonological processes, such as syncope).[69] For instance, the lack of mutated forms in the paradigm of the Old Norse feminine *i*-stems testifies to their early transition to the $\bar{o}$-declension, where they escaped *i*-mutation. This transition is not, however, shared by the *i*-stem nouns of masculine gender, where mutation is regularly attested in heavy-syllable stems (cf. *gestr* 'guest', vs. the light stem *staþr* 'place').

The mechanism as it relates to restructuring of the early Germanic nominal system may be summarised in the following way: the extensive phonological developments affecting unaccented syllables (*Auslautgesetze*) obscured morpheme boundaries in those syllables (Ringe 2006: 172), leading to the merger of distinct inflectional markers, which consequently induced confusion among different classes. The resulting inflectional instability encouraged the operation of analogical processes, which reduced the distinctiveness of individual classes and obscured the transparency of the original system of declensions. This last stage seems to belong to the historical period of the individual Germanic languages, where transfers among declensional classes are already well attested. The sequenced developments (excluding *i*-mutation) may be sketched as in Figure 2.

The emergence of syncretisms in the nominal inflection, some of which may be traced back to the Proto-Indo-European period, is considered to have been a feature "destined to have considerable impact on the subsequent development of the

---

67. Cf. also the presence of *i*-mutation in the paradigm of feminine stems which show *i*-mutated vowels not only in the plural, but also in the GEN. and DAT. SG., e.g. OHG *fart* 'journey' – (GEN./ DAT.) *ferti* – (NOM. ACC. PL.) *ferti* (Prokosch 1939: 247).

68. The fact that the *i*-mutated vowel is present in the paradigm of both the singular and the plural (e.g. OE *giest – gieste*, *dǣd – dǣde*, OS *seli – seli*) has no consequences for the pattern of restructuring in the sense that it does not work as a trigger for analogical levelling or as a factor conserving the inherited inflection. The potential link that could have emerged as a result of the presence of the *i*-mutated vowel in the paradigm was with the *ja-*, *jō*-stems, in which the *i*-mutated vowel was also present in the root. The formal similarity of the internal structure of these stems could have created the environment conducive to the operation of analogical processes and interdeclensional transitions (see Section 5.6.2).

69. For instance, the presence of *i*-mutated vowels in the consonantal stems in Old English and Old Norse indicates that the syncope of the ending in these stems was a fairly recent development.

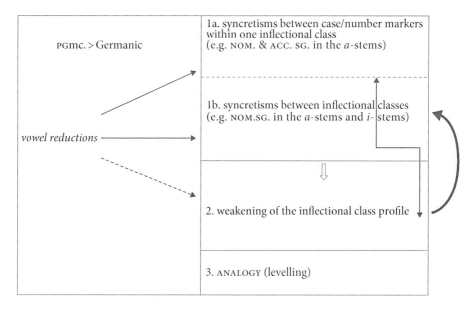

Figure 2. The mechanism of restructuring of the nominal inflection in early Germanic

daughters" (Ringe 2006: 41). However, not all case syncretisms emerged as a result of extensive weakening of inflectional syllables in early Germanic. Some of the syncretisms identifiable in the earliest Germanic material are clearly inherited from Proto-Indo-European, and thus predate the accentual changes of Proto-Germanic (Ramat 1981: 62). These include the syncretism of the nominative and vocative plural, as well as the syncretism of the nominative, accusative and vocative of both numbers in all neuter stems, which is shared by all other older Indo-European languages (Ringe 2006: 268).[70]

The growing lack of transparency in the inflectional system, induced by the presence of manifold syncretisms in and across paradigms, and the gradual loss of morphological distinctiveness and often functionality of the inherited declensional classes were the direct motivation for *inter*paradigmatic shifts in the early Germanic languages, as made explicit by Ringe (2006: 202):

> …because Germanic nouns were distributed among increasingly arbitrary inflectional classes with increasingly opaque endings, the transfer of individual nouns from one stem-class to another became a major trend in all the attested languages, including Gothic.

---

70. The nature of these syncretisms is systematic rather than random in that they emerge between cases which are semantically close to each other, e.g. between the NOM. and VOC., or the DAT. and INSTR. (Ramat 1981: 60).

The directions of these transfers were determined first of all by the productivity of some declensional classes, with the vocalic a-stem, $\bar{o}$-stem (and i-stem) declensions creating the template for analogical reshaping of the minor unproductive classes. A second factor influencing the direction of transition was gender, constituting at the same time a precondition for any inflectional interaction between paradigms, in prehistoric as well as historical Germanic. Even the earliest attested interdeclensional shifts tended to occur in compliance with gender; consequently, the default class for minor masculine and neuter nouns was the a-stem declension, and for the feminine nouns the $\bar{o}$-stem declension.

The three sets of inflections which turned out to be the most influential in the minor stem paradigms, i.e. the masculine and neuter a-stems and feminine $\bar{o}$-stems, are presented in Table 2.2 (Ringe 2006: 279; Bammesberger 1990: 39, 101).

Table 2.2 Inflection of the major productive nominal stem classes in Proto-Germanic

	a-stems masculine		a-stems neuter		$\bar{o}$-stems	
	SG	PL	SG	PL	SG	PL
NOM.	-az	-ōzes	-a^n	-ō	-ō	-ɔ̄z
GEN.	-as(a)	-ɔ̄n*	-as(a)	-ɔ̄^{n}	-ōz	-ɔ̄^{n}
DAT.	-ai	-amaz	-ai	-amaz	-āi	-ōmaz
ACC.	-a^n	-anz	-a^n	-anz	-ōn	-ōz
INSTR.	-ō	-amiz	-ō	-amiz	-ō	-ōmiz

* The symbol $\bar{ɔ}$ is used to denote the trimoraic nature of the inflectional vowel.

As the inflectional endings in the masculine and neuter paradigms are largely parallel, the restructuring process in these stems may be expected to follow similar paths of development. Among the earliest interdeclensional transfers assigned to the Proto-Germanic stage was the spread of the neuter a-stem NOM./ACC. PL. ending *-$\bar{o}$ (most likely followed by an extension of some other a-stem endings, such as the GEN. and DAT. SG. forms in the s-stems), which rendered the plural of neuter stems identical across all declensional classes. The GEN. SG. ending *-$as(a)$ has been commonly considered to continue PIE *-$osyo$ (Ringe 2006: 41, 201–202). Alternatively, the form may be an early analogical extension from the PIE pronominal ending *-$éso$ (> PGmc. *-esa), followed by a secondary development of *-es > *-as, entailing a spread of the thematic vowel -a- to the GEN. (Boutkan 1995: 177–178).[71]

The prevalence of these inflectional patterns continues into the subsequent stages of Germanic languages, but the early stages of restructuring involved

---

71. The origin of this form is fairly problematic and the attested Germanic languages testify to different variants of the original form. For a detailed discussion, see Boutkan (1995: 177–181).

transitions to a number of other declensions, including the *n*-stems (whose significance grew in the later historical stages), as well as other declensions which later became unproductive (e.g. *i*- and *u*-stems).

An important characteristic of the early stage of the restructuring of Germanic nominal declensions is the multidirectionality of interdeclensional transfers, evinced by the attestations of individual sister languages. Specifically, the nouns which originally belonged to an unproductive declension could follow different inflectional patterns in the various Older Germanic languages. This divergent development can be of a twofold nature, namely inflectional or derivational. The former refers to a context where the various attested forms derive from the same PGmc. stem, but follow different inflectional patterns in the different languages, as, for instance, the OE root noun *fōt* 'foot', OHG *i*-stem *fuoz*, Go. *u*-stem *fōtus* (< **fōz*, cf. Table 2.5); or the Go. root noun *spaúrds* 'racecourse' (f.), vs. OE and OHG *i*-stem *spyrd* and *spurt*, respectively (< **spurd-*). Here the divergence in inflection implies that the transition to the various declensional classes belongs to the prehistory of the individual languages. The divergent development of cognate forms in individual Germanic languages is not, however, always attributable to interdeclensional transfers, but also frequently results from the existence of parallel formations (stem derivations) in Proto-Germanic, which created the basis for disparate developments in the daughter languages. For instance, nouns which can be identified as historical *s*-stems based on the Gothic evidence (e.g. Go. *agis* 'fear', *hatis* 'hatred') are affiliated with the *i*-stem pattern in Old English and Old Saxon (OE *ege*, *hete*, OS *heti*), but with the *a*-stems in Old High German (*haz*), pointing to a dual development of the original PGmc. *s*-stem paradigm (**hat-iz-/hat-az-*). A parallel development may be found in the Germanic paradigm of the *s*-stem **sig-iz/-sig-az* 'victory', where Go. *sigis*, OE *sigor* and ON *sigr* (later reinterpreted as an *a*-stem) testify to the original *s*-stem inflection and originate in the NOM./ACC. **sig-az*, whereas OFris., OE *sige* and OS *sigi* are attested as regular *i*-stems, developing from the PGmc. oblique stem **sig-iz*. Not infrequently, the divergent development of forms based on parallel stems is accompanied by a change in gender class, e.g. Go. masculine *(t)u*-stem *luftus* 'air' vs. OE *lyft*, formed as a feminine *(t)i*-stem (< PGmc. **luf-ti*, with inconsistent gender), or Go. *faírhwus* 'world' (originating in PGmc. *u*-stem **ferhw-u-*) vs. ON *fjǫr* (n.), OE *feorh* (m. n.), OS/OHG *fer(a)h* (originating in PGmc. *wa*-stem/*wō*-stem **ferhw-a/-ō*). In fact, the coexistence of nouns built on two parallel PGmc. formations can be attested within a single language, e.g. OE *a*-stem *gāst* vs. *i*-stem *gǣst* 'ghost'. An example of a complex interaction between derivation and interdeclensional analogy is the development of PGmc. **aran-*, where the available evidence attests to the existence of two parallel forms in Proto-Germanic; accordingly, ON *are* 'eagle', Go. *ara* and OHG *aro* testify to a PGmc. *n*-stem preform **aran*, whereas the ON *u*-stem *ǫrn* 'eagle', OE *a*-stem *earn* and OHG *i*-stem *arn* go back to PGmc. *arnu-. Apart from pointing to different stem extensions, the comparison of the Old English and Old Norse forms indicates a discrepant development of the same stem form in the two languages, namely *u*-stem vs. *a*-stem (Kluge 2011, s.v. *Aar*; cf. *EWN*, s.v. *arend*).

Another potential effect of the activity of analogical restructuring is the occasional development of a hybrid inflection in some nouns (termed "heteroclitic" by Boutkan 1995: 241), as found, for example, in the Go. *háims* 'village', which retains the inherited *i*-stem inflection in the singular, while following the *ō*-stem pattern in the plural. Such bidirectional development of inflection within one paradigm may be observed in the later stages of the restructuring process in individual Germanic languages, as, for instance, in the OFris. *nd*-stems, where the singular entirely follows the *a*-stem pattern, while the plural largely retains the original *nd*-stem inflection. Such varied inflectional configurations across Germanic portend the later tendencies of morphological restructuring, and demonstrate that the process unfolded in largely language-specific ways. They also prove that a larger number of declensional classes had the potential to attract nouns at this early stage than in the later dialectal period, when the process of restructuring was characterised by the dominance of two or three major types as the "destination" for minor stems. The scale of "attractiveness" of individual classes in subsequent periods differed, depending partly on the dialect.

The examples adduced above demonstrate as well that the transformation of nominal inflection at the early Germanic stage was a complex, multi-layered development, which combined changes on the inflectional level with those of a derivational nature, and it is the interaction between them that contributed to the later shape of the nominal inflection in the various Germanic languages. When framing the process of restructuring of the nominal system in Germanic in the present study, a clear distinction must be made between processes of an inflectional and of a derivational nature. Many of the parallel existing formations which developed regularly in individual Germanic languages may at first sight be attributed to the operation of analogical processes, whereas their actual origin lies in derivation (e.g. stem extension). The major criterion distinguishing remodelling from derivational processes is the meaning (of the lemma), which is usually modified in the process of derivation. Given the scope of the present study, however, only the processes of an inflectional nature will be subject to close scrutiny and quantitative analysis.

2.2.3 Restructuring of the system: Minor declensional types

In order to investigate the reorganisation of the PGmc. minor paradigms effectively, the original system of inflection must first be presented in detail. Accordingly, the present section is devoted to a systematic overview of the PGmc. minor declensions, concentrating on the shape of the reconstructed paradigms and the general characteristics of each class. The directions of interparadigmatic realignments will be sketched, and close attention will be given to those inflectional features which rendered the unproductive paradigms either sensitive or resistant to the impact of analogical pressures from other, more productive declensions.

As the present investigation concentrates on the developments in the minor declensional types in Germanic, the productive types (i.e. the vocalic *a*- and *ō*-stems and the consonantal *n*-stems) have generally been excluded from the study. As types which exerted substantial influence on the minor stems from the PGmc. period onwards, they will nevertheless be present in the discussion (see also Table 2.2).[72]

The inflectional forms presented below for Proto-Germanic are standard reconstructions, based primarily on Ringe (2006) and Bammesberger (1990), supplemented with the information found in Krahe & Meid (1969), Boutkan (1995) and Lehmann (2005–2007). Some of these reconstructions turn out to be fairly problematic, and different (often discrepant) interpretations have been offered (e.g. the NOM. SG. ending in the root nouns). Although detailed discussion of these reconstructions is beyond the scope of the present study, cases in which their interpretation may have some bearing on its results will be treated in more depth. Note that the reconstructed forms of the DAT. PL. appear consistently with the ending *-miz*, which is an original INSTR. PL. marker (Ringe & Taylor 2014: 21).

2.2.3.1 i-*stems*
Of all minor declensional classes in Proto-Germanic, the *i*-stems constituted the largest group and despite being clearly a "declining category" (Boutkan 1995: 241), they managed to retain a degree of productivity in some dialects of Continental Germanic, most notably in Old High German and Old Saxon. Given the quantitative profile of the *i*-stem declension, the class is believed to have been a productive derivational pattern in Proto-Germanic (Bammesberger 1990: 128). The inclusion of the *i*-stems in the category of minor stems, as mentioned in Section 2.2.1, is not

---

72. The intrusion of the *a*-stem and *ō*-stem inflections is also well attested in the *n*-stems, which constituted a productive declensional type in Germanic (see Adamczyk 2007, Kroonen 2011). The analogical realignments in these stems remain beyond the scope of this study. The template ("locus") for the thematisation of these consonantal stems at the early stage (PGmc.) seems to be the GEN. (possibly SG.) (Kroonen 2011: 59).

entirely uncontroversial, yet given the comparative nature of the present study and
the lack of productivity of this class in North Sea Germanic (especially Old English
and Old Frisian), it offers an expedient method to organise the minor classes in a
transparent way for the purpose of a cross-linguistic comparison.

The *i*-stem declension comprised masculine, feminine and a few neuter nouns;
they may also be further subdivided into light- and heavy-syllable stems. This division with respect to the weight of the stem will turn out to be significant for
the pattern of reorganisation of inflection in individual languages, in particular
in the North and West Germanic languages.[73] An important characteristic of this
declension is the presence of a mutated vowel in the stem, which made the *i*-stems
distinct from the *a*-stems and *ō*-stems, and at the same time created parallels with
the *ja*- and *jō*-stems.[74]

The *i*-stems as a class are inherited from Proto-Indo-European, but most Germanic *i*-stems are of a secondary origin, resulting from modifications of other
formations, such as root nouns (e.g. PGmc. **kwēni-* > Go. *qēns* 'woman', ON *kván*,
OE *cwēn*, OS *quān*, based on the PIE consonantal stem **gʷen-* > **gʷēni-/gʷeni-*;
Bammesberger 1990: 128). From a derivational point of view, nouns belonging
to the *i*-stem declension were originally subdivided into two subgroups: *i*-stems
and **ti*-stems, the latter encompassing feminine nouns of the type **ris-ti* (e.g. OE
ǣ-rist 'resurrection'). In the context of the present investigation, this subdivision is
of no special relevance and no distinction will henceforth be made between these
two subtypes.

The Proto-Germanic *i*-stem paradigm may be reconstructed as presented
in Table 2.3 for the heavy-syllable masculine **gast-* 'guest' (Ringe 2006: 272;
Bammesberger 1990: 125; cf. Krahe & Meid 1969: 26–31; Boutkan 1995: 236;
Lehman 2005–2007: § 3.3.5).

Among the older Germanic languages, the category which retains a transparent
identity is the plural of Gothic *i*-stems, as well as the GEN. and DAT. SG. of feminine *i*-stems in West Germanic (Bammesberger 1990: 124; Hogg 1980: 132). All
other categories, to a greater or lesser extent, testify to the operation of analogical

---

73. As the early Germanic attestations indicate, the number of neuter *i*-stems was very limited
in Proto-Germanic, which is a continuation of the PIE state of affairs (Krahe & Meid 1969: 25;
Bammesberger 1990: 123; Ringe 2006: 196).

74. The presence of *i*-mutated vowels in the paradigm emerges as a crucial factor determining the
operation of the restructuring process. Given, however, that *i*-mutation was a dialectal phenomenon, operating differently (in terms of its extent and chronology) in the individual Germanic
languages, with divergent effects on the shape of the paradigms, the discussion of its significance
is relegated to individual chapters.

Table 2.3 Reconstructed PGmc. *i*-stem paradigm of **gastiz* 'guest'[*]

	SG	PL
NOM.	*gastiz	*gastīz
GEN.	*gastīz[**]	*gastiōⁿ
DAT.	*gastai, (-ī)	*gastimiz
ACC.	*gastiⁿ	*gastinz
INSTR.	*gastī	–

[*] Based on the evidence of endingless masculine forms in Gothic, Ringe (2006: 273) reconstructs also the form of the VOC. SG. in *-i*, which, however, as he notes, may have been an analogical formation from the *a*-stems (see also Boer 1924: 188). The form of the NOM./ACC. PL. *-īz* evolved from an earlier **-eiez* (Hogg & Fulk 2011: 39). The vowel length is questionable for Old High German, but not necessarily for Northern West Germanic languages (Boutkan 1995: 248–249).

[**] The evidence from the individual Germanic languages for the reconstruction of ablaut grade of the stem vowel in the GEN. and DAT. SG. is inconsistent. The ON and Go. material testify to **-aiz* as the original inflection in the GEN. SG., whereas the West Germanic forms attest to **-īz*. The origin of the DAT. SG. forms is even more unclear. The ON forms may be traced back to **-ī*, which may reflect an original instrumental, whereas the West Germanic dialects point to **-æi* (< **-ēi*). For details see Bammesberger (1990: 126), Boutkan (1995: 246) and Ringe (2006: 272).

processes in the paradigm. The primary trigger for the reorganisation of the *i*-stem paradigm was the merger of the NOM./ACC. SG. form with that of the *a*-stems, caused by apocope of the vowel in a word-final syllable in both classes (cf. PWGmc. *gasti vs. *daga > OS *gast* vs. *dag*) (Bammesberger 1990: 124; Ramat 1981: 1981). Given that apocope was a dialectal phenomenon (Boutkan 1995: 240), the transition of the *i*-stems to the more productive *a*-stems may be expected to have been more or less advanced, depending on the language. In contrast to East and North Germanic, where the loss of the unstressed vowel and the retention of the final consonant of the inflectional syllable (Go. *gasts*, ON *gestr* vs. OE *giest*, OHG/OS *gast*) point to an early date for this process, West Germanic data suggest that its occurrence there was relatively late. The late dating is confirmed by the fact that the final consonant **-z* was lost, but the inflectional vowels *-a* and *-i* were retained until shortly before the first attestations (cf. Runic Frisian *ko(m)bu* < *kamba, 7th/8th c.). In North and West Germanic (particularly in Old Saxon), aside from the impact of the pure *a*-stems, traces of interaction with the *ja*-stems are also evident, motivated by the similarities in the internal structure of these stems (e.g. ON *reykr*, *reykiar*, OS *hugi*, *hugies*, etc.).

With respect to the reorganisation of inflection, a clear dividing line may be drawn between the paradigms of the masculine and feminine *i*-stems, with the former tending to be more easily affected by analogical innovations. The most prominent consequences of these developments are to be seen in the shape of the masculine singular inflection, which has been almost entirely reshaped by analogy

in the older Germanic languages (e.g. Krahe & Meid 1969: 27). The transfer of
the masculine *i*-stems to the *a*-stem declension is attested already in the Gothic
material (e.g. Wright 1957; Braune/Heidermanns 2004), where the singular of the
heavy-syllable masculine stems has been entirely rebuilt on the paradigm of the
a-stems (in contrast to the plural, which somewhat more consistently retains the
historical inflection; Bammesberger 1990: 124). Extensive traces of interdeclensional realignments may be found in the GEN. SG. of masculine *i*-stems, where analogical forms were extended from the *a*-stems in all Germanic languages. Likewise,
the original shape of the DAT. SG. is recognisable only in some West Germanic
dialects in the attested material, but in general, the interpretation of these endings
as analogical or inherited turns out to be fairly problematic.[75] The INSTR. SG. form
in -*iu*, found in Old High German and Old Saxon, may be interpreted as an analogical formation modelled on the *a*-stem ending in -*u*[76] (Prokosch 1939: 246; Krahe
& Meid 1969: 28; Boer 1924: 189). Finally, intrusive analogy may be identified in
the forms of the NOM. SG. in Old High German, where the light stems, in which
a historical vocalic ending -*i* would be expected, are attested without an ending,
possibly on the analogy of the heavy-syllable stems (cf. OHG *slag, stat* vs. OS *slegi,
stedi*; Prokosch 1939: 246).[77] This attested large-scale reorganisation of the masculine singular *i*-stem paradigm was considered difficult to account for.[78] According
to Bammesberger (1990), a factor potentially contributing to the disintegration of
this class (apart from the formal similarity with the *a*-stems) may have been the
small number of these stems in Proto-Germanic (Bammesberger 1990: 124).

In contrast, the historical *i*-stem pattern is better preserved in the singular of
the feminine paradigm. The inherited inflections are retained in the GEN. and DAT.
SG. in almost all Germanic languages. A more advanced stage of the restructuring

---

75. The West Germanic DAT. SG. ending -*e* has been interpreted as original, i.e. as a regular
phonological development of -*i* which is found, for example, in the OS light-syllable *i*-stems (cf.
heavy-syllable stems in -*e*) (Fulk 1992: 421). Likewise, the light-syllable DAT. SG. ending -*i*, attested
in the earliest Old High German glossaries alongside -*e*, can be viewed as original rather than
analogical (cf. Table 2.12).

76. It is assumed that the analogical *a*-stem marker -*u* was attached to the original *-*i*-. Boutkan
suggests that the OHG -*iu* could potentially have been extended from the *u*-stems, where it was
a regular phonological development (Boutkan 1995: 248). For a discussion of this form, see
Section 5.6.2.1.

77. The explanation of these forms is not unproblematic and a number of alternative interpretations have been offered. For an overview, see Boutkan (1995: 242) and for a more recent
discussion Klein (2004b).

78. A parallel situation can be found also in Slavic, where masculine *i*-stems disappeared almost
entirely and were absorbed by the *yo*-stem declension, leaving only relics such as Pol. *gość* (GEN./
ACC. SG. *gościa*, etc. but INSTR. PL. *gośćmi*).

process is found in Old Norse, where most of the original feminine *i*-stem nouns have been transferred to the feminine *ō*-stems.[79] The greater archaism of the feminine *i*-stems has been ascribed to the fact that although these stems underwent syncopation parallel to the masculine stems (e.g. PGmc. **anstiz* > Go. *ansts* 'favour'), no merger with the feminine *ō*-stems (or feminine *n*-stems in -*ōn*-) followed (Bammesberger 1990: 124). This fact seems to validate the assumption that the developments affecting the NOM. (and ACC.) forms were the primary trigger for the large-scale transition in the masculine paradigm.

The scarcely attested neuter nouns largely follow the inflection of the masculine stems. The original inflectional features are attested only in West Germanic in forms of the NOM./ACC. SG. in -*i* (> -*e*) (OE *spere* 'spear', OS *urlagi* 'war') and the DAT. SG. in -*i* (OHG *meri* 'sea'). The origin of the attested neuter NOM./ACC. PL. forms in -*u* (OE *speru*, OS *aldarlagu*) may be sought in the productive paradigm of neuter *a*-stems (Krahe & Meid 1969: 29; Boutkan 1995: 249).

The inflection of the plural (both masculine and feminine) retains more features of the historical pattern, especially in the NOM. and ACC. (OS, OHG -*e*, -*i*), as well as occasionally in the GEN. (OHG, OS -*ie*, -*eo*; OE -*igea*). The historical inflections are best attested in Gothic and Continental West Germanic (except Old Frisian), where the DAT. PL. also continues the inherited pattern (Go. -*im*, OHG, OLF -*im*, -*in*). In Old Norse, traces of the inherited inflection are found in the NOM./ACC. PL., while the forms of the GEN. and DAT. PL. are analogical. The spread of *a*-stem inflection to the GEN. and DAT. PL. is also attested in Old English and Old Frisian.

The differentiation between light- and heavy-syllable stems is of particular importance to the analysis of the restructuring process in the historical period. Namely, the advancement of analogical levelling seems to have proceeded at a different pace in the light and heavy stems, with the former group being affected by the process at a later stage than the latter. It is most prominent in the NOM./ACC. PL. in West Germanic (notably in Old English), where the heavy syllable stems, both feminine and masculine, display predominantly analogical inflections from the *a*- and *ō*-stems (OE -*as*, m., -*a*, f.), whereas the light-syllable stems tend to partly retain the archaic inflectional pattern.

---

79. The transition in the opposite direction is also well attested in Old Norse. The most common feminine paradigm, i.e. the *ō*-stems, testifies to the influence of the *i*-stem inflection, resulting in a heteroclitic paradigm, where the *ō*-stem inflection prevails in the singular and the *i*-stem pattern in the plural: *gjof* < **gjafu* (NOM. SG.), *gjafer* (NOM. PL.) (Heusler 1977: 65). This points to an early productivity and expansion of the *i*-stem inflection to other classes, including the productive ones, which must have continued into Modern Icelandic, where a typical feminine paradigm is a hybrid based on these two inflectional patterns.

The original productivity of the *i*-stem declension is apparent from its considerable etymological heterogeneity, comprising nouns which were historically not
affiliated with the *i*-stem pattern. Such vestiges of prior productivity are especially
frequent in West Germanic, where a number of nouns which essentially follow
the inflection of the *i*-stems may be derived from the earlier (PIE) *-es-/-os* stems.
Their descent can easily be traced by external comparison, especially with cognate
forms in Gothic, e.g. OE *bere* 'barley', *eġe* 'terror' (cf. OE *egesa* 'terror' and the
verb *egsian* 'terrify', both testifying to an original *s*-stem), *hete* 'hatred', *sele* 'hall',
seġe 'victory' (cf. Go. *barizeins* adj. 'made of barley', *hatis* 'hatred', *sigis* 'victory';[80]
Bammesberger 1990: 134, 211). S-stem origin may also be detected in a number
of *i*-stems which show an alternation between the mutated and unmutated root
vowel in Old English, e.g. OE *ġefēġ* ~ *ġefōg* 'joint', *ġeheald* ~ *ġehyld* 'guard', *ġewealc*
~ *ġewylċ* 'rolling' (Campbell 1977: 244f). The attested etymological heterogeneity
of the *i*-stem declension is clearly indicative of the fact that this declensional pattern, capable of absorbing a considerable number of nouns from other declensional
types, must have been productive at an earlier stage of development. In contrast to
the other minor stems in Germanic, the *i*-stems did not entirely lose their productivity, and the Continental Germanic material provides ample evidence for retention and subsequent spread of *i*-stem inflection to other minor classes, especially
to the *u*-stems and root nouns.

Aside from the expected impact of the productive vocalic inflectional types
and the limited pressure of the *n*-stems, the early attestations of West Germanic,
in particular of Old Saxon, Old High German and occasionally Old Frisian, point
arguably to the presence of consonantal inflection in the *i*-stems, apparent in the
endingless forms of the DAT. SG. Such cases, reflected in synchronic alternations
in the early attested material, will be discussed in the chapters devoted to the individual older Germanic languages. In general, the presence of analogical features
other than those extended from the productive paradigms (e.g. of the *u*-stems or
consonantal stems) implies that the fluctuation of nouns among various paradigmatic types could also take place among the unproductive declensional paradigms,
some of which must have been relatively stable and productive in the early period
following the breakup of Proto-Germanic.

Finally, the class of *i*-stems and in particular their complex relation with the
a-stems at an early stage of development illustrates very well the potential complications in the interpretation of inflectional forms as analogical or inherited from the
parent language. The early Germanic data testify to the presence of related, parallel

---

80. Formally, all these forms are traditionally classified as strong neuter nouns (*a*-stems) in
Gothic (Wright 1957: 87). The *s*-stem origin of *sele* can be corroborated, in turn, by the OE *salor*
'hall, palace'.

forms, derived from the original -*i* and *a*-stem extensions: e.g. **gard-i/gard-a-* > Go. *gards* 'house, family' (*i*-stem with DAT. PL. *gardim*) vs. OE *geard*, ON *garðr* (*a*-stems), or **sangw-i-/sangw-a-* > Go. *saggws* 'song' (*i*-stem with DAT. PL. *saggwim*) vs. OE *sang* (*a*-stem; cf. Bjorvand 1995: 3; Bammesberger 1990: 128). These may be traced back to a common origin in PIE *s*-stems, where the *a*-stems are based on the original NOM./ACC. **-os* (> PGmc. **-az*), whereas the *i*-stems have been formed to the original oblique stem in PIE **-es-* (> PGmc. **-iz-*; Bammesberger 1990: 138–139). The existence of such cognate forms in different daughter languages could be potentially misinterpreted as a reflex of earlier analogical reshuffling between inflectional classes, where the Gothic form, being the earliest attested, would most likely represent the original class affiliation (cf. Go. *hatis* 'hate' vs. OE *hete*). Such developments, belonging to a very early stage of Proto-Germanic, are of a derivational nature (in the sense that they affect the stem suffix and not the inflectional ending) and need to be kept apart from inflectional realignments (cf. Section 2.2.2).

2.2.3.2 u-*stems*

The *u*-stem declension included all nouns originally containing a stem vowel **-u-*. In terms of their internal structure, the *u*-stems may be viewed as parallel to the *i*-stems in that they testify to the presence of etymological **-u-/-w-* in contexts where the *i*-stems invariably have **-i-/-j-*: hence PGmc. **sunuz*, **sunu^n* vs. **anstiz*, **ansti^n*, etc. Additionally, both offer evidence of an incipient lack of distinction between the masculine and feminine inflections (Bammesberger 1990: 150–151). The Proto-Germanic *u*-stems comprised nouns of masculine, feminine and neuter gender, yet this original distinction had largely been obscured by the time of the first written attestations. The forms of neuter *u*-stems are attested only in Gothic, and there only in the singular (e.g. NOM. *faíhu* 'cattle', GEN. *faíháus*, DAT. *faíháu*). In the other Germanic dialects, they survive only in relic forms, e.g. OE *feolu*, *feolo* 'much, many', OHG *fihu* 'cattle', OS *widu-* 'wood'.

The Proto-Germanic light-syllable masculine *u*-stem paradigm may be reconstructed as presented in Table 2.4 (Bammesberger 1990: 151; Ringe 2006: 272, cf. Boutkan 1995: 250; Krahe & Meid 1969: 33–94; Ramat 1981: 71).

Table 2.4 Reconstructed PGmc. *u*-stem paradigm of **sunuz* 'son'

	SG	PL
NOM.	**sunuz*	**suniwiz*
GEN.	**sunauz, -iz*	**sun(i)wō^n*
DAT.	**suniwi*	**sunumiz*
ACC.	**sunu^n*	**sununz*
INSTR.	**sunū*	

In West Germanic, the pattern of inflection was differentiated with respect to the weight of the stem. Accordingly, the distinctive final marker -*u*, which may be viewed as a hallmark of this declension, is preserved only in the NOM./ACC. SG. of light-syllable stems, whereas heavy-syllable stems are endingless in these two categories (e.g. OE *sunu* 'son', *wudu* 'wood', *duru* 'door' vs. *hond* 'hand', *feld* 'field', *ford* 'ford'; OHG *situ* 'custom', *fridu* 'piece', vs. *hant* 'hand'; OS *sunu*, *widu*- vs. *hand*, etc.), which parallels the pattern found in some other stems, for instance, the *ja*-stems or *i*-stems (e.g. OE *ja*-stem *here* 'army' vs. *secg* 'warrior', *i*-stem *wine* 'friend' vs. *wyrm* 'dragon', etc.).

Although the group of Proto-Germanic *u*-stems constituted (alongside the *i*-stems) a "substantial lexical class[es]" (Ringe 2006: 196), its productivity had declined considerably by the time of the first attestations of Germanic. An echo of the earlier productivity of this declensional pattern, no longer recognisable in Northwest Germanic, is to be found in Gothic, where the original *u*-stem inflection is well preserved. The status of this class as a productive declension was reinforced by a number of developments which contributed to the enrichment of the inventory of the *u*-stems in Gothic, the most important being: (1) the transfer of the original root nouns (e.g. *fōtus* 'foot', *tunþus* 'tooth') to the *u*-declension on the basis of the ACC. SG. $*-u^n$ ($< *-u-m$ or $*-m̥$) and the ACC. PL. $*-unz$ ($< *u-ns$ or $*-n̥s$), (2) the shift of the original *wa*-stems to the *u*-stem inflection due to their formal similarity (e.g. *u*-stem *sunus* 'son' vs. original *wa*-stem *skadus* 'shadow'), and finally (3) the adoption of the *u*-stem pattern by loanwords and names in Greek -ος and Latin -*us* (Schaffner 2001: 494).

In general, the *u*-stems show extensive traces of analogical intrusion of inflections from the productive nominal classes. The overall condition of the *u*-stem declension and the major directions of analogical transfers may be summarised as follows: "The *u*-class, which was never very numerous, is rather disintegrated even at the beginning of our tradition of the Gmc. languages. The masculines tend to go over to the *o*- or *i*- class, the feminines to the *ā*-class" (Prokosch 1939: 248; cf. Boutkan 1995: 253; Mottausch 2011: 25).[81] While the original pattern of inflection is still retained in masculine nouns in North Germanic, it is generally thought to be less well preserved in West Germanic. A clear dividing line emerges between the singular and the plural, with the former consistently continuing the original PGmc. pattern of inflection, and the latter showing considerable traces of analogical levelling. Alongside the prominent influence of the *a*-stems, attested in the GEN. PL.

---

81. The terms "*o*-stems" and "*ā*-stems" as used by Prokosch (1939) invoke the Indo-European situation, where the former denote masculine and the latter feminine inflection. In the present study the terms *a*-stems and *ō*-stems are used to refer to the regular Proto-Germanic development of Proto-Indo-European $*o$- and $*ā$-stems, respectively.

(*-a*, *-o*), the impact of the *i*-stem pattern is evident in the NOM. and ACC. PL. (OS, OHG, OLF -*i*), in both masculine and feminine stems and irrespective of the length of the stem vowel, and in the GEN. PL. (OS, OHG -*io*, -*eo*). In fact, the interpretation of the NOM./ACC. PL. marker -*i* in Continental West Germanic is not straightforward; potentially the form could be a reflex of the original PGmc. form, and this option is also taken into consideration in the present study (cf. the discussion in Sections 5.6.3.3 & 6.5.3.1). The assimilation of the *u*-stems to the *i*-stem declension in later stages is a phenomenon particular to (and well documented in) Continental West Germanic, and can be clearly attributed to the similarity of the phonological structure of these two classes, namely the presence of -*i* and -*j* in inflectional syllables (Voyles 1992: 233). A continuation of the inherited inflection may be sought in the DAT. PL. marker -*um*, -*on* (Krahe & Meid 1969: 35; Ringe 2006: 272), but due to its formal similarity with the DAT. PL. ending of *a*-stems, its origin cannot be unambiguously identified; the form can be alternatively interpreted as an analogical extension from the *a*-stems (Boutkan 1995: 258). Clearly analogical at any rate is the OHG marker -*im*, originating in the *i*-stems.

  Another form difficult to account for is the NOM./ACC. PL. marker -*a* attested in Old English and Old Frisian in place of the phonologically expected -*(i)u* (Bammesberger 1990: 153–154; Boutkan 1995: 84). Some scholars suggest tracing this ending back to the PIE NOM. *-*oues*- (> PGmc. *-*au̯iz* > *-*auz*), ablauting with *-*eu̯es*- (> PGmc. *-*iu̯iz*- Go. -*jus*; Campbell 1977: 246, cf. Krahe & Meid 1969: 34). An alternative hypothesis holds that this unexpected -*a* could be a continuation of an original dual ending (from PIE *-*ōu*-) which spread and "gradually came to be used as an ordinary NOM. ACC. PL. ending" (Dahl 1938: 182).[82] This interpretation seems conceivable, given the frequency of the dual number in such *u*-stems as in *hand* 'hand', *apple* 'eye-ball' or *duru* 'door', as well as *sunu* 'son' (with *suna* originally referring to two sons). Finally, the problematic ending has been viewed as an innovation occasioned by the internal analogical pressure of the other cases in the paradigm, namely the GEN. and DAT. SG. and GEN. PL. (Prokosch 1939: 249).[83] Given that neither Old English nor Old Frisian shows any traces of an alternative NOM./ACC. PL. ending in the *u*-stems, the development of this ending must in any case be dated relatively early. Accordingly, irrespective of the exact interpretation, the attested form -*a* will be treated as original, i.e. as a starting point for the quantitative investigation of inflectional changes in these two languages.

---

82. See Bammesberger (1985: 367ff.) for an investigation of the possibility of interpreting the irregular NOM./ACC. PL. ending as an original dual.

83. While the early influence of other declensional types is possible in the case of the feminine inflection (in particular of the *ō*-stems, whereby NOM. PL. *-*ōz* > OE -*a*) (Bammesberger 1985: 367), it cannot account for the ending in the masculine stems.

2.2.3.3   *Root nouns*[84]

Root nouns constituted the largest class of consonant stems among the minor declensions, comprising nouns of masculine, feminine and neuter gender. It has been assumed that masculine and feminine nouns followed an identical pattern of inflection in Proto-Germanic. At a later stage the original common paradigm was differentiated and, accordingly, the Germanic material testifies to the existence of two similar, yet independent inflectional patterns for masculine and feminine root nouns. Of the two genders, the feminine is considerably better preserved in Germanic, whereas the neuter paradigm is retained only vestigially (Bammesberger 1990: 188; Krahe & Meid 1969: 38).[85] In terms of their internal structure, root nouns were formations in which the inflectional ending was attached directly to the root, without an intervening stem extension. This particular structure determined their behaviour with respect to certain phonological processes, such as *i*-mutation, whose activity had consequently different effects here than in other paradigms where a stem-final vowel was present. As a result, the root nouns show considerable allomorphic variation in the paradigm, entailing the retention of mutated vowels which tended to develop into markers of case and number in some Germanic languages, such as in Old English.

As this declensional class was heavily influenced by analogical pressures from other classes from a very early stage, its original inflection is not easily determinable (Prokosch 1939: 256; Boutkan 1995: 259–260; Ringe 2006: 197). The reconstructed Proto-Germanic root noun paradigm is presented in Table 2.5 (Ringe 2006: 280, Bammesberger 1990: 188–190; cf. Boutkan 1995: 258–259; Lehmann 2005–2007: § 3.2.1).

The extensive analogical influence of the productive inflections on the root nouns most likely began with the transition of these nouns to the *u*-stem declension,

---

84. The terminology used with reference to root nouns is diversified. Campbell (1977: 251) refers to this declensional class as athematic nouns – a term which has been used also in a broader sense, especially when applied to the Indo-European nominal system, and could potentially cover vocalic *i*- and *u*-stems as well as consonantal *nd*-stems, neuter **-es-/-os-* stems, *þ*-stems and *r*-stems (Fortson 2010: 119–126). The transparent term "consonant stems", applied to this declensional type by Ringe (2006: 278), is used, for instance, by Lehmann (2005–2007: § 3.2.2) to refer to a different class of nouns, namely those originally built on the **-en-* suffix. In order to minimise the risk of terminological confusion, the term "root nouns", which appears to be least ambiguous, will consistently be used here, following the practice of Prokosch (1939) and Lehmann (2005–2007: § 3.2.1).

85. The prevalence of feminine nouns in this class has been explained on semantic grounds; firstly, as many root nouns denoted cattle, especially dairy animals, it can be expected that females were more common than males (Schwink 2004: 56).

Table 2.5 Reconstructed PGmc. root noun paradigm of *fōt- 'foot'

	SG	PL
NOM.	*fōz, *fōt[*]	*fōtiz
GEN.	*fōtiz	*fōtō^n
DAT.	*fōti	*fōt(u)miz
ACC.	*fōtu^n	*fōtunz
INSTR.	*fōt	*fōtiz

[*] The reconstruction of the NOM. SG. ending of the root nouns is problematic (Ringe 2006: 279). For a discussion of the potential forms and interpretations, see Bammesberger (1990: 190–192).

as suggested by the Gothic evidence.[86] The source of the analogical remodelling may be sought in the formal similarity of the forms of the accusative, both singular and plural, in the two declensional types in Proto-Germanic: PIE *-m̥ > PGmc. *-um > -u(n) (Ramat 1981: 62; Bammesberger 1990: 198; van Loon 2005: 179; cf. Lass 1986: 478). Traces of the u-stem inflection are also found in the Old Norse masculine singular paradigm of PGmc. root nouns, e.g. fótr, fót, fótar, fōte, along-side innovative a-stem forms, e.g. in maþr 'man' (Heusler 1977: 73). The other destination classes for root nouns were the masculine a-stems and feminine ō-stems and i-stems, with the transfers taking place in compliance with gender.

The pressure of the productive declensional types is most prominent in the GEN. SG. of masculine stems in all West Germanic dialects, as well as in the NOM./ACC. PL. in most of Continental Germanic (OHG, OS, OLF). The early impact of the feminine ō-stem pattern may also be identified in the endless form of the NOM. SG. in Old Norse (cf. Prokosch 1939: 257). The GEN. PL. endings may be interpreted as a regular phonological development of PGmc. forms (with the exception of the Gothic GEN. PL. -ē, on which see Ringe 2006: 279). The DAT. PL. forms in -in and -im, found in Gothic and Old High German, are clearly analogical formations on the pattern of the i-stems, whereas the most commonly attested endings -um and (Go.) -am are considered to be analogical to the a-stem inflections (Boutkan 1995: 262; Krahe & Meid 1969: 36–38) (cf. the discussion in Section 2.2.4).

The effects of intraparadigmatic pressure are visible in the NOM. SG. of Old English and Old Frisian light-syllable stems. Here, the origin of the marker -u may be sought in the form of the ACC. SG. (*-un) (Boutkan 1995: 260; cf., however, Prokosch (1939: 258) who postulates the opposite direction of analogical transition,

---

86. An early activity of the restructuring process can be found in particular in the two apparently aberrant Gothic forms of fōtus 'foot' and tunþus 'tooth', which, as nouns denoting parts of the body, followed the inflection of the u-stems, possibly on the pattern set by handus 'hand', with which they often occurred in fixed phrases, e.g., handuns jah fōtuns, but also liþus 'limb', kinnus 'cheek', giþus 'stomach' (Ramat 1981: 62).

attributing the forms of the ACC. SG. to the influence of the NOM. SG.).[87] Another example of intraparadigmatic pressure is the form of the ACC. PL., whose inflection was generalised from the NOM. PL. in all Germanic languages (Boutkan 1995: 261).

2.2.3.4 r-stems

The r-stems constituted a very small, semantically homogenous class in Proto-Germanic, comprising five kinship terms.[88] This set of basic and widely attested lexical items constitutes at the same time one of the historically more complex declensional types, both in terms of its origin as well as its subsequent development in the individual Germanic languages. As a semantically marked class, the r-stems were unproductive and their pattern of inflection could hardly attract any new nouns. This state of affairs was continued into the historical period of Germanic, with the notable exception of Gothic where the weak forms atta and áiþei (both n-stems) replaced the inherited Proto-Germanic forms fadar and *mō-dar, respectively.[89]

The PGmc. r-stem paradigm essentially continues the PIE inflectional pattern based on the formative element *-ter-, in which the vowel was subject to ablaut variation, with *-ter- appearing in the full grade, *-tēr- in the lengthened grade, and *-tr- (-tr̥-) in the zero grade.[90] Due to the working of analogy, the original distribution of these ablaut variants in Proto-Germanic is not easily reconstructible, yet it seems that most of the attested forms are built on the weak grade in North Germanic, and on the full grade in West Germanic (Krahe & Meid 1969: 38–39; cf. Ringe 2006: 276).[91] The original ablaut variation in the PIE paradigm of the r-stems was gradually reduced in Proto-Germanic, yet given the diversity of the

---

87. The process may have been enhanced by metrical constraints, whereby light stems show a preference for disyllabic structure (e.g. OE studu ← *stud 'pillar').

88. It is possible that the class of nouns of relationship included also MHG diehter 'grandson' (originating in PGmc. *þeuhtr-, related to Skt. tuc f. = tôká n. 'descendants, offspring', Avest. taoxma 'descendants'; Pokorny 1959: 1085; cf. Szemerényi 1977: 52).

89. The former is found only once in the Gothic material (excluding the derivative fadrein 'lineage, ancestors'), attested as a vocative singular in the following elevated context: aþþan þatei sijuþ jus gudis, insandida guþ ahman sunáus seinis in haírtōna izwara hrōpjandan: abba, fadar! (Galatians 4:6) (for a discussion see Stiles 1988: 117).

90. The *-ter/*-tor elements are known as "agent-noun" suffixes due to their original derivational function (Fortson 2010: 124).

91. The noun *swester can be traced back to a weak alternant *swesr- (Lat. soror, Skt. swasar) which developed into *swestr- (with an insertion of -t- between -s- and -r-, initially in the GEN. SG. and PL.) on the model set by the other nouns belonging to this declension (Kluge 1926: 3; cf. Wright 1957: 201, Bammesberger 1990: 208, and Boutkan 1995: 271, who reconstructs the noun as a "subtype" in *-ōr, i.e. *suésōr).

patterns still found in the individual Germanic dialects (related to the use of different ablaut grades in different cases), the levelling process was not yet completed in the Proto-Germanic period (Lehmann 2005–2007: § 3.2.4; cf. Bammeseberger 1990: 207).

The Proto-Germanic *r*-stem (masculine) paradigm can be reconstructed as presented in Table 2.6 (Bammesberger 1990: 155, Krahe & Meid 1969: 33–34, Ringe 2006: 276, 280; cf. Ramat 1981: 71):[92]

Table 2.6 Reconstructed PGmc. *r*-stem paradigm of **brōðēr* 'brother'

	SG	PL
NOM.	*brōðēr	*brōð(e)riz
GEN.	*brōðraz	*brōðrō^n
DAT.	*brōðri	*brōðrumiz
ACC.	*brōð(e)ru^n	*brōðrunz

Aside from the presence of ablaut variants, a characteristic feature of the *r*-stem paradigm is the appearance of *i*-mutated vowels in some Germanic dialects, namely Old Norse and Old English. They are attested consistently in the plural paradigm in Old Norse (NOM./ACC. PL. *feþr* 'fathers') as well as occasionally in the singular, alongside *u*-mutated forms (DAT. SG. *feþr/foþor*). In West Germanic, the *i*-mutated forms are to be found only in the DAT. SG. (e.g. OE *brēðer*) (Prokosch 1939: 256).

The extent of the analogical developments in the *r*-stems is fairly limited and the class remains synchronically more or less intact, with the original inflection relatively well-preserved in the Older Germanic languages. Nevertheless, the *r*-stem paradigm was also exposed to the pressure of internal analogy at the earliest stages of development. The analogical inflections emerging as a result of intraparadigmatic influences are found in the ACC. PL., where the inflectional forms attested in all Germanic languages except Gothic were extended from the NOM. PL. Likewise, the Gothic DAT. PL. in *-rum* may be attributed to the impact of the ACC. PL. (PGmc. **-r-unz* < PIE **-r-ns*) rather than external pressure from other paradigms (Boutkan 1995: 275, Ringe 2006: 276; cf. Lehmann 2005–2007: § 3.2.4). The intrusion of inflections from other declensional classes and the consequent lack of inflectional integrity of this class is, however, clearly a later phenomenon, which must have taken place in the individual Germanic languages. Some isolated early traces of the

---

92. The exact shape of the Proto-Germanic paradigm of *r*-stems is not unproblematic and several alternative interpretations have been offered (cf. Krahe & Meid 1969; Ramat 1981; Bammesberger 1990; Ringe 2006). The investigation of its origin, however, goes beyond the scope of the present study, and thus the presentation serves here only as a background for further discussion, and does not aim to be exhaustive (for details see especially Bammesberger 1989; also Lane 1951).

gradual loss of stability of this declensional type may be identified in the Gothic material, where the attested forms of the NOM. PL. *brōþrjus* and ACC. PL. *brōþruns* evince the early influence of the otherwise unproductive *u*-stem declension (Krahe & Meid 1969: 41; also Streitberg 1920: 112). Alternatively, the ACC. PL. may be interpreted as a regular development of the PGmc. forms which merged in both declensions due to their formal similarity (Wright 1957: 101). In West Germanic the earliest analogical forms appear in the GEN. SG. and NOM./ACC. PL., where they were extended from the productive *a*- and *ō*-stem declensions: hence OE *fæder*, OHG *fater* have GEN. SG. *fæderes, fateres* and NOM./ACC. PL. *fæd(e)ras, fatera*.

The attested forms of the GEN. and DAT. PL. may represent a regular phono-logical development (Ringe 2006), but may also be attributed to the operation of analogy, and accordingly interpreted as extensions from the *a*-stems in North and West Germanic (Lehmann 2005–2007: § 3.2.4) and from the *i*-stems in the Gothic GEN. PL. (Boutkan 1995: 275). The difficulty of unambiguous interpretation is par-ticularly evident in the DAT. PL. form, which even if developed regularly (PGmc. *-umiz > *-um(z)*) may have overlapped with the form of the DAT. PL. in the *u*-stems (Krahe & Meid 1969: 41) or the *a*-stems (see Tables 2.15 and 2.16).

2.2.3.5 *s-stems*

The Germanic *s*-stems (*-ez-/-oz*-stems) constituted a small group of neuter nouns and are vestiges of the original PIE *-es-/-os*- inflection.[93] The class is rather scantily attested in early Germanic, yet the inflectional pattern of the *s*-stems developed some secondary productivity in the plural, which continued into the later stages of development of Continental Germanic, especially of High and Low German. Three main criteria have been adduced to identify the PIE *-es-/-os*- stems in Germanic (Schlerath 1995: 255), namely:

a.   the ending *-ez > *-iz* in the NOM./ACC. SG.;
b.   neuter gender;
c.   the suffix *-iz*, Northwest Germanic *-ir*- in the GEN. and DAT. (INSTR.) SG., and in the plural.[94]

---

[93]. The *-es/-os* inflection in Germanic has occasionally been perceived as a Germanic innovation rather than a continuation of the PIE pattern. Such a premise is based on the fact that most of the alleged *s*-stems have no external (non-Germanic) cognates (Schenker 1971: 57). Crucial for this interpretation is a terminological distinction between the "*-es/-os* stems" and "*-es/-os* inflection" (for details see Schenker 1971: 50, 57).

[94]. The transparency of this fairly broad definition is complicated by (a) the possibility of tracing the NOM./ACC. SG. ending *-iz* to forms other than *-ez*, (b) frequent early shifts of nouns to the masculine gender, (c) the transfer of the *-ir*- formative to the plural of neuter *a*-stems and its subsequent dissemination in Old High German (Schlerath 1995).

Since the *s*-stems were originally declined according to the pattern of other conso-nantal stems, the Proto-Germanic *-*ez*-/-*oz*- stem paradigm may be reconstructed as presented in Table 2.7 (Ringe 2006: 278; Boutkan 1995: 265; cf. Lehmann 2005–2007: § 3.2.6).

Table 2.7 Reconstructed PGmc. *s*-stem paradigm of **lambaz* 'lamb'

	SG	PL
NOM.	*lambaz	*lambazō
GEN.	*lambezaz	*lambezōn
DAT.	*lambezi	*lambezumiz
ACC.	*lambaz	*lambazō

One of the early analogical developments affecting the paradigm of the *s*-stems was the redistribution of the original ablaut pattern in the inflectional suffix. As the NOM./ACC. SG. *-*az* (PIE *-*os*) was the only (certain) *o*-grade formation in the paradigm, it must have been exposed to analogical pressure of other categories, where the *e*-grade suffix *-*iz* (< PIE *-*es*) was found, in particular of the GEN. and DAT. SG. It is assumed that this analogical pressure eventually led to the replace-ment of the *o*-grade form by the dominant *e*-grade (Campbell 1977: 258, Boutkan 1992: 14; cf. Weyhe 1906: 89; Wright & Wright 1982: 213).[95] The occurrence of -*i*- in the Gothic NOM. SG. forms *hatis* and *sigis* (in place of the expected **hats*, **sigs*) has been adduced as a support for this assumption.

Further modification of the paradigm, entailing the operation of analogical processes, seems to have followed different pathways in the individual Germanic di-alects. Given the absence of the *s*-stem declension in Gothic and Old Scandinavian, the activity of interparadigmatic analogy must have taken place already before the first attestation of those languages.[96] This fact places the *s*-stems among the declen-sional types which were earliest affected by the restructuring process. In stark con-trast to Gothic and Scandinavian, West Germanic, and most notably Old English,

---

95. The incipient state of affairs is evident in the early Finnish loanwords where the forms in -*as* are attested: *kinnas* 'glove', *lammas* 'lamb', *lannas* 'beach', *mallas* 'malt', *porras* 'step', cf. ON *kinn*, OE *lamb*, OHG *lant*, *malz*, *bort* (Kluge 1913: 205).

96. The only exception here and the only residue of the historical pattern is arguably the Go. GEN. SG. *hatis* (Boutkan 1995: 264; Braune/Heidermanns 2004: 94), attested in the sentence: *jah wēsum wistái barna* hatis (Ephesians 2,3B) (alongside *hatizē*), where the marker -*is* may be considered a regular continuation of the *-*ez*- (< PGmc. **hatez-ez*). Counterevidence to this interpretation is offered by a parallel text (Ephesians 2,3A), and, accordingly, the form can be interpreted as a spelling error rather than an original GEN. SG. (Bammesberger 1990: 208; cf. Krause 1953:138; Schenker 1971: 52).

testifies to the retention of this inflectional type, despite its rather scant attestation, confined to the material affiliated with the Anglian dialects (Hogg & Fulk 2011: 58). The overall condition and the pattern of reorganisation of the *s*-stems in Germanic can be summarised as follows:

> Als Kategorie sind konsonantisch flektierende *s*-Stämme in den germ. Einzel-sprachen nur noch in Spuren zu erkennen, was mit dem Abbau der konsonanti-schen Flexion im Germ. allgemein im Zusammenhang steht. Meist flektieren sie thematisch oder sind in die *i*-oder *u*-Stämme übergetreten.
>
> (Casaretto 2000: 217)

A unique characteristic of the *s*-stems in West Germanic was the presence of the -*r*- formative (developed regularly from PGmc. suffixal *-*z*- < PIE *-*s*-) in cases other than the NOM./ACC. SG. In Old English, the profile of the paradigm was additionally complicated by the presence of a mutated vowel in the NOM. and ACC. SG. (as in *cælf*, *lemb*, *hrēð*, *dæg*), resulting from the impact of an earlier inflectional ending containing the high front vowel *-*i*- (PGmc. *-*iz*, e.g. in *calfiz*, *lambiz*). In Old High German, the original stem formative *-*ir*- underwent a process of morphologisation at a later stage, induced by the loss of the original phonological conditions, whereby it was reanalysed as a plural marker, which with time developed a substantial level of productivity.

Formally, the West Germanic *s*-stems may be divided into two subgroups: (a) nouns in which the NOM./ACC. SG. is attested without the *r*-stem formative (e.g. OE *lamb* 'lamb', OE *cealf*, OHG *kalb* 'calf', OE *dōēg* 'day', OE *hrēð* 'glory', OHG *huon* 'hen', OHG *(h)rind* 'cattle'), and (b) nouns in which the suffixal -*r* is consistently attested in all cases of the paradigm, including the NOM./ACC. SG. (e.g. OE *ēgur* 'sea', OE *hrīðer* 'horned cattle', OE *ēar*, OHG *ahir* (*ehir*) 'ear of grain', OHG *demar* 'twilight', OHG *liodar* 'noise'). In the latter case, their identity as former *s*-stems is based essentially on their etymological relationship to forms which did not preserve the -*r*- formative, as well as the occasional consonantal inflection of the DAT. SG. (Campbell 1977: 259). The NOM./ACC. SG. of the second subgroup (e.g. OE *dōgor*, *hālor* < *dōgr*, *hālr*) is believed to be an effect of *intra*paradigmatic levelling and, accordingly, its shape is determined by the structure of the oblique cases, where the -*r*- element was originally present (Wright & Wright 1982: 213; Hirt 1932: 59; Boutkan 1992: 12, 15; cf. Casaretto 2000: 219). This twofold development of the *s*-stems is significant from the perspective of the restructuring process: it may be expected that, due to the different structure of the nouns, the process unfolded differently in the two subgroups of *s*-stems.

The lack of vestiges of the *s*-stem inflection in Gothic and Old Norse is a direct result of the fact that both have no syncope of final *-*z* (Boer 1918: 204). The Old Norse material indicates that the *s*-stems were entirely integrated into the *a*-stem declension, whereas the Gothic attestation points to a bi-directional transfer of the original *s*-stems to the *a*-stem class (e.g. *agis* 'fear', *hatis* 'hatred', *riqis* 'darkness', *sigis* 'victory') and the *u*-stem class (e.g. *wulþus* 'glory', *sidus* 'custom', *faíhu* 'cattle', *liþus* 'member', *skadus* 'shade')[97] (Braune/Heidermanns 2004: 108; Streitberg 1920: 103; Prokosch 1939: 256; Schenker 1971: 51–52; Bammesberger 1990: 208).[98] The evidence of West Germanic testifies to two stages of transition of the *s*-stems, namely an early drift to the *i*-stem declension (e.g. OE *hete* 'hatred', *mene* 'necklace', *sele* 'hall', *sige* 'victory'), dated prior to the first attestations, and a later transition to the neuter *a*-stems, occurring partly in the historical period. The prehistoric shift of the *s*-stems to the *i*-stems has been explained in terms of a generalisation of the PIE *-es-* formative from the oblique cases to the entire paradigm, most importantly, to the NOM./ACC. SG., whereby the latter fell together with the NOM./ACC. SG. of the *i*-stems (cf. *sige* 'victory' < **segiz* and *i*-stem *wine* 'friend' < **weniz*; Casaretto 2000: 218). The interparadigmatic realignments which followed were apparently instigated by this formal coalescence of the NOM. SG. of the *i*- and *s*-stems. The analogical transfer of the *s*-stems to the *i*-stem declension in West Germanic must have been facilitated by the fact that these forms, just like the *i*-stems, were subject to *i*-mutation (Unwerth 1910: 2). A similar factor may have played a role in triggering the transference of the *s*-stems to the *ja*-stem declension, whose members regularly underwent *i*-mutation. The shape of the NOM./ACC. was also the direct trigger for the later extensive transition of the *s*-stems to the neuter *a*-stem declension. Once the NOM./ACC. SG. of the neuter *a*-stems became endingless, the form could fall together with that of the *s*-stems, and, as a result, the *s*-stem nouns tended to adopt the productive pattern of the *a*-stem declension (cf. GEN. SG. Go. *riqiz-is* [*s*-stem] and *barn-is* [*a*-stem]; Krahe & Meid 1969: 43).[99]

The wide spread of analogical *a*-stem endings in West Germanic is attested in the GEN. and DAT. SG., where only Old English and Old High German preserve residues of the original inflection. The other cases attest to a regular phonological development of the inherited inflections, even if preserved only vestigially in the earliest sources. The interpretation of the GEN. and DAT. PL. forms is not straightforward; they may be treated as hybrid formations in that the novel *a*-stem endings are attached to the inherited *r*-formative (e.g. OHG *lembiro*, *lembirum*). In both

---

97. The original PGmc. *s*-stem **kelb-*, which continues as the OE *cealf* and OHG *kalb*, *kilbur*, is preserved in Gothic as a feminine *n*-stem *kalbo*, showing no traces of the original affiliation.

98. For details concerning this class in Gothic, see Braune/Heidermanns (2004: 108–109), and Gordon & Taylor (1981) for an overview of inflectional patterns in Old Norse, where the *s*-stems are not treated as a separate declensional class.

99. For details concerning the problematic form of the NOM./ACC. SG. and its alternative interpretations, see Boutkan (1995: 266–267).

Old English and Old High German, the presence of -*Vr* in these cases may be attributed to *intra*paradigmatic pressure from the NOM./ACC. SG. (OHG -*ir*, OE -*or*) (Boutkan 1995: 268).

In contrast to other minor declensional classes, a significant characteristic of analogical restructuring of the *s*-stems was the fact that the change of paradigmatic affiliation was (usually) accompanied by gender reassignment (Schenker 1971: 53). Accordingly, the majority of the *s*-stems lost their original neuter gender and adopted the masculine pattern of inflection. This is particularly evident in Old Norse, where the shift of the *s*-stems was unidirectional, i.e. to the masculine *a*-stems. The factor clearly facilitating this direction of transfer in Old Norse was the formal similarity of the NOM. SG. form (*kalfr*) with that of the masculine *a*-stems, characterised by the presence of the ending -*r* (e.g. *ulfr*), which led to a reanalysis of the stem formative as the typically masculine NOM. SG. inflectional ending.[100]

2.2.3.6 nd-*stems*
The Germanic *nd*-stems were nominalised active participle formations of masculine gender, known also as *nomina agentis* (agent nouns), in which the original suffix **-nt* served as a formative element (cf. Lat. *ferēns, ferentis* 'bearing').[101] The type was fairly widespread in the early Germanic dialects, essentially retaining the original consonantal inflection of the PIE participles in **-nt-*, in marked contrast to productive participles which regularly lost their inherited consonantal inflection and joined the paradigms of the *ja-/jō*-stems or *n*-stems (Prokosch 1939: 259; Bammesberger 1990: 214).[102] Their substantival status in Proto-Germanic has occasionally been questioned and thus the postulation of a *class* of PGmc. consonant stems in **-nd-* is debatable. The fact that they formed a separate declension in the individual older Germanic languages does not necessarily mean that they constituted an independent inflectional class of nouns in the Proto-Germanic period. Alternatively, the PGmc. participial formations may be interpreted as consonant-stem adjectives

---

100. In this way, the original element **-az* is retained in a fossilised form in the NOM./ACC. SG. in North Germanic languages (**-az* > -*r*, but cf. ON *ax* 'ear of grain'), as opposed to West Germanic where it was lost (except in the subgroup of the *s*-stems where -*r*- was extended from the oblique cases throughout the paradigm).

101. In his study on the Old English *nomina agentis*, Kärre (1915: 9) defines these formations as "concrete nouns (or adj.) that express the active representative of an action or a condition. It is essential that they should express the performer of an action, not the bearer of a quality (...)". The distinction becomes particularly difficult in disyllabic *nd*-stems, where the connection to the verb appears to be fairly strong in all Germanic languages.

102. The transition of participial formations to vocalic inflectional types is not confined to the Germanic branch of Indo-European; for instance, in Latin these formations follow regularly the *i*-stem declension, and in Lithuanian and Old Slavonic they shift to the *ja*-stems.

terminating in *-nd-, with derived feminines in -nd-ī ~ *-nd-ijō- (Ringe 2006: 199). Notwithstanding the unsettled status of these formations in Proto-Germanic, their paradigm may be provisionally reconstructed on the basis of the material available from the daughter languages. As the nd-stems originally inflected according to the pattern of the other consonantal stems, the paradigm may have looked as in Table 2.8 (Ringe 2006: 274; cf. Krahe & Meid 1969: 42, Ramat 1981: 74, Boutkan 1995: 367, Lehmann 2005–2007: § 3.2.5).[103]

Table 2.8 Reconstructed PGmc. nd-stem paradigm of *frijōnd- 'friend'

	SG	PL
NOM.	*frijōnds	*frijōndiz
GEN.	*frijōndiz	*frijōndō^n
DAT.	*frijōndi	*frijōndmiz
ACC.	*frijōndu^n	*frijōndunz

As in the other consonantal classes, a distinctive feature of the nd-stem paradigm in North Germanic and parts of West Germanic (OE) was the presence of an i-mutated vowel in the DAT. SG. and NOM./ACC. PL. The reshaping of the inherited nd-stem paradigm appears to have been a relatively late phenomenon when compared to the other minor inflectional classes, as the archaic shape of the nd-stem paradigm is fairly well preserved in Gothic, except the forms of the GEN. and ACC. SG. and DAT. PL., which did not escape the influence of the a-stems (Braune/Heidermanns 2004: 107–108; Wright 1957: 101–102). In contrast, the paradigm was subject to extensive remodelling in North and West Germanic. In Old Norse, it is only the plural that retains features of the original nd-stem inflection (NOM./ACC. and GEN.), whereas the singular is consistently declined according to the n-stem pattern (e.g. NOM. SG. fiánde 'enemy'). In West Germanic, as a result of both phonological and analogical innovations, the major direction of transformation of the nd-stems, as with the other minor declensional types, is towards the masculine a-stems. The original consonantal inflection is recognisable only in individual cases, where it is attested alongside the a-stem forms, especially in the NOM./ACC. PL. The early influence of the productive inflections on the paradigm of the nd-stems in West Germanic is evinced in the GEN. SG. and DAT. PL., which consistently surface with

---

103. Two etymologically obscure nouns can be associated with this group, namely the OE tōþ (Go. tunþus, OS tand < *tanþ-/tund-, cf. Lat. dēns, dentis < *dent-) 'tooth' and sōþ 'truth' (ON sannr < *sanþ-). It is assumed that their original agential character had been lost before the pre-Germanic period, and as a result, they never went through the participial stage, but instead remained root formations (Kärre 1915: 77; Bammesberger 1990: 202; 2009: 111; Beekes 1995: 179; Ringe 2006: 198).

the productive markers (e.g. OE -*es* and -*um* respectively), extended from the *a*-stem declension. Early pressure of the *a*-stem and *i*-stem patterns is also attested in the DAT. SG. in Old Saxon, Old Frisian and Old Low Franconian (-*e*/-*a*/-*i*), which no longer shows traces of the inherited inflection. The remaining cases attest to the expected inflectional pattern, with endingless (and occasionally mutated) forms. Finally, in all languages, the ACC. PL. owes its shape to the activity of intraparadigmatic analogy, i.e. the extension of the NOM. PL. ending.

2.2.3.7 þ-*stems*

The *þ*-stems whose original inflection is attested vestigially only in West Germanic, constituted the smallest declensional class in Proto-Germanic. They are formed with the PIE suffix *-t-, which developed into the PGmc. formations *-*iþ*/-*aþ* and possibly *-*uþ* (Bammesberger 1990: 215). This inflectional class was unproductive already in Proto-Germanic, and given its scant attestation, its restructuring must have started very early (Boutkan 2003: 11). The reconstructed PGmc. nouns affiliated with this class include masculine *aluþ- 'ale', *halaþ- 'man', *mēnōþ- 'month', wītwōd- 'witness', feminine *magaþ- 'maid' and neuter *meliþ- 'honey' and possibly *ha(u)beþ- (*ha(u)buþ-) 'head' (Bammesberger 1990: 215–216; Ringe 2006: 279; cf. Boutkan 1995: 263; Voyles 1992: 237). Their inflection was parallel to that of the other consonantal stems. The *þ*-stems survived primarily in Old English, where vestiges of the original inflection, both masculine and feminine, are to be found in four nouns with the alternations of the type *hæle*, GEN. PL. *hæleþa* 'man' and *ealu*, GEN. PL. *ealeþa* 'ale' (cf. Section 3.5.8). In other Germanic dialects, these stems experienced a total transfer to the productive declensions, following different paths in the individual languages: some joined the *a*-stem declension, others the *i*-stem pattern (Prokosch 1939: 259; Thöny 2013: 241–244). An example of this diverse development may be *magaþ 'maid', which in Gothic and Old High German is attested as an *i*-stem (Go. *magaþs*, OHG *magad*), but in other Germanic languages follows the pattern of the *ō*-stems (see Sections 3.5.8, 4.5.8, 5.6.8).

2.2.4 Interparadigmatic realignments in Proto-Germanic:
A cross-declensional overview

The developments of the PGmc. inflections in the individual daughter languages are systematically summarised in Tables 2.9–2.16, each representing a different case/number category. In contrast to the presentation in Section 2.2.3, the present summary adopts a cross-declensional perspective, concentrating on the tendencies characteristic of a given case/number category across declensions. The systematisation of the nominal inflections is also intended to serve as a practical point of reference for the later discussions concerning individual Germanic dialects. As in the earlier sections of this chapter, the inflectional forms presented for Proto-Germanic are standard reconstructions, based primarily on Ringe (2006) and Bammesberger (1990), supplemented with information found in Krahe & Meid (1969), Boutkan (1995) and Lehmann (2005–2007). It must be observed that the interpretations and reconstructions of preforms offered by these authors frequently diverge or differ in detail. Unless indicated otherwise, the present study follows the traditional or rather majority-view reconstructions.

The forms presented in italics in the Tables refer to morphological innovations, i.e. forms which cannot be ascribed to regular phonological development. A distinction is made between forms which emerge as a result of *intra*pradigmatic analogy (light grey cells), i.e. the pressure of other case/number endings in the paradigm, and *inter*paradigmatic analogy (italics), i.e. the influence of inflections from other declensional types. All the other inflections (in bold) are considered to represent the regular (*lautgesetzlich*) continuation of the reconstructed PIE forms and are thus archaic. It is worth noting that the relevance of the early analogical reshufflings taking place within paradigms is fairly limited for the present investigation, which is mainly focused on the transitions of nouns among inflectional classes. For instance, the fact that the DAT. SG. form continues an original INSTR. SG. does not have a direct impact on the present analysis of the diffusion of productive inflections. As intraparadigmatic developments of this type occurred relatively early in the separate prehistory of Germanic, the restructured paradigm (incorporating these early changes) will be taken as a starting point for the quantitative investigation of interdeclensional transitions in the individual Germanic dialects. In other words, such forms will be interpreted as archaic in the analysis of the individual languages.

The inflectional endings given for individual languages presented in the Tables are the most archaic attested, and in many cases occur only sporadically in the available material. As this summary is intended to capture the earliest stages of the restructuring process, prior to the earliest attestations of the various Germanic languages, it largely ignores innovations belonging to the historical period, such as the spread of the *n*-stem inflection in West Germanic. Later analogical developments will be subjected to a detailed analysis and discussion in the chapters devoted to the individual languages. However, these later analogical forms do appear in the Tables when they constitute the prevailing pattern already in the earliest records (e.g. OFris. GEN. SG. *-ø* → *-es* in consonantal stems).

Some of the inflectional endings are typically hybrid formations in that they combine archaic features, continuing the PIE inflections, with analogically extended endings. These appear typically in the *s*-stem paradigm, where the forms of the GEN. and DAT. PL. (OE *-r-a, -r-um*, OHG *ir-o, -ir-um*) or the OHG DAT. SG. (*-ir-e*) are combinations of the archaic *-r-* element with the analogical *a*-stem endings *-a, -um* and *-e*. These *s*-stem hybrid forms are consistently marked as archaic in the Tables below.

In order to present a complete picture of the inflectional configuration in the oldest attested Germanic languages, the evidence of East and North Germanic – both staying beyond the focus of the quantitative study – was also included in the summary. As observed above, despite their generally more archaic character, these branches do testify to the presence of analogical pressures in the system of nominal inflection, pointing to an early date of restructuring in Germanic.

A distinction between light-syllable (L) and heavy-syllable (H) stems is consistently made for the NOM. and ACC. SG., since, as observed in the preceding sections, the reorganisation of inflection often followed different pathways in these two types of stems, especially in the West Germanic languages. Finally, a number of symbols used in the Tables require an explanation. A hyphen (–) is used for cases which are unattested in the available material; an asterisk (*) denotes forms which are unattested, but for which there is sound evidence (especially from present-day inflection) that they existed (e.g. the plural form -*eren* in Modern Dutch, not attested in the OLF material); a tilda (~) denotes forms for which there is positive evidence that they did not exist; the arrow (→) refers to analogical replacement of the historically expected form by a novel ending; it appears in cases where the original forms are only sporadically attested and the prevailing pattern is innovative.

Table 2.9 The development of PGmc. NOM. SG. inflections in the early Germanic languages

NOM SG	*i*-stems		*u*-stems		root nouns		*r*-stems	*s*-stems	*nd*-stems
	H	L	H	L	H	L			
PGmc.	-iz	-iz	-uz	-uz	-s	-s	-ø	-Vzø*	-s
Go.	-s		-us		-s		-ø	~	-s
ER	-iz		-uz		-z		-ø**	–	–
ON	-r		-r		-r m,f, -ø f		-ø	~	-e
OE	-ø	-e	-ø	-u	-ø	*-ø → -u	-ø	-ø + uml	-ø
OFris.	-ø	-e	-ø	-u/-e	-ø	*-ø (→ *-u/-e)	-ø	-ø	-ø
OS	-ø	-i	-ø	-u	-ø	*-ø	-ø	-ø	-ø
OHG	-ø	-i	-ø	-u	-ø	*-ø	-ø	-ø	-ø
OLF	-ø	-i	-ø	-u	-ø	*-ø	-ø	-ø	-ø

* As the quality of the vowel in this ending differs depending on the dialect and case (e.g. the *i*-mutated vowel is attested in the singular in OE, but in the plural in OHG), it will be marked consistently as -*V*-. As its exact quality has no direct effect on the interpretation of the data, it will not be explored further here. For details of the interpretation, see Boutkan (1995: 265) and Klein (2013).

** The ER forms in -*ar* and ON -*er* are difficult to account for. The former has been attributed to analogical pressure of other cases in the paradigm, in particular of the VOC. SG. (Stiles 1984) and ACC. SG. (Antonsen 1975). Alternatively, the forms can be viewed as a regular development of *-*ōr* and -*ēr*, respectively. The forms of the NOM. SG. found in Gothic and West Germanic can also be traced back to these two ablaut variants (Boutkan 1995: 272–273).

Table 2.10 The development of PGmc. ACC. SG. inflections in the early Germanic languages

ACC SG	*i*-stems		*u*-stems		root nouns		*r*-stems	*s*-stems	*nd*-stems
	H	L	H	L	H	L			
PGmc.	-i(n)	-i(n)	-u(n)	-u(n)	-u(n)	-u(n)	-u(n)	-Vzø	-u(n)
Go.	-ø		-u		*-u → -ø		-ø	~	-ø
ER	-i		-u		—		—	—	—
ON	-ø		-ø		-ø		-ø	~	-a
OE	-ø	-e	-ø	-u	-ø	-u	-ø	-ø + uml	-ø
OFris.	-ø	-e	-ø	-u/-e	-ø	*-u/-e	-ø	-ø	-ø
OS	-ø	-i	-ø	-u	-ø	*-u	-ø	-ø	-ø
OHG	-ø	-i	-ø	-u	-ø	*-u	-ø	-ø	-ø
OLF	-ø	-i	-ø	-u	-ø	*-u	-ø	-ø	-ø

Table 2.11 The development of PGmc. GEN. SG. inflections in the early Germanic languages

GEN SG	*i*-stems	*u*-stems	root nouns	*r*-stems	*s*-stems	*nd*-stems
PGmc.	-aiz, -īz	-auz	-iz	-(a)z	-Vzaz	-iz
Go.	-*is* [m], -**ais** [f]	-aus, -us	-s	-s	~	-*is*
ER	-az/-iz[*]	-ōz	—	—	—	—
ON	-*s* [m], -**ar** [f]	-ar	-r + uml	-ø	~	-a
OE	-*es* [m], -*e* [f]	-a	-ø + uml → -*es* [m], -*e* [f]	-ø	-ur	-*es*
OFris.	-*es* [m], -*e* [f]	-a	-*es* [m], -*ø* [f]	-ø	-*es*	-*es*
OS	-*es* [m], -*i* [f]	-*es* [m]	-*es* [m,f]	-ø	-*as*	-*as*
OHG	-*es* [m], -*i* [f]	-ō	-ø → -*es* [m], -*ø* [f]	-ø	-ires	-*es*
OLF	-*es* [m], -*i* [f]	-*is* [m,f], -*e* [f]	-*es* [m,f], -*ø* [f]	-ø	-*es*	-*es*

[*] The evidence provided by Early Runic is complicated and ambiguous, hence both variants of the GEN. SG. are mentioned (e.g. Boutkan 1995: 244–246).

Table 2.12 The development of PGmc. DAT. SG. inflections in the early Germanic languages

DAT SG	*i*-stems	*u*-stems	root nouns	*r*-stems	*s*-stems	*nd*-stems
PGmc.	-ēi/-ī	-Vw(i)	-i	-i	-Vzi	-i
Go.	-*a* [m], -**ai** [f]	-au	-ø	-ø	~	-ø
ER	—	-iu, -ō (?)	—	—	—	—
ON	-e, -ø [m,f]	-e + uml	-ø + uml	-ø + uml	~	-a
OE	-i, -e [m,f]	-a	-ø + uml	-ø (+ uml)	-ur	-ø + uml
OFris.	-e [m,f]	-a	*-ø + uml → -ø	*-ø + uml → -ø	-e	-e
OS	-i, -e [m], -i [f]	-o[*]	-ø	-ø	-a, -e	-a, -i
OHG	-e [m], -i [f,n]	-iu	-ø	-ø	-ire	-ø
OLF	-i, -e [m,f]	-e	*-ø	-ø	—	-i

[*] See the discussion in Section 5.6.3.3.

Table 2.13 The development of PGmc. NOM. PL. inflections in the early Germanic languages

NOM PL	*i*-stems		*u*-stems		root nouns		*r*-stems	*s*-stems	*nd*-stems
	H	L	H	L	H	L			
PGmc.	-īz	-īz	-iwiz	-iwiz	-iz	-iz	-iz	-Vzō-	-iz
Go.		-eis		-jus		-s	-jus	~	-s
ER		-		–		–	-iz	–	–
ON		-er		-er	-r + uml		-ø + uml	~	-r + uml
OE	-e → -*as* ᵐ, -*a* ᶠ	-e	-a⃰	-a	-ø + uml	-e + uml	-ø	-or, -ru	-ø + uml
OFris.	-e → -*ar* ᵐ, -*a* ᶠ	-e > -*ar* ᵐ, -*a* ᶠ	-a	-a	-ø + uml	–	-ø	-ar⃰⃰	⃰-ø + uml → -ø
OS	-i	-i	-i	-i	-ø → -i	–	-ø	-er	-ø
OHG	-i	-i	-i	-i(u)	-ø → -i	–	-ø	-ir	-ø
OLF	-i	-i	-i	-i	-ø → -i	–	-ø	⃰-ir	⃰-ø

⃰ Although these forms are marked as inherited here, the origin of this ending is problematic (see the discussion in Section 2.2.3.2).
⃰⃰ For a detailed discussion of this plural form and arguments for treating it as an inherited feature, see Section 4.5.6.

Table 2.14 The development of PGmc. ACC. PL. inflections in the early Germanic languages

ACC PL	*i*-stems		*u*-stems		root nouns		*r*-stems	*s*-stems	*nd*-stems
	H	L	H	L	H	L			
PGmc.	-inz	-inz	-unz	-unz	-unz	-unz	-(er)unz	-Vzō	-unz
Go.		-ins		-uns		-s	-uns	~	-s
ER		–		–		–	–	–	–
ON	-e ᵐ, -*er* ᶠ		-o		-r + uml		-ø + uml	~	-r + uml
OE	-e → -*as* ᵐ, -*a* ᶠ	-e	-u⃰ → -a	-u → -a	-ø + uml	-e + uml	-ø, -ru⃰⃰	-or, -ru	-ø + uml
OFris.	-e → -*ar* ᵐ, -*a* ᶠ	-e → -*ar* ᵐ, -*a* ᶠ	-a	-a	-ø + uml	–	-ø	-ar	⃰-ø + uml → -ø
OS	-i	-i	-i	-i	-ø → i	–	-ø	-er	-ø
OHG	-i	-i	-i	-u → -i	-ø → i	–	-ø	-ir	-ø
OLF	-i	-i	-i	-i	-ø → i	–	⃰-ø	⃰-ir	⃰-ø

⃰ The form is fairly speculative, based on only one attested form *flōdu*, the interpretation of which poses some difficulties. For a discussion see Section 3.5.3.2.
⃰⃰ The OE marker -*u* in this category (as in *brōþru*) has been interpreted as a regular development of PGmc. ⃰-*unz* (Kluge 1913: 196; Boutkan 1995: 275); it can be alternatively explained as an analogical extension from the *s*-stems or neuter *a*-stems (for a discussion see Section 3.5.5).

Table 2.15 The development of PGmc. GEN. PL. inflections in the early Germanic languages

GEN PL	*i*-stems	*u*-stems	root nouns	*r*-stems	*s*-stems	*nd*-stems
PGmc.	-ijō(n)	-iwō(n)	-ō(n)	-ō(n)	-Vzō(n)	-ō(n)
Go.	-ē*	-iwē	-ē	-ē	~	-ē
ER	–	–	–	–	–	–
ON	-a	-a	-a	-a	~	-a
OE	-igea → -a	-a	-a	-a	-ra	-a, -ra
OFris.	-a	-a	-a	-a	-ra	-a
OS	-io	-o	-o	-	-ero	-o, -ero
OHG	-eo	-eo	-o	-o	-iro	-o
OLF	-o	-o	-o	-o	-o	-o

* The origin of the Go. GEN. PL. marker -*ē* has been considered one of the most complex problems in Germanic historical morphology (Kortlandt 1978: 291; Beekes 1995: 117). The form has been interpreted as original (inherited) in the *i*-stems on account of the lack of the formative element before the ending (*-ejan* < *-ei-om*) (Kortlandt 1978: 291; Boutkan 1995: 249), but cf. Prokosch (1939: 246) and Ringe (2006: 273) who treat it as analogical, extended from the productive patterns.

Table 2.16 The development of PGmc. DAT. PL. inflections in the early Germanic languages

DAT PL	*i*-stems	*u*-stems	root nouns	*r*-stems	*s*-stems	*nd*-stems
PGmc.	-imaz/-imiz	umaz/-umiz	-maz/-miz	-umaz/-umiz	-(V)zmaz/-(V)zmiz	-maz/-miz
Go.	-im	-um	-im [f], -am [m]	-um	~	-am
ER	-umz	–	–	–	–	–
ON	-om	-om	-om	-om	~	-om
OE	-um	-um	-um	-um	-rum	-um
OFris.	-um	-um	-um	-um	-um	-um
OS	-iun	-un	-un	-un	-um	-un
OHG	-im	-um, -im	-um, -im	-um	-irum	-um
OLF	-in	-on	-on, -in	-on	-on	-on

A number of tendencies are easily identifiable when comparing the data from various declensional classes in the investigated early Germanic languages. Due to the widespread general syncretisms of the NOM. and ACC., and frequent parallelisms between the DAT. and GEN., both in the SG. and PL., the cases will be discussed in the following manner: NOM. and ACC. SG.; GEN. and DAT. SG.; NOM. and ACC. PL.; GEN. and DAT. PL.[104]

---

104. The summary does not include the INSTR. SG., occasionally attested in Germanic (OS and OHG). The inflections of the INSTR. SG. will be discussed in individual chapters when relevant.

NOM. & ACC. SG.

Most of the NOM. and ACC. SG. endings are regular continuations of the PGmc. inflections. Traces of analogical pressure are to be found only in the consonantal declensions (feminine root nouns and *nd*-stems) of Old Norse. The novel ending-less accusative forms of Gothic root nouns are believed to have been created either to avoid ambiguity with other cases in the paradigm or under the influence of the *u*-stems. The early shift of the Gothic root noun *fōtus* to the *u*-stems has been ad-duced as evidence for the earlier existence of the marker *-*u*- in the ACC. SG., where *-*u*- may have facilitated the transition to this declension (Boutkan 1995: 260). In general, the endingless form of the accusative fits into the overall synchronic pattern of distribution of the NOM. and ACC. SG. in nearly all declensional classes in Gothic, where the ACC. form equals the NOM. without the marker -*s*. Given this overall profile of the ACC. SG. in Gothic, the endingless ACC. SG. of root nouns may have emerged under the combined pressure of the other declensions, in particular the masculine *a*-stems.

The OE/OFris. NOM. SG. marker -*u* in light-syllable root nouns is an instance of early analogical extension from the ACC. SG. (Bammesberger 1990: 191; Boutkan 1995: 260). This paradigm-internal analogy has also been adduced to account for the novel zero ending (with *i*-mutation) in the NOM. SG. of the ON feminine root nouns. As this direction of intraparadigmatic transfer is not common in North Germanic, the endingless NOM. SG. may rather reflect the influence of the *ō*-stems (Prokosch 1939: 257).

It may be easily observed that the forms of the NOM. and ACC. SG. have become largely identical across different declensional types already in the earliest Germanic languages, as a result of phonological developments and the consequent reduction of endings. This lack of a distinctive NOM./ACC. SG. ending was one of the factors which triggered analogical transfers across inflectional classes in later periods.[105]

GEN. & DAT. SG.

Both the GEN. and DAT. SG. attest to the intrusion of analogical inflections, but to a varying extent. The GEN. SG. is the category which was most extensively affected by the working of analogical processes already in the earliest period. The impact is most prominent in the masculine paradigms in West Germanic, although neither Gothic nor Old Norse is entirely free from the analogical pressure of the *a*-stem inflection. The original inflectional pattern is better preserved in the feminine par-adigms. The contrast is particularly evident in the *i*-stems, where the masculine

---

105. On the significance of the shape of the NOM. SG. in the reorganisation of the Germanic nominal declensions, see Lahiri & Dresher (1984: 141, 148) (with reference to the OE *u*-stems and OHG and Go. *ja*-stems).

paradigm has been entirely restructured on the pattern of the *a*-stems, whereas the feminine inflection is consistently retained in all languages. The *r*-stems, *u*-stems and feminine root nouns emerge as the most archaic declensional types.

The complexity of the development of the DAT. SG. lies in the fact that the case was subject to both the pressure of the other declensional types, as well as that of the other cases in the paradigm, in particular of the INSTR. In fact, all the inherited DAT. SG. forms are secondary in Germanic in that they result from a merger of the inherited PIE dative with the locative, which was originally a more frequently occurring form (Prokosch 1939: 235; Boutkan 1995: 246, 256; Ringe 2006: 272). The merger of the locative and dative was a cross-declensional innovation, characterising all declensional types in Germanic, and was completed already by the Proto-Germanic period.

Altogether, the pattern found in the DAT. SG. appears to be more archaic than in the GEN. SG., with many endings continuing the PGmc. inflections. A complete analogical replacement of inflections is found in the *nd*-stems and *s*-stems in Old Frisian, Old Saxon and Old Low Franconian, and the impact of the *a*-stems is also evident in the *i*-stems in Gothic and in Continental Germanic. *Intra*paradigmatic pressure is evident in Old Frisian (root nouns and *r*-stems), where the unmutated forms appear under the influence of the other cases in the paradigm which showed no *i*-mutated vowels. The evidence of Old Norse *i*-stems poses a substantial interpretative difficulty and there seems to be little agreement as to the origin of the attested dative forms there, with contradictory opinions offered in the standard historical handbooks. In the summary above, which takes into account only the earliest attested inflections, the vocalic ending (-*e*) is interpreted as original and the endingless form as analogical, in compliance with the majority opinion; note, however, that Boutkan (1995: 247) argues that the marker -*e* as well as the endingless forms were inherited in the masculine paradigm but analogical in the feminine paradigm. Irrespective of the exact interpretation, the Old Norse data testify to the presence of analogical levelling in the paradigm at an early stage of North Germanic.

NOM. & ACC. PL.

A prominent feature of the NOM. and ACC. PL. inflection is the syncretism of their endings, which is partly phonological and partly due to analogical levelling. The original ACC. PL. marker was consistently replaced by the NOM. PL. in consonantal stems (i.e. root nouns, *nd*-stems and *r*-stems) in Northwest Germanic languages. Gothic shows traces of such analogical extension in the root nouns and *nd*-stems. All these forms are a reflex of intraparadigmatic analogy rather than external pressure from other declensional types.

As regards *inter*paradigmatic restructuring, the two cases show an almost identical pattern of reorganisation, with extensive analogical changes in the West Germanic languages. The earliest analogical inflections appear in the vocalic paradigms, i.e. the *i*-stems and *u*-stems, as well as in the root nouns. The early Germanic dialects testify to a two-way reorganisation of the inherited inflection of the vocalic stems, with the *a*-stems and *ō*-stem serving as a template for re-shufflings in Old English and Old Frisian, and the *i*-stems fulfilling this role in the remaining dialects of Continental Germanic. Such a distribution of analogical inflections will become even more prominent in the later period, with the *i*-stems constituting a declining category in the Ingvaeonic dialects, but becoming one of the major destination classes for minor stems in Inland Continental West Germanic. Another instance of early analogical extension is the Gothic NOM. PL. marker *-jus* in the *r*-stems, which testifies to the early impact of the otherwise unproductive *u*-stem inflection.

GEN. & DAT. PL.

Both the GEN. PL. marker *-a* and the DAT. PL. marker *-um* have traditionally been viewed as analogical extensions from the *a*-stem pattern rather than the result of a regular phonological development. However, there seems to be little consensus as to their origin in the individual inflectional classes. They may be partly attributed to intraparadigmatic analogy, as, for instance, the Gothic *r*-stem DAT. PL. ending *-(r)um*, which shows generalisation of *-u-* from the ACC. PL. *-r-unz* (Ringe 2006: 276). Similarly, the PGmc. root noun DAT. PL. ending *-u-miz* can be ascribed to the influence of the consonantal ACC. PL. *-unz* (Bammesberger 1990: 194). A major complication for the interpretation of these forms arises from the fact that even if the attested inflections are regular phonological developments in some minor classes, they most often happen to be homophonous with the inflections of the productive classes, so that an unambiguous assessment of their history becomes impossible. In the present summary, all forms which could potentially be a regular development from Proto-Germanic are interpreted as such (and marked in bold). Owing to this general syncretism of forms across classes (be it phonological or morphological) in both the GEN. and DAT. PL. at this early stage, these categories provide little information about the restructuring process in the later, historical period.

The category of GEN. PL. offers a complex and interesting case for analogical processes. In the standard view, espoused among others by Ringe (2006: 269, 272), the PGmc. ending *-ōn* is interpreted as inherited from Proto-Indo-European in all declensional classes, with a subsequent two-way development in the consonantal and vocalic classes in most daughter languages. While the endings in the consonantal types may be attributed to a regular phonological development of the original ending *-ōn,[106] they are replaced by analogical forms in the vocalic classes, i.e. the *i*-stems and *u*-stems (extended from the *a*-stems and *ō*-stems). An alternative interpretation is offered by Kortlandt (1978) and Boutkan (1995: 138 ff.), who treat the proto-form *-ōn in Northwest Germanic as an early analogical extension from the feminine *ō*-stems (*-ō-an) rather than a regular phonological development of the PIE form (Boutkan 1995: 143). On this interpretation, this form testifies to the double-layered nature of the restructuring process in the GEN. PL. Accordingly, the new analogical form of the GEN. PL. -ōn, emerging on the analogy of the feminine *ō*-stems, subsequently undergoes a second stage of analogical restructuring, whereby it either continues or is replaced by new analogical inflections, depending on the inflectional class. The presentation in Table 2.15 above follows the traditional phonological interpretation of *-ōn as a direct continuation of the PIE form.

Another problematic ending is the Gothic form in -ē in the consonantal stems, which is clearly analogical and is believed to have originated in the *i*-stems (Boutkan 1995: 140). The Gothic *u*-stem marker -iwē would represent a hybrid formation, where the -iw- element is inherited and -ē is analogically extended from the productive inflection (Boutkan 1995: 258). The OS and OHG forms -io and -eo likewise testify to the influence of the *i*-stem inflection on the *u*-stems.

The DAT. PL. is one of the categories where analogical restructuring must be dated early, with the *a*-stem pattern spreading across many paradigms in most Germanic dialects. The origin of the root noun inflections is unclear (Krahe & Meid 1969: 38; Campbell 1977: 252; Ringe 2006: 280). They are treated here as analogical in line with the majority opinion (Bammesberger 1990: 154; Boutkan 1995: 262); however, their interpretation as a regular phonological development cannot be excluded (Streitberg 1963: 249; implicitly Braune/Reiffenstein 2004: 204). The two classes which can potentially provide information about the process at the later stage of its operation are the West Germanic *i*-stems (OHG, OLF, OS) and *s*-stems (OE, OHG), where a contrast between the original inflectional pattern and the analogical forms is attested. The class of *u*-stems, which largely retains the original inflection, is likewise uninformative about the process of restructuring, as the ending coincides with that of the *a*-stems and hence cannot be unambiguously identified as inherited or analogical.

---

106. Campbell (1977), referring to the attestation of these forms in the Old English *i*-stems makes a distinction between light- and heavy-syllable stems, claiming that the GEN. PL. ending -a in heavy-syllable stems represents a Germanic formation, whereas in light-syllable stems it can be traced back to a combined influence of the heavy-stem paradigm and other declensional types (i.e. *a*-stems and consonantal stems) (Campbell 1977: 241).

The inventories of nominal inflection presented here will serve as a starting point for the discussion of the nominal systems in the individual Old Germanic languages, and, more importantly, as a reference point for identifying the traces of analogical realignments in the nominal paradigms.

2.2.5 Discussion

The data discussed above offer direct insight into the the mechanism of the process of analogical restructuring of the Germanic system of nominal inflection at an early stage of development. The earliest documented Germanic languages, Early Runic and Gothic, generally attest substantial inflectional archaism, but they too are not free from the impact of analogical remodelling. The West Germanic branch appears to have been more advanced in reorganising the inherited nominal inflection. It can be expected that the incipient tendencies discernible at the early stage of the restructuring process will continue into the subsequent period, i.e. the historical stage. The overarching tendency, clearly noticeable in the material above, is related to the direction of interdeclensional transfers. The data point to three dominant paths of transfer, with the *a*-stems, *ō*-stems and to some extent *i*-stems serving as the main destination classes for minor stems. A further direction of transfer, detectable especially in Old Norse, is towards the *n*-stems, which offered the pattern of analogical transformation for masculine and especially feminine nouns. This tendency will continue and the attractiveness (i.e. productivity) of this inflectional pattern will gradually increase at the subsequent stages of the development of West Germanic nominal inflection. Finally, the dialectally restricted popularity of the *i*-stem pattern will also play a significant part in the further reorganisation of the declensional system in Germanic. An evident forerunner of the inflectional patterns to be found in the later development of the Germanic languages is the emerging subdivision within West Germanic, whereby the coastal dialects (OE, OFris.) show an evident preference for the *a*-stems and *ō*-stems as the default classes for minor stems, while Continental West Germanic (OHG, OLF, OS) attests the spread of *i*-stem inflections.

A prominent characteristic of inflectional reorganisation at this early stage is the presence of both *intra*- and *inter*paradigmatic pressures, with the inflectional configuration attested in the early Germanic dialects being the result of an interplay of both these forces. While analogical shifts between classes are abundant both in the early as well as the later stages of the restructuring process, the pressure from within the paradigm seems to be more common in the early prehistoric stage, i.e. Proto-Germanic. The particular significance of this intraparadigmatic analogy lies in the fact that, by introducing syncretisms into certain paradigms, it often laid the ground for the reconfiguration of inflection through analogical shifts between declensional classes. The analysed material allows one to identify three layers of analogical developments, corresponding to the chronology of the process:

1. analogical extensions of inflections in Proto-Germanic
2. analogical extensions of inflections in the prehistoric stage of individual sub-branches (e.g. North Germanic, West Germanic), which do not emerge in the attested material in the form of variation between the inherited and innovative inflections (e.g. the spread of *i*-stem inflection to root nouns in OS and OHG)
3. analogical extensions dated to the (immediately pre-)historical stage, reflected in the form of synchronic alternations between inherited and novel inflectional patterns.

Note that these stages are not discrete, but gradual and that developments initiated at one stage tend to continue into the subsequent stage. At each of these stages, the interparadigmatic analogical developments interact with analogical pressures operating within inflectional paradigms. The first two stages belong to the prehistoric period and comprise innovations of a pan-Germanic nature as well as those occurring in individual sub-branches, whereas the last stage covers developments affecting individual Germanic languages, which may happen to be parallel across dialects. However, as we are dealing here with changes taking place at an early period of Germanic, including reconstructed stages, estimating the precise dating of these analogical processes or even their relative chronology is inevitably a challenging task. One safe assumption that can be made with reference to relative chronology is that those changes which are not reflected in synchronic alternations between archaic and innovative forms in the attested Germanic languages must have been completed in the prehistoric stage, i.e. prior to the first written attestations. Notwithstanding all these limitations, the following analogical innovations can be assigned to the respective Stages 1, 2 and 3.

Stage 1

The most prominent intraparadigmatic development belonging to this stage is the analogical extension of the NOM. SG. form in the root nouns. The process is pan-Germanic and given the available evidence, the attested form cannot be a regular phonological development, but an analogical formation involving a restoration of the root-final consonant, based on the shape of the other cases in the paradigm (hence **fōz/fōs* was replaced by **fōts*; Bammesberger 1990: 191; Ringe 2006: 280). The effect of intrapardigmatic pressure is also identifiable in the analogical extension of the NOM. PL. form to the ACC. PL. in consonantal classes, which is attested throughout Northwest Germanic and on a limited scale in Gothic (cf. Table 2.14).

An example of an early interparadigmatic transfer is the spread of the GEN. SG. marker -es (-is) from the a-stems to the i-stems.[107] Finally, another potential instance of an interparadigmatic change is the development of the GEN. PL. form in all minor stems in Northwest Germanic, which may be traced back to the feminine ō-stems (*-ō-an) on the assumption that the genitive form *-ōn is not original (see above Section 2.2.4).

Stage 2

The second stage of development, involving the changes in individual sub-branches of Germanic, abounds in both intra- and interparadigmatic developments. Probably the most important innovation which can be assigned to this stage is the syncretism of the NOM. and ACC. SG. in West Germanic. This development was phonological rather than an effect of analogical pressure and had far-reaching consequences for the operation of analogical levelling in the system of nominal inflection, such as inducing a parallel syncretism of the NOM./ACC. PL. The effects of *intra*paradigmatic analogy may be identified in the following developments:

–   the analogical redistribution of ablaut variants *-iz-/-az- (< PIE *-es-/-os-) in the s-stems in West Germanic, whereby the o-grade originally proper to the NOM./ACC. SG. (*-os) is replaced by the e-grade of the oblique cases
–   the syncretism of the NOM. and ACC. SG. in the light-syllable root nouns in Old English and Old Frisian, which results from analogical replacement of the original endingless NOM. SG. by the ACC. SG. in -u
–   the emergence of a syncretic NOM./ACC. PL. in West Germanic in all minor declensions (Table 2.13 and 2.14)
–   the levelling of i-mutation in the DAT. SG. in Old Frisian root nouns and r-stems (this process is not unique to Old Frisian, but on account of the late date of attestation of the Frisian material, the available sources do not testify to any traces of i-mutation; in the other Germanic languages this development takes place in historical times).[108]

---

107. The evidence of Early Runic is rather ambiguous, but it seems that an analogical form was present here as well. In fact, the feminine form may also be analogical, which would imply that the GEN. SG. was affected by very early levelling.

108. Note that the levelling of the i-mutated vowels could be an effect of intraparadigmatic pressure, but may also be ascribed to the influence of other declensions in which the i-mutated vowels are not present. The identification of the source of analogical levelling can be problematic and may vary depending on the declensional class. E.g. the lack of i-mutation in ON feminine i-stems (dāð 'deed' with unmutated vowel in place of the expected *dǣðr < *dāðiR, see Ramat 1981: 65) has been ascribed to the impact of the ō-stems rather than to the internal pressure of other cases in the paradigm.

The major *inter*declensional realignments belonging to Stage 2 include:

- the large-scale diffusion of the GEN. SG. ending -*es* to masculine *i*-stems, *s*-stems and *nd*-stems in West Germanic
- the analogical extension of the DAT. PL. marker -*um* in North and North Sea Germanic
- the extension of the *i*-stem (NOM./ACC. PL.) inflections to root nouns and *u*-stems in Old Saxon, Old High German and Old Low Franconian
- the spread of the *ō*-stem plural inflection to the feminine light-syllable *i*-stems in Old English
- the spread of the *a*-stem DAT. SG. ending to *nd*-stems in Old Frisian, Old Saxon and Old Low Franconian
- the extension of the ACC. SG. form to the NOM. SG. in root nouns in Gothic, under the influence of the *u*-stems
- the spread of the *a*-stem DAT. SG. to *s*-stems in Old Frisian and Old Saxon.

Stage 3
No intraparadigmatic analogical pressures can be assigned to Stage 3, which represents the beginning of the historical stage of the restructuring process. This is not to mean that such internal pressures were entirely absent, but rather that their effects are not observable at this stage. The activity of internal pressures will become more conspicuous again in the dialectal stage, i.e. in the individual Germanic languages. There, the shifts between declensions lead to a temporary enhancement of case distinctions (e.g. the introduction of the GEN. SG. marker -*es* to consonantal stems), which will eventually be largely abandoned with the gradual disintegration of the case system in many Germanic varieties. The interparadigmatic developments discernible in Stage 3 include the extension of the GEN. SG. ending to masculine root nouns and *r*-stems in West Germanic, which is a continuation of the earlier tendency affecting the other minor stems. Another analogical development is the spread of the *i*-stem inflection to the *u*-stems and root nouns in Old High German. In both categories, the attested pattern involves a fluctuation between the inherited and innovative inflections. In general, the analogical innovations attested in this period find a direct continuation in the subsequent stages, i.e. in the individual Germanic dialects, where their scope becomes even greater and more diversified.

As is clear from the above summary, although the earliest signs of restructuring may be traced back to the Proto-Germanic or Common Germanic stage, the large-scale restructuring of the inflectional system must be dated later, possibly to the period corresponding to the attestation of Early Runic, i.e. between the second and sixth centuries AD. Two of the earliest analogical shifts turn out to have clearly defined dialectal distributions: the extension of the GEN. PL. ending *-ōn (of whatever origin) is nearly complete in Northwest Germanic; the spread of *-um to the

DAT. PL. is likewise an areal feature, covering North and North Sea Germanic and Old Low Franconian, but leaving parts of Old Saxon and Old High German unaffected. Given the few developments which may be identified as common Germanic (stage 1), the bulk of the process must therefore postdate the stage of a uniform reconstructible Proto-Germanic.

When it comes to estimating the scope of *inter*declensional transfers, which are the focus of the present study, the analogical developments identified in the overview (Tables 2.9–2.14) indicate that the categories which were most extensively affected by the restructuring were the GEN. SG. and the GEN. and DAT. PL., whereas the categories which remained most resistant to the impact of analogical inflections were the NOM. and ACC. SG. More specifically, the following hierarchy of categories may be set up with respect to the number of analogical transfers attested, from most to least: GEN. SG. > GEN. PL. > DAT. PL. > NOM. PL. > DAT. SG. > ACC. PL. > ACC. SG. > NOM. SG.[109] Such a distribution of analogical inflections across cases shows a substantial correlation with the frequency distribution of individual cases in the paradigm, as deduced from the quantitative analysis of the early Germanic corpora. At one end of the scale are the GEN. SG. and PL., which are generally the least frequent categories and accordingly display a high number of interdeclensional shifts, while the other extreme of the scale is occupied by the NOM. SG. and ACC. SG., which are relatively frequent and thus resistant to external analogy. With respect to reshufflings caused by internal analogy, the category most sensitive to analogical pressure is the ACC. PL., which was analogically replaced by the NOM. PL. in the consonantal stems in most Germanic dialects. This analogical replacement may have been triggered or at least facilitated by the presence of phonologically motivated syncretism in the NOM. and ACC. SG.

Although a quantitative approach to the restructuring process was not the aim of the present chapter, the data presented in Tables 2.9–2.16 can tentatively be quantified to measure the amount of analogy (reflected in the number of analogical shifts) present in the paradigms of minor nominal declensions at the earlies stages of development. Accordingly, taking into account the process of *inter*paradigmatic restructuring, analogical inflections constitute around 35 percent of all the inflections in the minor paradigms.

With respect to gender, the presence of analogical tendencies is attested in the paradigms of nouns of all genders. At the same time, the material clearly indicates that the masculine paradigm tended to be more susceptible to the activity of analogical processes and the impact of the productive inflections than feminine paradigms. This tendency can be well captured in the GEN. SG. (especially in the

---

109. The number of interdeclensional shifts per case was the following: GEN. SG. 23, GEN. PL. 18, DAT. PL. 13, NOM. PL. 13, DAT. SG. 11, ACC. PL. 7, ACC. SG. 2, NOM. SG. 0.

i-stems and root nouns), where the masculine nouns are dominated by the marker *-es* originally proper to the *a*-stems, while the feminines largely continue the inherited inflections. Of some significance here is the morphological salience of the masculine GEN. SG. marker, which, coupled with its frequency profile, constituted an important factor in the restructuring process, as will become evident the later part of this study. Likewise, as the details of the distribution of analogical features across gender classes can be captured only through a systematic analysis of the data, more specific and exhaustive conclusions are reserved for Chapter 8, where the factors involved in the mechanism of the restructuring process will be discussed in detail.

2.3   Conclusion

The phenomena discussed in this chapter clearly indicate that Proto-Germanic nominal inflection was not a stable, unchanging entity, but rather an unsteady and dynamic system in a state of continuous transformation, entailing an array of phonological and morphological developments. These dynamics of the system, manifested most explicitly in the analogical realignments reviewed above, were guided by a number of principles, some of which appear to be of a more universal, pan-Germanic nature, while others are typically language-specific. A close inspection of the shape of the nominal inflection as attested in the earliest stage of the individual Germanic languages offers an insight into the complexity of the process of analogical restructuring already in the prehistoric period. This complexity involves two aspects of the process: one is the presence and interaction of internal and external analogical forces in the paradigm, both originating at the prehistoric stage of Germanic; the other is related to the interface of phonology and morphology, reflected in an interaction between the effects of phonological processes on the one hand and analogical levelling on the other. The cumulative effect of the activity and interplay of these processes is an obscuration of the origin of various inflectional forms. The ensuing diachronic ambiguity of individual inflections constitutes a major complication (and limitation) in interpreting and adequately modelling the reorganisation of the nominal system in early Germanic.

In summary, the shape of the nominal system in Proto-Germanic as well as in its daughter languages was largely determined by developments in the phonological system in that the emerging morphological adjustments were usually a reaction to phonological changes. This phonological conditioning turns out to have been crucial for the dynamics of the morphological restructuring in the individual Germanic languages. One of the major developments instigated in prehistoric times by early phonological reductions was the emergence of the formal identity of case forms across various declensional types, which turned out to be a critical factor inducing interdeclensional shifts. For instance, the formal coalescence of the NOM./ACC. SG. forms in the *i*-stems and *a*-stems created a basis for the transfer of nouns between these classes. The consequent ambiguity of such inflectional forms led to a more general confusion of inflectional exponents originally associated with a specific declensional type, as well as to a growing opacity of the declensional system. The lack of synchronic transparency – characteristic of nominal inflection in all the Old Germanic languages, even Gothic – is clearly a corollary of all these developments.

The restructuring of nominal inflection in Germanic was further conditioned by two variables, namely gender class affiliation and stem weight (relevant only in some classes, e.g. *i*-stems, *u*-stems and root nouns). Depending on these variables, the restructuring followed different paths at different times in the early Germanic languages. Given the significance of these two factors in the early period, they may be expected to be relevant in the later stage of the restructuring process, and, accordingly, they will be closely scrutinised in the analysis of the reorganisation of inflection in individual dialects.

The general diachronic trend which underlies the reorganisation of nominal inflection at the Older Germanic stage seems to be towards restoring or enhancing the functionality of the system. The original functionality of case-and-number endings was to a great extent disrupted by the operation of *Auslautgesetze*, which brought about firstly the fusion of the stem element with inflectional ending, and secondly the reduction and apocope of many inflections. The former development resulted in an increase in the number of declensional classes, which may be interpreted as a complexification of the system. The subsequent operation of apocope introduced considerable uniformity of inflectional exponents across paradigms, reducing many of the endings to zero, and jeopardizing the functionality of the inflectional system. The ensuing decline of declensional diversity, which may be viewed as a simplification of the inflectional system, was a response to these phonological developments, and the analogical reshuffling of nouns and case-and-number endings among declensional classes was a way to restore the original functionality of the system of nominal inflection, at least in part. These processes continue to play a role in the further development of the individual Germanic languages, which testify to drastically different levels of simplification, some reducing the number of inflectional paradigms fairly radically (e.g. English), others attesting to retention or even growth in declensional diversity (Icelandic, German).

The question essential to further investigation of the restructuring process is to what extent the tendencies and patterns identifiable at the earliest stage of Germanic (Proto-Germanic and Common Germanic) are continued and reflected in the subsequent development of the declensional systems in the individual Germanic languages. One of the basic assumptions underlying the present study is in line with

Kortlandt's observation that: "[a]t every stage of development we have to reckon with both phonetically regular and analogical forms. Analogy operates quite often along the same lines in different periods." (Kortlandt 1978: 281). Accordingly, as much as the phonological systems of individual Germanic languages have developed independently, it is to be expected that the analogical processes involved in the restructuring of the nominal inflection will be largely parallel and possibly similar to those found at the earliest stage in Proto- or Common Germanic. At the same time, as phonological processes play an important role in morphological restructuring, it can be expected that their independent operation in the individual Germanic dialects, with different conditioning factors, pace and scope, will lead to often strikingly discrepant results.

CHAPTER 3

Nominal inflection in Old English

3.1 Introduction

The Old English material constitutes the largest corpus investigated in the present study, covering the period between the seventh and twelfth centuries. Old English is at the same time one of the best-explored early Germanic languages, being the focus of an impressive number of studies also in the area of inflectional morphology, and therefore it needs little general introduction. The wide diversity of the corpus in terms of genre-composition is unparalleled by the other West Germanic languages, ranging from glossaries, poetic texts (often of a religious nature) to prose works, including chronicles, sermons, biblical translations or legal documents. The uniqueness of Old English among the West Germanic languages lies also in its isolated geographical position, which had considerable implications for the developments in its linguistic system. Many of the morphological or inflectional features characteristic of the Continental sister languages are not found in Old English and, as will also become evident from the present investigation, the dynamics of the phonological and morphological changes affecting the declensional system are partly divergent for these dialects. Geographically more distant, Old English displays a range of idiosyncratic traits pertinent to the nominal system, which allows one to expect that the transformation of the inflectional architecture took a unique pathway, ultimately with typological consequences.

It is essentially the phonological profile of the language that has a major bearing on the shape of the nominal inflection, constituting the trigger for the emergence of analogical reshufflings. In Old English, two phonological tendencies had a profound influence on the dynamics of the reorganisation of nominal paradigms, namely, the more or less consistent presence of i-mutation in certain minor classes (root nouns, nd-stems) and the progressive attrition of vowels in unaccented syllables, with its wider scope in the Late Old English period. The resultant changes in the inflectional system instigated a range of "transition phenomena which led to an internal differentiation of the system", with far-reaching consequences for the typological shape of the language (Bertacca 2009: 170; Ramat 1981: 60–63). A more direct consequence of these developments was the emergence of syncretisms across inflectional paradigms, which opened the way for interparadigmatic analogical interactions. A manifestation of these developments on the morphological level was a large-scale reconfiguration of nominal paradigms, with polarisation of the nouns to a few major inflectional classes. In Old English this polarisation entailed a gradual gravitation of nouns affiliated with unproductive classes (i.e. *i-*, *u-*, *r-*, *s-*, *ð-*, *nd*-stems and root nouns) towards the expansive masculine/neuter *a*-stems, and feminine *ō*-stems. The ensuing substantial reduction of the elaborate system of declensional classes, inherited from the Proto-Germanic ancestor, was an immediate corollary of these developments.

Given the scope and wide temporal time span of the Old English material, with the diverse dates of attestation and geographical provenance of the texts, it can be expected that the range and the dynamics of the reconfiguration of nominal inflection varied depending on the period and the dialect. The relative abundance of the available material allows us to incorporate both a diatopic and diachronic dimension into the study of the Old English nominal inflection. Such an approach, integrating a spatial and temporal perspective, guarantees a more transparent, detailed, and thus adequate picture of morphological realignments in the minor nominal paradigms, notwithstanding all the limitations that it at the same time inevitably entails (such as the under- or overrepresentation of texts affiliated with individual periods or dialects, or the imprecise dating of some texts).

As the Old English material is the most extensive in the present study, it can be expected to provide the most exhaustive information about the restructuring of nominal inflection, including its diversification with respect to period or dialect. The relatively high number of attested paradigms and forms (both in terms of token and type frequency) will facilitate identifying the tendencies and patterns, which will constitute a sound basis for drawing valid conclusions about the restructuring process. At the same time, the present study is not free from the obstacles and problems which any investigation of (in one way or another) limited data from historical corpora is bound to face.

3.2   Diatopic and diachronic dimension of the study

3.2.1   Early and Late Old English

For the purpose of the diachronic investigation, the Old English material was divided into two periods: Early and Late. The division into three groups of texts with respect to period – *Early*, *Indeterminate* and *Late* – found in the *Dictionary of Old English* Electronic Corpus (Healey et al. 2009), served as the basis for the classification into two periods, which included the *Early* stage covering the texts dated to the eighth to ninth centuries, and the *Late* one referring to the material from the tenth to early twelfth centuries. The inclusion of the diachronic dimension to this study was intended to enable capturing the restructuring process in the making. In light of the broad temporal span that the Old English material covers, such an approach was considered requisite. It is hoped to afford more insight into the dynamics of the process, revealing to what extent the restructuring of inflection was a gradual (or abrupt) development. The transparent division between *Early* and *Late* stages was essential also from the point of view of interpreting the inflectional forms, whose shape was intricately linked to the profile of the vocalic system in unstressed syllables, which was undergoing a continuous change. More specifically, while the system of vowels in unstressed syllables remained relatively stable in the *Early* Old English period, the later period witnessed a wide range of vowel reduction processes, which modified the shape of the inflectional endings. This fact is consequential when analysing the restructuring of inflection in vocalic stems, in particular in the *u*-stems, where many inflectional forms terminate in back vowels, which were the primary target of the reductions and were thus the most susceptible to confusion.

It must be emphasised that on account of the nature of the available material, the diachronic variation largely overlaps with the diatopic one. In order to keep the actual dialectal tendencies apart from those ascribable only to diachrony, a cross tabulation analysis was conducted, whereby the restructuring process in the Early and Late stages was investigated separately for the dialect groups. At the same time, such an approach admitted tracing the tendencies pertinent to a given dialect irrespective of the period.

Finally, the *DOEEC* comprises a substantial number of texts whose dating is not specified. They are classified in the corpus as *Indeterminate* and this category is used also in this study. The relevant forms found in these texts in the course of the investigation were consistently included in the quantitative analysis and the overall figures, but they were excluded from the figures referring specifically to the period. A parallel procedure was applied for the dialectal part of the study, i.e. the figures in the tables referring to the dialects do not include the forms attested in texts classified as *Unknown* (3.2.2).

3.2.2 Anglian and Saxon material

Given the extensive diatopic variation attested in the Old English material, it can be expected that the restructuring of the nominal inflection followed somewhat different pathways, or, at least, had different dynamics in the individual Old English dialects. Accordingly, in order to capture this diatopic variation, the investigation was conducted separately on the two larger groups of dialects, following a division applied in the *DOEEC* (Healey et al. 2009) into Anglian and Saxon. The former group comprised Northumbrian and Mercian texts, the latter included the scant

Kentish attestations and the abundant West Saxon material. Occasionally, where relevant, differences between Northumbrian and Mercian, or Kentish and West Saxon, will be made explicit. Any dialectal approach to the Old English material is bound to face a number of methodological problems related to such aspects as dialect mixture, scribal practices, or intrinsic limitations of the corpus. An investigation conducted on the complete corpus of the Old English texts, much as it can be exhaustive, is not free from such limitations pertinent to a historical corpus. An important facet of the diatopic approach is related to the composition of the corpus and, in particular the disproportions in the available material affiliated with individual dialects. In the case at hand, the extensive material of West-Saxon provenance is juxtaposed against the modest corpus of non-West-Saxon texts. This overrepresentation of the West Saxon data in the corpus must be taken into account when interpreting the findings. A further important aspect of the diatopic approach is related to the scope of the investigated material. In view of the profile of the present study which aims to be (as far as possible) exhaustive, the analysis encompasses all dialectally identifiable texts (as identified in the *DOEEC*) rather than a representative sample of texts from individual dialects, adjusted size-wise.

Another question that arises in the context of the dialectal investigation involves the precise identification of the dialect features in texts which are internally inconsistent, or of uncertain or much disputed origin. This dialect mixture problem concerns primarily, though not exclusively, Kentish and Mercian dialects, which among the established varieties of Old English, are the most difficult to define. Some of the texts ascribed to these dialects are linguistically inconsistent, showing a considerable amount of dialectal mixture, while others, though consistent linguistically, are poorly localised. Kentish texts, for instance, display a substantial admixture of West-Saxon as well as Mercian forms. The heterogeneous linguistic character of Kentish, probably best manifested in charters, has been viewed as directly correlated to Mercian political supremacy in the eighth and early ninth century. The Kentish charters of the Mercian period tend to display some unambiguously Mercian characteristics (e.g. the fluctuation of <a> vs. <o> before nasals) (Toon 1992: 450; 1987: 286; cf. Kitson 1995: 106; Colman 2004: 191–195; for the details on problems with identifying the Kentish material, see Lowe 2001). A similar interpretative problem is posed by the presence of West-Saxonisms in the Mercian texts, *Vespasian Psalter* and *Rushworth Gospels* (Ru[1]), such as the appearance of Saxon *wæron* vs. Anglian *weron*, or the inconsistent use of <æ> vs. <e> for reflexes of the WGmc. **a* and **e*, the interpretation of which can be problematic (Kitson 2004: 227; Toon 1987: 290–291). A closely related limitation regarding the nature of the available dialectal data is that of scribal interference and scriptorial convention, and more specifically the fact that the standard written languages "were sometimes used by clerks far beyond the bounds of the spoken dialects", with, for instance, Mercian written at Canterbury, or Late West-Saxon used at York (Crowley 1986: 99). The present study consistently follows the dialect labels of the texts and dialect information included in the *DOEEC*, with the subdivision into *Saxon*, *Anglian* and *Unknown*, as it is found there. The findings from the dialectal investigation presented in the respective sections discussing dialectal differences are based on the data from the two groups of texts, labelled as *Saxon* and *Anglian*. The attestations classified as *Unknown* are included in the overall figures presenting the identified tendencies in the corpus (without the dialectal information).

Given the wide scope of the present investigation, it can be expected that the study will not be devoid of some of the methodological problems that a diatopic account is inevitably fraught with. Some of the limitations of the traditional approach to dialectal variation, such as treating Old English dialects as "independent and discrete linguistic varieties" (Hogg 1988: 187), cannot be avoided in a study of this nature, and this fact needs to be allowed for when interpreting the findings. At the same time, the rationale behind the present enterprise is to explore the general tendencies pertaining to the restructuring of the Old English inflection, taking into account the dialects as they are defined in the traditional accounts. Accordingly, seeking strict demarcation lines between regions where the process of reorganisation had a different scope, or exploring the subtleties of the process in texts whose dialectal status is not clearly defined, remains beyond the purview of the present analysis. The same holds true for the diachronic aspect of the investigation, where the period labels assigned in the *Dictionary of Old English* are consistently adhered to in the present study.

3.3   Characteristics of the restructuring process in Old English

The Germanic nominal system underwent reorganisation at an early stage, dating back before the time of the first written attestations, with various subsequent pathways in the individual Germanic languages. The available Old English material indicates that many of the interdeclensional analogical realignments must have occurred at the prehistoric stage. Accordingly, in formal terms, two stages of reorganisation can be distinguished, including (1) the early, pre-Old English transfers of nouns to productive declensions and (2) the later, historical transfers, attested in the Old English period. Such a division has a purely practical rationale, and it is not to be interpreted in absolute terms: restructuring of inflection was a dynamic and continuous development that began at the prehistoric stage and continued into the historical period. The prehistoric dating of the process finds support in the Old English forms of the GEN. PL. and DAT. PL., which in many minor paradigms cannot be a continuation of the original forms, but must be interpreted as the effects of analogical remodelling on the pattern furnished by the expanding *a*-stems (Campbell 1977: 252, 258; Krahe & Meid 1969: 35ff; Boutkan 1995: 262, 268, 275). Another category where the early impact of the productive inflection is identifiable is the masculine GEN. SG., which, displaying very limited fluctuation between the inherited and innovative forms, surfaced predominantly with the expansive marker -*es*. The second stage of the restructuring process, which can be captured with all its complexity, belongs to the attested Old English period. The dominant pattern emerging from the textual material involves parallel interdeclensional shifts of masculine, feminine and neuter nouns to the productive (masculine and neuter) *a*-stems, (feminine) *ō*-stems, and, to a limited extent, to the increasingly expansive *n*-stems. The analogical remodelling of the paradigms operated on two distinct planes: within, and across paradigms, and the reconfiguration of the system is a result of an interplay of analogical changes on these two levels. The analogical pressures present within the paradigms reduced much of the allomorphy characteristic of some paradigms, resulting in their greater uniformity (especially in the singular), and thus triggered the changes on the *inter*paradigmatic level.

The developments in the Old English nominal inflection have traditionally been viewed as indicative of inflectional simplification. One of the early accounts of the changes was offered by Roedler (1916: 491), who observes:

> Seitdem die geschichte der englischen sprache an der hand einer mehr oder weniger reichen überlieferung verfolgt werden kann, stellt sich die entwicklung ihrer flexion als ein fortwährender vereinfachungsprozess dar nach dem grundsatz: the survival of the fittest. Schon im Ae., in einigen fällen sogar schon in vorliterarischer zeit, führte in der deklination der vokalischen stämme der verlust des sprachgefühls für die alten deklinationssklassen zur vereinfachung der flexion innerhalb der geschlechte, wobei z. b. die feminina der *i*- und *u*-stämme sich an die *ō*-stämme anschlossen etc.

The two adduced minor declensional classes, i.e. feminine *i*- and *u*-stems, were only two of a range of unproductive paradigms affected by analogical processes in Old English, which apart from vocalic stems of all genders (*i*- and *u*-stems) comprised also unproductive consonantal classes, i.e. root nouns, *s*-stems, *r*-stems, *nd*-stems and dental stems. All of them to a greater or lesser extent tended to succumb to the analogical pressure of "the fittest" inflectional types, which turned out to be the masculine *a*-stems and feminine *ō*-stems. The status of "fit" could be extended to the *n*-stems, which gradually emerged as an expanding type in the later stage of Old English, attracting nouns originally affiliated with minor declensions.

A significant characteristic of this "simplification" process, explicitly invoked in the above-quotation, is the consistent preservation of gender alongside the change of paradigmatic/declension class affiliation. On a closer examination, as will become apparent in the analysis, this gender consistency seems to be to some extent distorted, and consequently the influence of the masculine *a*-stem inflection in the paradigm of feminine nouns can frequently be observed (especially in the *u*-stems and root nouns). This refers in particular to the two most stable inflectional exponents, i.e. the GEN. SG. -*es* and the NOM./ACC. PL. -*as*, whose dissemination did not necessarily entail a change in gender affiliation, but testifies rather to the pervasiveness of these two remarkably stable inflectional markers (cf. Section 3.6).[110]

Many of these minor classes constituted more robust declensional types at an earlier stage. This is confirmed by some relics of patterns still retained in Old English (e.g. the occasional extension of root noun inflection to Celtic names, which may be indicative of its earlier productivity; see Hogg & Fulk 2011: 71), or by the material from other Germanic languages (e.g. the *u*-stems in Gothic). When seen from a more distant historical perspective, these minor classes, deriving from PIE athematic classes, which were essentially more complex in structure than the thematic paradigms, constituted the "more ancient layer of IE nominal and verbal derivation" (Fortson 2010: 84; cf. Szemerényi 1999: 164ff.). At some point, their earlier robustness shrank to the clear advantage of the less complex thematic paradigms, and their presence in the lexicon was by the time of the first attestations of Germanic confined to – from a Proto-Indo-European perspective – residual features.

3.4   Old English phonological developments in unstressed syllables

The phonological processes which occurred in the Old English period had a major impact on the shape of minor stem paradigms, obliterating their former consistency and leading to a substantial increase in syncretic forms across paradigms. This refers in particular to reduction-related developments affecting vowels in final unstressed syllables, which were consequential for the interpretation of inflectional forms in the context of the restructuring process. Many of the relevant inflectional endings found in the examined paradigms were vocalic, and were thus substantially disturbed by the reduction processes. This fact causes considerable interpretative problems, especially for the analysis of the Late Old English material where the reduction was fairly advanced.

---

110. The relative insignificance of the distinction between masculine and neuter in this context was invoked by Lass (1997b: 103) who points to the "text-indistinguishability" and the resultant "marginality" of the masculine/neuter opposition in this declensional class, viewing the *a*-stems as "gender-prototypical" (the only difference between the masculine and neuter paradigms being the endings in two categories, i.e. the NOM. PL. and ACC. PL.).

The inventory of Old English unstressed vowels appearing in inflectional suffixes included four vowels: *i, æ, a, u* (Hogg 1992b: 119–122). The front vowels gradually merged (/i/ > /e/ and /æ/ > /e/) and were represented in spelling by <e>, which resulted in a three-vowel system in the Classical Old English period, with one front and two back vowels (*e – a – u*) (Hogg 1992a: 241). This merger of front vowels influenced the shape of the inflectional paradigms, inducing an overlap of many of the inflectional markers of the *a*-stems, *ō*-stems and *i*-stems. Consequently, for instance, the DAT. SG. of masculine stems in these classes ended in *-e* both in the *a*-stems and *i*-stems, deriving from *-æ* in the former, and from *-i* in the latter (cf. footnote 118 and Section 2.2.3.1). Such an overlap of inflectional exponents diminished the transparency and distinctiveness of the paradigms, serving as a direct incentive for a confusion of inflectional features across declensional classes.

In the later period, the reduction processes continued, resulting in further mergers of unstressed vowels, in particular that of /o/ (< Classical OE /u/) and /a/, which rendered the two vowels interchangeable in spelling (Hogg 1992a: 239–241). The reduction of the unaccented back vowels /a/, /o/ and /u/ resulted in a confusion of the final <a>, <o> and <u> (in spelling) in inflectional syllables. The gradual elimination of the contrast in back vowels is well attested already in Kentish charters (9th c.) (where <a> is used for *-o, -u*). By the Late West-Saxon stage (11th c.), the process was advanced to such an extent that final <a>, <o> and <u> were used indiscriminately (Campbell 1977: 156–157; cf. Hogg 1997a: 101).[111] The result was a two-vowel system, with one front vowel /e/ contrasting with a back vowel. The process was followed by a large-scale coalescence of the unaccented *e* (< *æ, e, i*) and the unaccented back vowels, as a direct consequence of their phonological reduction to /ə/, dated to the eleventh century. It can be assumed that in the Late Old English period the vowels in the inflectional syllables largely represented the reduced vowel /ə/.[112]

All these phonological developments had serious morphological consequences, rendering the interpretation of the attested inflectional endings problematic, sometimes impossible. In many instances it is difficult to distinguish between forms which emerged as a result of purely phonological processes and those which appeared due to actual analogical pressure from other declensional types. The endings

---

111. An exception here is the inflectional <u>, appearing regularly as <o> in the later sources, which seems to have been more stable when preceded by an accented /u/ in the root syllable, reflecting a vowel harmony development (as in *sunu, wudu*; Campbell 1977: 136).

112. Not all the variation resulting from these developments is problematic from the point of view of the restructuring process. The development of the DAT. PL. *-um* > *-un* > *-on* > *-an* (later > *-en*), reflecting the weakening of /um/ > /ən/, does not affect the interpretation of the process. For details of this change, see Moore (1928) (cf. Griepentrog 1995: 158).

of the feminine *u*-stem paradigm may serve as an example: the innovative DAT. or ACC. SG. ending -*e* can be ascribed to the analogical pressure of the *ō*-stems, but it can well represent a reduced vowel /ə/, appearing due to the progressing attrition of the inflectional vowels that occurred towards the end of the Old English period. Given that these phonological developments progressed at a different pace in individual dialects of Old English, a workable solution for such problematic cases seems to be a precise identification of the literary source (text) in which the forms are attested, allowing for its exact dating and dialectal provenance (in those instances where identification is possible). Such a procedure has been applied in the present investigation for the sake of avoiding ambiguities and minimising the risk of drawing erroneous conclusions. Accordingly, in some paradigms the forms attested in the Late period had to be excluded from the investigation (cf. Section 3.5.3).

Another aspect relevant in the context of the restructuring process is related to the function of syllable weight in the reorganisation of inflection. The differences in the inflectional patterns of light- and heavy-syllable stems are a direct result of pre-Old English phonological developments, in particular the loss of /i/ and /u/ in final unstressed syllables when preceded by a heavy-syllable (Luick 1964: 282; Hogg 1992a: 222). Its consequence was the contrast evident in the NOM. and ACC. SG. of *i*-stems, *u*-stems, as well as root nouns, where light-syllable stems show a vocalic ending whereas heavy-syllable nouns are not marked by any inflection in these categories. As the present study will demonstrate, in most minor classes, the heavy-syllable stems tended to be more susceptible to analogical pressures than the light-syllable ones. This can largely be ascribed to the formal overlap of inflections in the NOM./ACC. SG. in the former, which subsequently triggered changes in the other categories in the paradigm.

3.5   Data analysis

3.5.1   Corpus and methodological considerations

The present investigation was conducted on the complete collection of Old English texts found in the *Dictionary of Old English* Electronic Corpus (Healey et al. 2009). The focus of the study was on the quantitative relation between the incidence of inherited and analogical (predominantly *a*-stem, *ō*-stem) inflections in the minor stem paradigms. The innovative forms brought about by the influence of the productive consonantal declension (*n*-stems), which also made their way into the minor paradigms, were included in the quantitative analysis as well, except for the forms of the GEN. PL. (see below). In order to capture fine details of the gradual reorganisation of inflection in these declensional classes, the masculine, feminine and neuter paradigms were examined independently, with a further subdivision into light- and heavy-syllable stems, where relevant. A few morphosyntactic categories were excluded from the quantitative study (i.e. from calculations) due to their ambiguous status with respect to the restructuring. This refers to the forms of the GEN. PL. (in -*a*) and DAT. PL. (in -*um*), which in most minor classes (except the *s*-stems) happened to be identical with the respective forms of the *a*-stems and *ō*-stems. The GEN. PL. forms in -*ena*, extended from the *n*-stem inflection, were not included in the overall figures showing the percentage distribution of archaic vs. innovative inflections as there is no unambiguous inherited form against which they could be compared. The results of the analysis for the categories which cannot provide any information about the restructuring process in the paradigm (very often also the NOM./ACC. SG.), either due to the early transition to productive inflectional classes, or on account of the impossibility to show the influence in an unambiguous way, are presented in italics. The attestations whose interpretation was problematic, ambiguous or hindered in any other way were also excluded from the calculations.

One of the more serious methodological problems emerging when investigating the restructuring of the nominal inflection is related to the formal classification of nouns. A number of forms are traditionally classified as belonging to two different lemmas with the same meaning, e.g. *andwlite* (*i*-stem) vs. *andwlita* (*n*-stem) 'face, countenance', *magu* (*u*-stem) vs. *maga* (*n*-stem) 'son, descendant', or *sige* (*i*-stem) vs. *sigor* (*s*-stem) 'victory', *sele* (*i*-stem) vs. *salor* (*s*-stem) 'hall'. The classification is in most cases based on the external (cross-Germanic) evidence, which renders such an approach justified. However, in some nouns the cross-Germanic evidence does not seem to provide sufficient justification for such a classification, and it seems feasible that such forms belong to one lemma and are thus variants testifying to an early analogical transition to another declensional type (in the aforementioned cases: an original *i*-stem and *u*-stem to *n*-stems, and *s*-stem to *i*-stems). This problem will be addressed and discussed in more detail in Section 3.5.3.2.

The inventory of minor stems which were included in the quantitative analysis was compiled on the basis of information found in standard historical grammars and dictionaries of Old English: Brunner (1965), Campbell (1977), Wright & Wright (1982), Hogg & Fulk (2011), historical dictionaries including the *Anglo-Saxon Dictionary* (Bosworth & Toller 1898) and the *Dictionary of Old English* (Healey et al. 2009). Only words unambiguous etymologically, whose affiliation can be traced back to minor classes in Proto-Germanic, were included in the study and their etymology was verified using information found in Bammesberger (1990), the *Oxford English Dictionary*, and Klein's *Comprehensive Etymological Dictionary of the English language* (1971). As the study is aimed to be nearly exhaustive (as far as possible), the quantitative analysis was based on the complete inventories of lemmas affiliated with a given class in all the minor declensions except the *i*-stems. For the *i*-stem declension, which constitutes the largest of all the minor classes, comprising a number of high frequent lemmas, and which shows a divergent pattern of restructuring depending on the subtype, the analysis was limited to a selection of nouns (cf. Section 3.5.2.2). Occasionally, some further limitations in individual classes had to be introduced; for example, the number of tokens in the *r*-stems, which are characterised by a remarkably high token frequency of occurrence, was limited to ca. 2000 per lemma. Such an approach, entailing some limitation on the scope of the analysed material, was considered sound and legitimate as the selected samples provided sufficient information for identifying the reorganisation patterns in the nominal paradigms. In view of the wealth of data, the tendencies recognised in the course of the investigation can be considered representative and well substantiated.

The paradigms referred to as 'archaic' in the tables depicting the competing inflections reflect mostly the Early West Saxon state of affairs. The paradigms denoted as 'innovative' present *hypothetical* novel forms, emerging under the analogical pressure of the productive inflections. Some of them are actually found in the examined material, but some remain *potential* variants, and are not attested in the corpus. The figures presented in tables depicting the distributions of forms in the respective morphosyntactic categories refer to the entire investigated material, including forms found in the texts labelled as *Unknown* and *Indeterminate* with respect to dialect and period in the *DOEEC*. This means in practice that the figures presented in these tables do not overlap with those showing the distributions with respect to dialect or period, where only the data from texts identifiable dialectally or diachronically were included. At the same time, on account of the evident dominance of the tenth- and eleventh-century West Saxon material in the corpus, most of the figures presented in the study reflect the time frame and the morphological shape of this dialect in large measure.

Given the rich spelling variation in Old English texts, the analysis of inflectional forms took into account a range of spelling variants of the relevant lemmas (forms). These spelling variants were retrieved from the *Dictionary of Old English* as far as it was possible (i.e. for nouns beginning with the letters A-G) and from other dictionaries of Old English (especially Bosworth & Toller 1898), as well as the standard historical grammars. Although many of the nouns subject to investigation were also found in compound formations (when used as the second element of the compound), these forms were not consistently included in the analysis of the material. As the scope of the quantitative investigation is very extensive, the number of attestations of simplex nouns found in the corpus was considered sufficient. This refers in particular to classes which contained lemmas of a very high token frequency, i.e. the *r*-stems and *i*-stems. Compound forms were consistently included in the analysis of the less frequently attested lemmas. The compounds where the original minor stems constituted the first element were irrelevant for the present analysis, as they could not provide any reliable information about the inflectional patterns; at the same time, due to their archaic nature, such forms will be occasionally referred to in the text.[113] Some of the minor stems are found in place and proper names, often constituting the second element of their structure, which could potentially qualify them as relevant for the analysis. However, these instances were not included in the quantitative investigation (unless specified otherwise), since being part of the onomastic material, they are likely to behave differently from the corresponding common nouns. In general, the morphological development of such onomastic forms was guided by independent rules, and they tended to display greater archaism than other formations (e.g. Mills 2011: xix).

Finally, the use of abbreviations in the present chapter follows the practice of Cameron (1973), who provides a complete list of texts cited in the *DOEEC*, with short titles and detailed bibliographic information. An updated, informative and easily accessible list of texts is also available on the homepage of the *Dictionary of Old English* project at: https://www.doe.utoronto.ca/pages/index.html.

3.5.2   *i*-stems

3.5.2.1   *General characteristics*
Of all the declensional types examined in the present study, the *i*-stem class constitutes the largest group, encompassing light- and heavy-syllable nouns of masculine, feminine and neuter gender.[114] The group of masculine nouns is the most extensive of the three, including a number of high frequent lemmas, whereas the neuter subtype is less abundantly represented and also less stable. The robustness of this declensional type, manifested in the high token and type frequency of lemmas affiliated with this class, contributes to a considerable diversification of the pattern of inflection depending on gender class (with three gender classes attested). At

---

113. It can be observed that the forms in such compound formations, independently of the declensional class, tend to be more conservative than simplexes, often preserving the inherited pattern, e.g. *æger-* in *aegergelu* 'yolk' or *calfur* (*cylfer*) in *cylferlamb*; (*i*-stems) *merestream* 'sea stream', *mereflōd* 'deluge', *metebælg* 'wallet'.

114. The class of neuter *i*-stems is believed to be non-original: the nouns which follow the neuter inflection in Old English are new acquisitions in the class, which transferred to it at a later stage, whereas the original neuter nouns did not survive (e.g. **mari* 'sea') (Brunner 1965: 216; Ringe 2006: 272). The origin of these nouns has been sought in the *s*-stem (**-es-/-os-*) declension, which comprised only neuter nouns (Hogg & Fulk 2011: 44). The low number of neuter *i*-stems in Old English has been interpreted as indicative of the fact that they originated in a different declensional type.

the same time, the substantial overlap with the productive inflections renders this inflectional pattern "dramatically ambiguous (…) already at the time of the invasions" (Bertacca 2009: 51).

From a synchronic Old English perspective, the *i*-stem declension was characterised by two major inflectional features, reflecting the original stem vowel *-*i*-, namely (a) the presence of an *i*-mutated vowel in the root – a major feature which renders this group of nouns distinct from the *a*- and *ō*-stems (but cf. *-*ja*- and *-*jō*-stems), and (b) the contrast between the NOM. SG. ending -*e* in light-syllable stems and an endingless form in heavy-syllable formations, as in: *wine* (< *weni-z*) 'friend', *byre* (< *beri-z*) 'son' vs. *ġiest* (< *gasti-z*) 'guest', *wyrm* (< *wurmi-z*) 'worm'.[115]

The lack of stability with respect to gender seems to be another characteristic of this declensional type, traceable to the prehistoric stage. Evident transitions between gender classes involved particularly neuter formations which tended to opt for masculine inflections (e.g. OE *mere* 'lake', *mene* 'mind', *ele* 'oil', *bere* 'barley', *eġe* 'ache', *hete* 'hate'), as well as feminine nouns, attracted by the otherwise scarcely attested neuter type (e.g. *gehygd* 'thought', *gemynd* 'memory') (Brunner 1965: 220, 222; Hogg & Fulk 2011: 44). The low number of light-syllable feminine nouns (e.g. *denu* 'valley, *fremu* 'benefit'), whose affiliation with *i*-stems can be verified solely by the presence of an *i*-mutated vowel in the root, can largely be accounted for by their complete early transfer to the *ō*-stem paradigm, dated to prehistoric times (Brunner 1965: 226; Campbell 1977: 242; Wright & Wright 1982: 188).

An important feature of the *i*-stem declension, which may have had some bearing on the pattern of restructuring of this paradigm, is the heterogeneity with respect to its etymological constitution. The declension comprises a number of nouns which, although classified as *i*-stems from the synchronic Old English perspective, derived from some other declensional types, and their origin can be traced down by external comparison. Accordingly, light-syllable masculine stems, such as *bere* 'barley', *eġe* 'terror', *hete* 'hate', *seġe* 'victory' and *sele* 'hall', originated as *-*es*-/-*os*- stems, as indicated by the cognate forms in Gothic: *agis* (cf. OE *egesa* 'terror', *egsian* 'terrify', both testifying to the *s*-stem origin; see Bammesberger 1990: 134, 211), *barizeins* (adj.)

---

115. No traces of *i*-mutation can be found in nouns such as the masculine tribe name *Seaxe* 'Saxons', feminine *ġesceaft* (*ġescæft*) 'creature', *ġeðeaht* 'idea, thought' (whose *i*-stem affiliation can be established on the basis of the endingless ACC. SG.), or *meaht* 'might, power' (*mieht*). The relative chronology of the operation of *i*-mutation and the analogical transference of the *i*-stems to productive inflectional types has been adduced to account for this pattern. Accordingly, it is held that the substitution of inflectional endings occurred earlier than *i*-mutation in these instances (Brunner 1965: 220; Campbell 1977: 84, 244; Hogg & Fulk 2011: 44–45). In the case of *Seaxe*, chronology played a role in an opposite way. The noun is considered to be an original *n*-stem (without *i*-mutation), which only at some point, due to its semantic characteristics, joined the *i*-stem paradigm (Hogg & Fulk 2011: 44–45).

'made of barley', *hatis* 'hatred', *sigis* 'victory' (cf. Section 3.5.6). The *s*-stem origin can also be identified in a number of feminine/neuter nouns with the prefix *ge-*, which evince an alternation between the *i*-mutated and unmutated root vowel, where the unmutated variant testifies to the historical *s*-stem affiliation (e.g. *ġefōg ~ ġefēġ* 'joint', *ġeheald ~ ġehyld* 'guard', *ġewealc ~ ġewylċ* 'rolling') (Campbell 1977: 244f). The attested etymological heterogeneity of the *i*-stem declension is indicative of the fact that this inflectional pattern must have been productive, i.e. capable of appropriating nouns affiliated with other declensional types, at an earlier stage. This assumption finds solid support in the evidence offered by the other West-Germanic languages, especially Old Saxon, Old High German and Old Low Franconian. Assuming that the internal stability of a nominal paradigm is to some extent dependent on its etymological uniformity (inasmuch as the latter functions potentially as a factor that secures greater stability of the paradigm), the attested lack of etymological homogeneity can be treated as a factor enhancing the analogical reorganisation of this declensional type. The fact that the *i*-stems were able to attract nouns from other declensional classes proves that the productivity of this otherwise unproductive pattern must have lasted for some time before it was eventually lost.

3.5.2.2   *Restructuring of the* i-*stem paradigm*

The group of Old English *i*-stems has been considered one of the declensions which was the most severely affected by analogical processes, as a result of which the original inflectional profile of the class was largely reshaped. The influence of the productive inflectional patterns on the *i*-stems can be dated to prehistoric times, as shown by the Gothic material, which testifies to the presence of the *a*-stem inflections in the paradigm of the singular. The consistently attested analogical *a*-stem inflections in the GEN. SG., GEN. PL. and DAT. PL. support this assumption (Campbell 1977: 241; Boutkan 1995: 244–245, 249; cf. Ringe 2006: 272). The analogical remodelling of the *i*-stem paradigm as attested in the earliest Old English sources involved parallel developments in the three gender classes, whereby the masculine and neuter *i*-stems were reorganised on the pattern of the masculine and neuter *a*-stems, while the feminine *i*-stems followed the feminine *ō*-stem declension. The presence of analogical pressure in the masculine paradigm is well attested in the NOM./ACC.PL. in light-syllable stems, which testify to a synchronic alternation between the inherited *-e* (< *-i*) and the innovative ending *-as* (e.g. *hyse* 'youth' – *hyssas*). The influence of the *ō*-stems can be seen in the ACC. SG. in heavy-syllable feminine stems, where the innovative marker *-e* is frequently found (e.g. *tīde* 'time', *cwēne* 'woman') alongside the expected endingless form (*tīd*, *cwēn*). Apart from these two major directions of interparadigmatic transition, the *i*-stems tended to follow the inflectional pattern of the *n*-stems (weak inflection), whose productivity started to grow in the (Late) Old English period. The *n*-stem inflection seems to have been particularly attractive to heavy-syllable masculine nouns denoting peoples or tribes, which exhibit the weak inflections already in Early West Saxon (i.e. by the tenth century), e.g. *lēodan* 'people', *waran* 'inhabitants', *Wihtwaran* 'inhabitants of the Isle of Wight', surviving in the Southern and West Midland dialects of Middle English. The impact of the *n*-stems is most evident in West-Saxon prose texts, especially in the GEN. PL. marker *-ena* (*-ana*, *-ona*) or the syncopated *-na*, as in: *-seaxna* (cf. footnote 115), *Francna, Longbeardna, Miercna, Sumursǣtna, Gotena, Iudena* (*-ana*) (Brunner 1965: 231) (cf. etymologically weak *gumena, heortena, namena*).

A significant characteristic of the restructuring of the *i*-stem paradigm is the discrepancy in the patterns attested for light- and heavy-syllable stems. While the vestiges of the original inflection of the *i*-stems can still be found in the light-syllable stems, the heavy-syllable stems of all genders attest to a much more innovative profile, with analogical inflections dominating their paradigms almost entirely. This discrepancy is to be ascribed to the divergent phonological development of light- and heavy-syllable stems, whereby the element *$-i(z)$ was lost after a heavy-syllable and retained after a light one (*$-iz > -e$), resulting in a "more thorough assimilation" of the heavy-syllable stems "into the category of *a*-stems" (Hogg & Fulk 2011: 38). In light of the fact that even the earliest Old English texts testify to the presence of analogical markers in the heavy-syllable paradigms (especially in the NOM./ACC. PL.), the beginning of the restructuring process in this subtype can be dated before the literary period. Consequently, when seen from a purely synchronic perspective, the heavy-syllable stems could essentially be classified as *a*- or *ō*-stems, since their inflectional profile almost entirely overlaps with that of the corresponding productive classes. This refers in particular to the masculine stems, where the overlap is complete (except for some vestigial forms still found in the noun *dǣl* 'part'). This divergent pattern of restructuring with regard to stem weight will have consequences for the quantitative investigation, which will (of necessity) be focused only on those paradigms which show some synchronic vacillation between the inherited and analogical inflections.

Exceptional with respect to the preservation of the inherited NOM./ACC. PL. ending *-e* is a group of masculine *i*-stems referring to the names of peoples and tribes (e.g. *Myrce* 'Mercians', *Seaxe* 'Saxons', *Norþymbre* 'Northumbrians'), the collectives denoting people (*lēode* 'people',[116]*ylde, ielde* 'men', Angl. *ældu*), as well as the suffixes denoting dwellers *-sǣte, -ware* (*Cantware, Wihtware*) and the noun *ælf* 'elf' (Dahl 1938: 156–158; Hogg & Fulk 2011: 45). The fact that this pattern

---

116. The noun is most likely an original plural form, with the singular as a secondary form (Lühr 1982: 464). The lack of an *i*-mutated vowel in this form is difficult to account for other than by analogy (Brunner 1965: 79; Hogg 1992b: 134; cf. Hogg & Fulk 2011: 45).

spread also to loanwords (from Latin and Brittonic, e.g. *Egypte* 'Egyptians', *Beornice* 'Bernicians', *Dēre* 'Deirans') may be interpreted as an indication of some restricted productivity of this otherwise unproductive type, confined to nouns denoting people or peoples. An alternative interpretation which also seems viable requires a recourse to the inflectional pattern found in Latin. The Latin tribal names inflected according to the second declension, with the NOM. SG. *-us* and the NOM. PL. *-i*, with the plural form synchronically corresponding thus to the Germanic *i*-stem plural ending. As tribal names are attested commonly in the plural, the final *-i* constituted an interface between these two declensions, allowing the loanwords to enter the *i*-stem declension in Old English. In other words, the presence of the marker *-i* in Latin nouns may have enhanced the retention of the final *-i* (later > *-e*) in nouns denoting tribal names in Old English.

As mentioned earlier, the methodological approach adopted for the quantitative analysis of the developments in this inflectional class differs from that applied to the other classes. This decision had two major motivations. Firstly, the *i*-stems were found to be too numerous to be considered in their entirety in the present analysis (both in terms of type and token frequency). Secondly, and more importantly, as the analogical remodelling of the *i*-stem inflection began and was largely completed at the prehistoric stage, the paradigms which can testify to synchronic variation between inherited and analogical inflections are in fact very few. Additionally, individual subclasses attest to entirely divergent patterns of restructuring, ranging from paradigms showing a complete submission to the productive inflection (e.g. heavy-syllable neuter stems), to those still retaining some vestiges of the original inflectional pattern (e.g. light-syllable masculine stems). Accordingly, the systematic quantitative investigation of this class could not cover all the subtypes and was confined to masculine and neuter light-syllable stems, and feminine heavy-syllable stems, where the alternation between inherited and analogical inflections is to some extent attested in the available material. Neither the heavy-syllable masculine nor neuter stems, although relatively well attested, show any synchronic vacillation in their paradigms, and thus they cannot provide any information about the restructuring process. A single exception is the paradigm of masculine *dæl* 'part', where, as the historical grammars observe, some alternation is attested in the NOM./ACC. PL. The quantitative analysis of the paradigm of *dæl*, nevertheless, had a limited scope and comprised only the forms attested in texts classified as *Early* and *Indeterminate* (cf. the discussion below). As regards the light-syllable feminine stems (e.g. *denu* 'valley', *fremu* 'benefit'), the dissemination of analogical *ō*-stem inflections in these nouns must have been completed by the time of the first attestations of Old English. The motivation behind the early restructuring of this subgroup of *i*-stems may have been functional, resulting from the need to avoid confusion with the light-syllable masculine paradigm; otherwise the two paradigms would have been indistinguish-able (Keyser & O'Neil 1985: 104). In terms of relative and absolute chronology, the merger of the *i*-stem feminine nouns with the *ō*-stems is considered to have been the first declensional class merger which occurred after the operation of *i*-mutation and prior to the first written attestations, i.e. in the seventh century, and was fol-lowed by a fusion of the masculine and neuter *i*-stems with the *a*-stems in the eighth century (Hogg 1992b: 134).

As the above-presented overview of the characteristics of the *i*-stems indicates, the *i*-stems (as a class) do not lend themselves easily to a quantitative analysis on account of the diversity and different chronology of the developments affecting individual (sub)types (subclasses). This fact does not allow one to make valid gen-eralisations about the entire class, and therefore the present section will focus on making more "local" observations about the paradigms in which the reorganisation of inflection can be quantitatively framed. Accordingly, only the (few) paradigms which provide the most reliable information about the restructuring process will be systematically examined and certain aspects of the reorganisation of this declen-sional class will be highlighted.

The synchronic alternation between inherited and analogical endings is attested in different categories depending on the weight of the stem and gender class. Given the overlap of inflections with those of the *a*-stems and *ō*-stems already in the early Old English period, occurring partly as the result of spontaneous phonological developments, the number of categories which can provide information about the restructuring process is limited (despite the abundance of the available material for this class). The alternations which attest to a competition between inherited and analogical inflections can be found in the following categories:

a. masculine and neuter *i*-stems
   - the endingless form of the NOM./ACC. SG. in place of the inherited marker *-e* (< *-i*) (light-syllable stems)
   - the NOM./ACC. PL. marker *-as* in place of the original ending *-e* (light- and heavy-syllable stems (*dǣl*))
b. feminine *i*-stems (heavy-syllable)
   - the ACC. SG. marker *-e* in place of the expected endingless form
   - the NOM./ACC. PL. marker *-a* in place of the inherited *-e* (< *-i*) (cf. the discussion below)

In both paradigms, traces of the *n*-stem inflection, especially in the NOM./ACC. PL. and the GEN. PL., are increasingly common. The feminine paradigm can also show traces of the influence of the *a*-stem inflection in the singular, where the marker *-es* appears in the GEN. SG. in place of the expected ending *-e* (e.g. *brȳdes*, *cwēnes*).

The potentially competing inflections in the paradigms of light-syllable masculine *i*-stems and heavy-syllable feminine *i*-stems are summarised in Table 3.1.

Table 3.1 The competing inflections in the OE light-syllable masculine and heavy-syllable feminine *i*-stems

	masc. *hyse* 'youth'				fem. *cwēne* 'woman'			
	archaic		innovative		archaic		innovative	
	SG	PL	SG	PL	SG	PL	SG	PL
NOM.	hyse	hyse	hys(s)	hys(s)as	cwēn	cwēne	cwēn	cwēna
GEN.	*hyse(s)*	*hysa(-iġa)*	*hyses*	*hys(s)a*	*cwēne*	*cwēna*	*cwēnes*	*cwēna*
DAT.	*hyse*	*hysum*	*hys(s)e*	*hys(s)um*	*cwēne*	*cwēnum*	*cwēne*	*cwēnum*
ACC.	hyse	hyse	hys(s)	hys(s)as	cwēn	cwēne	cwēne	cwēna*

* Cf. the discussion below.

The table does not present the forms of the (light-syllable) neuter *i*-stems, but their inflectional pattern is entirely parallel to that of the masculine *i*-stems, except that the analogical ending in the NOM./ACC. PL. is *-u*. As can be observed, the number of forms which are informative about the restructuring of inflection in this class is very limited. The most prominent residues of the historical inflectional pattern include the GEN. PL. *-iġa* (< *-ijō^n*), which survives exclusively in two nouns attested in poetic texts (*winiġ(e)a, Deniġa*). The early textual material testifies also to the presence of *-i* (later *-e*) as a marker of the NOM. and ACC. SG. (attested mainly in early Mercian texts, e.g. *cyri* 'choice', *caeli* 'keel', *meri* 'lake').[117] Another archaic feature is the occasional retention of the *i*-stem marker in the GEN. SG. and in the NOM./ACC. PL. in the earliest attested material. The old GEN. SG. is found in an isolated form *uyrdi*, attested in the Northumbrian *Leiden Riddle* (9th c.). The vestigial NOM./ACC. PL. ending *-i* (later *-e*) is attested in *hȳfi* 'hive' (CorpGl2) and in *me(h)cti, mæcti* (not included in the quantitative analysis), found in the Northumbrian version of *Cædmon's Hymn* (8th c.) (cf. Hogg & Fulk 2011: 43–44). Traces of the original *i*-stem inflection in feminine heavy-syllable stems are frequently attested in compound formations, where the stem formative *-i* is still preserved (e.g. in *brȳdiguma* 'bridegroom'). The endings of the (masc.) GEN. and DAT. SG. are assumed to have

---

117. Some of the examples found in the texts of Mercian provenance include: (1) stagnum staeg uel *meri* (ErfGl), (2) Rostrum neb uel scipes *caeli* (ErfGl), (3) Anetum *dili* (CorpGl 1), (4) Delectum *cyri* (CorpGl 1), (5) Passus faeðm uel tuegen *stridi* (CorpGl). For a detailed study of these early forms, see Dahl (1938), and for some more details on the influence of the productive inflections in the Anglian *i*-stems, see Adamczyk (2008).

originated in the *a*-stem declension already in prehistoric times.[118] The GEN. PL. ending *-a* in heavy-syllable *i*-stems is believed to represent a Germanic formation, while in light-syllable *i*-stems it can be traced back to the combined influence of the heavy-syllable stem paradigm and other declensional types (i.e. *a*- and consonantal stems) (Campbell 1977: 241; Hogg & Fulk 2011: 40–41). On account of the formal overlap with the endings of the productive declensions, this category was not included in the quantitative analysis.

Some of the innovative features present in the paradigm of the *i*-stems can be attributed to the influence of the *ja*-stem inflection. It is manifested in the presence of forms containing a geminate consonant, attested in the NOM./ACC. SG. and PL. in masculine light-syllable stems. They emerge as a result of a regular phonological development, whereby the stem formative triggered the gemination of the root final consonant in accordance with West Germanic Gemination (Campbell 1977: 167), e.g. *mettas* 'food', *hyssas* 'youths', *illas* 'soles of feet'.[119] The alternation between these geminated forms and the regular ones can be potentially informative about inflectional restructuring in the paradigm. This refers in particular to the NOM./ACC. SG., where the original ending *-i* (> *-e*) could be replaced by gemination of the stem-final consonant. In all other instances the alternation provides information about which productive inflectional type influenced the paradigm, namely, whether a given innovation appeared due to the influence of the *a*-stems or *ja*-stems (e.g. *metas* vs. *mettas*, *mete* vs. *mette*). The group of *i*-stems where this alternation

---

118. The forms of the DAT. SG. are not unanimously viewed as analogical and the ending has alternatively been interpreted as inherited. According to Fulk (1992: 421), in contrast to North and East Germanic languages, West Germanic dialects do not unambiguously point to an analogical origin of this ending. The DAT. SG. ending *-e* in Old Saxon is assumed to have developed from *-i*, which is the marker of light-syllable stems. Likewise, the DAT. SG. ending *-i*, attested in the earliest Old High German glossaries in light-syllable stems alongside *-e*, can be viewed as original rather than analogical. See also Krahe & Meid (1969): "Dat. Sg. Ahd. *meri* „dem Meer" hat gegenüber dem Masc. *gast* (…) die echte Dat.-Ending der *i*-Stämme (alter Lok. *-ēi*) bewahrt." (Krahe & Meid 1969: 29; cf. Braune/Reiffenstein 2004: 193). Due to this ambiguity of the DAT. SG. forms in *-e*, they are treated as inconclusive in the present analysis.

119. The relation between the *i*-stems and *ja*-stems turns out to be quite complex on account of their early history. The early Germanic data testify to the presence of related, parallel forms, deriving from the original *-i*- and *-a*- stem extensions: e.g. **gard-i-/gard-a-* > Go. *gards* 'house, family' (*i*-stem with DAT. PL. *gardim*) vs. OE *geard*, ON *garðr* (*a*-stems); **sangw-i-/sangw-a-* > Go. *saggws* 'song' (*i*-stem with DAT. PL. *saggwim*) vs. OE *sang* (*a*-stem) (Bjorvand 1995: 3; Bammesberger 1990: 128). Bammesberger (1990: 138f) considers the possibility of their common origin in the PIE **s*-stem formations, pointing to the original (PIE) NOM. (ACC.) SG. **-os* (> PGmc. **-az*), as the basis for the development of the *a*-stems, and the original oblique **-es-* (> PGmc. **-ez-* > **-iz-*) as the basis for the development of the *i*-stems.

could potentially occur was investigated separately and the results are discussed in Section 3.5.2.3.

The inflectional variation present in the plural paradigm of heavy-syllable feminine *i*-stems poses considerable interpretative difficulties, and in order to provide a viable interpretation, a number of factors needs to be taken into account, and the interpretative criteria explicitly defined. Of the two relevant categories, the forms of the NOM. PL. are less ambiguous: the ending -*a* can be considered an extension from the productive *ō*-stems and be contrasted with the (residual) inherited forms in -*i* or -*e* (-*i* > -*e*). However, such a contrast, in both the NOM. and ACC. PL. can be informative essentially only for the Early Old English period, as in the later stage (Late Old English), the confusion of the vowels, resulting from phonological reduction, rendered the forms in -*e* inconclusive. An additional difficulty for the interpretation of the NOM./ACC. PL. is the fact that the alternation between -*a* and -*e* was also dialect-specific, which is an immediate consequence of the dialectal distribution of inflections in the *ō*-stems. Namely, in Anglian the ending -*e*, which is the original ending of the ACC. PL. in the *ō*-stems, was levelled to the NOM. PL. and the dialect consistently shows the marker -*e* in these two categories (NOM./ACC. PL.). In contrast, already in Early West Saxon the ACC. PL. ending -*e* in the *ō*-stems tended to be replaced (by intraparadigmatic analogy) by the marker -*a*, extended from the NOM. PL. Consequently, the ACC. PL. forms in -*e* in the *i*-stems are even less informative when trying to understand the restructuring of inflection, as they may overlap (at least in the Early material) with the forms of the *ō*-stems (in -*e*). The consequences of this distribution for the present investigation are the following: in Anglian texts, the ending -*e* in the NOM/ACC. PL. is not informative as it can represent -*e* < -*i*, i.e. the original *i*-stem ending, as well as -*e* < -*æ*, i.e. the original ACC. PL. *ō*-stem ending, which had been levelled to the NOM. PL. In non-Anglian texts, the ending -*e* in the NOM. PL. must represent the original *i*-stem ending, as the *ō*-stems show only -*a* therein. In the ACC. PL., in turn, the ending -*e* may continue the original *i*-stem ending, but can well be an analogical extension from the *ō*-stems. However, given the fact that -*e* was a receding feature in the *ō*-stems, it is questionable whether it could influence the paradigm of the *i*-stems. As this direction of transfer is not very likely, the ending -*e* was considered to represent the inherited marker, and counted accordingly as archaic for both the NOM. PL. and ACC. PL. (It will become clear in the discussion of the corpus attestations that this assumption was reasonable.) Consequently, Anglian and Late forms of the NOM./ACC. PL. in -*e* were considered inconclusive, the former due to dialect-specific features, the latter due to the considerable phonological confusion of vowels in inflectional syllables in the Late Old English period; in the other categories (non-Anglian and non-Late), -*e* was interpreted as an archaic *i*-stem exponent of the NOM./ACC. PL.

3.5.2.3 *Results of the investigation*

Due to the formal features of the *i*-stem declension, discussed in the previous section (with the substantial size of this class in terms of type and token lemma frequency, and the divergent chronology of the restructuring process in individual subtypes), the scope of the quantitative analysis has been limited. Such an approach was considered sound and the selected material sufficient to identify major patterns. The complete inventory of lemmas covered in the quantitative analysis can be found in the Appendix section. As the masculine and neuter *i*-stems show parallel developments, the latter displaying additionally considerable confusion as to the gender (occasionally attaching masculine endings), the findings from the quantitative investigation in these two subtypes are presented in one table (Table 3.2).

Table 3.2 Distribution of archaic and innovative inflections in the OE light-syllable masculine and neuter *i*-stems

	archaic		innovative	
	SG	PL	SG	PL
NOM.	(293) 94%	(16) 33%	(18) 6%	(33) 67%
GEN.	*(171)*	*(55)*	–	–
DAT.	*(465)*	*(86)*	–	–
ACC.	(606) 95%	(35) 21%	(29) 5%	(133) 79%
Total	(950) 82%		(213) 18%	

The overall low level of innovation is clearly to be attributed to the singular, where the forms of the NOM. and ACC. SG. retain their original shape, whereas the plural turns out to be largely affected by analogical inflections. Such a pattern may be partly the consequence of the adopted method of quantification, which excludes categories where no synchronic alternation is attested due to early restructuring. The forms of the GEN. SG. show no archaic inflection by the time of the first attestation of Old English, which is interpreted as indicative of the early (prehistoric) interference of the analogical inflections in this category. If the forms of the GEN. SG. were included in the calculation, the archaism of the singular paradigm would drop from 95 percent to 80 percent. This adjustment is too insignificant to account for the discrepancy in the attested pattern.

A factor which seems to explain the attested distribution of forms much more adequately is the frequency of occurrence. It is evident from the data that the *i*-stems were much more frequently attested in the singular than in the plural. This refers not only to the paradigmatic categories that were included in the quantitative study, i.e. the NOM. and ACC., which in general tend to be frequent, but also to the GEN. and DAT., which were more frequent in the singular than in the plural. Accordingly, the archaism of the singular paradigm of the light-syllable *i*-stems may be interpreted as a reflex of the conserving effect of token frequency on the morphological patterns.

Another factor that must have played a role in the pattern of restructuring of these stems is related to the functionality of the system and, more specifically, the fact that the historical singular and plural forms of the NOM. and ACC. were identical. The presence of syncretic forms in the NOM./ACC. SG. and NOM./ACC.PL. constituted a serious threat to the retention of the opposition between singular and plural in the paradigm, jeopardizing thus the functionality of the paradigm. In order to retain the functional contrast between the singular and plural, a new, distinct, inflectional exponent was needed. In other words, the systemic require- ment of the functionality of the paradigms was an incentive for the extension of analogical inflections in the plural paradigm.

Yet another factor contributing to the retention of the archaic inflection in the paradigm is the lack of any phonological pressure on the syllable structure of light-syllable stems, which showed the preferred metrical pattern (i.e. the trochaic foot; Lahiri & Dresher 1991: 251).

The template for the restructuring in this subclass was created predominantly by the *a*-and *ja*-stem pattern. The innovative features in the paradigm of the sin- gular are the endingless (occasionally geminated) NOM./ACC. forms (*-wlitt*, *mett*), attested in Northumbrian and Mercian texts. They emerge specifically under the influence of the *ja*-stem inflection, whereby gemination of the final consonant oc- curs. Apart from these two categories, the intrusion of the *ja*-stems is more con- sistently attested in the plural, where the geminated forms can be found in all cases, including the GEN. and DAT. PL. (counted here as neutral). The attested distribution indicates clearly that gemination was a feature typical of the plural paradigm, where geminated consonants appear in 86 percent of forms (in nouns which formally could undergo the process), while it is not very common in the singular, where geminated forms constitute only 4 percent.

As regards the masculine and neuter heavy-syllable *i*-stems, which were not subject to a systematic quantitative analysis, it can be observed that they consist- ently follow the inflection of the *a*-stems. The paradigm of these stems is believed to have been remodelled after the separation of Old English from the Continental West Germanic dialect continuum, as the Continental sister languages testify (at least partly) to a distinct heavy-syllable *i*-stem paradigm (e.g. OHG *gast – gesti*, PL.; Braune/Reiffenstein 2004: 200–203; OS *wurm – wurmi*; Gallée 1993: 209–211), and after the advent of *i*-mutation, since the etymological *i*-stems which had shifted to the *a*-stem declension frequently contain an *i*-mutated vowel. The restructuring in the heavy-syllable masculine and neuter paradigm must have been completed prior to the first written attestations, i.e. by the second half of the seventh century. Such a relative chronology of analogical restructuring and *i*-mutation becomes problematic given the attested presence of such unmutated forms as *stapes, stapum* (vs. *stepe*), or *gasta* (vs. *giest*), which prove that in part of the lexicon the dissemination of the analogical inflections must have been an earlier development than the operation of *i*-mutation (Campbell 1977: 244; cf. Hogg & Fulk 2011: 39). Accordingly, this inconsistency in the attestation of *i*-mutated forms can be interpreted in a way that in part of the lexicon the restructuring began prior to the operation of *i*-mutation, but in most lemmas it was completed only afterwards.

As some occasional attestations to the archaic inflection in the heavy-syllable masculine *i*-stems could be identified in the corpus, their incidence relative to the analogical inflections was tested for the earliest attested period of Old English (*Early* OE) and the period labelled as *Indeterminate*.[120] The sample was confined to the forms of one of the better attested masculine *i*-stems: *dǽl* 'part' (cf. Hogg 1980: 282–283). The quantitative study into the pattern of inflections in the NOM./ACC. PL. of *dǽl* revealed that the inherited inflections in the paradigm constitute no more than 10 percent ($n = 31$) of all the attested forms. The figure is based on the forms of the NOM./ACC. PL. as they were the only morphosyntactic categories where some synchronic alternation (between the inherited -*e* and analogical -*as*) could be detected. This high level of innovation corresponds to the pattern found in the light-syllable *i*-stems, where the analogical forms in the plural amount to 76 percent. The inherited forms (of the NOM./ACC. PL.) were found in Early West Saxon texts and in the unlocalised CorpGl. Some other archaic forms are also attested in the DAT. SG. (*dǽli, daeli*) in the Mercian texts of EpGl and ErfGl.[121]

The second subclass of *i*-stems which showed synchronic alternation and could thus be systematically examined is the group of heavy-syllable feminine *i*-stems, which constitute the most numerous group of *i*-stems in the Old English material. The results of the investigation of this class are presented in Table 3.3.

The estimation of the level of innovation in this paradigm is based on three categories: the ACC. SG., NOM. PL., and ACC. PL. As can be observed, the plural paradigm emerges as largely innovative, with analogical inflections attested in 83 percent of forms, while the ACC. SG. remains fairly archaic. The analogical ending in the ACC. SG. (-*e*) appears sporadically in the early Mercian and early West Saxon material, dated to the ninth century, but more commonly in the later period, while

---

120. The *Late* stage was excluded from the investigation, since if there were any traces of the inherited inflection to be found in the paradigm, they would be more likely attested in the *Early* period.

121. Note that the DAT. SG. was counted as neutral due to the formal overlap of the ending -*e* (< -*i*) with the analogical *a*-stem endings.

Table 3.3 Distribution of archaic and innovative inflections in the OE heavy-syllable feminine *i*-stems

	archaic		innovative	
	SG	PL	SG	PL
NOM.	*(470)*	(7) 12%	–	(49) 88%
GEN.	*(86)*	*(65)*	–	–
DAT.	*(949)*	*(308)*	–	–
ACC.	(456) 74%	(26) 19%	(161) 26%	(111) 81%
Total	(489) 60%		(321) 40%	

the introduction of innovation in the plural is apparently an earlier phenomenon. The potential asymmetry in the distribution of the ending -*e* in the NOM. and ACC. PL., which could be expected from an etymological perspective (cf. *i*-stems NOM. ACC. PL. -*e* < PGmc. *-*īz*, *-*inz* vs. *ō*-*stems* NOM. PL. -*a*, ACC. PL. -*e* < PGmc. *-*ōz*; *-*ōns*; cf. Section 2.2.4), was not substantiated by the data: the difference between 88 percent of innovation in the former and 81 percent in the latter does not constitute a significant contrast. Such a parallel distribution of analogical forms in these two categories corroborates the assumption that the ACC. PL. forms in -*e* are a continuation of the former *i*-stem ending.[122]

The historical, phonologically-driven overlap between heavy-syllable feminine *i*-stems and *ō*-stems in the singular (NOM. GEN. DAT. SG.: -Ø, -*e*, -*e*) makes it nearly impossible to interpret the developments in this subclass of *i*-stems in terms of 'archaic' and 'innovative'. In all cases in the singular some deviating forms appear, including potential traces of the *n*-stem inflections (e.g. in *cwēn* 'woman': NOM. SG. *cwēne*, GEN. DAT. SG *cwēnan*;[123] in *tīd* 'time': GEN. PL. *tīdena*), or the incidental GEN. SG. forms in -*es* which appear in texts from the later period (e.g. *brȳdes* 'bride', *cwēnes*), attesting to the impact of the masculine inflection. Apart from these incidental deviations, the most systematic irregularities are manifested in the addition

---

122. If the appearance of -*e* in the ACC. PL. were due to the influence of the *ō*-stems, the percentage of forms in -*e* would be significantly higher in the ACC. PL. than in the NOM. PL. Note that only non-Mercian and non-Late forms could be included in the computation here (cf. 3.5.2.2).

123. The weak forms are commonly considered to belong to a related *n*-stem noun *cwene*, -*an* (cf. Go. *quinō*), attested alongside the *i*-stem *cwēn*. The analysed material shows that all the weak forms are attested in the singular and in the GEN. PL., and they are mostly found in Late Old English sources. Such a distribution may indicate that the forms of *cwēn* and *cwene* are part of one, mixed paradigm, where the weak forms are innovative in the mentioned categories (see the paradigm of *magu – maga*, Section 3.5.3.2) (cf. *OED*, s.v. *quean*). The forms belonging to these two lemmas were not kept apart in the present analysis. Excluding the instances in -*an* (*n* = 5) from the count lowers the percentage of innovation in the ACC. SG. of *cwēn* to 74 percent (Table 3.5).

(NOM./ACC. SG.) or apocope (DAT. SG.) of final -*e*. In the investigated sample, the analogical marker -*e* was found in 5 percent of the NOM. SG. forms and as much as 26 percent of all ACC. SG. forms, while 4 percent of the DAT. SG. forms are endingless.[124] The new shape of the ACC. SG. attested in nearly one-third of all forms contributes to the emergence of a paradigm of the type: NOM. GEN. DAT. ACC. SG.: -*Ø, -e, -e, -e*, which ideally corresponds to the *ō*-stem paradigm. Altogether 74 percent of the attested singular forms in the sample of heavy-syllable feminine *i*-stems matches the *ō*-stem paradigm. If the inflections are taken at face value, and the historically expected *i*-stem endings are counted as 'archaic', despite the potential overlap with the *ō*-stem forms, the level of archaism of the singular in the heavy-syllable feminine *i*-stems is very high, amounting to 88 percent. These two figures testify to a spontaneous, large-scale confusion of both paradigms, which was not so much a result of analogical processes, but rather an effect of the phonological overlap of forms across the two declensional classes.

A closer examination of the patterns found in the singular paradigm affords some further insight into the restructuring mechanisms in this subclass. The two cases to elaborate on here are the DAT. and ACC., which testify to a close interaction between the analogical levelling and phonological processes. The configuration of the inflectional endings in these two categories is presented in Table 3.4.

Table 3.4 The percentage of innovation in the DAT. SG. and ACC. SG. in the OE heavy-syllable femine *i*-stems

	i-stems	*ō*-stems	% innovative endings in the analysed *i*-stems
DAT.SG.	-e	-e	4% ("innovative" here = endingless)
ACC.SG.	-Ø	-e	26%

The interparadigmatic alternation can be captured only in the ACC. (SG.), where the *i*-stem inflections contrast with the ones of the *ō*-stems. The analogical pressure of the *ō*-stems is reflected in 26 percent of all the attested forms in this category. However, this figure is an effect of a range of diverse percentage distributions in individual lemmas; consequently, it conceals some relevant details of the distribution of the inherited and analogical forms in the category of the ACC. SG., as can be seen in Table 3.5.

---

124. These endingless DAT. SG. forms are not included in the estimation of the innovation level, in line with the criteria adopted for this study. They testify to a phonological innovation rather than analogical change. Needless to say, such phonological developments were essential for the unfolding of analogical processes in the paradigm. Likewise, the novel forms of the NOM. SG. are not included in the figure, as this extension is sporadic and largely lemma-specific, and moreover, it may testify to a gender-class change rather than a shift in the declensional class.

Table 3.5 The percentage of innovation in the ACC. SG. in the OE heavy-syllable feminine *i*-stems

ACC. SG	archaic (n)	innovative* (n)	% innovative
brȳd	10	21	68%
cwēn	10	34	77%
dǣd	13	10	43%
tīd	410	96	19%
dryht	13	0	0%
ēst	49	3	6%

* including a handful of instances in *-a* and *-an*; *hȳf* 'beehive' is not attested in the ACC. SG

As can be observed, the distribution of innovative inflections varies depending on the lemma and the most prominent feature of the attested pattern is the discrepancy in the level of innovation in individual lemmas, with *tīd*, *dryht* and *ēst* showing predominantly (or entirely) the archaic inflection. The attested distribution seems to be conditioned by two interacting factors, i.e. the frequency of occurrence and the phonological shape of the nouns. The former seems to account for the pattern found in the paradigm of *tīd*, which is frequently attested in the corpus, and this high token frequency may have worked as a factor conserving the original inflection, i.e. the endingless form of the ACC. SG. The other correlation identified in the data, i.e. between the level of innovation and the phonological properties of the nouns, involves final consonants. Specifically, the lemmas ending in a voiceless consonant cluster (*dryht*, *ēst*) are inclined to retain the endingless form in the ACC. SG. – an inclination also found in the Old Frisian *i*-stems (cf. Section 4.5.2).[125] An additional factor that may have contributed to the archaic profile of *dryht* and, to some extent, of *ēst* is the fact these these lemmas are attested only or predominantly in poetic texts, which tend to be morphologically more conservative.

A parallel pattern can be observed also in the DAT. SG., where, despite the fact that no systematic alternation between the *i*-stem and *ō*-stem inflections can be identified (both show the ending *-e*), the loss of *-e* is occasionally attested.[126] Also here, the phonological parameter turns out to be the most decisive factor, i.e. in *dryht* the loss of *-e* is attested in 69 percent (*n* = 13) of the tokens, while in the

---

125. Since *ēst* shows considerable gender confusion, the DAT. SG. ending *-e* cannot be unambiguously interpreted.

126. Not in all nouns though; for instance, *hȳf* consistently shows a voiced consonant in the DAT. SG. (with intervocalic voicing: *hȳfe* [hy:və]) despite its final voiceless consonant.

other nouns only in 0–5 percent of all DAT. SG. forms.[127] Frequency does not seem to have any effect on the pattern attested in the DAT. SG. (in instances where it interacts with the phonological factor), which may be explained by the fact that the DAT. SG. experiences two opposing effects of frequency, namely, on the one hand, the high frequency of occurrence protects the original form in -e, while on the other hand, it also encourages the apocope pressure (Reducing Effect of frequency, cf. Section 1.4.6.1) to which nouns ending in a voiceless consonantal cluster are more exposed. In consequence, the effect of frequency in the DAT. SG. seems to be levelled out.

Table 3.6 presents the distribution of analogical inflections in all the investigated *i*-stems with respect to the individual morphosyntactic categories and irrespective of the syllable weight. Only the categories considered conclusive for the present investigation were included.

Table 3.6 Overall distribution of innovative inflections in the OE *i*-stems*

	% innovative	% innovative
NOM. SG.	($n = 311$) 6%	($n = 1563$) 10%
ACC. SG.	($n = 1252$) 15%	
NOM. PL.	($n = 105$) 78%	($n = 410$) 80%
ACC. PL.	($n = 305$) 80%	
Total	($n = 1973$) 27%	

* The NOM. SG. is based on the masculine light-syllable stems. Compare the figures in Adamczyk (2011), where the forms of the NOM. SG. in the masculine *i*-stems were not included in the calculations.

The overall percentage of innovation cannot be interpreted at face value and is rather an abstraction; much more informative and representative are the figures showing the dissemination of analogical forms with respect to number. The figure for the singular is based entirely on the light-syllable masculine and neuter *i*-stems, which were only occasionally remodelled on the pattern of the *a*-stems (*ja*-stems). In order to account for the substantially higher level of innovation in the plural paradigm, a recourse to functional explanation is necessary: namely, the need to keep the contrast between the singular and plural must have worked as a trigger for

---

127. This contrast is statistically significant. A similar pattern can be observed in the Old Frisian material (see Section 4.5.2.3). In Old Frisian additionally the relative frequency of categories, i.e. the endingless NOM. ACC. SG. against the GEN. DAT. SG. in -*e*, seems to have played a role: nouns that appear more often in the NOM. ACC. SG. tend to generalise the endingless form throughout the singular, while those more often found in the GEN. DAT. SG. generalise the form in -*e*. This tendency was not found in the Old English data.

the adoption of the analogical ending in the plural. This is especially evident in the case of the light-syllable stems, where the substitution of the *a*-stem ending -*as* for the original -*i* may have been a change permitting to keep the contrast between the singular and plural (Hogg 1980: 283). In heavy-syllable stems, both masculine and feminine, the inherited plural marker -*e*, though contrasting with the zero ending in the singular, was exposed to the operation of apocope. The analogical ending -*a* was a slightly more salient inflectional exponent, and as such was better adjusted to allow retention of the distinction in number, at least in the Early Old English period (cf. Versloot 2008: 260–262).

Although the pattern of restructuring is largely parallel in the light- and heavy-syllable stems, there is a discernible difference between them in that the level of innovation is higher in the heavy-syllable stems (85% vs. 75%). Moreover, different levels of innovation are attested for individual lemmas, with the light-syllable lemmas showing a much lower range of percentages (28%–89%) than the heavy-syllable ones (68%–100%). Although this contrast between light- and heavy-syllable stems is rather subtle, it has certain implications: it implies that apart from the purely functional incentive involved in the mechanism of the process, i.e. the need to keep the SG./PL. contrast in the paradigm, the reorganisation of the nominal inflection was largely determined by phonological developments, in particular apocope, which worked towards the elimination of the vocalic endings in heavy-syllable stems. It can be concluded that the attested inflectional pattern is a result of an interaction between these forces. Moreover, the dispreference for the endingless NOM./ACC. PL. in heavy-syllable stems (attested in 2% of all forms), which emerged as a result of the apocope pressure, was apparently a stronger trigger for the adoption of the analogical inflection than the presence of an identical ending in the respective categories in the SG. and PL. in light-syllable stems.

With regard to the directions of interdeclensional transfers of the *i*-stems, the analysis clearly confirms the predominance of the two major productive classes, the *a*-stems and *ō*-stems, and a subtype of the former, *ja*-stems, attested only in light-syllable stems. The interference of the *n*-stem inflection is rather marginal and is best attested in the feminine *i*-stems in West-Saxon prose texts, especially in the forms of the GEN. PL. (e.g. *dēdana, tīdana, wyrtana*). The scale of restructuring in the *i*-stems varies, ranging from paradigms showing complete submission to analogical pressure, where the process of restructuring was completed prior to the time of the first attestations of Old English (heavy-syllable *i*-stems), to paradigms where the intrusion of analogical inflections is relatively limited (masculine light-syllable stems). The bidirectional transition of nouns to the productive declensions, *a*-stems and *ō*-stems, which began at the prehistoric stage and continued into the historical stage, rendered the paradigms increasingly opaque. Significantly, the unfolding of the restructuring process turns out to have been largely category-dependent, controlled by the morphosyntactic categories. As could be observed, analogical processes tended to affect the GEN. and DAT. (both SG. and PL.) earlier (at the prehistoric stage) than the NOM. and ACC., where synchronic alternation is, to a lesser or greater extent, still attested. Likewise, the plural turned out to be the category more extensively disturbed by the interplay of phonological and analogical developments and thus more easily transformed under the influence of the productive inflection.

Despite the considerable number of nouns originally affiliated with the class of *i*-stems, they constitute an unproductive declension in Old English, whose members gradually drifted to the productive inflectional types. This renders Old English remarkably different from its Continental sister languages, where this inflectional type became increasingly widespread (especially in Old and Middle High German). Clearly, the transformation of the *i*-stem class demonstrates that the remodelling of nominal paradigms was a multifaceted development, which had a different scope and chronology, depending largely on the original phonological and frequency profiles of the nouns.

3.5.3   *u*-stems

3.5.3.1   *General remarks*

The *u*-stem declension, characterised originally by the stem formative *-u*-, comprised in Old English light- and heavy-syllable stems of feminine and masculine gender. The residues of the neuter *u*-stem declension (NOM./ACC. SG.) can be found in *feolu, feolo* 'much', attested in PsGlA and in the corresponding West-Saxon *fela* and *feola*. The Old English equivalent of the well attested Gothic neuter *faíhu* 'cattle', *feoh* (Ang. *feh*) follows entirely the *a*-stem pattern (Brunner 1965: 198, 221).[128] In terms of their structure, the *u*-stems may be viewed as parallel to the *i*-stems in that they testify to the presence of etymological *-u-/-w-* in contexts where *i*-stems invariably evince *-i-/-j-* (*sunuz, *sunu^n vs. *anstiz, *ansti^n). Additionally, both attest to a lack of an original distinction between the masculine and feminine inflection (Bammesberger 1990: 150f.), notwithstanding their rather divergent subsequent development in the individual Germanic languages.

The class of Old English *u*-stems was synchronically unproductive, comprising a limited number of nouns; at the same time, some of the lemmas affiliated with this class were characterised by very high token frequencies (e.g. *sunu* 'son', *hond*

---

128. In Gothic the neuter *u*-stems are attested in the singular (NOM. *faíhu* 'cattle', GEN. *faíháus*, DAT. *faíháu*; Wright 1957: 95); in the other Germanic dialects they survive only in relic forms.

'hand', *feld* 'field' or *eard* 'country'), which had a bearing on the pattern of the re-organisation of inflection in their paradigms. Admittedly, the *u*-stem declension is believed to have been originally productive, or partially productive, at least within the semantic field of names of body parts. The support for this assumption comes from the Gothic material, where *fōtus* 'foot' or *tunþus* 'tooth' follow the paradigm of *handus*, although they originate as root nouns (< PGmc. **fōt-*, **tunþ-*); here belong also *kinnus* 'chin', *giþus* 'stomach', and *liþus* 'limb' (Ramat 1981: 62; Bammesberger 1990: 198).[129] The synchronic Old English data as well as the material from the other Germanic languages, however, do indicate that this once more widespread pattern had been repressed prior to the first attestations of Germanic; as a result, the *u*-stem paradigm displays evident signs of internal instability in the Old English period.

A number of historical *u*-stems had entirely shifted to other declensional types (primarily *a*-stems) in the prehistoric period, as they never appear with vestiges of the *u*-stem inflection in the attested Old English material. These early transfers involved the following *u*-stems: *ār* 'messenger', *dēað* 'death', *feorh* 'life, person' (Go. *faírhwus*), *flōd* 'flood', *hungor* 'hunger', *scield* (*sceld*) 'shield', *ðorn* 'thorn', deverbal nominal formations in *-(n)oð*, *-(n)að*, as well as *sceadu* 'shadow', attested as a *wa*-stem (GEN. SG. *scead(u)we*, alongside neuter *scead*) (Brunner 1965: 229). Bammesberger (1990: 155–160) adds to this list also *bōh* 'bough, arm', *cinn* 'chin', *cwidu* 'cud, quid', *cwiþ(a)* 'womb' (declined also as a masculine *n*-stem), *feoh* 'money', *grund* 'ground, foundation', *liþ* 'limb', *wāg* 'wall', *weþer* 'ram, wether' and the **-tu-* stems: *lust* 'desire, pleasure', *þurst* 'thirst'. It is essentially the evidence from sister languages, especially Gothic, that directly confirms the *u*-stem origin of these nouns.

The historical stage of the morphological reorganisation of the *u*-stem paradigms entailed bidirectional shifts, whereby the masculine *u*-stems were remodelled on the pattern of the *a*-stems, and feminine *u*-stems joined the *ō*-stems. Apart from these two directions of transfer, *u*-stems evince also a strong inclination towards the *n*-stem inflection, reflected primarily in the endings of the GEN. PL. *-ena* and the NOM./ACC. PL. *-an* (occasionally *-on/-en*). The inflectional irregularities which can emerge as a result of these analogical realignments in various morphosyntactic categories include:

---

129. The assumed prehistoric productivity of the *u*-stem formations and its subsequent loss was alluded to by Ramat (1981) and Bammesberger (1990), who observe: "Sowohl *u*-stämmige Substantiva als auch *u*-stämmige Adjektiva lassen sich in den altgermanischen Sprachen in beträchtlicher Zahl nachweisen. Sie scheinen aber im Laufe der Zeit ihre Produktivität verloren zu haben. Andere Bildungen tendierten dazu, an die Stelle ursprünglicher *u*-Stämme zu treten" (Bammesberger 1990: 154), and "… diese Produktivität erschöpfte sich jedoch bald und diese Klasse ist in keiner germ. Sprache produktiv geblieben" (Ramat 1981: 62).

a. masculine *u*-stems
   – the GEN. SG. marker *-es* in place of the inherited ending *-a*
   – the DAT. SG. marker *-e* in place of the inherited ending *-a*
   – the NOM./ACC. marker *-as* in place of the original ending *-a*
   – the *n*-stem ending *-an* in all cases in the singular except the NOM. SG., and in the NOM./ACC. PL.
   – the *n*-stem GEN. PL. marker *-ena*
b. feminine *u*-stems
   – the GEN. SG. marker *-e* (alternatively masc. *-es*) in place of the inherited ending *-a*
   – the DAT. SG. marker *-e* in place of the original ending *-a*
   – the ACC. SG. marker *-e* in place of the ending *-u* (in light-syllable stems) or zero ending (in heavy-syllable stems)
   – the *n*-stem ending *-an* in all cases in the singular except the NOM. SG., and in the NOM./ACC. PL.
   – the *n*-stem GEN. PL. marker *-ena*

Table 3.7 presents a summary of these potential analogical interferences in the paradigms of the light-syllable masculine (*sidu* 'custom') and feminine (*nosu* 'nose') *u*-stems.

Table 3.7 The competing inflections in the OE light-syllable masculine and feminine *u*-stems

	masculine				feminine			
	archaic		innovative		archaic		innovative	
	SG	PL	SG	PL	SG	PL	SG	PL
NOM.	sidu	sida	sida	sidas, -an	*nosu*[*]	nosa	*nosu*	nose, -an
GEN.	sida	*sida*	sides, -an	*sida (-ena)*	nosa	*nosa*	nose, -an	*nosa (-ena)*
DAT.	sida	*sidum*	side, -an	*sidum*	nosa	nosum	nose, -an	*nosum*
ACC.	sidu	sida	sida	sidas, -an	nosu	nosa	nose, -an	nose, -an

* The nouns *nosu* and *duru*, originated as root nouns, but they analogically formed new *u*-stem paradigms on the basis of the ACC. SG. PL. forms: **nos-uⁿ/-unz, *dur-uⁿ/-unz*. In the case of *nosu* the dual ending in **-a* (**nosa*) is additionally posited as a possible cause of the transfer to the *u*-stems (Bammesberger 1990: 197, 199; cf. van Helten 1911: 506).

In contrast to light-syllable stems, where the marker *-u* is preserved in the NOM./ACC. SG., heavy-syllable stems show no ending in these two categories. Such a distribution is a reflex of the phonological rule whereby the word final **-u* was apocopated after a heavy-syllable (e.g. *sunu* 'son', *wudu* 'wood', *duru* 'door' vs. *hond* 'hand', *feld* 'field', *ford* 'ford') (e.g. Campbell 1977: 144; Hogg 1992a: 223–224), and it is parallel to the condition found in some other classes, for example, *ja*-stems and *i*-stems, where the inflectional contrast between light- and heavy-syllable stems is also found (e.g. *ja*-stem *here* 'army' vs. *secg* 'sword, warrior'; *i*-stem *wine* 'friend' vs. *wyrm* 'dragon'). Accordingly, the category of the NOM./ACC. SG. will be relevant for the present analysis only in the light-syllable masculine *u*-stems; in the feminine stems only the ACC. SG. is relevant).[130]

The early Old English historical paradigm continues the Proto-Germanic inflections, with the exception of the NOM. and ACC. PL. ending -*a* which cannot be easily accounted for. The postulated hypotheses as to its origin involve: (a) a regular phonological development (*-o*u̯*es*- > PGmc. *-*awiz* > *-*auz*, cf. *-*eu̯*es*- > PGmc. *-*iwiz*-, Go. -*jus*) (Campbell 1977: 246; cf. Krahe & Meid 1969: 34), (b) intraparadigmatic innovation appearing due to the analogical influence of other cases, namely, the GEN. SG., DAT. SG. and GEN. PL. (Prokosch 1939: 249), or (c) a continuation of an original dual ending (from PIE *-*ōu*-) which gradually spread to the plural and was employed as a regular NOM./ACC. PL. marker (Dahl 1938: 182; Bammesberger 1985: 367ff., cf. Section 2.2.3.2).[131] This last interpretation seems conceivable given the frequency of the dual number forms in such *u*-stems as *hand* 'hand', *æpple* 'eye-ball' or *duru* 'door', as well as *sunu* 'son', with *suna* referring to two sons. Irrespective of the exact origin, the NOM./ACC. SG. marker -*a* is interpreted as archaic in the present study.[132]

In the context of the restructuring process and from the synchronic Old English perspective, the shape of the NOM./ACC. PL. poses a considerable interpretative problem in the feminine paradigm. The form overlaps with that of the feminine *ō*-stems (NOM. PL. *-*ōz* > OE -*a*, cf. e.g. *nosu: nosa* vs. *ō*-stem *lār: lāra* 'learning'), which renders this category inconclusive when it comes to interpreting the forms as inherited or analogical.

Likewise, the origin of the DAT. SG. is not entirely transparent and the ending can be viewed as a result of intraparadigmatic pressure, i.e. the analogical influence of the GEN. SG. (Brunner 1965: 229; van Helten 1911: 463). Here, however, the

---

130. Another important phonological feature involves the unaccented /u/ which tends to develop into /o/ (in later sources), except when preceded by an accented /u/ in the root syllable (as in *sunu*, *wudu*), where it seems to be much more stable (Campbell 1977: 136).

131. The form of the ACC. PL. *bordwudu*, attested in *Beowulf*, can arguably be interpreted as a residue of the original *u*-stem inflection (<*-*uns*) (Bliss 1967: 119; cf. Fulk 1992: 382–383, 422). Likewise, the forms in -*u* (-*o*), including the singly attested *flōdu* 'flood' (Franks Casket), can be interpreted as a continuation of the original ACC. PL. form, i.e. PGmc. *-*uns* (Boutkan 1995: 257).

132. The presence of the endings -*u* and -*o* in the NOM. PL. (*sunu*, *suno*) has been ascribed to the analogical intraparadigmatic pressure of the ACC. PL. (Prokosch 1939: 249). These forms are accordingly considered archaic in the present study, as they do not arise as an effect of the pressures from the productive inflectional types.

interpretation is rather unambiguous as the form does not overlap with the corresponding forms of the productive declensions (-*a* vs. -*e*). Accordingly, irrespective of the exact origin of this form, in the present study it will be interpreted as archaic against the analogical forms spreading from the productive paradigms. At the same time, a complication of a different nature comes into play, namely, the possibility that the non-original marker -*e* is a reduced variant of -*a*, emerging as a result of a regular phonological development, rather than an analogical form extended from the *a*-stems or *ō*-stems. This phonological development was a consequence of the confusion of the unaccented -*e* (< *æ, e, i*) and the unaccented back vowels, dated to the eleventh century, and it had a wide scope in the paradigm of the *u*-stems, characterised by vocalic endings both in the singular and plural (except for the DAT. PL. -*um*). Consequently, the original ending of the DAT. SG. in masculine and feminine stems became indistinguishable from the corresponding ending in the *a*-stems and *ō*-stems. Some other inflectional overlaps appeared in the GEN. SG. and NOM./ ACC. PL. in feminine stems, where the innovative -*e* can be ascribed to the pressure of the *ō*-stems, but can just as well represent a reduced vowel /ə/, appearing due to the progressing reduction processes in the inflectional vowels towards the end of the Old English period. Given that these phonological innovations progressed at a different pace in the individual Old English dialects and periods, the only methodologically sound approach to such problematic cases was the identification of the literary source in which the forms are attested, taking into account its exact dating and dialectal provenance. Such a procedure has been applied in the present investigation for the sake of avoiding ambiguities and minimising the risk of drawing invalid conclusions.

3.5.3.2 *Results of the investigation*

A complete list of *u*-stems subject to quantitative investigation can be found in the Appendix. Compound formations, where the *u*-stem constituted the second element of the compound, were included in the analysis in nouns of lower frequency and left out in high frequent items.[133] The two *u*-stem-based formations: *fri(o)þu* 'peace' and *leoþu* (*lioþu*) 'limb' (Go. *friþus, liþus*) are recorded as *u*-stems only as the first element of compounds and as such they are of no relevance to the present investigation, e.g. *friþusibb* 'protecting peace', *friþowebba* 'peace weaver,

---

133. Likewise, lemmas such as *ford* and *feld*, which were recurrently attested as the second element of place-names (many of them appearing typically in the *Charters* collection), were excluded from the counting (cf. Section 3.5.1 above), just like other place (or proper) names were. Interestingly, the attestations to *ford* (used as the second element of compounds in place names) testify to the spread of the *n*-stem inflection in the paradigm (e.g. *Brytfordan, wungyfe fordan, kælflæges fordan*).

angel', *Friþuweald* (proper name), *leoþucæge* 'limb key', *leoþucræft* 'bodily skill'. As independent lemmas they consistently follow the *a*-stem (*friþ, liþ*) or/and the *ō*-stem pattern (*friþu*) (Campbell 1977: 247; Hogg & Fulk 2011: 47).[134] Another *u*-stem noun which merits some consideration is the Old English *flōd* 'flood' which, in line with Brunner's (1965) classification, was not included in the quantitative investigation. Showing no inflectional endings of the historical *u*-stems, it has been considered a prehistorically transferred noun, and classified as a member of the masculine or neuter *a*-stem declension (Bosworth & Toller 1898). The once attested *flōdu* (*fisc flodu ahof on fergenberig*, ACC. PL.), found on the Franks Casket, is believed to be either an archaism (Dahl 1938: 18; Bammesberger 1985: 365, Boutkan 1996: 257; cf. PGmc. *-unz*, Go. *flōdus*), or an irregular [erroneous] formation[135] (Campbell 1977: 247; cf. Hogg & Fulk 2011: 48).[136]

In order to capture the details of the gradual reorganisation in the *u*-stem declension, and to make valid inferences about the attested developments, the quantitative analysis has been divided into four parts. Accordingly, the masculine and feminine stems were investigated independently and, additionally, anticipating quite discrepant patterns in the light- and heavy-syllable stems, the analysis was conducted separately on these two types of stems. The forms of the GEN. and DAT. PL. are of no relevance for measuring the level of innovation in the *u*-stems as they are identical with the respective forms of *a*-stems and *ō*-stems (except for the GEN. PL. ending -*ena* [-*ana*] which can be unambiguously identified as innovative). Likewise, the forms of the NOM. SG. (in contrast to the ACC. SG.) of the feminine stems are irrelevant for the analysis, since the influence of any other declensional type would not be reflected in the inflectional ending. To sum up, in the masculine light-syllable stems, both the NOM. and ACC. SG. were included (e.g. *wudu*) in the calculations, while in the light-syllable feminine stems only the ACC. SG., because

---

134. As these two lemmas show no traces of the inherited pattern in Old English, despite being well attested, they are considered to be early transfers and were thus not included in the quantitative investigation. On the potential close relation between *frīþ* and *freoþu*, see footnote 14 in Versloot & Adamczyk (2014: 547). See also Ross (1954: 92–93) for a discussion of the origin and cognates of Go. *leiþu*.

135. For a more detailed discussion, see Fulk (1992: 378–379), where a number of proposed interpretations are examined.

136. Another heavy-syllable stem which could (arguably) be included here is -*gār* 'spear', attested only as the second element of proper names, e.g. *Wihtgār* (cf. Campbell 1977: 247). Its affiliation with the *u*-declension, however, cannot be easily corroborated (Kluge 1913: 202; Brunner 1965: 220). A related form *aetgāēru* 'javelin', attested in early glossaries (EpGl, ErfGl, CorpGl), is equally difficult to interpret; the form has been considered to be a *jō*-stem (Dahl 1938: 148; Hogg & Fulk 2011: 35). Due to its ambivalent status, the form was not included in the present investigation.

the NOM. SG. overlaps with that of the ō-stems. In heavy-syllable stems, these categories are irrelevant in the masculine stems (e.g. *feld*), but the ACC. SG. is informative
(and thus included) in the feminine stems (e.g. *cweorn*).

Table 3.8 presents the distribution of inherited and analogical inflections in
the light- and heavy-syllable masculine stems. The figures for light-syllable stems
do not include the data from the investigation of *sunu*, which due to its very high
frequency of occurrence was analysed separately (cf. Section 3.5.3.3).

Table 3.8 Distribution of archaic and innovative inflections in the OE masculine *u*-stems[*]

	Light-syllable				Heavy-syllable			
	archaic		innovative		archaic		innovative	
	SG	PL	SG	PL	SG	PL	SG	PL
NOM.	(115) 84%	(4) 4%	(22) 16%	(95) 96%	(252)	(33) 36%	–	(58) 64%
GEN.	(22) 38%	(79)	(36) 62%	–	(12) 4%	(816)	(257) 96%	–
DAT.	(178) 83%	(122)	(37) 17%	–	(450) 46%	(201)	(525) 54%	–
ACC.	(121) 88%	(16) 17%	(16) 12%	(78) 83%	(533)	(64) 25%	–	(190) 75%
Total	(456) 62%		(284) 38%		(559) 35%		(1030) 65%	

[*] The scant *fala*, attested only thrice in the corpus as a gloss to *tabula* (*tubolo, tabulo*) has been viewed
as a DAT. SG. of an unattested *u*-stem **falχu-* 'pipe' (Dahl 1938: 178–179). Given the controversy over the
interpretation of these forms, the three instances found in the corpus were left out of the quantitative
investigation.

The examined material testifies to the presence of parallel tendencies in both paradigms, but, as can be observed, the reshaping of inflection had a different scope in
the two subtypes of the *u*-stems. While the light-syllable stems tended to be more
resistant to the influence of the productive inflections, the heavy-syllable stems
demonstrate greater vulnerability to analogical pressure, with the paradigm largely
dominated by innovative inflections. The conservatism of the light-syllable stem
paradigm is to be ascribed to the inflection in the singular, where the NOM. SG.,
showing the characteristic *u*-stem declension marker, is included in the calculations. The overall level of innovation in the singular amounts to only 20 percent and
it contrasts with the level of 90 percent in the plural, although it must be observed
that the figures for the plural reflect almost entirely the attestations to one lemma:
magu 'boy, servant'. The noun reveals a very interesting pattern of inflection, afford-
ing some more insight into the unfolding of the restructuring process. Although
the weak forms attested in the corpus are traditionally classified as belonging to
a different lemma, the *n*-stem *maga*, all its attestations, i.e. weak and strong, were
taken together here and interpreted as belonging originally to one lemma, i.e. the
u-stem *magu*. The *-an* forms in the paradigm are accordingly interpreted as innovative forms from the *n*-stem declension. Such an approach was considered legitimate

on account of the fact that in the other Germanic languages a corresponding weak noun is not attested (cf. Go. *magus*, ON *mǫgr*).[137] The assumption that all the attested forms belong to one lemma finds a confirmation in the inflectional pattern found in the material: the distribution of weak and strong forms turns out to be nearly complementary, with the singular being dominated by the weak inflections (*maga*) and the plural by the *a*-stem inflections (-*as*). This trend is consistent for both the Early and Late Old English periods. This nearly complementary distribution of competing inflections is illustrated in Table 3.9.

Table 3.9 Distribution of competing inflections in the paradigm of OE *magu*

	u-stem	*n*-stem	*a*-stem
NOM.SG.	35%	65%	0%
GEN.SG.	0%	100%	0%
DAT.SG.	0%	75%	25%
ACC.SG.	15%	85%	0%
NOM.ACC.PL.	1%	3%	97%
GEN.PL.	0%	0%	100%
DAT.PL	0%	0%	100%

The archaic *u*-stem NOM. SG. form *magu* is frequently attested as *mago* in Northumbrian; when used in poetic contexts (Beo) and in the sources not affiliated with Northumbrian, the form is nearly petrified and appears primarily as a fixed formula, e.g. *mago Ebrea, mago Hælfdenes*.

As regards the other nouns belonging to this subgroup, they are attested predominantly in the singular and some of them, including *bregu* (*breogo*) 'prince', *heoru* 'sword', *lagu* 'lake', are found only in the NOM./ACC. SG., which means that the observations about their pattern of inflection are inconclusive (see Hogg & Fulk 2011: 47).

Another characteristic of the light-syllable *u*-stem paradigm is the presence of the effects of extensive *intra*paradigmatic restructuring, manifested in a considerable confusion of vowels in the paradigm of the singular, not attributable to regular phonological developments. It can be seen, for instance, in the paradigm of *wudu* 'wood', where the marker -*u* is found also in the DAT. SG., while the ending -*a* is attested in the ACC. SG. The former has been ascribed to analogy from the NOM./

---

137. The OE form *mæcg* (*mecg) is considered to be a secondary formation based on an original *u*-stem, where the plural is a continuation of *mag-juz to which the ending -*as* was added as a marker of plurality (Bammesberger 1985: 368).

ACC. SG. or PL. (Griepentrog 1995: 125 with reference to *duru*), while the latter must be attributed to the pressure of the GEN./DAT. SG.[138]

The distribution of inherited and analogical inflections in the heavy-syllable *u*-stems attests to a fairly advanced stage of the restructuring. It is at the same time diversified on the lemma level in that certain nouns show a very high level of innovation (e.g. *eard* 'earth' 98%, *færeld* 'journey' 93%, *hearg* 'temple' 77%), while others remain much more archaic (e.g. *ford* 26%, *æppel* 37%, *sumor* 43%,[139]*feld* 52%). The most innovative category is, quite expectedly, the GEN. SG., and the incidence of analogical inflections is also high in the NOM. and ACC. PL. A correlation between the level of innovation and the frequency of occurrence can be observed on two interacting planes: the categorical and the lemma-level. The most innovative category – that of the GEN. SG. is at the same time the least frequent. The DAT. (SG.), which is in general a less common category than the NOM./ACC. (PL.), in this class of nouns turns out to be particularly frequent and, therefore, the level of innovation is lower than it could be expected given its generally lower frequency of use. For instance, lemmas such as *feld*, *ford*, *sumor* and *wald*, which are frequently attested in the DAT. SG. (respectively 43%, 65%, 41% and 50% of all forms), are all archaic in this category, showing the inherited inflection in ca. 80 percent of forms. The fact that the heavy-syllable *u*-stems were so commonly attested in the dative can be explained by recourse to their semantics: many of the *u*-stems are nouns denoting localisation, whether geographical or temporal, and accordingly they can be expected to be used frequently in the dative, which in Old English served to indicate (among other things) location. In other words, the high frequency of occurrence of these nouns in this category can be ascribed to their semantic properties. This correlation is not absolute (e.g. in *wald*, the innovation level in the DAT. SG. is higher, ca. 65%), but it seems to reflect a consistent trend in the restructuring of inflection in the *u*-stems. In the NOM./ACC. PL. the correlation with frequency is also clearly present. The relative frequency of these two categories is lower than expected, but the individual lemma frequencies correlate with the attested levels of innovation. Accordingly, lemmas which are very infrequent in these categories tend to show close to 100 percent of analogical inflections in their plural paradigms (e.g. *ford*, *sumor*, *wald*, *eard*), whereas in lemmas such as *hearg* or *færeld*, which are more often attested in the plural, the amount of innovative inflection in the NOM./ACC. PL. is slightly more moderate, reaching ca. 60 percent.

---

138. Cf. van Helten (1891: 480), who ascribed the ambiguous form of the DAT. SG. *sunu* to syncope of postconsonantal *-i* (*-j*) < **suniu*.

139. The noun is in fact not an original *u*-stem, but shows the *u*-stem inflection on the analogy of *winter* (Campbell 1977: 247).

The divergent tendency in the restructuring of the light- and heavy-syllable stems complies with an observation made by Suzuki (1996) with reference to the *u*-stems, who claims that "in certain morphological categories the inflectional endings otherwise generally employed (e.g. NOM. ACC. PL. ending -*as*) analogically attach to long stems more frequently than to short counterparts – for example, *suna*/(*sunas*) versus *felda*/(*feldas*)" (Suzuki 1996: 303–304). The statement has a more general relevance as can be seen also in the *i*-stems, where the heavy-syllable stems tend to show a less archaic inflectional profile (cf. Section 3.5.2.3). One feature of inflection which contributed to the more archaic shape of the light-syllable paradigm is the presence of final -*u* in the NOM. SG. (absent from heavy-syllable stems). This shape of the NOM. SG. (=ACC. SG.) was distinct from that of all the other masculine stems, and could render these stems more resistant to analogical remodelling on the productive patterns (cf. Lahiri & Dresher 1984: 143).[140] The retention of -*u* in this category, with the later development into -*o*, can be ascribed to a form of "vowel harmony", whereby the ending tended to stay more resistant to analogical levelling (cf. Campbell 1977: 155–156; Brunner 1965: § 44, 271; Luick 1964: § 326.1; see also footnote 111 in this study). Another factor which may have played a role in the preservation of the original inflection was the fact that some of these light-syllable stems, such as *bregu* (*brego*) 'prince, chieftain', or *heoru* 'sword', are words recorded predominantly (or exclusively) in poetic texts, which tend to exhibit greater archaism, and thus, to some extent, a higher level of archaic inflection in their paradigms can be expected. In contrast, the shape of the NOM. SG. of heavy-syllable *u*-stems was in no way different from that of the productive types.

In terms of directions of interparadigmatic transfers, the dominant trend in the *u*-stems was towards the *a*-stems, including the subtype of *wa*-stems. The influence of the latter type is found in the paradigm of *medu*, with the GEN. SG. and NOM. PL. *medewes* and *medewa* (respectively) (by analogy to, for instance, *bearu* 'forest', *bearwes*, *bearwas*) (cf. Campbell 1977: 231–232; Hogg & Fulk 2011: 131). Apart from the indisputable prevalence of the *a*-stem pattern among the analogical inflections, the inflection of the *n*-stems turns out to be relatively widespread, too. Although no quantitative analysis was conducted to estimate the incidence of the *n*-stem inflection relative to the *a*-stem inflection, it could be clearly observed in the examined material that the weak inflectional endings were relatively frequent, especially in the texts of West Saxon provenance. Their influence is well attested in the GEN. PL. (e.g. *applena*, PsGlI, cf. *æpilra*, DurRitGl1, *hergana*, *hærgana*, AldV), as well as occasionally in the ACC. SG. (in *fordan*) (not included in the calculations).

---

140. In fact, the marker -*u* is found also in the small group of *wa*-stems of the type *bearu* 'forest'. Given, however, the limited number of nouns affiliated with this class, their influence in the NOM. SG. of the *u*-stems is considered unlikely here.

The spread of weak inflections in other categories in the paradigm is limited. On the lemma-level, consistent dissemination of the *n*-stem features is attested in *feld* 'field' in the charter material, where alongside the analogical *a*-stem plural *feldas*, the form *feldan* is very frequent.

Another characteristic of the *u*-stems is the presence of some inflectional inconsistencies with respect to gender class affiliation. They are manifested in the appearance of occasional neuter *a*-stem inflections in *appel* 'apple', *færeld* 'journey' and *winter* 'winter', with the NOM./ACC. PL. in -*u*: *applu*, *færeldu* and *wintru*, alongside *applas* and *wintras*, as well as with no marking at all as in *winter*.[141]

Table 3.10 presents the findings from the examination of the light- and heavy-syllable feminine stems. As the feminine *u*-stem paradigms pose considerable interpretative difficulties, the details of the procedure applied for interpreting the attested forms need to be elucidated prior to the presentation of the results. The classification of forms (as archaic, innovative or neutral) was largely dependent on the dialectal provenance of the texts in which the relevant forms were found. Essential for their interpretation was the shape of the NOM./ACC. PL. of the *ō*-stems, which varied depending on the dialect. Accordingly, as in Anglian the expected NOM./ACC. PL. marker of the *ō*-stems was -*e*, the ending -*a* found in the *u*-stems can be unambiguously interpreted as archaic in these dialects, while -*e* must be attributed to the influence of the productive *ō*-stems. However, due to the more extensive confusion of inflections in the Late Old English period, the forms in -*e* attested in Late Anglian had to be excluded. In contrast, in West Saxon and Kentish, where -*a* was the typical marker of the NOM./ACC. PL. in the *ō*-stems (-*e* being attested exclusively in early texts), the ending -*e* must be interpreted as a phonological development of -*a* (ACC. PL.); since both -*e* and -*a* overlap in these dialects with the corresponding markers of the *ō*-stems, these instances had to be excluded from the calculations as well. The occasionally attested forms in -*u* and -*o* (in light-syllable stems), found primarily in the Early Old English texts, were interpreted as archaic. They are a result of analogical reshufflings within the paradigm rather than an effect of any external (interparadigmatic) pressure. As will become clear, the number of plural forms (NOM./ACC.PL.) which could be unambiguously identified as relevant, i.e. classified as archaic or innovative, is in fact very scarce, despite the relative robustness of these two subclasses. The criteria applied in the analysis rendered 542 forms found in the corpus neutral, i.e. ambiguous with respect to the restructuring process (excluding the GEN. and DAT. PL. which in all classes, except the *s*-stems, are not taken into account). Altogether, the feminine forms of the NOM. and ACC. PL.

---

141. Hogg & Fulk (2011: 47) after (Ross 1954: 47) point to some inconsistency in gender class affiliation also in *medu* attested in Lch II (2). The contexts found in the adduced texts in the corpus data do not explicitly attest the presumed neuter gender of this noun.

illustrate very well the fact that the ambiguity of paradigmatic forms (with respect to their interpretation as inherited or analogical) varies depending on the dialect.

As this dialectal distinction was not relevant for the singular, the forms of the GEN. and DAT. SG. in -*e* in feminine stems were interpreted as analogical on account of being consistent across all dialects.[142] Such an approach entails a degree of arbitrariness; however, it was deemed most adequate for the present analysis, especially in light of the widespread dissemination of the ending -*e* as an exponent of the DAT. SG. across various classes (both in feminine and masculine declensions).[143] The distribution of inflections in the light- and heavy-syllable feminine *u*-stems is presented in Table 3.10.

Table 3.10 Distribution of archaic and innovative inflections in the OE light- and heavy-syllable feminine *u*-stems

	Light-syllable				Heavy-syllable			
	archaic		innovative		archaic		innovative	
	SG	PL	SG	PL	SG	PL	SG	PL
NOM.	(56)	(5) 100%	–	(0) 0%	(131)	(13) 100%	–	(0) 0%
GEN.	(7) 87%	(2)	(1) 13%	–	(5) 38%	(104)	(8) 62%	–
DAT.	(106) 83%	(56)	(22) 17%	–	(334) 61%	(296)	(217) 39%	–
ACC.	(143) 97%	(5) 56%	(4) 3%	(4) 44%	(290) 94%	(42) 81%	(20) 6%	(10) 19%
Total	(266) 90%		(31) 10%		(684) 73%		(255) 27%	

The examination of the feminine *u*-stems reveals quite a different picture of the restructuring of inflection than that found in the masculine *u*-stems: the paradigms of both light- and heavy-syllable stems turn out to be noticeably less innovative than the masculine ones, preserving the archaic inflection in the majority of forms. Of the two types of feminine stems, the light-syllable ones, including only two nouns *duru* and *nosu*, quite expectedly, emerge as more conservative. The inherited pattern is well attested in both the singular and the plural, including the otherwise

---

142. The Kentish forms in /æ/ are interpreted as a variant of -*a* and are accordingly classified as archaic in the singular and as neutral in the plural (and consequently excluded due to the overlap with the *ō*-stems).

143. The complex encoding of the *u*-stem inflections in the individual dialects can be summarised as follows:

	archaic	innovative	neutral
GEN.DAT. SG.	-*a*, -*o*, -*u*; K: -*æ*	-*e*, -*n*, -*ø*, other: -*æ*	–
NOM.ACC.PL.	Angl. -*a*, North. -*o*, -*u*	non-Late Angl. -*e*, -*æ*;-*n*, -*as*	WS&K: -*a*, -*e*, -*æ*
			Late Angl: -*e*, -*æ*

usually very innovative GEN. SG. which could be expected to show a higher level of innovation.[144] However, the attested pattern of distribution needs to be interpreted with reference to the fact that many of the original feminine *u*-stem inflections spontaneously overlapped with the feminine *ō*-stem markers, and this overlap had a substantial influence on the developments in the paradigm. It seems feasible, although rather impossible to verify, that the preservation of the original marker *-a* was enhanced by the influence of the identical *ō*-stem marker (in the NOM./ ACC. PL.). Nevertheless, even if all these overlapping forms are considered inconclusive (and excluded from the figures), the overall profile of this subclass remains conservative. The paradigm attests as well to traces of *intra*paradigmatic pressure, which parallels the pattern found in the masculine light-syllable stem paradigm. Considerable confusion of inflectional endings is found especially in the paradigm of *duru*, where the marker *-u* is extended to the DAT. SG.

The heavy-syllable stems show likewise substantial inflectional archaism, which is to be attributed primarily to the frequently attested *hand*, where the level of innovation amounts to 23 percent (24% in the singular and 13% in the plural). The two other nouns, *cweorn* 'hand-mill' and *flōr* 'floor', are substantially more innovative, with the analogical inflections extended in ca. 50 percent of forms. The traces of innovation are concentrated in the GEN. and DAT. SG. The correlation of the attested pattern with frequency of occurrence appears to be relevant here as well, manifesting itself on the level of the lemma and paradigm category. Firstly, the highly frequent *hand* preserves the archaic pattern of inflection, whereas the much less frequently attested *cweorn* and *flōr* tend to follow the productive pattern. Secondly, the very low incidence of the GEN. SG. forms renders this category vulnerable to analogical pressures. The fact that the level of innovation in the GEN. SG. is lower than in the masculine stems indicates that apart from the significance of the frequency factor, also the salience of the inflectional exponent played a crucial role in the remodelling of the paradigms. More specifically, the salience of the masculine *a*-stem marker *-es* was higher than that of the feminine vocalic ending, be it the inherited ending *-a* or analogical *-e* (cf. the discussion in Section 3.6). The spread of the masculine inflections is only sporadically attested in the feminine paradigm, but found already in the Early West-Saxon material (e.g. *flōres*, Bede3).

The major direction of transition of the feminine *u*-stems was to the *ō*-stems, yet some less consistent inclination towards the feminine *n*-stem declension is well attested in both light- and heavy-syllable stems (DAT. SG. *cweornan, duran, (-)flōran, nosan*; ACC. PL. *duran, hændan, nosan*). The influence of the masculine *a*-stem inflection, which could potentially be expected given the expansiveness of the markers *-es* and *-as*, is confined to a few single instances of the GEN. SG. *-es* (*flōres*)

---

144. The singly attested innovative GEN. SG. *dure* is found in early Kentish glosses (OccGl49).

and the NOM./ACC. PL. -as ((helle)flōras). The occasional i-mutated forms dyre and dyru, found in the Late West Saxon material, can be attributed to the analogical influence of the feminine i-stems. Their origin has also been sought in the feminine light-syllable root nouns of the type hnutu - hnyte (Griepentrog 1995: 125; Hogg & Fulk 2011: 47), which seems rather unlikely in view of the marked lack of productivity of this class of nouns in Old English (cf. Section 3.5.4). As the alternation is only occasionally attested, it cannot be interpreted in terms of a general tendency.[145]

Table 3.11 presents the combined distribution of analogical inflections in the masculine and feminine u-stems with respect to individual morphosyntactic categories and irrespective of the syllable weight. Only the categories considered conclusive in the present investigation were included. As in the case of the i-stems, it must be emphasised that the figure showing the overall percentage of innovation represents an aggregated value and should not be interpreted at face value. At the same time, the presented figures are representative of the tendencies observed in the paradigms of the u-stems as attested in the analysed corpus.

Table 3.11 Overall distribution of innovative inflections in the OE u-stems[*]

	% innovative	% innovative
NOM. SG.	(n = 137) 16%	
GEN. SG.	(n = 348) 87%	
DAT. SG.	(n = 1860) 43%	40%
ACC. SG.	(n = 594) 7%	
NOM. PL.	(n = 208) 74%	
ACC. PL.	(n = 409) 69%	71%
Total	45%	

* The NOM. SG. is based on the masculine light-syllable u-stems. Compare the figures in Adamczyk (2010: 378), where the forms of the NOM. SG. in masculine stems were not included in the calculations (64% of analogical forms in the u-stem paradigm).

The pattern furnished by the data, with 45 percent of analogical inflectional forms present in the u-stem paradigms, indicates that the reorganisation of the u-stems was fairly advanced. The distribution of archaic and innovative inflectional endings is quite divergent for the singular and the plural, the latter tending to be significantly more innovative. The GEN. SG., quite expectedly, emerges as the most innovative morphosyntactic category. This high level of innovation can be ascribed to an

---

145. In the present study the shape of the root was not decisive for the classification of forms as archaic or innovative (but cf. root nouns, Section 3.5.4.1). An additional complication in interpreting the attestations of the noun duru is that in many cases it is impossible to decide whether a given form (duru, dura) is a singular or a plural, which renders the interpretation somewhat arbitrary (cf. Griepentrog 1995: 125).

interaction of two factors: the low frequency of occurrence of forms in this category and the strong salience of the competing productive masculine inflectional marker. In the other categories, the persistent correlation with frequency turns out to be the decisive factor, largely accounting for the attested levels of innovative inflection. This is particularly prominent in the DAT. SG. where the relatively limited amount of analogical inflection can be explained by the high frequency of forms in this category, characteristic of the *u*-stems on account of their semantics (cf. the discussion above). The combined figures for the plural obliterate the significant discrepancy in the level of innovation found in the masculine and feminine stems. While the former tend to follow the *a*-stem pattern in close to 80 percent of forms (90% and 72% in light- and heavy-syllable stems, respectively), the latter remain resistant to analogical pressure, retaining the inherited pattern in most of the attested forms (cf. Tables 3.8 and 3.10). The factor decisive for such a distribution seems to be the salience of the inflectional exponents in these two categories, distinctly different for the masculine and feminine stems. An aspect which may have partly contributed to the attested distribution may also be the methodological choice made as to the interpretation of the inflections in these two categories in the feminine stems, whereby the forms in -*a* are considered to be inconclusive (in West Saxon), or inherited, despite their formal overlap with the *ō*-stem forms (in Anglian) (cf. footnote 143). Most of the plural forms in feminine light- and heavy-syllable stems identified in the corpus had to be excluded from the calculation as they consistently overlapped with the inflections of the *ō*-stems.

The findings of the present study clearly depart from the descriptions of this declension in the traditional grammars of Old English, where, on the one hand, classical (Early Old English) paradigms are presented, while, on the other, the class is consistently recognised as being extensively affected by analogical developments. Admittedly, if only those forms which explicitly differ from the *a*- or *ō*-stems were interpreted as archaic (which was apparently the procedure applied in the earlier accounts), the level of innovation in the paradigms of the *u*-stems would be higher, since all the spontaneously overlapping forms would count accordingly as innovative. Such an approach may be referred to as a "narrow interpretation", and if applied, it would arrive at a substantially disintegrated *u*-stem paradigm. The disintegration would accordingly involve a spontaneous merger of certain paradigmatic forms with those of the dominant declensions (especially in the Late Old English period where the confusion of the unaccented vowels was advanced). In the methodological approach adopted in the present study, which can be designated here as a "broad interpretation", these overlapping forms were arbitrarily counted as inherited. This refers in particular to the NOM./ACC. PL. of feminine nouns, where the marker -*a* spontaneously overlaps with the *ō*-stem marker. The attested relatively high level of archaism of the *u*-stem paradigm, even if the overlapping forms are excluded, allows one to claim that these forms (despite the formal overlap) were most likely a continuation of the original pattern and thus can be classified as archaic. It seems conceivable that the formal overlap of these forms with the corresponding ō-stem inflections enhanced their status as exponents of the plural inflection in the *u*-stems, rendering them more stable and resistant to analogical pressure (e.g. from the *n*-stems) during most of the Old English period, until the moment when they were affected by phonological reduction processes (in Late Old English).

Some further insight into the restructuring of the *u*-stem inflection can be gained by focusing on the diachronic and dialectal distribution of analogical inflections in the paradigms, presented in Tables 3.12 and 3.13. Table 3.14 depicts the combined results for the two periods in the two investigated groups of dialects, allowing us to separate the tendencies which must be ascribed purely to dialectal and diachronic conditions.

Table 3.12 Diachronic distribution of innovative inflections in the OE *u*-stems

	Innovative inflection		
	SG	PL	Overall
Early Old English	(*n* = 370) 27%	(*n* = 95) 57%	(*n* = 465) 33%
Late Old English	(*n* = 1826) 47%	(*n* = 384) 75%	(*n* = 2210) 52%

The pattern in the analysed data is transparent and expected, testifying to a progressive increase in analogical inflections in the *u*-stem paradigm over time. This refers to both the singular and plural paradigms, with the plural showing a higher level of innovation in both periods. The earliest innovative endings can be found sporadically in the ninth-century interlinear glosses (the early Mercian *Vespasian Psalter*), West-Saxon *Pastoral Care* (9th/10th c.), *Junius Psalter* (PsGlB), *Regius Psalter* (PsGlD), or *Orosius* (9th/10th c.), and the percentage of analogical inflections increases in the texts dated to the tenth century (including the Anglian material, e.g. LkGl(Ru)). The Late West Saxon texts, especially the *Worcester Chronicle* (ChronD, mid-11th c.), *Peterborough Chronicle* (ChronE, 12th c.) and the *Lambeth Psalter* (PsGlI, 11th c.) show the highest percentage of analogical forms in the paradigms of the *u*-stems.

Table 3.13 Dialectal distribution of innovative inflections in the OE *u*-stems

	Innovative inflection		
	SG	PL	Overall
Anglian	(*n* = 176) 24%	(*n* = 88) 14%	(*n* = 264) 21%
Saxon	(*n* = 2559) 41%	(*n* = 487) 82%	(*n* = 3046) 47%

The Anglian material turns out to be significantly less innovative with respect to the reorganisation of the nominal inflection in the *u*-stems than the Saxon data. The difference is particularly manifest in the plural, but a largely parallel pattern is attested also in the singular. It can be concluded that while in Anglian the *u*-stem paradigm preserved a distinct inflectional profile, with a very limited amount of analogical inflection, in the Saxon dialects it was more extensively remodelled on the productive inflectional patterns. Table 3.14 illustrates to what extent the archaism of Anglian and the innovativeness of the Saxon dialects is to be attributed to the attestation dates of the texts affiliated with the respective dialects.

Table 3.14 Distribution of innovative forms in the OE *u*-stems with respect to dialect *and* period

period/dialect	Saxon	Anglian
Early	(*n* = 342) 41%	(*n* = 105) 10%
Late	(*n* = 2063) 53%	(*n* = 102) 36%

As can be seen, irrespective of the period, the Anglian paradigm shows greater conservatism than the Saxon paradigm, although this discrepancy decreases in the later period. The Early stage of Anglian comprises primarily Mercian glosses (dated to ca. 9th c.), whose morphological conservatism is widely recognised. Overall, the corpus data testify to a gradual dissemination of the analogical forms in the *u*-stems in both the Anglian and the Saxon material.

To conclude, the examination of the extant data revealed that the *u*-stem paradigm was significantly affected by analogical realignments. The spread of the productive inflections is well substantiated by the paradigm of the heavy-syllable nouns, whereas the light-syllable stems tend to be more resistant to the innovative inflection. Of significance is the fact that the class contained a number of high frequency items (such as *hand*, *winter* or *sunu*), which tend to be inflectionally more conservative than the low frequency items. This seems to be particularly prominent in the inflectional pattern of *sunu*, where the innovation level reaches no more than 7 percent (Section 3.5.3.3), as well as in *hand* attesting to 16 percent of analogical inflections in the paradigm. The incidence of analogical forms in the paradigms, apart from being largely dependent on the frequency of occurrence operating at different levels, was also determined by factors such as the salience of inflectional exponents, syllable weight, as well as the semantic profile of the class, or of individual lemmas, closely correlated with the frequency profiles. Another factor which emerges as relevant in the reorganisation of the *u*-stems is the functional strength of the inflectional markers. As in the case of the *i*-stems, the substitution of the analogical ending -*as* for the inherited -*a* in masculine stems can be viewed as a factor permitting to keep the distinction between the singular and plural. Given that the confusion of back vowels resulted in inconsistency in the paradigm of the *u*-stems (e.g. the NOM. SG. *sunu ~ suno ~ suna* vs. NOM. PL. *suna ~ suno ~ sunu*, etc.), it seems likely that the introduction of a distinct plural marker *-as* allowed the retention of the contrast in number. Such an interpretation allows one to view the operation of analogical processes in the minor vocalic classes (*i*-stems and *u*-stems) as encouraged by the need to mark the functional distinction between the singular and the plural.

The restructuring of the *u*-stem declension illustrates not only the complexity of the process, manifested in the interplay of the effects of phonological and morphological developments in the paradigm, but also the methodological problems involved in the analysis of the process, in particular the choices which have to be made to offer a consistent interpretation and account of the process.

3.5.3.3   *An excursus on* sunu

Given the remarkably high frequency of the OE *sunu*, the results obtained from its analysis were excluded from the figures presented in the previous section in order to avoid skewing the overall results for the *u*-stems and thus obliterating tendencies otherwise observable in the data. The examination of inflections in the paradigm of *sunu* revealed that the inherited pattern is remarkably well preserved, both in the singular and plural. Even if the categories of the NOM./ACC. SG. are excluded, the overall level of innovation amounts to 6 percent.[146] The attested pattern complies with the more general tendency which could be observed in the light-syllable masculine *u*-stems, where the spread of analogical inflections was limited. An essential factor responsible for the conservative profile of *sunu* is its high (token) frequency, coupled with its semantic properties. As a kinship term, *sunu* must have been frequent in use and was thus reluctant to change its paradigmatic affiliation. A parallel tendency can be observed in the Old English *r*-stems, i.e. nouns of relationship, which when compared to other minor paradigms exhibit a higher level of inflectional conservatism (cf. Section 3.5.5.2). The infrequent traces of analogical inflections in the paradigm of *sunu* are often built on the *n*-stem pattern, which can be seen especially in the later sources (e.g. NOM./ACC.PL. *sunan*, Rec 2.3 (Earle), ChronE, 12th c.), GEN. PL. *sunana* (MtHeadGl (Li), 10th c.). The appearance of the analogical NOM. SG. ending *-a* as a result of the *intra*paradigmatic reshufflings, and its formal overlap with the masculine *n*-stems (of the type *guma*), may

---

146. The figures for the amount of innovation in individual categories are the following: GEN. SG. 5% (*n* = 227), DAT. SG. 9% (*n* = 342), NOM. PL. 7% (*n* = 330), ACC.PL. 4% (*n* = 204). All these figures come from a separate study presented in Adamczyk (2010: 379–380), where the NOM. SG. was not considered as informative about the pattern of restructuring (cf. Krygier 2004).

have facilitated the encroachment of the weak inflectional endings in the paradigm (Brunner 1965: 229). In the longer perspective, the radical changes affecting the unaccented back vowels in the Late Old English period brought about a confusion of inflections in the paradigm of *sunu*, eventually facilitating its submission to the pressure of the *n*-stems and *a*-stems at a later stage, i.e. in Middle English (cf. the development of the paradigm in the Middle English period where the noun is attested predominantly as *-es* plural, but as *-en* plural in the Southwest: NEM *suness* (Orm.), NWM *sunez*, SWM *sones*, SW *sunen*, SE *zones*; Wełna 1996: 86–88).

3.5.4 Root nouns

3.5.4.1 *General characteristics*
The root noun declension comprised masculine and feminine nouns which in Proto-Germanic did not contain a thematic element (stem formative), but attached the inflectional ending directly to the root. This fact determined their behaviour with respect to some phonological processes, in particular *i*-mutation, which consequently had a different effect here than in the classes where the thematic vowel was present. The masculine and feminine nouns are assumed to have followed originally (in Proto-Germanic) an identical pattern of inflection. At a later stage, however, the original common paradigm was differentiated and, accordingly, the Old English material testifies to the existence of two similar, yet distinct inflectional patterns for the masculine and feminine nouns. Of the two subgroups, the feminine nouns are substantially better preserved in Old English (just as they are in the other Germanic languages).[147]

From a synchronic Old English perspective, the class-defining criterion is the presence of an *i*-mutated vowel as a case-and-number exponent in the DAT. SG. and the NOM./ACC. PL. The mutated vowel emerging from the impact of the Proto-Germanic inflectional **-i* (obscured prior to the first written attestations of English) assumed the function of earlier inflectional endings in the paradigm,

---

147. The only potential relic of the Germanic neuter inflection (whose status is not uncontroversial) is the Old English form *scrūd* 'garment', which can arguably be traced back to a PIE formation in **-t-* (> PGmc. **-d-*) (Brunner 1965: 236; Bammesberger 1990: 188; cf. Campbell 1977: 252; Nielsen 1985: 107–108). Its identity as a root noun is based on a single attestation of the *i*-mutated form *scrȳd*; otherwise, the noun declines as a neuter *a*-stem, with the endingless, unmutated NOM./ACC. PL. *scrūd*. The *i*-mutated form is attested in the Salisbury Psalter gloss (late 10th c.): *Todǽldan heom scryd min & ofer hrægel min hi sendon hlot* (PsGlK) ('They divided my clothes among themselves and over my robe threw dice'). Given, however, that the form is attested as *scrūd* in a parallel text (PsGlI (Lindelöf)), the *i*-mutated variant can well be attributed to a spelling variation or scribal error (Hogg & Fulk 2011: 10; cf. Griepentrog 1995: 490).

eventually becoming the exponent of plurality in this declensional class. A closely related inflectional property of the historical root noun paradigm, shared with the other minor consonantal declensions (*r*-stems, *s*-stems, *nd*-stems and dental stems) is the lack of inflectional suffixes in the singular, except in the GEN. SG. of masculine nouns, where the marker *-es* attests to an early extension of the productive inflection. Another characteristic of this declensional class is related to its quantitative profile, marked by low type frequency and high token frequency: the number of root nouns was relatively small (25 nouns altogether), but many of them were characterised by high frequency of occurrence (e.g. *mann* 'man', *bōc* book', *burh* 'town'). The latter, i.e. the high token frequency, can be viewed as a factor critical for the retention of the original inflectional pattern in these nouns in the plural (e.g. Hogg 1997a: 106; Adamczyk 2014; see also the discussion in Section 3.6). All of these formal features of the root noun paradigm are significant in the context of morphological restructuring, functioning as factors enhancing or inhibiting the activity of analogical processes in the paradigm.

Although the present study focuses on the historical stage of the restructuring of the Old English nominal inflection, the activity of analogical processes in the paradigm of root nouns can be dated to the prehistoric period, since many nouns originating in this paradigm decline consistently as *a*-stems or *i*-stems (e.g. *brēast* 'breast', *sōþ* 'truth', *spyrd* 'course'; cf. Appendix for a complete list). The overlapping NOM. SG. forms in the historical *a*-stems, *ō*-stems, *u*-stems and root nouns (with the marker *-u* in the light-syllable stems and zero marker in the heavy-syllable stems) may have been a factor facilitating analogical reshufflings in the root nouns (as was the case in the heavy-syllable *i*-stems and *u*-stems). The reorganisation of the inflection of root nouns in the Old English period involved the analogical transition of nouns to two major declensional classes, i.e. the masculine *a*-stems and feminine *ō*-stems. As it was the case in the two investigated vocalic classes, root nouns can be expected to show some inclination towards the *n*-stem inflection, manifested especially in the extension of the GEN. PL. marker *-ena* (*-ana*) and the NOM./ACC. PL. ending *-an* (occasionally *-on*/*-en*). These potential inflectional irregularities resulting from the analogical influence of the productive inflections may appear in the following morphosyntactic categories:

a.   masculine root nouns
  –   the GEN. SG. *a*-stem marker *-es* in place of the original endingless (occasionally *i*-mutated) form
  –   the DAT. SG. *a*-stem marker *-e* in place of the original *i*-mutated endingless form
  –   the NOM./ACC. PL. *a*-stem ending *-as* in place of the original *i*-mutated endingless form

b. feminine root nouns
    –   the GEN. SG. *ō*-stem marker *-e* (or alternatively the masculine marker *-es*) in place of the original endingless form (heavy-syllable root nouns)
    –   the DAT. SG. marker *-e* in place of the original endingless *i*-mutated form (heavy-syllable root nouns)
    –   the ACC. SG. *ō*-stem marker *-e* in place of the endingless form (heavy-syllable root nouns)
    –   the NOM./ACC. PL. *ō*-stem ending *-a/-e*, alternatively the *a*-stem marker *-as*, in place of the *i*-mutated endingless form (heavy-syllable root nouns)
    –   the NOM. SG. ending *-u* in place of the etymological zero ending (light-syllable)
    –   the elimination of the *i*-mutated vowel in light-syllable root nouns in the GEN., DAT. SG. and NOM./ACC. PL.

The potential traces of these morphological realignments which are expected to be found in the course of the investigation of the Old English material are summarised in Table 3.15 (masculine *tōþ* 'tooth' and feminine *bōc* 'book').

Table 3.15 The competing inflections in the OE masculine and feminine root nouns

	masculine				feminine			
	archaic		innovative		archaic		innovative	
	SG	PL	SG	PL	SG	PL	SG	PL
NOM.	*tōþ*	*tēþ*	*tōþ*	*tōþas*	*bōc*	*bēc*	*bōc*	*bōce, -a(n)*
GEN.	*tēþ*	*tōþa*	*tōþes*	*tōþa, -ena*	*bēc*	*bōca*	*bōce,-an*	*bōca, -ena*
DAT.	*tēþ*	*tōþum*	*tōþe*	*tōþum*	*bēc*	*bōcum*	*bōce,-an*	*bōcum*
ACC.	*tōþ*	*tēþ*	*tōþ*	*tōþas*	*bōc*	*bēc*	*bōce,-an*	*bōce, -a(n)*

The inflectional endings which can be viewed as a regular phonological develop-ment from Proto-Germanic are the *i*-mutated forms of the NOM. PL. and DAT. SG. The *i*-mutated form of the ACC. PL. is an effect of *intra*paradigmatic analogy, whereby the mutated vowel was extended from the NOM. PL. (Boutkan 1995: 261). The orig-inal PGmc. inflectional ending of the DAT. SG. continues as *-e* in the light-syllable (feminine) paradigm, but is absent from heavy-syllable nouns, where its earlier existence is signalled by the presence of an *i*-mutated vowel in the root. Likewise, the NOM. PL. ending *-e*, preserved in light-syllable formations (extended also to the ACC. PL.), is interpreted here as a relic of the original PGmc. ending **-ez > (*-iz)* rather than as an innovation (Bammesberger 1990: 193). The forms of the GEN. and DAT. PL., which can be viewed either as a continuation of the original paradigm, or as analogical formations based on the pattern furnished by the *a*-stems (Campbell 1977: 252–253, cf. Bammesberger 1984: 23), are considered neutral, as due to their formal overlap with the corresponding forms in the productive classes, they cannot be informative about the restructuring. The GEN. PL. forms in -*ena* constitute compelling evidence for the presence of analogical pressure from the *n*-stem inflection; however, owing to a lack of an unambiguous archaic form they were not included in the calculations in the present study.

A considerable interpretative challenge in the context of the restructuring process is posed by inflections in the light-syllable paradigm. The NOM. SG. marker -*u* preserved therein can arguably be interpreted as a residue of the original pattern (van Helten 1911: 510; Bammesberger 1984: 23). Alternatively, the ending can be attributed to an analogical influence of the feminine *ō*-stems (cf. *faru* 'journey') or *u*-stems (cf. *duru* 'door') (Campbell 1977: 252; Brunner 1965: 236; Bertacca 2009: 35). Boutkan (1996: 260; after Prokosch 1939: 257) postulates two potential sources for the NOM. SG. forms in -*u*, both analogical, namely: (a) the analogical extension of the feminine *ō*-stem pattern, and (b) the intraparadigmatic shift from the ACC. SG., where -*u* is the historically expected inflection. Given the reconstructed shape of the root noun paradigm (Section 2.2.3.3) and the attestations of a few isolated *endingless* NOM. SG. forms in Early Old English glosses, the interpretation of the ending -*u* as analogical was considered more feasible and thus adopted in the present study. The origin of the ACC. SG. marker -*u* is less problematic, as it has been commonly recognised as a regular phonological development of the PGmc. form (*-*u^n*) (hence interpreted here as archaic). The original inflections in the other relevant categories (i.e. the GEN. DAT. SG. and NOM./ACC. PL.) entirely overlap with the endings of the feminine *ō*-stems, except that in the original root noun forms an *i*-mutated root vowel can be expected.[148] Accordingly, the presence or absence of a mutated root vowel was considered the primary criterion for identifying these forms as archaic or innovative in this subclass. It must be observed that this small subclass of root nouns is the only declension where the shape of the root was taken as the major diagnostic criterion for estimating the level of innovation in the paradigm.

The fairly frequently attested unmutated forms of the DAT. SG. and NOM./ACC. PL. (especially *neaht* 'night' alongside *nieht*), which do not attach any novel inflectional markers, common especially in Late Old English texts, are not interpreted as *innovative* in the present analysis. The forms are clearly analogical, but emerge as a result of the *intra*paradigmatic rather than *inter*paradigmatic influence, i.e., the internal pressure of other (unmutated) case forms in the paradigm. The presence of this intraparadigmatic analogy is closely linked to the process of the disintegration of the original case marking system, dated before the beginning of the eleventh century, and well attested in the Late Old English material (Hogg 1997a: 106–107).

---

148. The overlap in the NOM./ACC. PL. refers to non-West Saxon forms only, where the *ō*-stems surfaced with -*e* as a marker of plurality; in West Saxon the standard ending in these cases was -*a*.

3.5.4.2 *Results of the investigation*

For the sake of capturing the fine details of inflectional reorganisation in this de-clensional class, the masculine and feminine root nouns were investigated sepa-rately, as were the light- and heavy-syllable subtypes. Given the compelling evidence from the other minor paradigms (*i*-stems and *u*-stems), where the heavy-syllable stems tended to succumb to the impact of analogical developments more easily and earlier than the light-syllable stems, one could expect the syllable weight to have had some bearing on the pattern of the spread of analogical inflections in the root nouns as well. The results of the investigation in masculine root nouns and feminine light- and heavy-syllable root nouns are presented consecutively in Tables 3.16, 3.17 and 3.18.[149]

Table 3.16 Distribution of archaic and innovative inflections in the OE masculine root nouns

	archaic		innovative	
	SG	PL	SG	PL
NOM.	(*157*)	(*167*) 95%	–	(8) 5%
GEN.	(1) 5%	(*199*)	(21) 95%	–
DAT.	(53) 82%	(*579*)	(12) 18%	–
ACC.	(*100*)	(494) 97%	–	(13) 3%
Total	(715) 93%		(54) 7%	

The historical root noun inflection turns out to be very well preserved in the para-digm of masculine nouns. The distribution patterns of analogical inflections do not follow the singular/plural division, but rather spread across the morphosyntactic categories. While the DAT. SG. and NOM. ACC. PL. remain remarkably conservative, the GEN. SG. is attested almost exclusively with the innovative marker -*es*, extended from the *a*-stem declension.[150] Accordingly, the level of innovation in the singular,

---

149. The figures for the masculine nouns exclude the occurrences of *mann* whose token frequency was much higher than the frequencies of the other nouns subject to the analysis, and their inclusion would be likely to skew the results for this class. For the two other frequent nouns, *burh* and *neaht*, the figures include all the occurrences found in texts labelled as *Early* and *Indeterminate*, while the attestations labelled as *Late* were limited to samples of ca. 1000 occurrences.

150. The singly attested form of the GEN. SG. (in: *Gyf þu swyftleras habban wylle, þonne sete þu þinne scytefinger uppon þinne fot and stric on twa healfa þines fet þam gemete þe hi gesceapene beoð* (Notes2) (*Monasterialia indicia*, Kluge 1885)) is ambiguous. The form is unusual given its late attestation date, i.e. mid-11th c. The interpretation as archaic is based on the Kluge's edition (1885) of the text, where the form shows an *i*-mutated vowel; it cannot be excluded that a refer-ence back to the manuscript (Cotton Tiberius A. iii) could give a different reading (M. Krygier, personal communication).

amounting to 38 percent, relies primarily on this category, which, as demonstrated also in the other declensional classes, was most easily and earliest affected by analogical pressures. The attested distribution of inflections in the paradigm shows a clear correlation with both the salience of the inflectional exponents, and with the frequency of occurrence. The former refers to the presence of the root vowel alternation (*i*-mutated vowel in the DAT. SG. and NOM./ACC. PL.), which was one of the most salient types of inflectional markers in Germanic (Section 1.4.6.2). With reference to the latter factor, it can be observed that the generally highly frequent NOM. and ACC. (PL.) continue the inherited pattern of inflection, whereas the GEN. and DAT. (SG.), being cases typified in general by lower frequency, tend to show a higher level of innovation. In the DAT. SG., which is still relatively archaic, frequency clearly interacts with the salience of the inflectional exponent, i.e. the *i*-mutated vowel, and their interaction turns out to have a neutralising effect (cf. Section 3.6). The overall conservative profile of this class must also be attributed to the fact that the nouns are attested predominantly in the plural, which is represented by the two highly frequent cases (NOM./ACC.), both characterised by a distinctive marker. The majority of the analogical forms which were identified in the paradigms of the masculine root nouns come from the *a*-stems, and only occasional traces of the *n*-stem inflection are attested in the GEN. PL. (in *-ana*), as well as in the ACC. PL. (in *-an*, e.g. *toðane, fotan*).

Table 3.17 Distribution of archaic and innovative inflections in the OE light-syllable feminine root nouns

	archaic		innovative	
	SG	PL	SG	PL
NOM.	(4) 13%	(2) 67%	(26) 87%	(1) 33%
GEN.	(1) 50%	*(6)*	(1) 50%	–
DAT.	(8) 67%	*(4)*	(4) 33%	–
ACC.	(8) 89%	(10) 91%	(1) 11%	(1) 9%
Total		(33) 49%		(34) 51%

As mentioned earlier, the interpretation of the patterns of restructuring of inflection in this subclass of root nouns is largely complicated by a lack of etymological transparency, i.e. ambiguity as to which forms should be interpreted as truly archaic and which as innovative. When compared to the masculine root nouns, the light-syllable feminines emerge as relatively innovative. The analogical inflections are concentrated in the NOM. SG., where the novel forms in *-u* compete with the endingless forms, which are assumed to continue the original inflection (*fēurstud, fērstud* 'buttress', *sweorhnit (suernit)* 'neck-nit', *durustod* 'pillar'). According to

Hogg & Fulk (2011: 68), the endingless forms are a result of apocope rather than a continuation of the original inflectional pattern. The major problem with this phonological interpretation and an argument in favour of treating them as inherited is the early attestation date of the sources in which these forms are found, i.e. the eighth century (ErfGl(2), CollGl(3)). An exception is the form *durustod* (*dorstod*) (ClGl1), attested later (mid-10th c.), and its status as an original form may indeed be disputed. If this problematic category of the NOM. SG. is excluded from the calculation, the level of innovation in the singular decreases to 22 percent. The other categories in the paradigm point to a limited dissemination of analogical inflections; however, the figures are altogether extremely low and the patterns found in the data must be evaluated with much caution. The novel forms are characterised by a lack of the *i*-mutated vowel in the root and occasionally a distinctive inflectional ending. The presence or absence of the *i*-mutated vowel is considered informative here, as it served as a systematic marker of inflection in this class of nouns; without this feature, the inflectional endings are ambiguous as they overlap with the endings of the productive ō-stems (e.g. GEN. SG. -*hnyte* vs. -*hnute* 'nut', DAT. SG. *styde* vs. *studa*, *stude* 'place', NOM./ACC. PL. *styde* vs. *stuðe*). This shape of the light-syllable paradigm, with a systematic overlap of inflections, must have been one of the factors which facilitated analogical developments in this declensional subclass, rendering it more vulnerable to the pressure of other inflectional types. It is worth noting that the dominant ending in the GEN. PL. is the weak marker -*ena*, attested in the Early Mercian (*eorðnutena*, Ch 216 (Birch 541)) and Late West-Saxon texts ((*pin-*) *hnutena*, PeriD, PsGlF). The predominance of this pattern may be, however, fortuitous, given the low number of attestations in this class, or may be a lemma-specific feature, as most of these forms belong to *hnut* (one of them to the formally similar *hnit* 'nit': *nitenu*).

As the group of heavy-syllable feminine nouns is very well attested in the corpus, containing several high frequency lemmas, the dynamics of the process of morphological restructuring can be well captured in their paradigms (see Table 3.18).

Table 3.18 Distribution of archaic and innovative inflections in the OE heavy-syllable feminine root nouns

	archaic		innovative	
	SG	PL	SG	PL
NOM.	(*745*)	(*240*) 94%	–	(14) 6%
GEN.	(82) 18%	(*262*)	(377) 82%	–
DAT.	(1227) 74%	(*671*)	(421) 26%	–
ACC.	(897) 97%	(351) 90%	(26) 3%	(40) 10%
Total	(2797) 76%		(878) 24%	

The paradigm testifies primarily to the analogical spread of the ō-stem inflections, but traces of the *a*-stem pattern are also attested, especially in the GEN. SG. (*-es*) and occasionally in the NOM./ACC. PL. The pattern closely resembles that found in the masculine root nouns in that the plural remains much more archaic than the singular, with the overall level of innovation amounting to 8 percent. The higher percentage of analogical forms in the singular (27%) is generated primarily by the GEN., which is the most innovative category in the paradigm, with analogical forms, be they feminine (e.g. *bōce*, *cue*) or masculine (e.g. *sules*, *burhges*), reaching over 80 percent. The archaic, i.e. endingless, forms are frequently attested without the *i*-mutated vowel in this category. It is disputable whether *i*-mutation was an original feature of inflection in the GEN. SG. (e.g. Boutkan 1996: 260–261; Ringe 2006: 280; Hogg & Fulk 2011: 67). The corpus distribution of forms in this category indicates that the *i*-mutated forms constituted only 16 percent and 17 percent of all forms in the Early and Late period, respectively. These low figures, however, do not necessarily speak in favour of the original absence of *i*-mutation, as the attested unmutated forms can be attributed to the activity of intraparadigmatic analogy, which worked against *i*-mutated forms in the paradigm. Some limited inclination towards the inflection of the *a*-stems (*-e*) is attested also in the DAT. SG., where the level of innovation reaches 26 percent, whereas the other categories, i.e. the ACC. SG. and NOM./ACC.PL. remain remarkably resistant to analogical pressures.

As with the masculine root nouns, the restructuring of the feminine paradigm appears to be guided by two factors: the token frequency of paradigm forms, combined with the salience of inflectional exponents. The original pattern of inflection is well retained in the relatively frequent NOM./ACC. PL., characterised originally by the *i*-mutated root vowel, as well as in the ACC. SG., which although not distinctly marked by *i*-mutation, is a very frequent category. The relatively low percentage of innovation in the DAT. SG. can be ascribed to both the consistent presence of the *i*-mutated root vowel and the exceptionally high frequency of occurrence of forms in this category (especially in *neaht* 'night' and *burg* 'town', where the DAT. SG. constitutes respectively 42 percent and 48 percent of all the forms in the paradigm). However, a closer look at the paradigms of individual lemmas reveals some further correlations, so other potential factors need to be considered when interpreting the findings. Accordingly, *neaht* and *meolc* 'milk' show a surprisingly high level of innovation in the DAT. SG. (51% and 95% respectively), which especially for *neaht* is not the expected outcome, given that the noun is frequently attested in this category. The morpho-phonological shape of these nouns, namely, the presence of *i*-mutation-alternation in the paradigm, seems to account for the attested pattern. In the case of *meolc* the reason for the absence of this morphophonemic alternation is purely phonological: the root vowel was not subject to *i*-mutation; in the case of *neaht*, the situation is more complex as the vowel could be mutated, but the paradigm was subject to internal analogical pressures (intraparadigmatic levelling), which rendered its shape inconsistent. Namely, alongside the form *neaht*, the *i*-mutated *niht* is frequently attested in the corpus, also in the category of the NOM. SG. This mutated form, originally proper only to oblique cases, was generalised throughout the paradigm, including the NOM. SG. (cf. Roedler 1916: 430). Consequently, the oblique cases could not be formally distinguished from the NOM. SG. by *i*-mutation, which led to analogical developments in the paradigm. In fact, the intraparadigmatic levelling, entailing the spread of the *i*-mutated forms throughout the paradigm, turns out to have been a more general phenomenon. It is attested also in the paradigms of other lemmas, including *āc* 'oak' (ACC. SG. *ǣc*) and *burg* (*byrig*), and at a later stage *brōc* 'breech', in which the *i*-mutated variant became eventually the basic paradigm form (PDE *breech*). In all these lemmas, *i*-mutation was, consequently, no longer distinctive (thus no longer a salient feature) and did not provide any protection from interparadigmatic analogical levelling, which rendered these nouns more susceptible to external pressures.

Another pattern which can be observed in the analysed data is the frequent attestation of the masculine GEN. SG. marker *-es* in the paradigm of feminine *neaht* (almost 100 percent of all the attested forms). The pattern is an idiosyncratic, lemma-specific development and may be attributed to the direct influence of the masculine *a*-stem *dæg*, with which *neaht* stays in a semantic relation when used in an adverbial function. Its frequent attestation in the collocation: *dæges and nihtes* (cf. OHG GEN. SG. *nahtes*; Go. *dagam jah nahtam* in place of the expected **nahtim*; Wright 1957: 103), found as early as in the text of *Vespasian Psalter* (PsGlA) (9th c.), must have triggered or at least furthered the extension of this inflectional marker.[151] At the same time, the corpus data clearly testify to the dissemination of the feminine *ō*-stem inflection in the GEN. SG. as well. The spread of the innovative DAT. SG. marker *-e* in this lemma (amounting to 51%) may have been enhanced by the presence of the masculine GEN. SG. marker and the formal identification of the paradigm with the masculine *a*-stem pattern, with 90 percent of ACC. forms remaining endingless, i.e. unaffected by the feminine *ō*-stem pattern, but rather imitating the masculine *a*-stem pattern (*neaht – neahtes – neahte – neaht*). The restructuring of the paradigm of *neaht* testifies to an interaction of a number of factors involved in the process, illustrating its complexity. It shows as well that these factors could work in a synergetic or neutralising way, enhancing or moderating the effects of their combined activity.

---

151. The pattern instantiates the rarely found, *immediate* model of analogy, where the two elements, the one exerting influence and the one being influenced, stay in direct proximity ("the same speech context") and their incidence as a phrase is frequent (Campbell 2004: 111).

The investigation of the root noun paradigms points to an evident discrepancy in the pattern of the spread of analogical inflections with respect to the weight of the root. The comparison of the data in Tables 3.17 and 3.18 allows one to conclude, somewhat superficially, that the heavy-syllable stem feminine paradigm turned out to be more resistant to the pressure of analogy. This situation is to some extent unexpected, given that in the *i*-stems and *u*-stems, the heavy-syllable stems tended to succumb to the impact of analogical developments more easily and earlier than the light-syllable stems. On closer inspection, it becomes clear that the innovativeness of the light-syllable stems is based essentially on the (controversial) NOM. SG., and it is precisely this category that cannot provide any reliable information about the restructuring process in the heavy-syllable stems (cf. Table 3.18). It can be concluded, accordingly, that stem/root weight in this class did matter in the sense that the pattern of retention of archaic features is discrepant for the two subgroups. Still, it cannot be viewed as a significant factor in the restructuring process in this class: there is no principled difference when it comes to weight-dependent bias to innovation, because the discrepancy is due to a category (NOM. SG.) which is inconclusive for the heavy-syllable stems. At the same time, observe that the masculine root nouns, which turned out to be the most conservative subclass, happened also to be heavy-syllable nouns. Again, a recourse to frequency of occurrence seems to bring some additional explanation for the attested distribution of forms. The data show a clear correlation with lemma token frequencies, which in this class were much lower for the light-syllable nouns than for most of the heavy-syllable ones. The more conservative inflectional profile of the latter, being largely a result of their high frequency of occurrence (on the lemma level), could accordingly be expected.

Table 3.19 depicts the overall distribution of analogical inflections in the root noun paradigm in the relevant (case/number) categories across all paradigms (excluding the problematic NOM. SG. in light-syllable feminines).

Table 3.19 Overall distribution of innovative inflections in the OE root nouns

	% innovative	% innovative
GEN. SG.	($n = 483$) 83%	
DAT. SG.	($n = 1725$) 25%	27%
ACC. SG.	($n = 932$) 3%	
NOM. PL.	($n = 433$) 5%	6%
ACC. PL.	($n = 911$) 6%	
Total		21%

As the data indicate, the dissemination of analogical inflections in the paradigm of root nouns is very limited, which proves that the reorganisation of this declensional type was not very advanced in the Old English period. Two intertwined features of the attested inflectional distribution deserve closer attention and elaboration, namely, the discrepancy with respect to: (1) individual morphosyntactic categories (paradigm forms) and (2) the category of number. A conspicuous feature of the distribution is the divergent development of the two most significant (when viewed from the present-day English perspective) categories: the GEN. SG. and the NOM./ACC. PL. The former succumbed to the pressure of analogy very early, whereas the latter turned out to be much more resistant, retaining residually the inherited pattern until present-day English. The archaism of the plural is clearly to be ascribed to the presence of the *i*-mutated vowel, which constituted a distinct and salient inflectional exponent, rendering the paradigm resistant to the influence of the productive inflections. The overall higher level of innovation in the singular is to be ascribed to the GEN., which turns out to be much more susceptible to the impact of the *a*-stem pattern than the other cases in the singular. The archaic inflections in the GEN. SG. are found primarily in the heavy-syllable feminine paradigm, where the inherited pattern (the endingless form) is still preserved in ca. 20 percent of forms. The fact that the salient marking was more consistently retained in the plural may indicate that the function of the *i*-mutated vowel as a marker of plurality was more prominent and distinct than its function as an exponent of case. This stays in line with the assumption about the functional-semantic status of the category of number, which, being a *semantic* paradigmatic category, is more important than a *syntactic* category of case (Plank 1987: 185; Plank 1991: 23; Kastovsky 1995: 234). The employment of the *i*-mutated vowel as an exclusive marker of plurality, which occurred with the disintegration of the case system, complies also with the "relevance principle" defined by Bybee (1985), whereby the more salient grammatical categories should be formally more differentiated.

The data reveals the significance of yet another factor involved in the process of the inflectional reorganisation, i.e. the frequency of occurrence operating at the level of the morphosyntactic categories. The unfolding of the process seems to be guided largely by the overall frequency of individual morphosyntactic categories: the GEN. SG., which comprises 7 percent of all the attested forms in the root noun paradigm, is a less frequent category than the NOM./ACC. SG., comprising 27 percent of forms, DAT. SG. comprising 24 percent, and the NOM./ACC. PL., embracing 19 percent of forms; accordingly, the higher level of innovative inflection in the less commonly used GEN. SG. is very much the expected result.

Another aspect of the correlation of the inflectional patterns with frequency is the effect of the singular/plural proportion of forms in the paradigms. The effect becomes most prominent when the distribution of forms is examined at the lemma level. The root nouns that show a very high proportion of plural forms in the paradigms (OE *tōþ* 86%, *fōt* 80%, *brōc* 75% and *lūs* 69%) tend to retain the inherited inflectional patterns, i.e. the *i*-mutated vowels.[152] The extreme effect of relative frequency can be observed in *brōk* 'breech': not only does it retain the *i*-mutated vowel in present-day English, but, on account of its semantic profile, the plural inflection of *brōk* is reinterpreted as the singular (cf. PDE *trousers, scissors*).[153] In contrast, the noun *burg*, attested much less frequently in the plural (12%) than in the singular, despite its high absolute token frequency in the Old English corpus, turned out to be more vulnerable to interparadigmatic analogy in the long run (with 44% of analogical forms found in the plural paradigm already in Old English).

Some further insight into the patterns of inflectional restructuring in the root nouns can be gained when examining the diachronic and diatopic distribution of the inherited and analogical inflections. The details of these distributions are presented consecutively in Tables 3.20, 3.21 and 3.22. Table 3.22 depicts the combined results for the two periods within the two investigated dialect groups. As in the other investigated classes, the combined results refer to the data culled from the Anglian and Saxon material, excluding the data from texts classified as *Unknown* and *Indeterminate* in the *DOE* corpus.

Table 3.20 Diachronic distribution of innovative inflections in the OE root nouns

| | Innovative inflection | | |
	SG	PL	Overall
Early Old English	(*n* = 572) 18%	(*n* = 145) 6%	(*n* = 717) 15%
Late Old English	(*n* = 1778) 30%	(*n* = 914) 5%	(*n* = 2692) 22%

Table 3.21 Dialectal distribution of innovative inflections in the OE root nouns

| | Innovative inflection | | |
	SG	PL	Overall
Anglian	(*n* = 222) 11%	(*n* = 107) 11%	(*n* = 329) 11%
Saxon	(*n* = 2667) 28%	(*n* = 1135) 6%	(*n* = 3802) 21%

---

152. For a statistical analysis of the significance of relative frequency for the retention of archaic patterns and the development of new morphological irregularities, see the study by Versloot & Adamczyk (forth.).

153. Cf. North Frisian (Sylt) *ted* 'tooth, teeth', where a parallel process of reinterpretation took place.

The pattern attested in the two periods of Old English is to some extent expected in that it reflects the gradual progression (albeit very limited) of the restructuring process. The gradual increase refers to the singular paradigm only, whereas the plural, with a remarkably low level of innovation, remains stable over the two periods. Such a pattern is clearly a forerunner of the tendencies to come in the subsequent stages in the history of English, most notably the preservation of the vestiges of the archaic pattern of the plural until present-day English. The earliest traces of analogical inflections can be found in the Mercian text *Vespasian Psalter* (PsGlA), dated to the mid-ninth century, a few early Mercian charters, and the West-Saxon *Cura Pastoralis*, dated to the late-ninth century. As regards the dialectal pattern, the restructuring turns out to have had hardly any geographical focus: analogical forms (scarce overall) are to be found in all dialects. On account of the nature of the Old English corpus, most of the evidence for the shifting of inflectional patterns comes from the West Saxon material, yet traces of the novel inflection are attested in Anglian texts as well (in the *Lindisfarne* and *Rushworth Gospels*).

The combined distribution of forms for the two periods in the two dialect groups, presented in Table 3.22, allows us to separate the dialectal and diachronic tendencies. The trends found in the Saxon material ideally correspond to the findings for the data in the entire corpus, with a gradual increase of innovative forms in the *Late* period. Anglian shows, quite unexpectedly, a slightly higher level of innovation in the *Early* period. This can be ascribed to the fact that the plural forms are largely underrepresented in the corpus (for this dialect) and, consequently, the figure refers primarily to the singular paradigm, which (for reasons discussed earlier) tended to be much more innovative.

Table 3.22 Distribution of innovative inflections in the OE root nouns with respect to dialect *and* period

period/dialect	Saxon	Anglian
Early	($n = 584$) 14%	($n = 86$) 17%
Late	($n = 2512$) 22%	($n = 143$) 13%

The underlying tendency of the early English nominal system towards a gradual reorganisation, which could be observed in the other minor classes, is only to a very limited extent reflected in the attested pattern of inflection found in the root nouns. The overall profile of the class remains undisturbed and distinct throughout the Old English period, despite the occasional traces of analogical influence. For some nouns this attested vacillation between inherited and innovative inflections was only a temporary phenomenon, which is confirmed by the preservation of the historical inflectional pattern in present-day English (in the plural) (e.g. *tēþ ~ tōþas* 'teeth', *fēt ~ fōtas* 'feet').[154]

As was pointed out earlier in this section, two factors emerge as decisive for the dynamics of restructuring in root nouns, and both work towards the preservation of the original shape of the paradigm: the salience of inflectional exponents (*i*-mutation) and the frequency of occurrence, operating at different levels. The significance of the former aspect has already been discussed in detail. As regards the latter factor, the high token frequency of lemmas and of individual paradigmatic categories turned out to be essential for the pattern of restructuring, working as a factor conserving the inherited inflection of the root nouns (on the conserving effect of frequency, see Section 1.4.6.1). Admittedly, the correlation between morphological (ir)regularity (here allomorphy in the paradigm) and frequency is not straightforward, and frequency does not seem to account for the inflectional pattern of all the root nouns. On the one hand, nouns such as *mūs* or *gōs* were rather moderately frequent in the texts, yet they managed to preserve their historical inflection in the plural until present-day English. On the other hand, the feminine *bōc* and *burg*, both extremely frequent in the Old English material, eventually joined the regular paradigm. Such deviations from an otherwise valid correlation demonstrate that the restructuring was determined by a range of interacting factors, both linguistic and extra-linguistic in nature, on some occasions enhancing, on others impeding the process (see Section 3.6 for a discussion). One of the factors of an entirely different nature, not inherent to the mechanism of the process but affecting the picture emerging from the analysis, is the text-type composition of the available corpora. Given the nature of the Old English corpus, consisting mainly of chronicles, homilies, sermons, poetic texts, etc., it seems feasible that the actual frequency of use of nouns was not perfectly reflected in their frequencies of occurrence in the corpus. Accordingly, nouns such as *fōt* 'foot', *mūs* 'mouse', *lūs* 'louse' or *gōs* 'goose', which represent a rather mundane, unsophisticated register, may have been in a relatively frequent use among actual speakers, without it necessarily being reflected in the textual material. In contrast, the well attested *bōc* 'book', expected to be found in the texts of higher register, need not have been frequently used among the masses, given the socio-cultural reality of mediaeval Europe (Adamczyk 2013: 293–294). This makes one acutely aware of the pragmatic limitations inherent in the nature of historical corpora, which impose a

---

154. Of the twenty well-attested root nouns in Old English, six (or seven if PDE *woman* and *man* are counted separately) still continue the original pattern, regularly preserving the *i*-mutated vowel in the plural in the standard variety of English. All the remaining nouns of this declensional type turned out to be more vulnerable to the influence of the productive inflection and were subject to the operation of analogical processes in the long run.

total reliance on a limited set of written material, and force one to draw sometimes speculative inferences as to the actual linguistic reality in mediaeval England.[155]

3.5.5   *r*-stems

3.5.5.1   *General characteristics*
The class of *r*-stems comprised the following nouns in Old English: *brōþor* (*-er*, *-ur*), *gebrōþor* (PL.) 'brother', *dohtor* 'daughter', *fæder* 'father', *mōdor* 'mother', *sweostor*, *gesweostor* (PL.) 'sister'. The two nouns *gebrōþor* and *gesweostor* were secondary formations and had some idiosyncratic inflectional features. Two characteristics of this class, the semantic relatedness of the nouns, all denoting kinship terms, and their high (token) frequency of occurrence were important from the perspective of the restructuring process, affecting the dynamics of the changes. With respect to the pattern of inflection, the paradigm of *r*-stems was characterised by the absence of inflectional endings in the SG. and (originally) in the NOM./ACC. PL., which rendered it very uniform. Another formal property of this declensional type in Old English, not found in the other West Germanic languages, was the presence of an *i*-mutated vowel in the DAT. SG. in *brēþer*, *dehter* and *mēder*, where originally **-i-* was present (**brōþr-i*, **dohtr-i*, **mōdr-i*). The rule did not regularly apply to *fæder*, where the *i*-mutated vowel in the DAT. SG. is attested only sporadically and is confined to the texts of Anglian provenance (both Mercian and Northumbrian). The *i*-mutated vowel could theoretically be expected in the NOM. PL., since the inherited PGmc. NOM. PL. ending was **-iz* (< PIE **-es*), yet, as no such forms are attested, the vowel must have been eliminated prior to the operation of *i*-mutation (Brunner 1965: 229). The mutated vowels which appeared regularly in the DAT. SG. were occasionally extended to the GEN. SG., primarily in the texts of Late West Saxon and Anglian origin.

---

155. The stability of this inflectional pattern is also reflected in its vestigial productivity. This consonantal pattern seems to have been extended to place names of Celtic origin, which tended to adopt the GEN. SG. marker *-e* and exhibit zero ending in the other cases, e.g. *Wiht* 'Wight' (DAT., ACC. SG.), *Wihte* (GEN. SG.), *Ī* (DAT., ACC. SG.), *Īe* 'Iona' (GEN. SG.) (Campbell 1977: 255; Brunner 1965: 229). Occasionally also the endingless DAT. SG. of the feminine *i*-stems (of the type *meaht* 'might, power') has been ascribed to the analogical influence of the root noun inflection, where the inherited DAT. SG. surfaces with no inflectional ending (notably van Helten 1911: 468). The presence of such sporadic analogical traces of root noun inflection in other paradigms can be interpreted either as a residue of its former productivity, or merely as the occasional and fortuitous influence of an otherwise unproductive pattern. Given that this trend can also be identified in the other West Germanic dialects, the former interpretation cannot be excluded.

As the class comprised masculine and feminine nouns, the restructuring involved analogical remodelling of the respective paradigms on the pattern of the *a*-stems and *ō*-stems, in accordance with gender class affiliation. Apart from the influence of the vocalic patterns, some inclination towards the *n*-stem inflection can be expected, especially in the GEN. PL. and NOM./ACC. PL., with the innovative endings *-ena* and *-an*, respectively. The following inflectional irregularities can be found in the *r*-stem paradigms:

a. masculine nouns
   - the GEN. SG. *a*-stem marker *-es* in place of the historical endingless form
   - the DAT. SG. marker *-e* in place of the historical endingless form
   - the NOM./ACC. PL. endings *-as* and *-u* in place of the historical endingless form (see further discussion)
b. feminine nouns
   - the GEN., DAT. SG. *ō*-stem ending *-e* and possibly GEN. SG. *a*-stem *-es* in place of the historical endingless form
   - the NOM./ACC. PL. markers *-a*, *-e* and *-u* in place of the historical endingless form

The competing inherited and analogical inflections in the paradigm of masculine and feminine *r*-stems are summarised in Table 3.23.

Table 3.23 The competing inflections in the OE masculine and feminine *r*-stems

	archaic		innovative		archaic		innovative	
	SG	PL	SG	PL	SG	PL	SG	PL
NOM.	*brōþor**	brōþor	*brōþor*	brōþ(o)ru, -as	*mōdor*	mōdor	*mōdor*	mōd(o)ru, -a
GEN.	brōþor	*brōþra*	brōþ(o)res	*brōþra*	mōdor	*mōdora*	mōdore, -es	*mōdora*
DAT.	brēþer	*brōþrum*	brōþ(e)r	*brōþrum*	mēder	*mōdorum*	mōdore	*mōdorum*
ACC.	*brōþor*	brōþor	*brōþor*	brōþ(o)ru, -as	*mōdor*	mōdor	*mōdor*	mōd(o)ru, -a

* The vowel of the final syllable in the historical paradigm tends to vacillate between *-er*, *-or* and *-ur*, especially in the texts of Mercian and Northumbrian provenance (e.g. Mercian GEN. SG. *feadur, mōdur*, North. *fador, fædur*, ACC. SG. *brōður, mōdur, dohtur*). The vowel is interpreted as a regular West Germanic development of the prehistoric syllabic *r* (in forms of the type **brōþr*) and its quality seems to have been determined (in Old English) by the quality of the root vowel (vowel harmony): hence the presence of harmonising vowels in *brōþor, mōdor, dohtor* on the one hand, but *brēþer, mēder, dehter* (and possibly *swiostor*) on the other (Prokosch 1939: 255; Hogg & Fulk 2011: 56; cf. Lane 1951: 525). The *-er* ending in *fæder* has been interpreted as original and the preservation of the short vowel *-e* is motivated by the presence of a preceding light-syllable, whereas in *mōdor*, which had originally contained a long root vowel, the suffixal vowel was lost and subsequently a secondary epenthetic vowel developed (**mōder* > **mōdr* > **mōdor*) (Krahe & Meid 1969: 40). All these phonological developments have no bearing on the results of the present investigation, as irrespective of the exact variant, whether *-or*, *-er* or *-ur*, the form is inherited and not extended from other declensional types.

Clearly, the original paradigm of the *r*-stems was characterised by considerable uniformity, manifested in the absence of a number distinction (i.e. the formal syncretism of the singular and plural), and case distinctions (i.e. the syncretism of the forms of NOM., GEN. and ACC. SG., and NOM./ACC.PL.). This uniform structure of the *r*-stem paradigm can be considered one of the major factors that contributed to the eventual demise of this inflectional type in early English. The only distinctive case exponent in the paradigm can be found in the DAT. SG., characterised originally by the presence of the *i*-mutated vowel in the root. As will be seen in the analysis, this inflectional feature had a bearing on the pattern of the restructuring of inflection in this category. The forms of the NOM. and ACC. SG. as well as the GEN. and DAT. PL. are not informative about the restructuring of inflection. In the case of the GEN. and DAT. PL., the forms overlap with those of the *a*-stems and *ō*-stems (except when the GEN. shows the *n*-stem marker *-ena*). An important characteristic of the restructuring pattern in this class is the presence of forms in which the NOM./ACC. PL. is marked by *-u*, frequently alternating with *-a* as in *brōþru, -a, mōdru, -a, dohtru, -a*, found predominantly in Late West Saxon texts, corresponding to Northern forms in *-o*: *brōðro, swestro, suoestro*. While the presence of the ending *-a* in feminine stems can be attributed to the influence of the *ō*-stems, the origin of the forms in *-u* is uncertain and a number of alternative views have been offered. The situation is complicated by the fact that in the Late OE period *-a* and *-u* tended to vary freely in inflectional syllables and thus commonly one explanation has been sought to account for both variants. According to Kluge (1926: 196), the ending *-u* could be regularly derived from the original PGmc. ACC. PL. ending **-unz* and subsequently extended to the NOM. PL. Much along the same line, van Helten (1911) claims that the irregular endings *-o* and *-u* can be derived from *-iu* which "auf eine linie zu stellen ist mit got. durch anlass von *-uns* des ACC. PL. entstandener endung von NOM. PL. *brōþrjus* etc." (van Helten 1911: 491). Another explanation was suggested in some earlier accounts, where the presence of such irregular forms was ascribed to the analogical influence of the *u*-stems (notably Primer 1881: 189). Alternatively, the forms in *-ru, -ra* (Northern *-ero*) have been viewed as an effect of the analogical influence of the *s*-stems (*lombru, -ra, -ero*), which display a parallel inflectional pattern. Finally, these irregular plural formations have been ascribed to the influence of the neuter *a*-stem inflection (most prominently Brunner 1965: 239)[156] and it is this interpretation, considered here most plausible, that has been adopted in the present study. A similar stance is taken by Wright & Wright (1982: 201) where the frequently attested NOM./ACC. PL. ending *-u* is explicitly ascribed to the neuter

---

156. "Der Akk. Pl. ist an den Nom. Pl. angeglichen; altws. *brōðru, mōdru* sind wohl analogisch zu den neutralen *o*-Stämmen gebildet (wegen *gebrōðru*) und nicht vom alten Akk. Pl. (got. *brôþruns*) abzuleiten, weil das auslautende *-u* abgefallen wäre" (Brunner 1965: 239).

collective nouns *gebrōþor* and *gesweostor*, declined originally like the neuter *a*-stems, with the plural forms: *gebrōþru* and *gesweostru*. This hypothesis accounts for the ending -*u* in *brōþor* and *sweostor*, and possibly their variants in -*a*. The presence of -*a* in *mōdra* or *dohtra* can be explained by recourse to the influence of the *ō*-stems (Hogg & Fulk 2011: 56–57). Given this wide range of potential interpretations of these forms, closer attention will be payed to the distribution of these forms in the corpus. It can be expected that if the form in -*ru* is an original ACC. PL., it should be attested primarily in the earliest sources.

3.5.5.2 *Results of the investigation*
The results of the investigation of the *r*-stems were grouped into three sets: masculine, feminine and the two nouns denoting siblings: *gebrōþru* and *gesweostru*, which show a different pattern of inflection from the other *r*-stems. An exhaustive investigation of the available data was conducted for all the lemmas except *fæder*, which is the most frequently attested *r*-stem in the corpus. Due to this high frequency of occurrence, the investigation of the inflection in *fæder* was limited, covering all attestations classified as *Early* and *Indeterminate*, and a selection of data from the *Late* Old English period, altogether amounting to ca. 2500 occurrences.[157] The three consecutive tables present the distribution of forms with respect to case and number for masculine (Table 3.24) and feminine stems (Table 3.25), and for the plural paradigms of *gebrōþru* and *gesweostru* (Table 3.26). The two nouns *gebrōþru* and *gesweostru*, by virtue of their semantics, appear only in the plural and their paradigm is very innovative. This high level of innovation complies with the pattern found in the plural paradigm of other *r*-stems, where the plural in contrast to the singular turned out to be, in general, more innovative.

Table 3.24 Distribution of archaic and innovative inflections in the OE masculine *r*-stems

	archaic		innovative	
	SG	PL	SG	PL
NOM.	(*1480*)	(*110*) 27%	–	(*295*) 73%
GEN.	(*501*) 77%	(*190*)	(*146*) 23%	–
DAT.	(*751*) 97%	(*345*)	(*20*)　3%	–
ACC.	(*620*)	(*34*) 28%	–	(*87*) 72%
Total	(*1396*) 71%		(*559*) 29%	

157.　In order to avoid any biases, the selection was based essentially on the syntactic context, i.e. demonstrative pronouns and a range of prepositions were used to specify the context.

Table 3.25 Distribution of archaic and innovative inflections in the OE feminine *r*-stems

	archaic		innovative	
	SG	PL	SG	PL
NOM.	*(989)*	*(27)* 42%	–	*(38)* 58%
GEN.	*(278)* 95%	*(164)*	*(14)* 5%	–
DAT.	*(341)* 98%	*(41)*	*(6)* 2%	–
ACC.	*(499)*	*(8)* 25%	–	*(24)* 75%
Total	*(654)* 89%		*(82)* 11%	

Table 3.26 Distribution of archaic and innovative inflections in OE *gebrōþru* and *gesweostru*

PL	archaic	innovative
NOM.	*(29)* 7%	*(397)* 93%
GEN.	*(77)*	–
DAT.	*(224)*	–
ACC.	*(7)* 5%	*(128)* 95%
Total	*(36)* 6%	*(525)* 94%

Both the masculine and feminine *r*-stem paradigms testify to parallel patterns of restructuring of inflection. The synchronic alternation between the two types of inflection is attested in the GEN. and DAT. SG. and NOM./ACC. PL. The prominent effects of the influence of the analogical inflections are attested in the plural only, but the overall amount of innovation in both paradigms is limited, with the feminine paradigm showing a slightly more archaic pattern. This higher percentage of analogical forms in the masculine paradigm is most evident in the GEN. SG. and the NOM. PL./ACC. PL., and can be attributed to the salience of the markers in the corresponding categories in the *a*-stems. Both the GEN. SG. ending *-es* and the NOM./ ACC. PL. marker *-as* were more distinct than their feminine *ō*-stem counterparts (*-e, -a*) and were, consequently, more expansive markers, whose productivity was steadily growing throughout the Old English period.

When it comes to the shape of the analogically reformulated paradigms, the paradigm of masculine *r*-stems was essentially dominated by the *a*-stem inflection, with the markers *-es* and *-as* extended to the GEN. and NOM./ACC. PL. The pattern is not entirely consistent as the innovative plural forms of *brōther*, in contrast to *fæder*, hardly ever show the *-as* marker (1x *brōðras*); instead the forms in *-u* prevail (*brōðru, -a*), alongside a few weak forms in *-an*. This pattern is unexpected in light of the fact that the form *brothers* became the ordinary plural form only in the seventeenth century, ousting the alternative *brethren*, which since then has been employed only with reference to a "spiritual, ecclesiastical or professional relationship" (*OED*, s.v. *brother*). The analogical inflections in the feminine paradigm in the plural are confined to the forms in -ra and -ru (e.g. mōd(e)ru, -a, doht(o)ru, -a), as well as occasional forms in -e, emerging as a result of the influence of the ō-stem declension (e.g. dohtre and dohtore).[158] The analogical marker -u in the NOM./ACC. PL., extended possibly from the neuter a-stems, is characteristic of both masculine and feminine paradigms. The hypothesis that the -(r)u form in the ACC. PL. (e.g. brōðru, sweostru) is an inherited ending is not supported by the data. Firstly, the ending is attested more often in the later sources and, secondly, it is not confined specifically to the ACC. PL. but is as common in the NOM. PL.

As regards the singular paradigm, the GEN. SG. a-stem marker -es is found also occasionally in the feminine r-stems: mōderes (mōdres), dohtres, and sustres (primarily in Late West-Saxon and Northumbrian). This analogical ending appears relatively early in mōder (mōdres), with the first attestations found in the Northumbrian texts of the second half of the tenth century. According to the OED, the masculine marker -es became a standard form only towards the end of the Middle English period, which corresponds to the scant attestation of innovative forms in the corpus in the feminine paradigm. The inherited endingless form of the GEN. SG. is still well preserved in the paradigm of the OE brōðor, and it turns out to have been resistant to analogical influence for a long time. In some dialects, forms without the marker -es are attested as late as until 1600, e.g. Scots brother son (nephew), broder bairn, broder wife, broder dochter (OED, s.v. brother). Another uninflected form, well preserved until the later stage, is the archaic endingless GEN. SG. of OE fæder, which survives occasionally until the fifteenth century, and that of mōdor, which is still amply attested throughout the Middle English period.[159] In general, it can be concluded that the influence of analogical inflections in the r-stems was not consistently guided by gender in that masculine and neuter inflectional markers were frequently found in the feminine paradigms. This pattern runs counter to the tendency observed in the other minor declensional types in which the interparadigmatic transfers were essentially observant of gender. A final remark about the distribution of forms in the r-stems concerns the traces of n-stem inflection, which are very limited and appear in Late West Saxon texts only (e.g. GEN. PL. fæderena (PsGlI (Lindelöf)).

Some further insight into the attested pattern can be gained by analysing the process on the lemma level. The paradigm of fæder testifies to a very high level

---

158. The earliest recorded masculine a-stem plural form in sweostor is dated to the late 12th c. and attested in the Ormulum in þa sustress. It has been argued that forms such as dohtres, and sustres start prevailing over the n-stem plurals only in the 14th c. (Krygier 1996: 50).

159. PDE expressions of the type mother tongue or mother wit can be viewed as remnants of the original unmarked GEN. SG. of this noun (OED, s.v. mother tongue, mother wit).

of innovation in the plural (97%) and can be considered the first noun to have transferred to the *a*-stem declension in this class. The remarkably high percentage of analogical forms in the plural paradigm of *fæder* indicates that the process of analogical remodelling was under way at an early stage and that the innovative plural endings (-*as*) were well entrenched in the paradigm, showing little synchronic vacillation. The singular paradigm of *fæder* remains much more archaic (86%), which corresponds to the pattern found in *brōðor*, with its innovative plural (61%) and predominantly archaic endingless singular (91%). The level of innovation in *mōder* and *dohter* is comparable, reaching 5 percent and 9 percent, respectively, while *sweostor* turns out to be more innovative, with 32 percent of analogical inflections attested in the paradigm. Both *mōder* and *dohter* show hardly any traces of analogical inflections in the singular (2%).

Table 3.27 depicts the distribution of innovative inflections in the *r*-stem paradigm, with respect to case and number, but irrespective of gender. The overall figures for the singular and plural as well as the total percentage of innovation in the paradigm are included.

Table 3.27 Overall distribution of innovative inflections in the OE *r*-stems

	% innovative	% innovative
GEN. SG.	(*n* = 950) 18%	10%
DAT. SG.	(*n* = 1118) 3%	
NOM. PL.	(*n* = 896) 81%	82%
ACC. PL.	(*n* = 288) 83%	
Total	36%	

The innovation level in the *r*-stems is relatively low and the data indicates clearly that it is to be attributed to the inflection in the singular, which, in contrast to the plural, remains remarkably stable. Irrespective of gender, it is the DAT. SG. that turns out to be the most resistant to analogical pressures. The attested inflectional stability of this category in the singular can be partly attributed to the presence of the *i*-mutated vowel, which was the most salient inflectional exponent in Old English. The use of *i*-mutated forms in the DAT. SG. decreases towards the end of the Old English period, and at the same time an opposite trend can be observed in the GEN. SG. where the *i*-mutated vowel is occasionally analogically extended from the DAT. SG. The analogical mutated forms in the GEN. SG. are found predominantly in the texts of Late West-Saxon provenance as well as those classified as *Indeterminate* (e.g. *mēder, dehter*). Occasionally forms doubly marked are found in the corpus (*i*-mutated vowel combined with an analogical inflectional ending): *dehtre* (DAT. SG.), *brēþ(e)re* (NOM. PL.).

Another factor which emerges as (partly) responsible for the attested distribution of forms is frequency of occurrence. The high innovation rate in the plural seems to correlate with the low incidence of plural forms in the paradigm, which amounts to 28 percent of all the attested forms. This correlation becomes even more explicit when the distribution of forms in individual lemmas is taken into account. A closer analysis of the figures for individual nouns reveals the significant role of the plural proportion in the reshaping of the *r*-stem paradigm. Table 3.28 illustrates a correlation between the spread of innovative inflections in the plural and the singular-plural proportion of forms (i.e. the percentage of plural forms in the paradigm relative to the singular ones).

Table 3.28 Distribution of innovative inflections in the plural and the proportion of plural inflection in the individual OE *r*-stems

r-stems	% innovative PL	% PL
mōdor	100%	($n = 1246$) 2%
fæder	97%	($n = 2507$) 16%
sweostor	69%	($n = 382$) 19%
brōþor	61%	($n = 2083$) 32%
dohtor	38%	($n = 801$) 26%

The data indicates clearly that the innovation level is the highest in nouns where the plural proportion is the lowest. Both *mōdor* and *fæder* are naturally infrequent in the plural and there the analogical features are found in almost 100 percent of plural forms. In contrast, with *sweostor* and *brōþor*, which tend to be used more often in the plural than in the singular, the innovation level is lower. *Dohtor* occupies here an intermediate position, with a lower percentage of analogical forms in the plural, but the figures do not contradict the general tendency. The attested distribution supports the assumption that high token frequency clearly has a conserving effect on morphological patterns, and implies that despite the fact that the plural inflection of the *r*-stems was not characterised by any salient exponent, it could survive due to mere frequency of use.

The pattern of reorganisation of inflection in the *r*-stem paradigms in individual periods and dialects is presented in Tables 3.29 and 3.30, respectively. The figures do not include the attestations to *gebrōþru* and *gesweostru*.

With regard to the diachronic distribution, it can be concluded that the inflection of the *r*-stems in the Early period is almost entirely archaic: the only exception is the noun *fæder*, where analogical (plural) forms are found already in the early Mercian and early West Saxon texts (mid-9th c.). A gradual increase in the percentage of analogical forms can be observed in the Late Old English period, although the overall level of innovation in this class of nouns is fairly limited. When it comes to the dialectal distribution, the level of innovation is generally somewhat higher in

Table 3.29 Diachronic distribution of innovative inflections in the OE *r*-stems

	Innovative inflection		
	SG	PL	Overall
Early Old English	($n = 157$) 4%	($n = 64$) 38%	14%
Late Old English	($n = 1344$) 10%	($n = 385$) 73%	24%

Table 3.30 Dialectal distribution of innovative inflections in the OE *r*-stems

	Innovative inflection		
	SG	PL	Overall
Anglian	($n = 367$) 27%	($n = 108$) 68%	36%
Saxon	($n = 1485$) 5%	($n = 507$) 72%	22%

the texts of Anglian provenance than in the Saxon material, both in the singular and the plural. At the same time, the fact that the figures for Anglian and Saxon in the plural are almost the same demonstrates that the contrast between Early and Late in the plural is not a result of a dialectal bias in the corpus, i.e. Early Anglian vs. Late West Saxon, but it rather reflects the actual diachronic contrast. Table 3.31 presents the combined distribution of analogical inflections for the dialect and period. As can be observed, in both dialects the trends are parallel irrespective of the period, and the greater inclination towards analogical inflections in Anglian is observable already for the Early period in this dialect. The higher level of innovation in the Late period in Anglian is largely the result of the spread of analogical inflections in the GEN. SG., where the expansive *a*-stem marker -*es* is found both in masculine and feminine paradigms.

Table 3.31 Distribution of innovative forms in the OE *r*-stems with respect to dialect *and* period

period/dialect	Saxon	Anglian
Early	($n = 178$) 11%	($n = 36$) 28%
Late	($n = 1418$) 21%	($n = 297$) 39%

Although the *r*-stems do exhibit a shift away from their original inflectional profile, the innovations progressed rather slowly, especially when compared to other minor classes. Despite a very small number of nouns affiliated with this declension, it remains fairly stable, preserving its distinct *r*-stem identity. This is unexpected, granted that the smaller declensions (with regard to the number of lemmas they contain) are potentially more likely to be the target of analogical pressures from the productive patterns. As could be seen in the examined material and the discussion, the attested conservatism of the *r*-stem inflection can be attributed to several factors. The most prominent of these is the frequency of occurrence of the *r*-stems, which as nouns denoting kinship terms, were frequent in use and thus resistant to analogical pressure. Apart from the frequency operating on the lemma level, the relative frequency (singular/plural proportion) turned out to be decisive for the restructuring of the *r*-stems. It was demonstrated that the frequency profiles of the *r*-stems were largely determined by their semantics, which could potentially have also another effect: the semantic homogeneity of the class may have been a factor contributing to the conservatism of the inflection. Such a conserving effect of semantics is seen in the heavy-syllable neuter *a*-stems of the type *dēor*, which, due to their coherent semantic profile, have resisted the pervasive influence of the productive masculine inflection until present-day English.

3.5.6   *s*-stems

3.5.6.1   *General characteristics*
The *s*-stems constituted a small group of neuter nouns in Old English, characterised by the presence of a consonantal alternation in the paradigm, i.e. the *r*-element in the GEN. and DAT. SG., and in all cases in the plural. With a single exception of the fossilised plural form *children*, where the historical *-r-* (OE *cildru*) has been preserved until present-day English, this inflectional type has been lost completely. In terms of its origin as well as its subsequent development, the class of *s*-stems constitutes one of the historically complex declensional types. Formally, from an Old English synchronic perspective, it can be divided into two subgroups:

a.   nouns in which the attested NOM. and ACC. SG. appear without the *r*-formative (as in *ǣg* 'egg', *cealf* (*cælf*) 'calf', *dōēg* 'day', *hrēð* 'glory', *lamb* 'lamb')
b.   nouns in which the suffixal *-r* is consistently attested in all cases in the paradigm, including the NOM./ACC. SG. (as in *alor* (*alr*) 'alder-tree', *dōgor* 'day', *ēar* (*eher*, *æhher*) 'ear of grain', *ǣgor/ēgur* 'sea', *gycer* 'acre', *hōcor* 'mockery', *hrīðer* (*hrȳðer*) 'horned cattle', *nicor* 'water-monster' (m.), *salor* 'hall', *sigor* 'victory', *wildor* 'wild animal').

The two groups will be referred to as the *lamb*-group and the *hrīðer*-group, respectively. In the latter group, the original *s*-stem affiliation of nouns can be recognised on the basis of their relationship to the forms which did not preserve the *r*-formative, often affiliated synchronically with the *i*-stems (e.g. *sigor* vs. *sige* 'victory', *salor* vs. *sele* 'hall'), and the occasional consonantal inflection of the DAT. SG., i.e. endingless form (Brunner 1965: 244, cf. Boutkan 1992: 12). The NOM./ACC. SG. in this subgroup (*dōgor* < **dōgr*, *hālor* < **hālr*) is believed to be an effect of intraparadigmatic levelling, whereby the *-r*-element was extended from the oblique cases, where it was regularly present (e.g. *dōgor(e)*, *dōgor(es)*; Wright & Wright 1982: 213; Hirt 1932: 59; Boutkan 1992: 15; cf. Casaretto 2000: 219). This different shape of paradigms in the two subgroups of the *s*-stems is significant in the context of the restructuring process: while the *lamb*-group can be expected to exhibit some synchronic variation between inherited and analogical inflections in the paradigm, the *hrīðer*-group, whose paradigm closely resembles that of the neuter *a*-stems, may be expected to be more exposed to the influence of the analogical inflections of the productive types.

The Old English *s*-stem inflection was characterised by a combination of two significant features which render it distinct from other inflectional types. One of them is the mentioned presence of the *-r*-element in cases other than the NOM./ACC. SG., which developed regularly from the PGmc. suffixal *-z* (< PIE *-s*) (e.g. the NOM./ACC. PL. *calfur*, *dōgor*, *lombur*, or the GEN. PL. *calfra*, *hrōðra*, *lombra*, etc.; cf. Table 3.32). The other property (relevant diachronically) is the presence of an *i*-mutated vowel in the NOM. and ACC. SG. (in the *lamb*-group) (as in *cælf*, *lemb*, *hrēð*, *dōēg*), resulting from the impact of the original inflectional ending containing a high front vowel *-i* (PGmc. *-iz*: *calfiz*, *lambiz*[160]). Since the *i*-mutated base form could be extended to other categories in the paradigm, *i*-mutated forms such as the GEN. SG. *celfes*, *cælfes*, etc. are to be sporadically found in the available material. While such intraparadigmatic extension of the *i*-mutated vowel is pertinent to the Anglian material, in the texts of West-Saxon provenance the *i*-mutated vowels tend to be levelled on the analogy of the unmutated forms from the oblique cases.

Given that a number of the original *s*-stems (whose *s*-stem class affiliation can be confirmed by the existing cognates in the other Germanic languages) do not show any residues of the historical *s*-stem inflection in the attested material, the restructuring of the *s*-stem paradigm must be dated earlier than the first attestations of English. These early transfers to other declensional types entailed shifts following two major pathways:

a. to the *i*-stem declension, where the transition was facilitated by the presence of the mutated vowel in the NOM./ACC. SG. (e.g. neut. *flǣsc* 'flesh', *flīes* (*flēos*) 'fleece', *geban(n)* 'summons', *gedyre* 'door-post', *gefōg* 'joint', *geheald* (*gehield*) 'keeping, guard', *gehlȳd* 'noise', *gehnāst* 'conflict, clash', *geswinc* 'toil, effort', *gewēd* 'rage, madness', *gewealc* 'rolling', *gehield* 'guard', *ofdele* (*ofdæle*) 'descent', *oferslege* 'lintel', *orlege* 'fate', *sife* 'sieve', *spere* 'spear'; masc. light-syllable stems: *bere* 'barley',

---

160. The NOM. SG. in *-iz* has been explained as an early analogical formation on the pattern of the GEN. and DAT. SG. The preservation of *-i-* in the Go. *hatis*, *sigis* (in place of the expected **hats*, **sigs*) is adduced as a corroboration of this assumption (Wright & Wright 1982: 213) (cf. Section 2.2.3.5 and Boutkan 1995: 266–267; Klein 2013: 172–175).

ege 'terror',[161]*hete* 'hatred', *mene* 'necklace', *sele* 'hall', *sige* 'victory'; as well as heavy-syllable stems *gǣst* 'ghost', *hǣl* 'health', *hilt* (*helt*) 'handle', *hlǣw* 'mound', *hrǣw* 'body', *lǣn* 'loan, grant', *sweng* 'blow') [162] (cf. Hogg & Fulk 2011: 61)

b. to the *u*-declension (*feoh* 'cattle', *liðu*-, *liðu* 'member', *lim* 'limb, part of body', *sidu*, *seodu* 'custom', *sceadu* 'shade'[163]) (cf. van Helten 1911: 502).[164]

The prehistoric shift of the *s*-stems to the *i*-stem declension has been explained in terms of the generalisation of the PIE *-*es*- formative in the NOM./ACC. SG., whereby this category fell together with the NOM./ACC. SG. of the *i*-stems (cf. *sige* 'victory' < *segiz, (*i*-stem) *wine* 'friend' < *weniz) (Casaretto 2000: 218). The *inter*paradigmatic realignments that occurred subsequently were apparently triggered by this formal similarity of the NOM. SG. of the *i*- and *s*-stems. Additionally, the analogical transference of the original *s*-stems to the *i*-stem declension must have been facilitated by the fact that these forms, just like the *i*-stems, were subject to *i*-mutation (Unwerth 1910: 2). A similar factor may have played a role in triggering the occasional transference to the *ja*-stem class, whose members regularly underwent the process of *i*-mutation (at a prehistoric stage). In these early analogical transfers, the change of paradigmatic affiliation was often accompanied by gender reassignment (Schenker 1971: 53). Such a shift in gender class is unsurprising given that the potential target group, i.e. the neuter *i*-stems, constituted a relatively small group of nouns, whereas the neuter *u*-stems were non-existent. Consequently, the nouns newly entering these declensional types were likely to change their inherited gender, being absorbed by a much better represented masculine subtype. To some extent, this characteristic of the restructuring process finds a continuation into the historical stage, where many of the *s*-stems lose their original neuter gender, and tend to follow the masculine pattern of inflection.

---

161. Cf. OE *n*-stem *egesa* (*egsa*) 'terror' (OHG, OS *egiso*).

162. As the existence of two parallel stems is a characteristic of Germanic languages (and of other Indo-European languages, too), for many of these nouns parallel *a*- (*ja*-) stem forms without a mutated vowel are attested in Old English, e.g. *gāst* 'soul, spirit', *sæl* 'hall', *hlāw* 'mound', *hrāw* 'corpse' (Campbell 1977: 259).

163. Cf. the Go. *wulþus* 'glory', *sidus* 'custom' which consistently follow the *u*-stem inflection.

164. The classification of these nouns is somewhat problematic, since standard historical grammars of Old English, as well as the major Old English dictionaries provide sometimes discrepant information as to the synchronic membership of individual *s*-stems. Tracing the exact paths of transition which occurred at the prehistoric stage stays beyond the scope of the present study (see Thöny 2013). The present list of the OE *s*-stems was compiled on the basis of the classification found in Brunner (1965), but cf. Campbell (1977), Wright & Wright (1982), Bosworth & Toller (1898).

The historical stage of the process is well attested in the Old English material and involves the remodelling of the inherited paradigm on the inflectional pattern of the neuter *a*-stems. At the same time, given the expansiveness of the masculine *a*-stems, with the salient NOM./ACC. PL. marker -*as*, the influence of this most productive declension is to be expected in the paradigm of the *s*-stems. In contrast, the traces of the neuter *n*-stem inflection are rather unlikely to be found in the *s*-stem paradigm as the neuter *n*-stems were not a productive inflectional type. Importantly, the *s*-stems are the single class where the GEN. and DAT. PL. can be considered informative about the restructuring process. The synchronic alternation between the inherited and analogical inflections in these categories can be tested in the *lamb*-group, where, in marked contrast to other minor classes, vestiges of the original inflectional pattern are unambiguously distinguishable from the features of analogical inflection.

The inflectional irregularities resulting from this analogical pressure can be expected to appear in the following categories:

- the GEN. SG. *a*-stem marker -*es* in place of the original endingless form
- the DAT. SG. *a*-stem marker -*e* in place of the original endingless form
- the NOM./ACC. PL. neuter *a*-stem zero marker (without *r*-extension), the masculine *a*-stem marker -*as* and/or the *n*-stem ending -*an*
- the DAT. PL. ending -*um* in place of the historical marker -*rum* (in the *lamb*-group)
- the GEN. PL. marker -*a* (in the *lamb*-group), or the *n*-stem marker -*ena* in place of the original ending -*ra*

Table 3.32 below depicts the two competing sets of inflections in the Old English *s*-stem paradigms, both in the *lamb*-group and in the *hrīðer*-group. The alternation of the root vowels in *cælf* (*æ/a* : *ea*) reflects the dialectal distribution of these vocalic elements in Anglian and West-Saxon, respectively, emerging as a result of divergent phonological developments in these two dialects. This contrast has no bearing on the results of the quantitative investigation of the interparadigmatic realignments.

Table 3.32 The competing inflections in the OE *s*-stems

| | lamb-group | | | | hrīðer-group | | | |
| | archaic | | innovative | | archaic | | innovative | |
	SG	PL	SG	PL	SG	PL	SG	PL
NOM.	*cælf*	calfur, -eru	*cealf*	cealf, -as, -an	*sigor*	*sigor*	*sigor*	*sigor(as)*
GEN.	calfur	calfra	cealfes	cealfa, -ena	sigor	sigora	sigores	sigora
DAT.	calfur	calfrum	cealfe	cealfum	sigor	sigorum	sigore	sigorum
ACC.	*cælf*	calfur, -eru	*cealf*	cealf, -as, -an	*sigor*	*sigor*	*sigor*	*sigor(as)*

The interpretation of some of these inflectional endings as they developed in Old English seems fairly problematic. This refers in particular to the GEN./DAT. SG. and NOM./ACC. PL. pre-Old English ending *-ur (OE -or > -er) and OE -(e)ru. According to Campbell (1977: 258), the -ur, -or endings found in the archaic forms, such as calfur or lombor, are a regular phonological development of an original WGmc. *-ar > -ur. Alternatively, the -u in *-ur has been interpreted as a parasite vowel, inserted in place of -e in the sequence *-er, which, once in the final position, was subject to the process of apocope (Boutkan 1995: 266; cf. Fulk 1988: 155–156; Schaffner 2001: 590ff.).[165] The development may well have involved vowel harmony, whereby the quality of the vowel in the inflectional ending was harmonised with that of the root vowel.[166] Irrespective of the exact source of this ending, it is clearly an archaic feature when seen in the context of the present study. A more problematic ending from the perspective of the present analysis is the NOM./ACC. PL. marker -(e)ru (e.g. ǣgru 'eggs', hrīðeru 'cattle'), frequently attested in the West Saxon texts. Its origin is not entirely transparent and it can be interpreted in two ways: (1) as a phonological development of the *-Vru, which was potentially the original plurality marker, where the medial vowel was lost as a result of syncope operating in disyllabic words; (2) as a morphological development, whereby the u-apocope did not operate in this group of nouns, and -r served as an additional marker of plurality. Alternatively, the form can be interpreted as emerging under the influence of the disyllabic neuter a-stems ending in a sonorant (Hogg & Fulk 2011: 94–95). In the present study, the ending is classified as an archaic feature, but given its uncertain status, closer attention will be given to the exact diachronic distribution of these forms in the material.

The archaic pattern presented in Table 3.32 is not very consistently preserved in the Old English material, as in consequence of the intraparadigmatic analogy the inherited r-formative was eliminated from the paradigm in many nouns originally affiliated with this class, consequently facilitating the transfer to other declensional types. The analogical endings from the productive declensions were essentially attached to the forms without the r-formative in the lamb-group, e.g. celfes, calfas, lombes, lambum. At the same time, the original stem formative was more consistently retained in the plural, where, in contrast to the singular, the analogical inflectional endings were typically attached to the r-formative. In the hrīðer-group, where the -r- formative is consistently preserved throughout the entire paradigm, both in the singular and plural, the analogical inflections are attached to the r-formative, as in dōgores, sigores, ehras.

---

165. For an informative overview of alternative opinions and an elaboration on this hypothesis, see Boutkan (1992: 16–18), and for the most recent summary of the problem, see Hogg & Fulk (2011: 59–60).

166. For details on the patterns of vowel combinations in West Germanic, see, e.g., Hogg (1992a) for Old English, Versloot (2008: 190–194) for Old Frisian.

3.5.6.2 *Results of the investigation*

The quantitative analysis examined the incidence of inherited and analogical inflections in the paradigm of the *s*-stems, taking into account the diverse shape of the paradigm in the two subgroups. The criteria for classifying the forms in *lamb*-group nouns were slightly different from those applied to nouns where the *r*-formative was extended to the NOM./ACC. SG. This refers in particular to the forms of the NOM./ACC. PL., where the presence of the *r*-formative and lack of analogical inflectional marker in the *lamb*-group is interpreted as archaic (*lamb – lambor*), but as neutral in the *hrīðer*-group, where it may be a regular phonological development, or a result of the reformulation on the pattern of the neuter *a*-stems (*hrīðer – hrīðer*). Likewise, due to the different shape of the paradigm in these two subgroups, the forms of the GEN. and DAT. PL. are relevant only for the *lamb*-group, where an alternation between *r*-full and *r*-less forms is attested (*lamba, lambum* vs. *lambra, lambrum*), and not in the *hrīðer*-group, where the *r*-formative is present throughout the paradigm. Accordingly, the quantitative investigation was conducted separately in the two subgroups of *s*-stems. Contrary to what could be expected, the findings from the two subparts of the investigation were largely parallel, testifying to identical trends present in the paradigms. Therefore, the cumulative results for the two subgroups are presented in one table (Table 3.33) without any further subdivision, and the minor discrepancies in the attested inflectional pattern are discussed below.

The interpretation of certain forms turned out to be fairly problematic or at least not straightforward. One such interpretative problem was posed by the noun *dōgor* 'day' which historically belongs to the same paradigm as the heavy-syllable stem *dōēg* – related to the light-syllable *a*-stem *dæg*. Bammesberger (1990: 213) postulates a PGmc. stem **dōg-uz-* as a point of departure for the OE *dōēg*, recognising its close relation to the PGmc. *a*-stem **dag-a-*. The NOM./ACC. SG. form *dōēg*, attested in the *Lindisfarne Gospels*, is a reflex of the original form **dōgiz* (e.g. Ross 1937, Brunner 1965, Hogg & Fulk 2011: 58; cf. Weyhe 1906: 85). The corresponding (Late) West-Saxon NOM./ACC. SG. forms appear as *dōgor* and testify to a consistent analogical spread of the *-r-* element from the oblique cases throughout the singular. Accordingly, in the present analysis, *dōgor* was interpreted as the oblique and plural form of *dōēg*, and included in the calculations only in the Northumbrian material, where the two variants belong to one lemma. In the other dialects, the NOM./ACC. SG. and PL. endingless forms are considered inconclusive and excluded.

A final qualification that has a bearing on the interpretation of the results concerns the original *i*-mutated forms, whose elimination from the paradigm of the *s*-stems, though clearly an innovation, is not interpreted as an *innovative* feature in the present investigation. The novel unmutated forms in the paradigm emerged due to the *intra*paradigmatic analogy, especially the pressure of the GEN. and DAT. SG., rather than the influence of other declensions. This type of internal restructuring is taken into account in the qualitative analysis in as much as it affected the shape of the paradigm – facilitating or inhibiting interparadigmatic changes – but it will not be quantitatively framed here.

The overall distribution of inherited and analogical inflections in the *s*-stem paradigm with respect to case and number is presented in Tables 3.33 and 3.34. The figures for the GEN. and DAT. PL. refer only to the forms from the *lamb*-group where the synchronic alternation between inherited and analogical inflections can be captured. The results for the noun *cild* were not included in the figures and will be presented and discussed separately in Section 3.5.6.3.

Table 3.33 Distribution of archaic and innovative inflections in the OE *s*-stems

	archaic		innovative	
	SG	PL	SG	PL
NOM.	(*128*)	(39) 67%	–	(19) 33%
GEN.	(6) 4%	(17) 40%	(140) 96%	(25) 60%
DAT.	(17) 18%	(7) 47%	(75) 82%	(8) 53%
ACC.	(*173*)	(55) 61%	–	(35) 39%
Total	(141) 32%		(302) 68%	

Table 3.34 Overall distribution of archaic and innovative inflections in the OE *s*-stems

	s-stem inflection	*a*-stem inflection
singular	(23) 10%	(215) 90%
plural	(118) 58%	(87) 42%
Total	(141) 32%	(302) 68%

Evidently, the paradigm of the *s*-stems is largely dominated by analogical inflections extended from the *a*-stems. The spread of innovative forms is well evinced in all categories, especially in the GEN. and DAT. SG. Also in the plural the percentage of analogical inflection is relatively high in these two categories. A striking characteristic of the attested distribution is the discrepancy in the percentage of analogical inflection in the singular (90%) and plural paradigms (42%). At least two factors may have played a role here. One of them is the salience of inflectional exponents and the fact that the -*r*-element is ranked high on the salience scale, constituting a marker which could compete with the analogical endingless *a*-stem forms. Another factor to be reckoned with is connected to the fact that the *r*-formative, although never generalised as a plural exponent in Old English, once eliminated from the singular did serve a distinctive function of marking plurality in this group of nouns. As a result, it tended to be preserved longer in the plural paradigm than in the singular. This tendency is reminiscent and parallel to the trend found in the root nouns, supporting the priority of the category of number, semantically and functionally more salient, over the category of case. Consequently, analogical levelling was more likely to operate within one number category (spreading across cases) rather than within one case category (spreading across number) (Kastovsky 1995: 234).

Evidently, the template for the reorganisation of the *s*-stem paradigm was created by the largely overlapping paradigms of neuter and masculine *a*-stems. The influence of the masculine inflections (in the NOM./ACC. PL.) is attested primarily in the Late Saxon material (e.g. *aelres, ceælfæs, cealfas, calfas, sigoras*) and singly in the Late Northumbrian *ehras*.[167] Although still sporadic and rather irregular at this early stage, it can be interpreted as a reflex of a combination of two interrelated developments, namely, the rapid expansion of the masculine *a*-stem inflection among ɪninor stems (attested especially towards the end of the Old English stage), and the gradual dissolution of the gender system, which had its beginnings in the Late Old English period (but with some fluctuation of nouns between genders found already in the tenth century, see Lass 1992: 107). The traces of the *n*-stem inflection are only sporadically found, which seems unexpected in view of the extensively attested Middle English forms of *calveren, lambren, ægeran*, or *eiren*. The rare exceptions here are the plural forms of *ēar* 'ear of corn' (*earan*) and *cild*, including the GEN. PL. *cildena* (DurRitGl1, North.), *stēopcildena* (ÆAbus (Warn), Late WS), as well as the ACC. PL. *cildræn* (ÆHomM 6 (Irv 1), Late WS) (cf. Section 3.5.6.3).

The attestations of *lamb* confirm the assumption that the ending *-ru* may have been an early extension from the *a*-stem declension, as the forms *lombor* are found only in the earliest material, while *lambru*, although attested also in the early stage, becomes evidently more widespread in the later period. Given the complexity of the restructuring process and the interaction between phonological and morphological developments, it seems feasible that the inherited form *lambru* emerged as a direct result of the interaction of these developments. In other words, the final vowel *-u* may have been a result of a regular phonological process (whereby *ō* > *u*), but its persistence may have been enhanced by the parallelism with the *a*-stem forms in *-u* (disyllabic ones) of the type *hēafod*: *hēafdu* (cf. Hogg & Fulk 2011: 101–102). The parallel metrical structure of these forms may have worked as a factor facilitating the interparadigmatic interaction in the Late Old English period (*lamb(o)ru – hēaf(o)du*).

---

167. According to Ross (1937: 97), the forms *ehher* and *æhher* 'ear of corn' continue into the later stage of English as the PL. *echirris* in Douglas and Modern Scots dialect *icker* (< OE *ehher*) and *acher, acre* (< *æhher*). The fluctuation between the neuter and masculine gender, attested in the paradigm, was ascribed to the analogical impact of the masculine *tahur* 'tear' (*tēar*) (van Helten 1911: 499) (cf. the feminine gender of present-day German *Ähre* < OHG neuter *ehir, ahar*).

An interesting pattern emerges from a comparison of the distribution of forms in the paradigms of two related nouns, i.e. *sigor* 'victory' and the corresponding *i*-stem *sige* 'victory'. As the two nouns have the same meaning, and similar structure, it seems feasible that they synchronically belonged to one lemma, forming one paradigm. The distribution of forms with and without the *r*-element lends credence to this assumption, as it turns out to be largely complementary, i.e. the *r*-less forms are found predominantly in the NOM./ACC. SG., while the forms with the *r*-element are typical of the GEN. SG., DAT. SG. and the plural. Such a distribution is reminiscent of the archaic *s*-stem paradigm, in which the NOM./ACC. SG. did not show the *r*-element, while the other categories in the paradigm were characterised by it.

It seems feasible that the impact of the endingless neuter *a*-stem inflection may have been enhanced by semantic factors. As the endingless plural was a salient feature of the heavy-syllable neuter *a*-stems denoting animals (e.g. *dēor* 'deer', *scēap* 'sheep'), the *s*-stems such as *lamb*, *cealf*, *hrīðor*, constituting a semantically coherent group, may have been more receptive to analogical pressure from this particular, semantically close subgroup of neuter *a*-stems. Also, the endingless NOM./ACC. PL. form *dōgor* could be explained by recourse to semantics: the noun, as a term referring to time measurement, could have followed the pattern of the neuter *a*-stem *ġēar* 'year', endingless in the NOM./ACC. PL. Another characteristic which may have had some bearing on the pattern of analogical restructuring in this class is related to the concept of plurality, which seems to be inherent in some of the nouns. The fact that some of the *s*-stems were used more often in the plural (e.g. *ēar* 'ear of grain', *ǣgor* 'sea', *hrīðer* 'horned cattle' or *hōcor* 'mockery') may account for the notable lack of an explicit plural marker in this group. In all these instances the semantic factor cannot on its own account for the attested distribution of forms, but it may have played a role as a factor enhancing the effects of other factors, such as frequency, salience or syllable structure.

A closer look at the distribution of analogical inflections in the two examined subgroups reveals that the restructuring of the *s*-stem inflection was minimally more advanced in the *lamb*-group than in the *hrīðer*-group. The overall percentage of innovation amounts to 70 percent in the *hrīðer*-group and 67 percent in the *lamb*-group. The only significant contrast between the two subgroups is found in the category of the DAT. SG: while the analogical inflections are present in 100 percent of forms in the *lamb*-group, they are confined to 75 percent in the *hrīðer*-group (in contrast, the amount of innovation is identical in both groups for the GEN. SG. reaching 96 percent). A factor which may be taken into account when explaining the divergent pattern of restructuring in the DAT. is the metrical structure. The standard Germanic foot structure (*Germanic foot*) was a trochee (a quantity-sensitive, left-to-right resolved moraic trochee) (Lahiri & Dresher 1991; Flikkert et al. 2009: 127). While a trochaic structure is preserved when the innovative inflection (-*e*) is attached to the DAT. SG. in monosyllabic *lamb*, the pattern becomes metrically less consistent, when the inflectional ending is attached to a disyllabic *hrīþer*:

H	L		H	L	Ļ
lamb	-*e*		*hrīþ*	*er*	-*e*

Consequently, the nouns from the *hrīðer*-group were more resistant to analogical pressures and tended to retain the inherited inflection in the singular more often than the nouns from the *lamb*-group.

Some further insight into the restructuring of the *s*-stems can be gained by looking at the diachronic and diatopic distribution of the inherited and analogical inflections in the paradigms. The details of these distributions are presented in Tables 3.35, 3.36 and 3.37. Table 3.35 depicts the combined results for the two periods within the two investigated groups of dialects. The *overall* results refer to the Anglian and Saxon material, excluding the data from texts classified as *Unknown* in the *DOEEC* (in contrast to the figures presented in Tables 3.33 and 3.34 above).

Table 3.35 Diachronic distribution of innovative inflections in the OE *s*-stems

	Innovative inflection		
	SG	PL	Overall
Early Old English	(*n* = 12) 75%	(*n* = 11) 27%	52%
Late Old English	(*n* = 116) 95%	(*n* = 150) 49%	69%

As could be expected, the more extensive dissemination of analogical inflections can be identified in the Late Old English period. This refers to both the singular and plural paradigms, although the percentage of analogical forms in the singular is already substantial in Early Old English. In contrast, the plural shows predominantly archaic inflection in the Early period, attested primarily in the ninth-century *Vespasian Psalter*. Traces of the historical inflection are still attested in the Late Old English period, for instance, in the Psalters from the mid-eleventh century (PsGlG, PsGlJ, PsGlD).

Table 3.36 Dialectal distribution of innovative inflections in the OE *s*-stems

	Innovative inflection		
	SG	PL	Overall
Anglian	(*n* = 34) 88%	(*n* = 28) 7%	52%
Saxon	(*n* = 183) 91%	(*n* = 167) 47%	70%

The original shape of the *s*-stem paradigm is much better preserved in the Anglian material, while the Saxon data exhibit substantial departures from the historical inflectional patterns. This greater archaism of Anglian in the analysed corpus does not come as a surprise in view of the descriptions found in the standard historical grammars. The most archaic paradigm is attested in the early Mercian glossaries, which retain the original inflection in nearly 85 percent of all the forms. The two dialect groups show an almost identical pattern in the singular, with a very high level of innovative inflection. The plural paradigm attests to a divergent pattern for the two dialects groups, with a remarkably archaic paradigm in Anglian, where the traces of analogical inflection are only sporadic, and a much more innovative Saxon, where almost half of all the attested forms are analogical. The combined results for the distribution of innovative forms with respect to dialect and period are presented in Table 3.37.

Table 3.37 Distribution of innovative forms in the OE *s*-stems with respect to dialect *and* period

period/dialect	Saxon	Anglian
Early	($n = 11$) 64%	($n = 8$) 13%
Late	($n = 221$) 71%	($n = 41$) 59%

The juxtaposition of the dialectal and diachronic patterns of reorganisation reveals that in the Saxon group, the *s*-stem paradigm was exposed to extensive analogical pressures already at the Early stage. In fact, the level of innovation is very similar in both examined periods and in general the paradigm emerges as largely disintegrated. In contrast, in Anglian the increase in the amount of innovative inflection between the Early and the Late Old English period is significant, which essentially reflects the contrast in the distribution of forms in early Mercian and late Northumbrian texts. At the same time, as the percentages for Anglian as well as for the Early Old English period are based on low numbers of attestations, the figures should be interpreted with caution, even if the contrasts as such are statistically significant.

A closer examination of the distribution patterns found in the individual dialects, including the subdivision within Anglian and Saxon, offers some further insight into the process of restructuring as it unfolded across the dialects and periods. For instance, the dialectal pattern of restructuring clearly reflects the different stages of the process. The amount of innovation found in individual dialects varies, ranging from 15 percent in Mercian, 55 percent in Northumbrian, 60 percent in Kentish and 67 percent in West Saxon (Adamczyk 2011: 400). In light of the available data, three stages of the development of the Old English paradigm can be distinguished, as presented in Table 3.38, corresponding largely to the dialects of Old English: Mercian, Northumbrian (late), and West-Saxon and Kentish (cf. Boutkan 1995: 264; Schenker 1971: 55 for Old High German).[168]

Table 3.38 Stages of the development of the OE *s*-stems

	I (Early Mercian)	II (Late Mercian, Northumbrian)	III (Saxon)
NOM. SG.	cælf	cælf	cealf
GEN.	calfur	calfes/cælfes	cealfes
DAT.	calfur	cealfe	cealfe
ACC.	cælf	cælf	cealf
NOM. PL.	calfur, -eru	cealfru, calfero	cealfas
GEN.	calfra	calfra	cealfa
DAT.	calfrum	cealfrum	cealfum, -on
ACC.	calfur, -eru	cealfru, calfero	cealfas

The paradigms presented above indicate that morphological restructuring in the *s*-stems involved three developments: (1) a gradual restriction of the forms containing the *r*-formative to the plural (Northumbrian), (2) an accompanying elimination of the *i*-mutated forms in the singular (partly Northumbrian, West-Saxon), and (3) a total eradication of the original stem formative from the plural (West-Saxon, Kentish) (Adamczyk 2011: 405). In other words, the process of disintegration ranges along a continuum where at one extreme there is the Saxon dialect with a highly innovative inflectional profile of the *s*-stems, attesting to their large-scale transference to productive classes, with analogical inflectional features appearing as early as in the ninth century. At the other extreme there is the limited set of Mercian forms, showing the original pattern of inflection, with the inherited *i*-mutated forms of the NOM. SG. (*caelf, ceolborlomb*) and endingless NOM./ACC. PL. and GEN., DAT. SG. (*calfur*). The space between these two extremes is covered by the Northumbrian material, where the original *s*-stems display a synchronic fluctuation between the inherited and innovative inflections (only when both the singular and the plural are taken into account). Such a distribution seems to a large extent expected on account of the dates of attestation of the individual dialects and the fact that the earliest attested Mercian glosses, dating back to the eighth and early-ninth centuries, are of necessity juxtaposed with the somewhat later Northumbrian (10th c.), and

---

168. Not all the forms of *cealf* presented in the paradigm are attested in the Old English material. The noun *cealf* serves here only as a representative of the *s*-stems, illustrating the inflectional profile of these stems in individual dialects.

West-Saxon material, going back to the tenth and eleventh centuries. The overall distribution of analogical and inherited inflectional features indicates clearly that the historical paradigm of the *s*-stems, as attested in the Old English corpus, was undergoing extensive restructuring, which eventually led to a total demise of this declensional type in English.

A final observation concerns the potential productivity of the *s*-stem inflection at an early stage of Old English. Representing one of the minor declensional types, the class of *s*-stems was synchronically unproductive, yet the pattern seems to have been attractive to some nouns which did not originate as *s*-stems, e.g. *brēadru* (*brēad*) 'bread crumbs', *hǣmedru* (*hǣmed*) 'married relationships', *hæteru* 'garments', *lēower* (*lēow*) 'ham, thigh',[169] *mǣdrum* (**mǣd, *mǣder?) 'measures', *scerero* 'shears' (*scear*), *speldra* (*speld*) 'torches', *stǣner* 'stone' (*stān*) (Brunner 1965: 244; cf. Campbell 1977: 259). Most of these nouns are attested in early Mercian material, dated to the eighth century, including the earliest glossaries: *Épinal* (early 8th c.), *Erfurt* (early 8th c.) and *Corpus Glossary* (late 8th c.), well-known for their conservative nature.[170] The presence of such forms in the corpus points to some early productivity of the *s*-stem inflection, parallel to that attested extensively in Old High German. As the extension of the *r*-formative is found only in the early material, this productivity must have been confined to this early stage. In contrast to High German, where the -*ir*- formative was morphologised and reinterpreted as a plural marker, the *r*-formative was never generalised as a plural marker beyond the *s*-stems in English; consequently, its potential to spread across other declensional types was limited. The explanation for such a state of affairs can be sought in the overall profile of the Old English nominal system, which, as a result of interacting phonological and morphological factors, lost the original declensional diversity. The predominance and rapid spread of one inflectional type in Old English (the *a*-stems) has been associated with a typological shift, whereby the inherited stem-based inflection was replaced by word-based inflection (Kastovsky 1995: 233; 1997: 67) (cf. Section 3.6). The newly emerging "monoparadigmatic, stem-invariant and word-based" inflection left consequently no chance for the extension of -*r*- as a

---

169. OE *lǣuw* 'thigh' is attested with plural forms *leower/lewera* (e.g. LorGl2). The word has a cognate in ON *lǣr* 'thigh' (with the -*r* element being part of the root), which supports its interpretation as an original *s*-stem (von Unwerth 1910: 3–4). Otherwise the form can be interpreted as one of the few instances of the productivity of the *s*-stem plural formative. A potential cognate is found in West-Flemish *lee* 'loin' (*EWN*, s.v. *lee*[II]), although this word has also been interpreted as a shortened form of *lid* < PGmc. **liðu*- 'limb, member' (van Veen & van der Sijs (1997), s.v. *lee* [*lende*]), which implies an entirely different path of development.

170. The dating of these glossaries is based on Hogg (1992a: 5) and Toon (1992: 427); an earlier dating (ca. 700) has been postulated by Brown (1982) (cf. Campbell (1977: 7).

plural marker in Old English, and all the nouns originally affiliated with the *s*-stems eventually joined the major inflectional pattern. Another crucial factor which may have prevented the functionalisation of the *r*-stem formative in Old English was an early phonemicisation of *i*-mutation. In contrast, in High German, the process of phonemicisation occurred relatively late (during the transition to the Middle High German period), facilitating the reinterpretation of the *r*-element (in combination with *i*-mutation) as a plural exponent (Kastovsky 1995: 236; Klein 2013: 184; for a further discussion of *i*-mutation, see Section 7.3).

3.5.6.3 *An excursus on Old English* cild

Due to its unclear etymological status, the noun *cild* was analysed separately and the findings from the investigation are presented in Tables 3.39 and 3.40. According to the *OED*, *cild* (< PGmc. **kilþoᵐ*) did not originate as an *s*-stem, but was towards the end of the Old English period partially assimilated to the inflection of neuter *s*-stems. This is substantiated by the widespread appearance of the NOM. PL. forms *cildru* or GEN. PL. *cildra* in the Late West-Saxon texts. Alternatively, the noun has been classified among the *s*-stems and derived from the PGmc. **kelþ-ez-* (cf. Go. *kilþei* 'womb', *inkilþo* 'pregnant') (Bammesberger 1990: 211). Given the uncertain etymological backround of this noun, the present quantitative analysis examined the incidence of the *s*-stem vs. *a*-stem inflection in the paradigm of *cild* rather than the degree of its archaism vs. innovation.

Table 3.39 presents the distribution of the *s*-stem vs. *a*-stem inflections in the paradigm of *cild* with respect to case and number, while Table 3.40 provides an overall percentage distribution with respect to dialect and period. The figures in Table 3.40 include the data for the plural paradigm only, i.e. where the vacillation between the two inflectional types can be captured.

Table 3.39 Distribution of archaic and innovative inflections in the paradigm of OE *child*

	a-stem inflection		*s*-stem inflection	
	SG	PL	SG	PL
NOM.	(282)	(76) 85%	–	(13) 15%
GEN.	(78) 100%	(65) 64%	(0)	(36) 36%
DAT.	(110) 100%	(123) 94%	(0)	(8) 6%
ACC.	(170)	(96) 89%	–	(12) 11%
Total	(548) 89%		(69) 11%	

The analysed material reveals that the paradigm of *cild* was dominated by the *a*-stem inflection, which is attested in 89 percent of forms and found even in the early sources (e.g. early-ninth century Mercian *Vespasian Psalter*). As can be observed, it is only the plural that shows a synchronic vacillation between the two inflectional types. The singular consistently displays features of the *a*-stem inflection, with the markers -*es* and -*e* in the GEN. and DAT., respectively.[171] Such a distribution of forms, i.e. the absence of any traces of the *s*-stem inflection in the singular (despite the overall high token frequency of the noun), can be interpreted as indicative of the fact that the noun belonged historically to the *a*-stem declension, and, consequently, that the *s*-stem inflection must have been an innovation in the paradigm of *cild* rather than a relic pattern.

The NOM./ACC. PL. turned out to be very resistant to the *s*-stem pattern, favouring either zero or the masculine *a*-stem ending -*as*. Traces of the *s*-stem inflection are most prominent in the GEN. PL., amounting to 36 percent, which is most likely attributable to the fact that the GEN. is one of the lower frequency categories and, consequently, favours more salient marking, which the *s*-stem inflection could offer (-*ra* vs. *a*-stem -*a*). Hardly any traces of *n*-stem inflection were found in the corpus, which may be surprising given their high incidence in the Middle English period, especially in the southern dialects, and later. The evident dearth of such forms in the Old English corpus suggests that the emergence of the weak inflection in the paradigm of *cild* can be dated no earlier than the Middle English or possibly Early Middle English stage. Another characteristic of the inflectional pattern found in the paradigm of *cild* is its (occasional) lack of stability with respect to gender, manifested in the vacillation between the neuter and masculine paradigm: accordingly, alongside the expected ACC. PL. neuter *cild*, the masculine forms *cildas* and *cildes* are attested (only in the Northumbrian material). The significance of these attestations lies in the fact that they may be viewed as a presage of the tendencies to come, whereby the masculine ending -*as* became the prevailing plural marker in the North (15th c. *childes*; cf. the related Scots *chield* 'chap, lad', with the regular plural form preserved as *chields*).[172]

Some further insight into the pattern of inflection of *cild* can be gained by looking at the details of the diatopic and diachronic distribution of the inflectional forms. The combined results for the distribution of *a*-stem forms in the *plural* paradigm with respect to dialect and period are presented in Table 3.40.

The patterns of distribution of plural inflections observable in Anglian and Saxon are largely parallel, with both dialect groups attesting to the dominance of the *a*-stem inflection. In terms of the temporal distribution, the *a*-stem inflection is more common in the Early period, whereas the later stage evinces some more traces

---

171. The single endingless form found in the material cannot be treated as entirely reliable, although the form is unambiguously a GEN. SG.: *Þa nam þæs cild modor þone deadan lichaman* (...) 'Then the child's mother took the dead body (...)' (Mart 1 (Herzfeld-Kotzor)).

172. The *s*-stem inflection is preserved in Middle English Northern and North Midland dialects, where the regular plural forms are *childer*, *childre* (*OED*, s.v. *child*; cf. Wełna 1996: 86–87), as well as later in the traditional Northern dialects (*LAE*, s.v. *children*).

Table 3.40 Distribution of the *a*-stem forms in the plural of *cild* with respect
to dialect *and* period

period/dialect	Saxon	Anglian	overall
Early	(*n* = 13) 92%	(*n* = 4) 100%	(*n* = 17) 94%
Late	(*n* = 344) 83%	(*n* = 13) 85%	(*n* = 357) 83%
overall	(*n* = 357) 84%	(*n* = 17) 88%	

of the *s*-stem pattern. In other words, in both dialects the tendency to develop the
r-formative in the paradigm of the plural increases with time, and the *r*-element
tends to become typically a marker of plurality. Given such a configuration of forms
in the paradigm of *cild*, it can be concluded that the introduction of the *r*-stem
formative in the plural, found primarily in the West-Saxon texts belonging to the
tenth and eleventh centuries, must have been typically a southern feature, from
where it only gradually spread into Anglian.

The distribution of forms across dialects and periods found in the material
investigated seems to lend credence to the assertion that *cild* did not originate as
an *s*-stem, but rather gradually adopted the *s*-stem inflection in the plural. Such a
distribution is markedly distinct from that of the plural forms in the other *s*-stems,
where the incidence of archaic inflections in Anglian dialects was remarkably high.

3.5.7 *nd*-stems

3.5.7.1 *General characteristics*
The class of *nd*-stems comprised a group of masculine nominalised participles,
known also as *nomina agentis* (agent nouns). A vestige of the original -*nd*- element
is still to be found in the PDE *friend* (< OE *frēond*) and *fiend* (< OE *fēond*). The Old
English *nd*-stems constituted a relatively numerous group of nouns which denoted
almost exclusively human beings, many of which appear as *hapax legomena* in the
Old English material.[173] According to Kärre (1915: 127), the number of *nd*-stems
with attested substantival forms amounts to two hundred (cf. Appendix for a list

---

173. The class comprised originally also single attestations of plant names, designations of concrete objects (e.g. *halettend* 'little finger'), or of groups of animals (e.g. *laguswimmend* 'fish', *flegend*
'bird'). As they consistently followed the *a*-stem inflection, they were not included in the analysis. Two other etymologically obscure nouns have been assigned to this group: *tōþ* 'tooth', Go.
tunþus, OS *tand* < **tanþ-/tund-*, cf. Lat. *dēns, dentis* < **dent-* and *sōþ* 'truth', ON *sannr* < **sanþ-*.
It is assumed that their original agential character had been lost prior to the Proto-Germanic
period, and as a result they never passed through the participial stage, but remained root formations instead (Kärre 1915: 77; Bammesberger 1990: 202; 2009: 111; Beekes 1995: 179; cf. Krahe
& Meid 1967: 141).

of lemmas found in the corpus of the present study). Formally, the class can be subdivided into two subgroups: (1) monosyllabic stems, i.e. *frēond* and *fēond* (and related compound forms), and (2) disyllabic stems of the type *hettend* 'enemy'. This distinct metrical shape of the stem will have a substantial bearing on restructuring, as will become evident in the course of the quantitative analysis. The monosyllabic nouns belonging to this inflectional type are characterised by the presence of the *i*-mutated vowel in the DAT. SG. and in the NOM./ACC. PL., which testifies to their original consonantal inflection (DAT. SG. **frijōndi*, NOM. PL. **frijōndiz*).[174] Another prominent trait of this declensional type, reflecting its origin in a participle formation, is the presence of adjectival inflection in the GEN. PL. (-*ra*) and NOM./ACC. PL. (-*e*) of disyllabic nouns, e.g. *hettendra, hettende*. The extension of the adjectival -*r*- to cases other than the GEN. PL. is well attested in Late West-Saxon texts, e.g. *wealdendras, wealdendrum* (Campbell 1977: 257), and can be considered an instance of intraparadigmatic analogy.

From a synchronic Old English perspective, the class can be subdivided into two distinct strata: (1) the archaic one, comprising lemmas affiliated with the *nd*-stems already in Proto-Germanic, and (2) the more recent one, including lemmas which followed the *nd*-stem inflection at some point at the Old English stage. Such a two-tier division implies that the -*nd*-suffix must still have been to a limited extent productive during the Old English period. According to Kärre (1915: 216), the productivity of the -*nd*-suffix can be viewed as "a literary one", since the new forms based on -*nd*- were most common in poetry, where they tended to be used in compound formations, which often and early acquired the character of kennings. Such an assumption seems to be validated by a wide range of new deverbial formations attested in the Old English material, but absent from any other Germanic language.

One of essential methodological problems involved in the analysis of this minor declensional class is the status of *nd*-formations. While establishing the agential character of these formations seems relatively unproblematic, the determination of their substantival status poses a greater difficulty. The source of confusion is the participial formations functioning potentially as (a) appositive participles, (b) adjectival participles, or (c) temporal verb forms, whose status cannot be unambiguously determined (Kärre 1915: 82). Much as the inflectional shape of these forms may be of help when deciphering their status, it is far from being conclusive, since the *nd*-formations, alongside the substantival inflection, display also adjectival features

---

174. The *i*-mutated form of the ACC. PL. is in fact an analogical formation based on the NOM. PL. The occasionally irregularly mutated forms of the GEN. and DAT. PL. (e.g. *fienda, fiendum* 'enemies') have been attributed to the impact of the participial ending (Campbell 1977: 81). It seems feasible that these forms emerged as a result of intraparadigmatic analogy, i.e. the influence of the NOM./ACC. PL.

(notably in the NOM./ACC. PL. in *-e* and GEN. PL. in *-ra*). This study covered only those *nd*-formations whose substantival status could be unambiguously identified (either by means of their inflectional makeup or, for example, by the presence of the accompanying modifier).

As the Old English *nd*-stems consisted of masculine nouns only, restructuring of this class occurred on the analogy of the masculine *a*-stems.[175] Given the pattern of restructuring found in the other consonantal stems, the *nd*-stems could also be expected to evince some inclination towards the *n*-stem inflection (the GEN. PL. *-ena* and NOM./ACC. PL. *-an*, occasionally *-on/-en/-æn*). Traces of the adjectival inflection can be expected in disyllabic nouns in the GEN. PL. (the *-r*-element) and in the NOM./ACC. PL. (the ending *-e*). The inflectional irregularities which can emerge as a result of these analogical realignments in the *nd*-stem paradigm include:

- the GEN. SG. ending *-es* in place of the original endingless form
- the DAT. SG. marker *-e* in place of the original endingless *i*-mutated form
- the NOM./ACC. PL. marker *-as* in place of the historical endingless *i*-mutated form
- the NOM./ACC. PL. marker *-ras*, with *-r* extended analogically from the adjectival inflection (disyllabic stems)
- the GEN. PL. marker *-ra* from the adjectival inflection in place of the ending *-a* (disyllabic stems)

All of these potential or expected influences are summarised in Table 3.41, where the two sets of competing inflections in monosyllabic *nd*-stems are presented.

Table 3.41 The competing inflections in the OE monosyllabic *nd*-stems

	archaic		innovative	
	SG	PL	SG	PL
NOM.	*frēond*	frīend, frȳnd	*frēond*	frēondas, -ras
GEN.	frīend, frēond	frēonda	frēondes	frēondra
DAT.	frīend, frȳnd	*frēondum*	frēonde	*frēond(r)um*
ACC.	*frēond*	frīend, frȳnd	*frēond*	frēondas, -ras

---

175. Although the class comprised of masculine nouns only, some *nd*-stems occasionally showed feminine features, e.g. *þēos wealdend* (ÆGram), *þēos fēond* (ÆGram), *to þǣre swelgende* (ChrodR1), *sēo timbrend* (Mart2.1). In some instances, e.g. in *fēond* or *wealdend*, the feminine forms were used as a direct translation of Latin expressions, which proves that the feminine construction of these words "was a possibility of the O.E. language", which was never developed (Kärre 1915: 193). It seems that the *nd*-stem nouns can be viewed as having epicene gender in that they are masculine in terms of form and inflection, but apply to both feminine and masculine nouns, denoting either sex.

The appearance of the NOM./ACC. PL. forms in -*ras* is confined to disyllabic stems only (hence the form *frēondras* is unlikely, but it represents the inflection widely attested in disyllabic stems, e.g. *hettendras*). It has been attributed to the *intra*paradigmatic influence of the GEN. PL., where the -*r*- element, extended from the adjectival inflection, originally belonged (cf. the OE adjectival inflection *blind-ra*). According to Boutkan (1995: 368), the GEN. PL. -*ra* should rather be attributed to the influence of the *s*-stem inflection, where -*r*- was originally present (cf. Section 3.5.6). Irrespective of the exact origin of these forms, traces of this adjectival inflection (-*ras*, -*ra*) are treated as analogical in this study on account of the -*r*-element introduced in the paradigm (in the GEN. PL.), combined with the innovative marker -*as* in the NOM./ACC. PL. This does not refer to the occasional traces of the -*r*-element in the DAT. PL., where they appeared as a result of *intra*paradigmatic analogical pressure from the GEN. PL. rather than *inter*paradigmatic interactions.

3.5.7.2   *Results of the investigation*

A complete inventory of *nd*-stems subject to investigation can be found in the Appendix. As the class of *nd*-stems is very large, the investigation did not cover all the compound formations (where the *nd*-stem constitutes the second element). Requisite for the preparation of the list and for the examination of the data was establishing the substantival character of *nd*-formations (i.e. distinguishing the nominal forms relevant for the analysis from the adjectival or verbal ones). The information found in the *Dictionary of Old English* (Healey et al. 2009) and Bosworth & Toller's (1898) *Anglo-Saxon Dictionary* served as the basis for identifying the *nd*-stems in the corpus. A number of *nd*-forms, including those which do not have an agential character (such as *borhhand* 'usurer', *elpend* 'elephant', *olfend* 'camel'), and those whose etymology is obscure (e.g. *ēowend*, *nōwend* 'sailor', *wāsend* 'throat') were excluded from the investigation (cf. Kärre 1915: 78–81). The analysis was conducted separately on monosyllabic and disyllabic stems, not only as they were expected to show somewhat different patterns of restructuring, but also because the restructuring of inflection was manifested in different paradigmatic categories. Accordingly, in contrast to the monosyllabic stems, traces of analogical inflection in the disyllabic stems could be detected also in the GEN. PL., where the spread of adjectival inflections is expected (-*a* vs. -*ra*). This category was included in the calculations in disyllabic stems only. At the same time, the figures do not comprise the potential alternation in the NOM. SG., where the adjectival ending -*e* is occasionally attested. The reason for such an approach was the shape of the NOM. SG. which can hardly be interpreted as a feature typical of *nd*-stems, being identical for all classes except for the light-syllable *i*-stems, *u*-stems and root nouns (*wine*, *sunu*, *hnutu*). The results of the quantitative investigation into the two types of *nd*-stems are presented in Tables 3.42 and 3.43, respectively. The figures for disyllabic stems include also the attestations to *hǣlend* 'saviour', which was one of the most frequently attested lemmas in this class. As the patterns found in the paradigm of *hǣlend* tally entirely with those found in the other disyllabic stems, there was no need to present the results of the investigation separately. The high number of tokens in the NOM. SG. is due to the high frequency of *hǣlend* in this category.

Table 3.42 Distribution of archaic and innovative inflections in the OE monosyllabic *nd*-stems (*frēond* and *fēond*)

	archaic		innovative	
	SG	PL	SG	PL
NOM.	(524)	(558) 93%	–	(42) 7%
GEN.	(14) 7%	(391)	(195) 93%	–
DAT.	(62) 62%	(526)	(38) 38%	–
ACC.	(254)	(455) 89%	–	(55) 11%
Total	(1089) 77%		(330) 23%	

Table 3.43 Distribution of archaic and innovative inflections in the OE disyllabic *nd*-stems

	archaic		innovative	
	SG	PL	SG	PL
NOM.	(2658)	(48) 47%	–	(54) 53%
GEN.	(14) 3%	(12) 9%	(505) 97%	(117) 91%
DAT.	(51) 14%	(218)	(323) 86%	–
ACC.	(436)	(11) 28%	–	(28) 72%
Total	(136) 12%		(1027) 88%	

The data indicate that the syllable structure of the nouns was an essential criterion in the restructuring process in this class. While an overwhelming majority of the disyllabic *nd*-stems succumb to the influence of the productive inflection, the monosyllabic stems tend to retain their original inflectional pattern. In both subgroups, aside from this discrepancy, a striking feature of the distribution is the divergence in the pattern of restructuring between the singular and the plural: while the former displays considerable vulnerability to analogical pressure, the latter tends to be more resistant to the influence of the productive inflections. In monosyllabic stems, where the plural is marked by the *i*-mutated vowel, the inherited inflection is preserved in 91 percent of all forms. The process of analogical dissemination of the new inflectional markers is clearly most widespread in the GEN. SG., where the inherited endings were almost completely ousted by the productive inflection, with the level of analogical inflections reaching more than 90 percent in both types of stems. This high percentage of analogical forms in the GEN. SG., with hardly any fluctuation between inherited and novel inflections attested, indicates that in this category the process of restructuring started prior to the first attestations.

The cumulative results of the investigation are presented in Table 3.44, which depicts the percentage of innovative inflection in the monosyllabic and disyllabic stems.

Table 3.44 Distribution of innovative inflections in the two types of the OE *nd*-stems

	Innovative inflection		
	SG	PL	Overall
monosyllabic	(*n* = 309) 75%	(*n* = 1110) 9%	23%
disyllabic	(*n* = 893) 93%	(*n* = 270) 74%	88%

A closer look at the distribution of analogical forms in the two subclasses allows one to conclude that the discrepancy between them involves primarily the plural inflection, which shows a divergent pattern in the two types of stems. Two interacting factors seem to have contributed to such a pattern of remodelling, i.e. the frequency of occurrence and the presence/absence of the *i*-mutated vowel in the plural paradigm. As regards the frequency of occurrence, both *frēond* and *fēond* are frequently attested in the plural, which largely follows from their semantics: in very many contexts these nouns were used in the plural. This high frequency level in the plural must have functioned as a conserving factor for the inherited inflectional pattern. In contrast, other frequent lemmas, such as *hǣland* and *wealdand*, which are even more frequently attested in the corpus, due to their semantic properties are found predominantly in the singular (especially in the NOM. SG.), and the low plural proportion renders them more vulnerable to external analogical pressures. The other factor that contributed to the retention of the historical inflection in monosyllabic stems was the presence of allomorphic variation in the NOM./ACC. PL., which was a salient and thus stable inflectional exponent (cf. the conserving effect of the *i*-mutated vowel in the root nouns). The absence of the *i*-mutated vowel in the paradigms of disyllabic stems, in turn, rendered them more prone to the influence of analogical inflections from the productive declensions.

Additionally, the higher level of innovation in disyllabic stems is a result of the dissemination of adjectival inflections in the paradigm in the GEN. PL. (*-ra*) and NOM./ACC. PL. (*-ras*). This development is characteristic especially of the Late Old English stage, and was triggered by the structure of disyllabic stems, which were formally similar to present participle formations, declining according to the adjectival pattern. A factor which furthered and enhanced the spread of adjectival declension in the paradigm was also the existence of the NOM. SG. agential formations in *-ere* (of the type *drincere* 'drinker, drunkard'), where the expected and attested plural ending was consistently *-eras* (according to the *a*-stem pattern). Occasionally, the intrusive *-r-* was analogically extended to forms of the DAT. PL. as in *hergendrum* 'plunderer', *fylgendrum* 'follower', *scēawigendrum* 'spectator', and *forsawendrum* 'one who despises', found in the Late Old English material, and, similarly, the adjectival -*e* is attested marginally also in the NOM. SG.

Another determinant of disintegration in the inherited inflection of disyllabic stems may be the fact that these nouns were hardly ever words of everyday (colloquial) use, but they had predominantly a literary character and were often used in poetic texts. Moreover, only some of them are recorded more than once in the available material; very many are *hapax legomena*, which could imply also their limited usage in spoken Old English. This has been made quite explicit by Kärre (1915: 229) who claims that the *nd*-stems "clearly bear the stamp of being occasional formations". Their low frequency of occurrence in the corpus, and its implications for the restructuring of the paradigm, is a direct consequence of this characteristic.

Given that even the earliest Old English texts attest to the presence of the *a*-stem GEN. SG. marker -*es* and NOM./ACC. PL. marker -*as* in disyllabic *nd*-stems, the beginning of the restructuring process in this subtype can be dated from before the literary period. The earliest traces of the novel inflection in monosyllabic stems can be identified as early as in the ninth century (for instance, in the interlinear glosses, including the early Mercian *Vespasian Psalter*), and the frequency of the innovative forms increases considerably in the texts dated to the tenth century and subsequently in the later sources.

The details of the chronological and dialectal distribution of the *nd*-stems are presented in Tables 3.45 and 3.46. As the discrepancies in the patterns of restructuring are substantial between the two types of stems, the results for the two subgroups are presented separately.

Table 3.45 Diachronic distribution of innovative inflections in the OE *nd*-stems

		Innovative inflection		
		SG	PL	Overall
Early Old	monosyllabic	(*n* = 36) 89%	(*n* = 100) 1%	24%
English	disyllabic	(*n* = 22) 100%	(*n* = 37) 81%	88%
Late Old English	monosyllabic	(*n* = 169) 68%	(*n* = 738) 6%	17%
	disyllabic	(*n* = 659) 93%	(*n* = 118) 90%	92%

Table 3.46 Dialectal distribution of innovative inflections in the OE *nd*-stems

		Innovative inflection		
		SG	PL	Overall
Anglian	monosyllabic	(*n* = 21) 95%	(*n* = 98) 40%	50%
	disyllabic	(*n* = 108) 76%	(*n* = 23) 96%	79%
Saxon	monosyllabic	(*n* = 268) 75%	(*n* = 975) 6%	21%
	disyllabic	(*n* = 693) 95%	(*n* = 227) 74%	90%

The diachronic and dialectal patterns attested in the *nd*-stem paradigms do not entirely comply with those found in the other minor stems. As regards the diachronic distribution, no rapid increase in the overall level of innovation can be observed across the two periods, either in monosyllabic or disyllabic *nd*-stems. The slightly lower percentage of innovation found in the Late Old English period in monosyllabic stems may be attributed to the absolute number of attested forms – much lower in the Early Old English period. The decrease in the level of innovation in the singular of monosyllabic stems is a result of the distribution of the DAT. SG. forms, which given the low number of attestations altogether, may be a limited, local phenomenon (the innovative inflections are found in two texts only, *Bede's Ecclesiastical History* and in *Cura Pastoralis*).[176]

As regards dialectal distribution, it can be observed that the overall innovation level is higher in the Anglian material, with the analogical forms present primarily in Northumbrian. Especially the difference in monosyllabic *nd*-stems is conspicuous, where the innovative forms amount to 50 percent in Anglian in contrast to 21 percent in Saxon, and in the Late Old English period the discrepancy is even larger (90% vs. 14%, cf. Tables 3.46 and 3.47). It seems that the relative frequency of the plural in Saxon was an important factor allowing the paradigm to retain a high level of archaism. Evidently, the plural forms in the paradigm are more frequent than the singular ones, and hence constitute the majority of all the attested forms in the paradigm. This trend shows a wider scope, because, irrespective of the dialect and period, the level of innovation is substantially higher in the singular, while the plural remains relatively conservative.

Table 3.47 Distribution of innovative forms in the OE *nd*-stems with respect to dialect *and* period

period/dialect		Saxon	Anglian
Early	monosyllabic	(*n* = 67) 36%	(*n* = 65) 14%
	disyllabic	(*n* = 53) 89%	(*n* = 6) 83%
Late	monosyllabic	(*n* = 867) 14%	(*n* = 40) 90%
	disyllabic	(*n* = 696) 94%	(*n* = 76) 76%

Some further insight into the patterns of reorganisation can be gained by examining the distribution of analogical inflections in Table 3.47, which presents a combined distribution of forms with respect to dialect and period.

A clear increase in the level of innovation can be observed only in monosyllabic *nd*-stems in Anglian, where the contrast between 14 percent and 90 percent for the

---

176. Another aspect to consider relevant here is the dating of the manuscripts of *Bede's Ecclesiastical History*, which poses some methodological problems (cf. Section 1.5.3).

Early and Late periods, respectively, is significant. The Saxon material evinces a higher level of innovation than Anglian in monosyllabic stems in the Early period, and a comparable rate of restructuring in disyllabic stems. The unexpected decrease in the percentage of innovative forms in monosyllabic stems in Saxon (36% > 14%) reflects again a difference in the absolute number of singular and plural forms in the two periods. While the Early Saxon period is dominated by forms attested in the singular, which tended to be more prone to analogical inflections, the plural forms, with their more archaic profile, are overrepresented in the Late Saxon period. The contrast represented by these figures is not meaningful, and it can be concluded that this dialect was stable with respect to the restructuring process.

Overall, the inflectional pattern of OE *nd*-stems complies with the general tendency present in the other minor classes, entailing a progressive erosion of the inherited inflectional paradigms. At the same time, substantial disparities are attested in the monosyllabic and disyllabic stems (in the plural). The significance of the frequency of occurrence and salience of inflectional marking in the pattern of restructuring in this class is manifest. The interaction between these factors is perfectly reflected in the divergent behaviour of the monosyllabic and disyllabic stems, where the high token frequency of the former and the salience of their inflectional exponents (*i*-mutation) have a strong conserving effect on the inflectional pattern, whereas the low token frequency and uniform historical paradigm of the latter rendered them vulnerable to analogical pressure.

The subsequent fate of the disyllabic *nd*-stems was determined largely by their formal character, in particular by the fact that as participial formations, *nd*-stems were closely related to the participial forms of the verb. Given that the formations in -*ende* were losing their productivity towards the end of the Old English period and were soon (i.e. in the Middle English period) to be replaced by -*ing* participles (Wełna 1996: 108–109), the corresponding *nomina agentis*, whose substantival status was increasingly flexible and gradually decomposing, followed suit, and very many of them became extinct by Middle English times.

3.5.8 Dental stems

Old English is the only West Germanic dialect where residues of the dental stems (PIE *t*-class) are consistently retained. The class of *þ*-stems in Old English comprised four nouns: *ealu* 'ale' (n.), *hæle* 'man' (m.), *mæg(e)ð* 'maiden' (f.), *mōnað* 'month' (m.), and the original inflectional pattern can be identified in their paradigms (Campbell 1977: 259–260; Boutkan 1995: 262–263; Hogg & Fulk 2011: 61–62; cf. Krahe & Meid 1967: 139–141). A characteristic feature of the paradigm was the presence of the intraparadigmatic alternation, which is a reflex of the original Proto-Germanic conditions, namely, the retention of the dental suffix in the GEN. and DAT. SG. and in the plural (e.g. *ealoð, ealoða*), and its absence in the NOM. SG. and (mostly) in the ACC. SG. (e.g. *ealu*). This original variation is still found in *ealu* and *hæle*, while in *mæg(e)ð* and *mōnað* the dental element was consistently extended to the NOM. and ACC. SG. In this respect, the *intra*paradigmatic reshaping of inflection resembles the early developments in the *s*-stems (of the *hrīðer*-type), in that the dental element present originally in the GEN. and DAT. SG. and in the plural was analogically restored to the NOM. and ACC. SG. As a result, the paradigm became very uniform and, most importantly, the contrast between the singular and plural was lost (*mōnað – mōnað*), which rendered the paradigm vulnerable to analogical pressures from the productive declensional types, especially in the plural. At the same time, the form without the dental formative, *mōna*, developed as a separate noun with a new meaning 'moon' (*OED*, s.v. *moon*; *EWN*, s.v. *maan*) (cf. footnote 349).

The expected destination classes for analogical transfers of the *þ*-stems were the *a*-stems, and in the case of the feminine *mæg(e)ð*, the *ō*-stems. The potential competing inflections in the paradigm of the Old English dental stems are summarised in Table 3.48, while Table 3.49 presents the incidence of analogical inflections in the individual morphosyntactic categories.

Table 3.48 The competing inflections in the OE *þ*-stems

	archaic		innovative	
	SG	PL	SG	PL
NOM.	*hæle*	hæleð	*hæle*	hæleðas
GEN.	hæleð	*hæleða*	hæleðes	*hæleða*
DAT.	hæleð	*hæleðum*	hæleðe	*hæleðum*
ACC.	*hæle*	hæleð	*hæle*	hæleðas

Table 3.49 Distribution of archaic and innovative inflections in the OE *þ*-stems

	archaic		innovative	
	SG	PL	SG	PL
NOM.	(*183*)	(51) 62%	–	(31) 38%
GEN.	(39) 13%	(*172*)	(272) 87%	–
DAT.	(95) 36%	(*147*)	(168) 64%	–
ACC.	(*121*)	(120) 61%	–	(76) 39%
Total	(305) 36%		(547) 64%	

The paradigm of the OE *þ*-stems is clearly dominated by analogical inflections, which is especially evident in the singular, where the level of innovation reaches 77 percent. The plural paradigm is moderately innovative and analogical inflections cover 38 percent of the forms, which complies with the trends observed in some other minor classes, where the singular tends to be more innovative and the plural retains more conservative features (e.g. root nouns, *s*-stems, *nd*-stems). The dental element present in the paradigm, just like the *r*-formative in the *s*-stems, was an inflectional exponent ranked very high on the morpho-phonological salience scale, and as such it had a potential to resist the analogical pressure of the productive inflection. However, with the extension of the dental element to the NOM. SG., its distinctive function was lost, despite its high ranking on the salience scale. Consequently, the dental stems could be easily reinterpreted as *a*-stems, and the *a*-stem marker -*as* was attached to the *þ*-formative (cf. the *hrīðer*-group in the *s*-stems). An additional factor accelerating the disintegration of the original inflectional pattern in the dental stems was their low type frequency: the class comprised four nouns only and accordingly the pattern had no productivity potential, despite the presence of the salient inflectional marker in the paradigm.

The details of diachronic and dialectal distribution of analogical inflections in the paradigm of the Old English dental stems are summarised in Table 3.50 and 3.51. Table 3.52 presents the combined results for the distribution of innovative forms with respect to dialect and period.

Table 3.50 Diachronic distribution of innovative inflections in the OE *þ*-stems

	Innovative inflection		
	SG	PL	Overall
Early OE	(*n* = 53) 81%	(*n* = 31) 3%	(*n* = 84) 52%
Late OE	(*n* = 423) 88%	(*n* = 152) 67%	(*n* = 575) 80%

The figures indicate a clearly divergent pattern of restructuring of the singular and plural inflection evident especially in the Early Old English period. While the singular shows predominantly analogical inflections at the Early stage, the plural remains almost entirely conservative (the singly attested innovative form is found in *Bede's Ecclesiastical History*). The spread of analogical inflections in the singular continues gradually towards the Late Old English period, while a more abrupt change can be observed in the plural, which testifies to a considerable increase in the number of analogical inflections in the Late period.

Table 3.51 Dialectal distribution of innovative inflections in the Old English *þ*-stems

	Innovative inflection		
	SG	PL	Overall
Anglian	(*n* = 9) 44%	(*n* = 5) 100%	(*n* = 14) 64%
Saxon	(*n* = 478) 87%	(*n* = 238) 37%	(*n* = 716) 71%

With respect to the dialectal distribution, the advancement of the process of restructuring is comparable for the two dialect groups, with the Anglian group remaining in general slightly more conservative. A striking feature of this distribution is the mirrored pattern attested for the singular and plural in the two dialect groups. While Anglian shows an entirely innovative plural paradigm, in Saxon it is the singular that turns out to be much more innovative. The five innovative plural Anglian forms belong to *mōnaδ* and are attested as *mōnoδas* in the *Rushworth glosses* (JnGl (Ru) and Lk(Ru) (*n* = 4)) and singly as *mōnδo* in the Northumbrian *Lindisfarne glosses* (JnGl (Li)). Given the overall low number of the plural forms in Anglian, the figures cannot be interpreted as entirely conclusive, all the more so as no plural forms are attested for this dialect in the Late Old English period.

Table 3.52 Distribution of innovative forms in the OE *þ*-stem paradigm with respect to dialect *and* period

period/dialect	Saxon	Anglian
Early Old English	(*n* = 73) 52%	(*n* = 5) 20%
Late Old English	(*n* = 571) 80%	(*n* = 2) 100%

The distribution of analogical inflections attested for the two periods in the two dialect groups is reminiscent of the distribution of forms with respect to the period, presented in Table 3.50. Both dialect groups show a considerable increase in the amount of analogical inflection over time. This increase is much more abrupt in Anglian; however, given the scant number of attestations in the Anglian dialect group (altogether 14 innovative forms), the figures should not be taken at face value, and accordingly little can be concluded about the restructuring process in this dialect. Consequently, the trends identified in the examined data are based largely on the distributions found in the Saxon material, which due to its wider scope turns out to be more reliable.

3.6   Summary of the results and overview of the tendencies

A comparison of the findings so far gives more insight into the prevailing patterns of the nominal inflection reorganisation in Old English. The present section offers an overview of these patterns and tendencies, attempting to provide some interpretations. A closer look is given to aspects such as the directions of interdeclensional transfers, the productivity of the *a*-stem inflection and the factors conditioning the restructuring process.

One of the overarching patterns identified in the examined material concerns the directions of the interdeclensional transitions of nouns. They are summarised in Table 3.53 for individual declensional classes, including gender and (where relevant) stem-type distinctions.

Table 3.53 Directions of interdeclensional transfers of minor stems in Old English

Historical declensional class	New declensional class
i-stems (m)	=> *a*-stems
i-stems (n)	=> *a*-stems
i-stems (f)	=> *ō*-stems
u-stems (m)	=> *a*-stems
u-stems (f)	=> *ō*-stems
root nouns (m)	=> *a*-stems
root nouns (f)	=> *ō*-stems
r-stems (m)	=> *a*-stems
r-stems (f)	=> *ō*-stems, *a*-stems
s-stems (n)	=> *a*-stems (m, n)
monosyllabic *nd*-stems	=> *a*-stems
disyllabic *nd*-stems	=> *a*-stems, adjectival inflection
þ-stems	=> *a*-stems

Clearly, the analogical transitions of nouns affiliated originally with minor classes turn out to be almost entirely polarised by two dominant classes, the *a*-stems and *ō*-stems, with the former increasingly prevailing with the gradual loss of stability of the gender system towards the end of the Old English period. The trend is a continuation of the analogical developments present already in the Proto-Germanic period, where the dissemination of the *a*-stem and *ō*-stem inflections began. This early spread is particularly visible in the categories of the GEN. SG., GEN. PL. and DAT. PL., all showing no or very limited synchronic variation (cf. Chapter 2). Another potential attractor of minor stems, the *n*-stem inflection, does not display extensive traces of productivity at this early stage, but weak inflections appear occasionally in the GEN. PL. (-*ena*) and NOM./ACC. PL. (-*an*). They seem to be in general more frequent in the feminine nouns and, in terms of the distribution across declensional classes, fairly frequent in the *u*-stem paradigm. Altogether, the influence of the *n*-stem inflection is fairly limited, especially when seen from a Middle English perspective, where this inflectional pattern was widespread, especially in the South. In terms of dialectal distribution, the *n*-stem inflections are more common in the texts of West-Saxon provenance, which is not surprising, given, firstly, the later date of attestation of these sources, and secondly, the fact that the dissemination of the *n*-stem inflections was a feature proper to the southern dialects of Middle English. Although no systematic quantitative analysis was conducted to estimate the exact scope of the spread of the *n*-stem endings relative to the *a*-stem and *ō*-stem inflections, it can be concluded (on the basis of the distribution of inflections in the examined paradigms) that the Old English stage witnessed a creeping, but relatively limited spread of the *n*-stem inflections in the minor paradigms.

Another characteristic of inflectional reorganisation, which the patterns presented in Table 3.53 demonstrate, is related to gender. The examined material allows one to claim that the remodelling of the inflectional system in Old English was governed by gender-based analogy, whereby the interparadigmatic reshufflings were congruous with the gender classes. In other words, gender served as a guiding factor for the major directions of noun transfers: the interdeclensional shifts occurred in line with the original gender class affiliation. However, the data indicate that this consistency in the preservation of gender-class affiliation was to some extent distorted, and some gender confusion did occur. This slight tendency can be found across various minor paradigms and it is a phenomenon occurring on the lemma- rather than class-level. The variation in the use of gendered forms, at the same time, does not reflect a systematic gender change. Although no consistent quantitative analysis was performed to chart the process of gender class change alongside the change of declensional affiliation, the spread of the masculine inflectional markers was noticeably more common in some classes than others. The attested examples of such a shift of gender class indicate that the change is unidirectional, with an evident preference for the masculine gender. This type of interaction, i.e. masculinisation tendencies, with the extension of masculine inflection to feminine (and neuter) nouns, is not necessarily a matter of change in gender class affiliation. Instead, such a process entails primarily a change of declensional class affiliation under the pressure of the most prevalent inflectional pattern, which happened to be masculine in Old English. Accordingly, the ubiquity of the masculine markers in most instances is not (or need not be) a manifestation of a change of gender affiliation, since any such change would require more than just the appropriation of a new masculine inflectional exponent. In fact, in many instances where the new inflectional masculine marker was attached to the noun, the original feminine or neuter demonstrative pronoun (or any other form of the attribute) was still retained, which does not fulfill the criteria of gender change.

Furthermore, one of the essential prerequisites for gender change is the extension of the unhistorical gender forms throughout the paradigm (Jones 1967: 291) rather than their confinement to one or two categories (especially the GEN. SG. or NOM./ACC. PL.), which was very often the case in the attested forms. Given that the adoption of masculine inflection was not very consistent, it can be concluded that the change of inflectional class affiliation did not involve a concomitant change in gender, and if it did happen, its extent was fairly limited (cf. Adamczyk 2011). Most cases reflect instead the prevalence of the new case-and-number exponent rather than the gender marker. Accordingly, the innovative GEN. SG. marker *-es* or the NOM./ACC. PL. ending -*as*, with their considerable analogical force, are not primarily indicators of gender in the nouns changing their class affiliation, but merely case-and-number exponents, emerging under the growing pressure of the most productive inflectional type, i.e. the *a*-stems.[177]

Table 3.54 presents an overview of the distribution of inherited and analogical inflections in individual declensional classes, irrespective of case and number or stem-type distinction. It must be emphasised that such a presentation of the re-sults of the investigation has many limitations – it is per definition oversimplified. The figures represent aggregated values and do not capture significant details of the distributions in individual classes and paradigms. The figures for the *i*-stems (marked italics), in contrast to the other examined classes, are not representative of the entire class, but only of the subtypes where residues of the original pattern were retained, i.e. where the synchronic alternation between inherited and innovative forms could be captured (cf. Section 3.5.2.3). Bearing in mind all these limitations, a few generalisations about the attested pattern of distribution can be ventured.

Table 3.54 Summary of the distribution of archaic and innovative inflections in the OE minor stems per class

	archaic	innovative
i-stems	*(1440) 73%*	*(533) 27%*
u-stems	(2327) 55%	(1585) 45%
root nouns	(3544) 79%	(940) 21%
s-stems	(138) 31%	(302) 69%
r-stems	(2086) 64%	(1155) 36%
nd-stems	(1225) 47%	(1357) 53%
þ-stems	(305) 36%	(547) 64%

Taking the figures at face value, the *s*-stems and the residual *þ*-stems, where the level of innovation reaches more than 60 percent, were the most innovative types. The root nouns and the *r*-stems turn out to have been the least conducive to ana-logical pressures from the *a*- and *ō*-stems. Nonetheless, in the *nd*-stems, the figures obscure the actual entirely divergent paths of inflectional development in the two

---

177. A systematic examination of the use of the attributives in the Old English root nouns cor-roborates this assumption. It reveals that in hardly any of the investigated root nouns is the new gender manifested by the application of a new demonstrative pronoun; the variation is predominantly expressed by the extension of the masculine *a*-stem markers to the head nouns (Adamczyk 2011). Accordingly, *Genuswechsel* is highly unlikely in these shifts, as no consistent transition or complete change to a new set of gender indicative modifiers in any one noun could be identified in the examined material.

types of stems, mono- and disyllabic ones, the former retaining the archaic inflection, the latter being substantially more innovative (cf. Section 3.5.7.2). Likewise, in the *r*-stems, the overall figure conceals the divergent paths of restructuring in the singular and plural, with the former remaining largely archaic, the latter being dominated by analogical inflections. The vocalic stems (*u*-stems), testify to a moderate level of innovation, but there again many significant details are obscured in these overall figures. Accordingly, instead of interpreting the patterns emerging from these figures on the class-level, closer attention will be given to specific aspects of this distribution, which can lead to a more adequate explanation of the attested patterns.

The attested diverse levels of innovation in the paradigms of individual classes can be attributed to a number of interrelated factors, three of which turn out to be decisive for the attested patterns: (1) the frequency of occurrence/use, (2) the salience of inflectional exponents and (3) the semantic makeup of classes, including the semantics of individual nouns. The attested inflectional profiles of the minor stem paradigms emerge as a result of a complex interaction between these controlling factors, which can either enhance or neutralise the effects of the activity of individual determinants. In order to gain a better understanding of the mechanisms involved in the restructuring process and the nature of the interactions between the factors mentioned, a closer examination of some details of the distribution of inflections is required.

One of the tendencies is the demonstrably divergent restructuring pattern in the singular and plural across all declensional classes. Table 3.55 depicts the distribution of analogical inflections in individual minor classes with respect to number. The figures in brackets refer to a total number of singular and plural tokens (n).

Table 3.55 Distribution of innovative inflections in the OE minor stems
with respect to number

	SG	PL
i-stems	(*n* = 1563) 10%	(*n* = 410) 80%
u-stems	(*n* = 2948) 40%	(*n* = 617) 71%
root nouns	(*n* = 2208) 27%	(*n* = 1344) 6%
r-stems	(*n* = 2057) 9%	(*n* = 1184) 82%
s-stems	(*n* = 238) 90%	(*n* = 205) 42%
mon. *nd*-stems	(*n* = 309) 75%	(*n* = 1110) 9%
dis. *nd*-stems	(*n* = 893) 93%	(*n* = 270) 74%
þ-stems	(*n* = 574) 77%	(n= 278) 38%

The pattern found in the data is not entirely straightforward, and generalisations above the class-level pose some difficulties unless the fine details of this distribution are taken into account. In general, it can be concluded that in most minor classes the paradigm of the singular tended to be more easily remodelled on the pattern of the productive classes than the plural. The high amount of innovation in the singular is to be ascribed predominantly to the category of the GEN. SG., which, irrespective of the class, was the most susceptible to analogical pressure from the productive inflection. This analogical pressure came primarily from the *a*-stem masculine marker -*es*, which emerges as a very stable ("super-stable" Wurzel 1987) and a very productive inflectional exponent, whose spread began at an early stage, prior to the first written attestations of Old English.

The factors responsible for the attested distributions of analogical forms with respect to the category of number differ, to some extent depending on the individual declension, but they essentially involve an interaction of the internal shape of the paradigms (salience), (token) frequency, and semantics. The correlation between the amount of innovative inflection in the paradigm and the salience of inflectional markers seems to be fairly straightforward. In root nouns, where the presence of allomorphic variation is consistent even in the singular (DAT. SG.), the amount of innovation is altogether very low, both in the singular and the plural. The vocalic stems (*i*-stems and *u*-stems), where the relevant categories both in the singular and the plural are marked with a vowel (-*e*, -*u* or -*a*) or a zero ending, show a much higher amount of analogical inflection in the paradigm, especially in the plural. In the other consonantal minor classes, the plural tends to remain altogether much more conservative, except in the *r*-stems, where the pattern is entirely opposite, despite the fact that the singular is not characterised by any distinct inflectional marker. Where the salience of inflectional marking does not account for the patterns found in the minor stem paradigms, recourse needs to be made to the other potential factors.

The correlation between the salience of inflectional exponents and the level of innovation is more direct if the plural paradigm on its own is taken into account, as presented in Table 3.56. The type of plural marker is juxtaposed with the percentage of analogical inflections in the plural paradigm in individual classes. The plural refers here to the forms in the NOM./ACC. PL., except in the *s*-stems, where the forms of all oblique cases were taken into consideration.

Evidently, the preservation of archaic inflection correlates strongly with the shape of the plural paradigm. The less distinctive (salient) the inflectional marker is, the more widespread the presence of analogical inflections in the paradigm. Accordingly, the *r*-stems and disyllabic *nd*-stems, where the plural is characterised by a zero ending, turn out to be the two most innovative plural paradigms.

Table 3.56 The correlation between the salience of plural markers and the innovation level in the OE minor stems

	plural marker(s)	% innovation in PL
i-stems (light-syllable)	vocalic marker -*e*, -*i*	76%
u-stems	vocalic marker -*a*	71%
root nouns	Ø + *i*-mutated vowel	6%
s-stems	*r*-marker	42%
r-stems	Ø marker	82%
mon. *nd*-stems	Ø + *i*-mutated vowel	9%
dis. *nd*-stems	Ø marker	74%
þ-stems	*þ*-marker	38%

A high percentage of analogical features is found also in the *i*-stems, where the plural is characterised by the ending -*e*, which served as an inflectional marker in many morphosyntactic categories across several declensional classes, and can thus be considered "the least useful marker" (Bertacca 2009: 49), susceptible to external influences. The other vocalic class, the *u*-stems, emerges as only slightly more conservative, with the vocalic marker of the NOM./ACC. PL. -*a*, showing some more resistance to the pressure of analogical inflections. In contrast, the presence of *i*-mutation in the paradigm as a distinctive case-and-number marker (though essentially a receding feature) turns out to have been a major factor which inhibited the activity of analogical processes in the paradigms. This is confirmed by the class of root nouns, as well as *nd*-stems, where the contrast between the nouns where the plural was marked by an *i*-mutated vowel and those without *i*-mutation is very sharp. Another relatively salient and distinctive marker of plurality is the *r*-formative present in the *s*-stems, which turns out to have a conserving effect as well. The spread of the endingless forms in the *s*-stem paradigm was enhanced by the fact that the default class for these nouns was endingless neuter *a*-stems. This conserving effect of a consonantal stem alternation is evident also in the dental stems, which, characterised by a distinctive dental marker (-*þ*), quite unexpectedly show a relatively low level of innovation. Given the scarcity of the attestations for this declensional class, the inferences can be only tentative. The marker is also subsequently extended to other cases in the paradigm, losing thus its original functional strength.

Another factor which turned out to be crucial is frequency, in particular token frequency, operating at the level of morphosyntactic category, class and lemma. The analysed data reveals a particularly heavy reliance of the patterns of restructuring on the relative frequency, in particular the singular-plural proportion (i.e. number of plural tokens as a proportion of all tokens). Table 3.57 illustrates the correlation between the plural proportion and the overall level of innovative inflection in the plural. Additionally, the type of inflectional exponent was presented to underscore the fact that these conditioning factors are not entirely independent of each other, but rather interact with each other, and that the final shape of inflection depends on this interaction.

Table 3.57 The correlation between the innovation level in the plural paradigms and the plural proportion

	plural marker	PL proportion	% innovation in PL
nd-stems (dis.)	Ø marker	11%	74%
r-stems	Ø marker	18%	82%
i-stems	vocalic marker -e/-i	20%	70%
u-stems	vocalic marker -a	40%	63%
s-stems	r-marker	41%	47%
þ-stems	þ-marker	41%	38%
root nouns	Ø + i-mutation	42%	8%
nd-stems (mon.)	Ø + i-mutation	65%	9%

As can be observed, the correlation between the amount of innovative inflection in the paradigm and the relative plural proportion holds for almost all the examined declensional classes. More specifically, the low level of plural proportion in the paradigms contributes to a considerable instability of the inherited plural inflection. Accordingly, the disyllabic nd-stems, r-stems and i-stems, which are less frequent in the plural, tend to show a very high level of innovation in their plural paradigms (≥ 70%). In contrast, the monosyllabic nd-stems, much more frequent in the plural, attest to hardly any traces of analogical inflection in the plural paradigms. In the other minor classes, the plural proportion oscillates around 40 percent, and their level of innovation in the plural is limited, although the range of percentages varies from very low in the archaic root nouns to relatively high in the u-stems. The divergent pattern found in these stems must be accounted for by the fact that the frequency factor is not the sole determinant of the attested pattern, but is accompanied by the activity of other factors, in particular the salience of inflectional marking. The presence of a salient exponent in the NOM./ACC.PL. in the root nouns clearly had a reinforcing effect, enhancing the retention of the i-mutated vowel in the paradigm. The much less salient vocalic marker in the NOM./ACC.PL. of the u-stems had an opposite effect, rendering the paradigm of the u-stems much more susceptible to analogical pressures.

The frequency of morphosyntactic categories also seems to have played a role in the attested inflectional patterns. In fact, the discrepancy between the figures in the singular and plural may be largely attributed to the fact that the figures for the plural are based on the two more frequent categories, i.e. the NOM. and ACC. (PL.), whereas the figures for the singular are based predominantly on the GEN. and DAT. (SG.), which are less frequent cases and thus more prone to analogical modification. Likewise, the GEN. SG., GEN. PL. and DAT. PL., which are in general the least frequent categories, turned out to be the categories most easily and earliest affected by analogical developments. The spread of analogical inflections in these categories, especially those of the GEN. PL. and DAT. PL. must be dated to the prehistoric stage.

The different frequency profiles of individual classes and paradigms are determined essentially by the semantics of the nouns affiliated with them. The fact that a given lemma was more commonly used in the plural than in the singular (e.g. nouns denoting small animals or certain nouns of relationship), or in a given morphosyntactic category, e.g. in the DAT. SG. (heavy syllable *u*-stems), or in the NOM./ACC. (*nd*-stems, referring to people), is entirely reliant on their meanings. In this sense, semantics affects the dynamics of the restructuring process in a significant but indirect way; namely, it translates into the frequency profiles of the lemmas, paradigms and classes. Some minor effect of semantics can also be expected in classes which form semantically coherent groups, which in turn enhances the retention of the historical inflection (cf. the PDE endingless plural in nouns denoting certain animals), but as the analysis demonstrated, this factor played a secondary role in inflectional restructuring (cf. the *r*-stems).

It becomes evident that the reduction of inflectional diversity was a cumulative effect of both interparadigmatic and intraparadigmatic developments. This refers in particular to the elimination of the *i*-mutated vowel from the paradigm and its replacement by the unmutated vowels from other paradigm forms (especially in the *s*-stems, but also in the singular paradigm of root nouns and in the *nd*-stems), as well as the elimination of the consonantal alternations (from the paradigms of the *s*-stems and dental stems). This levelling of the morphophonemic alternations, instigated by the working of *intra*paradigmatic analogy, rendered the paradigm more uniform and thus increased the susceptibility of individual cases/categories to external, *inter*paradigmatic analogical pressures, facilitating the attachment of new inflectional markers.

The levelling of allomorphic variation had also a different dimension: it involved a change in the status of the *i*-mutated vowel, whereby it became the exponent of the number only (Kastovsky 1985: 104). This refers in particular to the root nouns, where the irregular plural inflection is residually retained until present-day English. The development was enforced through the disintegration of the case marking system towards the end of the Old English period, and the concomitant intraparadigmatic processes. With the elimination of the allomorphy from the GEN. and DAT. SG., the *i*-mutated vowel started to function as the main feature disambiguating the singular from the plural, and gradually became a relatively stable plural marker in the root nouns.

Another tendency observable in the examined material is the divergent development of the restructuring process with respect to the weight of the syllable in the minor stems. The light-syllable stems tended to be more resistant to analogical pressures than the heavy-syllable ones. This can be seen in the classes of *i*-stems (18%), masculine *u*-stems (38%) and feminine *u*-stems (10%). The light-syllable root nouns do not entirely comply with this pattern, showing analogical features in 51 percent of forms, and thus a less archaic profile than the corresponding heavy-syllable nouns. Two factors emerge as responsible for such a distribution: (1) the less consistent presence of *i*-mutation in the paradigm due to *intra*paradigmatic reshufflings in the light-syllable nouns, and (2) the adopted interpretation of the NOM. SG. forms, where the endingless form is interpreted as archaic (cf. the discussion in Section 3.5.4.2).

Table 3.58 presents the overall distribution of historical and analogical inflections in the singular and plural paradigms of the Old English minor stems. Again, the emerging picture of the linguistic innovations is largely oversimplified, but it gives some indication as to the scope of the restructuring process. The presented figures do not have much relevance in *absolute* terms, but they gain meaning relative to the respective overall figures from the investigation of the other Northern West Germanic languages.

Table 3.58 Overall distribution of archaic and innovative inflections in the OE minor stems

	archaic	innovative
singular	61% (6233)	39% (3956)
plural	61% (3037)	39% (1971)
Total	61% (9270)	39% (5927)

Much as these figures cannot be taken at face value, they can be viewed as representative of certain general tendencies identified in the material. They unambiguously indicate that as a result of analogical processes affecting the nominal paradigms in the Old English period, the system of nominal inflections inherited from Proto-Germanic underwent a substantial reorganisation. The inflections of the productive declensional types constitute a considerable portion of all the inflections in the minor stem paradigms. The figures for the singular and plural represent here averages and are in fact somewhat misleading: as can be seen in Table 3.55, in none of the minor classes is the level of analogical forms the same for the singular and plural. In fact, in all the examined classes except the *r*-stems and *u*-stems the percentage of analogical forms is higher in the singular than the plural. In other words, the contrasts which could be observed in the individual classes are flattened in these combined figures. The major reason for this is the uneven (token) frequency distribution of the singular and plural forms, and especially the fact that the *u*-stems and *r*-stems, which are conservative in the singular, are also extremely frequent in the singular. Such a distribution of forms affects the overall figure for the singular, concealing the average higher level of innovation in this category (cf. Table 3.55).

The most prominent patterns of restructuring with respect to the dialectal and diachronic distribution are presented in Tables 3.59 and 3.60. It must be observed that the figures do not include a substantial number of forms from texts identified as *Indeterminate* in the corpus, and hence the they do not correspond directly to the figures found in Table 3.58.

Table 3.59 Diachronic distribution of innovative inflections in the OE minor stems

	Innovative inflection		
	Singular	Plural	Overall
Early Old English	26% (1222)	31% (483)	28% (1705)
Late Old English	44% (6315)	35% (2841)	41% (9156)

Table 3.60 Distribution of innovative features in the OE minor stems with respect to period

	% innovative inflection	
	Early Old English	Late Old English
u-stems	33%	52%
root nouns	14%	22%
r-stems	14%	26%
s-stems	52%	70%
mon. *nd*-stems	25%	23%
dis. *nd*-stems	88%	89%
þ-stems	50%	73%

The examined data reveals the gradualness of the process, demonstrated by the patterns found in all classes except the *nd*-stems, where the level of innovation is almost identical in the two periods. The figures prove that the restructuring of inflection in Old English was not a rapid development affecting the entire lexicon directly, and that its progression and tempo was determined especially by the unfolding of phonological processes. The contrast between the Early and Late Old English period is smaller than could be expected from the standard historical descriptions, where typically two extreme stages are presented, i.e. the Early Old

English stage, represented by a range of archaic forms, contrasted with the much more innovative features of the Late Old English period. The present analysis offers a refinement of such an approach, capturing and revealing the continuity and gradualness of inflectional restructuring.

As regards absolute chronology of restructuring, the influence of the *a*-stem and *ō*-stem inflections can already be found in the early Old English material, with forms such as *fōtas* and *tōþas*, attested in the *Vespasian Psalter*, dated to the mid-ninth century. Also the earliest glosses, CorpGl, EpGl as well as the texts of *Pastoral Care* (late 9th c.), or *Orosius* (9th/10th c.), show sporadic traces of analogical inflections in the paradigms of root nouns, *s*-stems or *u*-stems. However, the majority of innovative forms were found in prose texts of Late West Saxon provenance. This applies to the influence of both the productive vocalic and consonantal inflection, the latter attested predominantly in the GEN. PL. and NOM./ACC. PL. (*-ana -ena*, *-an*). Sporadic attestation of the analogical inflections in Late Anglian material (10th c.) was also identified in the examined material (*Lindisfarne* and *Rushworth Gospels*).

The details of the dialectal distribution of analogical inflections in the analysed material are presented in Tables 3.61 and 3.62, including the distributions for individual minor classes.

Table 3.61 Dialectal distribution of innovative inflections in the OE minor stems

	Innovative inflection		
	Singular	Plural	Overall
Anglian	33% (937)	36% (457)	34% (1394)
Saxon	40% (8333)	37% (3736)	39% (12066)

Table 3.62 Distribution of innovative features in the OE minor stems with respect to dialect

	% innovative inflection	
	Anglian	Saxon
u-stems	21%	47%
root nouns	11%	21%
r-stems	36%	23%
s-stems	52%	70%
nd-stems (mon.)	50%	21%
nd-stem (dis.)	79%	90%
þ-stems	64%	71%

As the data indicate, the general tendency towards adopting analogical inflections is attested in both dialect groups, with largely parallel patterns found in the individual classes. A higher level of innovation is found in the Saxon material and it is largely attributable to its dating. The dialectal discrepancies are most explicit in the *s*-stems, with West-Saxon displaying a highly innovative pattern, testifying to a large-scale transference of the original *s*-stems to the productive inflection (70%), and Anglian retaining a more archaic profile (52%), on account of the archaic vestiges in Mercian (cf. Section 3.5.6.2). Most of the other declensional types show a higher innovation level in the Saxon material. A converse pattern is found in the *r*-stems and the monosyllabic *nd*-stems, where a higher amount of innovative inflection is attested in Anglian. This higher level of innovation in Anglian is mostly due to the Late Northumbrian forms, which show a consistent expansion of the productive inflections across minor classes. In the *r*-stems, the pattern seems to reflect the dialectal contrast, i.e. the fact that the Anglian dialect was indeed more innovative from the earliest attestations onwards (cf. Table 3.31).

Overall, it can be concluded that the restructuring process was not dialect-specific, and that the dynamics of the changes were very much the same across the dialects of Old English. An exception here is the development of the *s*-stems, where the spread of innovative inflections is dialectally-conditioned. Also note that the dialectal contrasts found in the investigated material largely reflect the diachronic ones, which is not made transparent in the figures presented in Table 3.61 and 3.62. In other words, much of the attested dialectal variation can actually be explained diachronically. At the same time, as could be seen in the combined figures for individual classes, where these two dimensions were separated, the differences identified there turned out not to be significant either, except in the monosyllabic *nd*-stems (cf. Table 3.37 and Table 3.46).[178]

The primary cause for the expansion of the productive inflectional patterns can be sought in extra-morphological processes, namely, phonological reduction and deletion, characteristic of all Germanic languages (cf. Wurzel 1989: 102–103). These processes (especially, the attrition of the unaccented back vowels), occurring at the prehistoric stage, were the primary trigger for the reorganisation of the Old English nominal system, since they determined the shape of the nominal

---

178. Another aspect which may have had a bearing on the results of the investigation involves the labelling of the Old English texts as *Early* or *Late*, which of necessity entails an element of arbitrariness. As the dating is commonly based on philological criteria, it may not always correspond to linguistic reality. This aspect stays beyond the scope of the present study, but in light of the findings, the validity of the classification of some sources in the *DOE* (which is a heritage of the philological tradition), seems questionable and the classification itself may be in need of some revision or refinement (e.g. the labelling of *Bede's Ecclesiastical History* as an *Early* source despite its linguistic (here morphological) innovativeness).

paradigms. For instance, as a result of the loss of the original NOM. SG. exponents -*i*- and -*u*- in the heavy-syllable masculine *i*- and *u*-stems (respectively), these stems could no longer be distinguished from the *a*-stems in the NOM. SG., which triggered or at least furthered the expansion of the productive inflectional markers in their paradigms (for more details on the mechanisms of the restructuring, see the discussion in Chapter 8).

Alongside the more universal tendencies, a number of patterns identified in the Old English material turn out to be rather language-specific than cross-linguistic. This concerns in particular the gravitation of minor stems towards one declensional type, the *a*-stems, but also a few other related tendencies. Although the productivity of the *ō*-stems is well attested in the Old English corpus, the masculine *a*-stem inflection was more influential. The attested dominance and spectacular productivity of the *a*-stem inflection, whose scale of dissemination is unparalleled in the other investigated languages, can be ascribed to a number of formal features proper to this declensional type. One of them is (1) a relatively limited number of syncretic inflections in the paradigm, which was confined to the categories of the NOM./ACC. SG. and NOM./ACC. PL. (2) The presence of an explicit exponent in the plural (NOM./ACC. PL.) was another important characteristic which permitted to keep the functional contrast between the singular and the plural. Such a functional opposition was absent from the other minor classes, for instance, the light-syllable *i*-stems, where the ending -*e* served as an inflectional marker of the NOM., ACC. and DAT. SG., as well as the NOM. and ACC. PL., or in the *u*-stems, where the ending -*a* served as an exponent of the GEN. and DAT. SG., as well as the NOM. and ACC. PL. Of significance for the stability of the *a*-stem declension was also the fact that (3) the class contained two very salient inflectional exponents, i.e. the NOM./ACC. PL. marker -*as* and the GEN. ending -*es* (cf. Section 1.4.6.2). This morpho-phonological salience not only allowed these markers to spread widely to many minor inflectional paradigms in the Old English period, but it also rendered them persistent enough to survive as inflectional markers until present-day English. Additionally, two markers belonging originally to this declensional class, i.e. the GEN. SG. marker -*es*, common also in the neuter paradigm, as well as well as the DAT. PL. ending -*um*, had the status of *superstable* markers, being category markers across a number of inflectional classes. The *a*-stem DAT. PL. marker -*um*, as well as the GEN. PL. ending -*a*, are considered to have been one of the earliest inflectional markers to extend to the minor inflectional types (Bertacca 2009: 52; 2001; Wurzel 1987: 82–83).

Another important feature contributing to the stability of the *a*-stem pattern is related to the (4) typological status of the Old English morphological system, which can be viewed as heterogeneous (Kastovsky 1990: 262), given that stem-inflection, serving as the basic inflectional type, coexisted with word-inflection, proper to a portion of the Old English nouns. The *a*-stem declension is assumed to have represented word- rather than stem-based inflection (with a few exceptions), and was thus morphosemantically and morphotactically more transparent (Kastovsky 1997: 67). The typological shift, whereby the inherited stem-based inflection receded in favour of word-based inflection, could be one of the factors that contributed to the subsequent overwhelming spread of the *a*-stems as attested in Old English.

Two further features can be held responsible for the productivity of the *a*-stem paradigm in Old English, namely, (5) the lack of allomorphic variation in the paradigm and (6) "additive (i.e. iconic) encoding of all marked categories" (i.e. except the ACC. and NOM. SG.) (Bertacca 2009: 180–181). The former contributes to the greater transparency of the paradigm and complies with the rule that an invariant shape of the stem is perceptually more transparent and can thus be better memorised. The latter stays in compliance with the principle that the addition of morphological marking corresponds to an increase in meaning (Mayerthaler 1980: 25; cf. Section 1.4.4). Both vindicate the assumption that suffixation as a mechanism of expressing plurality or case relations tends to be preferred to internal stem alternation (in Germanic) (Dressler 1985a; cf. Bybee & Newmann 1995: 635ff.). The principle accounts for the fact that the *i*-mutated forms in the DAT. SG. tended to be eventually eliminated by the cumulative influence of both intra- and interparadigmatic analogy. An additional explanation for the widespread extension of the *a*-stem inflections in the vocalic classes involves (7) a change in the status of the stem formative, which was reinterpreted as an inflectional ending (e.g in the *i*-stems), leading eventually to a shift from stem- to word-based inflection (cf. Section 3.7). All these aspects will be the focus of a more detailed discussion in Chapter 7, and will be interpreted in a broader West Germanic context.

Overall, the expansion of the *a*-stem inflection can be viewed as a form of repair strategy, directed at restoring explicit category marking, i.e. replacing the obscure inflectional markers (such as the GEN./DAT. SG. -*ur* in the *s*-stems) by more transparent ones (-*es*, -*e*). The significance of this repair strategy becomes profound in the context when the essential contrasts in the paradigm are endangered, namely, the opposition between the singular and the plural. Given that the confusion of vowels in inflectional syllables brought considerable inconsistency into the paradigms of minor stems, it seems conceivable that the introduction of an ending as stable as the plural marker -*as* enabled retention of the most crucial distinction in the paradigm, i.e. the one in number. Such an interpretation allows one to view the operation of analogical processes as encouraged by the need to mark the functional distinctions between the singular and plural, as suggested by Hogg (1980: 283) with reference to the reshaping of the *i*-stem paradigm (cf. Kastovsky 1995).

Finally, the quantitative dominance of the *a*-stem declension, comprising close to 60 percent of Old English nouns, is highly significant. This proportion, however, is rather a consequence of the fact that this declension had the mentioned inherent characteristics which allowed it to have grown into a strong inflectional pattern, capable of attracting nouns originating in the less productive declensional types.

3.7 Taxonomic implications of the study

The basic criterion for establishing the paradigmatic affiliation of nouns in Old English (as well as in the other Germanic languages) is etymological, i.e. the type of stem, whereby the nouns were classified into a range of vocalic and consonantal declensions. This traditional approach to taxonomising nouns entails two underlying assumptions, i.e. the continuity of the earlier Proto-Indo-European and Proto-Germanic morphological realities, and the relevance of these realities for the descriptions of the nominal inflection in Older Germanic languages. However, the morphological structure of nouns inherited from the earlier stages had been obscured by the time of Early Old English, and, consequently, the adopted classifications turn out to be largely inadequate as was observed, among others, by Kastovsky (1995), Lass (1997b) and Krygier (1998, 2002, 2004).[179] The problem of the taxonomy of the Old English nominal system has also been addressed by Bertacca (2009), according to whom the major flaw in the traditional approach, apart from the fact that identical paradigms "are distinguished because of their different etymological thematic vowels", is treating the isolated, unproductive paradigms "on a par with all the others, despite their total marginality and lack of productivity" (Bertacca 2009: 138).

The phonological developments affecting inflectional paradigms over time led to a loss of the stem formatives, which used to form the basis for the classification of nouns, or their confusion with inflectional markers. As a result, the role of the inflectional ending increased considerably, to the extent that the inflectional paradigms came to depend on it rather than on the oblique etymological stem formative. As the unstressed vowels of inflectional syllables were particularly vulnerable to the reduction processes, the ambiguity of the inflectional endings tended to increase, inducing a growing number of paradigmatic syncretisms. Some of these syncretisms were inherited from Proto-West Germanic, where, for example, no formal

---

179. Apart from these theoretically-oriented considerations, Krygier (2004) offers a statistical underpinning of the restructuring of the paradigm of Old English *u*-stems. See also Steins (1998) for the argumentation against the use of arbitrary features in the analysis of inflectional systems.

differentiation existed between the NOM. and ACC. SG. in masculine stems, and where the process of progressive loss of transparency of the stem formative began.

Another development contributing to the gradual obliteration of the original morphological structure of Old English nouns, as observed by Kastovsky (1995) with reference to the *i*-stems, was the change in the status of the stem formative, which, if not lost, was reanalysed as a case-number exponent. Accordingly, the reflex of the original *i*-stem formative, the final vowel *-e* (as in OE *cyre*), was re-interpreted as part of the stem (understood here as the base form) (*cyre#*) on the template of the *a*-, *ja*-stems (cf. *here*) which had no marker in the NOM./ACC. SG. (referred to as the unmarked base form) (Kastovsky 1995: 228; Keyser & O'Neil 1985: 101).[180] A parallel interpretation can be applied to the Old English *u*-stem declension. The pattern which created the template for the reinterpretation was that of the *a*- and *wa*- stems (*bearu*, PL. *bearwas*), characterised by a lack of the case-number exponent in the NOM./ACC. SG. The status of the reflex of the original *u*-stem formative (*-u*) changed, as it was accordingly reinterpreted as a part of the stem (*sunu#*). Such a change in the status of the stem formative led to a situation where class affiliation was "no longer marked explicitly by a morphological segment, but became an implicit morphological property of the stem, i.e. was largely unpredictable" (Kastovsky 1995: 228; cf. Hogg 1980: 282). This change in the morphological structure of nouns is believed to be one of the most significant developments contributing to the morphological reanalysis of the nominal system.

The inadequacy of the traditional classifications of Old English nouns can be viewed as a direct consequence of the opacity of the early English declensional system, attributable to its three major characteristics: (a) the lack of transparency of the etymological stem formatives, (b) the lack of uniqueness of the inflectional markers, and (c) the homophony of inflectional markers of different classes (Bertacca 2009: 49; cf. Krygier 1998, 2002; Hogg & Fulk 2011).

Another question to consider is whether the inflectional criterion can be better fitted as the basis for an accurate classification of the paradigms. Two more recent attempts at a systematic reclassification of the Old English nouns according to the inflectional ending parameter were made by Bertacca (2009) and Hogg & Fulk (2011), both drawing on the earlier, more formalisation-oriented proposal by Krygier (1998, 2002). In the treatment offered by Krygier (2002), who concentrates on the productive declensional types, the basic classificatory criterion is

---

180. The evidence for such an interpretation comes from compounding, e.g. *winescipe* 'friend-ship', *wineleas* 'friendless', *spereleas* 'without a point', and *sperenīþ* 'spear strife', where the first element of the compound, containing the once inflectional ending *-e*, constitutes the stem form (Keyser & O'Neil 1985: 101).

paradigm unity, and the GEN. SG. exponent serves as an effective parameter whose "distribution (…) aligns neatly with paradigm boundaries" (Krygier 2002: 316). Accordingly, the postulated system consists of three declensional types and, significantly, grammatical gender does not play any role in the paradigm assignment. A more complex system is offered by Bertacca (2009), who applying the Natural Morphology framework, groups paradigms into a range of classes in a hierarchical structure (i.e. from macroclass to microclass), which is based on the principle of default inheritance (Corbett & Fraser 1993; cf. Dressler 2003). According to this rule, "a node may have an obligatory or a default property, and this property is inherited by its inferior nodes", where a *default property* refers, for instance, to the unmarked zero marker in the NOM. SG., proper to most nouns in a given declensional class (Bertacca 2009: 138–139). Accordingly, three macroclasses are postulated, each of them comprising respectively 13, 5, and 6 microclasses. The general threefold subdivision complies roughly with the categorisation proposed by Hogg (1992b: 137) on the basis of the NOM./ACC. PL. form, or by Krygier (2002), with the GEN. SG. serving as the basis for the division. The categorisation proposed by Hogg & Fulk (2011) is based on the assumption that "a noun [can] be assigned to a particular declension by virtue of the inflexions which it takes" (Hogg & Fulk 2011: 69). The nouns are classified into three major groups partly correlating with gender, with the NOM./ACC. PL. inflection serving as the basis for the labelling (*as-*, *a-* and *an-*declension). The remaining classes are subsumed under the term "minor declensions" and divided into three further types, where also the type of plurality marker is used as the main criterion (*a*-plurals, mutation plurals and *e*-plurals, kinship terms and zero plurals). The threefold subdivision is supplemented with a range of subtypes or subclasses, which account for the further variation present in the paradigms.

The declensional systems emerging from these alternative classifications turn out to be still fairly complex, and in fact the new classes largely correspond to the divisions which are based on the diachronic criteria. The three main classes postulated by the authors refer largely to the same three groups of nouns; accordingly, class 1 comprises historical *a*-stems, both masculine and neuter, class 2 historical feminine ō-stems, and class 3 historical *n*-stems. The minor paradigms require a more elaborate classification: although they do not represent prevalent or frequent inflectional patterns, the variety of inflections they display is too extensive to subsume them under the label of exceptions. This is particularly visible in the categorisation proposed by Bertacca who in an attempt at a systematic formalisation of the inflections arrives at a very elaborate declensional configuration. Undoubtedly, the added value of all these synchronic treatments is the new synchronic perspective, which more adequately illustrates (or rather gives an idea of) the actual linguistic situation that the learner of Old English had to face. However, given the complexity of the offered synchronic classifications, one can wonder whether such formalisations can be considered more efficient descriptions of the Old English nominal inflection.

The quantitative distribution of inflections, as mapped in the analysis, proves that none of the minor paradigms was free from the analogical features, with most of them showing a novel pattern in 35 to 70 percent of forms (cf. Table 3.54). Consequently, the paradigms described in the present study as "archaic" must be viewed as idealistic representations, in some instances (classes) hardly reflecting the actual shape of the early English inflection. In light of this, a diachronic approach, using the stem formative as the basic parameter for the classification of Old English nouns, seems far from being adequate. At the same time, the level of this inadequacy varies from class to class, and accordingly, if the inflectional ending were taken as the primary parameter of classification, the number of minor paradigms could be theoretically reduced, with traces of the inherited inflection viewed only in terms of some residual features.

One of the classes which could be easily subsumed under the productive inflectional paradigms of the *a*- or *ō*-stems is the class of *i*-stems. The findings from the investigation indicate that the traditional stem-class labels are obsolete from a synchronic point of view and a postulation of an independent *i*-stem class turns out to be synchronically unjustified. The sporadic historical features found in the paradigms of nouns originally affiliated with the *i*-stem declension (the marker -*e* in the NOM./ACC. PL. in masculine light-syllable stems, and the endless ACC. SG. in feminine heavy-syllable stems) should rather be interpreted as vestiges of the original *i*-stem pattern. Referring to the nouns showing these vestiges as the *i*-stems is inaccurate synchronically, since such an assignment bears no actual relation to their morphological properties as attested in Old English.

Another class which could be dispensed with is the group of the *s*-stems, which except in Anglian, decline predominantly according to the *a*-stem inflection. As the singular is almost entirely dominated by the *a*-stem inflection, the class could be viewed as a subtype of the neuter *a*-stem paradigm, with several lexicalised plurals retaining the *r*-formative. A similar status could be assigned to the dental stems, where a number of petrified features were preserved only in the plural. While the disyllabic *nd*-stems can be entirely subsumed under the *a*-stem pattern, the monosyllabic stems show a distinct profile with *i*-mutated vowels, parallel to that of the root nouns. Likewise, as the data presented in Table 3.54 indicate, the *u*-stems cannot be subsumed under any other declension as the attested pattern of inflections in their paradigms is fairly chaotic, and assigning them to the productive types would generate too many exceptions. The situation looks very different in the root nouns, where the innovation level in the paradigm is limited, and the class, although fossilised and entirely unproductive, is far from losing its identity as an independent declensional type. The presence of the *i*-mutated vowels in the DAT. SG. and the NOM./ACC. PL. renders the paradigm distinct and inhibits a large-scale analogical reshaping. Accordingly, root nouns could not be subsumed under any productive pattern and thus deprived of the status of an independent declensional type. In turn, the *r*-stems, where the disintegration of the inherited inflection is much less advanced in the singular, could be viewed as an independent class, with a distinct archaic singular and analogical plural, largely determined by gender. In other words, three minor declensions, i.e. *i*-stems, *s*-stems, and disyllabic *nd*-stems, can be reinterpreted and reclassified as subtypes of productive declensional types. The other classes, i.e. *r*-stems, root nouns and monosyllabic *nd*-stems, retain their distinct declensional profiles in Old English, with the root nouns and monosyllabic *nd*-stems sharing synchronically the same paradigm.

The investigated material allows one to conclude that much as a revision of the traditional taxonomy of Old English nouns is needed if it is to reflect the synchronic state of affairs, the level of innovation found in some of the classes does not admit of a radical reduction in the number of declensional classes. Clearly, the interplay of phonological and analogical developments disrupted the paradigmatic coherence of the minor classes, to the extent that some classes can be considered only vestiges of the original patterns (e.g. *i*-stems, dental stems, disyllabic *nd*-stems). On closer inspection, however, rather than conceiving of the changes as an elimination of *declensional classes*, one should approach the changes in the system in terms of an elimination of *paradigms*. As could be observed, in some classes the paradigm of the singular shows predominantly analogical features, while the plural retains traces of the inherited pattern (e.g. monosyllabic *nd*-stems); in others, an opposite distribution is found (e.g. *r*-stems – conservative in the singular and innovative in the plural). Altogether, given the figures presented in Tables 3.54 and 3.55, the overall picture of the early English nominal system remains considerably diversified, with a number of paradigms retaining a distinct inflectional profile. This refers in particular to the root nouns and monosyllabic *nd*-stems, where both paradigms turn out to be remarkably stable, and which consequently can be viewed as a coherent declensional type. At the same time, the evident discrepancy in the patterns found in the singular and plural across different classes, mostly with a conservative plural and very innovative singular, allows one to postulate the plural marker as the primary criterion for the classification of Old English nouns, as has been done, for instance, by Hogg & Fulk (2011).

The inflectional patterns found in the investigated material clearly prove that the reorganisation of the declensional system inherited from Proto-Germanic was advanced to such an extent that the traditional (etymological) stem class organisation has a limited relevance for the Old English linguistic reality. The system as presented in the traditional historical accounts does not adequately reflect the synchronic state of affairs (as attested in the corpus) and thus does not sufficiently capture the actual morphological structure of the idiom used in mediaeval England. The traditional labelling is synchronically inadequate as the paradigms do not consistently demonstrate clear evidence of stem marking, which would correspond to the assigned labels. The declensional class assignment of any given noun is predominantly lexically conditioned. However, as vestiges of the former stem types are easily identifiable in individual paradigms, it is justifiable to make synchronic morphological distinctions, acknowledging their existence. Another related problem is that of the formal criteria of class affiliation: many scantily attested nouns cannot be synchronically assigned to a declensional class with certainty, as there is no formal characteristic of the noun (root) that would suggest an affiliation with any given class. The problem of the lack of transparency of class affiliation is additionally enhanced by the extensive interparadigmatic inflectional syncretism, which generates many inflectional overlaps between classes.

Although the present study did not aspire to offer a revised classifcation of Old English nouns, the findings allow for some refinement of the existing diachronically-oriented descriptions. At the same time, the analysis of the minor paradigms has shown that despite the fact that the traditional stem-class labels are largely obsolete, the traditional distinction finds some synchronic support, as it partly corresponds to the synchronic classifications. It can be concluded that the most accurate classification of declensional classes in Old English would require an intermediate approach which mediates between the reality of the still existing inherited inflection as well as the reality of novel patterns, introduced through extensive analogical reshufflings.[181]

---

181. According to Hogg (1997b), the question of taxonomy exemplifies a more general problem of approaching the historical data. Namely, the descriptions or classifications of paradigms and forms found in the traditional accounts, while giving the impression of directly representing the textual evidence, are in fact not free from a theoretical bias. They are instead "representations of one type of theoretical analysis of the textual material." In other words, "the apparently theory-neutral approach of the standard handbooks conceals a very strong theoretical approach which has major implications for the presentation of the data (…)" (Hogg 1997b: 118).

3.8   Conclusions

The investigated material testifies to substantial inflectional variation in the minor paradigms, which indicates that the Old English nominal system was far from being stable. This lack of equilibrium is to a varying extent demonstrated in all minor paradigms, ranging from classes (or paradigms) which show an overall archaic profile (e.g. root nouns or monosyllabic *nd*-stems) to those displaying a much higher level of inflectional innovation (e.g. dental stems, *u*-stems, disyllabic *nd*-stems). The tendency to change the inflectional patterns, which resulted in wide-range interdeclensional shifts, determined the shape of the early English declensional system, working essentially towards reducing inflectional diversity. The wide-ranging consequences of such system dynamics, entailing a gradual elimination of the minor classes and the eventual reduction of the number of inflectional types, can be found in the makeup of the present-day English nominal system, where only residues of the original elaborate inflectional configuration are identifiable.

The Old English material, with its extensive temporal span, allows us to capture the dynamics of these developments, which are a continuation of the restructuring processes from the unattested stages (Proto-Germanic). One of these gradual changes was the gravitation of nouns towards the *a*-stems, which constituted a template for the reformation of other nominal paradigms even prior to the East/North-West Germanic split. The expansion of the *a*-stem pattern can be viewed as one of the most prominent tendencies in the remodelling of the minor stem inflection in Old English.

The underlying mechanism of the restructuring process, regulating the level of innovation in the paradigms, is the interaction between the phonological and analogical developments. It is the phonological changes that largely determined the shape of the inflectional paradigms, rendering them either more resistant (e.g. root nouns) or more susceptible (e.g. vocalic stems) to analogical pressures. In some minor paradigms, i.e. in the *i*- and *u*-stems, the effect of the phonological processes is even more consequential in that the analogical changes are largely enhanced by their phonological profiles. The loss of the original inflection in these classes cannot be ascribed solely to a large-scale morphological levelling, but to a combination of morphological levelling and phonological coalescence, with the latter factor being equally or perhaps even more important than the former.

Although the Old English material abounds in competing inflectional forms in the minor paradigms, the process cannot be viewed as an impetuous development, permeating the entire lexical stock. As could be observed in the diachronic part of the study, the restructuring of the nominal inflection was a gradual process. The frequent fluctuation of forms between the inherited and analogical inflections points to a continuous expansion of the latter, whereby the minor classes gradually lost their earlier distinct profiles. The process seems to conform to the mechanism of restructuring described within the Natural Morphology framework (Wurzel 1989), whereby inflectional classes which lack stability are inevitably eliminated as their members are transferred to more stable inflectional patterns (cf. Section 1.4.5).

The changes in the declensional system were "driven by well-defined internal forces whose dynamics followed universal preferences, typological adequacy and system adequacy" (Bertacca 2009: 184). A range of factors which turned out to have had an impact on the reshaping of the nominal inflection were identified in the present study. The reduction of inflectional diversity in the nominal system was a cumulative effect of both *inter*paradigmatic and *intra*paradigmatic analogical adjustments. The analysis has revealed the importance of the shape and strength (salience) of individual morphological exponents, including the stem-vowel alternation. The elimination of internal allomorphy from the paradigms had major implications for the reorganisation of nouns across declensional classes. The other major factor guiding the restructuring of the inflectional system was frequency of occurrence/ use, operating on different levels, including the level of morphosyntactic category, class and lemma, working towards the preservation of the original shape of the paradigm. This conserving effect may have been to some extent reinforced by semantics, whether of classes or of lexemes (kinship terms, collective nouns).

A significant role in the process of restructuring must be assigned to the category of gender, which determined the directions of interdeclensional transitions, in that the transfers mostly occurred according to gender class. While the material does show some variation in the use of gendered forms, the attested irregularities are far from reflecting a systematic gender change. Some masculinisation tendencies are manifested in the extension of the masculine *a*-stem forms to feminine and neuter paradigms; however, the attested variation reflects primarily the reorganisation of the formal system (case system), with the growing syncretism of nominal categories, and the competition between declensional types, rather than any major reorganisation occurring within the category of gender.

The findings from the present investigation indicate that the Old English period was a stage where the restructuring of the nominal inflection was fairly advanced. The developments resulting from an interaction of phonological and morphological factors were a continuation of the processes occurring already at the prehistoric stage, and gained some momentum especially in the Late Old English period, where the restructuring had a much wider scope. Many of the minor paradigms were apparently on the verge of losing their transparency and consequently their identity as separate declensional types. The wide range of analogical processes which affected the nominal inflection had the effect of re-establishing the transparency and functionality of the system, which had been largely shattered by the activity of phonological processes. The new architecture of the inflectional system was based on those inflectional paradigms which due to their transparency and functionality were able to maintain a distinct inflectional identity and thereby tended to polarise the nouns whose original paradigms became increasingly opaque.

The process of the reorganisation of the inflectional system found its continuation in the later stage of development of English, leading to an almost complete elimination of the inherited inflections. Of the six minor classes, only the vestiges of the root noun declension (with a stable inflectional profile in the Old English period) and the etymologically problematic *s*-stem *children* (OE *cild*: *cildru*) survive until present-day English as residual plural formations.

CHAPTER 4

Nominal inflection in Old Frisian

4.1 Introduction

Each of the Germanic languages investigated in the present study is unique, be it in the peculiarities of their existent records, their specific developmental features, their relations with the sister languages, or their geographical positioning with its often far-reaching linguistic consequences. The uniqueness of Old Frisian involves the nature of the available material, as well as its close linguistic bonds with the Anglo-Saxon idiom, which date back to the pre-invasion period, when the cultural interchanges were characterised by considerable intensity.[182] To what extent this close relationship with Old English is reflected in the investigated morphological developments will become evident in the present chapter, where a detailed examination of the Old Frisian material forms the background for a later comparison with the findings from the abundant corpus of its closest relative. The nature of the available Old Frisian material has constituted a challenge for comparative studies of Older Germanic languages, marginalising it essentially to the status of "the Cinderella of Germanic philology" (Nielsen 1990: 349). Nevertheless, problematic as the analysis of the material and interpretations may be, Old Frisian affords an invaluable perspective on the phonological and morphological evolution of Germanic (van Helten 1890), and the dynamics of the developments it testifies to offer a better insight into and understanding of the mechanisms involved in the inflectional restructuring in Northern West Germanic.

One of the problematic aspects of the investigation of the Old Frisian material from a comparative Germanic perspective is the considerable gap in the dates of attestation, which has been a widely disputed matter in the Frisian scholarship. Despite the relatively late attestation date of Old Frisian (when compared to the other West Germanic languages), the language recorded in the earliest Frisian sources (i.e. the thirteenth century) is still considered to represent a late Old Germanic stage (e.g. Århammar 1990: 13; Boutkan 2001: 621; Versloot 2004; for

---

182. Traditionally, the early contacts have been described in terms of the Anglo-Frisian unity hypothesis, but it has essentially been contested by more recent scholarship, and the similarities between Old Frisian and Old English are interpreted rather in terms of convergence or/and language continuum (Kuhn 1955, Nielsen 1985, Stiles 1995, Fulk 1998).

an overview, see Bremmer 2009: 119–128). This relative antiquity is reflected both in the phonology, where full final vowels are usually still retained (notably in the Riustring variety[183]), and morphology, where the original conjugational and declensional patterns, though largely modified, are easily identifiable (cf. Section 4.2).

In contrast to the neighbouring idiom of Old Saxon, Old Frisian remained resistant to the spreading Franconian linguistic influence, preserving its original Ingvaeonic character. It was, however, not entirely free from the Franconian impact: the process of Franconisation in South-Holland is dated to the eighth century and, given the insights of the theory of contact-induced language change, would be manifested primarily in the phonology and the lexicon (rather than morphology and syntax) (Bremmer 2008: 295–296). In light of the extensive Franconisation of the language continuum in the Low Countries region, Old Frisian (alongside the insular Old English) can be viewed as representing an Ingvaeonic relic area (Stiles 1995: 212). Its emergence as an independent language has been attributed to non-linguistic factors, partly cultural and partly geographical (Århammar 1990: 13). The former involved the "deingvaeonicization" of Low German, associated with the subjugation of the Saxons by Charlemagne (Århammar 1990: 21; Nielsen 2001: 513). The latter is linked to the geographical isolation of Old Frisian, which must have contributed to the conservation of its Ingvaeonic features. The "peripheral geographical location of the Frisian area" has also been adduced by Markey (1981: 100–101) in order to account for the archaic nature of Frisian laws, and is considered "comparable to that of Iceland in its role as a conservatory of older tradition in North Germanic, on the edge of the Frankish empire". This special status of Old Frisian as a repository of Ingvaeonic characteristics may find its reflection in the restructuring patterns of the nominal system, especially when seen from a broader West Germanic perspective. In this context also comes the justification for assigning the name *old* to mediaeval Frisian which, as expressed by Århammar (1990: 13), "in seiner letzten hoch- und schriftsprachlichen Ausformung im Vergleich zu den kontemporären Kultur- und Verkehrssprachen Mittelniederdeutsch und Mittelniederländisch zu Recht der Name Altfriesisch zukommt."

The archaism of Old Frisian understood as a conservation of Ingvaeonic features is, however, not equivalent to its linguistic archaism. In the traditional historical grammars, especially when compared to the other Germanic languages, Old Frisian emerges as a dialect characterised by considerable innovation. In the area

---

183. This is not to be taken to mean that the text in the Riustring manuscripts (especially R_1) is older than the other sources – they all come from the turn of the 13th and 14th century – but some of the typological features represent a less modern version of Old Frisian than that found in the other manuscripts. At the same time, as has been pointed out by Bremmer (2007), the language of Riustringen is innovative in other aspects.

of the nominal inflection, it is notorious for the presence of formal syncretisms across declensional classes, resulting in a reduction of the wide variety of historical paradigms. In hardly any Germanic language is this fact as explicitly reflected in the taxonomy of nouns as in Old Frisian. In marked contrast to Old English, where the stem criterion emerges as the dominant one in the traditional treatments, the Old Frisian declensional system has often been described in synchronic terms, with a twofold division into strong and weak declensions, and a further subdivision into gender classes. This shape of the Old Frisian declensional system, adopted in a number of morphological descriptions (e.g. Sjölin 1969; Boutkan 1996, 2001), was first postulated by Heuser (1903: 24), who found the activity of analogical levelling and phonological weakening consequential for the eventual makeup of the system, stating:

> Die Deklination der Substantiva ist durch Analogiewirkung und Schwächung der Endungen stark vereinfacht und läßt sich im Wesentlichen in den beiden Hauptformen der starken und schwachen Deklination unterbringen, mit einigen Besonderheiten, welche sich als Reste der alten *i-*, *u-*, oder consonantischen Stämme erklären.

The diachronic perspective is still present in the earlier treatments of van Helten (1890), Siebs (1901) and Steller (1928), who adhere to the classification which takes the Proto-Germanic linguistic reality as a starting point. Adopting a historical perspective on the nominal system results in distinguishing seven minor, unproductive paradigms in Old Frisian, including: *i*-stems, *u*-stems, *r*-stems, root nouns, *s*-stems, *nd*-stems and vestigial dental stems – most of them rather scantily attested in the available material. Each of these minor declensional types was represented by a relatively low number of nouns, often compensated for by their high frequency of occurrence (token frequency), which turned out to have been consequential for the reorganisation of the system. Despite the fact that their existence as independent declensional types in Old Frisian can be questioned, this historical perspective, in compliance with the treatment of the other Old Germanic languages, will consistently serve as the organising principle for the presentation of the Old Frisian material.

As regards the morphological constitution of Old Frisian, the picture which emerges from the available descriptions is one of a relatively innovative Germanic language. The apparent morphological innovativeness of Old Frisian, however, can be to some extent illusory and consequently constitutes an inadequate description of the Old Frisian linguistic reality. This illusoriness may be a result of the very nature of the available textual material; more specifically, the scarcity of archaic features in the nominal inflection may be attributed to corpus limitations rather than certain inherent tendencies present in the language. It is one of the aims of the present quantitative study to reevaluate the status of Old Frisian with respect to its level of morphological archaism/innovation, taking into account all the constraints resulting from the nature of the available corpus.

4.2   Corpus and methodological considerations

A number of features of the Old Frisian corpus are crucial for the interpretation of the data in the context of other West Germanic languages, most notably the age and the genre composition of the Old Frisian texts. Both seemingly create a limitation for a linguistic analysis of a comparative nature, inhibiting any straightforward juxtaposition of the data from the sister languages. With regard to the age of the available material, the traditional approach in Frisian philology has been to assign the common term *Old Frisian* to all Frisian manuscripts and charters created in the mediaeval tradition (i.e. before 1550). While the linguistic shape of the oldest sources of Old Frisian (before 1400) testifies to a close affiliation with the *old* stages of the other Germanic languages, the later sources are typologically more innovative. Their linguistic profile corresponds rather to that found in contemporaneous languages from the surrounding areas, namely, Middle Dutch, Middle Low Saxon, or Middle English, which attest a more advanced stage of phonological, morphological and, more generally, typological development. Given this evidence, the validity of the label *Old Frisian* may be questioned and the actual delimitation of the periods in the history of Frisian turns out to be partly dependent on the chosen classificatory criteria (Bremmer 2009: 125). The traditional view has been challenged on several occasions, most notably in the discussions by de Haan (2001) and Versloot (2004) who, respectively, provide arguments against and in favour of the conservative character of the Frisian language from the fourteenth century. Both evaluate the linguistic character of Old Frisian by comparing it with the other Old and Middle Germanic languages. The linguistic comparison of the available material leads de Haan (2001: 201) to conclude, partly in line with some previous scholarship (e.g. Siebs 1901), that the language traditionally referred to as *Old Frisian* should be re-labelled as *Middle Frisian*, and to postulate a periodisation in which there appears to be no longer space for an *old* stage.[184] Versloot (2004), employing a much wider choice of diagnostic criteria, argues in favour of retaining the traditional label *Old*

---

184.   The periodisation according to de Haan (2001: 201) comprises the following stages: prior to ca. 1275 Ante-Middle Frisian, ca. 1275–1550 Middle Frisian, ca. 1550 – present Modern Frisian, where 1275 refers to the dating of the oldest Frisian law manuscript.

Frisian to refer to the texts written in the thirteenth and fourteenth centuries.[185] Significantly, the original interpretation of linguistic variation in Frisian (dating back to the nineteenth century) was diatopic rather than diachronic, with a twofold division into Old East Frisian and Old West Frisian. Old East Frisian was viewed as the most archaic variety of Frisian, whereas Old West Frisian was interpreted as more innovative (Siebs 1901; cf. Nielsen 1994). The chronological interpretation of the differences was first advocated by Sjölin (1966, 1969, 1984), who pointed to the presence of archaic features in some Old West Frisian texts on the one hand, and, on the other, identified quite unexpected innovative features in the Old East Frisian material. Consequently, the labels *classical* and *post-classical* Old Frisian were adopted, the former to refer to the material originating in the East, the latter in the West, with a few archaic Old West Frisian texts being classified as *classical* and some late Old East Frisian texts as *post-classical*. Altogether the language of these two periods (taken together) seems to represent some typological hybrid, consisting of two major varieties, defined in both diatopic and diachronic terms.

Naturally, one needs to bear in mind that any periodisation of language has an arbitrary nature and depends largely on the adopted classificatory criteria. Consequently, establishing clear-cut boundaries in the language history can often be a problematic task (e.g. Fisiak 1994, Lass 2000, Lutz 2002, with reference to the periodisation of English). The periodisation accepted for the purpose of the present study, while staying close to the approach (dating) proposed by Sjölin (1966), essentially follows Versloot's (2004: 288) linguistic periodisation, where the definition of Old Frisian is narrower in that it covers the period between ca. 1200 and ca. 1400. Accordingly, the present study is based on manuscripts which constitute the core of the oldest Frisian material, associated primarily with the "classical" stage, including: the *First Brokmer Manuscript* (B_1) (ca. 1300), *First Riustring Manuscript* (R_1) (ca. 1300), *Second Riustring Manuscript* (R_2) (1327),[186] *Fourth Riustring Manuscript* (R_4) (early 14th c.),[187] *First Hunsingo Manuscript* (H_1) (ca.

---

185. The linguistic periodisation proposed by Versloot (2004: 288) involves the following stages in the history of Frisian: prior to 1100 – Runic Frisian, ca. 1200–ca. 1400 Old Frisian; ca. 1440–1550 Middle Frisian; 1550–1800 Early Modern Frisian; 1800 – now Modern Frisian.

186. The archaism of Old Frisian is primarily associated with the Riustring variety, which displays a number of conservative features, notably phonological ones, such as the preservation of the full vowels /u/, /i/, /a/ in unstressed final syllables. As some of these traits find their continuation in modern dialects descending from the Riustring area, they have been viewed as a dialectal characteristic rather than a chronological archaism (Bremmer 2007: 36; 2009: 121; cf. de Haan 2001: 183).

187. The manuscript R_4 is only a 35-line fragment, overlapping with the text found in R_1. For a discussion, see also Bremmer (2007: 32).

1325–1350), *Second Hunsingo Manuscript* (H$_2$) (ca. 1325–1350),[188] *First Emsingo Manuscript* (E$_1$) (ca. 1400), fragments of *Codex Unia* (U) (ca. 1477) and the Psalter fragments.[189] The corpus selected for the present study corresponds largely to the selection of manuscripts made by Sjölin (1969: 17), which represents a language characterised by remarkable linguistic homogeneity, deserving the name of "klassisches Altfriesisch".[190] It must be emphasised that the Old Frisian texts are believed to have originated earlier than the manuscripts they are attested in, with the dates of composition estimated by some to belong to the eleventh and twelfth centuries (e.g. Sjölin 1969: 9–11). An important characteristic of this corpus, especially in the context of morphological restructuring, is the preservation of full vowels in inflectional syllables, as well as the consistency in the orthographic layer, which managed to escape the impact of late-mediaeval spelling practices. Importantly, the overall linguistic profile of post-classical Frisian is substantially different from

---

188. The two manuscripts are presumably copies from the same exemplar, made by one scribe, the difference between them being the order of the included items. There is, accordingly, hardly any textual difference between the two manuscripts and those sporadic ones can be explained as scribal errors (Bremmer 2007: 55). The countings are based essentially on H$_2$ and only incidental forms deviating from H$_1$ are added.

189. The use of abbreviations of Old Frisian texts consistently follows the practice of Hofmann & Popkema (2008) who in "Siglenliste zum *Altfriesischen Handwörterbuch*" provide a complete list of all texts used in their *Altfriesisches Handwörterbuch*, including the short titles and detailed bibliographic information. For detailed descriptions of the Old Frisian law texts and manuscripts, see Johnston (2001) and Bremmer (2009: 13–14).

190. Sjölin's (1969) selection includes additionally the slightly younger Emsingo manuscripts (E$_2$ [ca. 1450] and E$_3$ [ca. 1450]), manuscript F (copied ca. 1440) and manuscript B$_2$. The last one was not included in the present study due to the fact that it represents almost an exact copy of the material found in the fifty-year older manuscript B$_1$ (Sjölin 1969: 17). Reference to manuscript B$_2$ will be made whenever it provides additional information about the paradigms. Manuscripts E$_2$, E$_3$ and F, although considered to be written in classical Old Frisian (Sjölin 1969: 17; 1970: 228), were not included in this study on account of their less consistent spelling of unstressed syllables; see van Helten (1890: 49–52), where they are consistently ranked on the side of the manuscripts showing innovative phonological features. Despite the relatively late dating of manuscript U (*Codex Unia*) (the text of the codex dated to 1477 is preserved only in a 17th-c. copy by Franciscus Junius), it was included in the corpus because of the very archaic nature of some of its parts (predominantly found in Junius' *Apographa*; Sytsema 2012). The texts of this codex represent a number of "linguistic 'layers'", including relatively archaic ones, most of which can with certainty be dated to earlier than 1410, the oldest parts perhaps to the late 13th c. (Versloot 2008: 7, 70). Admittedly, an analysis of individual texts/fragments from the manuscript, which would eliminate the younger parts, could offer even more nuanced results, but it was hindered by the nature of the edition used for this study (Sytsema 2012). Given that these younger fragments constitute a minor part of the manuscript (ca. 15%), it did not have a serious bearing on the results of this study. The parts of *Unia* that are only fragments from Druk are explicitly not included in this analysis.

its classical ancestor, representing a later stage of phonological and morphological development. The more radical changes in phonology as well as the growing influence of Middle Low German and Middle Dutch in the post-classical period, both consequential for inflectional morphology, would offer a considerably different picture of the restructuring of the early Frisian nominal system. In contrast, the earliest stage of attestation of Frisian reflected in the selected material seems to be compatible with the state of affairs attested in the oldest stages of the other investigated West Germanic languages. It is precisely on account of this cross-Germanic compatibility that the confinement of the study to this stage was considered rational and desirable.

Although the evidence provided by the runic inscriptions (dated between 400 and 800; see Page 2001) and place-names could potentially be revealing, since in terms of attestation dates it corresponds to the material from the other West Germanic languages, its linguistic value is largely limited due to the serious interpretative difficulties it poses. More importantly, as no relevant morphological forms which could be informative about analogical restructuring are attested in the available runic material, its inclusion into the study would not bring any additional insights (cf. Hofstra 2003: 78).[191]

Despite its limited size, the Old Frisian corpus is not an entirely homogenous entity and the diatopic variation, just as it is the case in Modern Frisian, is relatively rich. Apart from the traditional division into East and West Old Frisian, which, as mentioned before, largely overlaps with the chronological distribution, some variation is found within Old East Frisian, reflected also in the selection of manuscripts for the present study. Accordingly, the selection comprises texts representing three different dialects, in line with the division proposed by Siebs (1901), i.e. Ems Old Frisian (western branch) (E, H$_1$/H$_2$, B$_1$), Weser Old Frisian (eastern branch) (R$_1$ and R$_2$) as well as Old West Frisian (U). At the same time, it must be noted that a systematic dialectal investigation, involving the study of discrepancies on the manuscript-level, remains beyond the purview of this study for two major reasons. Firstly, given the focus and the wide scope of the present comparative analysis, such an approach could result in a too fragmented description of the examined developments and consequently blur the more general picture needed for a comparison with the other languages. Secondly, with respect to the features relevant for the restructuring of the early Frisian declensional system, the presence of diatopic variation in the Old Frisian material turned out in the course of the analysis to have little bearing on the final results: the dialectal discrepancies were too insignificant to affect the major developmental tendencies (cf. Section 4.6).

---

191. This early Runic Frisian evidence, albeit of limited value for the investigation of morphological innovations, turned out to be particularly informative for the chronology of phonological developments in early Germanic (see Section 2.2.2).

Another peculiarity of the Old Frisian corpus concerns its text-type composition, namely, the fact that it is essentially confined to one genre, comprising predominantly legal prose texts. At first glance, such a limitation constitutes a serious obstacle for any investigation of a comparative nature, where a homogenous corpus is to be juxtaposed with more genre-diversified corpora, such as the corpus of Old English. A parallel difficulty emerges in relation to the size of the Old Frisian corpus, which is rather modest when compared to the impressive size of the Old English corpus. One of the consequences of this largely limited size of the corpus was the fact that many missing forms in Old Frisian had to be extrapolated from the corresponding paradigms in Old English, which can often be a complicated endeavour (Nielsen 1991). In this respect, however, Old Frisian is not an isolated instance, as some other West Germanic corpora, i.e. Old Low Franconian and Old Saxon, are burdened with the same predicament. All the above-mentioned features of the corpus may have some bearing on the results of the comparative analysis and need to be taken into account when interpreting the findings (for details see Section 7.2).

4.3 Restructuring process in Old Frisian: Emerging patterns

The restructuring of the Old Frisian nominal inflection comprised both prehistoric and historical shifts of nouns between declensional classes. Many nouns historically affiliated with minor classes do not show any vestiges of the original inflection in the attested Old Frisian material, which indicates that they had entirely transferred to other declensional types (mainly masculine and neuter *a*-stems) in the prehistoric stage. The analogical developments occurring prehistorically are identifiable primarily through the evidence provided by cognate forms found in the sister languages (e.g. OFris. *hunger* 'hunger' (*a*-stem) vs. Go. *hūhrus* (*u*-stem); OFris. *dāth* 'death' (*a*-stem) vs. Go. *dáuþus* (*u*-stem); OFris. *sige* 'victory' (*i*-stem) vs. Go. *sigis* (*s*-stem); cf. Appendix). The focus of the present investigation, however, is on the interdeclensional shifts which are manifested in the synchronic alternations between the inherited (from Proto-Germanic) and innovative (analogical) paradigmatic forms. Analogical remodelling of the declensional system entailed two main directions of the transition of nouns affiliated originally with minor declensions, namely to the masculine *a*-stems and feminine *ō*-stems, which occurred largely in compliance with gender. Aside from these two paths of reorganisation, traces of the *n*-stem inflection and sporadic features of the *i*-stem pattern (e.g. in the root nouns and *nd*-stems) are also attested. Of particular significance is the spread of the NOM./ACC. PL. marker -*an* in Old West Frisian (*Codex Unia*), and in the western parts of Old East Frisian (H$_2$, F) in all masculine paradigms, which, in contrast to Old English, did not originate in the *n*-stem declension. Its origin is sought in the contamination of the regular ending -*a* and the *n*-stem marker -*en*, borrowed from Middle Low Saxon and Middle Dutch (Bremmer 2009: 60). It is believed that in (western) Old East Frisian this marker appeared first in the *i*- and *ja*- stems (both ending in -*e* in the NOM. SG.), whence it spread to other declensional classes (Versloot 2004: 277, 300).

One of the innovative productive endings in the NOM./ACC. PL., frequently found in minor stems, is the marker -*ar* (-*er*), associated with the masculine *a*-stem inflection. Given the Old English and Old Saxon evidence, the expected NOM./ACC. PL. marker in this declensional type could be the ending -*as*, which is, however, never attested in the corpus. The marker -*ar* (-*er*) is most common in manuscripts of the Old East Frisian provenance[192] and its origin is rather unclear.[193] From the perspective of the present investigation, the essential point is that the forms with this suffix are interpreted as innovative, since the ending is evidently analogical in minor paradigms, irrespective of its exact origin (cf. *s*-stems).

As the findings from the analysis of the Old English material reveal, the inter-declensional transfers tended to occur in line with gender class affiliation, and this pattern is expected to be found also in the Old Frisian material. At the same time, given the expansiveness of the masculine *a*-stem inflections, some departure from this tendency can be expected, especially in the feminine stems, where also some further dialectal differences involving gender class shift are detectable.

4.4 Old Frisian phonological developments and their morphological implications

The phonological processes which occurred in the Old Frisian period had a direct impact on the shape of the nominal paradigms, leading to the reinterpretation of paradigmatic contrasts, and consequently obliterating the former consistency of the inflectional system. Essential from the point of view of inflectional

---

192. Scant attestations of the marker -*ar* are found also in Old West Frisian. For a discussion see Versloot (2014).

193. For a survey of various explanations of the provenance of this inflectional marker, see Meijering (1989). The interpretation as a late borrowing from North Germanic, introduced to preserve or restore category distinction between the NOM./ACC. PL. and GEN. SG. (which otherwise would have merged), was dismissed by Philippa (1987: 89–105) (cf. Nielsen 2000: 253–254). An alternative account ascribes this ending to a PGmc. form *-*ōzes*, which is a Vernerian alternant of the old NOM. PL. form *-*ōses*, corresponding to Indo-Aryan *-*āsas* (Siebs 1901: 1340; Krogmann 1969: 203; Boutkan 2001: 622; Bremmer 2009: 60). Given, however, that the related forms in the other Germanic languages can all be derived from the non-Vernerian variant, it seems fairly far-fetched to adduce the Vedic form only to account for the Frisian irregularity.

restructuring were the developments affecting final unstressed syllables that were subject to a number of phonological reductions, beginning already at the prehistoric stage. The Old Frisian system of vowels in unstressed syllables, as attested in the most archaic sources (notably in the Riustring dialect), consisted of three vowels represented graphemically by <a>, <i~e> and <o~u>, where the alternation between the variants expresses a complementary distribution of /i/, /u/ and /e/, /o/, in compliance with the vowel harmony and vowel balance (Boutkan 1996: 26–32; cf. Sjölin 1969: 22). In the other Old Frisian dialects this system is further reduced; however, the distinction between /e/ and /a/ is consistently retained (Versloot 2004: 271–272). The major phonological developments in unstressed (inflectional) syllables that were significant for the inflectional shape of nominal paradigms included:

- the development of /i/ > /e/ and /u/ > /e/ (e.g. *breki* > *breke*; *sunu* > *sune*) (in all Old Frisian dialects except $R_{1,2}$)
- the development of the DAT. PL. *-um* > *-em* > *-en*
- the weakening of the vowels to *schwa* (late/post-classical Old Frisian).

Some of these variations, although well attested in the material (e.g. the DAT. PL. ending where *-um* tended to alternate with *-en*), are not relevant in the context of the restructuring process as defined in this study, and thus remain beyond the scope of the analysis. Other developments, however, in particular the reduction of vowels in word-final position, had far-reaching consequences for the restructuring of the paradigms, as demonstrated for Old English. The direct morphological consequence of these phonological developments were the mergers of inflectional exponents across different declensional types, which in the longer run led to the obliteration of class distinctions, and rendered an adequate interpretation of forms problematic. An example of such an interpretative difficulty is the DAT. SG. form *breke* in the *i*-stems, where the word-final *-e* may be a phonological continuation of the historical ending on the one hand, and an analogical extension from the *a*-stems on the other (see Section 4.5.2).

An even more essential problem for the present investigation emerges at the point of the interaction between phonology and morphology, i.e. when it comes to the interpretation of forms as an effect of phonological or morphological developments. Such is, for instance, the case with the NOM. SG. marker *-e* in the light-syllable *u*-stems (e.g. *nose*), which, on the one hand, can be attributed to a regular phonological development (*u* > *e*), but on the other, can be ascribed to the analogical pressure of the productive declensions, most likely of the *ō*-stems (or feminine *n*-stems). Although such cases very often remain inconclusive (and thus need to be dismissed from the analysis), crucial for disentangling such puzzles is the dating of the operation of phonological processes, especially of the weakening of vowels in unstressed syllables. In contrast to Old English, the levelling of final unstressed vowels seems to have been a late development in Old Frisian and, accordingly, the confusion of the vowels in inflectional endings was rather limited in classical Old Frisian. Most importantly, the unaccented /e/ and /a/, i.e. the potential source of confusion, are consistently distinguished in the classical Old Frisian material. The loss of the phonological opposition between /a/ and /e/ in word-final position is dated only to the middle of the fifteenth century (Versloot 2008: 215).[194] This fact is essential in the context of the present investigation where the interpretation of vowels in inflectional syllables is decisive for classifying a given form as archaic or innovative. Given that the corpus used for the present study is confined to the oldest layer of the Old Frisian material, it can be assumed that the word-final <e> did represent the phoneme /e/, which was distinct from /a/ and cannot be interpreted as a subsequent development of /a/ (i.e. its weak variant). Accordingly, the vowel contrasts which are found in the inflectional endings are interpreted as meaningful in this study.

Finally, important for the changes in the nominal inflection were the developments affecting the root syllable, in particular the elimination of the historically motivated vowel alternation from the paradigm (*i*-mutation). The mutated vowel can be expected to appear in the DAT. SG. and the NOM./ACC. PL. in root nouns, *r*-stems and *nd*-stems. The loss of these morphophonemic alternations rendered the Old Frisian paradigms more uniform (in terms of inflectional marking) and possibly more vulnerable to the impact of analogical pressures from other declensions (cf. Section 4.6). Importantly, this internal reshaping of the paradigm, resulting from the activity of intraparadigmatic analogy, remains without any direct bearing on the measuring of the level of archaism/innovation.

4.5 Data analysis

4.5.1 Methodological considerations

The quantitative study involved analysing the incidence of archaic and innovative forms in the paradigms of individual minor declensional types. Essential for the quantitative analysis was the identification of the attested forms as archaic, i.e. continuing their PGmc. antecedents, or innovative, i.e. emerging as an effect of external analogical pressure from the productive declensions. The difficulty inherent in this procedure is the potential ambiguity of the attested forms which, depending on

---

194. For the discussion of alternative interpretations, see Versloot (2008: 205–208), Boutkan (2001: 619) and de Haan (2001: 189).

the criteria of interpretation applied, can be identified as archaic or innovative (cf. Section 4.4). For Old Frisian this difficulty turned out to be particularly evident in the vocalic stems, especially the feminine *i*-stems and *u*-stems (cf. 4.5.2, 4.5.3). A prominent but problematic ending is the GEN. PL. marker -*(e)na*, extended from the *n*-stem paradigm. Although unambiguously innovative, the marker cannot serve as a reliable measure of the level of innovativeness in the paradigm, as it can be tested only against the GEN. PL. marker -*a*, which is a generalised ending in all declensional classes (cf. Section 2.2.4). The situation is parallel to that in Old English, where likewise a competition took place between two innovative endings: one extended at the prehistoric stage, the other in the later, historical period. In compliance with the investigation procedure applied to Old English, these forms were excluded from the quantitative analysis, but will occasionally be referred to when of significance for the completeness of the description of the restructuring process. Another category excluded from the study was the DAT. PL., with the marker -*um* being one of the earliest analogical extensions in all declensional types, except the *s*-stems (cf. Section 2.2.4).

Due to the scarcity of the available data, for some lemmas there is no positive synchronic evidence of their affiliation with a given historical class. For instance, the OFris. *u*-stem *nose* 'nose' is attested only with endings which do not show the historical *u*-stem pattern. Their original affiliation with the *u*-stems can be confirmed only by the evidence from the other Old Germanic languages (e.g. OE *nosu*). On account of the cross-Germanic comparison, which necessitated consistent treatment of inflections, such forms were included in the quantitative study as long as a form testifying to the historical inflection could be found in any of the sister languages. A similar problem is posed by the NOM./ACC. SG. forms, which are mostly (not in all declensions though) inconclusive with respect to the restructuring (e.g. *dōk* 'cloth').

As discussed in Section 4.4, crucial for the interpretation of all forms was the chronology of phonological developments affecting the unstressed syllables, in particular the late dating of the weakening of /a/ > /ə/, and apocope, which in the period (and dialects) represented by the selected Old East Frisian manuscripts (R_1, R_2, B_1, H_2, and E_1) occurred only sporadically (van Helten 1890: 146). The same is true of the fragments of the Old West Frisian manuscript of *Unia*, where apocope is dated to between the middle of the fourteenth and late fifteenth century (Versloot 2008: 160–161).

Aside from the dating of phonological processes, an additional check on the status of attested forms was applied, taking into account the entire profiles of the paradigms. It involved controlling the sensitivity of forms, potentially purely phonologically-conditioned, to case and number. Accordingly, if only phonological conditioning were at stake, the final vowels would be expected to disappear (or be reduced) systematically throughout the entire paradigm rather than in selected categories in the paradigm, as is frequently the case (see, for instance, the paradigm of the *i*-stem *breke*). This implies that an interplay of phonological and morphological factors was crucial in the restructuring of the nominal inflection, and that both need to be taken into consideration in order to arrive at an adequate interpretation of the data.

For reasons of clarity, several technical details deserve a brief commentary before the material and the findings of the investigation are presented. Firstly, all the forms cited in the tables in this chapter (as well as those presented in the Old Frisian section of the Appendix) are consistently based on the shape they have in the *Altfriesisches Handwörterbuch* by Hofmann & Popkema (2008) (cf. *friōnd*, R$_{1,2}$ vs. *friūnd* H$_2$, E$_1$, B$_1$). Secondly, not all the forms presented in the tables in the present section are actually attested in the analysed corpus (e.g. the GEN. SG. **fōt*, **brōther*, **clāther*, the NOM./ACC. PL. *clāthar*); the depicted paradigms are "reconstructed" on the basis of the entire available inventory of a given class, and the chosen lexemes serve to represent a given declensional type. Thirdly, italics were used to present the findings for those categories which cannot provide any information about the restructuring in the paradigm. This practice refers to both the forms in the tables depicting the competing paradigms, as well as those showing the percentage distributions.

4.5.2   *i*-stems

4.5.2.1   *General characteristics*

In contrast to other unproductive declensions, the *i*-stems were relatively well attested (both in terms of token and type frequency). Despite this relatively high number of *i*-stems (high type frequency, 80 lemmas, cf. 21 *u*-stem lemmas), which is one of the classificatory criteria for productivity, the class was characterised by an extensive restructuring of the inherited paradigms of all three genders. The original affiliation of nouns with the *i*-stem declension is reflected in the presence of the *i*-mutated root vowel or a palatalized final consonant (Bremmer 2009: 63), while their set of inflectional endings corresponds largely to that of the productive declensions. The dominant innovative inflections found in the paradigm are those of the masculine and neuter *a*-stems, feminine *ō*-stems, as well as of the *n*-stems. The picture emerging from the few available descriptions of the OFris. *i*-stems is one of a substantially disintegrated declensional class, with the historical pattern of inflection retained only residually in the paradigm (e.g. Steller 1928: 39; Bremmer 2009: 63).[195] On closer inspection, however, the pattern of attestation of archaic and

---

195. Cf. van Helten's (1890: 140–148) detailed description of the *i*-stems, where they emerge as a well attested, internally diversified, but still independent inflectional class, albeit subject to much analogical pressure.

innovative forms turns out to be much more complicated than expected, with fine details of the distribution revealing the complexity of the restructuring process. In analogy to Old English, one could expect a discrepant distribution of the original *i*-stem features in light- and heavy-syllable stems, with a further diversification depending on gender. Given the original shape of the *i*-stem paradigms, the most prominent and unambiguous reflexes of the historical inflections can be identified in the masculine and neuter light-syllable stems as well as in the feminine heavy-syllable stems, with other subtypes being much less informative about the restructuring on account of the ambiguity implicated in the attested inflections.

The major difficulty in analysing the attested forms involved the classification of inflectional endings as archaic or innovative, many of which turned out to be ambiguous in this declensional class, because Proto-Fris. *-æ* and *-i* merged, resulting in OFris. -*e*. The interpretation varies depending on the weight of the stem as well as the gender. Many of the attested forms remained obscure and were thus considered inconclusive, and consequently excluded from the quantitative investigation. Apart from the expected ambiguity of the GEN. and DAT. PL. inflections, equivocal are also most of the singular inflections in the masculine and neuter stems (cf. Table 4.1 and 4.3), where the attested markers may be a continuation of the Proto-Germanic forms, but may well represent analogical inflections extended from the *a*-stems. The situation looks the least prosperous for the heavy-syllable masculine and neuter stems as well as the light-syllable feminine stems, where unambiguous alternation is confined solely to the plural.

The inventory of features that can unambiguously be identified as innovative includes the following inflections:

- the endingless NOM./ACC. SG. form (light-syllable masculine and neuter stems)
- the NOM./ACC. SG. marker -*e* in heavy-syllable feminine stems
- the marker -*a* in the entire singular paradigm of light- and heavy-syllable stems, extended from the *n*-stem declension (all genders)
- the endings -*a*, -*ar*, -*an* in place of the expected marker -*e* (-*i*) in the NOM./ACC. PL. in masculine stems (light- and heavy-syllable stems)
- the NOM./ACC. PL. marker -*a* in place of the expected -*e* (-*i*) in feminine stems (light- and heavy-syllable)

The forms in -*a* appearing in the GEN., DAT. and ACC. SG. are clearly analogical and testify to the impact of the *n*-stem inflection. The inclusion of these forms in the quantitative analysis, however, turned out to be problematic, especially in feminine stems, since their alternating variants in -*e* could not always be unambiguously identified as archaic; potentially they could represent innovative forms emerging under the influence of the *a*- and *ō*-stems. An adequate interpretation of these forms was possible in heavy-syllable stems on some assumptions involving the entire paradigm of the singular. Accordingly, the forms of the GEN. and DAT. SG. in -*e* can be interpreted as archaic only if the NOM./ACC. SG. are endingless, i.e. continue the original Proto-Germanic inflection. Such an approach necessitated a closer scrutiny of the entire singular paradigms of individual lexemes rather than a general treatment. In the following section these instances will be treated separately, whereas the results presented in Tables 4.5 and 4.6 refer only to the entirely unambiguous instances of interparadigmatic alternations.

As the inflectional profiles of light- and heavy-syllable *i*-stems differ, the competing archaic and analogical inflections found in their paradigms are presented separately for these subtypes, with a further subdivision with respect to gender. Accordingly, Tables 4.1, 4.2, 4.3 and 4.4, respectively, present the potential variation in the light-syllable masculine and neuter nouns, light-syllable feminine nouns, heavy-syllable masculine and neuter nouns, and heavy-syllable feminine nouns.[196]

Table 4.1 The competing inflections in the OFris. light-syllable masculine and neuter *i*-stems

	archaic		innovative	
	SG	PL	SG	PL
NOM.	breke (-i)	breke (-i)	brek	breka, -ar, -an
GEN.	*brekes*	*breka*	*brekes, -a*	*brekena*
DAT.	*breke* (-i)	*brekum* (-on)	*breke, -a*	*brekum*
ACC.	breke (-i)	breke (-i)	brek, -a	breka, -ar, -an

Table 4.2 The competing inflections in the OFris. light-syllable feminine *i*-stems

	archaic		innovative	
	SG	PL	SG	PL
NOM.	*stede* (*stidi*)	stede (-i)	*stede*	steda
GEN.	*stede* (-i)	*steda*	*steda, (-es)*	*stedena*
DAT.	*stede* (-i)	*stedum*	*steda*	*stedum*
ACC.	*stede* (-i)	stede (-i)	*steda*	steda

---

196. The forms in brackets refer to the attestations from the dialect of Riustringen. Note that the forms in -*i* in these manuscripts are not necessarily etymological, but a result of further phonological developments proper to this dialect.

Table 4.3 The competing inflections in the OFris. heavy-syllable masculine and neuter *i*-stems

	archaic		innovative	
	SG	PL	SG	PL
NOM.	*dēl*	dēle	*dēl*	dēla, -ar, -an
GEN.	*dēles*	dēla	*dēles, -a*	dēlena
DAT.	*dēle*	dēlum (-*on*)	*dēle, -a*	dēlum
ACC.	*dēl*	dēle	*dēl, -a*	dēla, -ar, -an

Table 4.4 The competing inflections in the OFris. heavy-syllable feminine *i*-stems

	archaic		innovative	
	SG	PL	SG	PL
NOM.	dēd	dēde	dēde	dēda
GEN.	*dēde*	*dēda*	dēda, -e, dēd	dēdena
DAT.	*dēde*	dēdum	dēda, -e, dēd	dēdum
ACC.	dēd	dēde	dēde, -a	dēda

As can be observed, many forms in the above-presented paradigms are indeterminate and therefore they do not offer reliable information about the inflectional restructuring. This ambiguity stems from two facts: firstly, from the early extension of analogical endings in the paradigms, and the ensuing lack of synchronic alternation attested (e.g. in the GEN. and DAT. PL.); secondly, from the syncretic shape of inflections, irrespective of their origin, i.e. the overlap of forms that continue the original pattern and those which come from the productive paradigms (e.g. the GEN., DAT. SG. in feminine stems). In effect, despite the rich attestation of this class, the number of forms which could be informative about the restructuring and hence eligible for inclusion into the quantitative analysis was rather limited.

4.5.2.2 *Results of the investigation*
The presentation of the results in a tabular form for this declensional class is confined to two types of *i*-stems, where the alternation between archaic and innovative inflections can be relatively well captured. Tables 4.5 and 4.6 depict the distributions of inflections in the masculine and neuter light-syllable stems, and feminine heavy-syllable stems, respectively. The figures for masculine and neuter *i*-stems are assembled into one table, since the pattern these stems displayed turned out to be identical.[197] As the light-syllable feminine stems and heavy-syllable masculine

---

197. Only one light-syllable neuter noun, *spere* 'spear' ($n = 3$), was found in the analysed material, with a single ACC. SG. form following the archaic pattern (*spere*).

stems show hardly any synchronic alternation, or because the alternating forms cannot be unambiguously classified as either archaic or innovative, the findings from the quantitative examination of these two types will be presented in a non-tabular form and discussed in detail.

Table 4.5 Distribution of archaic and innovative inflections in the OFris. light-syllable masculine and neuter *i*-stems

	archaic		innovative	
	SG	PL	SG	PL
NOM.	(111) 87%	(1) 11%	(16) 13%	(8) 89%
GEN.	(16)	(1)	–	–
DAT.	(22)	(2)	–	–
ACC.	(21) 81%	(0)	(5) 19%	(5) 100%
Total	(133) 80%		(34) 20%	

Table 4.6 Distribution of archaic and innovative inflections in the OFris. heavy-syllable feminine *i*-stems

	archaic		innovative	
	SG	PL	SG	PL
NOM.	(111) 64%	(7) 15%	(63) 36%	(40) 85%
GEN.	(28)	(13)	–	–
DAT.	(233)	(46)	–	–
ACC.	(107) 58%	(2) 3%	(79) 42%	(69) 97%
Total	(227) 47%		(251) 53%	

Although the details of the distribution of analogical forms in these two subtypes of the *i*-stems vary, the overall tendencies seem to be largely parallel. In both types, the inflectional archaism is concentrated in the singular (NOM./ACC.), while the plural turns out to be substantially innovative. Whereas the lack of inflectional ending in the NOM./ACC. SG. in the masculine *i*-stems is a paradigmatic innovation, emerging under the pressure of the endingless NOM. SG. of the *a*-stems, its absence in the feminine heavy-syllable *i*-stems is interpreted as an archaic feature, as it is a continuation of the original Proto-Germanic inflection, resisting the pressure of the marker -*e* from the *ō*-stems.[198] The innovative plural inflections appear as -*a* (especially in R$_1$, R$_2$, E$_1$), -*ar* (especially in H$_2$, B$_1$) and -*an/-en* (especially in U) in the

---

198. The -*e* in the NOM. SG. of the *ō*-stems is analogical, built on the pattern of the ACC. SG.; the original endingless form is attested only sporadically (van Helten 1890; Siebs 1901; cf. Versloot 2016b).

masculine stems, spreading from the *a*-stems, whereas in the feminine paradigm they come predominantly from the *ō*-stems. The masculine forms in *-ar* and *-an* are also occasionally attested, notably in the light syllable feminine *i*-stems, which tend to show a gender shift towards masculine inflection in some dialects. The substantial conservatism of the masculine *i*-stems can be compared to the pattern found in Old English (cf. Section 3.5.2), where this subclass of *i*-stems is the only type still displaying the inflectional features of the original *i*-stems. A factor which must have played a role in the reorganisation of the light-syllable *i*-stems was the formal similarity of the NOM./ACC. singular and plural, which were characterised by identical inflectional endings. The substitution of the productive markers for the inherited ending permitted to keep the distinction between the singular and the plural. Specifically, the proneness to adopt new analogical markers in the plural was in a way induced by the need to mark the functional distinction between the singular and the plural.

In the two remaining subclasses, the shape of the singular paradigm was entirely inconclusive and the level of archaism/innovation could be tested only for the NOM. and ACC. PL. In both subtypes the transition to the productive classes was almost complete, which corresponds to the figures presented in Tables 4.5 and 4.6, where the plural turned out to be more innovative than the singular. In the light-syllable feminine *i*-stems the rate of innovation reaches 97 percent ($n = 34$) (93% in the NOM. PL. and 100% in the ACC. PL.), with a single NOM. PL. showing the archaic pattern (*urkere* 'superior statutes', E_1), whereas in the heavy-syllable masculine stems the innovative inflection was found in 92 percent of forms ($n = 51$) (96% in the NOM. PL. and 88% in the ACC. PL.).

An entirely opposite pattern is found in the heavy-syllable neuter stem *liude* 'people', which consistently retains the final vowel (< Proto-Fris. *-ī). The innovative inflection is attested in two instances only, namely, in the NOM. and ACC. PL. (*liuda*), in manuscripts H_2 and U (which constitutes 2% of all forms). In contrast to Old English, where the final vowel *-e* was preserved in the group of nouns denoting tribes (*Dēne*, *Seaxe*, etc.) (cf. 3.5.2.2), *liude* is the only noun in this declensional class in Old Frisian which consistently shows this archaic inflection. A potential explanation of this form requires a broader perspective, entailing the study of the inflectional pattern in other classes, where similar irregularities are attested. Given the Old English evidence and the pattern of attestation found there, it seems justified to assume the existence of a common template for plural inflection in nouns denoting collective concepts, which, to some extent, may have been productive, potentially spreading across the minor declensional types. The evidence provided by the other minor classes seems to give ample support to this hypothesis (see Sections 4.5.5, 4.5.7 and Versloot & Adamczyk 2013).

Some interpretative difficulties are posed by the occasionally attested ending-less forms of the NOM./ACC. PL. in heavy-syllable *i*-stems (*dēl* 'part', *kest* 'choice', *kerf* 'cut', *liud*, *wald* 'power'). They can hardly be attributed to the analogical pressure of other paradigmatic patterns but rather could arguably be interpreted as phonologically reduced variants of archaic *-e*. Given that *liude* is a neuter noun and *dēl* displays traces of neuter inflection as well, one could potentially attribute the endingless forms to the impact of neuter *a*-stems, where the NOM./ACC. PL. are endingless. The evidence, however, is so limited that such a conclusion seems to be unwarranted (explicit positive evidence is found only for *ōrdēl* 'verdict', which is consistently attested as a neuter noun with endingless plurals). The phonological interpretation in turn is problematic in view of the dating of apocope in early Frisian (cf. Section 4.4). Accordingly, the six tokens found in the analysed material were considered inconclusive and have been excluded from the total calculation.

A further characteristic of the attested pattern is related to gender and the apparent gender confusion found in the examined material. This feature is most evident in light-syllable feminine stems, which especially in U and partly H_2 and B_1 show a wholesale transfer to the masculine gender, with the masculine endings attested in the GEN. SG. and NOM./ACC. PL. (GEN. SG. *stedes* (U), NOM. PL. *keran* (H_2), ACC. PL. *kerar*, *keran* (B_1, H_2)). Given the principle of gender preservation as formulated by Carstairs-McCarthy (1994), where gender-class affiliation does not change with the change of declension, the shift of many feminine *i*-stems to the masculine (or neuter) paradigms is an unexpected tendency. It is all the more unexpected in light of the Old English evidence, where the departure from the original gender-class affiliation was minimal in this class as well as in the other minor declensions. A parallel tendency can also be observed in the Old Frisian feminine root nouns which tend to adopt masculine inflections (for details see Section 4.5.4).

Table 4.7 presents a summary of the distribution of archaic and innovative forms in the *i*-stems, with respect to the category of number and irrespective of the syllable weight and gender. The figures refer to the results for all stem types, including the light-syllable feminine stems and heavy-syllable masculine stems, which were not presented in a tabular form.[199]

---

199. The table does not include the attestations of *liude* 'people' which show a very unique, idiosyncratic pattern, with an almost complete retention of the historical inflection. Its inclusion in the overall calculation would skew the results and thus obscure the pattern of inflectional restructuring in this class.

Table 4.7 Overall distribution of archaic and innovative inflections in the OFris. *i*-stems

	i-stem inflection	innovative inflection
singular	(350) 68%	(163) 32%
plural	(14) 7%	(201) 93%
Total	(364) 50%	(364) 50%

An evident tendency in the distribution of forms is the discrepancy in the amount of innovation in the singular and plural paradigms. It is precisely due to the singular that the overall percentage of innovation is relatively low in the *i*-stems. Although such a discrepancy is frequently to be found in other declensional types, and as such is not unusual, the remarkably high percentage of archaism in the singular is unexpected, especially in view of the descriptions of this declensional class found in the standard historical grammars. As the details of this distribution in the singular can offer further insight into the mechanism of the restructuring, they deserve some additional attention. They will be discussed in Section 4.5.2.3 below, which will also illustrate some methodological problems entailed in the study.

4.5.2.3 *An excursus on the alternation in the singular paradigm of heavy-syllable feminine stems*

The pattern of alternation found in the singular paradigm of heavy-syllable feminine *i*-stems turned out to be the most problematic in this class and thus worth a separate treatment, since it illustrates the complexity of the restructuring pattern of the *i*-stems. Due to their ambiguous status with respect to the restructuring, the alternating forms in the GEN. and DAT. SG. could not be considered conclusive in the present study, as the origin of the attested inflectional endings could not be unambiguously traced back to one type of inflection (cf. Table 4.4). A closer look at the distribution of archaic and innovative inflections on the lemma level allows one to identify three different patterns of inflection present in the singular, with a twofold division into lemmas which show an alternation between the forms in -*e* in the GEN. and DAT. SG. and endingless forms in the NOM./ACC.SG. within the paradigm, such as *nēd(e)* 'need' and *wrald(e)* 'world', and lemmas with very limited or no alternation, such as *plicht* 'duty' and *dēde* 'deed'. The limited alternation pattern refers both to nouns which display no ending throughout the entire paradigm (*plicht* 'duty') and those which predominantly show -*e* (*dēde* 'deed'). The pattern with the alternation between the endingless forms in the NOM./ACC. SG. and the forms in -*e* in the GEN. and DAT. SG. reflects the shape of the original *i*-stem paradigm. Tables 4.8, 4.9 and 4.10 present the (token) distribution of inflections in three nouns, each representing one of the three inflectional patterns mentioned. The grey cells mark the etymologically expected forms and the most frequently attested forms appear in bold face.

Table 4.8 The attested singular forms in the paradigm of OFris. *wrald* 'world'

	wrald	*wralde*
NOM.SG.	(6)	(1)
GEN.SG.	(0)	(8)
DAT.SG.	(2)	(9)
ACC.SG.	(9)	(0)

The data indicate that the alternation in the paradigm of *wrald* (*wrald*/*wralde*) is largely in line with the expected historical pattern (92% of forms correspond to the archaic paradigm), reflected in the endingless NOM./ACC. SG. and the marker *-e* in the GEN./DAT. SG. The interpretation of the GEN./DAT. SG. forms as archaic is conditioned by the shape of the NOM./ACC. SG., i.e. its endingless form. If the ending *-e* were the consequence of levelling from the *ō*-stems, one would expect the extension of the pattern also to include the NOM./ACC. SG., and consequently an even distribution of *wralde* over all four cases, which is not attested in the available material.

Table 4.9 The attested singular forms in the paradigm of OFris. *dēde* 'deed'

	dēd	*dēde*	*dēda*
NOM.SG.	(1)	(19)	(1)
GEN.SG.	(0)	(10)	
DAT.SG.	(0)	(16)	(1)
ACC.SG.	(0)	(14)	(4)

The paradigm of *dēd(e)* testifies to hardly any synchronic alternation, with *dēde* being the prevalent form. The minor variation found in the paradigm is due to the impact of the *n*-stems, and the single instance of endingless *dēd* appears in the NOM. SG., where it is historically expected. The archaism of the paradigm increases if the GEN. and DAT. forms are included, reaching then 41 percent (with 27 forms showing the historical inflection). The extension of the forms in *-e* appears to be common in nouns ending in a voiced consonant.

Table 4.10 The attested singular forms in the paradigm of OFris. *plicht* 'duty'

	plicht	*plichte*
NOM.SG.	(0)	(0)
GEN.SG.	(0)	(0)
DAT.SG.	(2)	(0)
ACC.SG.	(8)	(0)

Another pattern is found in nouns of the type *plicht*, where no variation of forms is attested and the prevailing form is the endingless variant. Given such a distribution of forms, 80 percent of the tokens (8 forms) still match the historically expected forms. This 'archaism' of the paradigm results from the fact that the noun is attested almost exclusively in the NOM./ACC. SG., which by regular phonological development was endingless. This pattern appears to be common in nouns ending in a voiceless consonant.

The consequences of the two approaches, i.e. one including, the other excluding the GEN. SG. and DAT. SG. forms, for the interpretation of the data are presented in Table 4.11. The figures refer to the overall percentage of the archaic inflection in the singular, found in the three paradigm types analysed.

Table 4.11 The effect of different interpretations on the level of archaism of the paradigms

% archaic forms	*wrald*	*dēde*	*plicht*
when all cases are included	92%	41%	80%
when the 'standard procedure' is applied (without the GEN. SG. and DAT. SG.)	93%	3%	100%

An inescapable conclusion from the above-presented figures is that both methods of interpreting the data have their flaws. Of the three lemmas analysed, only *wrald* consistently follows the archaic pattern in the singular, and may thus be called a genuine conservative representative of the *i*-stems. The applied interpretation, where the GEN. SG. and DAT. SG. are considered inconclusive ('standard procedure'), gives a realistic percentage for nouns of the type *wrald* and *dēde*, but not for the type *plicht*. In nouns of the latter type the amount of archaism is largely overestimated, no matter whether one includes or excludes the results for the GEN. and DAT. SG. What can be concluded from the above considerations is that (a) some lemmas positively attest to the persistence of the archaic pattern, with alternating forms in -Ø and -*e*; that (b) the methodological procedure applied, being largely restricted by the ambiguity of the inflectional endings, in this particular case, leads to an underestimation of the innovation in the singular of heavy-syllable feminine *i*-stems.

In order to reduce the bias and increase the accuracy of the interpretation, an additional calculation was made, excluding the nouns ending in a voiceless consonant, such as *plicht*, from the group of heavy-syllable stems. By applying this procedure, the overall percentage of archaic inflection in the singular (including the NOM. and ACC. SG.) drops from 60 percent to 48 percent (cf. Table 4.6), which means a reduction from 48 percent to 37 percent of archaic features for the entire paradigm (i.e. including the plural inflection).[200]

---

200. Notice that Table 4.6 presents separately the figures for the NOM. SG. and ACC. SG.; however, the accumulated percentage of archaism in the singular amounts to 60.5%.

Many of the interpretative difficulties result more or less directly from the scarcity of the available Old Frisian material, which frequently does not provide complete paradigms and thus renders many inflectional forms inconclusive. There seems to be no effective systematic solution to restore the balance in the data other than excluding the entire subclass(es) from the analysis. The obvious disadvantage of such an approach, however, is that it rids the study of important details which do throw light on the mechanisms of the restructuring. Therefore, the interpretation of the data in cases such as the heavy-syllable feminine *i*-stems calls for much caution and attention to detail. The lemma-by-lemma approach to analysing the data presented above could be a way to help such a predicament. However, such an approach is beyond the scope of this study, and, more importantly, still remains limited by the nature of the available material, since many lemmas are attested only in one or two paradigmatic categories, and do not allow one to draw any conclusions about their full paradigmatic patterns.

4.5.3   *u*-stems

4.5.3.1   *General characteristics*

The *u*-stems constitute another minor class in Old Frisian which in the traditional accounts has been viewed as extensively affected by the analogical influence of the productive declensions (Siebs 1901: 1343; Steller 1928: 40). As implied by the evidence provided by the other Older Germanic languages, a number of transfers from this class occurred already at the prehistoric stage, prior to the first attestations of Old Frisian (e.g. *dāth* 'death', *hunger* 'hunger', *lust* 'lust', *sāth* 'stream', *side* 'custom', compounds in -*hēd*).[201] The major destination classes for these *u*-stems were the *a*-stems and sporadically the *n*-stems. This direction of reorganisation of the *u*-stem declension continued into the historical stage of Old Frisian, where the *u*-stems tended to shift to the *a*-stems, *ō*-stems and to some extent the *n*-stems, and these transfers occurred in compliance with gender-class affiliation. The dissemination of the *n*-stem inflections in the *u*-stems was enhanced by the presence of a number of inflectional endings which these two classes shared, most notably of the GEN. and DAT. SG., as well as the NOM. and ACC. PL. markers in -*a*. These formal syncretisms rendered the interpretation of many forms of the original *u*-stems problematic.

---

201. An early transfer to the *n*-stems can be postulated for *hūswerda* 'guard' (< *werdu; Go. *waír-dus*), where the final -*a* in the NOM. SG. (attested once in B₁) and in the DAT. SG. (attested twice alongside *huswerde* found in B₂) is a clear indication of the *n*-stem inflection. Van Helten (1890) posits the original *u*-stem affiliation also for the noun *haet* (*hāt*) 'hatred' (attested in the ACC. SG. in E₃) (cf. Go. *hatis*, OE *heti*). Given the scarcity of the data, no definitive statement can be made about the affiliation of this noun in Old Frisian. Its *u*-stem origin is, however, difficult to confirm in view of the evidence from the other Germanic languages. The Gothic material points to its *s*-stem origin, and its instability is well evidenced in the transfer to the *i*-stems in Old English.

The pattern of reorganisation of the *u*-stem paradigm is reminiscent of that found in the *i*-stems, with a divergent development in the light- and heavy-syllable stems. As the class comprised nouns of masculine, feminine and neuter gender, one can expect different paths of development in these subclasses. The historical inflection is vestigially preserved in the light-syllable masculine nouns, where a competition between the inherited and analogical inflections can be captured. The heavy-syllable paradigm, in turn, as a result of the early loss of the inflectional vowel in the NOM. SG. (e.g. *feld* 'field' < PGmc. **felþu*, *wald* 'wood' < PGmc. **walþu*) was much more exposed to the impact of the productive inflections, and the process of restructuring cannot be well captured therein. The most prominent effects of analogical pressure of the productive inflectional types are found in the following categories:

a. masculine and neuter *u*-stems
   - the NOM. SG. ending -*a* (from the *n*-stems) in place of the historical ending -*u* (> -*e*) (light-syllable stems)
   - the GEN. SG. marker -*es* (-*is*) in place of the historical ending -*a*
   - the DAT. SG. marker -*e* in place of the historical ending -*a*
   - the NOM./ACC. PL. markers -*ar* and -*an* (-*en*) in place of the original ending -*a*
   - the *n*-stem GEN. PL. marker -*ena*
b. feminine *u*-stems
   - the GEN. SG. ō-stem marker -*e* or the *a*-stem marker -*es* (-*is*) in place of the historical ending -*a*
   - the endingless DAT. SG. in heavy-syllable *u*-stems in place of the original ending -*a*
   - the *n*-stem GEN. PL. marker -*ena*

A summary of these analogical influences can be found in Table 4.12 which presents the two competing inflectional patterns in the masculine light- and heavy-syllable *u*-stems.

Table 4.12 The competing inflections in the OFris. light- and heavy-syllable masculine *u*-stems

	Light-syllable masculine				Heavy-syllable masculine			
	archaic		innovative		archaic		innovative	
	SG	PL	SG	PL	SG	PL	SG	PL
NOM.	sunu, -e	suna	suna	sunar, -an	*feld*	felda	*feld*	feldar, -an
GEN.	suna	*suna*	sunes	*sunena*	felda	*felda*	feldes	*feldena*
DAT.	suna	*sunum*	sune	*sunum*	felda	*feldum*	felde, feld	*feldum, -em*
ACC.	sunu, -e	suna	suna	sunar, -an	*feld*	felda	*feld*	feldar, -an

The archaism of the *u*-stem paradigm is manifested in the retention of *-e* (< **-uz*) (*-u* or *-o* in the Riustring manuscripts) in the NOM./ACC. SG., as well as the marker *-a* in the remaining categories of the paradigm. The synchronic alternation between the inherited NOM./ACC. SG. marker *-u* and analogical endingless form can be found in light-syllable stems, whereas no parallel alternation appears in the heavy-syllable stems, which by a regular phonological development had no ending in these categories.[202] In general, the interpretation of inflections found in the paradigms of *u*-stems poses a number of interpretative difficulties resulting from several overlaps in inflectional markers. One such problematic inflection is the NOM. SG. marker *-e* in the light-syllable feminine *u*-stems (e.g. *nose* 'nose'), which can be considered a regular phonological development, i.e. an effect of the weakening of /u/. However, the forms can equally well be attributed to a morphological development, i.e. the analogical pressure from the *ō*-stems, where it was extended from the ACC. SG. (Steller 1928: 41; Griepentrog 1995: 339; Versloot 2016a: 12–15).[203] Due to this ambiguity, the NOM./ACC. SG. forms were considered inconclusive and were excluded therefore from the quantitative investigation.

On account of the impossibility of unambiguous interpretation, a number of other forms had to be discarded as well. This is especially true of the feminine heavy-syllable paradigm, where only the singular can provide reliable information about inflectional restructuring. The NOM./ACC. PL. ending *-a* (*honda*) may be a regular continuation of the PGmc. form, but may as well represent an analogical extension of the *ō*-stem plural marker *-a* (cf. *ieve* 'gift' – PL. *ieva*), being thus inconclusive. In the GEN. PL. the synchronic alternation takes place between two non-etymological forms: one extended from the *a*-stems and the other from the *n*-stems, and therefore the form is not relevant for the present investigation. Although the singular paradigm turns out to be more informative about the restructuring, the interpretation of the inflectional endings is not entirely straightforward. The endingless NOM./ACC. SG. forms are interpreted as archaic and are juxtaposed with the innovative forms of the *ō*-stems, characterised by the presence of the marker *-e*. A potential problematic case is the endingless DAT. SG. form in heavy-syllable stems (*hond*), which may represent an old instrumental (see Versloot 2017c). This form is attributed to

---

202. Another potential alternation in the paradigm is that of the root vowel, as in *durun* (DAT. PL.) vs. *dora* (ACC. PL.), found in the Riustring manuscripts. Attributed to the Riustring *a*-mutation (Löfstedt's Law) (Bremmer 2007: 49), this intraparadigmatic alternation has no bearing on the findings of the present quantitative analysis.

203. The NOM. SG. form *nosi*, attested in manuscripts R_1, R_2, R_4 ($n = 5$), can be interpreted as a morphological innovation, as it is not a reflex of the original pattern in these stems (its expected phonological development would have been **noso) (cf. Steller 1928: 41). Boutkan (1996: 29–30), adducing evidence from Middle and Modern Dutch (*nese, neus*), sees the origin of this irregular form in *nosi, which would imply that the form was affiliated with the *i*-stems at an early stage.

morphological innovation, i.e. to the influence of the *i*-stems, and interpreted in the present study as innovative (van Helten 1890: 147). Arguably, the endingless form could be ascribed to the pressure of consonantal declensions; however, given that the consonantal pattern was unproductive, this interpretation seems unlikely. Equally improbable seems the phonological explanation, entailing the need to postulate a loss of the final vowel in this inflectional ending. In light of the dating of the texts incorporated in the analysed corpus and the chronology of the apocope of /a/, which did not take place in Old Frisian before the end of the fifteenth century (van Helten 1890: 49–53; Versloot 2008: 160–161), the morphological explanation seems justifiable. By the same token, the DAT. SG. marker -*e* is not interpreted as an effect of a phonological development (weakening of the final vowel), but ascribed to the impact of the *ō*-stems, where -*e* was the dominant DAT. SG. ending. The justification for such a treatment comes again from the dating of the phonological processes, and in particular the fact that the final vowels remained distinct at this stage.

The presence of the marker -*a* in the NOM./ACC. PL. in masculine stems is interpreted in this study as a conservative feature and contrasted with the innovative, productive endings -*ar* and -*an*. A problematic aspect of such an interpretation is the formal similarity of this marker and the masculine *a*-stem (in R_1, R_2) or possibly *n*-stem ending -*a*, which rendered the *a*-plural forms ambiguous. As the dominant endings in the masculine paradigm in most of the investigated manuscripts were -*ar* (B_1) and -*an* (H_2, U), it can be assumed that the ending -*a* reflects an original formation (cf. van Helten 1890: 148; Siebs 1901: 1344). The situation looks more complex in the case of the Riustring manuscripts, where the masculine *a*-stems show both the ending -*ar* (only in R_1) as well as -*a* as plural markers (see also Versloot 2017b, cf. Bremmer 2007: 45). The decisive factor working in favour of interpreting -*a* as an original inflection is the overall shape of the *u*-stem paradigm in the Riustring manuscripts, which turned out to be very conservative, retaining the historical inflections in all other categories. Accordingly, this form was consistently treated as archaic in the present study.

Likewise, the marker -*a* present in the GEN. and DAT. SG. (of both masculine and feminine stems) was interpreted as a vestige of the historical *u*-stem inflection rather than an effect of the influence of the *n*-stem inflection. Although formally the ending overlaps with that of the *n*-stems, its treatment as due to analogy is excluded on account of the overall shape of the paradigm and the fact that the NOM. and ACC. SG. forms do not testify to the extension of the *n*-stem marker -*a* in the paradigm (cf. Siebs [1901: 1344] who leaves the interpretation of this ending open and van Helten [1891: 481], according to whom forms such as *forda* 'ford', *hūswerda* 'landlord' and *fretha* 'peace' testify to a transition to the *n*-stems).[204]

---

204. Cf. DAT. SG. *fon ongesta*, *in ongesta*, vs. ACC.SG. *umbe* (…) *ongest* (ms. E_4, not included in the present study).

Another morphological innovation in this paradigm is the presence of the vowels -*e* and -*i* in the NOM./ACC. PL. of the light-syllable neuter *lith* 'member'. Although the ending -*i* (found in R$_1$, *lithi*) has been viewed as a continuation of the PGmc. NOM. PL. (Siebs 1901: 1344), it can also be interpreted as a new formation based on the *i*-stem pattern. The latter interpretation seems feasible in view of the evidence from other declensional types in which forms in -*i* (-*e*) appear in nouns denoting the collective plural (e.g. *r*-stems, *nd*-stems).[205]

4.5.3.2   *Results of the investigation*

The distribution of inherited and analogical inflections in the masculine light- and heavy-syllable *u*-stems is presented in Table 4.13. Given that different paradigmatic categories could each be informative about the restructuring patterns in these two stem types, the analysis was conducted separately in these two subtypes.

Table 4.13 Distribution of archaic and innovative inflections in the OFris. light- and heavy-syllable masculine *u*-stems

	Light-syllable MASC.				Heavy-syllable MASC. (SG.)	
	archaic		innovative		archaic	innovative
	SG	PL	SG	PL	SG	
NOM.	(98) 97%	(4) 67%	(3) 3%	(2) 33%	*(5)*	–
GEN.	(10) 91%	*(0)*	(1) 9%	–	*(0)*	(9) 100%
DAT.	(101) 93%	*(5)*	(8) 7%	–	(24) 77%	(7) 23%
ACC.	(131) 92%	(3) 25%	(12) 8%	(9) 75%	*(12)*	–
Total	(347) 91%		(35) 9%		(24) 60%	(16) 40%

In the light-syllable *u*-stems, the retention of the inherited inflection is best evinced in the NOM./ACC. SG., where most of the forms show the historical endings -*u* or -*e* (the latter being a regular phonological development of -*u*). Also the oblique cases in the singular testify to a very high level of archaic inflection. Much more innovative is the paradigm of the plural, where the analogical forms extended from the *a*-stems (NOM./ACC. PL. in -*ar* and -*an*) amount to 61 percent. This discrepancy in the singular and plural paradigms can be ascribed to their different frequency profiles (cf. Section 4.6). The heavy-syllable masculine *u*-stems are very scantily attested in the investigated material. Hardly any conclusions can be drawn about the plural paradigm, which is represented by a single form *ettekere* (PL. of *(et)gēr* 'spear'). The pattern attested in the singular testifies to a considerable amount of

---

205. See Versloot & Adamczyk (2013) for details of the distribution of the *e*-plurals in Old Frisian.

inflectional conservatism retained in the paradigm, which is to be attributed to the DAT. SG, with the GEN. SG. being entirely dominated by the productive inflection.

Table 4.14 presents the findings from the quantitative analysis of the feminine u-stems. As the feminine paradigm is represented by four nouns only (*dure* 'door',[206] *nose* 'nose', *hond* 'hand' and *quern* 'hand-mill'), the results for these stems were assembled in one table, irrespective of the stem weight.

Table 4.14 Distribution of archaic and innovative inflections in the OFris. feminine u-stems

	archaic		innovative	
	SG	PL	SG	PL
NOM.	(28) 100%*	(4)	(0)	–
GEN.	(0)	(27)	(3) 100%	–
DAT.	(8) 12%	(58)	(60) 88%	–
ACC.	(39) 87%	(29)	(6) 13%	–
Total	(75) 52%		(69) 48%	

* The figure comprises the attestations of heavy-syllable stems (*hond*) only; 10 light-syllable forms (of *nose*) were not included for reasons discussed in Section 4.5.3.1.

As can be seen, the evidence offered by the feminine u-stems is fairly inconclusive, with the plural comprising forms which provide no reliable information about the innovative inflection in the paradigm. The attested inflectional markers, e.g. the NOM./ACC. PL. *dura*, *honda*, are ambiguous as they can be analogical innovations, emerging under the influence of the ō-stems, but they may just as well be vestiges of the original u-stem inflection. Accordingly, the level of innovation can be estimated only on the basis of the singular paradigm, where the amount of analogical forms reaches almost 50 percent. The incidental spread of the masculine inflection in this paradigm is evinced in the GEN. SG. *handis*, attested in manuscript U. The archaism of the paradigm relies primarily on the endingless forms of the NOM. and ACC. SG. In contrast, the alternation in the DAT. SG. takes place between the archaic forms in *-a* and the analogical endingless forms, extended from the i-stems (e.g. *querna* 'hand-mill' vs. *quern*). Alternatively, the endingless forms could be interpreted as an effect of *intra*paradigmatic pressure from the historical INSTR. SG. forms. The attested pattern of inflection in heavy-syllable stems is reminiscent of a sub-pattern found in the feminine i-stems, characterised predominantly by the absence of an inflectional exponent in the singular. Given the numerous developmental parallelisms between the i-stems and u-stems, it seems feasible that the feminine stems tended to stay closer to the i-stem rather than ō-stem pattern. The feminine i-stem

---

206. The alternation between *dore* and *dure* is difficult to account for. The form *dore* has been ascribed to analogical development on the pattern of other words where *u* is retained instead of *o*, especially in front of a nasal, or to the presence of a parallel neuter a-stem (Griepentrog 1995: 129).

paradigm (with endingless NOM./ACC. SG.) may have worked as a factor enhancing the retention of the endingless NOM./ACC. SG. in the *u*-stems.

Table 4.15 depicts the distribution of archaic and innovative forms in the scantily attested neuter nouns. The paradigm is dominated by the innovative inflections extended from the *a*-stems, and occasionally *i*-stems (*lithi* 'members'). The few archaic forms attested in the paradigm are confined to the NOM./ACC. PL. (*litha*) and a singly attested (archaic) form in the singular (*felo* 'multitude').[207]

Table 4.15 Distribution of archaic and innovative inflections in the OFris. neuter *u*-stems

	archaic		innovative	
	SG	PL	SG	PL
NOM.	(15)	(1) 20%	–	(4) 80%
GEN.	(0)	(20)	(3) 100%	–
DAT.	(0)	(14)	(3) 100%	–
ACC.	(1) 25%	(2) 18%	(3) 75%	(9) 82%
Total	(4) 15%		(22) 85%	

Table 4.16 presents a summary of the results for the masculine, neuter and feminine *u*-stems, irrespective of their syllable weight. The overall distribution of archaic and innovative inflections with respect to number is presented in Table 4.17.

Table 4.16 Distribution of archaic and innovative inflections in the OFris. masculine, feminine and neuter *u*-stems

	archaic	innovative
masculine	(364) 89%	(45) 11%
feminine	(75) 52%	(69) 48%
neuter	(4) 15%	(22) 85%
Total	(443) 77%	(136) 23%

Table 4.17 Overall distribution of archaic and innovative inflections in the OFris. *u*-stems

	u-stem inflection	innovative inflection
singular	(433) 79%	(112) 21%
plural	(10) 29%	(24) 71%
Total	(443) 77%	(136) 23%

---

207. Another *u*-stem, *fiā* 'cattle', which originally belonged to this declension was not included due to the ambiguous status of the final vowel, which merged with the root vowel, and consequently the identification of the inflectional ending as archaic or innovative became impossible. The final vowel *-a* in the GEN. & DAT. SG. is the original inflectional ending which had become part of the root (e.g. GEN. SG. *fia-s*) (cf. Siebs 1901: 1344).

The *u*-stems turned out to be remarkably conservative and a clear distributional variation with respect to gender can be observed, with the masculine nouns being the most resistant to analogical pressures from other declensions. Another clearly identifiable pattern involves the number: the plural turned out to be much more innovative than the singular, showing predominantly the influence of the *a*-stems. Such a distribution is parallel to the pattern found in the *i*-stems, where the amount of innovation in the plural reached 94 percent. The high percentage of innovation in the plural paradigm of the *u*-stems is largely owed to the neuter *u*-stems, whose inflectional profile was overall very innovative (also in the singular).

In the light-syllable *u*-stems, where the innovation in the plural paradigm reaches ca. 60 percent, the underlying motivation for the spread of the new inflections could be (as in the case of the *i*-stems) the need to restore a contrast in number (cf. GEN. DAT. SG., NOM., GEN., ACC. PL. in -*a*). Furthermore, the relative conservatism of the class must be attributed to the fact the final inflectional vowels were still well preserved in the classical period of Old Frisian, and were resistant to confusion through analogical pressures. This fact is all the more important as the contrast could be maintained in the NOM. SG., which has a special status in the paradigm, determining or in a way protecting its shape. As was made clear in Chapter 2 and will become evident in the course of the investigation, the primary trigger for the reorganisation of the paradigms (already in Proto-Germanic) were the phonological changes affecting the NOM. SG., resulting in the overlap of inflectional exponents and leading to confusion across declensional classes. The retention of the original vowel -*u* (> -*e*) in the NOM. SG. of light-syllable *u*-stems rendered this subclass particularly immune to analogical pressures (at least until the encroachment of further phonological weakening).

A final observation refers to the frequency of occurrence at the lemma-level. Although in terms of type frequency the class of *u*-stems was very modest, the nouns which retain traces of archaic inflections are quite frequently attested (e.g. *sunu, frethe, hond*), which may have helped preserve the archaic inflectional characteristics in their paradigms (see Section 8.6.1).

4.5.4   Root nouns

4.5.4.1   *General characteristics*
From a historical perspective, the major feature of this declensional class was the presence of the *i*-mutated vowel in the DAT. SG. and in the NOM. and ACC. PL. The attested Old Frisian state of affairs, however, testifies to a gradual elimination of this morphophonemic alternation from the paradigm of root nouns, and consequently to an increase in the uniformity of the paradigm. While the root vowel

alternation is still occasionally preserved in the plural, it is absent from the singular, being replaced by analogical inflections from the productive declensional classes. The gradual disappearance of *i*-mutated vowels from the paradigm seems to have been consequential for the sensitivity of root nouns to analogical pressures, and the eventual shape of the paradigms. As the class of root nouns comprised nouns of masculine and feminine gender, parallel transitions to the *a*-stems and *ō*-stems are to be expected. Although the present study explores the pattern of gradual morphological restructuring from a synchronic perspective (i.e. Old Frisian), it must be noted that the root noun paradigm had been under the influence of other declensional types relatively early. On account of a rather limited attestation, very little can be concluded, however, about the earliest stages of the restructuring. Some of the nouns affiliated originally with the root nouns are attested as *a*-stems (e.g. *briast*, *brust* 'breast'), or *u*-stems (*dore* 'door'), showing no vestiges of the original inflection.

The presence of analogical pressure from the productive declensions in the paradigm of root nouns is reflected in the following paradigmatic irregularities:

a. masculine root nouns
   - the GEN. SG. marker *-es* (*-s*) in place of the original endingless form
   - the DAT. SG. ending *-e* in place of the original *i*-mutated endingless form
   - the NOM./ACC. PL. markers *-a*, *-ar* and *-an* in place of the original *i*-mutated endingless form
b. feminine root nouns
   - the GEN. SG. *ō*-stem ending *-e* or *a*-stem ending *-es* (*-is*, *-s*) in place of the endingless form
   - the DAT. SG. ending *-e* in place of the original *i*-mutated endingless form
   - the ACC. SG. ending *-e* (or *-a*) in place of the original endingless form
   - the NOM./ACC. PL. ending *-a* in place of the original *i*-mutated endingless form.[208]

Table 4.18 presents competing inflections in the paradigms of masculine and feminine root nouns. The forms of the GEN. and DAT. PL. are not informative, although it must be noted that they have occasionally been interpreted as a continuation of the original consonantal inflection (Griepentrog 1995: 160).

---

208. Assuming that the innovative inflection in the feminine root nouns derives from the *ō*-stems, one could expect the NOM. SG. to be potentially involved in the alternation as well (cf. *wund(e)* 'wound', where the marker *-e* is present by analogy to the ACC. SG.; Bremmer 2009: 62). Given, however, that the occurrence of this analogical formation was very limited, and that the latter analogical form was not found in the examined material, this potential alternation was not considered part of the restructuring process (cf. Section 4.5.3.1).

Table 4.18 The competing inflections in the OFris. masculine and feminine root nouns

| | MASCULINE | | | | FEMININE | | | |
| | archaic | | innovative | | archaic | | innovative | |
	SG	PL	SG	PL	SG	PL	SG	PL
NOM.	*fōt*	*fēt*	*fōt*	*fōta*, -e(n), -an	*burg*	*burg*,*berg*	*burg*	*burga*
GEN.	*fōt*	*fōta*	*fōtes*	*fōtena*	*burg*	*burga*	*burge*,-es	*burga*, -ena
DAT.	*fōt*,*fēt*	*fōtum*	*fōte*	*fōtum*	*burg*,*berg*	*burgum*	*burge*,-a	*burgum*
ACC.	*fōt*	*fēt*	*fōt*	*fōta*, -e(n), -an	*burg*	*burg*,*berg*	*burge*,-a	*burga*

In the context of the restructuring process understood as *inter*paradigmatic an-alogical realignments, the lack of *i*-mutated forms in the DAT. SG. is a secondary development, occurring as an effect of analogical *intra*paradigmatic pressures, most likely of the generalisation of the NOM./ACC. SG. form across the entire paradigm of the singular. The potential analogical influence of the *a*-stem inflection, with a sec-ondary endingless variant in the DAT. SG., is considered unlikely here (Griepentrog 1995: 160, 240). A number of root nouns, at the same time, exhibit an extension of the *i*-mutated forms to categories where the *i*-mutated vowel was not originally present. This refers in particular to the NOM./ACC. SG. *men* (B_1), *man* (R_1), *dēc* 'cloth' (E_2) as well as the scantily attested *bē* 'dwelling' (F).[209] According to van Helten, these forms may be instances where the *i*-mutated vowel was extended from other categories in the paradigm, most likely from the NOM./ACC. PL. (*men*) (van Helten 1906: 179) and possibly DAT. SG. (*bē* and *dēc*) (van Helten 1890: 157; Sjölin 1970: 177–179).[210] The lack of *i*-mutated vowels in the NOM./ACC. PL. in the archaic paradigm of feminine root nouns cannot be considered a definitive proof that the process was absent in these categories. Although the available Old Frisian material does not attest to any *i*-mutated feminine forms, the forms found in late mediaeval and present-day Frisian dialects testify to the presence of *i*-mutation in the plural (see Section 4.5.4.2 below).

4.5.4.2 *Results of the investigation*
The quantitative investigation was carried out separately for the masculine and feminine root nouns. The neuter subgroup is very scantily attested, comprising two

---

209. The context in which *dēc* is attested is ambiguous and the form can be interpreted as both singular and plural.

210. The original distribution of *i*-mutated forms is attested in the paradigm of *mon* in the eastern dialects of Old Frisian, with the contrast between the singular and plural reflected in the oppositions: *mon – man* (R_1), *mon – men* (B_1, H_2). In the western dialects (U), the contrast is largely neutralised, with partly non-alternating forms *mon/man – man*.

nouns only: *skrēd* 'cut' and *bē* 'dwelling'.[211] The noun *bē* 'dwelling' was not found in the examined material, and *skrēd* is attested once as a DAT. SG. *skrēde* in manuscript U, testifying to no traces of the inherited inflection.[212] The results of the investigation are presented in Tables 4.19 and 4.20, with the distributions for the masculine and feminine paradigms, respectively.[213] Table 4.21 presents the overall incidence of archaic and innovative inflections in the root nouns, including the distribution with respect to the category of number.

Table 4.19 Distribution of archaic and innovative inflections in the OFris. masculine root nouns

	archaic		innovative	
	SG	PL	SG	PL
NOM.	(*365*)	(61) 90%	–	(7) 10%
GEN.	(0)	(*65*)	(72) 100%	–
DAT.	(10) 8%	(*79*)	(117) 92%	–
ACC.	(*163*)	(27) 87%	–	(4) 13%
Total	(98) 33%		(200) 67%	

Table 4.20 Distribution of archaic and innovative inflections in the OFris. feminine root nouns

	archaic		innovative	
	SG	PL	SG	PL
NOM.	(*14*)	(1) 33%	–	(2) 67%
GEN.	(2) 8%	(*12*)	(23) 92%	–
DAT.	(29) 71%	(*14*)	(12) 29%	–
ACC.	(34) 100%	(2) 18%	(0)	(9) 82%
Total	(68) 60%		(46) 40%	

---

211. Scantily attested in the analysed corpus is also the feminine noun *ē*, *ā* 'river'. The noun appears in compounds related to the names of rivers (*Wiserē*, E₁, H, DAT. SG. *Wisurā*, R₁) and other compound formations (e.g. *ēmutha* 'Emden'), and therefore it was not included in the quantitative analysis (cf. later sources 1476: *OFO* II, 82: *ee*, 1453: *OFO* IV, 18: *ee*, 1381: *OFO* III, 1: *estrasil*; Gildemacher 1993).

212. The etymology of OFris. *skrēd* is unclear (cf. Section 3.5.4.1); the noun may be related to MLG *schrāt* which is not affiliated with root nouns (Holthausen & Hofmann 1985, s.v. *skrēd*; Nielsen 1985: 108).

213. The OFris. *tusk*, *tosch*, *tusch* (< *tunþ-ska-*) is not an original root noun, but a root noun-based derivative (*tōth*) (Bammesberger 1990: 202); accordingly, it was not included in the present investigation. The NOM. PL. form *tēsch* (attested in ms. E₂), which shows traces of *i*-mutation, originates in a combination of forms belonging to the two nouns: *tōth* and *tusk* (*tēth* and **toskar*; Griepentrog 1995: 481).

Table 4.21 Overall distribution of archaic and innovative forms in the OFris. root nouns

	root noun inflection	innovative inflection
singular	(76) 25%	(224) 75%
plural	(90) 80%	(22) 20%
Total	(166) 40%	(246) 60%

As the data indicate, the overall inflectional profile of the class was largely modified under analogical pressures, with ca. 60 percent of forms showing innovative inflections. The most prominent feature in the distribution of forms in this class is the discrepancy between the singular and the plural. While the former is substantially more innovative (with analogical inflections found in close to 75% of forms), the latter remains predominantly conservative (with archaic inflection in over 80% of forms). The pattern of restructuring is reminiscent of the situation found in the Old English root nouns, and different from that found in the other investigated classes (i.e. the vocalic stems). The factor which contributes to the archaism of the plural is the occasional presence of the morphophonemic alternation in the paradigm, i.e. a salient inflectional marker. Given that the *i*-mutated vowel was absent from the singular while present in the plural in many lemmas, it may have functioned as the main feature disambiguating the singular from the plural, serving as a relatively stable and clearly distinctive plural marker. The morpho-phonological salience of this marker rendered it (at least for some time) resistant to analogical pressures, as it was the case in the Old English root noun paradigm.

The data indicate that the predominant direction of transfer for the root nouns was towards the *a*-stems and *ō*-stems, with some features of the masculine inflection spreading also to the feminine paradigms (the GEN. SG. marker *-es*, *-is*). The sporadic NOM./ACC. PL. forms in *-an* (*-en*), such as *tōthan*, *fōten*, *mannen*, attested in manuscripts H₂ and U, emerge as a result of the influence of the *a*-stems (where the marker *-an* is a borrowing from Middle Dutch or Middle Low German). Some of the attested innovative forms cannot be unambiguously recognised as representing one specific inflectional pattern. An example here may be the NOM./ACC. PL. ending *-a* found in the feminine paradigm, which can be attributed to the pressure from the *ō*-stems, but could well be a feature extended from the *n*-stems.

Another pattern emerging from the data is related to the greater conservatism of the feminine paradigm, where roughly 60 percent of forms retain the inherited inflection. The bulk of this archaism is to be ascribed to the DAT. and ACC. SG., where, in contrast to the GEN. SG., forms without an inflectional ending are still prevalent. The lack of the *i*-mutated vowel in the singular in the feminine stems has occasionally been ascribed to the influence of the *ō*-stem inflection (Griepentrog 1995: 66). Yet, the unmutated endingless forms are interpreted in this study as

conservative, since the innovation (the loss of the *i*-mutated vowel) emerges as a result of *intra*paradigmatic analogical pressures. The archaism of the endingless DAT.
SG. may have been enhanced by the singular inflection of the heavy syllable feminine *i*-stems and *u*-stems, where endingless forms are frequent (cf. Section 4.5.2 and
4.5.3).[214] The pattern identified in the feminine singular paradigm is all the more
interesting as it implies that the innovative inflection found therein is owed to the
influence of the masculine rather than the feminine paradigm: the few forms which
are attested with analogical endings appear in nouns whose gender is rather unstable (*bōke, nachte*) and they may well be extensions from the masculine *a*-stems.
The total absence of the *i*-mutated vowel in the plural forms, in turn, appears to
have been consequential for the pattern of restructuring in the feminine paradigm,
since it facilitated the spread of analogical forms, rendering it nearly complete. The
masculine paradigm is characterised by greater consistency in that the singular
is very innovative, while the plural is considerably archaic. The fact that the GEN.
SG. testifies to no synchronic alternation can be ascribed to an early, prehistoric
intrusion of the *a*-stem inflection. The encroachment of the *a*-stem ending -*es* is
attested also in the feminine paradigm in two nouns: *nachtis, nachtes* 'night' (in all
manuscripts) and *bokis* 'book' (U). The presence of this inflectional ending in the
two nouns can be attributed to two different developments. With *naht*, a combination of syntactic and semantic factors must have played a role, namely the fact
that the noun frequently appeared in an adverbial phrase with the masculine *dag*
'day'. Given the evidence from the later period, as well as from the neighbouring
languages, the OFris. *bōc* could potentially testify to gender vacillation. The endingless ACC. PL. form in manuscript H$_2$, as well as the marker -*is* found in the GEN.
SG., can be considered innovative features, extended from the neuter *a*-stems. The
endingless ACC. PL. form is ambiguous as it could well be a continuation of the
original root noun inflection. In the present study the latter interpretation was
adopted and the single endingless ACC. PL. form was considered archaic.[215] There
are no unambiguous traces of the pressure of the *ō*-stem inflection in the singular
of feminine root nouns. The dominant analogical ending in the DAT. SG. is -*e* (occurring alongside sporadic -*a*), which could be an extension from both masculine
or feminine inflection. Theoretically, such an extension from the *ō*-stems could also

---

214. The view that these endingless forms served as a template for the reorganisation of the
singular paradigm of the *u*-stems is considered unlikely here (cf. Section 4.5.3.1).

215. The form is found in the following context in ms. H$_2$: *and efter inda bokem scriwen thet ma
tha boc minnie ende tha gerne lese* 'and afterwards it is written in the books so that one remem-
bers the books and reads them eagerly', and it is classified as an ACC. SG. in the glossary to this
manuscript. It seems, however, that the ACC. PL. reading is more adequate, given the preceding
DAT. PL. *bokem*, and accordingly the form was classified as an ACC. PL.

be expected in the ACC. SG., yet no innovative features were identified in the corpus. This pattern of distribution of innovative forms indicates that the feminine root nouns were characterised by a lack of consistency in their gender class affiliation. This tendency towards confusion of gender is also found in the feminine root nouns in Modern Frisian dialects (e.g. in the Mooringer dialect of Coastal North Frisian), where, for instance, *burg* is both masculine and feminine.

Although the historical inflection is not well attested in the Old Frisian material, vestiges of the archaic plural pattern re-emerge in present-day dialects of Frisian, where the following forms can be found: WFris. *ko* 'cow' – *kij*, Wang. *kuu* – *kiier*, Föhr-Amr. *kü* – *ki*, WFris. *goes* 'goose' – *guozzen*/†*gies*, Föhr-Amr. *gus* – *ges*, Sylt *guus* – *gös*, Sylt/Föhr-Amr. *fut* – *fet*; Moor. *fötj* – *fätj*; *göis* – *gäis*, *kü* – *kee* (cf. *lüs* 'louse', *müs* 'mouse', with endingless plural) (Århammar 1967: 8–9; 1969: 14; Jörgensen 1978; Walker 1990; Hoekstra 2001: 777). As can be seen, many of these forms are original feminine root nouns which were not attested in the Old Frisian material. The fact that these forms retain the historical inflection in present-day Frisian implies that the pattern with *i*-mutation must have been continuously present in the language; however, on account of the nature of the Old Frisian corpus, both its size and genre composition, these nouns did not stand a chance of being attested (denoting often names of animals, they could hardly fit in the register of legal texts).

Significantly, when inflectional restructuring is analysed on the lexeme level, it becomes evident that there are substantial differences between individual lexemes. Given the nature of the restructuring, with its gradual diffusion throughout the lexicon, such differences are only to be expected. Accordingly, while the paradigm of *kū* 'cow' appears to be entirely archaic, preserving the mutated form in the plural (*kī*; not in pre-1400 Old Frisian, but in the younger sources rendered as <ky>, e.g. *OFO* I, 253, 1474) as well as endingless GEN. and DAT. SG. (*kū*),[216] *burch* 'city' (PL. *burga*) seems to have followed entirely the pattern of the ō-stems and testifies to hardly any synchronic alternation (except the endingless GEN. SG. *seburch* 'seawall').

A root noun that deserves a separate treatment is *merk* 'coin', which shows an interesting pattern of inflection and whose etymological status is somewhat ambiguous. It is closely related to the OFris. *merke*, which is a feminine ō-stem, meaning 'boundary, territory' (< *markō-*) (*EWN*, s.v. *mark*; cf. Boutkan & Siebinga 2005, s.v. *merk* vs. *merke*), cognate with the Old Norse *mǫrk* 'boundary, wood', and it can be considered an early extension of the original root noun *merk (Griepentrog 1995: 273–275). The feminine noun *merke* shows consistently the ō-stem inflection

---

216. The archaic endingless forms of *kū* (GEN. & DAT. SG.) are retained, e.g., in SkRa (ca. 1300), *...than hi mith ku and mith ey gelda mei* '...than he can pay out of cattle and sheep' (DAT. SG.) (SkRa, LI, 12); *...ther cu bote thes livis thritich panninga* '...the wergeld of a cow, thirty pence' (GEN. SG.) (SkRa, LVII, 2; Sytsema 2012).

and is attested only in the plural in the Old Frisian corpus (NOM./ACC.PL. *merka*, *n* = 8). The forms of *merk* 'coin' found in the corpus (*n* = 570) with endingless GEN. and DAT. SG. and NOM./ACC. PL. testify clearly to a consonantal pattern of inflection (SG. *merk, merk, merk, merk*, PL. *merk, merka, merkum/-on, merk*). Griepentrog (1995: 275), following earlier studies, interprets some occasional instances with the ending -*a*, found alongside the endingless forms, as ACC. PL., ascribing them to the analogical influence of the *ō*-stem inflection. Given the context in which these -*a* forms are attested, i.e. after higher numerals (≥ 20), it seems more likely that these forms represent the original GEN. PL. rather than ACC. PL. As the Old Frisian evidence indicates, case marking on measure terms like *merk* was determined by the numeral cooccurring with these terms. The lower numerals required the use of the NOM./ACC. PL., whereas the higher numerals that of the GEN. PL. (Hofmann 1982; Bremmer 2009: 127. Accordingly, the forms in -*a* comply with this more general pattern, constituting part of the original inflection of the GEN. PL. rather than an analogical extension of the ACC. PL. forms of the *ō*-stems. This pattern appears to be consistent in all the manuscripts except R$_{1,2}$, where the NOM./ACC. PL. forms are used also with numbers above 20, competing there with the GEN. PL.[217]

An alternative interpretation of the attested forms of *merk* is based on the assumption that the noun is an *ō*-stem and may even have originated in the *ō*-stems. It is classified as such in the grammars of van Helten (1890: 135) and Siebs (1901: 1341–1342). In order to account for the attested inflectional pattern under such an interpretation, one needs to take recourse again to the context in which the endingless forms are attested. They appear predominantly after numerals, which means in a context where nouns were frequently found without a plural ending (van Helten 1890: 139). Accordingly, the lack of ending especially in the plural can be interpreted as analogical, corresponding to the pattern found in the other nouns following a numeral. In other words, the shape of the paradigm of *merk* is interpreted as the result of analogical processes rather than a continuation of the original inflection. However, given the consistency with which the root noun inflection is attested in the paradigm of *merk*, it seems more likely to interpret the paradigm as a continuation of the original pattern, which was in a way fossilised, most likely because of the context in which the noun was frequently used. A factor which contributed to the preservation of the historical inflection may have been also the frequency of occurrence, with its conserving effect. On account of the considerable genre bias in the Old Frisian corpus, which rendered the attestations to *merk* very frequent (in particular in the registers of compensations), the noun was not included in the overall count for the root nouns to avoid skewing the results of the investigation.

---

217. The compounds, such as *hemrik, himmerik* were consistently declined as the *ō*-stems (also Griepentrog 1995: 275).

4.5.5 *r*-stems

4.5.5.1 *General characteristics*

This semantically coherent group of nouns is relatively well attested in Old Frisian, though confined to five nouns only (see Appendix).[218] The *r*-stem paradigm resembles the Old English pattern in that it is relatively undiversified in the singular, not only lacking internal allomorphic variation, but also showing no class-specific inflections. This original uniformity, enhanced by the loss of the *i*-mutated vowel in the DAT. SG., made the paradigm of the *r*-stems prone to the influence of analogical pressures. As the class comprised nouns of masculine and feminine gender, the restructuring followed the two expected parallel paths, with the *a*-stems and ō-stems emerging as the major destination classes for the *r*-stems. Accordingly, the influence of the productive inflectional types is manifested in the presence of the following irregularities, potentially to be found in the paradigms:

a.   masculine *r*-stems
   – the GEN. SG. marker *-es* (*-is*, *-s*) in place of the original endingless form
   – the DAT. SG. ending *-e* in place of the original endingless form
   – the NOM./ACC. PL. markers *-a, -ar, -an* (*-en*) in place of the original endingless form
   – the presence of the *n*-stem marker *-(e)na* in the GEN. PL.
b.   feminine *r*-stems
   – the GEN. SG. ending *-e* and/or the *a*-stem marker *-es* (*-is*, *-s*) replacing the original endingless form
   – the DAT. SG. ending *-e* in place of the historical endingless form
   – the ACC. SG. ending *-e* or *-a* in place of the historical endingless form
   – the NOM./ACC. PL. endings *-a, -an* (*-en*) in place of the original endingless form
   – the presence of the *n*-stem marker *-ena* in the GEN. PL.

The above-mentioned expected analogical influences are summarised in Table 4.22, where the competing inflections in the masculine *r*-stem paradigm are presented. Since the innovative inflection in the feminine paradigm departs

---

218. Apart from the five expected nouns denoting kinship terms, this group comprised, arguably, also the masculine *sunder* 'son' (*sunder*), attested in the NOM. PL. in B₁ and E₂ as *sundre* and *sunder*, respectively (van Helten 1890: 159). As the etymology of this noun is rather dubious, it was not included in the quantitative analysis. The two attested forms *sundre* (B₁) and *sunder* (E₂) testify respectively to the innovative and archaic pattern of plural inflection. Another noun which could be considered an original *r*-stem is *taker* 'brother-in-law', which is attested once in the GEN. SG. as *takeres* (U). The form was not included in the study.

from the masculine one only in the GEN. SG. (in -*e*) and ACC. SG. (in -*a* and -*e*), no separate table showing the competing inflections was considered necessary for the feminine paradigm.

Table 4.22 The competing inflections in the OFris. masculine *r*-stems

	archaic		innovative	
	SG	PL	SG	PL
NOM.	*brōther*	brōther	*brōther*	brōthera(n), -en
GEN.	brōther	*brōthera*	brōther(e)s	*brōther(e)na*
DAT.	brōther	*brōth(e)rum, -em*	brōthere	*brōth(e)rum, -em*
ACC.	*brōther*	brōther	*brōther*	brōthera(n), -en

The historical paradigm of the singular is very uniform and the intrusion of intra-paradigmatic analogy at an early stage is manifested in the absence of the *i*-mutated vowel in the DAT. SG. The lack of this feature does not directly affect the interpretation of the forms in the present study, but is a factor contributing to the pattern of morphological restructuring, as could be seen in the root nouns.[219] In contrast to masculine stems, feminine *r*-stems show synchronic alternation in the ACC. SG. between the inherited zero marker and the innovative endings -*a* and -*e*. The NOM. SG. of feminine *r*-stems, which could potentially show the influence of the ō-stems by attaching the marker -*e*, was not included in the study as a category informative about the analogical restructuring, because the original form in this category in the ō-stems was endingless, and the marker -*e* is considered to be a later analogical development (van Helten 1890: 137; Siebs 1901: 1341; Bremmer 2009: 62; cf. Versloot 2016b).

4.5.5.2 *Results of the investigation*
The quantitative analysis was conducted separately for the masculine and feminine nouns, and the results showing the distribution of archaic and innovative inflections in the masculine and feminine *r*-stems are presented in Tables 4.23 and 4.24, respectively.

---

219. The alternation of the root vowel -*a*- and -*e*- found in the paradigm of *feder* (cf. E₂ *fader*, F *fadir*), where -*e*- was originally interpreted as a reflex of *i*-mutation once present in the paradigm (van Helten 1890: 159), reflects an alternation between two chronologically (or dialectally) different forms. The forms with -*a* are found in the younger sources (not in the analysed selection of texts), and can be ascribed to borrowing from Low German or Middle Dutch, while the forms in -*e* are a regular phonological development, i.e. the fronting of WGmc. **a* > Proto-Fris. **æ* (> /æ/ <e>), parallel to that found in Old English (Bremmer 2009: 29; cf. Campbell 1977: 52ff).

Table 4.23 Distribution of archaic and innovative inflections in the OFris. masculine *r*-stems

	archaic		innovative	
	SG	PL	SG	PL
NOM.	(*73*)	(5) 16%	–	(27) 84%
GEN.	(6) 21%	(4)	(23) 79%	–
DAT.	(1) 11%	(6)	(8) 89%	–
ACC.	(*30*)	(1) 33%	–	(2) 67%
Total		(13) 18%		(60) 82%

Table 4.24 Distribution of archaic and innovative inflections in the OFris. feminine *r*-stems

	archaic		innovative	
	SG	PL	SG	PL
NOM.	(*50*)	(0) 0%	–	(5) 100%
GEN.	(14) 61%	(2)	(9) 39%	–
DAT.	(12) 80%	(2)	(3) 20%	–
ACC.	(29) 97%	(0) 0%	(1) 3%	(1) 100%
Total		(55) 74%		(19) 26%

The pattern of distribution presented above testifies to a greater proneness of the masculine *r*-stems to submit to the influence of the productive declensions. The analogical inflections seem to be more or less equally distributed in the singular and the plural of the masculine stems. In contrast, the feminine paradigm turns out to be more resistant to external influences, and the incidence of archaic and innovative inflections is markedly different depending on the number. While the plural submits to the analogical pressure entirely, the singular remains conservative. This tendency continues into the later stages, with the feminine *r*-stems remaining indeclinable in the singular even in one of the youngest Old Frisian texts, *Thet Freske Riim*, dated to the early sixteenth century (Campbell 1952: 46). The endingless singular of feminine *r*-stems corresponds to the pattern found in the feminine *i*-stems and root nouns (and partly heavy-syllable *u*-stems), which seems to have developed into a common feature of the feminine nouns. This common inflectional pattern may have enhanced the retention of the original endingless inflection in the feminine *r*-stems. Another factor of importance for the discrepancy in the restructuring pattern of the masculine and feminine paradigms is the shape of the innovative inflectional markers in the two paradigms, with the masculine GEN. SG. *-es* (*-is*, *-s*) being more prominent (salient) and thus expansive than the feminine marker *-e* (for a discussion of the salience of inflectional exponents, see Section 8.6.2). Table 4.25 presents the overall distribution of archaic and innovative inflections in the masculine and feminine *r*-stems, including the incidence of forms with respect to number.

Table 4.25 Overall distribution of archaic and innovative inflections in the OFris. *r*-stems

	r-stem inflection	innovative inflection
singular	(62) 58%	(44) 42%
plural	(6) 15%	(35) 85%
Total	(68) 46%	(79) 54%

The data indicate that the *r*-stems stayed under the moderate pressure of the productive declensional types. The nearly equal distribution of archaic and innovative features shows that although reshaping of the paradigm was already well underway, the original shape of the *r*-stem inflection is still detectable in the Old Frisian material. This refers in particular to the singular which turns out to be much more archaic than the plural, with 58 percent of forms retaining the inherited inflectional pattern, as compared to 15 percent in the plural (where the archaism relies entirely on the noun *brōther*, relatively frequent in the plural). The categories which turned out to be the most vulnerable to analogical pressures were the NOM. and ACC. PL., where the innovative inflection is attested respectively in 87 and 75 percent of forms. The data testify to the presence of three innovative inflectional markers in the masculine plural paradigm: the endings -*a* (*brōthera*) (extended from the *a*-stems or *n*-stems, depending on the manuscript/dialect), -*en*/-*an* (*federen*), found only in manuscript U, as well as the ending -*e* (*brōthere*), whose interpretation is problematic. The plural ending -*e* is occasionally found also in the feminine paradigm (*sustere*), where otherwise the analogical *ō*-stem marker -*a* is attested. According to Siebs (1901: 1346), the NOM./ACC. forms in -*e* may have two sources, namely (a) they may result from the regular phonological development (weakening) of -*a* > -*e*, where -*a* itself is a morphological innovation in the paradigm, extended from the productive vocalic declensions, or (b) they may be a continuation of the old ACC. PL. form in -*u*, in which case they are to be viewed as an archaic feature in the paradigm (Versloot & Adamczyk 2013: 432; cf. van Helten 1890: 159–160; Steller 1928: 44; Boutkan 1995: 275). Given that the scope of the study is limited to the material which shows hardly any confusion between final -*e* and -*a*, the interpretation of -*e* as a reduced variant of -*a* seems less likely in these forms (van Helten 1890: 49–51).[220] It seems feasible that the ending -*e* could be a consequence of the spread of the *i*-stem

---

220. Van Helten (1890), postulating the ending -*u* to be the source of the irregular marker -*e*, draws a parallel with the Northumbrian forms *faedero, dohtero, mōdero, brōþero*, equally problematic in terms of their origin (van Helten 1890: 159–160; cf. Section 3.5.5).

inflection, or at least a sub-pattern developed therein, proper to nouns denoting the collective plural (cf. OFris. *liude*). Both *brōthere* and *sustere* fit the pattern very well in that they tend to appear in the plural more often, in particular in texts of a legal nature (e.g. dealing with succession). Irrespective of whether of phonological (*-a* > *-e*) or morphological origin, these irregular forms are interpreted as innovative in this study, because they emerged due to the analogical pressure of other declensions, be it of the *a*-stems (with a further phonological modification) or the *i*-stems (cf. Section 4.5.7 for a parallel development in the *nd*-stems).[221]

As regards the distribution of innovation with respect to case, as could be expected, the most innovative case in the singular was the GEN., where analogical inflections constituted over 60 percent of the attested forms. Apart from the expansive *a*-stem marker *-(e)s* found in both masculine (*federes, brōderis*) and feminine stems (*mōders*), the *ō*-stem ending *-e* is attested in the feminine paradigm (*fulsustre, sinsustere, dochtere*). The fluctuation between archaic and innovative inflections is also well attested in the DAT. SG., with an almost equal share of both features. Finally, although the GEN. PL. is excluded from the counting (for reasons discussed in Section 4.5.1), the influence of the *n*-stem inflection is sporadically attested here, with forms such as *susterna*, found in manuscripts U and in B₁.

The shape of the *r*-stem paradigm, with a moderate scope of the effects of the operation of analogical processes, could theoretically be attributed partly to the semantic constitution of this class, comprising nouns denoting kinship terms. The semantic uniformity of the class may have constituted an effective barrier for the operation of analogy. However, as shown also for the Old English material, where this declensional class is much better attested, the eventual shape of this declension was determined by an interplay of a number of factors, the most prominent of them being the frequency of occurrence (cf. Section 3.5.5.2). The semantic profile of the class was crucial in the sense that it determined the frequency profiles of the lemmas and their use in individual paradigmatic categories. The lack of salient inflectional exponents in this class was another factor contributing to the remodelling of the paradigm.

Interestingly, the vestiges of the original plural inflection of the *r*-stems can be found in modern North Frisian dialects, where the plural is characterised by a zero ending and additionally the presence of the *i*-mutated vowel, e.g. *bruler - brääler* (Föhr).

---

221. The sporadically attested NOM. PL. form *feders*, reminiscent of the Old English plural *fæderas*, is not attested in the material investigated, but is found in Codex Roorda (ca. 1500) (Cummins 1887: 46). The presence of the *s*-plural marker in Frisian was common in the later period (in particular in West Frisian) and has been attributed to the impact of the inflectional pattern of Middle Low German (Steller 1928: 44; Markey 1981: 119; Hoekstra 2001: 777) or Middle Dutch (Bremmer 1989).

4.5.6 *s*-stems

4.5.6.1 *General characteristics*

Most of the historical *s*-stems had entirely shifted to other declensional types at the prehistoric stage, and consequently they never appear with vestiges of the consonantal inflection in the attested Old Frisian material. The main destination classes for the early shifts of the *s*-stems were the neuter *a*-stems and *i*-stems. These earliest transfers involved the following nouns in Old Frisian, which no longer show vestiges of the historical inflection:

a. shifts to the *i*-stems: *hei* (< *hugi*) (m.), *hat* 'hatred' (possibly a *u*-stem; van Helten (1890: 148); Go. *hatis*), *sīde* 'side' (m.) (Go. *sidus*)
b. shifts to the *u*-stems: *feld* 'field', *fiā* 'cattle'
c. shifts to the *a*-stems: *del* 'valley' (n.), *sted* 'bank' (m.)

The original affiliation of these nouns with the *s*-stem declension is confirmed by the evidence provided by the other Older Germanic languages, in particular by Gothic and North Germanic.

Only in a few nouns was this historical pattern residually retained in Old Frisian, and scant traces of synchronic alternation are attested, for instance, in *kind* 'child', with the plural vacillating between *kind-er(-a)* and *kinda*, or *klāth* 'cloth(es)', with the plural *klāthar* vs. *klātha*.[222] A factor which may have facilitated the large-scale transfer of these nouns to the productive inflectional types was the inherited NOM./ ACC. PL. element *-r-*, which rendered these forms indistinguishable from the NOM./ ACC. PL. of the *a*-stems, where the plural was marked by the ending *-ar*.

Although nouns originally affiliated with the *s*-stems are only scantily attested in the Old Frisian material, the restructuring of their paradigms can be systematically framed. The following analogical inflectional features can be found in the paradigms of the *s*-stems:

–   the *a*-stem GEN. SG. marker *-es* (*-is*, *-s*)
–   the *a*-stem DAT. SG. ending *-e*
–   the NOM./ACC. PL. markers *-a* and *-an*
–   the endings *-a* and *-um* in the GEN. and DAT. PL., respectively, without the *-r*-element
–   the *n*-stem ending *-ena* in the GEN. PL.

---

222. As has already been mentioned (cf. OE *cild*), the etymology of *kind* is not entirely transparent and its affiliation with the *s*-stems can be questioned. In the case of Old Frisian, it seems likely that *kind* was borrowed from Low German (Meijering 1985). Since in all the modern Germanic languages this noun does show features of the *s*-stem inflection, it is discussed with these stems.

All these innovative inflections appear in place of forms which were originally characterised by the presence of the *r*-element. As the historical *r*-formative was eliminated from the singular in most nouns at an early stage, the innovative inflectional endings were attached to the forms without the *r*-extension. An exception here is the noun *(h)rīther* 'cattle', where the original stem formative was consistently retained in the entire paradigm and analogical inflections were attached to it (e.g. *hrītheres*). These forms were, accordingly, interpreted as innovative in the present study.

In the *s*-stems the alternation between archaic and innovative inflections can be captured also in the DAT. and GEN. PL., with the archaism reflected in the retention of the *r*-element. Formally, the inflectional endings in these two categories, whether attached to a bare stem (e.g. *clatha*, *clathum*), or to the stem element *-r-* (e.g. *clathra*, *clathrum*), can be ascribed to the prehistoric influence of the *a*-stems. In the present investigation, however, the forms of the GEN. and DAT. PL. which preserve the *r*-formative (*-ra*, *-rum*) will be considered archaic and, accordingly, counted against the plain forms without the stem formative (*-a*, *-um*). Such a synchronic approach to this inflectional pattern seems legitimate on account of the status of the *r*-formative as a hallmark of the West Germanic *s*-stem inflection. Table 4.26 presents the potential competition between archaic and innovative inflections in the *s*-stem paradigms.

Table 4.26 The competing inflections in the paradigm of the OFris. *s*-stems

	archaic		innovative	
	SG	PL	SG	PL
NOM.	*clāth*	clāthar	*clāth*	clāth(a), -**an**
GEN.	clāther	clāthra	clāthes	clātha,-**ena**
DAT.	clāther	clāthrum	clāthe	clāthum
ACC.	*clāth*	clāthar	*clāth*	clāth(a), -**an**

The archaic paradigm of the OFris. *s*-stems is largely reconstructed as the inherited forms are only sporadically attested in the corpus, which will become evident in the following section. Although some internal stem-vowel alternation could be expected in the paradigm given the Old English evidence, no consistent morphophonemic alternation was found. A single exception here is the presence the NOM. SG. form *clēth* (of *clāth* 'cloth') in manuscript H$_2$ (alongside the NOM. PL. *clāthar*), which is reminiscent of the Old English situation and the distribution of *i*-mutated forms there (with *i*-mutated singular vs. unmutated plural, e.g. OE *cælf – calfur*, Angl. *lemb – lombor*, *dōēg – dōgor*). This alternation has no bearing on the interpretation of forms in the present study.

4.5.6.2 *Results of the investigation*

The results of the analysis of the *s*-stems are demonstrated in Table 4.27 and 4.28, with the former depicting the distribution of archaic and novel inflections with respect to case and number, and the latter showing the overall distribution of forms, including the pattern for the singular and plural.

Table 4.27 Distribution of archaic and innovative inflections in the OFris. *s*-stems

	archaic		innovative	
	SG	PL	SG	PL
NOM.	(*65*)	(4) 33%	–	(8) 67%
GEN.	–	(1) 8%	(32) 100%	(11) 92%
DAT.	–	(0)	(9) 100%	(34) 100%
ACC.	(*32*)	(15) 56%	–	(12) 44%
Total		(20) 16%		(106) 84%

Table 4.28 Overall distribution of archaic and innovative inflections in the OFris. *s*-stems

	s-stem inflection	innovative inflection
singular	(0) 0%	(41) 100%
plural	(20) 24%	(65) 76%
Total	(20) 16%	(106) 84%

The data clearly indicate that the restructuring was very advanced in the *s*-stems both in the singular and plural. The vestiges of the inherited pattern are confined to the plural (23.5%), whereas the singular turned out to be dominated by analogical inflections. The vacillation between archaic and innovative forms attested in the plural, especially in the NOM. and ACC., involves primarily the extension of the *a*-stem markers *-an* (*-in*) and *-a* (e.g. *āra, kinda, clātha, clāthan, claen, kindyn*). A single form unambiguously showing the influence of the neuter *a*-stems is the NOM. PL. form *kind*, attested in manuscript B$_1$. A clear pattern of distribution of these markers emerges across individual texts, with the *-en* (*-an*/*-in*) forms being confined only to the relatively young manuscript U. The singly attested ACC. PL. form *clāthera* (R$_2$) is a hybrid formation in that the historical plural exponent is retained and at the same time a new analogical ending from the *a*-stems is attached (Klein 2013: 191). It is interpreted as an archaic form in the present investigation as the retention of the *r*-element is a feature of the plural paradigm only, not of the singular (cf. *hrīther*). Traces of archaic inflection were also found in the GEN. PL. in manuscript B$_1$, attested as *clātha* (*n* = 1). Although no instances of archaic DAT. PL. were found in the investigated corpus, they are attested for the noun *clāth* as *clāthrum* (*clatrum*) in manuscript B$_2$ (32.15, 44.13), which, on account of its relation with B$_1$, however, remained beyond the scope of the present quantitative study (cf. footnote 190).

The interpretation of the ending -*ar* as an archaic plural marker (e.g. in *clāthar*, *kindar*) is not entirely unproblematic: as the marker -*ar* was a widespread plural ending in the *a*-stem declension, its appearance in the largely disintegrated *s*-stem paradigm could equally be ascribed to the impact of the *a*-stems.[223] Also, the quality of the vocalic element, i.e. -*a*- instead of the expected -*e*-, could point to the fact that the ending was an early extension from the masculine *a*-stems (-*ar* < *-*ōz*) (Schlerath 1995: 262; cf. van Helten 1890: 129). One of the arguments against such an interpretation, however, is related to the fact that the -*ar* exponent was a characteristic of the masculine stems and not of neuter ones. Given that the preservation of gender was one of the guiding principles in the mechanism of analogical restructuring, the expected direction of transfer of the *s*-stems would be towards the neuter *a*-stems, where the plural form was endingless. This renders the interpretation of -*ar* as an archaic feature in this declensional type more convincing. Secondly, the quality of the vowel in the -*ar* element can be attributed to the original stem-vowel alternation (*-*es*-/-*os*-) in these nouns, and its origin in the *-*os*- form, which is reflected in the absence of the *i*-mutated vowel in the NOM./ACC. PL. (in contrast to the occasionally mutated singular) (cf. also the unmutated forms in Modern Frisian dialects where the ending is retained as -*er*: Amrum *kualew:kualwer*, *lum:lumer*; Siebs 1901: 1347).[224] Another piece of evidence comes from the diatopic distribution: the -*ar* plural marker is attested primarily in manuscripts B$_1$ and E$_1$, which can be associated with the present-day East Frisian Saterland dialect, characterised by the absence of the -*er* ending in masculine nouns. In light of the presented evidence, the interpretation of the marker -*ar* in Old Frisian as a continuation of the historical paradigm appears more adequate, and is adhered to in the present study (cf. Klein 2013: 190–191).

The assumption that the plural paradigm of some of the Old Frisian *s*-stems was archaic, although not supported by the available Old Frisian material, finds its confirmation in the later attestations of the nouns belonging originally to this declension. The plural forms found in (early) Modern Frisian dialects closely related to Riustringen Old Frisian testify to a former presence of the archaic plural

---

223. To what extent the NOM./ACC. PL. ending -*ar* was widespread in the *a*-stems is a matter of dispute: it has been viewed as a pan-Frisian ending or as a dialectal feature confined to Ems Old Frisian (notably Bremmer 2009). For discussions, see Århammar (1995: 77), Nielsen (2000: 253), Bremmer (2009: 60) and Versloot (2014, 2017b).

224. Alternations of the type -*ar*/-*er*, -*an*/-*en* are found occasionally in classical texts, such as E$_1$ and U, resulting from an early reduction of /a/ > /e/ in the protected position after a heavy-syllable (Versloot 2008: 144, 155).

pattern in Old Frisian, and the lack of such forms in the OFris. material should be attributed to the nature of the available corpus rather than to some exceptionally progressive morphological development of early Frisian; cf. Wursten Frisian *kláed*, PL. *kliar* 'clothes'; Wang. *kleet* (< LG, OFris. *klēth* > Wang. **kleid* or **kleið*), PL. *kloo$_e$der* 'clothes', Harlingerland Frisian *klaadersphine* 'wardrobe' (Möllencamp 1968: 106; Ehrentraut 1968: 375; Cadovius-Müller & Kükelhan 1875: 44). Traces of the etymological plural marker *-r* are also found in North Frisian, e.g. Sylt *kualw – kualwer* 'calf', *kluad – kluader* 'cloth', Föhr-Amr. *ai – aier* 'egg', *kualew – kualwer* 'calf', *kleet – kluader* 'cloth/clothes', *lum – lumer* 'lamb'.

4.5.7 *nd*-stems

4.5.7.1 *General characteristics*

This small declensional class consisted of masculine nouns only and therefore the reorganisation in this class occurred according to the pattern of the masculine *a*-stems. The prehistoric dating of the influence of analogical pressures in the paradigm of *nd*-stems is supported by the presence of the GEN. SG. *-es*, the GEN. PL. *-a* and the DAT. PL. *-um*, all deriving from the *a*-stems. Traces of analogical influence can potentially be detected in the forms of the DAT. SG., where the innovative marker *-e* replaces the original endingless forms. The expected analogical inflections in the plural are the NOM./ACC. endings *-a*, *-ar* or *-an*, extended from the *a*-stem inflection. The impact of the *n*-stem inflection can be seen in the forms of the GEN. PL., where the weak marker *-ena* appears in place of the expected ending *-a* (which, as in the other classes, was not taken into account in the quantitative study). The competing archaic and innovative features in the paradigm of *nd*-stems are presented in Table 4.29.

Table 4.29 The competing inflections in the paradigm of OFris. *nd*-stems

	archaic		innovative	
	SG	PL	SG	PL
NOM.	*friōnd*	friōnd	*friōnd*	friōnda, -ar, -an
GEN.	friōnd	*friōnda*	friōndes	*friōndena*
DAT.	friōnd	*friōndum,-em*	friōnde	*friōndum,-em*
ACC.	*friōnd*	friōnd	*friōnd*	friōnda, -ar, -an

The paradigm of the Old Frisian *nd*-stems, in marked contrast to the Old English paradigm, was characterised by considerable uniformity, with no morphophonemic alternation present. The *i*-mutated vowel, which in Old English could be found in monosyllabic stems in the DAT. SG. and NOM./ACC.PL., is entirely absent from the

Old Frisian paradigms. The lack of *i*-mutation renders the two types of stems that the class comprised – monosyllabic and disyllabic – identical in terms of their (inherited) inflectional pattern. Significant is the lack of contrast between the singular and plural in the nominative and accusative. Both features, i.e. the absence of *i*-mutated vowels in the paradigm and the lack of a distinct plural exponent influenced the pattern of reorganisation of the *nd*-stem paradigm, rendering it more vulnerable to interparadigmatic analogical pressures.

4.5.7.2 *Results of the investigation*
Table 4.30 presents the distribution of archaic and innovative inflections in the paradigm of *nd*-stems. The categories which provide no information about the restructuring in this class are the NOM. and ACC. SG., as well as the GEN. and DAT. PL.

Table 4.30 Distribution of archaic and innovative inflections in the OFris. *nd*-stems

	archaic		innovative	
	SG	PL	SG	PL
NOM.	*(11)*	(20) 95%	–	(1) 5%
GEN.	(0)	*(17)*	(3) 100%	–
DAT.	(0)	*(22)*	(14) 100%	–
ACC.	*(18)*	(2) 25%	–	(6) 75%
Total	(22) 48%		(24) 52%	

The paradigm of the singular does not testify to any synchronic fluctuation; both the GEN. and DAT. SG. show a pattern reminiscent of the Old English pattern, with the *a*-stem markers found consistently in all the attested instances. A striking characteristic of the plural paradigm is the discrepant pattern of distribution in the NOM. and ACC., which is fairly unexpected in view of the evidence from the other investigated classes, where no such correlation seems to hold. In fact, there seems to be a straightforward correlation involving the following pattern: while the nominative forms are attested in the older East Frisian manuscripts ($R_{1,2}$, H_2, E_1), the accusative ones appear only in the younger manuscript U, representing West Frisian. Consequently, the incongruity in the pattern is more a direct effect of an uneven distribution of forms across the manuscripts, with their different attestation dates (and indirectly of the scarcity of the data), rather than some systematic paradigmatic phenomenon. This pattern of distribution has no special significance for the overall picture of the inflectional reorganisation of the *nd*-stems.

Table 4.31 presents the overall percentage distribution of the competing inflections in the *nd*-stem paradigm, including the incidence of forms with respect to number.

Table 4.31 Overall distribution of archaic and innovative inflections in the OFris. *nd*-stems

	nd-stem inflection	innovative inflection
singular	(0) 0%	(17) 100%
plural	(22) 76%	(7) 24%
Total	(22) 48%	(24) 52%

The data indicate that the original inflectional pattern was to a large extent remodelled in this declensional class. A prominent feature of the distribution of archaic and innovative inflections is the discrepancy between the singular and plural paradigms, with the former being entirely innovative, the latter remaining archaic. The conservatism of the plural inflection is unexpected, given the morphological shape of the NOM./ACC. PL. lacking any salient marking (whether inflectional or root internal), which could otherwise render the pattern immune to the impact of analogical pressures. Some explanation comes from a closer inspection of the frequency of occurrence on the lemma-level, although it must be noted that this class is not very well attested in Old Frisian and the figures are altogether low. The attestations to the NOM. and ACC. PL. are confined to two nouns only, *friōnd* and *fiūnd* (except for a single *berinda* 'carrier'), and their frequency of occurrence in the plural is higher than in the singular. The evidence from Old English, where this class is much better attested, points to such a correlation more straightforwardly. The relative high token frequency of these nouns in the plural may have had a conserving effect for the entire paradigm, working as a factor fending off the pressure of analogical inflections, and facilitating a temporary fossilisation of the original endingless plural.

As regards the innovative forms in the plural, apart from the expected presence of the *-an* ending, found in manuscript U (NOM. PL. *fiandan*), there is a single attestation of the marker *-a* in *berinda*, which indicates the impact of the adjectival inflection. These novel forms are attested only in manuscript U, while in the other manuscripts the archaic inflection is consistently retained. The ACC. PL. forms in *-e* (*fiunde* = 2, *fiande* = 3), which appear to be the dominant forms in manuscript U, seem to correspond to the pattern found in the *r*-stems, and accordingly can be interpreted as an extension of the *i*-stem sub-pattern, encompassing the nouns frequently attested in the plural and denoting groups of people. Although the interpretation of these forms may be problematic, they are clearly analogical formations, resulting from the extension of a new inflectional pattern rather than a phonological process. As these instances are attested in the older text layers of manuscript U, their interpretation as an effect of a phonological weakening of a final *-a* (**fiunda* > *fiunde*) seems unlikely. Moreover, this interpretation does not seem feasible in light of the fact that the ending *-a* was not the default marker for the masculine nouns in this manuscript. In conclusion, the *nd*-stem inflection was reorganised on the pattern of the *a*-stems (in the singular) and partly *i*-stems (in the plural). The class turns out to have been almost entirely free from the influence of the *n*-stem inflection, showing no traces of weak pattern even in the GEN. PL., relatively widespread in other minor declensional types.

4.5.8   Dental stems

Although this group of nouns can hardly be considered a separate declension from the Old Frisian perspective, the original affiliation of the nouns in Proto-Germanic allows one to group them under one heading. Two nouns attested in the analysed Old Frisian corpus can be identified as originating as dental stems: *mōnath* 'month' and *megith* 'maid' (**magaþ ~ *magiþ*; Boutkan 2003: 25). A third noun originally belonging to this class, *hel(e)de* 'hero', was not found in the analysed material, but is attested in the younger Old West Frisian chronicles (CrK and Rom) (Hofmann & Popkema 2008, s.v. *helede*). All of these original dental stems shifted to the productive declensions and decline according to the *a*-stem (*mōnath*) or *ō*-stem (*megith*) patterns, showing no vestiges of their original inflection (e.g. NOM. PL. *mōnathar*, B_2, ACC. PL. *megitha*, R_1). It can be assumed that the shift took place in compliance with gender, although in *megitha*, the ending *-a* found in R_1 may not be conclusive. Strong support for this assumption comes from manuscript E_2, where *megitha* points unambiguously to feminine inflection (otherwise the ending *-ar* would be expected): *Alsa helpe thi god, and sente Katerina and alle godis megetha, and alle sine helga* (A1.7) 'So help thee God and Saint Catherine and all God's virgins and all his saints'. A single form which could be interpreted as archaic is the endingless ACC. PL. *monat*, attested in manuscript E_1 in: *thet thet kind andere modere bilethad werthe niughen monat* 'So that the child be formed in the mother for nine months' (E_1 V. 62). The lack of inflection in this category seems to point to a fossilised feature of the original consonantal pattern.[225]

---

225. This form is not mentioned as a dental stem relic by Boutkan (2003) in his analysis of the dental stems in Old Germanic (alongside the Old English and Old Saxon evidence) (cf. van Helten 1890: 157).

4.6   Summary of the results and overview of the tendencies

This section presents an overview of the patterns and major tendencies in the reorganisation of the Old Frisian nominal inflection. Table 4.32 summarises the most prominent trends in the restructuring with respect to the major directions of interdeclensional transfers.

Table 4.32 Directions of interdeclensional transfers of minor stems in Old Frisian

Historical declensional class	New declensional class
i-stems (m, n)	=> *a*-stems
i-stems (f)	=> *ō*-stems
u-stems (m)	=> *a*-stems
u-stems (n)	=> *i*-stems
u-stems (f)	=> *i*-stems
root nouns (m)	=> *a*-stems, *i*-stems
root nouns (f)	=> *ō*-stems , *a*-stems
r-stems (m)	=> *a*-stems, *i*-stems
r-stems (f)	=> *ō*-stems, *i*-stems, *a*-stems
s-stems (n)	=> *a*-stems (n, m)
nd-stems (m)	=> *a*-stems, *i*-stems
þ-stems (m)	=> *a*-stems
þ-stems (f)	=> *ō*-stems

The substantial impact of the *a*-stem inflection on the shape of the minor paradigms, as attested in the Old Frisian material, was to be expected given the productivity of this inflectional class. The influence of the feminine *ō*-stems, although clearly present in the minor paradigms, is much less extensive. This is especially true of the singular paradigms in the feminine *i*-stems, *u*-stems and root nouns, which show a clear preference for zero marking. This trend may indicate an emerging predilection of the feminine stems to develop a typically word-based inflection, the development of which occurred at a later stage in the masculine paradigm. In marked contrast to the Old English data, the early Frisian material testifies to some expansion of the *i*-stem inflection, and its spread seems to be conditioned largely by semantic factors. This development is reminiscent of the tendencies present in the other West Germanic languages (i.e. in Old Saxon, Old Low Franconian and Old High German) which also show productivity of the *i*-stem inflection, associated primarily with the feminine paradigms (although the scale of these phenomena cannot be compared). A less expected feature is the limited expansion of the *n*-stem inflection, confined mostly to the plural paradigm (GEN. PL. -*ena*). What may be partly responsible for the limited scope of the spread of this inflectional type is the relatively uniform shape of the *n*-stem inflection in Old Frisian. In contrast to the other West Germanic languages, the OFris. *n*-stems were not characterised by a very salient inflectional marker in the singular (cf. OE -*an* found in most of the cases in the singular and consistently in the NOM./ACC. PL.). In other words, the salience of the vocalic exponents was too low to achieve the level of expansion comparable to that of the *a*-stem markers, such as the GEN. SG. -*es* or the NOM./ACC. PL. -*ar*/-*an*. Another well attested feature of the distribution of analogical inflections is the expansion of the plural marker -*an* in the West Frisian material, i.e. in *Codex Unia*, which testifies to a generalisation of the ending -*an* in the masculine plural in all minor declensions, except the *nd*-stems and root nouns. Although reminiscent of the situation in (Early) Middle English, the marker -*an* did not derive from the historical *n*-stems in Old Frisian; it is instead an effect of the dissemination of the *a*-stem inflection. Finally, another tendency that could be observed in the material involves the shift of gender-class affiliation occurring alongside the shift of nouns to another declension. Although for the majority of interdeclensional shifts gender remains the guiding parameter, some deviation from the original gender class was detectable in the feminine stems, especially in root nouns and light syllable *i*-stems, which tended to decline according to masculine or neuter inflection.

An overview of the distribution of inherited and analogical inflections in individual declensional classes is presented in Table 4.33. Admittedly, such a presentation gives an oversimplified picture of the reorganisation of the Old Frisian nominal inflection. Given the complexity of the process and the interplay of factors involved in its mechanism, it is hardly possible to interpret these generalised figures at face value. The overview is rather to serve as a general indication of the extent to which the new analogical inflections were present in the minor paradigms, and the figures will become more meaningful in the comparison of the tendencies across the investigated Old Germanic languages.

Table 4.33 Summary of the distribution of archaic and innovative inflections in the OFris. minor stems per class

	archaic	innovative
i-stems	(364) 50%	(364) 50%
u-stems	(443) 77%	(136) 23%
root nouns	(166) 40%	(246) 60%
r-stems	(68) 46%	(79) 54%
s-stems	(20) 16%	(106) 84%
nd-stems	(22) 48%	(24) 52%

The data clearly indicate that the degree of reorganisation of the original inflectional pattern differs considerably in individual declensional classes, ranging from the most advanced in the *s*-stems, to the least advanced in the *u*-stems. Such a pattern of distribution is to be attributed to a number of interacting factors. Although some of these factors are class-specific and can be decisive about the fate of a given class in general (e.g. phonological profile and the semantic make-up which may influence the frequency profiles of nouns), many of them operate across class boundaries (e.g. the morpho-phonological salience of markers and frequency profiles), and the eventual shape of a given class is most often an effect of their interaction and accumulation.

An examination of the details of the distribution, including the variation in the inflection of the singular vs. plural, and in the type of stem (the significance of which was signalised already in the discussion of individual classes) can offer further insights into the patterns of morphological restructuring. The results of a closer scrutiny of the distribution with respect to the type of stem are presented in Table 4.34. It depicts the details of the arrangement of inflections in the two types of minor stems, vocalic (*i*-stems, *u*-stems) and consonantal (root nouns, *r*-stems, *s*-stems, *nd*-stems), in which the attested pattern of restructuring turned out to be discrepant.

Table 4.34 Distribution of archaic and innovative inflections in the OFris. vocalic and consonantal stems

	archaic	innovative
vocalic stems	(807) 62%	(500) 38%
consonantal stems	(276) 38%	(455) 62%

The bulk of the inflectional archaisms is concentrated in the vocalic stems (61.7%), whereas the consonantal stems testify to the considerable pressure from the productive inflectional classes (62.2%). In order to account for this discrepancy and to gain a better insight into the mechanism of the restructuring, closer attention needs to be paid to the distribution of analogical inflections in the singular and the plural. A striking discrepancy in these figures can already be detected when analysing the overall distribution of the Old Frisian inflections with respect to number, irrespective of the declensional type, as presented in Table 4.35.

Table 4.35 Overall distribution of archaic and innovative inflections in the OFris. paradigms minor stems

	archaic	innovative
singular	(921) 61%	(601) 39%
plural	(162) 31%	(354) 69%
Total	(1083) 53%	(955) 47%

The deviation of inflections from the historical pattern is moderate, but a clearly divergent pattern is found in the singular and plural inflection. One of the reasons for this is the disproportion in the number of attested vocalic and consonantal stems, the former being much better represented in the investigated corpus. It is especially true for the singular, which turned out to be the better attested category in the vocalic stems. The pattern becomes more transparent when the figures for the singular and plural in the two types of stems mentioned are compared, as demonstrated in Table 4.36.

Table 4.36 Distribution of archaic and innovative inflections in the OFris. minor stems with respect to number

	archaic		innovative	
	SG	PL	SG	PL
vocalic stems	(783) 74%	(24) 10%	(275) 26%	(225) 90%
consonantal stems	(138) 30%	(138) 52%	(326) 70%	(129) 48%

The substantial percentage of conservative inflection in the singular of the vocalic stems (74%) is contrasted with a very high percentage of innovative inflection in the plural (90.4%). A mirrored pattern is to be found in consonantal stems, with a highly remodelled paradigm of the singular (70.3%) and a relatively well-preserved inflection in the plural (51.7%). Two factors seem to have played a significant role here. One of them was the frequency of occurrence of forms in the singular in vocalic stems. As the figures indicate, the forms of the vocalic stems occurred more frequently in the singular than in the plural and this high frequency may have worked as a factor conserving the inflection in the singular. Secondly, a prominent feature of the singular paradigm in vocalic stems was the presence of endingless dative and accusative forms, which were very frequently attested. This endingless pattern in the singular emerges as a template for feminine stems, spreading also to consonantal declensions, and was evidently strong enough to resist the potential influence of the ō-stems, which, as the figures show, was very limited in the vocalic stems. Another factor which may also have contributed to the conservation of the historical pattern in the singular of the vocalic stems is the presence of consistent vocalic contrasts in unstressed syllables, which prevented a potential confusion of inflectional endings; especially the retention of marking in the light-syllable stems in the NOM. SG. may have enhanced the stability of the class. None of these features was a prominent characteristic of the consonantal stems, whose paradigms in the singular tended to be much more uniform, often lacking specific case marking, and whose frequency profiles showed yet a different distribution. The relative conservatism of the plural inflection in the consonantal stems and the realignments occurring in the plural paradigm will be given closer attention in the subsequent paragraphs, as they turned out to be consequential for the later shape of the Frisian nominal inflection (cf. Table 4.37).

With regard to dialectal variation, the patterns of restructuring are similar in that no striking discrepancies can be observed in the levels of innovation in individual manuscripts. For most of the manuscripts dated around 1300 the overall amount of innovative inflection oscillates around 45 percent ($R_{1,2}$ 40%, H_2 46%, U 48%, B_1 51%). An exeption is the youngest manuscript E_1 (ca. 1400), where the level of innovation reaches ca. 62 percent.

As the Old English data has revealed, the scope of the restructuring was strongly dependent on the salience of inflectional exponents. This is particularly conspicuous in the plural paradigm, as the contrast in the category of number was more essential than in the category of case, and the changes in the nominal system were in most instances guided by the functionality principle. The relation between the salience of plural markers in individual classes and the level of innovation in the plural paradigms (based on the NOM./ACC. PL.) is presented in Table 4.37.

Table 4.37 The correlation between the salience of plural markers and the innovation level in the OFris. minor stems

	plural marker(s)	% innovation in PL
i-stems	vocalic marker -*e*, Ø	94%
u-stems	vocalic marker -*a*	71%
root nouns	*i*-mutation	20%
r-stems	Ø marker	85%
s-stems	*r*-formative	51%
nd-stems	Ø marker	24%

A clear correlation emerges between the type of inflectional exponent (its morphophonological salience) and the level of innovation in the plural paradigm. The paradigms where the marking of plurality was confined to a vowel (*i*-stems, *u*-stems), or, alternatively, was not signalled by any specific inflectional exponent (some *i*-stems, *r*-stems) were most easily reorganised under the analogical pressure of the productive declensions, showing hardly any traces of the original pattern of inflection. In contrast, the paradigms where the inflectional markers were more prominent (especially the *i*-mutated vowel) tended to resist the impact of analogical inflections. In other words, the paradigms where the inflectional exponent was more salient were also more transparent, and thus more likely to fend off analogical pressures. Accordingly, in the paradigm of root nouns, which were often characterised by the presence of the *i*-mutated vowel, the archaic inflection was retained in 80 percent of forms. The correlation is to some extent evident also in the *s*-stems, and becomes even more conspicuous if one takes into account only the data from the East Old Frisian dialects where the amount of innovation in the *s*-stem plural paradigm reaches no more than 17 percent. In contrast, the low salience of markers (vocalic or zero markers), especially in the *i*-stems (and possibly *u*-stems), and thus the proneness to analogical pressures, was additionally triggered by the lack of distinction between the singular and plural. The introduction of a new inflectional marker in the plural thus served the function of restoring the paradigmatic contrast between the singular and the plural.

Clearly, the reorganisation pattern attested in the *nd*-stems cannot be accounted for by the salience of the inflectional marker. The low amount of innovation in the paradigm is unexpected, given that the plural was not marked by any prominent inflectional feature. Accordingly, other factors need to be taken into account when interpreting these figures, especially frequency of occurrence and, indirectly, semantics. In particular, as the attested *nd*-stems denoted concepts which can be expected to be used more often in the plural than in the singular, their higher frequency of occurrence in the plural may have worked towards the retention of the historical pattern.

The frequency of occurrence, operating on different levels, and in particular the relative frequency of the singular and plural inflection in paradigms emerged already as a significant factor in the Old English material. The correlation found in the data involved the following pattern: the lower the percentage of the plural inflection in the paradigm, the more likely it is that the paradigm would be subject to analogical remodelling under the influence of the productive declensions. Table 4.38 presents the potential correlation between the percentage of innovative inflection in the Old Frisian plural paradigms and the relative frequency of the plural inflection (plural proportion).

Table 4.38 The correlation between the percentage of innovative inflection in the plural and the proportion of the plural inflection

	plural marker(s)	PL proportion	% innovation in PL
r-stems	Ø	18%	85%
i-stems	-e, Ø	34%	94%
u-stems	vocalic (-a)	23%	71%
s-stems	r-formative	38%	51%
nd-stems	Ø	58%	24%
root nouns	*i*-mutation	25%	20%

As the data indicate, the percentage of the plural inflection accounts for the pattern of distribution found in the *nd*-stems, where 58 percent of all the attested forms are plural tokens and the plural paradigm remains remarkably archaic. In the *r*-stems and light-syllable *u*-stems, both infrequently attested in the plural, this factor rein-forces the spread of analogical forms in their plural paradigms, which were char-acterised by fairly non-salient marking. An exactly opposite effect of the relative frequency can be observed in the *s*-stems, where the relatively high percentage of plural inflection (38%) may have worked as a factor inhibiting analogical pressures, supported by a fairly salient *r*-formative as a plural marker.[226] Clearly, the local frequency effects could be easily detected in the corpus and they turn out to have played an important role in the reorganisation of the paradigms of minor stems, with the higher frequencies of forms serving as a factor conserving the archaic inflection in the paradigms.

A more direct effect of semantics can be observed in the pattern of extension of the original NOM./ACC. PL. *i*-stem marker *-e* in minor stems. The dissemination of this marker seemed to be dependent on the semantics of the nouns, affecting primarily nouns denoting people or groups of people. To what extent these indi-vidual factors contributed to the final shape of the inflectional paradigms will be the subject of a more extensive discussion in Chapter 8, where the broader West Germanic perspective will make it possible to compare their impact on the shape of declensional systems in the investigated languages.

When looking at the restructuring of the nominal inflection from a present-day perspective, it is the changes in the plural inflection (i.e. NOM./ACC. PL.) that are particularly significant. Given that the case system of Frisian had entirely disin-tegrated by the sixteenth century, it is only in the variation of the plural markers that the earlier patterns of reorganisation can be detected.[227] As the distinction of number is essentially more crucial than that of case, the inflectional contrasts tend to be more consistently retained in number. This could already be observed in the spread of uniform, endingless forms in the singular paradigm of the feminine *i*- and *u*-stems, which obliterated case marking, in contrast to the introduction of explicit inflectional exponents in the NOM./ACC. PL. in classes where the plural was not originally marked. The original complex declensional system was reduced to two major plural allomorphs in present-day West Frisian, namely *-en* and *-s*, distributed according to specific phonological rules. A threefold system, with the ending *-er* typical of the masculine nouns, is still preserved in the dialects of Insular North Frisian (e.g. Hoekstra 2001).

---

226. This discrepancy in the relative frequency for the plural seems to hold also in the larger Early Modern Frisian corpus, where the plural forms constitute 26% of all the instances in the historical *nd*-stems and 5% in the *r*-stems.

227. The disintegration of the case system in West Frisian is essentially dated to the late 15th and early 16th c., possibly mid-16th c. in the north-eastern part of the West Frisian area (Hoekstra 2001: 776; Versloot 2004, 2008: 160, 178, 273–274).

Concluding, the analysis of the material revealed the importance of two major causal factors in the restructuring of the Old Frisian nominal system: the salience of inflectional markers (determined essentially by phonology) and the relative frequency of nouns. Some additional effect comes from semantics, for instance, in the spread of the *e*-plural pattern, but also on a more local level, when semantics defines the frequency profiles of the lemmas. A further factor involved in the restructuring process was gender, which to a large extent, although not as consistently as in Old English, regulated the directions of transfers between classes. Significantly, the maintenance of the functionality of the system emerges as the most important driving force behind the analogical changes, which is manifested, above all, in the retention of inflectional contrasts in number to the detriment of the distinction in case. It is an interplay of all the factors mentioned and their accumulated effect that determined the patterns of the restructuring of the Old Frisian nominal paradigms.

4.7   Taxonomic implications of the study

Much as the examination of the Old English material confirmed the need for a revision of the way the declensional system is presented in standard historical grammars, the pattern attested in Old Frisian leads to a more moderate conclusion. The available descriptions of the declensional system in Old Frisian have not been entirely dominated by the anachronistic stem-based perspective, so evident in the major treatments of Old English nominal morphology. This may be partly due to the nature of the available corpus of Old Frisian, characterised by relatively scant attestations of the minor stems, whose inflectional patterns have not so far been given much attention. It seems that the awareness of the fact that the analogical remodelling of the declensional system in Old Frisian was fairly advanced must have been firmly present in the studies of Frisian historical morphology. As mentioned in the introduction to this chapter, with a notable exception of the early treatments by van Helten (1890), Siebs (1901) and Steller (1928), the more recent descriptions of the morphological structure of Old Frisian do not take the Proto-Germanic system as a template for the presentation of the Old Frisian declensional system, offering instead classifications allegedly closer to the actual state of affairs reflected in the available material, with a twofold division into weak and strong nouns, and a further subdivision into gender types (Boutkan 1996, 2001). An important synchronically oriented account was offered by Sjölin (1969) (followed by Markey 1981: 119), who presented a threefold subdivision of the declensional system using gender as the primary criterion, with a further subclassification into types where the inflectional marker served as the basic criterion (Sjölin 1969: 31–32). The most recent systematic treatment of Old Frisian morphology by Bremmer (2009), although essentially following the diachronic path, leads the author to conclude that it is the twofold division of Old Frisian nouns that most adequately reflects the attested state of affairs.

The results of the quantitative analysis show that the analogical inflections were present in more than 50 percent of forms in most declensional classes (except the conservative *u*-stems). Such a distribution of archaic and innovative inflections implies that the strictly diachronic approach to nominal inflection in Old Frisian based on stem-type criterion can hardly be viewed as adequate. On the other hand, the picture of Old Frisian inflectional morphology that emerges from the present investigation is substantially different from the one sketched in the earlier descriptions. The number of archaic features found in the paradigms turns out to be higher than could be expected from the available synchronic accounts of Old Frisian nominal morphology. The attested state of affairs allows one to conclude that the generalisation of the nominal inflection to two major inflectional types is an oversimplification when referring to the Old Frisian material attested prior to 1400, in that it discounts a number of important features of inflection which reach beyond the status of the relics of the historical pattern. The present analysis reveals that Old Frisian (prior to 1400) still shows some declensional diversity which points to its relative morphological conservatism. The discrepancy between the traditional accounts and the results of the present study can be explained by the fact that the mentioned synchronic descriptions of Old Frisian cover the entire timeframe between 1250 and 1550. In this context, one of the implications of the present study is that for the analysis of the early Frisian morphology a fine-grained periodisation, with early/classical Old Frisian and late/post-classical Old Frisian, is a methodological necessity.

4.8 Conclusions

The examination of the Old Frisian material has revealed that its nominal system was exposed to intense analogical pressures, which considerably changed the shape of the inherited nominal paradigms. The interaction of these analogical developments with phonological processes led to an increase in syncretism across paradigms, and consequently to a reduction of declensional class diversity. The two major types serving as a template for the reorganisation of the declensional system were the *a*- and *ō*-stems, and, to some extent, the *i*-stems; traces of the spread of other inflectional types are rather limited. At the same time, the amount of inflectional archaism still retained in Old Frisian in its classical stage is much higher than expected in light of the existing accounts and its late attestation date.

A prominent feature of the pattern of restructuring is an apparent lack of gradualness of the process, understood as the presence of synchronic variation between competing forms (e.g. in the GEN. and DAT. SG. in the *nd*-stems or in root nouns). This lack of attested synchronic alternations, which otherwise allows one to capture the restructuring as a progressing development, on the one hand, points to the fact that certain lemmas/paradigms must have yielded to the influence of the productive inflection more radically and earlier than others; on the other, it may be attributed to the nature of the corpus with a limited number of fully attested paradigms for individual lemmas available.

The restructuring of the Old Frisian nominal inflection can be interpreted also in the context of the long-standing controversy over the periodisation of Frisian. The findings from the present study testify to a relatively high amount of morphological archaism of pre-1400 Old Frisian, providing yet another argument that the earliest attested stage of Frisian is linguistically more compatible with the *old* stages of the development of English, German or Dutch than with their *middle* stages.

The findings from the present research at the same time seem to have some methodological implications for the study of Old Frisian in general. They demonstrate, namely, the significance of the heterogeneity of the Old Frisian corpus, understood as a combination of classical and post-classical sources, for the interpretation of the material. Most of the generalisations made about the Old Frisian morphology found in historical grammars are based on the findings from the treatments which incorporate classical and post-classical sources as a whole. The picture of Old Frisian morphology emerging from such descriptions seems to be biased towards the evidence offered by the later sources (post-classical), representing a fairly advanced stage of phonological development, with its wide-ranging morphological consequences. The present study, confined to the examination of the oldest stage of Old Frisian, indicates that separating the two sub-corpora and analysing each as a homogenous entity allows one to capture the fine details of morphological processes, and avert the danger of potential oversimplifications of the linguistic description.

Finally, it must be emphasised that the attested pattern of restructuring of the Old Frisian nominal inflection is a reflection of the shape of the available corpus, with all its limitations, primarily those of size and genre. Therefore, the vestiges of the historical patterns found in present-day Frisian dialects in some nouns (historical root nouns or *s*-stems) are an invaluable source of information in completing the picture of the restructuring process in Old Frisian. They prove that the absence of certain features in the investigated material is not to be attributed to some particular morphological advancement of Old Frisian, but rather to the scant attestation of the language. In a broader perspective, it clearly testifies to the value of the Modern

Frisian internal variation for the uncovering of linguistic (in this case morphological) features of Old Frisian. At the same time, the analysis has demonstrated that some of the tendencies found in the material of Old English – much richer and extended over a longer period – could largely be identified in a smaller and much more genre-undiversified corpus of Old Frisian.[228]

---

228. For a corpus study on the validity of findings based on a comparative analysis of corpora of different sizes and genre-composition, see Versloot & Adamczyk (2014).

CHAPTER 5

Nominal inflection in Old Saxon

5.1 Introduction

Old Saxon, representing the oldest stage of the development of Low German, exhibits a typological profile that constitutes a challenge for any linguistic investigation. Its complex linguistic shape reflects the special position that the language occupies in the West Germanic linguistic continuum. On the one hand, in terms of its genetic affiliation, Old Saxon can be classified as one of the North Sea Germanic dialects, sharing a range of characteristics with Old English and Old Frisian; on the other, due to the geographical vicinity of High German dialects and the ensuing linguistic influences, its typically Ingvaeonic nature is to a large extent obscured, being overlaid with a Franconian component. This intermediate position of Old Saxon among the West Germanic dialects is reflected especially in its phonology and morphological structure, including the complex system of inflections. The heterogeneous linguistic profile resulting from a combination of Franconian and Ingvaeonic traits renders Old Saxon unique among its sister languages. In this context, the present investigation into the restructuring of the Old Saxon nominal inflection can gain an additional dimension in that the findings can offer some insight into the positioning of Old Saxon within the West Germanic dialect continuum.

The attestation of Old Saxon extends between the ninth (ca. 800) and twelfth centuries (ca. 1150–1200), and can be subdivided into two stages depending on the type of textual evidence combined with the attestation dates: (1) the ninth century with the two major literary monuments, *Heliand* and *Genesis*, and (2) the tenth/ eleventh century with the remaining minor prose texts, both religious and secular, and glosses, which attest partly to the Ingvaeonic characteristics, partly to the transition to Middle Low German and the interference of the southern features (Klein 2000a: 1245–1246). The fragmentary evidence which can be considered pre-Old Saxon or early Old Saxon is dated between the fifth and eighth centuries, and encompasses some onomastic data, as well as the runic inscriptions on the Weser bones (Weser runes), whose authenticity is, however, debatable (e.g. Looijenga 2003: 23, 268; cf. Pieper 1989: 41–43; Krogh 1996: 112–113), and two further runic inscriptions dated before the sixth century (Libenau and Wremen) (Sanders

1983: 33; Krogh 2013: 141).[229] When compared to the corpora of Old English or Old High German, the corpus of Old Saxon is a *relatively* homogenous entity in that the available textual material testifies to a moderate dialectal diversification and a very modest text-type (genre) variation. This is hardly surprising given that the majority of textual material comes from two poetic texts, complemented by rather limited evidence from a number of minor prose documents and glosses. While some differences between the language represented in *Genesis* and *Heliand*, on the one hand, and the idiom of the minor documents, on the other, are identifiable, their scope cannot be compared to the more explicit discrepancies existing between, for instance, Anglian poetic texts and West-Saxon prose texts – not because such differences did not exist, but because the scarcity of the available material precludes their identification in Old Saxon. An aspect which is comparable is the nature of the variation; more specifically, the discrepancies are not purely stylistic (or diatopic for that matter), but also diachronic, with the language attested in the two poetic sources representing an earlier stage than the idiom found in the minor documents.

The scant amount of available material limits also the access to information about the diatopic diversity of Old Saxon. In fact, in no other Old Germanic language (except Gothic) are the available sources so much concentrated in only one part of the language area. It can be assumed, however, that no uniform idiom was spoken in the Old Saxon linguistic area and that dialectal variation did exist. This was made explicit by Stiles (1995: 202), who asserts that the language "was never a monolith, rather, it was a dialect continuum." Therefore, Old Saxon as it is known from the available attestations must be conceived of as an abstraction of the dialectal variation existing in the area where the Saxon settlement can be identified (Sanders 1983: 32). The abundance of features testifying to external (Franconian) interference has occasionally been interpreted as evidence that Old Saxon, as it is attested in the available documents (especially in *Heliand*), functioned as a *koiné* of Saxon dialects (Cathey 2000: 14). Although such a hypothesis is difficult to verify, the Old Saxon material amply illustrates the scope and complexity of the continual interaction and mutual influence of Germanic dialects in the area of northern Germany (Kufner 1972: 92).

One of the notorious characteristics of the Old Saxon texts is the presence of considerable spelling variation, which can be attributed to two circumstances: firstly, the fact that the extant documents are attested in a number of manuscripts originating from different scriptoria and different geographical areas (cf. the different

---

229. As the town of Wremen belonged to the Frisian language area until the 18th c., the Wremen inscription can just as well be considered pre-Old Frisian. Given its early attestation date, it is fairly speculative to assign it to any of the languages which emerged only a few centuries later (Versloot 2016a: 2).

manuscripts of *Heliand*); and, secondly, the fact that a large portion of the Old Saxon material was strongly influenced by Franconian linguistic traits, including Franconian scribal practices. The impact of the southern features is more evident in the literary texts (i.e. *Heliand* and *Genesis*) whose origin is commonly ascribed to High German speaking regions (with Fulda and Werden postulated as the likely places of origin, e.g. Cordes 1973: 15–17; Krogmann 1973: 25–27), whereas at least part of the non-literary pieces tends to preserve a more Ingvaeonic character. The interpretation of the variation resulting from the Franconian influence has posed a number of difficulties, the major question being whether the existing contrasts should be interpreted on the graphematic or the phonemic level, but also whether (or to what extent) the variation is a consequence of language contact in the written language or in the spoken idiom of that period.

The geographically intermediate position of Old Saxon within the West Germanic linguistic continuum led to the emergence of various phonological and morphological correspondences – with Old English and Old Frisian, on the one hand, and Old High German and Old Low Franconian, on the other. Some of the best known phonological features of Old Saxon shared with Old English and Old Frisian include the loss of a nasal before spirants with a compensatory lengthening of the vowel (e.g. MLG *gōs*, OE *gōs* vs. OHG *gans*), and monophthongisation of PGmc. **ai* > *ē/ā*. The close phonological affiliation of Old Saxon with Old High German, in turn, is manifested in the parallel developments of vowels in final syllables, or the presence of Franconian graphemes <ie> for *ē* and <uo> for *ō*. The latter testify presumably to the process of diphthongisation in Old Saxon (*ē* > *ia*, *ō* > *uo*), corresponding to that found in Old High German (Klein 2000a: 1250).[230] The most important phonological feature which creates a sharp boundary within the West Germanic dialect continuum is the implementation of *i*-mutation, with respect to which Old Saxon complies with the Old High German pattern (cf. Section 5.5). As regards morphological correspondences, the OS DAT. SG. in *-o* < **-au* attests to a development parallel to that in Old English and Old Frisian with **-au* > *-a*, in contrast to OHG *-iu*, which testifies to the origin in **-æu* (Krogh 2013: 152) (see Section 5.6.3). Another morphological feature is the syncretism of the present and preterite indicative endings in the plural (present ind. OS *-ath* vs. OHG *-mēs*, *-et*, *-ant*). In contrast, the presence of the marker *-i* in the NOM./ACC. PL. of the masculine and feminine *u*-stems testifies to a parallel with Old High German (< **-ewez*), against the Old English and Old Frisian marker *-a* (< **-awez*). A consequence of these bidirectional linguistic correspondences is that Old Saxon displays an appreciable

---

230. Whether the digraphs <ie> and <uo> should be considered a result of diphthongisation in Old Saxon has been a matter of dispute; arguably, they could represent monophthongal values, close to *ī* and *ū*, respectively. For details, see Krogh (1996: 257–262).

amount of heterogeneity when it comes to its linguistic profile, to such a degree that the language has traditionally been described in terms of a *Mischsprache*.

With regard to this heterogeneous profile, there is a consensus among linguists that the originally Ingveaonic Old Saxon was in one way or another affected by Franconian through cultural and political influences. According to some linguists (notably Klein 2000b; Stiles 1995), this interaction was even a longer-standing phenomenon and the source of the contacts is to be sought already in the Merovingian era. The most prominent external influences and the ensuing gradual typological change in the Ingvaeonic profile of Old Saxon towards a High German one came with the political, cultural and religious integration of the Saxons into the Carolingian empire (Sanders 1983: 31; McKitterick 2008: 103–106). The attested variation in (chiefly) morphological forms has brought scholars to emphasise the double-layered nature of Old Saxon (*Zwiegesichtigkeit*; Wolff 1934: 151, or *Zweischichtigkeit*; Dal 1954: 74). This duality involves a combination of the (autochthonous) northern Ingvaeonic traits, on the one hand, and the features attributed to the southern, High German/Franconian influence, on the other. The twofold nature of the Old Saxon language was alluded to by Rooth (1932) who interprets the Ingveaonic traits as genuinely Old Saxon ("echtsächsische Volksprache") and views the southern characteristics present in the material as an orthographic phenomenon, ascribing them to Franconian scribal practices (Rooth 1932: 40; 1949: 23). In contrast, Dal (1954, 1983) attributes the southern bias to a genuine linguistic influence of Old High German phonology and morphology rather than to orthographic variation, and this view appears to be endorsed in the subsequent studies. Evidently, Old Saxon as attested in the available sources represents no uniform system and this lack of uniformity is very well evinced, among other aspects, in the inflectional morphology (Krogmann 1970: 216; Dal 1983: 80). Significantly, the divergent linguistic features belong to two chronological layers: the period when Old Saxon was more closely bound with Old English and Old Frisian, and the younger stage, characterised by the influence of Franconian linguistic features (cf. Markey's [1976] distinction between "genuine Old Saxon with distinctively Ingvaeonic features" and "Old Saxon influenced by High German").[231] Accordingly, the features shared by Old Saxon exclusively with Old High German must be considered secondary developments (Nielsen 2001: 513).

---

231. A formal distinction has occasionally been made between two terms used to refer to the language spoken by the Saxon tribes: Old Saxon (*altsächsisch*) and Old Low German (*altniederdeutsch*). The former would refer to the earlier period, when the language had a purely North Sea Germanic character, while the latter refers to the later stage, when the language was affected by the Franconian features (Dal 1983: 78 after Bischoff 1956–1957; Krogh 1996: 83–84). In the English tradition of describing the earliest stage of the development of Low German, the term *Old Saxon* has consistently been used, but cf. the use of both terms in Besch et al. (2000) and the respective discussions in this volume, e.g. by Klein, p. 1241, Sanders p. 1288, Scheuermann, p. 1283.

The two chronological layers vary also with respect to the nature of the interdialectal relations. While the affiliation with Old English and Old Frisian can be characterised as *adstratal*, with the three Ingvaeonic dialects constituting no more than a "loosely knit linguistic community within West Germanic" (Nielsen 1989: 78), exhibiting both common inherited traits as well as independently developed innovations and retentions, the southern affiliation of Old Saxon is commonly defined in terms of *interference* (Rauch 1992a: 108–109). In order to gain a better understanding of this heterogeneous linguistic nature of Old Saxon, its position among the West Germanic sister languages will be discussed in more detail.

5.2   The placement of Old Saxon in West Germanic

The positioning of Old Saxon among the West Germanic languages has been viewed as one of the most difficult and challenging problems of comparative Germanic linguistics (Krogh 1996: 138–140). The difficulty is related to the fact that on the phonological and morphological level Old Saxon exhibits features characteristic of both the northern and southern division of West Germanic. Consequently, the major controversy centres around the question whether Old Saxon should be considered, alongside Old High German and Old Low Franconian, a Franconian dialect, or rather, alongside Old English and Old Frisian, an Ingvaeonic one. In the former view (espoused most notably by Holthausen 1921, Kuhn 1955, Cordes 1956, Rösel 1962, Lasch 1974), Old Saxon is believed to have originated as a Franconian dialect and the Ingvaeonic features are viewed as secondary, ascribed either to Anglo-Saxon scribal practices or a contact situation. The linguistic influence of Old English and Old Frisian is accordingly dated to the period after the emigration of the Anglo-Saxon tribes from the Continent. The alternative view, known as the Ingvaeonic theory, dates back to Wrede (1924) who believed that the Ingvaeonic features had originally a much wider scope on the Continent (extending also to southern Germany). The Ingvaeonic theory (in its more moderate version) was later advocated among others by Rooth (1932, 1949), Dal (1934, 1983), Sanders (1982) or Århammar (1990) (cf. Nielsen 1994: 197–198). The core of the hypothesis is that Old Saxon originated as an Ingvaeonic dialect and that at some point, as a consequence of the socio-political and cultural conditions, the language came gradually under the influence of Franconian in the Lower Rhine region, which resulted in the emergence of its hybrid linguistic structure. In other words, Old Saxon can be conceived of as a vestige of an Ingvaeonic idiom, demonstrating evident features of a language staying within the Franconian linguistic realm, but escaping its total domination (Wolff 1934: 129ff). Much along the same line, with reference to the geographical dissemination of the North Sea Germanic characteristics, Århammar

(1990: 10) concludes that while these features could freely develop in England and Friesland, their further development in the Saxon region was disturbed by the impact of the Franconian linguistic element, which effectuated a "diastratisch und diatopisch partiellen Verdrängung wichtiger ingwäonischer Züge des Altsächsischen". This stance constitutes the mainstream view with respect to the dialectal position of Old Saxon within the West Germanic language continuum (Nielsen 2001: 513).

The positioning of Old Saxon is a multifaceted problem, encompassing also the question of the early separation of Old Saxon from its common West Germanic ancestor, as well as the dialectal relations within the Old Saxon linguistic area. It has been a matter of debate whether the phonological features which Old Saxon shares with the Anglo-Frisian branch should be viewed as old *Gemeinsamkeiten*, or rather as independent Old Saxon innovations which happened to have led to very similar results as in Old English and Old Frisian (Klein 2000a: 1249). Klein (2000b, 2001, 2004), favouring the former interpretation, postulates, as a subsequent stage of the development, the existence of a Continental West Germanic innovation community (*Neuerunggemeinschaft*) in the Merovingian period, which encompassed Old High German, Old Low Franconian, Old Saxon and partly also Old Frisian. Accordingly, the emergence of some of the Old Saxon (morphological) features shared with Old High German or Old Low Franconian can be ascribed to this period (Klein 2000b: 24ff). In contrast, Krogh (1996, 2002, 2013), claiming that there are not enough indications for the existence of such an extensive innovation community, posits a more limited community confined to Old High German and Old Low Franconian (Krogh 2013: 158). Old Saxon, in turn, is viewed as representing an independent sub-branch of West Germanic, whose heterogeneous linguistic nature is an effect of later diversification. More specifically, Old Saxon is not viewed as a *Mischsprache*, which would imply the presence of allochthonous features in the system, but is regarded instead as an independent entity, which developed its own distinct (heterogeneous) profile in the same way as its sister languages did. This distinct linguistic profile, reflected also in inflection, is believed to have emerged through an independent selection of allomorphs from the reconstructable Proto-Germanic inflectional system (Krogh 2013: 152). The possibility of *Sprachmischung*, occurring as a result of the incorporation of foreign elements, is relegated to the very last stage of the development of Old Saxon, namely the end of the eighth century, when the language, due to the changed socio-political circumstances, became exposed to the impact of Franconian (Krogh 1996: 404).[232] In other words, notwithstanding

---

232. Krogh (1996) distinguishes three stages in the evolution of Old Saxon: (1) independent selection of forms from old allomorphs, (2) common development of Old Saxon with Old Frisian and Old English (shared innovations), (3) infiltration of Old Saxon with Franconian features (*Sprachmischung*) (Krogh 1996: 403–404; Krogh 2002, cf. Klein's criticism of this stance (2000b, 2004a)).

the considerable variation in phonology and morphology, evident in the attested material, Old Saxon is interpreted as an originally uniform, homogeneous idiom, which, according to Krogh, very early, i.e. before the year 0, separated from the West Germanic continuum, and only at a later stage underwent diversification (Krogh 2013: 162). This early dating of the emergence of Old Saxon is not supported by other studies exploring the nature of linguistic relations in the West Germanic dialect continuum. According to Nielsen (2000: 291), the separation of Old Saxon from Continental North Sea Germanic should be dated much later, i.e. around 500 AD. Likewise, Klein (2000b, 2004a) in his polemic against Krogh's theory adduces a list of arguments against considering the selection of allomorphs as uniquely Old Saxon, and postulates a later chronology for the emergence of Old Saxon, with the decisive stages of the development dated not earlier than the fourth/fifth century AD (Klein 2004a: 21). In turn, the process of the franconisation of the language is more commonly considered to be a fairly old development, "beginning prehistorically and continuing to the present day, affecting phonology, morphology and lexis." (Stiles 1995: 202).

An aspect relevant to the positioning of Old Saxon in the West Germanic linguistic continuum is its diatopic variation. When compared to the dialectally diversified Old English or Old High German, the corpus of Old Saxon can be viewed as relatively uniform, with little diatopic diversification present. On closer inspection, however, considerable phonological contrasts emerge between the western texts from Werden and Essen, the more eastern varieties, including minor documents, such as the Merseburg texts and the onomastic material, or the non-localised Straubing fragment of *Heliand* (Århammar 1990: 2). The original concern of the studies examining the dialectal aspect was whether the mixture of features attested especially in literary texts is a reflection of the actual dialectal situation on the Old Saxon territory, or whether it reflects merely scribal conventions (Rooth 1932). The prevailing view nowadays seems to be that the discrepancies reach far beyond the graphematic layer and reflect, thus, actual linguistic variation (e.g. Stiles 1995).[233] The most general division of the Old Saxon linguistic area is the one based on the grouping of Saxon tribes, with a basic distinction made between Westphalian, Engrian and Eastphalian (e.g. Sanders 1983: 32–34). Most of the Old Saxon texts derive from the Westphalian region which can be further subdivided into East- and West-Westphalian. An early attempt at a dialectal division of the Old Saxon material was made by Foerste (1950: 154–155), who distinguished between East-Westphalian

---

233. Apart from the Franconian graphematic interference, the Anglo-Saxon influence is sporadically evident in the *schrift* in the use of the graphemes <æ>, <ea> and <eo> for <a> and <e>, as well as <f> for <b> and <u> (ms. C and Werdener Urbare (rent rolls)). The impact may not have been direct, but may be attributed to the practices of the scribes or monks who were trained in the Anglo-Saxon tradition (Gallée 1993: 11).

(where the language of manuscript M belongs), West-Westphalian, which remains closest to the dialects of Central/Rhine Franconian, and Engrian, represented in place names. Much along the same lines, Klein (1990) makes a distinction between the extensively franconised south-west-Westphalian sources, associated with Werden and Essen, and the "engere" group, encompassing East-Westphalian, Engrian and Eastphalian. The latter group shows a more Ingvaeonic nature and, apart from ms. S of *Heliand* (with a hypothesised origin in northern Engrian), comprises a number of glosses. Most of the minor Old Saxon documents can be identified as south-west Westphalian and dated to the tenth century.[234] The material showing a typically Ingvaeonic linguistic profile includes primarily onomastic data, death registers, tax lists (*Heberegister*), as well as collections of glosses, in particular those localised in Merseburg, Lamspring, Oxford (the Vergil glosses) and Leipzig, and some further less easily localisable glosses (Klein 1990: 201–202; cf. also Sanders 2000c: 1291). A diatopic subdivision into the eastern (Hildesheim, Halberstadt, Merseburg) and western varieties (Essen, Werden, Corvey) has been postulated by Klein (1977) on the basis of the vocalism in final syllables, with a third variety not assigned to any particular region, but represented by ms. M of *Heliand*. It is assumed that the graphemically varied idiom of ms. M testifies to the indigenous Old Saxon state of affairs (cf. Sections 5.5 and 5.6.3).[235] At the same time, on account of the nature of the Old Saxon corpus, part of the attested dialectal variation may, in fact, be a reflection of variation in time (Scheuermann 2000: 1283); accordingly, the younger texts of eastern provenance can be expected to show fewer archaic morphological features than the older material from the southwest.

The presented diatopic distribution corresponds to the division of the Saxon settlement area into four major regions including Westphalia, Angria, Eastphalia and Northalbingia. A conspicuous feature of this dialectal distribution is that the North Sea Germanic traits are located in the east and are nearly absent from the sources affiliated with south-west Westphalia. Such a distribution of the northern (Ingvaeonic) features, extending deep inland (as far as Magdeburg and Merseburg) seems fairly unexpected and counter-intuitive given their coastal origin and accumulation in the north. It becomes much more intelligible if the regions are reinterpreted in terms of river catchment areas, which, given the extensive forest and peatbog areas in the North German Plain, may have functioned as traffic routes and thus linguistic communication paths (Versloot & Adamczyk 2017). From this perspective, four main regions can be identified:

---

234. For details on the dialectal subdivision in the minor documents, see Cordes (1973: 16) and Klein (1990: 201–202).

235. The attested variation between the graphemes <a> and <e> is believed to have served to render /æ/ in this manuscript (Klein 1977: 416). For a summary of the problem, see Boutkan (1995: 152–162).

- the Rhine valley with Werden and Essen, and the Lower Rhine – the core of the Franconian realm
- the Ems river valley, comprising central Westphalian
- the Weser valley, comprising the Engrian region
- the Saale-Elbe valley (and the Aller branch of the Weser), comprising the East-phalian region.

It is in particular the Rhine valley where the Saxon tribes entered into closer contacts with the Franconian idiom, whereas in the other regions the orientation was much more towards the north (including the Frisian area), alongside the natural river flows. Just as such channels could facilitate the spread of the North Sea Germanic features, the natural boundaries could also have formed linguistic boundaries. This may have been the case with Eastphalian, where most of the Ingvaeonic-oriented material is found, and where the Harz mountain range must have formed a natural boundary, inhibiting the contacts with High German dialects. The underlying assumption of such an interpretation is that linguistic boundaries correspond very often to natural boundaries and that linguistic changes can be accordingly hindered or facilitated by natural/geographical factors (König 2001: 143; Nerbonne 2010).

The problem of the Old Saxon dialectal diversity was made particularly conspicuous with the discovery of the Straubing manuscript (S), which confirmed the assumption that the language was far from being uniform or standardised. The manuscript S (mid-9th c.) is unique among the other extant fragments in that linguistically it is much more Ingvaeonic than the other manuscripts which were characterised by a more prominent High German tinge (Taeger 1983: 960; Taeger 1979–1984).[236] Because of its Ingvaeonic character, the text has been hypothesised to be an Old West-Frisian translation with some influences of Old Low Franconian (Huisman 1986), or, alternatively, to represent a Proto-Frisian or coastal Saxon (*küstensächsische*) stage, which later developed into Old Frisian (van Weringh 1984). According to Klein (1990: 199), who criticised both hypotheses, the language of the S fragment represents "ein stark nordseegermanisch gefärbtes Altsächsisch", which, on the one hand, is very close to Old Frisian, but on the other, complies with the "südwärts gewandten Zügen vor allem der altsächsischen Flexionsmorphologie" (Klein 1990: 219; cf. also Krogmann 1970: 218). The presence of southern features

---

236. The following phonological characteristics have commonly been included among the "North Sea Germanic evolutionary features" (Nielsen 2001: 516) of the mentioned manuscript: the fronted reflexes of WGmc. $\bar{a}$ and Gmc. *a* (as in *uuerun* 'were', *creht* 'power', *gest-seli* 'hall'); the rounding of $\bar{a}$ and *a* before a nasal (> $\bar{o}$ and *o*) (e.g. *monn* 'man'); $\bar{a}$ as a reflex of Gmc. *au* (e.g. *harian* 'hear'). Another conspicuous phonological discrepancy involves the vowels in unaccented syllables, where the Ingvaeonic spellings *-e*, *-a* appear alongside the more southern *-a*, *-o*, respectively (e.g. ms. S *thiorne* 'maiden', *uuillia* 'will' vs. ms. C *thiorna*, *uuilleo*) (Nielsen 2001: 516; cf. Klein 1990).

in this particular variety of Old Saxon is interpreted as a confirmation of the fact that the drift of the genuine Old Saxon variety ("das Echtaltsächsische") from its North Sea Germanic character had begun already in pre-Carolingean times (Klein 1990: 220; Stiles 1995: 202; cf. Dal 1954: 74–75). In general, the language of this manuscript has been interpreted as closely reflecting the regional vernacular variety of north-west Old Saxon (Sanders 2000c: 1291). It can be concluded that the three major manuscripts of *Heliand* form a continuum with respect to the Ingvaeonic nature of the text, with ms. C being the least Ingvaeonic, ms. S showing the Ingvaeonic features most extensively, and ms. M occupying an intermediate position. A clear correlation with the dating of manuscripts emerges, since both mss. M and S, attesting to a more Ingvaeonic character, are dated earlier (9th c.) than ms. C (10th c.) (Nielsen 1994: 201). The distinct linguistic profile of ms. S proves that various manuscripts of *Heliand* can potentially show a more extensive dialectal variation than that found in mss. M and C, which can be interpreted as indicative of the fact that the variation attested in the extant Old Saxon material reflects only a fragment of the variation that must have actually existed in the language, for which, however, no sufficient evidence is available.

In the context of this study, some contrasts with respect to the shape of the nominal system and its reorganisation can potentially be expected between the material of south-western (Werden/Essen) and eastern (Merseburg, Magdeburg) provenance. In a broader perspective, the study of inflectional variation, including the identification of patterns and directions of interdeclensional shifts, can shed some more light on the question of the (morphological) affinity of Old Saxon with the neighbouring sister languages. On account of the limited scope of the extant material, the number of such inflectional differences turned out to be very limited.

5.3   Corpus and methodological considerations

The total number of lemmas in the existing Old Saxon corpus is estimated to be ca. 4,000 (Sanders 2000a: 1257), which when compared to the corpus of Old English or Old High German may not look impressive. As the study was intended to be as exhaustive as possible in terms of the selection of the material, the investigation collated the data from the two Old Saxon biblical epics *Heliand* and *Genesis*, and from most of the minor documents. The majority of the data come from *Heliand*, which constitutes around 80 percent of the Old Saxon material (Sanders 2000a: 1259; Sanders 2000b: 1277). As regards the genres represented in the available sources, a clear distinction emerges between the early poetic texts and the few younger prose texts, including a number of glosses. In contrast to the poetic idiom found in *Heliand* and *Genesis*, the language found in the religious and secular minor Old

Saxon texts is believed to represent the so called "verschriftlichte a[lt]n[ieder]-d[eutsche] Normalsprache" (Sanders 2000b: 1279).

The text of *Heliand*, consisting of 5,983 lines of alliterating verse, is dated between the years 822 and 850 on the basis of the Latin *Praefatio et Versus*, which, although not physically attached to any of the manuscripts, was linked to the text (Cathey 2000: 18–19). The text of this Saxon poem has been preserved in two major manuscripts: M (Cgm. 25, Staatsbibliothek, Munich, first-half of the 9th c.) and C (Cotton Caligula A.vii, British Library, London, second half of the 10th c.).[237] Fragments of the poem have survived in four other manuscripts: V (Palatinus Latinus 1447, Biblioteca Apostolica Vaticana, Città del Vaticano, lines 1279–1358), dated to the third quarter of the ninth century; P (R 56/2537, Museum für deutsche Geschichte, Berlin, ex cod. XVI D 42, Universitní Knihovna, Prague, lines 958–1006), dated to the mid-ninth century; S (known as "Straubing Fragment", ll. 351–722, discovered in 1977), dated to the ninth century; and the most recently found (in 2006) manuscript L, known as the "Leipzig Fragment", dated to the ninth century (Schmid 2006, 2007). The preservation of the text of *Heliand* in a number of manuscripts from various geographical locations is a particularly fortuitous circumstance in light of the fact that the language is scantily attested. The two major manuscripts of the text, M and C, differ not only in terms of their dating, but also in their linguistic consistency, with the former written most likely in two or three hands and being the more reliable of the two (with fewer corrections) (Krogh 1996: 115; Cathey 2010: 27).

The other major source of information about the Old Saxon language is the text of *Genesis* – a work of alliterative scriptural poetry (330 alliterating lines), belonging to the first half of the ninth century (the surviving manuscript is dated to the second half of the ninth century; Vatican Library, MS Palatinus Latinus 1447). The three existing extracts of the Old Saxon *Genesis* amount to a total of 337 lines. Apart from the two major documents, the minor attestations of Old Saxon include tithing lists, blessings, church calendars, a confession of faith, a renunciation of the devil, tax rolls, glosses (including psalm glosses, e.g. the Lublin Psalms, PsLub), place names and personal names (Krogh 1996: 111–138; Tiefenbach 2010: XIII–XXXVIII). The special value of the minor sources lies in the fact that they are believed to represent the "genuine" Old Saxon, as opposed to the larger monuments characterised by a heavy overlay of Franconian features.

The database for the present investigation of the material was composed on the basis of the material from the *Altsächsisches Handwörterbuch* by Tiefenbach (2010) and the *Vollständiges Wörterbuch zum Heliand und zur altsächsischen Genesis* by

---

237. A more precise dating was postulated in Behaghel & Taeger (1984: XVI), where the text is placed between 814 and 840 and possibly after 821.

Sehrt (1966), supplemented by the information found in *Altsächsisches Wörterbuch* by Holthausen (1967) and *Altsächsisches Wörterbuch* by Köbler (2014a). A few editions of *Heliand* and *Genesis* were consulted, including the Behaghel & Taeger's (1984), Sievers' (1878) and Piper's (1897) editions, which have been considered standard in the linguistic studies of Old Saxon. As the Sievers' (1878) edition of *Heliand* is unique in providing facing pages with matching lines of mss. M and C, reference to it was made in particular with a view to finding discrepancies between the manuscripts in the relevant forms. For the language in the minor documents, three sources were consulted, including Wadstein's *Kleinere altsächsische Sprachdenkmäler* (1899), Gallée's *Altsächsische Sprachdenkmäler* (1894) and Köbler's *Sammlung aller Glossen des Altsächsischen* (1987).

The modest size of the Old Saxon corpus confined to ca. 4,000 lemmas has implications for the results of the present study and their interpretation. One of the clear limitations is the genre bias inherent in the Old Saxon corpus, with literary epics constituting the majority of the material. One potential consequence of such a bias is that words of high frequency of use in daily speech will not necessarily be attested in the corpus dominated by texts written in a more elevated register. As Old Saxon is available to us primarily through two larger texts of a religious nature, little genre diversification can be expected. In the context of the present cross-Germanic study, this problem has a wider scope and applies also to the corpus of Old Frisian, confined essentially to the legal register, or to the corpus of Old Low Franconian, representing the smallest of all the investigated corpora (cf. Section 1.5.2; also Versloot & Adamczyk 2014).

5.4 Restructuring process in Old Saxon: Patterns

Just like its sister languages, Old Saxon underwent a range of developments in its nominal morphology, with the declensional system exposed to a range of analogical processes. Despite the parallel mechanisms involved, the dynamics of these developments, largely conditioned by phonology, resulted in the Old Saxon nominal system gaining a distinct inflectional profile. With reference to the changes in the Old Saxon declensional system, Sanders (1983: 47) concludes:

> Im Zuge eines durch die neue Initialbetonung ausgelösten germ. Schwundprozesses, in dem ursprünglich selbständige Flexionsgruppen durch Endungszusammenfall allmählich in andere, produktive Klassen übergingen, sind die vokal. *u*- und – mit Ausnahme der *n*-Dekl. – alle konsonant. Stämme für das As. nicht mehr vollständig paradigmatisch zu belegen.

A more recent statement to the same effect can be found, for instance, in Rauch (1992a): "While signs of genetically stem-unique case inflections are observable, the (…) heterocliticity observable in the suffix variations (…) attests to the ongoing syncretism and resultant destruction of the genetic stem class distinctions." (Rauch 1992a: 49–50). Much along the same lines, when referring to the idiom attested in *Heliand*, Schwink (2004: 55), concentrating essentially on the developments in the gender system, describes the system as being "in a state of considerable disarray and confusion, reflecting (…) a breakdown of the older declensional patterns, and a shift to *i*-stems that are not declensionally clear". To what extent these statements correspond to the linguistic reality as attested in the Old Saxon material will become evident in the present quantitative investigation.

The early prehistoric interdeclensional transitions in minor declensional classes followed three major paths, with the shifts to the *a*-stem declension in masculine nouns, and *ō*-stem and *i*-stem declensions in feminine nouns (cf. early transfers in the Appendix). The pattern found in the historical stage shows largely similar developmental tendencies, enhanced by the productivity of the *ja*- and *jō*-stems. The significance of these two subclasses for the inflectional restructuring is a unique feature of Old Saxon and can be attributed in the first place to a phonological development, whereby the -*j*- element was retained in the *ja*- and *jō*-stems, in contrast to other Germanic languages where it was consistently reduced (cf. Section 5.5). Apart from these directions of transfer, the material testifies to an increasing importance of the *i*-stem inflection. The numerous inflectional parallels in the paradigms of the *i*-stems and *ja*- and *jō*-stems result in a complex interaction between them, leading to the emergence of a more general inflectional pattern. This new common inflectional paradigm, which is an amalgamation of inflections of the *ja*- and *jō*-stems on the one hand, and *i*-stems on the other, emerges as a template for the restructuring of the minor stems (cf. a similar development in Old English, where the *a*-stems overlapping inflectionally with *ja*-stems, developed features of a "super class"). Subsequently, the common pattern forms a new destination class for many minor stems and its productivity gradually increases.

Another characteristic of the restructuring is its multi-layeredness which entails two stages: one that can be dated to the prehistoric period, and the other reflected in the fluctuation between inherited and analogical inflections in the attested material. An example can be the category of the GEN. SG. of masculine *i*-stems, whose marker -*es* is an early (prehistoric) extension from the *a*-stems (cf. Table 2.11), and the most frequent forms in the paradigm, -*ies*, -*ias*, emerge under the later (historical) pressure of the *ja*-stems.

The inflections of the productive declensions (*a*- and *ō*-stems) which served as templates for the restructuring of the minor stem paradigms are presented in Table 5.1. The three potential sets for individual gender classes are included, assuming that, just as in the other investigated languages, the interdeclensional transfers occurred essentially in compliance with gender. At the same time, the presented paradigms serve as general guidelines, and some nuances relevant from the perspective of the interaction with minor paradigms, such as the differences between light- and heavy-syllable stems, are not captured in this summary. All the relevant details will be discussed in the respective sections devoted to individual classes. Likewise, the class of *i*-stems, including its interaction with the *ja*- and *jō*-stems and its productivity potential, is treated separately in Section 5.6.2.2.

Table 5.1 The productive paradigms serving as templates for the restructuring of the OS minor stems

	masculine *a*-stems		neuter *a*-stems		feminine *ō*-stems	
	SG	PL	SG	PL	SG	PL
NOM.	dag	dagos, -as, -a	word	word	geba, -e	geba,-e
GEN.	dages,-as	dago	wordes,-as	wordo	geba, -e, -u	gebo,-on
DAT.	dage, -a	dagun, -on	worde,-a	wordun, -on	geba, -e, -u	gebun, -on
ACC.	dag	dagos, -as, -a	word	word	geba, -e	geba,-e
INSTR.	dagu,-o	–	wordu	–	gebu	–

The alternation between -*as*, -*os* and -*a* in the NOM./ACC. PL. of the masculine *a*-stems illustrates the duality of the Old Saxon morphological system, with its Ingvaeonic and Franconian layers. The ending -*a* (-*e*), attested in the younger texts only (e.g. in the Werden and Freckenhorst glosses), is most likely an innovation, but its origin is not entirely transparent. It has been attributed either to Franconian influence (where -*a* is the only marker in this category), or interpreted as a "bodenständige Variante des Altsächsischen" (Quak 1989: 51; Krogh 1996: 302; Versloot 2017a). Given that this inflectional ending is not found in the linguistic system of *Heliand*, and appears only in the younger sources of southern or south-western provenance, the impact of High German seems to be the most viable explanation (cf. Gallée 1993: 197; Holthausen 1921: 96). The distribution of forms in -*as* vs. -*os*, which is not relevant from the perspective of the present study, is believed to be genre-dependent, but corresponds also to the geographical origin of the textual sources, with -*os* appearing in the early texts affiliated with Werden and Essen, and -*as* in the east (Magdeburg, Merseburg) (Quak 1989: 48–49). The variation cannot be attributed to the influence of Frisian or Old Low Franconian, where this ending surfaced as -*a* (competing with -*ar* in the former, and possibly also with -*as* in the latter dialect) and thus must be treated as a typically Old Saxon feature (Klein 1990: 216). Another inflectional characteristic of Old Saxon is the preservation of the instrumental form in the singular of masculine and neuter nouns (*a*-, *ja*- and *i*-stems), marked by the ending -*u* (cf. the OHG instrumental in -*u*). As will become clear in the later discussion, the interpretation of this ending in the context of inflectional restructuring is not entirely unproblematic and will be treated in Section 5.6.2.1.

In view of the patterns found in Old English and Old Frisian, as well as the subsequent inflectional development in Middle Low German, one could expect to find traces of the *n*-stem inflection in the minor paradigms as well. This direction of analogical transition of minor stems is hardly explicitly referred to in the treatments of Old Saxon morphology (except the weak adjectival inflection in the *nd*-stems) and, therefore, weak inflections are rather unlikely to appear frequently in the corpus.

Finally, a recourse to some younger data, including the Middle Low German evidence, as well as the data from modern dialects, can potentially turn out revealing for the interpretation of the patterns observed in Old Saxon. In particular, the vestiges of the historical inflection attested in Middle Low German may shed some light on the inflectional configurations in classes which are not well attested in the early material and thus on the status of some declensional types in Old Saxon. At the same time, it must be emphasised that the Saxon language did have an evident southern bias at the later stage of its development, and therefore, the interpretation of archaic forms found in the two consecutive stages (Old Saxon and Middle Low German) as a direct continuity of patterns cannot be taken for granted.

5.5   Phonological developments in unstressed syllables

As in the other Germanic languages, the dynamics of the changes in the nominal inflection in Old Saxon depended primarily on the developments affecting the phonological system. The phonological processes influenced both the scope and tempo of the restructuring processes, potentially facilitating or inhibiting analogical pressures from productive paradigms, and thus eventually (indirectly) determining the shape of the nominal inflection. Of primary importance here were the phonological changes affecting vowels in unstressed syllables, including phonetic attrition. The resultant configuration of unstressed vowels in inflectional syllables is crucial for the interpretation of the changes in the inflectional system. Another development consequential for the reshaping of inflectional paradigms was the operation of *i*-mutation, which in Old Saxon had only a limited scope.

The major problem with the interpretation of vowels in inflectional syllables is the wide graphemic variation present in the Old Saxon material. A further complication is that part of this spelling variation can be ascribed to the Franconian scribal tradition and thus the interpretations may vary, depending, to some extent, on the dialectal provenance of the texts or manuscripts. In fact, the Old Saxon spelling system is believed to have developed from the Old High German graphemic system (with some adaptations and modifications) (Klein 2000a: 1248), and the different scope of this High German influence is evident even in the individual manuscripts of *Heliand*. Overall, the Old Saxon phonological system as reflected in the complex but consistent spelling variation emerges as remarkably conservative. It is assumed that in ms. C of *Heliand*, a five-vowel system can be reconstructed for unstressed syllables (i.e. *i, e, a, o, u*), with a distribution approximately parallel to that found in the Franconian material. The evidence offered by ms. M turns out to be more problematic to interpret, but the system found there is believed to reflect the oldest situation in Old Saxon.[238] Most difficult to account for is the spelling variation between <e>, <o> and <a>, which, in Klein's (1977) systematic analysis, represents different vocalic systems attested in the available material, depending on the dialect. The postulated system contains four unstressed vowels /i, æ, å, u/, rendered by the graphemes <i>, <e>, <o>, <u>, where /æ/ is a result of a merger of the WGmc. /æ/ < */a/ and /æ/ < */ai, ē/. The system has been referred to as the "*e,o*-system" (where /æ/ is rendered by <e>) and is one of the three grapho-phonemic systems postulated by Klein (1977) to explain the wide spelling variation in the Old Saxon material (Klein 1977: 390ff.). The two remaining systems are the "*a, o*-system", attested in the South-Westphalian area, where the /æ/ is rendered by <a> and /å/ by <o>, and the "*e-,a*-system", found in the Engrian-Eastphalian region, where /æ/ is rendered by <e> and /å/ by <a> (Boutkan 1995: 159–160). Further alternations involve the less frequent interchange between <i> and <e>, which emerged as a result of the weakening of unaccented *-i* to *-e*, and the sporadic alternation between <u> and <o>, which reflects no phonemic contrast (Holthausen 1921: 53–56; Boutkan 1995: 156–157, 254). This extensive spelling variation poses problems also for analysing the restructuring of inflection inasmuch as it induces some formal overlap of inflectional markers which consequently cannot be unambiguously interpreted as historical or analogical features. The details of these interpretative difficulties are

---

238. The greater inconsistency of vowels in final syllables attested in ms. M (9th c.), as observed by Schlüter (1892), Foerste (1950) or Rooth (1956), has occasionally been interpreted in a way that the unstressed syllables of ms. M favoured the Old English and Old Frisian "orthography and perhaps even phonology", whereas those of ms. C are reminiscent of the Old High German state of affairs (Rauch 1970: 368). Such an interpretation seems fairly far-fetched, especially with reference to Old Frisian, where the spelling practices can hardly be analysed in terms of orthography, and the interference in phonology would require an intense language contact situation, which is not well documented for the post-migration stage (e.g. Århammar 1990: 13). Likewise, adducing the influence of Old English and Old Frisian orthographic practices as an explanation for the presence of the *i*-mutated vowels and their conditioning vowel in ms. M is considered unsound (cf. Rauch 1970: 370).

discussed in the respective sections devoted to individual stem classes. Table 5.2 offers a brief summary of the grapho-phonemic correspondences and individual morphological categories in which spelling variation may affect the interpretation of inflectional forms.

Table 5.2 Grapho-phonemic correspondences and their morphological consequences

phoneme	graphemic rendering	morphological consequences
/i/	<i> ~ <e>	DAT. SG. in *i*-stems
		NOM./ACC. PL. in *i*-stems
/æ/	<e> ~ <a>	DAT. SG. of *u*-stems (cf. Section 5.6.3)
/å/	<a> ~ <o>	DAT. SG. of *u*-stems (cf. Section 5.6.3)
/u/	<u> ~ <o>	–

The ambiguity as to the exact phonological value of the graphemes is most prominent in the distribution of the graphemes <e>, <a> and <o>. Accordingly, the interpretation of the vowel -*e* in the DAT. SG. poses a problem in the *i*-stems, where, on the one hand, it can be treated as a historical marker of the *i*-stems, i.e. a reduced variant of -*i*, and on the other, it can be ascribed to the analogical influence of the (*j*)*a*- and (*j*)*ō*-stems, where -*e* was the commonly expected marker in the DAT. SG. The alternation which is least problematic in the context of the present investigation is the variation between <o> and <u>, in which <o>, although potentially ambiguous, does not reflect any inflectional contrast understood as a competition between historical and analogical inflections (e.g. both NOM. SG. forms *suno* ~ *sunu* are interpreted as inherited; likewise, the alternation between -*on* and -*un* (-*un* > -*on*), attested in the DAT. PL., is not meaningful from the perspective of the present study).

As regards the operation of *i*-mutation, its range in Old Saxon is fairly limited and so is its significance for morphological restructuring. The available evidence testifies only to primary *i*-mutation, indicated in spelling for *a* > *e* (in front of the mostly preserved *i* and *j*). It parallels accordingly the unfolding of *i*-mutation in Old High German, and must be dated later than its operation in Old English and Old Frisian, and certainly later than the loss of -*i* after a heavy syllable (Krogh 1996: 176; 2013: 154). At the same time, it can be assumed that on the phonetic level the process was operative earlier and that the umlaut allophones had emerged already in the Old Saxon period. The sporadic vestiges of the older (North Sea Germanic) stage of *i*-mutation ("ältere Umlautschicht" or primary *i*-mutation), confined to the mutation of the short vowel *a* before *i*, are retained in some isolated forms, such as heavy-syllable *menn* 'men', *leng* 'longer', *gestseli* 'hall', as well as in the preterite forms of heavy-syllable *jan*-verbs (e.g. *kenda* 'understood', *hefta* 'bound', *felda* 'threw'), and neuter *ja*-stems of the type *bed* 'bed', *flet* 'floor' (Klein 1977: 207; Klein 2000a: 1249; cf. Prokosch 1939: 258; Krogh 1996: 180; 2013: 154). Such instances testify to an earlier dating of the process in Old Saxon than in Old High German, and demonstrate its gradual propagation from north to south.[239] In terms of absolute chronology, the operation of secondary *i*-mutation in Old High German is dated either to the 9th century (Gütter 2011) or ca. 1000 (Braune/Reiffenstein 2004: 55–56). This divergent chronology of the application of *i*-mutation across West Germanic and in particular the fact that umlaut was introduced later in Old Saxon (and Inland West Germanic) than in Old English and Old Frisian turned out to be crucial for the morphological developments in the later stages of the respective languages (Prokosch 1939: 247; Buccini 1995; Krogh 1996: 210–212). The use of the *i*-mutated vowel to mark the contrast between the singular and plural in the *i*-stems and *u*-stems (and minor classes that merged with them) in the subsequent stage of the development of Old Saxon, Old Low Franconian and Old High German, on the one hand, and the fossilisation of *i*-mutated vowels in consonantal stems in Old English and Old Frisian, on the other, had a considerable influence on the inflectional restructuring in these languages. At the same time, the direct significance of *i*-mutation for the reshaping of the Old Saxon inflection is fairly limited, being confined to the *i*-stems and, to some extent, the *u*-stems (cf. Sections 5.6.2, 5.6.3). In the consonantal stems, especially in the paradigm of root nouns, the *i*-mutated vowel is sporadic and turns out to have had no particular effect on the inflectional shape of this class (cf. the Old English root nouns, where *i*-mutation played a crucial role in the dynamics of inflectional reorganisation).

Another phonological development which influenced the patterns of inflectional reorganisation was the preservation of **-j-* as *-i* in inflectional syllables in both light- and heavy-syllable stems across various grammatical categories (Holthausen 1921: 62; Boer 1924: 152).[240] The retention of this semivowel was decisive for the *ja-* and *jō*-stem inflection. The most conspicuous consequence of this development was the interaction of the *i*-stems with *ja-* and *jō*-stems, leading to numerous inflectional overlaps between these classes (cf. Section 5.6.2). The development rendered the classes of *ja-* and *jō*-stems productive in Old Saxon and their inflections tended to disseminate across the minor paradigms.

---

239. Cf. an alternative interpretation of the process by Rauch (1970), according to whom such inconsistencies testify to a dialect mixture and, accordingly, the original layer of *i*-mutation goes back to the earliest contact situation with the Frisians and Anglians, prior to the migration of the latter group from the Continent. In formal terms, the process is interpreted as the rephonemicisation of a prehistoric *i*-mutation (which had been earlier dephonemicised), taking place under the influence of the Old High German *i*-mutation conditioning (Rauch 1970: 370–371).

240. The retention of this semivowel is, for instance, a characteristic of weak verb infinitives in *-ian* (*ō-*) (with the original stem suffix **-j-*), e.g. *fremmian* 'accomplish, make', *nerian* 'save', *uuonian* 'dwell', cf. 1st person SG. OS *fremmiu* vs. OE *fremme*.

All in all, Old Saxon did not witness large-scale reduction processes in unaccented syllables and its phonological profile remains very stable when compared to the sister languages. According to Sanders (1983: 40–41), the reduction of the unaccented vowels to *schwa* took place only towards the end of the Old Saxon period, ca. 1100, and although some reductive processes may have been present earlier, the consistent variation in spelling does not unambiguously reflect the allophones of *schwa*. Given this phonological stability and the fact that the dynamics of phonological developments tend to correlate with the dynamics of changes in the morphological system (especially in inflectional syllables, which are the most susceptible to changes), the scope of analogical restructuring in Old Saxon may be expected to be moderate, or at least less extensive than in the sister languages.

5.6   Data analysis

5.6.1 Methodological considerations

The procedure applied for the investigation of the Old Saxon material was parallel to that used for the study of the Old English and Old Frisian data, and accordingly the quantitative analysis examined the incidence of the original inflectional endings relative to the analogical inflections in the minor stem paradigms. The inventory of relevant lemmas was compiled on the basis of the information found in Bammesberger (1990), and in standard historical grammars of Old Saxon, including Gallée (1993) and Holthausen (1921), and was supplemented by the data from the comprehensive Old Saxon dictionaries: *Altsächsisches Wörterbuch* by Holthausen (1967), *An Etymological Glossary to the Old Saxon Heliand* by Berr (1971), *Altsächsisches Handwörterbuch* by Tiefenbach (2010) and *Altsächsisches Wörterbuch* by Köbler (2014a). All the identified compound forms (in which the relevant nouns constituted the second element of the compound) were included in the analysis. At the same time, nouns which are attested in glosses in the Latin context were not taken into account as their forms could not be unambiguously interpreted (mostly due to the potential influence of Latin; e.g. the ACC. PL. form of *askmann*: *ascomannos*, AdamII, 31.77.IV, 6; GEN. PL. *ascomannorum*, AdamII, 32).[241] Likewise, forms found in glosses which were identified by Tiefenbach (2010) as unambiguously Old High German or Old English were excluded from the counting.

---

241. All the abbreviations as well as line numbering and text citations used in this chapter follow consistently the conventions applied in Tiefenbach (2010).

As in the other investigated corpora, some of the nouns were attested in forms which are not informative about inflectional restructuring, testifying to no variation between inherited and analogical inflections. For example, the root noun *ēk* 'oak', attested only in the NOM. SG., cannot be unambiguously assigned to any declensional type (from a synchronic perspective), as this NOM. form allows one to affiliate it potentially with two different classes: feminine root nouns or the *i*-stems (cf. Griepentrog 1995: 22). Such forms, although included in the study, are counted as neutral, i.e. inconclusive. In contrast to the other investigated languages, where the forms of the GEN. and DAT. PL. were considered inconclusive, in Old Saxon they are potentially informative about the restructuring in most declensional classes. Apart from the *s*-stems, where the *r*-formative can be interpreted as a vestige of the original inflection, the synchronic alternation in the DAT. PL. can also be captured in the *i*-stems (where the contrast of the type *trahnin ~ trahnun* 'tears', *liudim ~ liudon* 'people' reflects a variation between the inherited and analogical inflections), and to some extent in the *u*-stems and root nouns. An additional complication for interpreting the attested inflectional endings as archaic and innovative is related to the aforementioned pervasive spelling variation in the Old Saxon material. Not only does it call for careful sieving through the data, but also necessitates a number of *a priori* assumptions about the grapho-phonemic correspondences (cf. Section 5.5). Some of the spelling discrepancies stem from the differences between individual texts or manuscripts (in particular between individual manuscripts of *Heliand*) and reflect inflectional contrasts. More specifically, while one manuscript shows forms testifying to the historical inflection (e.g. *i*-stem NOM. PL. *hornseli* 'gabled houses', ms. M), the other may display an analogical ending in the corresponding forms (NOM. PL. *hornselios*, ms. C). Given that such discrepancies affect the interpretation of inflectional changes, they were taken into account in the present study. Accordingly, the forms which testify to such contrasts between the manuscripts were included in the quantitative analysis with both variants. Such an approach, entailing a comparison of individual manuscripts, was feasible only on account of the relatively small size of the Old Saxon corpus.

Finally, it must be observed that not all the forms presented in the tables depicting the sample paradigms for individual minor declensional types are actually attested in the Old Saxon material (cf. especially the *s*-stems). The presented paradigmatic forms serve rather as an illustration of the general pattern attested for various other nouns belonging to a given declensional class. Only forms which are not attested for any noun affiliated with a given declension are marked with an asterisk (*) (unless specified otherwise). Likewise, the innovative forms are in some instances purely hypothetical and do not always correspond to the actually attested novel forms found in the corpus, but they serve to indicate the *potential* direction of analogical pressures to be tested in the analysis. All the forms which do not provide information about inflectional restructuring are consistently italicised in all tables.

5.6.2 *i*-stems

5.6.2.1 *General characteristics*

The *i*-stems constitute one of the largest declensional types in Old Saxon, comprising nouns of all three genders, with a further differentiation between light- and heavy-syllable stems retained. While the masculine and feminine formations are well attested, the neuter category is limited to a few nouns which show considerable instability when it comes to gender. The best attested subgroups are the heavy-syllable masculine and feminine stems, the latter constituting the majority of the *i*-stems. With regard to their descent, the *i*-stems form a rather heterogeneous group, encompassing nouns originating in various declensional types, including the *u*-stems (e.g. *hugi* 'mind') and neuter *s*-stems (e.g. *heti* 'hate', *sigi*- 'victory', *seli* 'hall') (cf. Sections 5.6.3 and 5.6.6). Also the adjectival abstracts in -*i* (< *-īn*) and deverbal formations in -*īni*, having merged with the feminine *i*-stems, followed this declension, forming a subclass or a satellite class, with an overlapping inflectional pattern (e.g. *diupi* 'depth', *huldi* 'grace', *meginstrengi* 'mighty power', *hrōri* 'stirring', *dōpi* 'baptism', etc.) (Foerste 1950: 53; Sanders 1983: 49; Tiefenbach 2000: 1252).[242] This etymological heterogeneity indicates that the class must have been productive at an early stage, attracting nouns from the less productive declensions. In this respect the *i*-stems are unique among the other declensional types investigated in the present study. This early productivity of the *i*-stem inflection continues into the later historical stage, where the pattern begins to disseminate among the *u*-stems and (possibly) root nouns, with *i*-stem inflections attested alongside the inherited features both in the singular and plural (e.g. DAT. SG. *hendi*, or NOM./ACC. PL. *burgi*). The early productivity of the *i*-stem pattern is reflected also in the inflection of two nouns originally affiliated with the productive classes: the *ja*-stem *segg* 'man' and *a*-stem *locc* 'hair, curl', which consistently follow the *i*-stem declension in the plural (NOM. PL. *seggi* and *loc*[*k*]*i*, cf. OE *loccas*, OHG *lochā*). Such an analogical extension attests to quite an unexpected direction of interdeclensional transition (i.e. towards the less productive paradigm) and clearly testifies to the stability of the *i*-stem inflection.

---

242. The nouns of the type *huldi* 'tribute' (< *hulþī-*, *hulþīn*) represent original feminine stems in -*ī*, equivalent to the Gothic feminine *Verbalabstrakta* in -*eins* (e.g. *manageins* 'multitude') and in -*ī* in Old High German (e.g. *hōhī*, *hōhīn*); the group comprised also *Adjektivabstrakta* in -*ei* (e.g. *diupei* 'depth'). The original paradigm looked as follows (Gallée 1993: 62; cf. Braune/ Heidermanns 2004: 105–106; Braune/Reiffenstein 2004: 211–212):

SG	PL
NOM.ACC. huldi	NOM.ACC. huldī
GEN. huldī	GEN. huldī, -io
DAT. huldī	DAT. huldīon

A significant characteristic of the Old Saxon *i*-stem paradigm is the pattern of preservation of *i*-mutation. Old Saxon, just like Old High German, shows only traces of primary *i*-mutation (short *a* > *e*), as in *anst* – *ensti* 'grace' (but *wurm* – *wurmi* 'serpent'), and, in contrast to Old English, the mutated vowels do not permeate the whole paradigm, because *i*-mutation operated later (cf. OE *giest*: *giestas*) (cf. Section 5.5). Accordingly, while the plural of masculine heavy-syllable stems testifies to earlier *i*-mutation, the singular, due to an early loss of the inflectional vowel, which eliminated the environment conducive to the operation of *i*-mutation, is left unaffected by the process. In this way, *i*-mutation can be viewed as a functional device serving to differentiate between the singular and plural in these stems, as in *gast* (SG.) – *gesti* (PL.) (Prokosch 1939: 247; Salmons 2012: 123, 152), creating a paradigm which finds its continuation on a larger scale in present-day German. Conversely, the light-syllable stems, in which the inflectional *-i* is preserved, consistently show mutated vowels across the paradigm, e.g. *seli* 'hall' (masculine), *stedi* 'stead' (feminine) (irrespective of gender). In heavy-syllable feminine stems the reflex of *i*-mutation surfaces not only in the plural, but also (occasionally) in the GEN. and DAT. SG., hence the alternation of the type *fard* – (DAT. SG.) *ferdi* 'journey'.

The pattern of restructuring of the *i*-stems varies depending on the gender and syllable weight; at the same time, the analogical features in the masculine and neuter paradigms are largely parallel. The analogical inflections in the paradigm emerge under the pressure of the *a*-stems, *ō*-stems and, not infrequently, their two subclasses: *ja*- and *jō*-stems, the latter manifested in the spread of endings *-(i)es*/*-(i)as*, *-(i)e*, *-(i)o*, *-(i)un*, etc. The extension of these two sub-patterns seems to be a uniquely Old Saxon feature, not found in the other Germanic languages, so it will be examined more closely. Some of the interdeclensional reshufflings date back to an early Common Germanic stage, and seem to be shared by all or most of the daughter languages (cf. Section 2.2.5). The earliest analogical change in the paradigm of the *i*-stems was caused by the apocope of *-i* in the inflectional syllable, whereby the NOM. and ACC. SG. of the *i*-stems and *a*-stems became homophonous, constituting a trigger for the subsequent reformulation of the entire paradigm (Boutkan 1995: 240). The Old Saxon material, and in particular the attestations to the *i*-stems, testify to a double-layered nature of inflectional restructuring with respect to the chronology of analogical realignments. On several occasions this fact renders the interpretation of the attested inflectional variation problematic. Not all of the synchronic attestations found in the Old Saxon material can be viewed as "innovations" in the sense adopted for the present study. In line with the applied criteria, genuinely innovative are, for instance, the new inflectional endings in the NOM. and ACC. PL., *-os*, *-ios*, extended from the *a*- and *ja*-stem declensions, which compete with the etymological *i*-stem ending (*-i*). In contrast, the alternations attested in the GEN. SG. in the masculine stems give evidence to a competition between two analogical endings: one extended from the *a*-stems in prehistoric times (*-es*), the other adopted more recently from the *ja*-stems (*-ies*). As such, they do not provide information about the competition between the historical (*i*-stem) and analogical inflections; instead they testify to a complete, two-stage submission of these stems to the productive inflectional pattern (see further discussion in this section).

The features that can unambiguously be ascribed to analogical pressure in the paradigms of *i*-stems are found in the grammatical categories enumerated below. The inflectional features which are more problematic to interpret (with respect to the restructuring process) will be discussed in more detail in sections devoted to individual classes.

a. masculine and neuter stems
   - the NOM./ACC. SG. endingless form in place of the historical ending *-i* in light-syllable stems
   - the DAT. SG. markers *-(i)a, -ie, -ea* in place of the historical ending *-i*
   - the NOM./ACC. PL. masculine marker *-(i)os* and neuter *-(i)u* in light-syllable stems
   - the NOM./ACC. PL. masculine marker *-(i)os* and neuter endingless form in heavy-syllable stems
   - the DAT. PL. marker *-(i)un (-on)* in place of the historical marker *-in*
b. feminine stems
   - the GEN. SG. masculine marker *-(i)es* in place of the historical ending *-i*
   - the DAT. SG. marker *-u, -o, -a* in place of the historical ending *-i*
   - the NOM./ACC. PL. marker *-a, -ia* in place of the historical ending *-i*
   - the DAT. PL. marker *-(i)un (-on)* in place of the historical marker *-in*

Tables 5.3 and 5.4 below present competing inflections in the masculine (light-syllable) and feminine (heavy-syllable) *i*-stems, respectively. As the class of feminine *ī*-stems cannot be treated as a productive declensional type, the overlap of inflections from this class is not taken into account.

Table 5.3 The competing inflections in the OS light-syllable masculine *i*-stems

	archaic		innovative	
	SG	PL	SG	PL
NOM.	hugi	hugi	*hug	hugios
GEN.	*huges*	*hugio*	hugies, *-ias*	*hugio*
DAT.	hugi	hugin	hugie, *-(i)a, -ea*	hugiun, *-ion*
ACC.	hugi	hugi	*hug	hugios
INSTR.	hugi	–	hugiu	–

Table 5.4 The competing inflections in the OS heavy-syllable feminine *i*-stems

	archaic		innovative	
	SG	PL	SG	PL
NOM.	*anst*	ensti	*anst*	ensta
GEN.	ansti, ensti	*enstio*	anstes, -ies, -eas	*enstio*
DAT.	ansti, ensti	enstin	anste, -(i)u, -(i)a	enst(i)un, -(i)on
ACC.	*anst*	ensti	*anst*	ensta
INSTR.	ansti	–	anstu, -o	–

The *i*-stem declension is one of the few classes in Old Saxon (alongside *a*- and *ja*-stems) preserving the historical instrumental case; it is attested only in the singular and primarily in masculine nouns. This category may potentially attest to the influence of the productive inflections. In consonance with the Old Saxon phonological developments, the unaccented -*i*, serving as a marker of the NOM./ACC. SG. and PL., and DAT. SG., was commonly weakened to -*e*, e.g. *ferde, liude, hôhe* (Gallée 1993: 90); consequently, the marker -*e* could be interpreted as a feature of historical inflection as well. The basic problem with unambiguous interpretation of this ending is that it overlaps with the *a*-stem and *ō*-stem markers, and thus from a synchronic perspective its status is obscure. It seems feasible that this form, continuing the original inflection, was at the same time reinforced by the identical inflection of the productive declensions, and it can, accordingly, be ascribed to a combined effect of phonological development and analogical levelling. The non-transparent status of these forms rendered them inconclusive and they were excluded from the calculations. Another interpretative problem is posed by the endingless forms of the NOM./ACC. SG. in heavy-syllable feminine stems. While in heavy-syllable masculine nouns this lack of ending is considered uninformative about the inflectional restructuring, in feminine stems it is a feature which could be considered inherited, since otherwise the influence of the productive inflections would be manifested in an extension of the *(j)ō*-stem endings. Such an interpretation of the endingless forms gains support from the fact that, apart from the *i*-stems, the only class where these categories show no ending is the root nouns, whereas all the productive types have an ending in these two categories. Due to the ambiguity of the NOM./ACC. SG. forms, the analysis of the heavy-syllable feminine stems took into account the two alternative interpretations (cf. Table 5.8). Some other inflectional forms posing interpretative difficulties belong to the following grammatical categories:

GEN. SG.
The status of the marker -*es* in masculine nouns is not entirely clear: the ending is not the original *i*-stem marker, but it is most likely an early transition from the *a*-stems (Boutkan 1995: 245–246). The variation takes place between the -*es* and -*ies*/-*ias* endings, the former testifying to the influence of the *a*-stems, the latter of

the *ja*-stems. As both endings originate in the productive declensions, the competition between them reflects two stages of the restructuring: one going back to Proto-Germanic (as evinced by the sister languages), the other taking place later, as a part of the more general spread of *ja*-stem inflections in the (pre-) Old Saxon period. In other words, the variation reflects a synchronic alternation between the two productive inflectional patterns rather than a factual alternation between the inherited and analogical inflections. On account of the overlap with the corresponding forms of the *a*-stems, the GEN. forms were not included in assessing the innovation level (in masculine stems). In the feminine stems, the situation is more transparent as the analogical markers compete with the inherited ending *-i*. Occasionally, the marker *-es* (*-is*) in feminine stems has been interpreted as inherited rather than analogical (e.g. *werildi-s*) (Heyne 1873: 75). The only forms which could be considered historical under this interpretation are those in *-is*; however, given the absence of such forms in the available material and the instability of the unaccented *-i* and *-e* in inflectional syllables, the interpretation of *-es* as inherited was not considered sustainable. In the present study the majority view is adhered to, i.e. the forms in *-es* were interpreted as resulting from the analogical pressure of the masculine inflection (*a*-stems) (cf. Gallée 1993: 210; Sanders 1983: 48).

GEN. *and* DAT. PL.

The forms of the GEN. PL. evince likewise two chronological layers of the restructuring process in Old Saxon. The GEN. PL. endings *-io* and *-o* are not historical from the Proto-Indo-European point of view. The former is a result of an early Proto-Germanic extension of the general GEN. PL. ending *-ōn* to the stem formative of the *i*-stems (cf. Section 2.2.4). The ensuing form *-io*, which from the Old Saxon perspective could be viewed as inherited, overlaps with the potential innovative form *-io* levelled from the *ja*- and *jō*-stems, whose influence was present also in other categories in the paradigm. The incidental instances in *-o* point to a relatively recent influence of the *a*- and *ō*-stems. In compliance with the procedure applied for the other investigated languages, due to the overlap of forms, this category is not considered informative about the restructuring. The picture looks somewhat different in the DAT. PL., where the historical ending *-im* (*-in*) is sporadically found alongside the forms in *-iun*, *-ion*, originating in *ja*- and *jō*-stem declensions, and the less frequent *-un*, *-on*, resulting from the influence of the pure *a*- and *ō*-stems.[243]

---

243. The DAT. PL. forms sporadically show also an older variant *-um* (> *-un*). The infrequently attested form *-in*, found twice in ms. C, was ascribed by Holthausen (1921: 19, 103) to the Franconian influence. It cannot be excluded that the vicinity of Franconian dialects played a role in that the retention of the ending in Old Saxon may have been enhanced by its more common use in the related dialects of High German. In this study these forms are interpreted as archaic and counted accordingly.

As sporadic traces of the original pattern are attested, the DAT. PL. forms were considered conclusive and included in the quantitative investigation.

INSTR. and DAT. SG.

There seems to be a general consensus on the point that the INSTR. SG. ending *-iu* represents an analogical form, while the marker *-i* is the historically expected ending (Gallée 1993: 209; Boutkan 1995: 248). Likewise, the ending *-iu* in the DAT. SG. is viewed as attesting to the influence of the productive *ja*-stem inflection. As the findings of the present quantitative analysis reveal, the ending *-iu* is only sporadically found in the DAT., while it is the most common marker in the INSTR. It seems feasible that these two categories were at a stage of a gradual functional merger as a result of which the distinction between them was no longer clear-cut in Old Saxon. Accordingly, the presence of the marker *-iu* in the DAT. may alternatively be interpreted as a result of intraparadigmatic restructuring, i.e. the pressure of the instrumental, rather than the influence of the *ja*-stems. Yet another phonological treatment of these endings was offered by Heyne (1873: 74), according to whom the instrumental in *-iu* testifies to the origin in the *i*-stem declension, whereas the forms in *-i* are to be ascribed to a phonological development, i.e. the loss of the final vowel /u/. Taking into consideration more recent reconstructions of this grammatical category (Ringe 2006: 272; Boutkan 1995: 248), the interpretation of *-i* as a result of the phonological reduction of the final vowel is not considered a likely scenario for the INSTR. SG. The ending *-iu* has also been interpreted as a hybrid, in which the *-i* element is a reflex of the original instrumental, while *-u* is the analogically extended *a*-stem ending (Boer 1924: 190; Boutkan 1995: 248). Such an alternative interpretation, postulating an amalgamation of the historical and innovative inflections in one form, could theoretically be extended to other cases in the paradigm, resulting in a reinterpretation of the mechanism involved in the restructuring (see the discussion in Section 5.6.2.2). Finally, unambiguous traces of analogical influence in the DAT. SG. can be found in forms in *-u* and *-o*, attested in the feminine stems.

NOM./ACC. SG.

The forms of the NOM. and ACC. SG. in light-syllable masculine and neuter stems in *-i* overlap entirely with those of the *ja*-stems (*hirdi* 'shepherd', *rīki* 'kingdom'). This formal similarity poses some problems for interpreting the marker *-i* as an archaic characteristic of the *i*-stems and raises the question whether they should be included in the calculations. The essential difference between these forms in the two classes lies in their syllable structure as the masculine *ja*-stems are predominantly (although not exclusively) heavy-syllable stems. It seems that the interpretation of the *i*-forms in the *i*-stems as inherited is possible on the assumption that the syllable structure constituted a barrier for interdeclensional shifts in the same way as gender did (which seems to be the case in most transfers). It cannot be excluded at the same time that such a formal similarity of the NOM. SG. form across classes led to the enhancement of *-i* as an exponent of the NOM. SG., reinforcing the integrity of the light-syllable *i*-stem paradigm and possibly creating a constraint on further restructuring of the paradigm. These forms were accordingly counted in the present study as *i*-stem class markers.

5.6.2.2 *Results of the investigation*
As the differences resulting from alternative treatments of forms in individual grammatical categories can be significant, two different ways of interpreting the inflections were applied in a few instances: (1) a narrow interpretation (in terms of the adopted criteria), which excludes any overlapping inflections, and (2) a more moderate, broader interpretation, where endings which *could* be a continuation of the *i*-stem inflection are interpreted as inherited. The results presented in the consecutive tables refer to the findings from the broader interpretation, but, where relevant, references are also made to the results obtained from the narrow treatment. In all the subclasses, the forms in *-e* attested in the DAT. SG. and NOM. and ACC. PL., which could be interpreted as etymological (*i > e*), were excluded from the counting on account of the overlap with the analogical forms from the (*j*)*a*- and (*j*)*ō*-stems (*n* = 25).

The results of the quantitative analysis of the masculine and neuter light-syllable *i*-stems, which show largely parallel patterns, are presented collectively in Table 5.5.[244] The figures include also the attestations to *hugi* 'mind', which, despite its very high frequency, shows an inflectional pattern parallel to that found in the other nouns in this subgroup, and thus its inclusion did not skew the overall findings for this subclass.[245]

---

244. The *i*-stems, and especially the feminine heavy-syllable *i*-stems, constitute a large class of nouns in Old Saxon. As the present quantitative analysis was aimed to be a comprehensive one, it attempted to include all the nouns affiliated with this declensional class. Note, however, that not all the nouns classified as *i*-stems in Tiefenbach (2010) and Köbler (2014a) were included. The original affiliation of nouns was verified in the etymological dictionaries (primarily Kroonen 2013, Boutkan & Siebinga 2005, Berr 1971) and only if confirmed there, were the nouns included. Given that the class was to some extent productive, the nouns, for instance, of Latin origin are also classified as *i*-stems in the mentioned sources, as they most likely followed the *i*-stem inflectional pattern. The nouns whose affiliation with the *i*-stems declension is more recent were not considered relevant for the present study. A more general problem with assigning nouns to a given class was that many of them are attested in forms entirely inconclusive with respect to the restructuring process (e.g. the NOM. or ACC. SG.), and if their original affiliation cannot be corroborated by external (Germanic) evidence, their status remains largely unclear.

245. The proportion of archaic forms in the paradigm of *hugi* amounts to 98 percent, being thus slightly higher than the overall percentage of archaism for the light-syllable stems, which may reflect the correlation with the frequency of occurrence (cf. Section 8.6.1). Following the procedure applied in the Old English analysis, the compound formations in *-scepi*, *-scipi* were not included in this investigation.

Table 5.5 Distribution of archaic and innovative inflections in the OS masculine and neuter light-syllable *i*-stems

	archaic		innovative	
	SG	PL	SG	PL
NOM.	(87) 97%	(12) 92%	(3) 3%	(1) 8%
GEN.	(3)	–	–	–
DAT.	(62) 85%	(0)	(11) 15%	(5) 100%
ACC.	(105) 100%	(15) 79%	–	(4) 21%
INSTR.	(16) 55%	–	(13) 45%	–
Total	(297) 89%		(37) 11%	

A cursory look at the data suffices to notice that the Old Saxon light-syllable masculine and neuter *i*-stem paradigms were only to a very limited extent susceptible to the influence of the *a*- and *ja*-stems. The light masculine and the scantily attested neuter nouns pattern alike, displaying considerable archaism in the singular and plural (9% and 27% of analogical inflections, respectively), where the original stem formative *-i* functions as an inflectional exponent in most of the cases. The paradigm of the singular is altogether much better attested than the plural, and some inclination towards the productive inflections is evident in the DAT. and INSTR. SG., and only sporadically in the NOM. SG. ((-)*slag* 'blow', (-)*sif* 'sieve', (-)*stad* 'place'). Traces of analogical inflections are well attested also in the DAT. PL., where all the forms appear with the *ja*-stem ending *-iun* (*-ion*). The infrequent traces of innovation in the NOM./ACC. PL. are manifested in the extension of the markers *-a* and *-ios* from the *a*- and *ja*-stems, respectively (*muthbita* 'mouthful', *grurios* 'terror', *hornselios* 'gabled house'; the latter two attested only in ms. C of *Heliand*), and in the ending *-u* extended from the neuter *a*-stems (*aldarlagu* 'lifetime'). Furthermore, considerable synchronic fluctuation is attested in the INSTR. SG., where the competition takes place between the forms in *-i*, considered here original, and the forms in *-iu*, interpreted as analogical. Given the complexity of the interaction between the DAT. and INSTR., and the fact that the original functions of these two cases tended to merge gradually, one could conclude that the alternation reflects an internal development within the paradigm rather than an actual interdeclensional transition. Irrespective of the exact interpretation of the instrumental forms, the paradigm of the light-syllable masculine and neuter stems remains overall stable.

The results of the investigation of the scantily attested feminine light-syllable stems are summarised in Table 5.6. The majority of the forms in this subgroup belong to the lemma *stedi* 'town' and its compounds.

Despite the scant attestation, it can be concluded that the overall inflectional profile of this subclass remains unchanged and the pattern corresponds largely to that found in the masculine and neuter light-syllable stems. The alternation in the

Table 5.6 Distribution of archaic and innovative inflections in the OS light-syllable feminine *i*-stems

	archaic		innovative	
	SG	PL	SG	PL
NOM.	(3) 60%	(7) 100%	(2) 40%	(0)
GEN.	–	–	–	–
DAT.	(9) 82%	(1) 50%	(2) 18%	(1) 50%
ACC.	(6) 86%	(2) 100%	(1) 14%	(0)
Total	(28) 82%		(6) 18%	

NOM./ACC. SG. is attested only in compounds, while the base noun is consistently found with the historical pattern. A further inflectional irregularity is the lack of the *i*-mutated vowel in the (endingless) NOM. SG. in the paradigm of *(-)stedi* 'town' (e.g. *hofstedi* ~ *hofstad*, GlMarf and UrbWerdTrad; cf. a parallel pattern in OLF *stat*; Section 6.5.2). No synchronic alternation is found in the NOM. or ACC. PL. where the *i*-stem ending is consistently retained. The alternation in the DAT. PL. is found in one lemma (*snarin* ~ *snariun* 'strings'), and, given the number of attested forms, its value is considerably limited. At the same time, *snarin* is one of the very few instances where the original *i*-stem inflection is attested for the DAT. PL. The analogical forms found in the light-syllable feminine stems can generally be ascribed to the influence of the *jō*- and *ō*-stems.

Table 5.7 depicts the incidence of archaic and innovative forms in the heavy-syllable masculine and neuter *i*-stems. The variation in the GEN. SG. involves the markers *-es* and *-ies*, the former, potentially interpretable as original, but overlapping with the ending of the masculine *a*-stems, and thus considered inconclusive.

Table 5.7 Distribution of archaic and innovative inflections in the OS heavy-syllable masculine and neuter *i*-stems[*]

	archaic		innovative	
	SG	PL	SG	PL
NOM.	*(31)*	(93) 100%	–	(0)
GEN.	*(9)*	*(114)*	–	–
DAT.	(8) 80%	(2) 2%	(2) 20%	(97) 98%
ACC.	*(50)*	(56) 95%	–	(3) 5%
INSTR.	(1) 14%	–	(6) 86%	–
Total	(160) 60%		(108) 40%	

[*] Two nouns in this subgroup show considerable lack of stability with respect to gender: OS *wiht* (Go. *waíhts*, feminine) is attested as masculine in the NOM./ACC. PL. with the meaning 'ghost, demon', but as neuter when denoting 'thing, something'; likewise OS *thionost* 'service' appears as feminine in ms. C of *Heliand* (line 2905: *an thia godes thionost*), but as neuter in ms. M (line 2905: *an that godes thionost*).

Traces of analogical inflections in the singular are confined to a few instances in the DAT. and INSTR., which testify to an entirely divergent pattern, the former retaining the original inflection, the latter showing primarily analogical endings. Given the interaction between these two cases, the attested alternation cannot be viewed as entirely reliable. Unambiguous traces of analogical inflections are found in the plural, but they are essentially limited to the DAT. The scant novel forms in the ACC. PL. are, apart from the masculine marker -os, the endingless neuter forms (*gibend* 'bond', *uuik* 'village'), emerging under the pressure of the neuter *a*-stems. Altogether, the heavy-syllable masculine and neuter nouns show more bias towards the *a*-stem and *ja*-stem inflection than the light-syllable stems, but at the same time the inherited pattern of inflection is not entirely abandoned. The paradigm of masculine heavy-syllable stems turns out to exhibit fewer innovative features than could be expected from the treatments of inflectional morphology found in the historical handbooks and overviews (e.g. Gallée 1993, Cordes 1956, Tiefenbach 2000).

Table 5.8 depicts the distribution of forms in the paradigm of heavy-syllable feminine stems. As the status of the NOM. and ACC. SG. with respect to the inflectional restructuring is ambiguous, the table presents two alternative interpretations: one including these forms as markers of the *i*-stem pattern, the other considering them inconclusive.

Table 5.8 Distribution of archaic and innovative inflections in the OS heavy-syllable feminine *i*-stems

	archaic		innovative	
	SG	PL	SG	PL
NOM.	(*126*) 100%	(37) 97%	(*0*)	(1) 3%
GEN.	(10) 26%	(*36*)	(28) 74%	–
DAT.	(151) 83%	(1) 1%	(30) 17%	(81) 99%
ACC.	(*243*) 100%	(77) 100%	(*0*)	(0)
INSTR.	(0)	(0)	(13) 100%	(0)
Total	(*645*) *81%*		(*153*) *19%*	
excl. NOM./ACC.SG.	(276) 64%		(153) 36%	

The distribution of forms testifies to a considerable archaism of inflection, which is largely a result of the attestations in the NOM. and ACC. SG. Given the high token frequency of forms in these two categories and their partly ambiguous status, their significance in estimating the extent of reorganisation of the paradigm deserves closer inspection. On the one hand, the inclusion of these forms in the calculations seems legitimised, because none of the productive classes was characterised by a zero ending in the NOM./ACC. SG. Accordingly, traces of analogical pressure from the *jō*-stems could be expected here, with competition from the markers -*e* and -*a*.

On the other hand, a major argument against such an interpretation is connected to the nature of the attestations. A close examination of the NOM. and ACC. SG. forms reveals that they are very often the only forms a given noun is attested in. An attestation pattern confined to these two categories cannot constitute positive evidence that a given noun actually consistently followed the *i*-stem inflection in the other cases in the paradigm. Although such a possibility cannot be excluded, on account of the scarcity of the available material, the affiliation with the *i*-stems cannot be unambiguously corroborated. Given this ambiguity, the two-way interpretation was considered necessary and eventually the findings excluding the NOM./ACC. SG. were found more reliable in estimating the extent of analogical reformulation of the paradigm. If these two categories are excluded, the level of innovation increases to 36 percent, corresponding to the figures obtained for the masculine and neuter heavy-syllable stems.

As regards the other cases in the paradigm of feminine stems, unambiguous traces of interference from *jō*-stems are found in the GEN., DAT. and INSTR. SG. The innovative inflections in the GEN. SG. are almost exclusively the masculine markers -*es* and -*ies* (e.g. *giburdies*, -*eas* 'birth', *kustes* 'choice', *gisiunies* 'sight', etc.), which clearly attest to gender confusion (e.g. in *craft* 'power'), or possibly to the extensive productivity of this marker irrespective of gender. This "heteroclicity" (Rauch 1992b: 251) of the paradigms of nouns such as *craft*, which combine the features of masculine and feminine inflections, is well attested also in the other minor classes and seems to have had a broader scope in Old Saxon than in the other investigated languages. This development may be partly responsible for the instability of the paradigm and the gradual gender shift to the masculine type. The retention of this masculine marker in the GEN. SG. of feminine stems at a later stage (i.e. Middle Low German) indicates that it must have represented a rather stable inflectional pattern (Foerste 1950: 54; Lasch 1974: 201). Occasional signs of innovation can be seen in the DAT. SG. which shows analogical endings of the *jō*- and *ō*-stems (-*iu*, -*a*). Apart from the expected *jō*- and *ja*-stem inflections, the GEN. and DAT. SG. show also forms without an ending (e.g. *craft*, *maht*, *giuuald*, *uuerold*). These endingless forms have been ascribed to the impact of consonantal inflection, in particular of the root nouns (Holthausen 1921: 103; Sanders 1983: 48; Boutkan 1995: 241). This direction of transition is unlikely given that the requirement for a declension to become productive is its stability, which was clearly not a characteristic of the root noun declension, itself largely influenced by productive inflections (cf. Section 5.6.4). At the same time, some other parallels between the *i*-stems and root nouns did exist, including the lack of an ending in the NOM./ACC. SG., which may have triggered some interaction between these stems, but with a more likely direction of shift to the *i*-stems. The absence of an inflectional ending in these two categories can be interpreted as a reflex of a more general tendency of feminine stems to favour a syncretic singular paradigm (Rauch 1992a: 64). No synchronic alternation was found in the INSTR. SG. where the only attested ending is the analogical *jō*-stem marker -*iu*. As regards the plural paradigm, there is hardly any alternation attested in individual cases: while the NOM. and ACC. PL. retain the historical inflection, the DAT. shows exclusively novel endings.[246] The singly attested NOM. PL. form *tida* testifies to the influence of the *ō*-stem inflection. The low percentage of analogical forms in these categories parallels the pattern found in the (heavy-syllable) masculine paradigm, where the NOM. and ACC. PL. show only inherited inflections. Of significance for such a distribution is the contrast between the singular and the plural. In heavy-syllable stems this contrast is retained, with the NOM. SG. characterised by a zero ending and the NOM. (ACC.) PL. by the *i*-ending, the latter being a sufficiently distinct exponent of the plural. No such contrast is found in light-syllable stems, where -*i* is the marker in both the singular and plural, and the need to mark the contrast in number renders the paradigm more susceptible to the influence of the productive inflections (cf. Table 5.5).

Table 5.9 shows the summary results from the investigation of the incidence of archaic and analogical features in the *i*-stem paradigm, irrespective of the syllable weight, case or gender. The figures do not include the NOM./ACC. SG. forms in heavy-syllable feminine stems.

Table 5.9 Overall distribution of archaic and innovative inflections in the OS *i*-stems

	i-stem inflection	innovative inflection
singular	(458) 80%	(111) 20%
plural	(303) 61%	(193) 39%
Total	(760) 71%	(304) 29%

As the data indicate, the extent of analogical pressure in the *i*-stems is fairly limited and the class can be considered one of the more stable declensional types in Old Saxon. The drift away from the inherited inflectional pattern is more discernible in the heavy-syllable stems than in the light-syllable ones. The relatively high percentage of innovation in the plural is unexpected in light of the fact that in general it tended to remain more conservative than the singular. The high percentage of innovation is owing to the DAT. PL., while the NOM./ACC. PL. remain very conservative. If only the figures for the NOM./ACC. PL. were taken into account (as it was the case in Old English and Old Frisian, where the DAT. PL. was not informative in this class), the innovation level in the plural drops to 3 percent (*n* = 308). In

---

246. Some forms cited by Gallée (1993) as the original DAT. PL. forms (-*in*) are attested in (parts of) glossaries considered Old High German (*halfthruin* (*halsthrūh*) 'collar', GlPrudF1 93,10; Tiefenbach 2010) and accordingly they were not included in the calculations.

consequence, the paradigm of *i*-stems emerges as even more conservative, with the overall amount of innovation reaching 14 percent, which proves that this inflectional pattern was very stable. The perseverance of the historical inflection in these two categories (NOM./ACC. PL.) can be ascribed to the presence of the vocalic marker (-*i*), frequently accompanied by the mutated root vowel. This double way of marking the plural rendered the paradigm more resistant to analogical restructuring, contributing to the overall conservative profile of the class. The category where the spread of analogical features is slightly more noticeable are the light-syllable stems, where the ending -*i* served as a marker of both NOM./ACC. SG. and PL., being thus indistinctive. Consequently, the introduction of a new inflectional ending can be interpreted as a means of retaining the essential functional contrast between the singular and the plural. Finally, no traces of the influence of the *n*-stems were found in the investigated material.

As regards the mechanisms underlying the transformation of this class, a prominent feature is the interaction of the *i*-stems with the *ja*- and *jō*-stems. Although the influence of the pure *a*- and *ō*-stem inflections is also present, its scope is fairly limited. Such a pattern of restructuring, with *ja*- and *jō*-stems playing an important role, is an Old Saxon idiosyncrasy; but rather than being a morphological peculiarity, it seems to have a clear phonological basis and is related to the phonological conservatism of Old Saxon. In contrast to Old English, Old Saxon retained the original -*j*- in inflectional syllables, both after light- and heavy-syllable stems across various grammatical categories (cf. Section 5.5). Significant for the restructuring of inflection is the consistent retention of the -*i*- element throughout the *ja*- and *jō*-stem paradigms, e.g. *hirdi, hirdies* 'shepherd', *kunni, kunnies* 'race', etc. (Gallée 1993: 200). Its consequence is the interaction of the *ja* -and *jō*-stems with the *i*-stems (where -*i*- was also present as a result of a regular phonological development) and the emergence of a number of inflectional parallels between these stems. Table 5.10 presents formal overlaps between these stems, contrasting them with the inflections of the *a*- and *ō*-stems. The overlapping forms are marked in bold; italics refer to an alternative interpretation, with the extension of pure *a*-stem markers (see below). The table presents the masculine paradigms only, but parallel correspondences are to be found in the neuter and feminine paradigms as well.

The above-presented correspondences shed some light on the question why the pure *a*-stems (and *ō*-stems) were less likely to exert influence on the *i*-stems than the *ja*-stems (and *jō*-stems). The parallelisms with the latter class are straightforward and compelling. Of special significance for the restructuring of the paradigms are the parallels in the NOM. SG., which can easily function as the category triggering analogical transitions between classes. Clearly, the phonological developments, inducing a formal overlap of inflections, created conditions conducive to the analogical transition of nouns to the *ja*- and *jō*-stems.

Table 5.10 The overlapping inflections in the OS *i*-stem, *ja*-stem and *a*-stems

	i-stems		*ja*-stems	*a*-stems
SG.	*light-syllable*	*heavy-syllable*		
NOM.	-i	-ø	-i	-ø
GEN.	-i(s)	-i	-i*as*, -i*es*	-as, -es
DAT.	-i	-i	-i*a*, -i*e*	-a, -e
ACC.	-i	-ø	-i	-ø
PL.				
NOM.	-i		-i*os*, -i*as*	-os, -as
GEN.	-io		-i*o*	-o
DAT.	-in		-i*un*	-un
ACC.	-i		-i*os*, -i*as*	-os, -as

Alternatively, the analogical reorganisation of this class can potentially be interpreted as an expansion of the *a*-stems and *ō*-stems, whereby the inflections of these stems were attached to the *i*-stem formative -*i*-, resulting in forms homophonous with those found in the *ja*- and *jō*-stems. In other words, while superficially the reanalysis appears to be an analogical extension of the *ja*- and *jō*-stem inflections, factually the novel forms may be interpreted as reflecting an amalgamation of the *a*- and *ō*-stem endings with the original *i*-stem markers. This interpretation seems to find support in the form of the INSTR. SG., where such an amalgamation of endings took place at a prehistoric stage (Boutkan 1995: 248). Irrespective of the exact mechanism involved, a consequence of these developments is that the inflections of the *i*-, *ja*- and *jō*-stems overlapped extensively. A further corollary of this inflectional overlap was the emergence of a fairly stable, common inflectional pattern, based on a mixture of *i*-stem and *ja*-/*jō*-stem features, which became increasingly competitive and tended to disseminate to other declensions.

Overall, the class of *i*-stems emerges as a remarkably stable declensional type, with a potential to become productive (as will become evident in the investigation). This state of affairs is reminiscent of the conditions found in Old High German (and in Old Low Franconian), where this declensional type was one of the most productive classes, continuing the historical pattern with the *i*-mutated vowel serving as a plural marker until the present-day. The inflectional shape of the *i*-stems clearly positions Old Saxon closer to its Inland Germanic neighbours (OHG, OLF) and away from its coastal Ingvaeonic sisters (OE and OFris.). The attested stability of the *i*-stems will be consequential for the pattern of inflectional restructuring in the other minor classes, where the *i*-stem inflection can serve as a potential template for the reorganisation of paradigms.

5.6.3 *u*-stems

5.6.3.1 *General characteristics*

The *u*-stems constitute a relatively well attested minor class in Old Saxon, comprising nouns of masculine, feminine and neuter gender. The affiliation of nouns with this class is often reflected in a vestigial variation between *e* ~ *i* and *o* ~ *u* present in the root, for instance, in *frethu* ~ *frithu* 'peace', *fehu* ~ *fihu* 'cattle'. The alternation involved vowel harmony or height harmony (Krogh 1996: 253–256; cf. Buccini 1995: 23), which was fairly widespread in Continental Germanic, whereby the quality of the root vowel was adjusted in height to that of the inflectional vowel (Holthausen 1921: 32, 33, 105; Salmons 2012: 121). A feature characteristic of this paradigm is also the occasional presence of a mutated vowel in the plural (e.g. *hand*: *hendi*), which constituted a formal parallelism with the *i*-stems, and may have facilitated the early transfer of these stems to the *i*-stem declension. The original inflections of the *u*-stems are retained primarily in light-syllable masculine and neuter stems; otherwise the paradigm shows many external influences, both in the plural and the singular, testifying to the impact of the *a*-stem and *i*-stem inflections. A number of nouns originally affiliated with this class transferred to other declensional classes at an early stage, showing exclusively the *a*-stem features (e.g. *hungar* 'hunger', *dōð* 'death', *skadu* 'shadow', *wethar* 'ram') or the *i*-stem inflections (e.g. *ēr* 'messenger', *bōg* 'bough'). At the same time, many *u*-stems are attested only in the NOM. and ACC. SG., i.e. in categories that are often (e.g. in heavy-syllable stems) inconclusive about the actual affiliation of these nouns.

As in the other minor declensional classes, the restructuring of the *u*-stem paradigm was sensitive to stem type. Accordingly, a divergent pattern is to be found in light- and heavy-syllable stems, the former tending to be more conservative, the latter more prone to the influence of analogical inflections of the *a*-stems and *i*-stems. The predominant pattern of transfer in this declensional type involved parallel shifts in the three gender groups, with the masculine and neuter nouns drifting towards the *a*-stems, and the feminines adopting the *ō*-stem and partly the *i*-stem inflections (Gallée 1993: 211).

The inflections in the *u*-stem paradigm illustrate the complexity of the Old Saxon spelling and phonological system, posing a number of interpretative difficulties. As the inflectional variation in the paradigm is abundant, many endings are ambiguous and not easily interpretable. In order to estimate the scale of the reorganisation in the *u*-stem paradigms, some decisions as to how to interpret the problematic endings had to be made and accounted for. For the sake of transparency, the details of analogical realignments in individual morphosyntactic categories are discussed before presenting the competing paradigms.

1. *NOM./ACC. SG.*

Traces of analogical pressure can be detected here only in the light-syllable stems, with the alternation between the historical endings -*u*, -*o* and analogical ending-less forms. In the heavy-syllable stems, these two categories are not informative about the reorganisation. The spread of analogical inflections in the paradigm (in neuter and masculine nouns) has been viewed as an effect of the loss of the ending after a heavy-syllable, whereby the form became identical with that of the *a*-stems (Boutkan 1995: 255). Potentially, the ACC. SG. could also testify to the *n*-stem influence.

2. *GEN. SG.*

The historically expected ending would be -*o*, from PGmc. **-auz* (cf. Table 2.11; Boutkan 1995: 256), and the analogical forms derive from the *a*-stem (-*es*) and *ja*-stem declensions (-*ies*) in masculine stems and potentially from *ō-/jō*-stems or *i*-stems in feminine stems.

3. *DAT. SG.*

The attestations to the DAT. SG. are probably the most problematic to interpret. The abundant spelling variation results in a considerable diversification in inflectional endings and, therefore, some preliminary assumptions need to be made in order to apply a consistent analysis. As some endings are entirely ambiguous and thus uninterpretable, they had to be dismissed from the analysis. For the forms which can be interpreted, two scenarios of historical development seem plausible and their interpretation as historical or analogical depends on which of the scenarios is adopted. The basis for the two alternative treatments is the PGmc. form and its two variants: the "high reflex" **-ēu* > -*iu* > -*i*, which constitutes the basis for the DAT. in Old Norse and Old High German, and the "low reflex" **-ēu* > -*ǣu* > -*ō* > -*o*, found primarily in Old English and Old Frisian (Boutkan 1995: 256) (corresponding to the two PGmc. variants **-iwi* and **-awi* postulated by Ringe 2006: 272–273). Although the Old Saxon forms have been traditionally interpreted as a continuation of the "low reflex", the complexity of inflectional marking found in the material allows one to assume that most of the forms may go back to the "high reflex", in line with the pattern found in Old High German (cf. Prokosch 1939: 248–249). Accordingly, while the ending -*i* attests to the "high reflex" interpretation of the original *u*-stem marker (PGmc. **-iwi*), the ending -*a/-o* points to the "low reflex" interpretation (Boutkan 1995: 258; Krogh 1996: 303–305). An additional complication is related to the fact that the form of the DAT. is an amalgamation of the original LOC. and INSTR. forms, and some intraparadigmatic analogy between these cases must be reckoned with. Table 5.11 presents the inflectional variants in the DAT. SG. and their interpretations under the two potential scenarios of development. The

Table 5.11 The interpretation of inflections in the OS DAT. SG.

DAT SG	<e>	<a>	<ie>	<u>	<i>	<o>	<o>
high reflex: $*-\bar{e}u > -iu > -i$ expected ending <i>	–	–	–	–	+	–	–
low reflex: $*-\bar{e}u > *-\bar{æ}u > -\bar{o} > -o$ expected ending <o>~<a> (overlap with <e>~<a> = /æ/)	–	+	–	–	–	+	–
analogical extension from:	a-stems $*$/æ/ <e>~<a>	a-stems + $*$/æ/ <e>~<a>	ja-stems	intra. ← INSTR.SG. or NOM./ACC.SG. +	–	–	(a) intra. ← INSTR. SG. $*u$ > ø (heavy syll.) (b) root nouns
"high reflex" interpretation	I	I	I	N	A	I	N
"low reflex" interpretation	I	N	I	N	I	A	N

Read: 1. The ending <e> cannot be a continuation of the PGmc. form, either according to the "high reflex" interpretation or in the "low reflex" interpretation, the form is innovative. In other words, irrespective of the chosen historical interpretation, the form is innovative. 2. The ending <a> cannot be a continuation of the PGmc. form according to the "high reflex" interpretation, but it is inherited according to the "low reflex" interpretation; at the same time, it can be an analogical extension from the a-stems. The overlap renders the forms neutral if the "low reflex" interpretation is adopted, but innovative if the "high reflex" interpretation is adhered to, etc.

overview reveals the complexity of the Old Saxon spelling variation and is intended to clarify the interpretative choices made for the quantitative analysis. The basis for the examination of the spelling variation is the detailed treatment offered by Klein (1977), who postulates a system where /å/ can be rendered by <a> and <o>. The <o> is unambiguous, despite the existing spelling variation of <o> ~ <u> (as in the NOM./ACC. SG.), which is not interpreted as being meaningful in this study. More problematic is the spelling <a>, since it overlaps with the spelling for the phoneme /æ/, which was rendered by <e> or <a> (cf. Section 5.5). The abbreviations *A*, *I* and *N* refer to "archaic", "innovative" and "neutral", respectively.

The marker which poses little interpretative difficulty is -*ie*, which, irrespective of the chosen interpretation, is an analogical extension from the *ja*-stems. Likewise, the ending <e> is innovative under both interpretations. If the "high reflex" interpretation is adopted, the only unambiguous archaic ending in the DAT. SG. is <i>. If the "low reflex" hypothesis is adhered to, the instances with -*i* have to be considered analogical, built on the template of the *i*-stems, and, consequently, the only genuine (historical) inflection is the ending <o>. In the present study both options will be considered: the "low reflex" interpretation is included in the regular analysis (in compliance with the mainstream view) and the "high reflex" interpretation will be discussed in an excursus (Section 5.6.3.3). In a few instances, the variation can be ascribed to internal, intraparadigmatic pressure; for example, the zero ending has been explained as an original INSTR. SG. (with a regular phonological change of **-u* > ø in heavy-syllable stems) and the marker <u> as a result of the pressure either of the INSTR. or the NOM./ACC. PL. (Boutkan 1995: 257). The intraparadigmatic pressure of the GEN. SG. and the ablaut grade therein (**-auz*) has also been postulated by Ringe (2006: 273) to account for the endless DAT. SG. Alternatively, these endingless forms have been interpreted as evidence of the consonantal inflection influence (Holthausen 1921: 106) (cf. Section 5.6.2). As the investigation into the *intra*paradigmatic interactions remains largely beyond the scope of this study, these endingless forms were considered inconclusive and are classified as neutral.

4. NOM./ACC. PL.

These two categories, characterised by formal syncretism in many classes, reflect the double-layered nature of the inflectional reorganisation and attest to its early date. The problematic ending here is the marker -*i*, found in both feminine and masculine stems. The form is interpreted as inherited, although from the Proto-Germanic point of view it could be treated as analogical from the *i*-stems (cf. Tables 2.13, 2.14). In the historical period, the ending can potentially be exposed to further restructuring under the influence of the *a*-stems, *ō*-stems, or possibly *i*-stems. In the last case, the shape of the ending is indistinguishable and thus inconclusive (cf. Section 5.6.3.3 for a potential *u*-stem origin of this ending). The forms of the ACC.

PL. are a result of intraparadigmatic analogy, i.e. the pressure of the NOM. PL., dating back to the prehistoric stage (cf. Table 2.14).

5. GEN. PL.

The GEN. PL. forms are considered inconclusive as the original endings overlapped with the inflections of the productive vocalic declensions at a prehistoric stage (Proto-Germanic). A trace of analogical inflection is the marker -*io*; however, given that there is no unambiguous historical *u*-stem form to juxtapose it with, this grammatical category was not included in the calculations.

6. DAT. PL.

In the DAT. PL. the synchronic variation between historical and analogical inflections can be identified with greater reliability. As the reconstructed ending of the DAT. PL. is *-*umaz*/-*umiz*, the attested forms in -*on* and -*un*, *could* potentially be a continuation of the historical inflection. However, they are not entirely unambiguous due to the overlap with identical markers from the productive classes (Boutkan 1995: 258). The analogical inflections are extended from the *i*-stem or *ja*- and *jō*-stem paradigms, and appear as -*ion*, -*iun*, as opposed to the (potentially) historical -*on*, -*un*. Because of the mentioned formal overlap, the DAT. PL. forms were not included in measuring the incidence of archaic and novel inflections in the paradigm. Their potential significance for the restructuring process will be considered separately (Section 5.6.3.2).

All these considerations lead to identifying a set of inflectional irregularities, which can be interpreted as features of the non-historical inflectional pattern in the paradigm of *u*-stems. If the rigid criteria of interpreting inflectional endings as historical and analogical are applied, only few cases are unambiguously informative about the inflectional reorganisation in the *u*-stem paradigms. They include:

a. masculine and neuter *u*-stems
    – the NOM./ACC. SG. zero marker in the light-syllable stems in place of the historical endings -*u*, -*o*
    – the GEN. SG. marker -*es*/-*ies* extended from the *a*- and -*ja*-stems respectively in place of the historical marker -*o*
    – the DAT. SG. markers -*e*/-*ie*/-*i* extended from the *a*- and *ja*-stems in place of the historical marker -*o* (-*u*)
    – the NOM./ACC. PL. *a*- and *ja*-stem ending -(*i*)*os* in place of the historical marker -*i*
b. feminine *u*-stems
    – the GEN. SG. ō-stem endings -*a*, -*e* in place of the historical marker -*o*
    – the NOM./ACC. PL. ō-stem endings -*a*, -*e* in place of the historical marker -*i*

Tables 5.12 and 5.13 below present the reorganisation scheme of the *u*-stem paradigms, showing the competing inflections in the masculine and (heavy-syllable) feminine nouns, respectively. The light-syllable feminine stems are not attested in Old Saxon and the attestations to neuter nouns are confined to two nouns (discussed further in the section). In the heavy-syllable masculine nouns (e.g. *uuald* 'wood'), no alternation is identifiable in the NOM./ACC. SG.

Table 5.12 The competing inflections in the OS light-syllable masculine *u*-stems

	archaic		innovative	
	SG	PL	SG	PL
NOM.	sunu, -o	suni	sun, -e	sun**os**, -a
GEN.	suno	*suno*	suneas, -ies	*sunio*
DAT.	suno, -u	*sunun, -on*	sune, -ie, -i	*sunion*
ACC.	sunu, -o	suni	sun, -e	sun**os**, -a

Table 5.13 The competing inflections in the OS heavy-syllable feminine *u*-stems

	archaic		innovative	
	SG	PL	SG	PL
NOM.	hand	handi, hendi	hand	handa
GEN.	hando	*hando*	handes, -ies	*handio*
DAT.	hando	*handun*	handi, hendi, hand	*handiun*
ACC.	hand	handi, hendi	hand	handa

The allomorphic variation in the paradigm of *hand* reflects traces of *i*-mutation; much as the process is significant for the mechanism of inflectional restructuring, it is of limited value for the estimation of the scope of analogical changes. The origin of the DAT. SG. forms in *-o* in masculine stems, such as *suno* (*Heliand* C 2269, 5946) and neuter *feho* (M 1841), attested alongside forms in *-u* (*sunu Heliand* M 2815, *frethu* PsGern 5,2), turns out to be problematic (Krogh 2002: 11). It has been viewed as a formation based on **-ou-i*, resulting from the influence of the GEN. SG. with the ablaut grade **ou* (Prokosch 1939: 248). Alternatively, the ending *-o* may be interpreted as a variant of *-u*, parallel to an alternation found also in the NOM./ACC. SG. (cf. Klein 2000b: 9 for potential explanations of this alternation).[247] In the present analysis, these forms are counted on the archaic side, as opposed to the potential

---

247. The presence of the <u> ~ <o> alternation is attested in mss. P (9th c.) and C (10th c.) as well as in the *Hildebrandslied* (9th c.) and *Sächsisches Taufgelöbnis* (late 8th c.). The question of its origin in *Sächsisches Taufgelöbnis* has been addressed in Krogh (1995), where the hypothesis of the Old English influence is confronted and excluded on account of the chronology of the <o> and <u> attestations in the Anglo-Saxon sources (Krogh 1995: 144).

forms in *-i, -ie, -e*, emerging under the pressure of the *i*-stems and *a*-stems, or end-ingless forms whose origin is obscure. The marker *-a* (*-e*) in the NOM./ACC. PL. of the *a*-stems (alongside the expected form *-os*) is an innovation attested only in the younger south-Westphalian texts. The ending has been attributed to the influence of Old High German or alternatively viewed as an autochthonous variant, not found in *Heliand* (except a single form in ms. C). An argument against treating the *-a* forms as secondary (analogical) is related to the salience of inflectional markers: such an interpretation would imply that a more salient ending (*-os/-as*) would be replaced by a less salient one (*-a/-e*) (Krogh 1996: 302–303).[248] This would run counter to the assumptions of morpho-phonological salience, whereby the more salient markers are preferred in the paradigm (for a theoretical discussion, see Section 8.6.2). In the context of the present study, both endings, irrespective of their exact origin, are considered innovative when they appear in the paradigms of minor stems.

5.6.3.2 *Results of the investigation*

The results of the quantitative investigation are presented separately for masculine and feminine stems, with a further subdivision into stem types. The details of inflectional distribution in the paradigms of two attested neuter nouns will be discussed separately. Table 5.14 presents the results for the masculine light- and heavy-syllable stems. As the most frequently attested noun *sunu* shows a distribution entirely parallel to that found in the other light-syllable stems, the results of its analysis were also included in the figures.

Table 5.14 Distribution of archaic and innovative inflections in the OS light- and heavy-syllable masculine *u*-stems

	Light-syllable				Heavy-syllable			
	archaic		innovative		archaic		innovative	
	SG	PL	SG	PL	SG	PL	SG	PL
NOM.	(91) 93%	(6) 100%	(7) 7%	(0)	(6)	(0)	–	(1) 100%
GEN.	(0)	(3)	(2) 100%	–	(0)	(8)	(3) 100%	–
DAT.	(1) 8%	(5)	(11) 92%	–	(0)	(0)	(3) 100%	–
ACC.	(56) 97%	(4) 100%	(2) 3%	(0)	(2)	(0)	–	(3) 100%
Total	(158) 88%		(22) 12%		(0) 0%		(10) 100%	

---

248. The findings from a diatopic investigation of the distribution of Ingvaeonic features clearly support the interpretation of the ending *-a* as an innovative feature, which emerged in the intensive contact zone with Franconian in the south-west. The distribution of *-os* and *-a* in various nouns shows, moreover, no indication that *-a* would have been an original ACC. PL. ending, as has occasionally been claimed (Versloot 2017a).

The attested pattern of distribution shows that the paradigm of light-syllable *u*-stems remained largely conservative, both in the singular and the plural. An evident bias in the attested distribution is found with respect to individual cases, namely the majority of etymological *u*-stem endings are concentrated in the frequently attested NOM. and ACC. SG., while the more scantily attested GEN. and DAT. SG. are almost entirely innovative. Again, the correlation with frequency of occurrence and its conserving effect can be evoked to account for the attested distribution (see Section 8.6.1). The novel forms in the NOM. SG. are the endingless forms in compounds based on *sunu*, attested in the younger sources (glossaries) (*fedironsun* 'son of father's brother' (GlTrSem, GlMarf), *swestarsun* 'sister's son' (GlTrSem), *brōtharsun* 'brother's son) (GlMarf), *kevissun* 'illegitimate son' (GlMarf)). The dominant analogical pattern in these stems is the *a*-stem (*ja*-stem) inflection, with the GEN. and DAT. SG. endings (-*i*)*es*, -(*i*)*e*. The heavy-syllable stem *wald* 'woods' is attested once as a DAT. SG. with an analogical *ja*-stem ending -*ie* (*sinuueldie* 'wilderness') in ms. C, and with the ending -*i* (*sinuueldi*) in ms. M. The mutated vowel in the root syllable can be explained in two ways: (1) as indicative of the transition of this noun to the *i*-stems or *ja*-stems, or (2) as a regular phonological development of the "high reflex", whereby the vowel is mutated.

As the figures indicate, the heavy-syllable masculine stems are scantily attested and many of them must be considered early transfers in line with the assumptions made for the present cross-Germanic investigation (cf. Section 1.5.3). The early transition of heavy-syllable stems to productive declensions was facilitated by the loss of the inflectional ending after a heavy-syllable, which rid the NOM. (ACC.) SG. of a vocalic ending and thus rendered the shape of this category indistinctive (i.e. identical with the shape of the NOM. SG. in other classes). The few attested forms testify to a large-scale transfer to the *a*-stem and *ja*-stem declensions. This is manifested especially in the forms of the GEN. SG. (*uualdes, uualdies*) and the NOM./ACC. PL. (*uualdas, uuerdos*).

Table 5.15 presents the distribution of the inflectional forms in the feminine stems. As the attestations to this subclass are very limited, the results of the investigation for light- and heavy-syllable stems were combined in one table.

Table **5.15** Distribution of archaic and innovative inflections in the OS light- and heavy-syllable feminine *u*-stems

	archaic		innovative	
	SG	PL	SG	PL
NOM.	(*2*)	(*2*) 100%	–	(0)
GEN.	(0)	(*1*)	(0)	–
DAT.	(0)	(*74*)	(1) 100%	–
ACC.	(*18*)	(8) 80%	–	(2) 20%
Total	(10) 77%		(3) 23%	

The low number of attestations in this subgroup renders the interpretation problematic, and the conclusions ventured are fairly tentative. The figures refer primarily to heavy-syllable feminine stems; the only attested original light-syllable stem is *duru* 'door', whose inflections testify to a rather inconsistent pattern (NOM. PL. *duru, duri*, DAT. PL. *duron*).[249] The NOM. PL. *duri* points to the *u*-stem inflection, which tallies with the pattern found in the other Continental Germanic languages, but the irregular plural *duru* may potentially be interpreted as a dual form. In compound formations (when used as the first element) the noun still shows traces of the original inflection (*duruwarderi* 'doorkeeper', 10th c.). The attestation and thereby the archaism of the class is confined to the plural, where the ending -*i* is consistently preserved. The singly attested DAT. SG. *hendi* testifies to a combined effect of *i*-mutation and the analogical pressure from the *i*-stems, and is accordingly interpreted as innovative. Some further traces of *i*-mutation are found in the NOM. PL. *hendi* (in *Heliand*); the form is consistently interpreted as inherited (cf. Section 5.6.3.1) and the *i*-mutated vowel is viewed as a reflex of the original ending **-iwiz*. The noun *winter* is attested once without an ending in the ACC. PL., with the meaning 'year'. Given the context in which the form is found, i.e. referring to years not the season, it is most likely an analogical formation on the neuter *a*-stem *jār* 'year', where the NOM./ACC. PL. forms are endingless. Alternatively, the form could be interpreted as a "super" archaic formation, which goes back to an old ACC. PL. form **uns* (cf. ON *vǫllu* 'field', *fiǫrðu* 'fjord'). On account of a lack of compelling evidence from the corpus data, the latter hypothesis cannot be convincingly supported.

Theoretically, the DAT. PL. can be informative about the restructuring, since the data show an opposition between the ending -*on* (-*un*), which could be interpreted as a continuation of the *u*-stem pattern, and the marker -*ion* (-*iun*), which points to the influence of the *i*-stems or possibly *jō/ja*-stems. The major argument in favour of treating the ending -*on*, -*un* as historical is that there is hardly any impact of the pure *ō*-stems in the paradigm, and thus the DAT. PL. marker -*on* would be the only inflection systematically extended from the *a*-stems and/or *ō*-stems. Accordingly, if the attestations to the DAT. PL. are included in the analysis on the assumption that the ending is a continuation of the original PGmc. form, the conservatism of this class increases by 3 percent (amounting to 86 percent). On account of the ambiguity entailed in the interpretation of this ending, these attestations were, however, considered inconclusive and were thus excluded from the figures.

---

249. The noun originated, in fact, in the root noun class, but transferred at an early stage to the *u*-stems (Griepentrog 1995: 130; cf. Kroonen 2013, s.v. *durī*- where also the origin in the old dual form **dhur-ih₁* is postulated for a related neuter noun **dura*- 'single door, gate' < **dhur-o-*). According to Griepentrog (1995: 130), the inflections of *duru* in Old Saxon allow one to view it as a continuation of the proto-West-Germanic root noun rather than a *u*-stem. The related forms *doru, doru, doron* are interpreted as belonging to a parallel neuter *a*-stem *dor* denoting 'gate' (Tiefenbach 2010; Gallée 1993: 212; Griepentrog 1995: 130–131; Köbler 2014a, s.v. **dor* 'gate'; cf. Sehrt 1966).

The attestation of the neuter *u*-stems is confined to the singular paradigm only, with archaic forms found in the NOM., ACC. and INSTR. SG. ($n = 5$) and innovative *a*-stem forms attested in the GEN. and DAT. SG. ($n = 12$, e.g. *fehes* 'cattle', *feldes* 'field') (with four forms in the paradigm being inconclusive). Analogical inflections are found in 67 percent of forms. A number of neuter *u*-stems show historical inflections only in compound formations, where they are attested as the first element of a compound, as in: *uuidu-* 'wood' (*widubill* 'hatchet'), *heru-* (*herugrimm* 'fierce'), *lagu-* (*lagulīthandi* 'seafarer'),[250] *lithu-* (*lithubendi* 'shackles'). As these forms do not provide information about the inflectional endings, they could not be included in the quantitative investigation.

The overall results for the distribution of archaic and innovative inflections in the paradigm of *u*-stems, irrespective of the syllable weight, case or gender, are summarised in Table 5.16. The meaning of the consolidated results in this class is rather limited and the figures cannot be interpreted at face value, without taking into account all the nuances of the distribution discussed earlier. The figures reflect essentially the situation in the light-syllable stems, with the archaism concentrated primarily in the NOM./ACC. SG.

Table 5.16 Overall distribution of archaic and innovative inflections in the OS *u*-stems

	archaic	innovative
singular	(148) 84%	(29) 16%
plural	(20) 77%	(6) 23%
Total	(168) 83%	(35) 17%

The attested distributional pattern is unexpected in light of the distributions found for Old English and Old Frisian. The infiltration of analogical inflections into the paradigm of the *u*-stems is considerably limited, with an almost identical distribution of archaic and innovative inflections in the singular and the plural. This low incidence of analogical features can be attributed to two major factors: firstly, the complex interaction with the class of *i*-stems and the natural synchronic overlap with the *i*-stem inflections; secondly, the bias in the data towards the light-syllable stems, as most of the heavy-syllable stems had transferred to other classes at an earlier stage and thus remained beyond the scope of the investigation. The formal similarity of the NOM./ACC. PL. in the two classes must have acted as a factor enhancing the position of the ending *-i* as a plural marker, and consequently rendered it resistant to the pressure of other vocalic patterns (*a*-stems, *ō*-stems).

---

250. The noun *lagu* is, in fact, singly attested as a name of one of the runes in ABC 13.

5.6.3.3 *Excursus on the* i-*marker in the* DAT. SG. *and* NOM. PL.

The complexity of the problem of accounting for the *-i* form of the DAT. and NOM. PL. is evidently reflected in the lack of unanimity among the authors of major historical comparative grammars (cf. Table 5.17). While all seem to agree that the *u*-stems in Old Saxon stay largely under the influence of other declensional types, the opinions as to the origin of the marker *-i* seem to vary and, in fact, are sometimes not explicitly expressed. The core of the discussion is whether the *i*-marker is a regular phonological development of the original *u*-stem ending or rather an analogical extension from the *i*-stems. An additional complication in the DAT. SG. is the fact that two potential paths of phonological development of the original PGmc. form are identifiable: the "high reflex" *-ēu* > *-iu* > *-i*, and the "low reflex" *-ēu* > *-ǣu* > *-ō* > *-o*, which are dialectally distributed across Germanic (the former constitutes the basis for the DAT. in Old Norse and in Old High German, the latter in Old English and Old Frisian; Boutkan 1995: 256). Neither the "high" nor the "low reflex" are explicitly discussed in Streitberg (1963: 245–246) with reference to Old Saxon. According to the author, given that the Old High German DAT. SG. form in *-i* is derived from an original LOC. SG. in *-iu* (< *-ēu)* (with a subsequent regular phonological development of the *-iu* > *-i*), it seems feasible that the parallel Old Saxon form in *-i* (*suni*) has the same origin (which corresponds to the "high reflex" interpretation). At the same time, the only DAT. SG. form presented in the Old Saxon paradigm (p. 245) is a form in *-o* (*suno*), which could theoretically point to the alternative "low reflex" interpretation. As no explicit explanation for this form is offered, one has to rely on the references made to the corresponding forms in the sister languages. Given that the OE DAT. SG. in *-a* is explained as a consequence of intraparadigmatic levelling from the original GEN. SG., and that the OHG archaic GEN. SG. ends in *-o*, it can be hypothesised that the rare Old Saxon DAT. SG. ending *-o* could also have originated in the GEN. SG. The NOM. PL. form in *-i* is interpreted by Streitberg (1896) as inherited, with a parallel development, i.e. *iu* > *-i*, postulated for both Old Saxon and Old High German. Much along the same line, Boer (1924: 191) interprets the OHG DAT. SG. "*-iu*, jonger *-i*" as a continuation of the original LOC. SG. The same marker in the plural, however, is interpreted as analogical (this time explicitly for Old Saxon as well): "[d]e os. ohd. vorm op i schijnt wel uit de i-declinatie te stammen, daar de DAT. s. nog -iu uit -eui kent." As *-iu* survives in the DAT. SG., but not in the NOM. PL. in Old High German, Boer concludes that the NOM. PL. *-i* must have another origin; otherwise one could expect *-iu* also there. Yet, it seems probable that the lack of simultaneous attestations of the two forms may be due to chronological and not etymological differences, because the DAT. SG. *-iu* is attested solely in the older sources, while the NOM. PL. only in the younger ones, and hence only as *-i*.

Table 5.17 Interpretations of the DAT. SG. and NOM. PL. inflections in the OS *u*-stem paradigm

	Streitberg (1896)	Boer (1924)	Prokosch (1939)	Krahe & Meid (1969)	Bammesberger (1990)	Boutkan (1995)	Braune/Reiffenstein (2004)
DAT. SG. "HIGH REFLEX" -*i* < *-*iu* (< *-*ēu*)	inherited (?)	inherited	inherited	not explicit	–	inherited	inherited
DAT. SG. "LOW REFLEX" -*o* < -*ō* < *-*ǣu* < *-*ēu*	inherited (?)	inherited	inherited	inherited	inherited	inherited	–
NOM. PL. *i* < *-*iu* < *-*iwiz*	inherited	< *i*-stems	< *i*-stems	inherited	inherited	inherited	< *i*-stems

An interpretation entailing the two reflexes of the original Proto-Germanic form is found in Prokosch (1939: 248–249). Taking recourse to intraparadigmatic analogy, the author explains the DAT. SG. form in -*o* as a continuation of *ou-ei*, emerging under the influence of the GEN. SG. The DAT. SG. form in -*i* is ascribed to a regular phonological development of the "high reflex", while the NOM. PL. forms are interpreted as analogical from the *i*-stems. According to Krahe & Meid (1969: 33, 34), the OHG -*iu* is the regular form of the DAT. SG. (< LOC. SG.), while the frequently attested ending -*e* (in the masculine stems) is analogical, extended from the *a*- (or *i*-) stems. This leaves the DAT. SG. forms in -*i* unaccounted for. The Old Saxon form(s) in -*o*, alongside the Old English ones in -*a*, are interpreted as a regular continuation of the "low reflex" variant. The NOM. PL. -*i* in Old Saxon and Old High German, in turn, is explained as an effect of the reduction of -*iu* > -*i* (*suniuz* > *suniz*), where the -*u*-element is regularly lost (cf. ON *syner*, where *-*i* is retained as -*e*). Bammesberger (1990: 151–153) derives the DAT. SG. form in -*o* from the PGmc. *-au* (< *-*ēu*) (the variant in -*i* is not explicitly discussed). The Early Runic form -*iu* (> -*e*) is explained as a shortening of *-*ēu*, while the NOM. PL. is traced back to *-*juz* (< *-*ewez*) (except the Old English forms). Boutkan (1995: 256) interprets the DAT. SG. as an original LOC. SG., which derives from *-*ēu*. The diphthong is preserved in OHG -*iu*, with a later phonological development into -*i*, and accordingly the Old Saxon form in -*i* could be interpreted in the same way. The form in -*o* is analysed as a "low reflex" of *-*ǣu* (cf. OE -*a*) or as a result of intraparadigmatic transfer from the INSTR. SG. (*-*u* > -*u*, -*o* in light-syllable stems and *-u > ø in heavy-syllable stems). The NOM. PL. -i is treated as a regular reflex of *-eues (with a dialectal variation in the development of *-e- before *u, resulting in OS/OHG -iu vs. OE -a) (Boutkan 1995: 84–86). The treatment of the Old High German forms found in Braune/Reiffenstein (2004) may also shed some light on the Old Saxon state of affairs. The DAT. SG. form in -i is explained therein as a reduced continuation of the original locative ending -iu ("mit Abfall des u"), while the ending -e is viewed as levelled from the a- or i-stems. The i-marker in the NOM. PL. is considered to be an analogical extension of the i-stem ending rather than a continuation of PGmc. *-iwiz. Finally, the cryptic description found in Gallée (1993: 211) is confined to a general statement that most of the original u-stems follow the i-stem pattern, and that the original inflection is mostly retained in light-syllable stems, but no explicit interpretation of individual forms is offered.

A summary of the adduced opinions on the origin of the inflectional forms of the DAT. SG. and NOM. PL. is provided in Table 5.17. It presents the two alternative historical sources of the DAT. SG. forms as defined by Boutkan (1995: 256), i.e. the "high" and "low reflex".

As becomes clear from the overview presented above, the predominant view seems to be that the ending -i, being a younger variant of -iu (formally PIE LOC. SG.), is the inherited u-stem ending in the DAT. SG. in Old Saxon (and in Old High German). The Old Saxon DAT. SG. seems to be a hybrid in that, in contrast to other Germanic languages (perhaps excluding Early Runic), it testifies to two variants of the original DAT. SG. form, namely its "high" and "low reflex". The "low reflex", which it shares with Old English and Old Frisian, is attested as -o (in fact rarely), and the "high reflex", which places it closer to Inland Germanic, appears as the i-marker. The opinions as to the origin of the plural marker seem more divided, and in the treatments where the marker is interpreted as analogical the original form is not explicitly mentioned. Assuming that the form is analogical, the interdeclensional shift must have taken place at a very early stage. On account of the parallelisms with the i-stems, it turns out to be quite problematic to trace the exact development of this inflectional ending. In the present study it is consistently interpreted as inherited, following the majority view.

These considerations have one main implication for the reorganisation of inflection: if the ending -i is a regular development of the earlier -iu in the DAT. SG. and NOM. PL. (and consequently also in the ACC. PL. through intraparadigmatic levelling), the actually attested paradigm shows only one "genuine" shift to the i-stems – in the GEN. SG. If the ending -i in these categories is not a continuation of the historical ending, but an analogical form extended from the i-stems, then the impact of the i-stem inflection in the u-stems is much more profound. As mentioned earlier, the interpretation of the i-marker as analogical in the NOM. PL. is considered here less plausible and excluded; the results of interpreting the DAT.

SG. marker -*i* as analogical are presented in the tables in Section 5.6.3.2. As the interpretation of the *i*-marker as a "high reflex" in the DAT. SG. is considered a likely possibility, an alternative analysis of forms was conducted, where the ending -*i* was interpreted as inherited (while the other endings were analysed as in Tables 5.12 and 5.13). The recounting of forms produces similar results to those obtained from the analysis where the DAT. in -*i* was considered analogical: the overall percentage of innovative inflections in the paradigm amounts to 18 percent. This lack of more spectacular results can be ascribed to the low number of the DAT. SG. forms and the fact that in the "high reflex" interpretation the ending -*a* is counted as innovative instead of neutral (cf. Table 5.11 and 5.14, 5.15).

Clearly, the paradigm of the *u*-stems poses interpretative difficulties for the investigation of inflectional restructuring. The major reason for the confusion is the early stage of development of this declensional class, which followed a pathway entirely parallel to that of the *i*-stems (see Thöny 2013: 50 for a discussion of these two declensional classes in PGmc. and PIE, and the interaction between them). In consequence, a number of inflections in the *i*-stem and *u*-stem paradigms overlapped and this overlap rendered many forms inconclusive regarding the (synchronic) declensional affiliation. In this respect, the Old Saxon *u*-stem paradigm can be interpreted as a hybrid, combining the historical inherited *u*-stem features with the novel *i*-stem characteristics, the latter induced not so much by analogy but largely by the entirely parallel phonological development of these two declensional classes. Accordingly, it can be concluded that the nature of the influence of the *i*-stem inflection in the *u*-stems is different from that in the other classes, where the expansive *i*-stem markers simply replaced the original endings. In the *u*-stems, the endings largely overlapped with those of the *i*-stems and this formal congruence served as a factor triggering, or perhaps enhancing, further analogical replacements. More specifically, if the original markers of the *i*-stems and *u*-stems (e.g. in the NOM. PL.) happened to be identical through phonological development, the resulting form was reinforced, on the one hand, facilitating the merger of the two classes, but on the other hand, remaining fairly resistant to the pressure from other productive types. In consequence, the numerous parallelisms between the *i*-stems and *u*-stems led to a development of a "super" class or an overarching paradigm, comprising a substantial number of nouns whose inflectional pattern was largely the same, irrespective of their etymological origin. In this pattern *i*-mutation had a significant role to play in the succeeding period, with the *i*-mutated vowel developing (alongside the inflectional ending) as a distinctive plurality marker. This complex interaction between the *u*-stems and the *i*-stems gives some further insight into the status of the latter class in Old Saxon. The interplay between these two inflectional types substantiates the unique status of the *i*-stems, which due to their inflectional profile served as an interface, with links to the *u*-stems, on the one hand, and to the *ja-* and *jō-*stems, on the other. Consequently, the *i-*stems emerged as a stable and highly productive declensional type, whose productivity rendered them one of the major destination classes for minor stems in Old Saxon (cf. Section 5.6.2.2).

5.6.4 Root nouns

5.6.4.1 *General characteristics*

The class of root nouns in Old Saxon comprised nouns of masculine and feminine gender, with the former being only fragmentarily preserved in the existing material. No nouns of the neuter gender are attested in the corpus. According to the descriptions found in historical grammars, morphological restructuring of the paradigm was fairly advanced in this declensional type and the original inflectional profile is to a large extent disintegrated, with many nouns following the *i-*stem inflectional pattern. The only noun attested in all its inflectional forms is the masculine *man(n)*, which testifies to a synchronic vacillation between historical and analogical features.

The reorganisation of the root noun inflection can be expected to have followed three major paths, with the masculine nouns shifting to the *a-*stem (*ja-*stem) inflection and the feminine nouns yielding to the pressure of the *ō-*stems (*jō-*stems) and *i-*stems. Potentially traces of the masculine *a-*stems (and *ja-*stems) can be expected to appear in the feminine paradigm (as it was the case in the other classes), and additionally, both paradigms may show traces of the *n-*stem inflection. The pressure of the productive inflectional types is manifested in the following inflectional irregularities:

a. masculine root nouns
   - the GEN. SG. ending *-as*, *-es* in place of the original endingless form
   - the DAT. SG. marker *-e* (*-a*) in place of the original endingless form
   - the NOM./ACC. PL. ending *-a* (from the *a-*stems) and *-i* (from the *i-*stems) in place of the expected endingless form
   - the GEN. PL. ending *-eo/-io* in place of the original ending *-o*
   - the DAT. PL. ending *-eon/-ion* in place of the inherited marker *-un*
   - the NOM./ACC. PL. *n-*stem ending *-on* in place of the expected endingless form
b. feminine root nouns
   - the GEN. SG. marker *-i* extended from the feminine *i-*stems, and the marker *-(i)es* from the masculine *a-* and *ja-*stems
   - the DAT. SG. marker *-i* and the *ō-*stem marker *-a*, *-e* in place of the historical endingless forms

- the NOM./ACC. PL. ending -i extended from the i-stems, or the marker -a from the a-stems
- the GEN. PL. ending -eo/-io in place of the original ending -o
- the DAT. PL. marker -eon/-ion in place of the inherited marker -un

All these potential traces of analogical pressures are summarised in Tables 5.18 and 5.19, where the two competing sets of inflections are presented for the masculine and feminine paradigms, respectively.

Table 5.18 The competing inflections in the OS masculine root nouns

| | archaic | | innovative | |
	SG	PL	SG	PL
NOM.	*man*	man, men	*man*	manna, -on
GEN.	man	manno	mannes, -as[*]	manneo, -io
DAT.	man	mannun, -on	manne	manneon, -ion
ACC.	*man*	man, men	*man*	manna, -on

[*] The frequently attested ending -as, extended from the a-stems, is viewed as a secondary development from -es (Prokosch 1939: 234).

Table 5.19 The competing inflections in the OS feminine root nouns

| | archaic | | innovative | |
	SG	PL	SG	PL
NOM.	*burg*	burg	*burg*	burgi, -a, -e
GEN.	burg	burgo	burges[*]	burgeo, -io
DAT.	burg	burgun, -on	burgi, -a, -e	burgion, -iun, -eon
ACC.	*burg*	burg	*burg*	burgi, -a, -e

[*] The singly attested irregular GEN. SG. burgo (*Heliand* 5407, C) is difficult to account for; it can be interpreted as a spelling error (for burges which is attested in ms. M) or attributed to a "Sproßvokal" u > o (Griepentrog 1995: 100).

The historical paradigm of root nouns was uniform, with little allomorphic variation and most of the categories lacking an inflectional exponent. In contrast to the pattern found in the Ingvaeonic sister languages, traces of i-mutation in the root noun paradigm in Old Saxon are confined to occasional instances of the NOM./ACC. PL. *men* found in *Genesis*, in glosses (GlLam) and in the Straubing manuscript of *Heliand*. The presence of these forms in ms. S is interpreted as yet another reflex of its typological proximity to Ingvaeonic Germanic. Such sporadic presence of i-mutation corresponds to the pattern found in Inland West Germanic dialects (OLF and OHG) and can be explained by the different dating of i-mutation in these dialects (cf. Section 5.6.4.2).

5.6.4.2 *Results of the investigation*

The results of the analysis are demonstrated in Tables 5.20 and 5.21, the former presenting the incidence of archaic and innovative endings in the masculine paradigm, the latter in the feminine paradigm. Table 5.20 includes also the distribution of forms for the noun *mann*, which turned out to be much more frequent than the other masculine nouns.

Table 5.20 Distribution of archaic and innovative inflections in the OS masculine root nouns, including the paradigm of OS *man(n)*

	masc. root nouns				*mann*			
	archaic		innovative		archaic		innovative	
	SG	PL	SG	PL	SG	PL	SG	PL
NOM.	(2)	(0)	–	(0)	(168)	(102) 100%	–	(0)
GEN.	(0)	(1) 100%	(0)	(0)	(0)	(149) 100%	(32) 100%	(0)
DAT.	(0)	(10) 100%	(13) 100%	(0)	(16) 31%	(54) 100%	(35) 69%	(0)
ACC.	(2)	(0) 0%	–	(8) 100%	(45)	(39) 100%	–	(0)
Total	(11) 34%		(21) 66%		(360) 84%		(67) 16%	

Table 5.21 Distribution of archaic and innovative inflections in the OS feminine root nouns

	archaic		innovative	
	SG	PL	SG	PL
NOM.	(45)	(1) 6%	–	(16) 94%
GEN.	(0)	(21) 87%	(16) 100%	(3) 13%
DAT.	(49) 87%	(9) 53%	(7) 13%	(8) 47%
ACC.	(46)	(11) 73%	–	(4) 27%
Total	(91) 63%		(54) 37%	

Despite the limited data, two general qualitative trends can be identified in the analysed material: while the singular consistently shows the *a*-stem pattern, the plural adopts the *i*-stem inflection. The analogical pressure is manifested in the *a*-stem marker in the DAT. SG. and the marker *-i* in the ACC. PL., extended from the *i*-stems (*fuoti*).[251] The attested archaism of the paradigm is based on the forms

---

251. With reference to *fōt*, Griepentrog (1995: 153, 163–164) postulated that the transfer of masculine nouns to the *i*-stem declension was preceded by analogical restructuring of the plural on the pattern of the *u*-stems (DAT. PL.). As the class of *u*-stems was on the decline, the noun followed the more productive *i*-stems (cf. the Go. *u*-stem paradigm of *fōtus*, and the corresponding Old Norse forms where the singular shows *u*-stem inflections). Given the lack of traces of productivity of the *u*-stems at the historical stage, this explanation is arguable.

of the GEN. and DAT. PL., both showing the endings which could be viewed as a continuation of the historical inflection.[252] At the same time, as these inflections are homophonous with the corresponding endings in the *a*-stems, their status is not entirely transparent. It seems conceivable that this homophony had some reinforcing effect and accordingly these two categories were resistant to the *i*-stem inflections (in contrast to the ACC. PL.). The major reason to include them in the counting is that the ACC. PL. attests to the spread of the *i*-stem inflections, and thus these inflections would be expected in the other cases in the plural as well (cf. the feminine paradigm). If these two categories are excluded from the calculations, the masculine paradigm emerges as entirely innovative. Given the limited amount of the available data, these figures should not be interpreted at face value, but rather as an approximation of some more general tendencies present in the paradigms, in this case, indicative of a substantial submission of the paradigm to the productive inflectional patterns.

The distribution of inflections looks entirely different for the most frequently attested masculine noun *mann*, as presented in Table 5.21. The described state of affairs relies primarily on the interpretation of the grammatical forms of *mann* as provided in Tiefenbach (2010) and Sehrt (1966) (for *Heliand* and *Genesis*). The interpretation becomes more problematic when it comes to the glosses, which by nature are more ambiguous with respect to inflectional morphology, and accordingly, a few forms have received various interpretations. According to Gallée (1993: 219), two forms of *mann* attest to a transition to productive declensions in the NOM. PL.: *waldmanna*, showing the influence of the *a*-stems, and *thienestmannon* 'servants' (RegFrek), with the ending *-on* extended from the *n*-stems (also Boutkan 1995: 295). The former was found neither in Tiefenbach (2010), nor Wadstein (1899) and considered "nicht auffindbar" by Köbler (2014a); the latter, following Tiefenbach and Köbler, was interpreted as a DAT. PL. in the present study. Likewise, the forms *offerman* 'sexton' and *wichman* 'warrior', viewed as an archaic DAT. SG. in Gallée (1993: 219), are counted as NOM. SG. forms after Tiefenbach (2010) (the third DAT. SG. form, *spiloman*, was not found in the corpus).

The paradigm of *mann* turns out to be remarkably conservative, with entirely divergent patterns attested for the singular and plural, the former testifying to the presence of analogical *a*-stem inflections, the latter remaining consistently archaic. Such a pattern of attestation is found more commonly also in the other classes and in the other investigated languages, and seems to be linked to the relative frequency

---

252. The GEN. PL. *fuoti*, attested singly in ms. C, corresponding to a regular *fōto* in ms. M, is most likely a spelling error. It could be alternatively interpreted as an ACC. PL. form, although the evidence of ms. M speaks clearly against such an interpretation (Tiefenbach 2010, s.v. *fōt*; cf. Boutkan 1995: 262).

of forms in the relevant morphosyntactic categories (frequent NOM./ACC.PL. and less frequent GEN./DAT. SG.) (cf. the discussion in Chapter 8). The only category which testifies to a synchronic alternation in the paradigm is the DAT. SG., where the endingless forms compete with the analogical endings -*e* and -*a*. The paradigm of *mann* remains conservative even if the questionable categories of GEN. and DAT. PL. are excluded from the counting, with the amount of archaism reaching 70 percent. As will become evident in the later part of the study, the frequency of occurrence with its conserving effect can be considered the major factor that determined the shape of the paradigm of *mann* (and other root nouns as a matter of fact).

The plural paradigm was not characterised by *i*-mutation and mutated forms were in general rare in Old Saxon, yet some occasional instances of the NOM./ACC. PL. *men* were found in *Genesis* (*n* = 3), in glosses (*ashmen*, GlLam, *n* = 1) and in the Straubing manuscript (*n* = 9). Aside from testifying to the Ingvaeonic character of Old Saxon, they also have a special relevance for the interpretation of morphological *i*-mutation in West Germanic. As noted already, for instance, in Bucinni (1995: 32, 40; 2003) and Krygier (1997), the process of morphologisation of *i*-mutation had a different scope and different chronology in North Sea Germanic (OE, OFris.) and Inland Germanic (OLF, OHG) languages. The discrepancy entails in particular the different chronology of the operation of *i*-mutation and the apocope of PGmc. /i/. While the process of *i*-mutation generally preceded the reductions of final high vowels in North Sea Germanic, in Continental (Inland) Germanic both primary and secondary umlaut followed the developments in final syllables. The irregular mutated form *menn* found especially in the Straubing fragment attests to primary *i*-mutation, while the other forms found in the same text indicate that secondary *i*-mutation had not been implemented (perhaps except for /a:/ which shows a somewhat mixed pattern) (Klein 1990: 205, 207). The presence of the mutated plural forms implies that in the more North Sea Germanic-oriented part of Old Saxon the order of primary mutation and the reduction of final high vowels was inverted. In other words, at the time of a complete application of *i*-mutation in North Sea Germanic, at least primary *i*-mutation must already have reached parts of the Old Saxon linguistic territory, prior to the apocope of the short word-final /i/.[253]

The feminine paradigm shows more synchronic variation, both in the singular and the plural. On the lemma level, the alternation between archaic and innovative inflections can be identified in *bōc* 'book', *burg* 'town', and *naht* 'night'. In line with the tendencies observed in the paradigm of masculine root nouns, the feminine nouns testify to a bidirectional restructuring of the inherited paradigm, which is

---

253. Cf. the later *i*-mutated forms *men* and *menne* attested in Middle Low German in the Eastphalian dialect (Lasch 1974: 202).

evident both in the singular and the plural. Accordingly, traces of the influence of *i*-stems and *ō*-stems are attested in the DAT. SG. where alongside *burgi* and *idisi*, the forms *nahta*, *aho* (*-u*), *alaha*, *-e* are found.[254] The presence of the masculine inflections in the DAT. SG. can be attributed to the intraparadigmatic pressure of the GEN. SG., where the masculine *a*-stems consistently serve as a template for analogical restructuring (*burges*, *nahtas*, *milukas*) (cf. Griepentrog 1995: 478). The masculine endings present in the paradigm could potentially indicate a change in gender affiliation; however, they can also be ascribed to some contextual conditioning, which becomes more evident in the analysis on the lemma-level. The spread of *-as* in *naht* was a common tendency in other Germanic languages as well, especially when the noun appeared in phrases with *dag* 'day'. Likewise, *miluk* attested in the GEN. SG. with a masculine ending *-as* (GlPrudF1, 96,34) has been explained as analogical to the neighbouring form in *-as* (*bluodas*) (Griepentrog 1995: 295). However, out of nine instances of *nahtes* attested in the corpus, five occur without the accompanying *dages*, which proves that the original contextual/semantic conditioning must have been lost at some point, and that the form *nahtes* emerged as the default shape of the GEN. SG. in this lemma.

The paradigm of the plural shows an evident preference for the inflections of the *i*-stems (NOM./ACC.PL. *burgi*, *koii*, *buoki*), although single forms such as *idisa* or *nohte* indicate the influence of the *ō*-stems. The archaic inflections are attested primarily in *Heliand*, where additional contrasts occasionally emerge in individual manuscripts. Accordingly, while *bōk* follows the novel pattern in ms. C (*buoki*), it remains archaic in ms. S, fitting into the general profiles of the two manuscripts, with the Straubing text showing a more Ingvaeonic and conservative character (9th c.) than the more franconised ms. C. Likewise, the NOM. PL. form of *idis* 'maid' is attested as *idisa* in ms. M, but as *idisi* in ms. C, pointing to the influence of the *ō*-stem inflection in the older ms. M (in line with the OE/OFris. pattern) and the pressure of the *i*-stems in the younger ms. C (in line with the OHG/OLF pattern). The discrepancy between the NOM. and ACC. PL. is not meaningful as most of the instances are attested in glosses where precise identification of case is problematic (this refers in particular to the paradigm of *kō* 'cow' where the interpretation of forms varies depending on the dictionary/glossary, cf. Wadstein 1899, Tiefenbach 2010, Köbler 2014a, Griepentrog 1995). Significantly, the contrast between inherited and novel inflections can be identified in the GEN. and DAT. PL. in feminine root nouns. The latter, i.e. *-io*, *-eo*, *-ion*, *-iun*, originated most likely in the *i*-stems or *jō*-stems. Irrespective of their exact origin, these forms are clearly analogical and are counted as such in the present study. Their status as analogical inflections is much

---

254. The form *ala* (Gen), attested alongside *alaha*, *alahe* (H), testifies to a simplification of the root structure.

more transparent than in the masculine nouns, as the rest of the plural paradigm (and in fact largely the singular) shows the *i*-stem inflections. The singly attested DAT. PL. form *musin*, found in glosses (GlPrudBr II, 574,12), points unambiguously to the spread of the *i*-stem pattern. Overall, the level of innovation in the GEN. and DAT. PL. corresponds to the general tendencies identified in the paradigm.

A prominent feature of the attested distribution is the high level of innovation in the root nouns in general, and in particular, the higher amount of innovation in the NOM./ACC. PL. than in the GEN. and DAT. PL. Both seem to be an irregularity given the overall trends in the restructuring of the Old Northern West Germanic paradigms. A potential explanation for such a distribution may come from the frequency profiles of individual lemmas and the assumption that the apocope of final vowels was largely a frequency-dependent process, affecting first high frequency lemmas. Accordingly, the presence of -*i* in low frequency lemmas (e.g. *burgi*) can be considered a retention of the original inflection (< PGmc. *-iz*), which was not affected by apocope. In other words, the distribution of the -*i* endings in the NOM./ACC.PL. of root nouns may be viewed as a result of a partly implemented *i*-apocope, controlled by frequency, rather than as an analogical extension of the *i*-stem inflection. Such a scenario in which the -*i* endings are a continuation of the original PGmc. forms, could account for the high level of "innovation" in the Old Saxon root nouns when compared to the sister languages.

The distribution of inherited and analogical inflections in the root nouns, irrespective of case and gender, is presented in Table 5.22 (excluding the forms of *mann*). For reasons of consistency (with the results from the other classes), the figures do not include the attestations to the GEN. and DAT. PL.

Table 5.22 Overall distribution of archaic and innovative inflections in the OS root nouns

	archaic	innovative
singular	(49) 58%	(36) 42%
plural	(53) 58%	(39) 42%
Total	(102) 58%	(75) 42%

The data presented above indicate that the Old Saxon root nouns were fairly innovative. The bias towards the novel inflectional patterns is evenly distributed with respect to number. It must be noted, however, that the conservatism of the singular is built exclusively on the feminine paradigm, in particular, on the endingless forms of the DAT. SG.

A minor sub-pattern can be identified in the distribution of forms in individual manuscripts of *Heliand*, which, however, is not entirely consistent. A number of historical consonantal forms identified in mss. M or S (especially in the DAT. SG. and NOM. PL.) correspond to innovative forms in ms. C, extended from the *i*-stems, e.g.

burg (M) vs. *burgi*; *bōk* (S) vs. *buoki* (cf. Griepentrog 1995: 99–100). Such a distribution reflects the different age of the manuscripts, and additionally the dominance of the *i*-stem inflection in ms. C points to its affinity with the patterns found in the High German dialects (cf. also NOM. PL. *idisa* (M) vs. *idisi* (C)). The correlation does not seem to hold for the frequently attested noun *mann*, where the distribution of forms across manuscripts testifies to little systematicity (except for the presence of *i*-mutation, which is found in the sources of a more Ingvaeonic character).

5.6.5 *r*-stems

5.6.5.1 *General characteristics*
As in the sister languages, the Old Saxon *r*-stems, denoting kinship terms, constituted a closed class of nouns, with the following inventory of feminine and masculine nouns: *fadar* 'father', *brōthar* 'brother', *gibrōthar* 'siblings', *mōdar* 'mother', *dohtar* 'daughter', *swestar*[255] 'sister', *giswestar* 'sisters', most of which appeared also in compound formations, such as *godfadar* 'godfather', *spunnibrōthar*[256] 'foster-brother', *stefmōdar* 'stepmother', *uōstmōdar* 'fostermother', *steefdohtar* 'stepdaughter'.[257] The historical paradigm of the *r*-stems is characterised by a substantial inflectional homogeneity, both in the singular and the plural, with all categories (except the GEN. and DAT. PL.) lacking an inflectional exponent and showing no root vowel alternation (Gallée 1993: 217–218; Cordes 1973: 91).

The restructuring of the *r*-stems involved potentially, as in the other minor classes, an interaction with the *a*-stem, *ō*-stem and *i*-stem patterns. The effects of analogical pressures can be reflected in the extension of the following inflectional endings, all replacing the historical endingless forms:

255. A derivative formation built on *swester* – **gisustruhoni* 'siblings' (**gisustrithi, gisustrōni*; Holthausen 1967: 72) – is attested as a DAT. PL. *gisustruonion*, H ms. C 1264; according to Gallée (1993: 218), it is a DAT. PL form of *giswester*, equivalent to *suuestron*, attested in the same line in ms. M (1264). The form is classified as a neuter *ja*-stem by Tiefenbach (2010, s.v. *gisustruhoni*). The forms are not semantically equivalent, since *geswister* refers to siblings of any gender. As the text fragment refers exclusively to males, the form *suuestron* in ms. M does not seem to be semantically adequate in this context, but given that it formally represents the word 'sister', it was included in the counting here as an attestation to *swestar*. In contrast, the form *gisustruonion* was not included in the analysis (cf. Versloot & Adamczyk 2013: 432–433).

256. The compound *spunnibrōther*, related to OHG *spunnibruoder*, which can alternatively be interpreted as belonging to the Old High German lexical stock, was included in the analysis. It is attested once in the corpus as a NOM. SG. (Gl MarfIII); Tiefenbach 2010, s.v. *spunnibrōther*, cf. Holthausen 1967: 70; Köbler 2014a: 1039).

257. The forms in -*or* attested in ms. C of *Heliand* and in *Genesis* (*brothor, muodor*) have been attributed to the influence of Old English forms (cf. OE *brōþor, mōdor*) (Holthausen 1921: 45; Boutkan 1995: 273–274).

a. masculine *r*-stems
  - the GEN. SG. marker *-as*
  - the DAT. SG. endings *-a, -e*
  - the NOM./ACC. PL. endings *-os, -a*
b. feminine *r*-stems
  - the markers *-a, -e* in the GEN. and DAT. SG.
  - the endings *-a, -e* in the NOM./ACC. PL. extended from the ō-stems, and the marker *-i* extended from the *i*-stems.

In view of the later historical development of the Low German nominal system, where the *n*-stem inflection was widespread, the influence of the weak inflections could be expected in both paradigms (especially in the plural). Additionally, the feminine paradigm can be expected to show some masculine (*a*-stem) inflections. The potential inflectional irregularities resulting from the analogical pressure in the paradigms of the *r*-stems are presented in Table 5.23 (for masculine stems).

Table 5.23 The competing inflections in the OS masculine *r*-stems

| | archaic | | innovative | |
	SG	PL	SG	PL
NOM.	*brōther*	brōther	*brōther*	brōthera,-os
GEN.	brōther	*brōthero*	brōtheres, -as	*brōthero*
DAT.	brōther	*brōtherun, -on*	brōthere	*brōtherun*
ACC.	*brōther*	brōther	*brōther*	brōthera, -os

5.6.5.2 *Results of the investigation*

Although the standard historical grammars of Old Saxon do not mention any un-historical inflections in the *r*-stem paradigm, the class was subjected to a quantitative analysis and the findings are presented in Table 5.24 below.[258] Even if the *r*-stem paradigms show no traces of analogical inflections, the inclusion of the figures from the quantitative investigation was essential for estimating the overall level of archaism/innovativeness of the Old Saxon nominal inflection. As no distinction in the patterns of attestation between the masculine and feminine stems was detected, the figures for both paradigms are presented jointly in one table.

---

258. The form *fadera patris*, attested in Psalm 67,6, is difficult to interpret. According to Heyne (1873: 80), it can be ascribed to a scribal error, and, therefore, it cannot be concluded whether it stands for the innovative GEN. SG. *faderis* or *faderin*, both induced by the influence of productive (respectively) vocalic or consonantal declensions.

Table 5.24 Distribution of archaic and innovative inflections in the OS *r*-stems

	archaic		innovative	
	SG	PL	SG	PL
NOM.	(*49*)	(9) 100%		
GEN.	(12) 100%	–	*not attested*	*not attested*
DAT.	(21) 100%	(*2*)		
ACC.	(*27*)	(7) 100%		
Total	(49) 100%		–	

No traces of analogical inflections were found in the examined material. Although the lack of inflectional diversification in the historical paradigm of *r*-stems might be viewed as a factor rendering it conducive to external analogical pressures, the class turned out to have been entirely resistant to the influence of other declensional types. The high level of archaism does not comply with the patterns found in this class in the other investigated languages, where the presence of analogical inflections was fairly widespread. The limited amount of data does not allow one to draw conclusions about the correlation between the level of archaism and frequency of occurrence, as it was the case in Old English and Old Frisian, where relative frequency (plural proportion) turned out to have had a significant influence on the restructuring of the *r*-stem paradigm.

A significant feature of the distribution, given the patterns found in the sister languages, is the lack of analogical forms in the plural paradigm of *fader* (*gisunfader* = 1). As in all the other examined languages, *fader* tended to be more innovative than the other *r*-stems, it could be expected that if any analogical forms were to emerge in this class, the paradigm of *fader* would be the first to show such traces. The absence of analogical inflections in this paradigm, especially in the plural, corroborates the premise that the Old Saxon inflectional system was characterised by a greater level of archaism than the systems of the sister languages.

Some insight into the inflectional development of the *r*-stems can be gained by taking recourse to the Middle Low German *r*-stem paradigm. The available material indicates that the class long remained resistant to the analogical pressure of the productive inflections, retaining the endingless GEN. SG. form (alongside the novel -*s* formations) and the endingless plural forms well into the fourteenth century (especially *brōder, vader*). It is only in the later material that the *r*-stems show innovative vocalic and *n*-stem inflections in the plural, as in: *vedere, süstere, vadern, süstern*, etc. (Lasch 1974: 203).

5.6.6 *s*-stems

5.6.6.1 *General characteristics*

The *s*-stems are preserved vestigially and are attested in the younger texts only (except *kind*), i.e. the minor Old Saxon monuments, especially in glosses. The scant remnants of this declensional type can hardly be viewed in terms of a fully-fledged paradigm; in fact, the standard historical handbooks on Old Saxon present no complete paradigm for this declensional type, concentrating primarily on the directions of transfers of these stems to other declensional classes (Heyne 1873: 71; Holthausen 1921: 112–113; Gallée 1993: 57). An exception is the treatment in Boutkan (1995: 264), who reconstructs the paradigm of *s*-stems on the basis of the scant attestations, providing the following set of forms: NOM./ACC. SG. *ehir*, NOM./ACC. PL. *huaner*, GEN. PL. *hōnero/ei(i)ero*.[259] Using these forms as the point of departure and relying on the shape of the paradigms attested in the other West Germanic languages, the competing archaic and innovative paradigms could tentatively be reconstructed. Accordingly, most of the forms denoted as archaic in Table 5.25 are not attested, but as far as possible, they are "reconstructed" on the basis of the existing forms of other lemmas affiliated with the *s*-stem declension. For instance, the attested form *eiero* is the basis for reconstructing forms with the *r*-formative in the other cases in the plural. The forms marked with an asterisk are genuine reconstructions in the sense that none of them is found in the available corpus in any noun.

Table 5.25 The competing inflections in the OS *s*-stems

	archaic		innovative	
	SG	PL	SG	PL
NOM.	ei	eiiru	ei	ei, eios
GEN.	*eiir	eiero	eies, -as	eio
DAT.	*eiir	eirun, -on	eie, -a	eiun, -on
ACC.	ei	eiiru	ei	ei, eios

As the class comprised neuter nouns only, the major destination paradigm for analogical shifts was that of the neuter *a*-stems and possibly, less frequently, of the masculine *a*-stems. Given the evidence from other West Germanic languages, the process of remodelling of the *s*-stems and the transition to other declensional

---

259. The NOM. PL. form *huaner*, treated as Old Saxon also by Gallée (1993: 200), is attested in a glossary from the abbey of St. Peter, which is largely Old High German (GlSpet). The form is classified as High German in Tiefenbach (2010) and this interpretation is adhered to here (and the form thus excluded).

classes must be dated earlier than the first attestations of Old Saxon. These early, prehistoric transfers to other classes entailed shifts following two major pathways: most of the original *s*-stems transferred to the neuter *a*-stems, others, with a change of gender, followed the pattern of the masculine *i*-stems. In more detail, these early analogical realignments included transitions to (Unwerth 1910: 1–5; Casaretto 2000: 215ff.):

a.   the neuter *a*-stems (e.g. *dal* 'dale', *brōd* 'bread', *flēsk* 'flesh', *hēl* 'health', *lēhan* 'feud', *sper* 'spear')
b.   the neuter *wa*-stems (e.g. *hlēu* 'grave', *hrē(u)* 'body')
c.   the masculine *a*-stems (e.g. *gēst* 'ghost')
d.   the masculine *i*-stems (e.g. *heti* 'hatred', *seli* 'hall', *sigi-(drohtin)* 'victory').

As many of these nouns are affiliated with the productive declensions also in the other investigated languages, it can be assumed that these interdeclensional transitions took place earlier than at the pre-Old Saxon stage, possibly in common-West Germanic or Common Germanic.

5.6.6.2 *Results of the investigation*

Despite the limitations resulting from scant attestations, the incidence of inherited and analogical forms in the residual paradigms was examined. Given the comparative nature of the present study, the inventory of nouns subjected to the investigation comprised nouns whose identity as 'active' *s*-stems (i.e. testifying to a synchronic alternation) is confirmed by the attestations from the other West Germanic languages. Because of the scant documentation of the *s*-stems, their relevance for the quantitative investigation may seem limited; however, including the information on the distribution of archaic/innovative features was essential in the context of examining the overall scope of the inflectional restructuring in Old Saxon. The following nouns were included in the quantitative study (most of which are not attested in their basic forms): **kalf* 'calf', **ei* 'egg', *ehir* (< *ēr*) 'ear (of corn)', *hōn* 'hen' (*berk-* 'quail', *feld-*, *watar-*, *reba-*),[260] **hrīth* 'cattle', **hrīs* 'twig', *kind* 'child', *lamb* 'lamb'. Owing to a lack of etymological transparency of *kind*, the attestations to this noun were counted separately. The results of the analysis, excluding the attestations to *kind*, are presented in Table 5.26.

Both the scarcity of the data as well as the consequent fragmentary picture which emerges from the analysis, allows one to draw only tentative conclusions about the transformation of this declensional class. When taking the results at

---

260. Most of these compound formations (including also *erdhōn* 'partridge', *hasalhōn* 'hazel hen') turned out to be attested in the Old High German material and were thus not included in the calculations.

Table 5.26 Distribution of archaic and innovative inflections in the OS *s*-stems

	archaic		innovative	
	SG	PL	SG	PL
NOM.	(*10*)	–	–	–
GEN.	–	(14) 100%	(1) 100%	(0)
DAT.	–	–	(4) 100%	–
ACC.	(*1*)	(1) 50%	–	(1) 50%
Total		(15) 71%		(6) 29%

face value, it can be inferred that the *s*-stems display a pattern similar to the other minor classes, in that the historical inflections are better preserved in the plural than in the singular, which is entirely innovative. The only noun where synchronic alternation could be found is **ei* 'egg', retaining the *r*-formative in the GEN. PL. and showing an analogical form in the DAT. SG. The archaic plural forms include: GEN. PL. *ei(e)ro* 'eggs', GEN. PL. *hōnero* 'hens', ACC. PL. *kaluiru* 'calves'.[261] The form *hrītherīnon* 'cattle', found in Prudentius Glosses (10th c.) and considered an archaic DAT. PL. by Gallée (1993), was not included, as it most likely represents an adjectival formation (Cordes 1973: 90–91; Tiefenbach 2010). The forms *hrithas* (GEN. SG.), *rise* (DAT. SG.) and *lamb* (ACC. PL.), all singly attested, show analogical inflections of the neuter *a*-stems. Another singly attested form, the NOM. SG. *ehir* (< *ēr*) 'ear (of corn)', attests to analogical intraparadigmatic levelling from the oblique cases (cf. Boutkan 1995: 267), as was the case in Old English. Given the relatively archaic profile of this class in Old English, it can be assumed that also in Old Saxon the -*ir*- formative was originally present in the GEN. and DAT. SG., whence it could spread to the NOM. and ACC. SG. (although no such form is found in the corpus) (cf. Section 3.5.6).

Significantly, the archaisms such as the GEN. PL. *ei(e)ro* and *hōnero* are found in the glosses, dated to the later stage of Old Saxon, i.e. the tenth/eleventh century. The explanation for the attested textual distribution involves stylistics, and more specifically, the fact that these words belong to the vocabulary that would not be expected in the more elevated register of poetic texts (cf. Tiefenbach 2000: 1253). With reference to the vocabulary attested in the minor Old Saxon texts, Sanders (2000a: 1259) concludes: "Die kleineren Texte, die sich im großen und ganzen der Normalsprache zuordenen erhalten dadurch ihren besonderen Wert, daß sie trotz ihres vergleichsweise geringen Umfangs zahlreiche in der Dichtung nicht vorkommende Wörter überliefern." (cf. Sanders 1983: 61). This statement is especially

---

261. According to Klein (2013: 177), it can be assumed that the form *kaluiru* belongs to the Old High German part of the text (Lublin/Wittenberg Psalter) and is built on the pattern of OHG *kelbir*. It is considered here Old Saxon after Tiefenbach (2010).

relevant for the interpretation of the developments in the vestigial *s*-stems for which these minor documents turn out to be the only source of information. The evidence from the other Germanic languages, in particular Old English, provides rather reliable information as to the semantic constitution of this class, which comprised agrarian vocabulary (notably nouns denoting animals; cf. *Hühnerhof* group; Kürschner 2008; Dammel et al. 2010). Therefore, it should come as little surprise that the *s*-stems were preserved in the minor Old Saxon documents rather than in the poetic texts that are characterised by vocabulary belonging to a more elevated register. Altogether, the scarcity of the forms hardly allows for conclusive statements about the changes in this declensional class in Old Saxon.

As regards the paradigm of *kind*, it is attested in the GEN. and DAT. SG. and in all cases in the plural except the DAT.: in total there are 16 attestations. All the attested forms are analogical and in light of the obscure etymology of this noun, it can be concluded that there is no positive evidence that it was ever affiliated with the *s*-stems in Old Saxon. The later Middle Low German evidence indicates that the plural forms in -*r* were not attested before the thirteenth century (Lasch 1974: 198). If the attestations of *kind* are included in the counting, the overall innovation level in the *s*-stem paradigm increases to 59 percent (15:22). In contrast to Old English, where *cild* could be considered an *s*-stem at least from a synchronic perspective, there is little justification for treating *kind* as one of the *s*-stems in Old Saxon.

Given that compound formations or derivations are characterised by greater archaism, several such conservative forms are attested in the Old Saxon material. The original inflectional element is retained in an adjectival formation based on *ehir* (< *ēr*) 'ear (of corn)': *a(h)arin* (< **ahar*) 'spiceus', as well as in *hūnrepenninge* (Prepos.) (Gallée 1903: 146; cf. Tiefenbach 2010, s.v. *hōnpenning*, where *hunpenninga* appears without the -*r*- element, UrbWerdF). Another form which testifies to the presence of the *r*-formative is *rother-stidi* 'cattle pasture' (Lat. *saltus*) (GlLam 67,15), whose interpretation is fairly problematic (cf. Tiefenbach (2010) where it is glossed as a 'grubbed woodland' rather than 'cattle pasture', related to *roth* 'clearing'). At the same time, place names such as *Calbesloge, Caluaslogi*, both recorded in *Werdener Heberegister*, point to a lack of the *s*-stem inflection, which may imply that the *r*-formative was lost at an early stage.

In contrast to Old High German where the *r*-formative became with time a widespread plurality exponent, the plural marker of *s*-stems in Old Saxon shows hardly any traces of expansion to other stems. The only form which may be interpreted as testifying to some productivity of the pattern is *hūser* (Werdener Heberegister, 10th c.) (Gallée 1993: 200). The fact that the -*er* ending is found in *hūs* in relatively late records supports the assumption that it may have been to some extent productive as a plurality marker, disseminating to nouns whose *s*-stem origin cannot be confirmed. Alternatively, the form may be attributed to Old High

German influence, where the number of *r*-plurals tended to increase and the suffix became gradually a productive plural formation pattern. The lack of compelling evidence for a wide expansion of the *r*-formative as a plurality marker in Old Saxon complies with the pattern found in the Middle Low German material, which testifies only to a limited spread of this inflectional marker. Apart from *kint* and *clet* 'cloth', where the *r*-plural has been attested since the thirteenth century, forms such as *dörpere* 'villlages', *hūsere* 'houses', *boker* 'books', *lendere* 'lands', and *graver* 'graves' attest to a much later extension of this marker. Many of these nouns, including those originally affiliated with the *s*-stems, show double plural marking in Middle Low German, with the *r*-formative attested alongside the mutated vowels, e.g. *hønere* 'hens', *lemmere* 'lambs', *kelvere* 'calves', *lendere* 'lands' (Lasch 1974: 198).

5.6.7 *nd*-stems

5.6.7.1 *General characteristics*
The class of *nd*-stems is relatively well attested in Old Saxon, with 19 lexemes identified as belonging to this declension in the investigated material (including compound formations, see Appendix; cf. Prokosch 1939: 259).[262] Despite the fact that their token frequencies are not too high, *nd*-stems provide valuable information about inflectional restructuring, evincing considerable variation in the paradigm. As the *nd*-stem declension comprised only masculine nouns, the morphphological reanalysis involved the reshaping of the inherited inflection on the pattern of the masculine *a*- and *ja*-stems, and potentially the *i*-stems. Apart from analogical inflections of the productive declensions, the *nd*-stem paradigm testifies also to the adjectival inflection in the GEN. PL. (-*ero*, e.g. in *hettendero*, *hēlendero*), which is a prominent trait of this declensional type across (West) Germanic, reflecting its origin in participle formations.[263] It is at the same time a feature that distinguishes

---

262. The number of attested *nd*-stems in Continental West Germanic is very low when compared to the Old English attestations. This scarcity of *nd*-formations can be ascribed to a lack of productivity of the *nd*-suffix in these languages at the prehistoric stage. Problematic in such an interpretation are the nouns denoting deity, which must have been relatively new given their semantics, and accordingly it is difficult to view them as inherited from some earlier stage of Germanic (e.g. OHG *heilant*, *neriand*, *scepfant*). An alternative interpretation could be to view these words as loan translations from Old English, disseminated on the Continent through the missionary activity of the Anglo-Saxon monks (Kärre 1915: 216).

263. According to Holthausen (1921), the adjectival influence can also be sought in the sporadic NOM./ACC. PL. ending -*a* (e.g. *friunda*, *fianda*) (Holthausen 1921: 110). In the present investigation, this novel ending is interpreted as originating in the masculine *a*-stems, which seems more likely given that the alternative new marker -*os* is also found in this category.

the monosyllabic nouns of the type *friund* 'friend', *fiond* 'fiend' from the dissyllabic formations (*hettiand* 'enemy', *waldand* 'ruler'), where the adjectival ending is the default marker in the GEN. PL. On account of the inflectional differences between paradigms of monosyllabic and disyllabic stems, and in particular the fact that the information about analogical realignments is provided by different categories in the two subgroups, the two types were examined separately. Much as the category of the NOM./ACC. SG. can be informative about analogical changes in the disyllabic nouns, where the historical endingless form competes with the novel adjectival inflection (e.g. *heliand ~ helandi ~ heleando* 'saviour'), it does not provide any information about the inflectional restructuring in monosyllabic *friund* or *fiond*. The influence of the productive declensions, potentially detectable in both monosyllabic and disyllabic nouns, is reflected in the following inflectional irregularities:

–   the GEN. SG. *-as/-es* ending in place of the historical zero ending
–   the DAT. SG. *a*-stem marker *-e* (*-a*) and the *i*-stem ending *-i* in place of the historical zero ending
–   the NOM./ACC. PL. markers *-os* and *-a* instead of the historical endingless forms

Additionally, the following alternations can be expected in the paradigms of disyllabic *nd*-stems:

–   the NOM./ACC. SG. adjectival ending *-i* or *-o* in place of the historical endingless form
–   the adjectival marker *-ero* in the GEN. PL. in place of the historical *-o*
–   the DAT. PL. ending *-iun* in place of the historical *-un*.

These potential influences are summarised in Tables 5.27 and 5.28, the former presenting the competing inherited and analogical inflections in monosyllabic nouns, the latter in disyllabic nouns.

Table 5.27 The competing inflections in the OS *nd*-stems (mon.)

	archaic		innovative	
	SG	PL	SG	PL
NOM.	*fiond*	fiond	*fiond*	fiond**os**
GEN.	fiond	*fiondo*	fiond**es**, -**as**	*fiondo*
DAT.	fiond	*fiondun*, -*on*	fiond**e**, -**a**	*fiondun*, -*on*
ACC.	*fiond*	fiond	*fiond*	fiond**os**

Table 5.28 The competing inflections in the *nd*-stems (dis.)

	archaic		innovative	
	SG	**PL**	**SG**	**PL**
NOM.	heliand	heliand	heliand**o**,-**i**	heliand**os**, -**ia**
GEN.	heliand	heliand**o**	heliand**es**, -**as**	heliand**ero**
DAT.	heliand	heliand**un**, -**on**	heliand**e**, -**i**, -**a**	heliand**iun**
ACC.	heliand	heliand	heliand**o**, -**i**	heliand**os**, -**ia**

As can be seen, both historical paradigms are very uniform, showing no root vowel alternation and hardly any contrast between the singular and the plural. Most importantly, no contrast existed originally between the NOM. SG. and PL. which, given the fact that the retention of this functional opposition is one of the forces largely determining the dynamics of changes in the paradigm, must have rendered the latter more susceptible to analogical pressures. The analogical endings in the NOM. SG. *-o, -i* as well as the GEN. PL. *-ero* can be ascribed to the influence of the adjectival inflection. Alternatively, they have been interpreted as resulting from the pressure of the *r*-stems (Boutkan 1995: 368).[264] The presence of the adjectival inflection can be explained by the very nature of these stems, i.e. their historical relatedness to present participles which inflected like adjectives. The shape of the *nd*-stems, with the participial *-nd-* element fossilised therein, may have rendered them vulnerable to the pattern of regular participles inflecting like adjectives.

Another inflectional feature of *nd*-stems is the presence of synchronic alternation in the NOM. SG. in disyllabic stems. The archaic NOM. SG. endingless forms are attested alongside analogical formations in *-eo*, *-io* and *-i* (*helandi, heleando, uualdandeo, uualdandio*) in *Heliand*. While the endings *-eo*, and *-io* can be attributed to adjectival declension, the marker *-i* could potentially be interpreted as a *ja*-stem feature (cf. heavy-syllable *hirdi, kunni*). Given, however, the general bias of the paradigm towards the adjectival inflection, it seems more probable that the marker *-i* has the adjectival origin as well. Irrespective of their exact source, the forms in *-i* are clearly analogical and hence counted on the innovative side.

---

264. The forms of the GEN. PL. **fadero* or **mōdero* are not attested in the corpus, which does not necessarily exclude the *r*-stem influence. However, given that the same pattern is attested in Old English, where the adjectival character of this ending can be better confirmed, it is more likely that the ending originates in the adjectival inflection (cf. Boutkan 1995: 368 who ascribes also the GEN. PL. ending *-era* in Old English to the pressure from the *r*-stems). The assumption of the *r*-stem origin of the ending *-ero* is particularly problematic as the *r*-stems were an entirely unproductive and closed class, with no traces of expansiveness found in any other stem type.

The forms of the GEN. PL. are taken into consideration only in the investigation of the disyllabic nouns, as they show an alternation between the earlier historical forms and the new adjectival ones (-o vs. -ero). The forms of the DAT. PL. in these stems were also included in the calculations, with the ending -iun ascribed to the influence of the ja-stems. As the original ending -un in the DAT. PL. is, in fact, an early analogical formation (cf. Table 2.16), the alternation reflects a competition between two non-original forms, one extended at an early prehistoric stage, the other in the historical period. They were considered relevant for assessing the innovation level in the disyllabic paradigm, but were excluded from the counting of the overall distribution of inflections in the nd-stem paradigm (Table 5.32).

5.6.7.2 Results of the investigation

Tables 5.29 and 5.30 demonstrate the results of the quantitative investigation of the monosyllabic and disyllabic nd-stems, respectively. A complete list of nouns subjected to the analysis is presented in the Appendix. It was essential for the examination of the data to establish the substantival character of the nd-formations, i.e. to distinguish the nominal forms, relevant for the present analysis, from the adjectival or verbal ones (which in fact turned out to be less problematic than in the case of Old English that abounds in such novel formations; cf. Appendix).

Table 5.29 Distribution of archaic and innovative inflections in the OS monosyllabic nd-stems

	archaic		innovative	
	SG	PL	SG	PL
NOM.	(15)	(8) 100%	–	(0)
GEN.	(0)	(24)	(2) 100%	–
DAT.	(1) 20%	(15)	(4) 80%	–
ACC.	(3)	(11) 79%	–	(3) 21%
Total	(20) 69%		(9) 31%	

Table 5.30 Distribution of archaic and innovative inflections in the OS disyllabic nd-stems

	archaic		innovative	
	SG	PL	SG	PL
NOM.	(121) 88%	(3) 37%	(16) 12%	(5) 63%
GEN.	(0) 0%	(0) 0%	(54) 100%	(15) 100%
DAT.	(3) 18%	(4) 67%	(14) 82%	(2) 33%
ACC.	(38) 97%	(2) 67%	(1) 3%	(1) 33%
Total	(171) 61%		(108) 39%	

The level of innovation in the two types of stems is comparable and the major tendencies are parallel. The main difference between them lies in the directions of transition and the presence of adjectival inflection in the disyllabic stems. In both subclasses the singular is more innovative, with the GEN. and DAT. SG. showing an almost identical distribution in mono- and disyllabic stems. The incidence of analogical forms in the NOM./ACC. SG. is limited. It may be related to the fact that the NOM. SG. is largely dominated by the forms of one noun, *uualdand* 'ruler', and accordingly, the high percentage of archaism in the NOM. SG. can be ascribed to the conserving effect of frequency in this category. The reluctance to adopt analogical inflections is particularly evident in the plural paradigm of monosyllabic nouns, where the majority of forms are endingless. In contrast, the disyllabic nouns turn out to be more susceptible to analogical pressures, especially of the adjectival inflection.

As the examination of the two types of stems required taking into account different categories, the overall incidence of the inherited and innovative inflections presented in Table 5.31 comprises only those categories which were relevant and unambiguous for both subclasses, namely the GEN. and DAT. SG. and NOM./ACC. PL. The assessment of the overall level of innovation in the *nd*-stems was made also on the basis of these four categories only, and the results are presented in Table 5.32.

Table 5.31 Overall distribution of archaic and innovative inflections in the OS *nd*-stems

	archaic	innovative
GEN. SG.	(0)	(56) 100%
DAT. SG.	(4) 18%	(18) 82%
NOM. PL.	(11) 69%	(5) 31%
ACC. PL.	(13) 76%	(4) 24%

Table 5.32 Overall distribution of archaic and innovative inflections in the OS *nd*-stems

	archaic	innovative
singular	(4) 5%	(74) 95%
plural	(24) 73%	(9) 27%
Total	(28) 25%	(83) 75%

The figures indicate that the inherited paradigm was largely modified under the analogical pressure of the productive inflections. The distribution of forms with respect to number complies with the trends present also in the other classes, with the singular being very innovative and the plural retaining to a large extent the historical inflection. The factor that could account for the attested pattern is the frequency of individual morphosyntactic categories: the less frequently used GEN.

and DAT. SG. should be more prone to external influences than the more common NOM./ACC. (SG. and PL.) (see Section 8.6.1). This correlation has been found in the Old English and Old Frisian data, and is not surprising given that the *nd*-stems were nouns denoting people, and thus functioned in the sentence mostly as agents. However, this correlation does not find exact confirmation in the number of attested tokens for individual categories; given the scant attestations of Old Saxon, this can be attributed to a lack of one-to-one relation between the frequency of use and frequency of occurrence in the texts.

Another prominent feature of the distribution is the absence of historical inflections in the GEN. SG., which consistently shows the expansive marker *-as*/*-es*. It implies that the GEN. SG. was exposed to analogical pressures prior to the first attestations of Old Saxon and, in a broader context, it indicates that the restructuring began earliest in this category. In contrast, the synchronic alternations between the inherited and innovative inflections attested in the other categories testify to a later dating of the restructuring, i.e. at the historical stage.

Although the destination class for the *nd*-stems was the *a*-stem declension and the adjectival pattern, traces of the *n*-stem inflection are occasionally attested. The weak inflectional markers appear in the GEN. SG. (a single instance found in the younger minor documents: *nerion(do)n salvatoris* PsGern 13, 5), and ACC. SG. (*helandean*, H), as well as in the NOM. and ACC. PL., where alongside the novel *a*-stem markers (*fianda, fiundos, uuigandos*), the weak inflections *-on*, *-ean* are attested in *sēolithandiun/sēolidandean*, and *uuigandon* (H). The single attestation of the marker *-i* in the DAT. SG. (*uualdandi* ms. C 260 vs. *uualdande* ms. M), alongside the most common endings *-a, -e*, could be attributed to the influence of the *i*-stems. This interpretation seems problematic, because the DAT. SG. form would be then the only one in the *nd*-stem paradigm testifying to the spread of the *i*-stem inflection. An alternative explanation may come from spelling practices, and the form may be interpreted as a spelling variant of *-e*, or as a scribal error. On account of the limited amount of the available data, none of these hypotheses can be sufficiently supported.

The paradigm of *nd*-stems provides no transparent pattern when it comes to the spread of analogical features in individual texts or manuscripts. Innovative forms are to be found in both the minor Old Saxon texts of the tenth and eleventh centuries and in the earlier poetic sources. Quite expectedly, most of the *nd*-stems are attested in the latter category. In conclusion, the number of categories where synchronic alternation is attested in the *nd*-stem paradigms allows one to consider this declensional type as one which provides relatively reliable information about the morphological restructuring in Old Saxon.

5.6.8 Dental stems

Only vestiges of this declensional type are attested in the Old Saxon material and all of the archaic features belong to one noun, i.e. the feminine *magad* 'maid'. There are seventeen tokens attested, with the NOM. SG. ($n = 5$) and the ACC. SG. ($n = 5$) being inconclusive with respect to the inflectional restructuring. The remaining forms are the endingless and thus archaic DAT. SG. ($n = 5$), one archaic NOM. PL. and one innovative ACC. PL. (*ēkmagadi* 'wood-nymph'). The noun *mānuth* 'month' testifies to a transition to the *a*-stems, with a singly attested DAT. SG. (*mānutha*). The few analogical forms point to a two-way influence in the paradigm, depending on gender, with the masculine nouns (*mānuth*) following the *a*-stems and the feminines (*magad*) the *i*-stems. Another noun originally affiliated with this declensional type, *helith* 'man, warrior', transferred entirely to the productive declension and inflects as a masculine *a*-stem. Given the residual nature of this declensional type, the attestations were not included in the overall results presented in Section 5.7. Significantly, the fact that vestiges of the dental stem inflection are retained in the small Old Saxon corpus at all indicates that, when compared to the other early West Germanic languages, Old Saxon represented an archaic dialect with respect to inflectional morphology.

5.7 Summary of the results and overview of the tendencies

The present section offers an overview of the major tendencies identified in the investigation of the Old Saxon material. The dominant tendencies with respect to the directions of interparadigmatic transitions are summarised in Table 5.33 for individual declensional classes, including gender-class and stem-type distinctions where relevant. Some minor features, such as the presence of the masculine *a*-stem inflections in the feminine root nouns, were not included in this overview.

In terms of directions of transition, Old Saxon shows a pattern largely parallel to that found in Inland West Germanic (cf. Chapter 6 on Old Low Franconian), primarily in that the reshaping of the declensional system was not mono-directional – as it is largely the case in Old English and (partly) Old Frisian. The wide scope of the dissemination of the *a*-stem inflections is well evinced in the available material, yet the inflectional reorganisation is not dominated by the expansion of this single declensional type; instead, a few productive inflectional patterns affect the minor stem paradigms. This is especially true of the feminine stems, where both *ō*-stems (*jō*-stems) and *i*-stems constitute attractive inflectional patterns for the minor stems. A prominent feature of the inflectional reorganisation is the spread

Table 5.33 Directions of interdeclensional transfers of minor stems in Old Saxon

Historical declensional class	New declensional class
i-stems (m)	=> *ja*-stems, *a*-stems
i-stems (f)	=> *jō*-stems, *ō*-stems
i-stems (n)	=> *ja*-stems, *a*-stems
u-stems (m)	=> *(j)a*-stems, *i*-stems
u-stems (f)	=> *i*-stems, *ō*-stems
root nouns (m)	=> *a*-stems, *i*-stems
root nouns (f)	=> *i*-stems
s-stems (n)	=> (neuter) *a*-stems
r-stems (m, f)	no innovative features
nd-stems (monosyllabic)	=> *a*-stems
nd-stems (disyllabic)	=> *a*-stems, adjectival inflection
þ-stems (m)	=> *a*-stems
þ-stems (f)	=> *i*-stems

of the *ja*- and *jō*-stem inflections, especially in the *i*-stems, where many inflectional parallels between these classes existed. The presence of adjectival inflection in the *nd*-stems complies with the pattern found in this class in the sister languages (especially in Old English). It can be assumed that the divergent tendencies in the inflectional reorganisation across West Germanic were delineated already at an early (prehistoric) stage, and in the historical period the restructuring continued alongside parallel pathways of development. An example may be the small class of abstract feminine *-īn*-stems (Go. *managei, manageins*), which in Old English and Old Frisian was entirely reorganised on the pattern of the *ō*-stems, while in Old Saxon on the pattern of the *i*-stems (in line with the development in Old High German), reflecting the divergent preferences of the Coastal vs. Inland Germanic for the respective inflectional patterns.

Another characteristic of the restructuring is the presence of masculine inflections in the paradigms of feminine stems, attested especially well in the *i*-stems and root nouns. The presence of these forms can be interpreted not only as a reflex of the "syncretisation" of the feminine paradigm with the masculine (and neuter) types, but also as an indication that the "neutralisation" of the contrasts tended to take place between grammatical gender types as well (Rauch 1992b: 251).

Table 5.34 juxtaposes the results of the quantitative investigation for individual minor classes. It must be emphasised that such an approach has many limitations, resulting in an oversimplified picture and the overall figures do not capture details of the distributions in individual classes. The figures for the *i*-stems depict the distribution which excludes the attestations to the NOM./ACC. SG. of heavy-syllable feminine stems (cf. Section 5.6.2). Due to their residual nature as a class, the dental stems were excluded, and for reasons discussed in Section 5.6.6, the figures for the *s*-stems do not include the lemma *kind*.

Table 5.34 Summary of the distribution of archaic and innovative inflections in the OS minor stems per class

	archaic	innovative
i-stems	(761) 71%	(304) 29%
u-stems	(168) 83%	(35) 17%
root nouns	(102) 58%	(75) 42%
s-stems	(15) 71%	(6) 29%
r-stems	(49) 100%	(0) 0%
nd-stems	(28) 25%	(83) 75%

The paradigm of *nd*-stems was the most conducive to analogical pressures from other declensions, with 75 percent of forms showing innovative inflections. At the other end of the spectrum is the class of *r*-stems, which is remarkably stable, also when compared to the other investigated Old Germanic languages, consistently retaining the inherited pattern both in the singular and plural. This resistance to external influences could be attributed to the semantic profile of the class, and possibly to the high frequency of nouns denoting kinship terms, which is not reflected in the material (but largely confirmed by the evidence from Old English and Old Frisian). Given, however, the overall innovative inflectional profile of the *r*-stems in the other examined languages, the semantic factor does not convincingly account for the conservatism of the Old Saxon paradigm (cf. the distribution of forms in the singular and plural in the other languages, which seems to be largely determined by token frequency; see also Table 5.37). Instead, the conservatism of this class can be ascribed to the overall archaic inflectional profile of Old Saxon, resulting from the early attestation date of the sources (cf. Chapter 7). The evidence provided by the *s*-stems is of a limited value given the number of attested forms. The *i*-stems and *u*-stems testify to a similar amount of innovation in the paradigms, which is not entirely surprising as the two classes showed largely parallel inflectional profiles. In the root nouns the results of the competition between the inherited and analogical inflections are numerically balanced. The presence of analogical inflections in ca. 40 percent of forms indicates that the class, although still characterised by a fairly distinct inflectional profile, was at a stage of gradual transformation, facilitated by a lack of a distinctive marker in the plural.

Although the attested distribution testifies to considerable dynamics of restructuring, with synchronic alternations well attested across paradigms, the variation is often not found within the paradigms of individual lemmas, but is a cumulative effect, emerging from the distributions for all nouns affiliated with a given class. For instance, some of the original *u*-stems show only the inflections of the *a*-stems, others of the *i*-stems, while still others are attested in the archaic forms only, or in forms which do not admit an unambiguous identification of any pattern. These circumstances, which result in particular of minor stems attested (in terms of tokens), need to be taken into account when interpreting the findings.

Some more insight into the patterns of inflectional restructuring can be gained from a comparison of the innovation levels for the singular and plural in individual classes, as demonstrated in Table 5.35. The numbers in brackets refer to the total number of singular and plural tokens (n).

Table 5.35 Distribution of innovative inflections in the OS singular and plural paradigms

	% innovative singular	% innovative plural
i-stems	(569) 20%	(496) 39%
u-stems	(195) 21%	(26) 23%
root nouns	(85) 42%	(92) 42%
r-stems	(33) 0%	(16) 0%
s-stems	(5) 100%	(16) 6%
nd-stems	(78) 95%	(33) 27%
Total	(965) 28%	(679) 37%

The percentage of analogical inflections in the singular and plural paradigms is comparable, which is unexpected in view of the evidence from the sister languages, where the prevalent pattern involves a higher innovation level in the singular and greater archaism of the plural. The high level of conservative inflection in the singular may be ascribed to the distributions in the *i*-stems and *u*-stems, where the NOM. and ACC. SG. forms were included in the calculation. If the figures from these two categories were excluded, as was the case in the other investigated classes, the overall amount of innovative inflection in the singular would increase to 47 percent (*n* = 692).

As the plural markers constitute the basis (in the present study) for testing the relation between the salience of inflectional markers and the scope of the restructuring, Table 5.36 gives an overview of the plurality patterns found in the analysed material, juxtaposing the type of plural marker with the incidence of analogical features in individual classes. As the salience of the plural markers is tested in the forms of the NOM. and ACC. PL., the figures include only the attestations to these categories, except the *s*-stems, where also the GEN. PL. and DAT. PL. (the latter in fact not attested) were included (for reasons discussed in Section 5.6.6). The numbers in brackets refer to the total number of singular and plural tokens (n).

Table 5.36 The correlation between the salience of plural markers and the innovation level in the OS minor stems

	plural marker	% innovation in PL
i-stems	vocalic marker -*i* + umlaut	(308) 3%
u-stems	vocalic marker -*i* + umlaut	(26) 23%
root nouns	Ø marker	(40) 70%
r-stems	Ø marker	(16) 0%
s-stems	*r*-formative	(16) 6%
nd-stems	Ø marker	(33) 27%

In contrast to Old English and Old Frisian, the postulated significance of the salience of inflectional markers is not straightforwardly reflected in the patterns of restructuring found in Old Saxon. No traces of analogical inflections were found in the paradigms of the *r*-stems, where the zero ending in the plural can be considered a feature with little salience. The vulnerability of this marker to analogical pressures, well evinced in the other examined languages, is not consistently confirmed in the Old Saxon data (cf. root nouns and *nd*-stems). Accordingly, the immunity of the *r*-stems to analogical pressures must be accounted for by factors other than salience, which again supports the premise that the changes in the inflectional profile of any declensional class are determined by a range of interacting factors, including, for instance, the semantic constitution of the class. The correlation between the innovation level and salience is evinced in the *s*-stems, where the *r*-formative was a marker of plurality. However, given the scant attestation of the *s*-stems, the evidence can hardly be treated as conclusive. The confirmation for such a correlation can be sought in the later Middle Low German period, where the *r*-plural forms are frequent in nouns originally affiliated with the *s*-stems. The two vocalic classes, where the plural is marked by the same vowel, and occasionally supported by *i*-mutation of the root vowel, testify to a largely parallel pattern, with the *u*-stem plural being somewhat more affected by analogical inflections. The source of this minor discrepancy may be the presence of the *i*-mutated vowel, which is only sporadic in the *u*-stems, while more consistent in the *i*-stems. Clearly, the presence of a double exponent of plurality, involving an inflectional ending and a mutated vowel, renders the paradigm (of the plural) resistant to external analogical pressures. What is certainly less expected in the attested distribution is the divergent pattern found in the *nd*-stems and root nouns. These two consonantal classes, in which the historical plural shows no salient markers, could be expected to follow parallel paths of development. Neither the type of plurality marker nor frequency of occurrence can straightforwardly account for the attested distributions. Significantly, if the forms of the most frequent root noun *mann* are included in the calculations, the overall share of innovative inflections in the root nouns (in the NOM./ACC. PL.) drops to 16 percent. The correlation with the frequency factor is evident in the case of *man*, which as a frequent lemma (and, in addition, occasionally marked by a mutated vowel in the plural) does not testify to any traces of innovative inflection in the plural. These refined figures correspond (approximately) to the distribution in the *nd*-stems, yet the question why the amount of innovation in the *nd*-stems is low still remains unanswered. A closer look at the distribution allows one to conclude that the dissemination of analogical inflections is more evident in the disyllabic nouns than in the monosyllabic ones. The juxtaposition of the percentages of innovation for the NOM./ACC. PL. in these two subgroups results in quite a divergent pattern: while the less frequently attested disyllabic nouns show analogical inflections in 55 percent of forms ($n = 11$), the two monosyllabic nouns, *fiund* and *friond*, which turn out to be more frequent (in the plural), show innovation in only 14 percent of forms ($n = 22$). Although the number of attestations is low and the assumption that the monosyllabic nouns were more frequent in the plural and thus more conservative is not sufficiently substantiated, the explanation seems at least to some extent feasible. It is all the more likely as a parallel distribution is found in Old English, with *frēond* and *fēond* being much more frequently attested (in the plural) than the disyllabic nouns. Incidentally, such an approach to the available data reveals also the importance of and, consequently, the need for a micro-level analysis, i.e. on the lemma level, which in many cases turns out to be revealing and often the only way to account for the attested inflectional patterns.

Finally, worth emphasising from the perspective of the further development of plural inflection in (Low) German is the absence of the weak inflections in the plural paradigm. It is the evidence of Middle Low German that clearly suggests that the competition between the vocalic plural markers and *n*-plural inflections was eventually won by the latter, with the majority of Middle Low German forms showing *-en* endings.

The overall incidence of inherited and analogical inflections in the Old Saxon material, including the distribution with respect to number, is presented in Table 5.37.

Table 5.37 Overall distribution of archaic and innovative inflections in the OS minor stems

	archaic	innovative
singular	(698) 72%	(267) 28%
plural	(431) 63%	(248) 37%
Total	(1129) 69%	(515) 31%

The figures indicate that the overall amount of analogical inflection in the minor stems is very limited, especially when compared to the corresponding figures for Old English and Old Frisian. This substantial inflectional archaism may be partly attributed to the nature of the available material and the fact that the major sources are poetic, while the non-poetic evidence is scarce. Moreover, the major two textual sources date to the ninth century, and this early dating to a large extent accounts for the conservatism of the paradigms. The scope of the restructuring process is comparable to that found in the Early Old English stage, where the overall amount of innovative inflection reaches 28 percent (see Table 3.59).

The overarching tendency identifiable irrespective of class is that the inflectional restructuring was determined largely by the frequency of use/occurrence, operating on various levels (lemma, morphosyntactic category, paradigm). Admittedly, this tendency could be much better captured in the distribution of analogical forms in the minor paradigms of the sister languages. The underlying mechanism involved the unfolding of the restructuring process with respect to case/number category and its correlation with case/category frequency. Across classes, the GEN. SG. and DAT. SG., which are the less frequent categories in the paradigm, tend to be more susceptible to the influence of analogical inflections. This tendency is even better manifested in the development of these two cases in the plural, which were the first categories to be restructured on the analogy of the productive patterns, already at the prehistoric stage (cf. Table 2.15, 2.16). In turn, the NOM. and ACC., both singular and plural, which are essentially the more frequent cases in the paradigm, attest to the relative conservatism across classes. This general observation finds additional support in the data: if only the figures for the GEN. and DAT./INSTR. are taken into account in the singular, the overall share of innovative inflections increases to 47 percent ($n = 692$), with 87 percent ($n = 167$) in the former category and 34 per-cent ($n = 525$) in the latter. The overall amount of innovation in the NOM./ACC. SG. reaches 4 percent only ($n = 913$). A parallel discrepancy is found in the plural, where the overall level of innovation in the NOM./ACC. PL. amounts to 11 percent ($n = 576$), while in the DAT. PL. (the GEN. counted only for the s-stems) it reaches 71 percent ($n = 274$). Such a refinement in the calculation, taking into account the frequencies of individual cases/categories, reveals a clear correlation between the level of innovation and the frequency of individual categories. Furthermore, it be-comes evident that the restructuring of inflection occurred primarily above the level of the declensional class and class-specific features were of secondary importance (see the discussion in Chapter 8).

Finally, as the sources examined in the present study showed some variation with respect to attestation date and dialect, it can be expected that the patterns of restructuring of the nominal inflection in these sources differed. As the literary texts tend to be more conservative than the more utilitarian or prosaic ones, one could expect them to favour the inherited inflectional pattern. This potential variation was tested in the present investigation and the figures for the amount of analogical inflection in three subgroups of texts, i.e. the two major texts and the group of minor documents, are depicted in Table 5.38, showing the distribution of archaic and analogical inflections irrespective of the declensional class and the category of case and number.

Table 5.38 The percentage of archaic and innovative inflections in minor stems in individual OS sources

Genesis (9th c.)		Heliand (9th–10th c.)		minor sources (10th–11th c.)	
archaic	innovative	archaic	innovative	archaic	innovative
(36) 69%	(16) 31%	(1041) 70%	(439) 30%	(101) 56%	(79) 44%

The distribution indicates that although the restructuring trends remain parallel in all three sources, the scale of the inflectional reorganisation differs slightly. The material represents a clear continuum in which the dating of the source plays a crucial role: the minor documents attest to a more extensive pressure of analogical inflections. This straightforward correlation between the amount of innovative inflection and the dating of the text may be potentially enhanced also by the genre these texts represent. The incidence of analogical inflections in the two alliterative poems contrasts with the distribution found in the minor documents, dominated by glosses. Altogether, the discrepancy in the quantitative distribution of archaic and analogical forms in these two groups of texts is statistically significant. At the same time, when it comes to qualitative interpretation, no clear differences can be recognised in the restructuring tendencies, and the attested trends are identical in the three sources, differing only in the scope and the rate of advancement.

Likewise, hardly any conclusive statements can be made about the dialectal distribution of analogical forms on the basis of the investigated material. No straightforward patterns emerge and the discrepancies between the major (south-western) and minor (central and south-eastern) Old Saxon texts with regard to the examined morphological features are insignificant. Some discrepancies in the extant manuscripts of Heliand are identifiable, but it can be concluded that they essentially correspond to the chronological ordering of the manuscripts rather than their dialectal provenance. Theoretically, these differences could correspond to some diachronic contrasts, yet the attested variation is not consistent. The Straubing fragment which could potentially show greater variation due to its geographical location does not contain many forms that would allow us to make claims about the restructuring process, except the retention of a mutated vowel in the root nouns, unattested in the other manuscripts. Much as a comparison of the manuscripts could be revealing, the limited amount of the available material did not admit of identifying any consistent patterns with respect to the restructuring process. Given the relatively small size of the available Old Saxon corpus, it is most likely that the language viewed from the extant sources reflects only a fragment or a sample of a larger linguistic reality, characterised by a similar variation as that found in the better attested sister languages.

5.8   Taxonomic implications of the study

The classification of Old Saxon nouns in the standard historical grammars parallels largely the approach adopted for Old English, with a clear bias towards etymologically-oriented treatments in the earlier publications and more synchronically-oriented descriptions in the later ones. The oldest treatments of Old Saxon morphology, i.e. Roediger (1893), Gallée ([1910]1993), Holthausen (1921) and Foerste (1950), adhere to a historical approach, presenting a division of nominal classes according to the etymological criteria and the original (Proto-Germanic) stem-affiliation. As could be expected, the overlap of case-and-number inflections across declensional types, induced by phonological developments, rendered the stem-type criterion less relevant for the presentation and description of the Old Saxon nominal system. Accordingly, the later publications, notably Cordes (1973) and Rauch (1992a), acknowledge the need to reanalyse the nominal system from the synchronic Old Saxon perspective and advocate alternative, synchronically-oriented classifications, employing the "Flexions-Morphemzeichen" as the primary criterion (Cordes 1973: 90).[265] Cordes (1973: 90–93) distinguishes two major nominal classes, alongside a third class consisting in adjectives and pronouns, which correspond to the "strong" and "weak" types in the nomenclature of the diachronic approach. A further differentiation is made into gender subclasses as well as into subtypes, depending on the shape of the infix/suffix in the morpheme structure. Accordingly, Type 1, characterised primarily by a lack of inflectional exponent in the NOM. SG. and the marker *-es* in the GEN. SG., is subdivided into four subgroups, whereas Type 2, distinguished by a vocalic ending in the NOM. SG. and the presence of *-n* in all other paradigm cells, into two subgroups. The adopted approach results in a fairly complex configuration of declensional types, with a system of eight inflectional sub-patterns, and testifies to a considerable complexity of the inflectional

---

265. For a synchronic classification of nouns in 9th/10th c. Old High German see Klein (1987) and for a more extensive discussion of the development of German nominal morphology, see Harnisch (2001).

system altogether, even if seen from the unhistorical perspective. In fact, a very similar result is obtained in the study by Rauch (1992a), who approaches the Old Saxon inflectional morphology from the perspective of diachronic synchrony (xxvi). The author aims at presenting an ahistorical classification of nouns, and postulates a base form inflection for the Old Saxon nominal system. The system presented by Rauch (1992a) is based primarily on the shape of the plural marker and gender of nouns. In most general terms, the proposed classification draws a sharp dividing line between strong and weak declensions, with a further subdivision into gender classes. Within the masculine type, the division into three types of plural endings is posited, i.e. *os*-plural, *i*-plural and *ø*-plural (Rauch 1992a: 50). In the strong neuter class, a distinction is made between the two plural ending types: zero and -*u* markers (p. 55). For the feminine strong nouns, likewise, a twofold division is posited, with a differentiation in the plural between zero and -*i* markers (p. 63), and an additional subclass which testifies to the neutralisation of the grammatical gender (p. 67–68). The irregularities which are vestiges of the historical inflectional patterns are explained in terms of anomalies (e.g. *fehu*) (p. 56).

Although such synchronic approaches to the diversity of nominal inflections are evidently not more economical or expedient descriptions of the attested state of affairs, they do reflect more adequately the linguistic reality that a "synchronic" speaker of Old Saxon had to face. At the same time, in both synchronic treatments references are consistently made to etymological stem classes. Clearly, the attested diversity of inflectional patterns that need to be captured in a synchronic treatment is very wide and substantiates the complexity of the Old Saxon declensional system, irrespective of whether it is framed in a diachronic or synchronic perspective.

Although the present study is not aimed at postulating a new classification of Old Saxon nouns, the findings from the quantitative analysis allow a refinement of the classifications found in the standard historical descriptions. As could be observed in the analysed data, many of the etymological stem classes retain their distinct inflectional profiles, although none of them, except the *r*-stems, is entirely free from the influence of analogical inflections. The major discrepancy between the traditional handbook descriptions and the findings of the present study relates to the inflectional profile of the *u*-stem declension, which is commonly believed to be fairly disintegrated, as observed, for instance, by Sanders (1983: 49): "Die in allen germ. Sprachen rezessive *u*-Dekl. (…) hat sich im As. aufgelöst". The examined material allows one to claim that the inherited pattern remains relatively archaic when compared to the shape of inflection in the sister languages. The archaism of this class, however, may be attributed to the inflectional overlap with the *i*-stems (especially in the NOM. and ACC. PL.). Another refinement of the model involves the class of *i*-stems, whose productivity is well attested in the examined material and, in fact, the class can hardly be considered a minor declension in Old Saxon. An evident complication for tracing the dissemination of the *i*-stem inflections is the formal congruity with the inflections of the *ja*-stems, and consequently the impossibility to distinguish between these two sets of endings. Taking into account the overlapping inflections, one common, overarching inflectional pattern, combining the inflections of the *u*-stems and *i*-stems, can be postulated for heavy-syllable stems, serving as an alternative template for the analogical transformation of minor paradigms (alongside the productive pattern of the *a*-, *ja*-stems and *ō*-, *jō*-stems). These overlapping inflections in the masculine and feminine heavy-syllable stems are summarised in Table 5.39.

Table 5.39 Common inflectional pattern based on the OS *u*-stems and *i*-stems

	masculine stems		feminine stems	
	SG	PL	SG	PL
NOM.	–	-i	–	-i
GEN.	-(i)es	-(i)o	-i	-(i)o
DAT.	-(i)e	-(i)on	-i	-(i)on
ACC.	–	-i	–	-i

5.9 Conclusions

The overall morphological profile of Old Saxon emerging from the present study of the nominal inflection is one of a remarkably conservative Old Germanic dialect. The dissemination of analogical inflections affects 31 percent of forms in minor stems. This conservative nature of Old Saxon is manifested especially in the inflectional profile of the *r*-stems and *i*-stems, which largely retain the inherited inflection. The antiquated shape of the nominal inflection can be ascribed to a number of interacting factors, whose share in contributing to the archaism varies. The decisive determinant was the shape of the Old Saxon phonological system, in particular the vocalism of unstressed syllables, which remained relatively conservative. This phonological archaism is in turn to be ascribed to two facts: firstly, the relatively early dating of the textual sources in comparison to the sister languages (except the early Old English sources), and secondly, the genre represented in the available material, i.e. alliterative epic poetry, which by definition is more conservative than prose. The preservation of /j/ in *ja*- and *jō*-stems and its significance for the transformation of the *i*-stem paradigm, or the retention of the instrumental case, are further characteristics contributing to the overall archaic (morphological) profile of the language.

In formal terms, the inflectional archaism of Old Saxon is to be ascribed in particular to the shape of inflection in the NOM./ACC. SG. and PL. With respect to declensional classes, it is concentrated in the *r*-stems and the two vocalic classes *u*-stems and *i*-stems. The conservatism of these classes has its own motivations on the declension-level as well. Accordingly, factors such as the semantic constitution of the class or the presence of allomorphic variation in the paradigm had some influence on the dynamics of the restructuring. When compared to the other examined languages, Old Saxon emerges as the most conservative dialect, preserving the original inflectional pattern largely intact; at the same time, the major restructuring trends can easily be recognised as parallel to those observed in the sister languages.

A prominent feature of the restructuring process in Old Saxon relates to the direction of interdeclensional transitions of minor stems. Much as the Old English and Old Frisian minor nouns were polarised by two main inflectional types, the *a*-stems and *ō*-stems, the polarisation in Old Saxon is more varied, and aside from these two directions of transfer, the nouns are largely attracted by the *i*-stem declension as well as the two sub-patterns, i.e. *ja*- and *jō*-stems. Especially the dissemination of the *ja*-stem and *jō*-stem inflections, not found in Old English or Old Frisian, is a typical feature of the inflectional restructuring in Old Saxon. In turn, the productivity of the *i*-stem pattern is especially well attested in the *u*-stems and root nouns, where it emerges as the predominant inflection in feminine nouns. The gradual dissemination of the *i*-stem inflections in Old Saxon is a forerunner of the patterns found in present-day German, where the vocalic ending accompanied by a mutated vowel, characteristic of the historical *i*-stems, is one of the major plural formation patterns. This diversification of productive declensional types is also reminiscent of the situation in Old High German and partly in Old Low Franconian. In fact, the divergent direction of transition in Inland vs. Coastal West Germanic is well reflected already in interdeclensional shifts dated to the prehistoric stage: the small class of abstract feminine *-īn*-stems was absorbed by the *ō*-stems in Old English and Old Frisian, but by the *i*-stems in Old Saxon. It must be emphasised that the diverse paths of the inflectional restructuring across Northern West Germanic are a direct effect of the differences in the phonological developments that affected the respective systems. The expansion of the *ja*-stem (*jō*-stem) inflection in Old Saxon, as a consequence of the retention of the *-j*- element, is the most illustrative example of this effect.

Notwithstanding the limitations of interpreting the younger data as a continuation of an earlier situation, the evidence from Middle Low German and modern dialects can shed some more light on how to interpret the level of archaism found in Old Saxon. This refers in particular to the interpretation of the scant data from the *s*-stems. The presence of the *r*-plural forms in Middle Low German and present-day German indicates that the pattern must have been fairly widespread at an earlier stage. Admittedly, the bias towards High German, attested in the Middle Low German data, may be an obstacle for such an interpretation, as the *r*-plural forms were widespread already in Old High German, and the pattern found in the later period may have been enhanced by the influence of the High German inflection. Another example involves the abundance of the *n*-stem inflections in Middle Low German and their only sporadic presence in the minor stems in Old Saxon, which indicates that the large-scale dissemination of this pattern must be dated later.

Finally, the analysed material admits of making some observations about the placement of Old Saxon in the West Germanic language continuum. It has commonly been acknowledged that Old Saxon occupies (structurally) the position between Inland West Germanic and the Coastal West Germanic (Ingvaeonic). The examination of the material with respect to the restructuring of the nominal inflection allows one to place Old Saxon much closer to the Franconian than to the Ingvaeonic dialects. This closeness is demonstrated on two planes: firstly, in the directions of the transition of minor stems (with a special position of the *i*-stems), and secondly, in the scope of the restructuring in individual inflectional classes. The typological proximity to High German is reflected in the multidirectionality of interdeclensional transfers, as well as in the inflectional profile of the *i*-stems, which turned out to be a conservative declensional type, with a potential to spread to other declensions, and to become productive (in the plural) at the later stage (see also the discussion in Chapter 7).

The results of the present research lend credence to the general trends signalised partly in the standard historical handbooks; yet, the examination of the available material (in the methodological framework adopted) reveals that the scope of the restructuring was more limited than could be inferred from the available descriptions. The retention of the distinct inflectional profiles of classes such as the *i*-stems and *r*-stems, and the relatively low percentage of innovative inflections in individual declensional types allows one to claim that much as the process of reorganisation of nominal inflection was in progress, it was evidently not very advanced in Old Saxon in the 9th–10th c. At the same time, given the limitations resulting from the scope of the available material, it needs to be emphasised that the picture obtained from the investigation is, and will remain, a largely fragmented one.

CHAPTER 6

Nominal inflection in Old Low Franconian

6.1   Introduction

Old Low Franconian has not received extensive treatment in comparative Germanic studies, for long remaining a "blinder Fleck der Altgermanistik" (Pijnenburg 2003: 7). The absence of references to and discussion of the Old Low Franconian material in the major comparative handbooks (e.g. Hirt 1931, 1932; Prokosch 1939; Krahe & Meid 1969) can hardly go unnoticed (cf. Buccini 1995: 9). The major reason for such a state of affairs is the very fragmentary and, in many respects, complex nature of the sources in which the language is attested. Despite many corpus-related limitations, the inclusion of Old Low Franconian material into the present comparative study was considered essential, since the valuable evidence it offers supplements the picture of the reorganisation of the nominal inflection in the western branch of Germanic, and is crucial for gaining the desirable comparative perspective, not least because Old Low Franconian is the only language in this study which (traditionally) represents Inland Germanic, and which can be thus expected to show a different path of inflectional development than the Ingvaeonic dialects.

The analysis of Old Low Franconian, which is morphologically closer to Old High German than to any of the investigated Ingvaeonic languages, is fraught with a number of difficulties related to the character of the textual material.[266] It is not

---

266. In compliance with the traditional approach, the term *Old Low Franconian* is used in the present study to refer to the earliest attested stage of Dutch; however, occasionally the term *Old Dutch* will also be employed, without the intention to mark any specific difference. The preference for the former denotation in standard historical texts (*altostniederfränkisch* or even *altniederdeutsch*) (Heyne 1867; van Helten 1902) has its source in the fact that the language of the psalms, which constitute the major source of information about early Dutch, was originally viewed as a dialect of Low German. The term *Old Dutch* was first used by Cowan (1957) (*Oudnederlandse [Oudnederfrankische] psalmenfragmenten*), but has largely been resented by linguists (cf. the later consistent use of *Old Low Franconian* by Kyes 1969 or Quak 1973a, 1992) (Pijnenburg 2003: 10). The relation between these two designations was explicated by van Loey (1970) who considers the term *Old Dutch* to be more appropriate: "Da wir vom Altniederfränkischen (…) vor dem 9. Jh. nichts wissen, das Sprachmaterial in und nach dem 9. Jh. hingegen schon niederländische Merkmale aufweist (…) mitsamt Ingwäonismen, ist (wie "altenglisch" statt "angelsächsisch") "altniederländisch" eine geeignetere Benennung als "altniederfränkisch" (van Loey 1970: 253). The resentment toward using the term *Old Dutch* seems related to the fact that present-day Dutch is not a direct continuation of the language found in the *Wachtendonck Psalms*, which is the main source of information about the earliest attested stage of this language.

only the remarkably limited size of the available corpus, but also its heterogeneous nature that constitutes a challenge for any linguistic investigation. The latter feature is clearly related to the positioning of Old Low Franconian among the other Old Germanic languages, and more precisely, within the Continental West Germanic dialect continuum. The heterogeneous nature of the earliest attested Dutch language is commonly attributed to the extensive linguistic impact of the neighbouring Franconian variety, which encroached on the territory of the autochthonous Ingvaeonic idiom (Århammar 1990: 13). In this respect, its position is reminiscent of the situation in Old Saxon in that it was also exposed to external linguistic influences from the south and the west, which came with conflicting cultural alignments (Kufner 1972: 92).

Attestations of Old Low Franconian date from between the eighth and twelfth centuries (1150) and consist, apart from personal and place names, in a fragmentary interlinear translation of psalms, known as the *Wachtendonck Psalms* (WPs), dated to the tenth century (Quak 1992: 81). These fragments were translated in or near southern Limburg and testify to a stage preceding Middle Dutch. The other two sources traditionally considered Low Franconian are the *Leiden Willeram* (LW), dated to the eleventh century, and the Middle Franconian *Rhyming Bible* (RB), belonging to the twelfth century, both displaying a substantial influence of High German (Central Franconian) features (cf. Section 6.2). The scarce attestation of Old Low Franconian to a large extent impairs the investigation of its nominal inflection, potentially affecting the soundness of conclusions. For the study of the declensional system in particular, the limited textual material means that many lemmas or inflectional forms are not attested (e.g. in the *s*-stems) and thus the scope of the analysis is necessarily limited, especially when contrasted with the richer and more diversified corpora of languages such as Old English.

The principal difficulty with the available Old Dutch material lies in delimiting its scope, i.e. the range of sources which should actually be considered Old Dutch. A number of sources which have traditionally been subsumed under the term Old Dutch are fairly difficult to classify, firstly on account of their linguistic heterogeneity, and secondly, due to the fragmentary attestation of linguistic features (Klein 2003: 21). The heterogenic nature of the mediaeval sources is admittedly a more general phenomenon, characterising also the other investigated languages. However, combined with the fact that the attestations to Old Low Franconian are so meagre, it becomes an even more acute problem for the interpretation of the available data. What certainly works to the benefit of the present study is that this linguistic diversity, which results largely from the inconsistencies between the language of the original and the idiom of the scribe or the editor, is most evident at the graphemic and phonological level, while the morphological layer and lexicon seem less susceptible to *Sprachmischung* (Klein 2003: 22).[267] In light of this fact, the investigation of the reorganisation of the Old Low Franconian nominal system is a task worth undertaking, and the material, although very limited, is believed to offer insights into the mechanisms of inflectional changes in Northern West Germanic.

An essential aspect in the discussion of the inflectional development of early Dutch is its linguistic identity, seen in the context of its relation to Old High German. Formally, the most prominent feature distinguishing Low Franconian from Central Franconian was the Germanic *Lautverschiebung*; however, as noted by Klein (2003: 19), the two languages form a Franconian dialect continuum, within which "lässt sich andererseits mit rein linguistischen Mitteln keine klare Abgrenzung zwischen einem niederfränkisch-altniederländischen und einem oberfränkisch-ahd. Sprachraum treffen." At the same time, there is no doubt about the Franconian status of Old Dutch, as was explicitly expressed, among others by Krogh (1997), who grounding his conclusions on the morphological profile of the language, states: "Über den fränkischen Grundcharakter des Altostniederfränkischen dürfte somit kein Zweifel herrschen. Dasselbe gilt vermutlich auch für das restliche Binnenniederländische." (Krogh 1997: 25). Evidently, none of the Old Dutch texts is free from traces of the High German influence. This influence was consequential for the linguistic profile of the Old Dutch material and in particular for its phonological shape. This state of affairs is to be attributed not only to the geographical vicinity of High German dialects and their genetic closeness (Inland West Germanic), but also to the circumstances surrounding the creation of the texts, namely the fact that the extant Old Dutch texts are translations (or a reworking) of the High German originals (cf. Section 6.2). In practice this means that when examining the linguistic structure of these texts, attention should be given to distinguishing the original Dutch features from those that can be ascribed to the impact of High German. In many instances such a separation is problematic and a potential admixture of features of various origin in the linguistic layer needs to be reckoned with. In the context of this study, this admixture renders the analysis more complicated, as some of the archaic inflectional features may potentially appear because of external influences, either geographical (the vicinity of morphologically more conservative High German dialects) or "encrypted" in the original texts (older and thus more archaic High German originals), one way or the other reflecting the archaism of the Old High German inflection.

---

267. Cf. Sanders (1974) who, with reference to *Leiden Willeram*, claims that the impact of High German was most conspicuous at the grapho-phonemic level, where some amount of systematicity attributable to this influence is detected in the consonantal system (Sanders 1974: 287ff.).

On account of these close linguistic bonds between Old Dutch and Old High German, including the nature of the corpus, some tendencies present in the Old High German nominal inflection will be discussed in this chapter. In this respect, the relation between Old Low Franconian and Old High German can be compared to the one between Old Frisian and Old English. In both cases the small corpora provide limited information on inflectional restructuring when compared to their richly attested closest relatives. In both cases, the larger corpora can be viewed as a "supplement" to the data provided by the smaller ones in the sense that if the broad array of data from the better attested languages is superimposed on the scant material provided by their modestly attested sister languages, a comprehensive picture (or at least an approximation) of the developments in the latter can be obtained. In other words, just as the Old English material can be informative about the Old Frisian "missing" data, the Old High German material can serve a similar function for Old Low Franconian.

The discussion of the heterogeneous nature of the Old Dutch corpus leads directly to the more general and, in fact, complex question of the genesis of Dutch. Although early Dutch was not an Ingvaeonic dialect, it did display some Ingvaeonic traits (phonological, morphological and lexical), which, however, were not "gemeinniederländisch" (Krogh 1997: 27). It is believed that the western dialects of Old Dutch were de-Ingvaeonised as a result of the extensive impact of the Franks – in that the Franconian linguistic structure was imposed on the original Ingvaeonic layer (Heeroma 1965, 1972). The presence (or absence) of the Ingvaeonic features has been interpreted as an effect of language contact taking place between the coastal Frisian and Franconian (Heeroma 1951; Buccini 1995, 2003; Bremmer 2008; de Vaan 2010, 2017), and partly explained by recourse to the language contact theory advocated by van Coetsem (1988, 2000). The application of this theory is discussed in detail in the 2003 paper by Buccini in which the author advocates the view that the emergence of Dutch can be attributed to the contact situation in the late-seventh and early-eighth century between the speakers of Ingvaeonic and Franconian, and an imperfect acquisition of the Franconian idiom by the Ingvaeonic speakers of the coastal areas. The new language which emerged in consequence of this contact was "a form of Franconian but one with ultimately markedly individual phonological and morphological characteristics." (Buccini 2003: 195). This hypothesis accounts for the lack of secondary umlaut in Modern Dutch as well as explains the presence of many relic Ingvaeonic characteristics in Dutch, which is a combination of features otherwise difficult to account for, especially given that *i*-mutation was a very regular process in the Ingvaeonic dialects (Buccini 2003: 205).[268] The claim seems to be confirmed by both the toponymic evidence as well as the data from

---

268. Cf. Goossens (1980), according to whom the secondary umlaut occurred in Dutch, but its phonemicization was confined only to the eastern part of the area.

Middle and Modern Dutch dialects, attesting to the Frisian or "frisophone" linguistic character of the coastal region of Holland prior to the year 1100 (Bremmer 2008: 290–295; de Vaan 2010: 315).[269] A further complication of the origin question is related to the fact that modern standard Dutch, which is essentially believed to be based on the dialects of (South) Holland and Brabant, shows a number of features which are absent from the eastern Franconian dialects (in particular Limburgian). Given that the language found in the earliest attested material represents usually the local dialect of the author, the translator, or the copyist, it can be assumed that Old Dutch was probably also dialectally diversified. This dialectal diversification cannot be captured due to the limited amount of the available material, yet it must be emphasised that the idiom found in the earliest records represents a variety which is not the direct ancestor of present-day Dutch. While present-day standard Dutch is most likely a descendant of Old West Low Franconian, the earliest attested material, i.e. the *Wachtendonck Psalms*, is formally classified as Old East Low Franconian, which finds its continuation in the modern Limburgian dialect (Cosijn 1896; van Helten 1902; Cowan 1959; cf. Sanders 1974).[270]

The complex linguistic situation described above and reflected in the textual material can affect the evaluation of the material in the present study insofar as the present-day linguistic situation is used to supplement the meagre Old Dutch attestations. This essentially means that it is the morphological 'irregularities' of present-day East Low Franconian dialects (i.e. Limburgian), such as the presence of *i*-mutated plural forms, rather than the (morphological) regularities of standard Dutch that can provide information about the earliest stage of the morphological development of Dutch.

6.2   Corpus and methodological considerations

The corpus of Old Low Franconian texts is the smallest of all the corpora analysed in the present work (and in fact of all Old Germanic corpora), hence the relevant material is much more limited than that from the other examined languages. The textual evidence comes from three major documents: (1) the *Wachtendonck Psalms*

---

269. For an extensive recent treatment of this problem, see de Vaan (2017), who offers a refinement and partly revision of the views presented by Buccini and Heeroma.

270. The surviving material from Old West Low Franconian is limited only to onomastic evidence from Latin texts, and a single sentence dated to the 11th c. (de Grauwe 2004). Unfortunately, none of these can provide any relevant information for the study of the nominal inflection in early Dutch. Accordingly, the present study covers in fact the material from the Old East Low Franconian variety.

(10th c.[271]), i.e. a collection of Latin Psalms translated into Old Dutch,[272] (2) *Leiden Willeram* (11th c.), i.e. a Low Franconian version of the Old High German commentary on the *Song of Solomon* by a Bavarian abbot, Williram of Ebersberg, and (3) the *Rhinelandic Rhyming Bible* (early 12th c.), which is a fragmentarily attested verse translation of Biblical stories, characterised by a substantial dialect mixture. The difficulty in interpreting the linguistic layer of these texts lies in their considerable heterogeneity with respect to dialectal traits, with many High German features found in the phonological, morphological, syntactic and lexical layers. This lack of linguistic consistency is most conspicuous in the *Rhyming Bible*, where, alongside the Old Dutch features, both Low and High German (Rhine-Franconian) traits are evident.[273] Similarly heterogeneous is the Old Dutch idiom of *Leiden Willeram*, referred to as "Umschreibungsdialekt", which displays an admixture of East Franconian and Hollandish features.[274] Even the material of the *Wachtendonck Psalms*, considered to be the most Dutch-like of the three, reveals a combination of Low and Central Franconian linguistic features (Smith 1976: 67).[275] At the same

---

271. An earlier dating of the original manuscript, i.e. the 9th c., was suggested by Gysseling (1964: 36); most of the phonological and morphological features point to its later origin, i.e. the 10th c., as has been purported by Sanders (1968: 87–88).

272. The text is attested in a number of fragments including the Lipsius Glosses (a list of 822 Old Low and Central Franconian words with their Latin equivalents, which is a copy of a 10th c. original text, dated to ca. 1600), the *Diez Psalms* (a 16th c. copy of a 10th c. translation of 21 psalms) and a 17th c. version of Psalm XVIII (see Quak 1975, 1981).

273. According to Willemyns (2013), the *Rhyming Bible*, originally Dutch, was "transposed into southern German" (Willemyns 2013: 42). The detailed study of its linguistic profile by Klein (2003) led the author to conclude that the original text is "eindeutig nördlich der Lautverschiebungsgrenze entstanden" and that it exhibits many north-western features, particularly in the lexicon. In fact, its north-western orientation (with respect to lexicon) is even stronger than in the *Leiden Willeram* and the number of (South) Low Franconian-Lower Berg and Low German-Westphalian features allows one to classify the language of this text as Low Franconian or Low German, originating most likely in Werden (Werden Abbey) (Klein 2003: 43).

274. The text is believed to have been originally written in East Franconian and translated into Dutch in the abbey of Egmond in North-Holland (Sanders 1970: 415). Lexically, the text is clearly Old Dutch, but on the morphological level, it shows many East Franconian characteristics (Sanders 1974: 164).

275. The text is a reworking of an Old High German (Middle Franconian) original and preserved in manuscripts from the 16th and 17th c. (Quak 1992: 81). It appears to be double-layered in terms of its linguistic structure in that the first part of it (Psalms 1–9) shows a more Central Franconian character, whereas the second part (from Psalm 10 onwards) is linguistically Low Franconian, which most likely indicates that the original text was Central Franconian, while the editor of the text must have been a speaker of Low Franconian (Sanders 1974; Quak 1973b: 33–34; cf. Cowan 1959; van Helten 1902).

time, the lexicon of the *Psalms* is "ausgesprochen nordwestlich geprägt und kann daher (…) als (auch) anl. betrachtet werden." (Klein 2003: 23). The problem is further complicated by the transmission of the texts, i.e. (1) the fact that the major texts are translations of non-Dutch originals and (2) that the *Wachtendonck Psalms* are transmitted only in copies from the sixteenth century. The absence of the Old Dutch originals reveals a more general characteristic of the early history of the Dutch language; it can be interpreted namely as an indication that no writing tradition existed before the twelfth century and the beginning of the thirteenth century. This has been made explicit by Klein (1979: 428; cf. Kyes 1967: 668) who states:

> Daß es aber vor dem ausgehenden 12. oder beginnenden 13. Jahrhundert tatsächlich keine volkssprachige nl. Sprachtradition gab und der Mangel an anl. Sprachquellen also nicht nur die Folge einer besonders verlustreichen Überlieferungsgeschichte ist, erweist die Eigenart der wenigen vorhandenen Zeugnisse. Sie (…) beruhen meist auf fremden Vorlagen und sind teils sogar in der Fremde geschrieben (…).

The fact that the texts are transmitted in later copies may cause an extra problem for the reliability of the attested forms, including the interpretation of the phonological contrasts. Aside from the three major sources, the Old Dutch corpus comprises also a number of vernacular glosses in Latin texts, runic inscriptions, dated between the sixth and ninth centuries, as well as (relatively well-attested) place and personal names, dated between the ninth and eleventh centuries. Most of this material is, however, fragmentary. Much as the onomastic evidence can be valuable for the study of phonology or the lexicon, its use in the investigation of morphological developments, such as the analogical restructuring of the inflectional system, is largely limited, which has explicitly been expressed by Quak (2003: 309) with reference to place names: "Auf dem Gebiet der Morphologie bringen die Ortsnamen in allgemeinen nicht viel. Nur ab und zu lässt sich vermuten, dass sich in der lateinischen Umgebung germanische Kasusfromen erhalten haben".[276] Due to this unreliability and consequently its limited value for morphological investigation, the relatively rich onomastic (especially toponymic) evidence was not included in measuring the scope of the inflectional reorganisation, which also stays in line with the procedure applied in the investigation of the sister languages.[277] The categories which can occasionally be unambiguously identified as showing Germanic inflection are the GEN. SG. in the first element of the compounds, and the DAT. SG. and PL. (Quak 2003: 309). Given that the onomastic material generally tends to retain considerable

---

276. Cf. Quak (in preparation) where an attempt is made at an interpretation of the GEN. and DAT. PL. forms attested in the Old Dutch toponymic material.

277. Another aspect complicating the interpretation of the Old Dutch place names is that it is difficult (and often impossible) to distinguish them from the Old Frisian names (Quak 2003: 281).

archaism, displaying vestiges of inherited inflection, reference will be made to it when relevant.

Note that many of the relevant forms were found in a Latin context, attested in between Latin words. The attested inflectional endings seem to largely reflect the Latin inflections, and the extent to which this inflection contributed to the shape of the Old Low Franconian paradigms cannot be precisely estimated. Consequently, these forms remain mostly ambiguous and they were not taken into account in the present quantitative study.

The present qualitative and quantitative investigation was conducted on the corpus of the earliest attested Dutch texts as collected in the *Oudnederlands Woordenboek* (*ONW*), which covers the period between 500 and 1200, and comprises ca. 4,500 entries (26,000 attestations and around 15,000 toponyms). It includes the three major texts discussed earlier, as well as some shorter texts and fragments. The scope of the dictionary is relatively extensive in that it encompasses the entire extant material that can be localised in both the historical and present-day Dutch-speaking territory, which means that, for instance, some Frisian runic inscriptions and psalm glosses are also included. The inflectional forms identified in these sources were excluded from this analysis. Given the limited size of the corpus, not all declensional types are well-represented in the extant sources and some are almost non-existent (e.g. *s*-stems). Also, many lemmas are attested in inflectional forms which cannot be sufficiently informative about the restructuring. Consequently, the (type and token) frequencies of individual nouns may be expected to differ substantially from those found in the analyses of the Old English or Old Saxon material. The list of nouns included in the quantitative investigation is presented in the Appendix.

6.3   Restructuring process in Old Low Franconian: Patterns

In his overview of early Dutch nominal inflection, Quak (1992) concludes that the tendency towards simplification and uniformisation of the declensional system is clearly discernible ("deutlich spürbar") (Quak 1992: 82). As in the other languages, the reshaping of the nominal system involved transitions of nouns across declensional classes, with the productive vocalic paradigms serving as the templates for analogical restructuring. Although the interdeclensional migrations affected primarily minor classes, the fluctuation between the inherited and novel inflections is also well attested in the productive paradigms. While the details of analogical developments in the productive declensions (*a*-stems, *ō*-stems and *n*-stems) stay beyond the scope of this study, they can be of significance for the description of the restructuring in the minor declensions, since the analogical reshufflings in these productive paradigms influenced the directions and rate of transfers in the minor classes. One such large-scale development which is not found in the other investigated languages, and thus makes the restructuring process in Old Low Franconian distinctive in the cross-Germanic context, is the merger of two productive feminine classes – the *ō*-stems and *n*-stems (Quak 1992: 87). As a result of this fusion, a new feminine class emerged, where both weak and strong inflections could appear as markers of individual categories; for instance, the NOM./ACC. PL. tended to alternate between the strong -*a* and weak -*on* endings (*geva* 'gift' ~ *gevon*). Consequently, the analogical endings that can be expected to appear in the unproductive feminine paradigms (alongside the historical ending) are the markers extended from the historical *n*-stem inflection and the historical *ō*-stems. Although this tendency corresponds to the patterns found in Old English or Old Frisian, its scope is incomparable in these languages.[278]

Another evident tendency which makes the restructuring process in early Dutch distinct from that of the other investigated languages is the attested productivity of the *i*-stem pattern, which was an unproductive paradigm in the Ingvaeonic dialects (with some marginal productivity confined to the collective plurals in Old English (Section 3.5.2) and a more frequently attested productivity in Old Frisian and especially in Old Saxon). Consequently, the reorganisation of the declensional system was more diversified in Old Low Franconian in that it involved more trajectories of analogical transfers: apart from the two most productive declensions, i.e. the *a*-stems and the combined inflection of feminine *ō*-/*n*-stems, also the *i*-stems served as a destination class for the minor, especially feminine, stems. In this respect, Old Low Franconian shows a pattern corresponding to that found in Old High German, where the spread of the *i*-stem inflection is well-attested, and the *i*-stems constitute a productive inflectional pattern. Additionally, granted that in Middle Dutch the *n*-stem inflection gained the upper hand, the impact of the *n*-stems can be expected in the Old Dutch period as well, not only in the feminine stems but also in the masculine ones.

The productive paradigms which served as templates for the inflectional restructuring in the three gender classes are demonstrated in Table 6.1 (after Quak 1992: 82–91; Quak & van der Horst 2002: 37–41). As with the other investigated languages, it is assumed that the interdeclensional transfers occurred in compliance with gender, but some divergence from the original gender class is not excluded. It must be observed that the model paradigm for the feminine stems does not represent a pure *ō*-stem, but is a hybrid pattern which combines the historical inflection of the *ō*-stems (*jō*-stems) and *n*-stems.

---

278. The study of the spread of the *ō*-stem inflections in the feminine *n*-stems, conducted on a selection of the Old English material, reveals that analogical inflections are attested in approximately 35% of forms (Adamczyk 2007).

Table 6.1 Productive paradigms serving as templates for the restructuring of inflection in OLF

	masculine		neuter		feminine	
	SG	PL	SG	PL	SG	PL
NOM.	dag	daga	wort	wort	tunga	tunga,-on
GEN.	dagis,-es*	dago	wordes	wordo	tungon	tungono
DAT.	dage, -i	dagon	worde	wordon	tungon	tungon
ACC.	dag	daga	wort	wort	tungon, -a	tunga,-on

* The alternating vowels <i> and <e> are believed to represent two variants of the same phoneme (Quak 1992: 83); cf. Section 6.4.

In contrast to early Old Saxon and Old English, the exponent of the NOM./ACC. PL. in the masculine stems is vocalic (-*a* > MDu. -*e*), which places Old Low Franconian in one line with part of the Old Frisian and late Old Saxon inflectional pattern (as well as that of Old High German). This lack of a more salient or distinctive plural marker may have been the reason why the *a*-stem inflection was not as dominant as in Old English and had to compete with two comparably productive types, i.e. the *n*-stems and *i*-stems.

Given the limited scope of the available Old Dutch corpus, little can be established about the developments in neuter nouns. The neuter inflection is attested vestigially in the historical *u*-stems (*fē* 'cattle') and in two *s*-stem nouns, *kalf* 'calf' and *kind* 'child'. It can be assumed that the major destination class for these nouns was the class of neuter *a*-stems, although a different inflectional pattern can be diachronically observed for the historical *s*-stems (cf. Section 6.5.6).

Another limitation resulting from corpus size is the restricted amount of information that can be retrieved about the prehistoric transitions of nouns. Many nouns which show only inflections of non-original classes could theoretically testify to such early, prehistoric transfers; however, as their absolute numbers are very low, the evidence does not exceed a mere chance level. An example may be the singly attested ACC. PL. form *coi* 'cows', which testifies to a shift from the root noun inflection to the *i*-stems. As it is the only attestation to the lemma *kuo*, the possibility that the historical root noun inflection was still present as well at that time, though not reflected in the small corpus of Old Dutch, cannot be excluded. Consequently, there are only few instances where it can be positively stated that a noun had earlier followed a different pattern of inflection and transferred to another class prior to the first attestations of Dutch (see Section 6.5.2 for examples).

As in the other investigated languages, the restructuring of the nominal inflection in Old Low Franconian was guided by gender in that the nouns changing their declensional affiliation retained their original gender. In fact, the affiliation of nouns with a particular class was strongly dependent on gender. At the same time, as Table 6.1 demonstrates, some parallels across gender classes can easily be detected: the masculine and neuter nouns tend to show a considerable overlap of inflections in the singular, while the masculine and feminine nouns show more correspondences in the plural. The importance of gender is also reflected in the merger of the feminine ō- and n-stems, as a result of which a new distinct, feminine class emerges in opposition to the masculine and neuter a-stems. In his discussion of the development of the Old Dutch plural, Kürschner (2008) emphasises the significance of gender in the separation of declensional types. He points to the discrepant patterns in the neuter vs. non-neuter nouns and the gradual dissolution of the "Koalition der Maskulina und Feminina" in the plural (Kürschner 2008: 156). This strong dependence of the classification of nouns on gender was lost in (late) Middle Dutch, where the inflectional classes tended to merge independently of gender (Kürschner 2008: 157).[279] This original stability of gender class affiliation despite interdeclensional reshufflings is reflected in the taxonomy of nouns and the treatments of declensional classes in the grammars, where gender distinction emerges as a primary criterion (e.g. Quak 1992).

The descriptions of the Old Low Franconian declensional system in the historical grammars present it as a system whose reorganisation involving analogical realignments was considerably advanced. Despite this assumed advanced stage of inflectional reorganisation, the present analysis, in compliance with the methodology applied in the other chapters, will consistently take the historical classification of nouns based on the stem criterion as the starting point, trying to identify vestiges of the historical inflection. It can be expected that, just as in Old English or Old Frisian, the etymological stem criterion is no longer relevant for the synchronic classification of inflectional types.

6.4   Phonological developments in Old Low Franconian

The heterogeneity of the Old Low Franconian material becomes particularly prominent when considering the phonology of unstressed syllables. Due to geographical, chronological and consequently linguistic discrepancies between the three major sources, the phonological developments influencing the reorganisation of the nominal inflection need to be discussed separately for individual texts. According to Quak (1992: 81), the use of full vowels in unstressed syllables was an inherent feature of Old Low Franconian, distinct from Middle Dutch (as with the sister languages, especially Old vs. Middle English and Old Saxon vs. Middle Low German). The attested alternations, such as between <e> and <i> in the i-stem inflections,

---

279. For a detailed treatment of these developments in Middle Dutch, see Marynissen (1996).

can potentially be ascribed to the phonological context (Quak 1992: 89).[280] Alternatively, this alternation can be interpreted as indicative of a merger of *e* and *i*, parallel to the alternation between the vowels *u* and *o* (de Vaan 2017: 96; cf. Borgeld 1899: 15). The exact phonological values of these vowels are not of primary concern for the present study inasmuch as they represent a single phoneme. As regards the status of the other vowels, the ending <a> is scarce in the material provided by the minor classes; it is not a historical ending in any of the instances, but originates in the NOM./ACC. PL. of the masculine *a*-stems (*fadera* 'fathers', *fiunda* 'enemies'). The ending <o> is common in the GEN. PL. (*hando* 'hands', *manno* 'men') and alternates also with <u> in the NOM./ACC. SG. in the *u*-stems: *fritho* ~ *frithu* 'peace', *fio* ~ *fiu* 'cattle', and in the DAT. PL. in all classes except the *i*-stems (e.g. *fiundon* ~ *fiundun* 'enemies'). The ending <o>, consistently applied in the GEN. PL., may represent a long vowel /o:/ < PGmc. *-ōn, while the alternation between <o> ~ <u> in the *u*-stems and in the DAT. PL. of other stems may reflect a short vowel /ʊ/ (< PGmc. *-u). In other words, the attested distribution of vowels represented by <o> and <u> indicates a phonemic contrast between /o:/ and /ʊ/.

Even though the contrasts are not always consistent, they are frequent enough to justify a postulation of a variety of distinct phonemes in unstressed syllables.[281] The following set of unstressed vowels could be identified in the text of WPs: /ɪ/ rendered by <e/i>, /a/ rendered by <a>, /ʊ/ rendered by <o~u> and possibly /o:/ rendered by <o>.[282] Although the phonological reduction of final vowels to *schwa* is dated later (the beginning of Middle Dutch; van Bree 1987: 79), a potential trait

---

280. Some regularity in the distribution, depending on the weight of the stem, can be detected. Accordingly, the (scantily attested) light-syllable masculine stems show consistently the marker *-e* (*stede, beke, slege*), whereas in the heavy-syllable stems the alternation between <i> and <e> is regularly found (*crefte, -i, thurste, -i*). The former consistency could be attributed to vowel harmony, regularly found in Old Frisian (cf. Versloot 2008).

281. For a discussion of the spelling variation, and in particular the question of allophonic and phonemic contrasts in unaccented syllables, see, e.g., Hogg (1992a: 214–245, with reference to Old English), Versloot (2008: 205–212; 215, with reference to Old Frisian), and Klein (1977, with reference to Old Saxon).

282. Such an interpretation is reminiscent of the treatment found in Borgeld (1899: 14–30), who refers to the Old High German vowels in order to render the Old Low Franconian correspondences. The phonological status of the spellings is not considered; they are taken at face value and a nearly one-to-one relation between character and sound is assumed. His comparison reveals that there is a fairly high correlation between the vowels in Old High German (*a, e, i, o, u,* short and long) (Braune/Reiffenstein 2004: 61) and the way they are represented in WPs. The attested irregularities are explained as levellings from other paradigms or in terms of a phonetic detail, as in the case of the alternating <i> and <e> spellings in the *i*-stems, where the alteration is believed to represent "(…) een tusschen *-e* en *-i* liggende vocaal (…)" (Borgeld 1899: 15).

of such a reduction in WPs is reflected in the singly attested irregular form of the GEN. PL. *berge* 'mountain' (instead of **bergo*), which may, however, equally well represent a scribal error (Quak 1992: 83).[283]

The situation in Rb is considerably different, which comes as little surprise given that the source is younger than WPs. The text has been included in the Old Dutch corpus (*ONW*) primarily on account of the phonological criteria and correspondences with the other sources. However, the present analysis of the vowels in inflectional syllables (confined to minor stems) indicates that full vowels were no longer present in inflectional syllables. As the most common character used in the inflectional endings is <e>, it can be assumed that it had the phonological value of /ə/, cf. WPs *hendi*, Rb *hande* 'hand' (DAT. SG.); WPs *handun*, Rb *handen* 'hand' (DAT. PL.). This assumption complies with the claim that *schwa* can be reconstructed for the Late Old Dutch period, with different realisations depending on the dialect and phonetic conditioning (de Vaan 2017: 248–249). Such a state of affairs was consequential for the interpretation of the inflectional endings (as archaic or innovative), and rendered many forms inconclusive (especially in the *i*-stems) (cf. Section 6.5.2).

Finally, the text of LW exhibits an intermediate stage with respect to the development of inflectional vowels between the one observed in WPs and the one found in Rb. In LW a clear contrast between a front vowel, rendered by <e>, and back vowels, spelled <a> and <o>, is retained. At the same time, nearly all inflectional endings can also be represented by <e>, which indicates that [ə] was already a potential realisation. Accordingly, a vowel system with two unstressed vowels can be reconstructed, with /e/ represented by <e>, and /ɔ/ represented by <a> ~ <o>, where both phonemes could alternate with the [ə] realisation.

The free interchange between <e> and <i>, and the growing tendency to use <e> as an inflectional marker leads to a situation where many inflectional endings become opaque and cannot be unambiguously interpreted as historical or analogical. For instance, the presence of <e> in the GEN. and DAT. SG. in masculine and neuter nouns can point to both *i*-stem or *a*-stem inflection, and accordingly, the exact declensional source of forms such as the innovative *u*-stem *uualde* 'forest' cannot be unambiguously identified.

---

283. A more widespread presence of the *schwa* in Old Low Franconian inflectional syllables was postulated by Cowan (1961), according to whom alternations such as the one between <i> and <e> testify to the presence of a reduced vowel /ə/, which is not interpreted as a phoneme, but rather as a reduced (unstressed) allophone of the stem vowel (as in *uuatir* ~ *uuateres* 'water', NOM.SG. ~ GEN.SG.) (Cowan 1961: 9). Much in the same vein, Kyes (1969) ascribes the inconsistent spelling of unstressed (inflectional) vowels to a lack of phonemic contrast and the presence of one reduced vowel /ə/. The author claims that the vowels in inflectional syllables coalesced into one phoneme before the first attestations of Dutch, adducing the Middle and modern Limburgian vowel systems as evidence for this interpretation (Kyes 1967: 670).

Apart from the developments in unstressed syllables, another factor significant for the reorganisation of inflection in Old Low Franconian was the process of *i*-mutation. The unfolding of the process corresponds to the pattern found in Old High German (and largely Old Saxon), where *i*-mutation is not yet morphologised and is hardly reflected in spelling (i.e. it is graphically rendered for instances of primary umlaut of PGmc. */a/). The *i*-mutated vowels are regularly attested in the *i*-stem paradigms in compliance with the expected development, while their presence in the other minor classes is a consequence of the analogical extension of the *i*-stem inflection rather than a trait of the original pattern. Accordingly, the presence of *i*-mutated vowels in the paradigms of the *u*-stems (e.g. *hand* – *hendi*, DAT. SG. and NOM. PL.) or root nouns (e.g. *tand* – *tende*, NOM./ACC. PL.), attested alongside the analogical *i*-stem markers, is a feature which points to the influence of the *i*-stem pattern. Significantly, in contrast to Old English or Old Frisian, which attest to *i*-mutation in the DAT. SG. and NOM./ACC. PL. of root nouns and *nd*-stems, no *i*-mutated vowels were originally present in the paradigms of nouns historically affiliated with consonantal declensions in Old Dutch (e.g. *man* – *man, naht* – *naht*). The absence of the *i*-mutated vowel in consonantal declensions, which could otherwise have served as a distinctive inflectional feature, may have had some impact on the tempo of the restructuring process, facilitating the encroachment of analogical inflections into the paradigm.[284]

6.5   Data analysis

6.5.1 Methodological considerations

In compliance with the procedure applied in the investigation of the sister languages, the tendencies present in the Old Dutch nominal inflection were also framed quantitatively. Accordingly, the study examined the quantitative relation between the incidence of the inherited (archaic) and analogical (innovative) inflectional endings (i.e. *a*-stem, *ō*-stem, *i*-stem, *n*-stem) in the paradigms of minor stems. Given the limited scope of the available corpus and the scant attestations to minor stems, the results of the present investigation should not be interpreted in absolute terms. It is assumed, however, that despite the low figures retrieved from

---

284. A few instances, e.g. the *i*-stems: *enst* (WPs) and MDu. *ghewelt* can be interpreted as vestiges of *i*-mutation before *-*i* which is no longer regularly attested in Old Low Franconian (Krogh 1996: 181). Essentially *i*-mutation operated after the apocope of *-i* following a heavy-syllable, but, as these few isolated examples indicate, the chronology of primary *i*-mutation and apocope must have been occasionally reversed (in contrast to Old High German).

the available data, the quantitative investigation conducted on a corpus as small as that of Old Low Franconian can still be informative about the predominant tendencies identifiable in the language.

A few morphosyntactic categories, although included in the quantitative study, were considered uninformative about the restructuring on account of their ambiguous status. This refers in particular to the GEN. PL. (in -*o*) and DAT. PL. (in -*un*, -*en*), which (with a few exceptions, i.e. the *s*-stems and the *i*-stem DAT. PL. in -*in*) happened to be identical with the respective forms of the *a*-stems and *ō*-/*n*-stems. This does not refer to the *s*-stems, where vestiges of the historical pattern are potentially identifiable. Theoretically, in classes where traces of the *i*-stem inflection are present in the paradigm, the DAT. PL. could be informative in that the endings -*un*, -*on*, as opposed to analogical -*in*, could be interpreted as a continuation of the original inflection rather than as a result of the influence of the *a*-stems or *ō*-/*n*-stems. This is especially relevant for the material attested in WPs, which consistently displays the spread of the *i*-stem inflection, but it is less conclusive for the evidence from the other sources, where the phonological developments in inflectional syllables (such as the reduction of unstressed vowels in Rb) need to be taken into account. An example here is the DAT. PL. form of the root noun *mannon*, attested in WPs, which could be interpreted as a continuation of the historical inflection (rather than as a single instance of the *a*-stem inflection), since all the other forms in the plural paradigm point to the analogical extension of the *i*-stem pattern. Such potential instances which could continue the historical inflection will consistently be referred to in the discussion, though, as mentioned earlier, they are not considered conclusive in the analysis.

Not all the forms in the tables presenting the paradigms are actually attested in the corpus. The depicted paradigms are "reconstructed" on the basis of the entire available inventory of a given class and the chosen lexemes serve to represent a given declensional type. Because of the scarcity of the available material, recourse was occasionally made to the Old High German evidence, which stays morphologically closest to Old Dutch. The forms quoted in this chapter (as well as those in the Old Low Franconian section of the Appendix), unless shown in a context, are consistently presented in the shape that they are cited in the *Oudnederlands Woordenboek*.

On account of the linguistic heterogeneity of the texts included in the analysis, some discrepancies in the inflectional patterns between individual texts can be expected. Therefore, attention will be given to such potential inflectional divergences, especially in light of the fact that some of them, in particular those attested in Rb, but also in LW, could be ascribed to the influence of Central Franconian. Another problem related to the heterogeneous nature of the textual material is posed by the spelling variation of vowels in inflectional syllables, e.g. -*es*, -*is* (GEN. SG.), -*en*, -*in*,

-*on* (*n*-stem DAT. SG.). This spelling variation can to some extent be used to recon-struct phonemic contrasts in that the spelling variants are used to render a limited (and gradually diminishing) set of phonemes in unstressed syllables. The variation affected the interpretation of spelling especially in cases where the phonological analysis led to the conclusion that phonemic contrasts were (almost) entirely lost (Rb); in other instances its effects on the morphological analysis are limited.

Finally, it must be observed that all forms that were ambiguous, whether due to the phonological shape, problematic identification of case/number, or unclear origin, were considered inconclusive and excluded from the calculations (ca. 40% of all forms).

6.5.2   The status of the *i*-stems in Old Low Franconian

As can be inferred from the treatments found in the standard historical grammars, the class of the OLF *i*-stems can hardly be treated as unproductive. Already in the prehistoric stage, the *i*-stem inflection attracted nouns originally affiliated with the *s*-stem pattern, as evidenced by the sister languages. In the later period, the *i*-stem pattern spread to the original heavy-syllable feminine *u*-stems, root nouns and feminine *r*-stems. In this respect, Old Low Franconian matches Old High German, where the productivity of the *i*-stem inflection had a very wide scope. As the pre-vious chapters have demonstrated, some productivity of this inflectional type is observable also in Coastal West Germanic, especially in Old Saxon and vestigially in Old Frisian. Although the presence of analogical inflections from other produc-tive types in the paradigms of *i*-stems can occasionally be detected, the class can be viewed as representing a productive declensional type, and the fact that traces of analogical features can be identified in the *i*-stem paradigms does not undermine its status as a stable declension.[285]

The *i*-stem pattern had certain distinctive features which rendered it productive and attractive to minor stems. Formally, the historical *i*-stems were characterised by the ending -*i*/-*e* in the NOM./ACC. PL. as well as the effects of *i*-mutation in the root vowel. The presence of *i*-mutated forms in the paradigm can be viewed as a hallmark of the *i*-stem inflectional pattern, both in the masculine and feminine paradigms. The distribution of *i*-mutated forms corresponds closely to that found in the Old English root nouns, where the *i*-mutated vowels are found in the GEN. and DAT. SG. (e.g. NOM. SG. **scaft* 'spear', DAT. SG. *scepte*; SG. **slag* 'stroke', DAT. SG. *slege*) as well as potentially in all cases in the plural, but most commonly in the NOM./ACC. PL.

---

285. Cf. the feminine paradigm of Old English *n*-stems, considered a productive declension, which is itself to some extent influenced by the *ō*-stems.

In contrast to Old High German, and in line with the Ingvaeonic dialects, Old Low Franconian retains the distinction between light- and heavy-syllable *i*-stems, although the former are only vestigially attested in the material (except the DAT. SG. *slege* 'stroke' and ACC. PL. *beke* 'brook') and, consequently, it is difficult to make any conclusive statements about their inflection (Quak 1992: 85). Assuming that the Middle Dutch attestations, where the light-syllable *i*-stems are well represented (e.g. *bete* 'bite', *beke* 'brook', *broke* 'breach', *hate* 'hatred', *mere* 'sea', *orloghe* 'war', *screde* 'step', *spere* 'spear', *sproke* 'saying', *trede* 'step', etc.), can to some extent be informative about the earlier stages, it can be concluded that the class was more numerous than evidenced in the available material and that the limited number of attested lemmas is due to the nature of the corpus.

A typical paradigm of heavy-syllable masculine and feminine *i*-stems is presented in Table 6.2 (the light-syllable *i*-stems show -*i* throughout the paradigm of the singular). The presented masculine paradigm is largely reconstructed as this inflectional subtype is only scantily attested.

Table 6.2 The OLF heavy-syllable masculine and feminine *i*-stems

	masculine *i*-stems		feminine *i*-stems	
	SG	PL	SG	PL
NOM.	*scaft*	scefti	craft	crefte, -i
GEN.	scefte,-i	*scefto*	crefte, -i	*crefto*
DAT.	scefte,-i	sceftin	crefte, -i	creftin,-on
ACC.	*scaft*	scefti	craft	crefte, -i

The unsystematic alternation between -*e* and -*i* in the GEN. and DAT. SG. probably involves variants of the same phoneme (Quak 1992: 90), and it is as such of no significance for the present morphological analysis. The feminine inflection, with its *i*-mutated root vowel and the distinctive inflectional markers both in the singular and the plural, is clearly distinct from the productive ō-/*n*-stem inflection. The presence of inflectional -*i*- in the DAT. PL., attested in the feminine stems, is also a unique feature of this inflectional type, which Old Low Franconian shares with Old Saxon and Old High German (in contrast to the rest of West Germanic). The status of the masculine *i*-stems is somewhat more ambiguous, largely due to their limited attestations. Although the class is not very large (19 attested nouns), the *i*-stem declension features, i.e. *i*-mutated vowels and the NOM./ACC. PL. marker -*e*/-*i*, are consistently attested in the paradigms (NOM. PL. *scefte*, *sceifte*, ACC. PL. *scepfti* 'arrows', *trani* 'tears'). The available evidence indicates that *i*-mutation was present also in the GEN. and DAT. SG., which, given the shape of the historical *i*-stem paradigm, can be interpreted as a regular phonological development (DAT. SG. *thursti* 'thurst', *tuni* 'fence') (cf. Table 2.12). An opposite view is espoused by Borgeld (1899: 70), who ascribes the occasional *i*-mutated vowel in the singular (DAT. SG. *scepte*) to *intra*paradigmatic pressure, i.e. an analogical extension from the plural. This interpretation corresponds to the treatment of the Old High German *i*-stems found in Braune/Reiffenstein (2004: 201), where the singular of masculine nouns is consistently presented without the *i*-mutated vowel. The forms which show no *i*-mutated vowel in the DAT. SG. are indistinguishable from the *a*-stem forms and are thus considered inconclusive in this study.

As has already been mentioned, it is generally assumed that the presence of the NOM./ACC. PL. in -*e*, -*i* in the root nouns, *u*-stems and *r*-stems testifies to the analogical spread of the *i*-stem inflection in their paradigms. In view of this wide scope of analogical expansion of the *i*-stem inflections to other declensions, attesting to the productivity of this pattern, a systematic and exhaustive quantitative investigation involving the entire inventory of the *i*-stems, parallel to that conducted for the unproductive paradigms, was considered superfluous. Such an extensive spread of inflectional features to other declensions would be unlikely if the *i*-stems themselves were affected by extensive analogical levelling from other productive classes, i.e. the *a*- and *ō*-/*n*-stems – as it was the case in Old English and Old Frisian. The productivity of the *i*-stem inflection presupposes that the historical *i*-stems constituted a stable class, in which the influence of other inflectional patterns was insignificant. Given, however, the empirical orientation of the present study as well as the fact that the status of the masculine *i*-stems is somewhat less unambiguous with respect to productivity, the assumption that *i*-stems represented a stable class was subjected to a quantitative analysis, with a view to estimating the extent of potential analogical pressures in their paradigms. Accordingly, the investigation was conducted on a representative and nearly exhaustive set of historical *i*-stems, including 38 masculine and feminine nouns, amounting to 257 tokens altogether. The list included 19 masculine nouns, which constituted an exhaustive inventory of masculine stems, and 19 (most common) feminine stems (see Appendix). The inventory was compiled on the basis of the lists of *i*-stems available for the other Old Germanic dialects, in particular Old Frisian and Old Saxon. The information was supplemented by the instances of historical *i*-stems found in the grammars of Continental West Germanic languages, especially of Old Saxon and Old High German. Essential for the analysis were the discrepancies between the three major textual sources, which due to their diverse origin could be expected to differ with respect to the preservation of the *i*-stem inflection. The investigation of the inflectional patterns found in the *i*-stems led to a number of observations which can be summarised as follows:

1. The inflections in the singular of heavy-syllable feminine stems

While the NOM. and ACC. SG. are regularly endingless in all sources, the GEN. and DAT. SG. show predominantly -*e*, -*i* endings, which constitute respectively 83 percent (*n* = 30) of all the attested forms in WPs and 86 percent (*n* = 21) in the LW. In Rb the endingless singular appears to be the rule in the feminine. The endingless forms in the GEN. and DAT. SG. which do not show *i*-mutated vowels can be attributed to *intra*paradigmatic levelling, i.e. the influence of the (unmutated endingless) NOM. and ACC. SG. forms (Sanders 1974: 202; cf. Marynissen 1996: 290, with reference to Middle Dutch).

2. The inflections in the light-syllable stems (masculine and feminine)

The final vowel -*e*, -*i* is regularly preserved in WPs (only 4 tokens attested), both in the singular (DAT.) and plural (ACC.), and to some extent also in LW (50%, *n* = 32); the Rb shows predominantly apocope of the vowel (92%, *n* = 13). Endingless forms appear in the NOM. SG. for *stad* 'place'[286] in both LW and Rb, and the former text attests as well to the spread of the *n*-stem inflections in *wine* 'friend' (ACC. SG. *winon*).

3. The ending of the DAT. PL.

The expected *i*-stem ending -*in* is found only in WPs in feminine stems (*misdadin*, *creiftin*); the archaic ending is not attested in the other textual sources, where the common markers are -*on*, -*an* and -*en* (*crafton*, *woledadan*, LW). The presence of the latter, attested especially in Rb, may be indicative of the process of phonological weakening.

4. The NOM./ACC. PL. inflections

The historical NOM./ACC. PL. marker -*e*, -*i* is found in 92 percent (*n* = 12) of all forms in WPs, but only in 27 percent of forms in LW (*n* = 11), where the marker -*a*, spreading from the *a*- and *ō*-/*n*-stems, is dominant both in masculine and feminine paradigms. In Rb the attested forms are inconclusive due to the phonological reduction that rendered the historical contrast between -*i* and -*a* no longer visible, as well as the lack of the forms with /a/, where *i*-mutation could be reflected. With respect to gender differences, in the feminine paradigm the historical inflection is attested consistently in WPs, whereas LW shows analogical forms in 67 percent (*n* = 6) of all attestations. In masculine nouns the historical ending is attested in 62 percent of inflections, with WPs showing a much more archaic pattern than LW, the former covering 88 percent (*n* = 8) of forms, the latter only 20 percent (*n* = 5) of forms.

---

286. Cf. the DAT. SG. *stede* and a potential NOM. SG. *stede* instead of *stat* as attested in place names *Hemstede* vs. *Blindenstat* (Quak 1992: 90); cf. OHG *stad* (Braune/Reiffenstein 2004: 202).

5.   *i*-mutation

The *i*-mutated vowels are attested in all three sources, with the most consistent pattern of distribution found in WPs and a less regular pattern in the other sources, which can be ascribed to the extension of the non-mutated vowels from the NOM./ACC. SG. While the original vowel /a/ is regularly preserved in the NOM./ACC. SG. (*n* = 18), the *i*-mutated variants are consistently attested in the GEN. and DAT. SG. in WPs (*n* = 17), and in 60 percent of forms (*n* = 5) in LW. The GEN. SG. form *epheles* 'apple' (LW) is a hybrid formation, showing both the historical *i*-mutated vowel and the non-original ending -*es*, and was accordingly considered inconclusive in the present study. Hardly any *i*-mutated vowels were found in the singular paradigm in RB (8%, *n* = 13). In the NOM./ACC. PL. *i*-mutation is common (*n* = 7) in WPs and LW, and occasionally appears in forms which show no historical inflections (e.g. *eppela* 'apples', LW). The *i*-mutated vowel is attested also in the DAT. PL. (*creiftin*, WPs; *eppelon*, LW; *benthen* 'bounds', Rb), alongside the more common unmutated forms found in sources other than WPs (*crafto, crafton*, LW; *balgun* 'bellies', other sources).

The quantitative investigation reveals that the text of WPs testifies to the most conservative pattern with respect to the preservation of the *i*-stem inflection: the *i*-stems show historical inflections in both gender classes, including the archaic DAT. PL. ending -*in* and the *i*-mutated vowels in all instances where they could be historically expected (except the GEN. PL. where no instances of historical **-ion* were found). The other sources, i.e. the LW and Rb, display a more innovative profile, with a tendency towards apocope of -*e* in the singular. In the plural, Rb tends to show a pattern of (respectively) -*e*, -*e*, -*en*, -*e*, while LW testifies to traces of analogical *a*-stem and *ō*-/*n*-stem inflections.

Overall, the results of the investigation corroborate the status of the feminine *i*-stems as a stable class in Old Low Franconian, which was hardly affected by interparadigmatic levelling. This complies with the assumption that the origin of the plurals in -*i* in feminine minor classes (in root nouns, *u*-stems and *r*-stems) must be sought in the *i*-stem declension. The stable status of the *i*-stem inflection attested in early Old Low Franconian (WPs) fulfills the condition (sine qua non) for the productivity of this pattern, the effects of which are clearly visible in the WPs material. When it comes to the distribution of inflections in the masculine *i*-stems, it can be concluded that the plural inflection is mostly archaic, in particular in WPs, whereas for the singular the data is largely ambiguous and the conclusions are fairly tentative. It can be assumed that by the time of the first attestations of Old Low Franconian, many paradigmatic syncretisms between the masculine *i*-stems and *a*-stems existed, especially in the singular. The difference between the two paradigms was primarily in the forms of the NOM./ACC. PL. (and occasionally DAT. PL. -*in* vs. -*un*, -*on*), while the rest of the inflections overlapped with the *a*-stems, which facilitated the merger of these two inflectional paradigms at a later stage. In the

Middle Dutch period, due to the formal similarity of the (heavy-syllable) *i*-stem and *a*-stem paradigms, enhanced by the elimination of *i*-mutated vowels from the *i*-stem paradigm, these classes tended to merge (Franck 1883: 122). Generally, the evidence for the inflections of masculine stems turns out to be less conclusive than for the feminine stems.

To conclude, in contrast to the situation in the Ingvaeonic dialects, and in compliance with the Old High German pattern, the *i*-stem declension cannot be treated as an unproductive type in Old Low Franconian. The attested material indicates clearly that this declensional class constituted an attractive inflectional pattern for minor stems. The expansion of the *i*-stem inflection to other declensional types is unambiguously reflected in the spread of the following features, to be found potentially in the paradigms of minor stems:

a.   the *i*-mutated vowel in the GEN./DAT. SG. and in all cases in the plural
b.   the NOM./ACC. PL. ending -*e*/-*i* (but see also the discussion in 6.5.3.1)
c.   the DAT. PL. marker -*in* (in place of the -*on*, -*un*).

6.5.3   *u*-stems

The process of reorganisation of the *u*-stem paradigm must be dated early, since many of the nouns originally affiliated with this declension inflect entirely according to the patterns of the productive classes, typically of the *a*-stems and *i*-stems. Given the formal similarities between the *u*-stems and *i*-stems at an early stage (Bammesberger 1990: 150; Krahe & Meid 1969: 33–34), it is hardly surprising that their paradigms tended to merge at some point, which is well evinced in the Old Low Franconian material. Complying with the patterns found in the Old High German dialects, the *i*-stem inflection in Old Low Franconian absorbed most of the nouns affiliated originally with the *u*-stems, and the features of the historical inflection can be expected to appear only as vestiges. A number of early analogical transfers can be identified on the basis of the evidence provided by the other Old Germanic languages, including the following nouns: *thurst* 'thirst' (*i*-stem), *grunt* 'ground' (*ja*- or *i*-stem), *appel* 'apple' (*i*-stem, cf. the *i*-mutated vowel in the GEN. SG. and in the plural: *epheles, ephela*), *thorn* 'thorn' (*i*-stem).[287] The paradigm of *feld*

---

287. The noun is an original *u*-stem and is attested in glosses (MSS Paris, BN lat. 8670, dated to the 9th c.) as *thorni*, which complies with the Old Saxon state of affairs, where it tended to oscillate between the *a*-stem and *i*-stem patterns (in contrast to Old High German where it consistently displays *a*-stem inflections, OHG *dorn*; Braune/Reiffenstein 2004: 201–202); cf. DAT. PL. of OS *thornion* (Heliand M, 1741) vs. *a*-stem *thornon* (C, 1741) and the other forms in the paradigm following the *a*-stem declension as well (Gallée 1993: 210). See also Blech (1977: 142, 145) for an alternative interpretation of *thorni* in Old Low Franconian.

'field' can arguably be considered an early transfer to the *a*-stems, with a simultaneous change of gender to neuter in all the attested forms. According to the *EWN*, the noun may be traced back to two PGmc. forms: **felþa-*, **felþu-*. Assuming that the OLF *feld* developed from PGmc. **felþa-*, its affiliation with the *u*-stems in Old Low Franconian may be questioned.

In spite of meagre attestations, nouns of all three genders, including light- and heavy-syllable stems, are recorded in the available material, with the neuter confined to one noun only (*fio* 'cattle'). As in the other investigated languages, restructuring affected the light-syllable and heavy-syllable stems in different ways, with the latter being more prone to analogical pressures. The historical heavy-syllable *u*-stems tended to follow the pattern of the *i*-stems, which was manifested in the extension of the ending *-i/-e* in the NOM./ACC. PL. as well as the presence of the effects of *i*-mutation (Quak 1992: 84). The two attested light-syllable *u*-stems, *fritho* 'peace' and **sido* 'custom', retain some vestiges of the historical inflection in the singular, although they essentially follow the inflection of the *a*-stems (*frithis, frithe*[288]) and *n*-stems (the GEN. SG. *sidin*, WPs 67,7) (Quak 1992: 87).

The effects of analogical pressure of the productive inflectional types are found in the following categories, summarised also in Table 6.3:

Table 6.3 The competing inflections in the OLF light-syllable masculine *u*-stems

	archaic		innovative	
	SG	PL	SG	PL
NOM.	frithu, -o	frith(i)u	frith	frithi, -e
GEN.	fritho	*fritho*	frithis,-(e)n	*fritho*
DAT.	frithiu	*frithun*	frithe(n)	*frithen*
ACC.	frithu, -o	frith(i)u	frith	frithi, -e

a.   masculine stems
   – the NOM. SG. zero ending in place of the historical *-u* (> *-o*) (light-syllable stems)
   – the GEN. SG. *a*-stem marker *-is* and the *n*-stem marker *-(e)n* in place of the historical ending **-o*
   – the DAT. SG. *a*-stem marker *-e* and the *n*-stem marker *-(e)n* in place of the historical ending **-iu*
   – the NOM./ACC. PL. marker *-i* (*-e*) in place of the historical ending **-iu*

---

288. According to Quak (1992: 87), the DAT. SG. form *frithe* is ambiguous. In the context of the present study it is clearly analogical, irrespective of whether it is to be attributed to the influence of the *a*-stems or *i*-stems.

b. feminine stems
  - the NOM./ACC. SG. marker -*a* in place of the original ending -*u* (in light-syllable stems) and an endingless form (in heavy-syllable stems)
  - the GEN. SG. marker -*e*, the *a*-stem marker -*es* (-*is*) and the *n*-stem marker -*(e)n* in place of the historical ending *-*o*
  - the DAT. SG. marker -*e* (-*i*) and the *n*-stem marker -*(e)n* in place of the historical ending *-*iu*
  - the NOM./ACC. PL. marker -*e*, -*i* in place of the historical ending *-*iu*.

The archaism of the *u*-stem paradigm is reflected most prominently in the singular in the retention of the marker -*u* (< *-*uz*) or -*o* in the NOM. and ACC. in light-syllable stems. Accordingly, the lack of this original ending (e.g. *sun(u)*) is interpreted as an analogical feature.[289] The influence of the *i*-stems, apart from being reflected in the extension of the respective inflectional endings, can be expressed also in the root structure, with the presence of the *i*-mutated vowel. Consequently, root vowel alternations of the type *hendi/hande/heinde* 'hand' in the NOM./ACC. PL. testify to the influence of the *i*-stem inflection, where the *i*-mutated vowel was regular in the plural (but see Sections 5.6.3.3 and 6.5.3.1).

As the token frequencies of individual nouns in this class are very low, no distinction was made between the masculine and neuter paradigms, with the latter attested only for the noun *fē* 'cattle'. The noun is recorded in WPs and shows historical inflections in the NOM./ACC. SG. (*fio, fiu*). The combined results for masculine and neuter *u*-stems as well as for the feminine *u*-stems are presented in Table 6.4. The tendencies identifiable for individual gender classes are discussed below. Table 6.5 presents the overall distribution of archaic and innovative features in the *u*-stem paradigm, as well as their distribution with respect to number.

The data indicates that the historical paradigm of the *u*-stems was largely disintegrated by the time of the first attestations of Old Low Franconian. This holds true for the masculine (neuter) and feminine paradigms, the latter testifying to no traces of the archaic inflection whatsoever. The dominant pattern of inflection in the paradigm of the *u*-stems is that of the *i*-stems, accompanied by the *a*-stem inflections in the masculine stems. The influence of the latter is in fact fairly limited; it shows in the inflections of the GEN. SG. (*frithis*) and DAT. SG. (*frithe, fluode*). As no masculine forms of the NOM./ACC. PL. are attested in the corpus, little can be said about the spread of analogical forms in the plural. The expansion of the *i*-stem inflections is

---

289. This tendency towards reduction of final vowels in the NOM./ACC. SG. is well attested in Old High German, where the nouns such as *sunu* (*suno*) 'son' or *lidu* 'member' are found most frequently without a final vowel in these categories: *sun, lid*, testifying thus to a complete transition to the *i*-stem declension (Braune/Reiffenstein 2004: 205; Franck 1909: 190–191).

Table 6.4 Distribution of archaic and innovative inflections in the OLF masculine, neuter and feminine *u*-stems

	Masculine & neuter				Feminine			
	archaic		innovative		archaic		innovative	
	SG	PL	SG	PL	SG	PL	SG	PL
NOM.	(1) 6%	(0)	(16) 94%	(2) 100%	(0)	(0)	(1) 100%	(6) 100%
GEN.	(0)	*(3)*	(3) 100%	–	(0)	*(3)*	(2) 100%	–
DAT.	(0)	*(1)*	(6) 100%	–	(0)	*(5)*	(9) 100%	–
ACC.	(6) 40%	(0)	(9) 60%	(0)	(0)	(0)	(1) 100%	(8) 100%
Total	(7) 16%		(36) 84%		(0)		(27) 100%	

Table 6.5 Overall distribution of archaic and innovative inflections in the OLF *u*-stems

	u-stem inflection	innovative inflection
singular	(7) 13%	(47) 87%
plural	(0) 0%	(16) 100%
Total	(7) 10%	(63) 90%

attested especially in the feminine paradigm. The two attested heavy-syllable feminine nouns, i.e. *fluot* 'flood' and *hant* 'hand', largely follow the *i*-stem pattern, which is reflected in the GEN. SG. (*fluodi*) and DAT. SG. (*henti*). Another innovation in the paradigm of feminine heavy-syllable stems is the presence of endless forms in the DAT. SG., attested in LW and Rb. The form is reminiscent of the endless forms in the feminine *i*-stems, and can be attributed to the influence of intraparadigmatic levelling, i.e. the extension of the form of the NOM./ACC. SG. The analogical plural forms (in -*e* and -*i*) are found only in the feminine paradigm (for *hant* 'hand' and *dura* 'door'), and derive from the *i*-stem inflection. The DAT. PL. *handun* can potentially be interpreted as archaic as it shows no effects of *i*-mutation, which would be otherwise (i.e. under the influence of the *i*-stems) expected in the plural (cf. NOM. PL. *hendi*). The NOM./ACC. SG. ending -*a* in *dura* is interpreted as novel and ascribed to the influence of the productive *ō*-/*n*-stems.

As regards the spread of the process with respect to morphosyntactic categories, it can be concluded that the GEN. and DAT. are the most innovative cases in the singular. The analogical GEN. SG. marker -*is*/-*es* prevails in the masculine paradigm, and the ending -*e* in the feminine paradigm. The novel inflection in the DAT. SG. of masculine nouns originates in the *a*-stems, and in the feminine nouns either in the productive *ō*-/*n*-stems (*dure*) or the *i*-stems (*hendi*).

Given the later spread of the *n*-stem pattern (in Middle Dutch), traces of this declension in the *u*-stem paradigm are not unexpected. The weak inflections are found in LW and Rb, but not in the earlier attested WPs. They are relatively well-attested in the singular (e.g. GEN. SG. *sidin* [*sido 'custom'], DAT. SG. *friden, duren, spizzon,* ACC. SG. *uriden*).

The archaic inflection is attested in light-syllable stems, especially in the NOM./ ACC. SG., where forms in *-u, -o* appear (*suno, fritho, fio*). Vestiges of historical inflection can potentially be found also in the GEN. and DAT. PL. which, in contrast to the NOM./ACC. PL., show no traces of *i*-mutation (*hando, handun, -on*) (cf. Quak 1992: 90). The problem with interpreting these forms as historical is familiar from the discussions of similar forms in the other investigated languages: on account of their formal similarity across declensional classes, they cannot be unambiguously distinguished from the forms of the *a*-stems or *ō-/n*-stems. Accordingly, they were considered inconclusive in the present study and excluded from the overall counting, in compliance with the treatment they received in the other investigated languages. Among the archaic forms identified in the corpus, one instance of the original DAT. SG. ending *-u* was found, namely the form *wudu* 'wood'. The form points clearly to the historical *u*-stem inflection; however, the interpretation is fairly problematic due to the origin of the source it is attested in and its possibly ambiguous reading.[290]

Finally, a number of historical inflections could be identified in compound formations (as the first element) and in toponyms (as the first or the last element), which tend to retain more archaic features, e.g. *widumānōth* 'September', *widubruok* 'Widdebroek', *marowidu* '*Maarwede'. Likewise, the form **haru-* 'hill' (f.) is attested in the NOM. as *-hara*, with the DAT. SG. in *-i*: *-heri, -here*, which shows the original *u*-stem inflection (*ONW*, s.v. *hara, heri*).[291] For reasons discussed in Section 6.2, such forms were excluded from the quantitative investigation.

In consequence of the analogical developments, the paradigm of the *u*-stems lost its original identity primarily to the benefit of the *i*-stem inflection. The parallel historical profile of these two classes was a factor triggering and enhancing this direction of analogical reshaping (cf. Section 6.5.3.1).

---

290. The form is found in a runic inscription which is commonly affiliated with the early Frisian material. It is attested in the following context: **anwudu kiri þu**, with the following translation provided: 'turn to the wood(s)', ca. 800 (*ONW*, s.v. *wudu*) (Quak 1991b: 19–21). As the material used in the *Oudnederlands Woordenboek* has a wide geographical scope, covering the present-day Dutch-speaking area, texts or inscriptions whose descent is not entirely transparent, but which derive from that region are also included (cf. Pijnenburg 2003: 14–16). Another problem is posed by the exact interpretation of this runic inscription which is not unambiguous, and alternative readings, where the form is not interpreted as an independent lemma but possibly as *æwudu* (cf. OE *æwda* 'witness') or proper noun *æludu* (< **aluða(z)*), have also been postulated (Looijenga 2003: 314–316; Looijenga & Knol 1990). The form was accordingly excluded from the calculation.

291. I would like to thank Professor Arend Quak for drawing my attention to these forms.

6.5.3.1   *An excursus on the* DAT. SG. *and* NOM. PL.

On the assumption of the validity of the claims concerning the origin of the DAT. SG. and NOM. PL. endings, presented in Section 5.6.3.3, an alternative interpretation of the *u*-stem inflection can be offered in compliance with the argumentation presented there.

Firstly, given the overall linguistic profile of Old Low Franconian and in particular the parallelisms of morphological developments it shows with Old High German, the general opinion that the OHG ending *-i* in the DAT. SG. and NOM. PL. is a younger development of the original *-iu* (Braune/Reiffenstein 2004: 205–206) can be extended to Old Low Franconian as well. In other words, the inflectional marker *-i* found in the DAT. SG. can be interpreted as a continuation of the historical ending. Likewise, the plural forms such as *duri* (ACC. PL.) and *hendi* (NOM. PL.) may represent a continuation of the original *u*-stem plural marker on the assumption that the ACC. PL. was built by analogy to the NOM. PL., which is a likely direction of intraparadigmatic levelling (cf. Section 2.2.2). As the contrast between *-i* and *-e* is not phonemic in Old Dutch, both vowels can be interpreted as inherited (e.g. *frithe*, *hendi*), but they cannot be distinguished from the *i*-stem endings.

The implications of this theory are significant for the interpretation of inflectional forms in the Old Low Franconian corpus. Namely, if the DAT. SG. and NOM./ACC. PL. forms in *-i/-e* are considered inherited, then the inflection of the *u*-stems needs to be compared to that of the *i*-stems on the one hand, and to the *a*- and *ō*-/*n*-stems on the other. The reason for a separate comparison is that, depending on the class the *u*-stems are compared to, different cases will be informative about the restructuring in the paradigms. Accordingly, when the *u*-stems are compared to the *i*-stems, only the GEN. SG.[292] and the DAT. PL. are conclusive. If they are compared to the *a*- and *ō*-/*n*-stems, the GEN., DAT. and ACC. SG. are informative for the feminine stems, and the GEN. SG. and possibly DAT. SG. (when *i*-mutation is visible, i.e. in roots with *-a-*) for the masculine ones. In the plural, the NOM. and ACC. are conclusive and theoretically also the GEN., with a potential *i*-mutation in the root. For instance, the DAT. SG. *hendi* is inconclusive when compared with the *i*-stem inflection, but it is conclusive when compared with the *a*- and *ō*-/*n*-stems, and is then interpreted as an archaic form. The results of this twofold comparison are presented in Table 6.6, which depicts the overall percentage of analogical inflections in the *u*-stems in individual texts. The table does not present the directions of the transition of nouns, but refers to contrasts between inflectional patterns (i.e. which paradigmatic forms are treated as informative/non-informative about the restructuring). The three sources were treated separately, since it could be expected

---

292. There is one interpretable GEN. SG. feminine *u*-stem, which shows an *i*-stem ending: *fluodi* (WPs).

that the two texts staying linguistically closer to Central Franconian could show the more extensive impact of the *i*-stems, complying with the pattern similar to the one found there.

Table 6.6 The interpretation of the OLF *u*-stems in two different perspectives

	u-stem vs. *i*-stem inflection		*u*-stem vs. *a*-, *ō*-/*n*-stem inflection	
	archaic	innovative	archaic	innovative
WPs	55%	(11) 45%	79%	(24) 21%
LW	23%	(13) 77%	33%	(12) 67%
RB	7%	(29) 93%	22%	(32) 78%
other	100%	(2) 0%	100%	(3) 0%
Total	24%	(55) 76%	46%	(71) 54%

As becomes evident, the interpretation of endings of the DAT. SG. and NOM. (and ACC.) PL. as inherited rather than analogical yields quite a different picture of inflectional reorganisation in the *u*-stems. The level of innovation is comparable to that in Table 6.5 when the point of reference is the paradigm of *i*-stems, but it is considerably lower when the point of reference is the paradigms of *a*- and *ō*-/*n*-stems. A substantial part of the archaism in the latter case must be attributed to the NOM. and ACC. PL. The lower number of analogical inflections in these two categories indicates that the salience of plural markers (NOM./ACC. PL.) played an essential role in the retention of the historical endings (cf. Table 6.22). The vocalic marker (*-i*, *-e*), although not as salient as the presence of allomorphy (*i*-mutated vowels), tended to show greater resistance to analogical pressures than a zero marker (e.g. in consonantal stems).

The comparison with the *i*-stems reveals a profound influence of this inflection in the *u*-stems in the NOM./ACC. PL. Given the overlap of endings in the remaining categories (which were considered inconclusive here), it can be concluded that these two classes show nearly identical inflectional profiles. In light of their historical development, which points to many parallels existing already in Proto-Germanic, this tendency to merge can hardly be surprising. Even if the overall shape of the *u*-stems is to be attributed to analogical reshaping on the pattern of the *i*-stems rather than to a historical development, parallel to that found in the *i*-stems, it must be concluded that the restructuring took place at a prehistoric stage. A consequence of it was the obliteration of the boundary between the *i*-stem and *u*-stem patterns, and the emergence of a "super-class" or "super-inflection", whose growing productivity is well attested in Old Low Franconian and the rest of Inland West Germanic. Finally, the anticipated discrepancies between the sources turn out to be prominent, reflecting a departure from the historical pattern of inflection in line with the chronology of their attestations.

6.5.4 Root nouns

Root nouns are a *relatively* well attested group of nouns in Old Dutch, both in the singular and the plural. Their paradigms bear no traces of internal vowel alternation (*i*-mutation) as was the case in the other investigated languages. Traces of the original consonantal pattern of inflection are still to be found in the paradigm of *man*, especially in the plural, where endingless forms appear in the NOM. and ACC. As regards the novel pattern of inflection, the masculine nouns are attested predominantly with the inflections of the *a*-stems, whereas the feminine nouns show predominantly inflectional features of the *i*-stems. The analogical pressure from the productive declensions is reflected in the following paradigmatic irregularities:

a. masculine nouns
    –   the GEN. SG. marker *-es* (*-is*) in place of the original endingless form
    –   the DAT. SG. ending *-e* in place of the original endingless form
    –   the NOM./ACC. PL. markers *-a*, *-i* and *-an* in place of the original endingless form
b. feminine stems
    –   the GEN. SG. ending *-e* (*-i*) in place of the original zero ending (extended from the *ō-/n*-stems or *i*-stems)
    –   the GEN. SG. *a*-stem ending *-es* (*-is*)
    –   the DAT. SG. ending *-e* (*-i*) in place of the historical endingless form
    –   the NOM./ACC. PL. markers *-a* or *-i* in place of the original zero ending

Tables 6.7 and 6.8 present competing inflections in the paradigms of masculine and feminine root nouns, respectively. Due to the scant attestation of Old Dutch, not all the forms which appear in the tables are actually attested in the available material. This refers in particular to the archaic paradigm (see footnote 45). The distinction between light- and heavy-syllable stems is irrelevant in this declensional class (in the context of inflectional restructuring).

Table 6.7 The competing inflections in the OLF masculine root nouns

	archaic		innovative	
	SG	PL	SG	PL
NOM.	*fuot*	fuot	*fuot*	fuota, -i
GEN.	fuot	*fuoto*	fuotis	*fuoto*
DAT.	fuot	*fuotan, -en*	fuote, -i	*fuotan, -en*
ACC.	*fuot*	fuot	*fuot*	fuota, -i

Table 6.8 The competing inflections in the OLF feminine root nouns

	archaic		innovative	
	SG	PL	SG	PL
NOM.	*naht*	naht	*naht*	nahta, -i
GEN.	naht	*nahto*	naht(e)s, -e, -i	*nahto*
DAT.	naht	*nahtan, -en*	nahte, -i	*nahtan, -en*
ACC.	*naht*	naht	*naht*	naha, -i

Although the default paradigm for the analogical transfers in feminine nouns was the *i*-stem and partly ō-/*n*-stem declension, the presence of traces of the *a*-stems cannot be excluded. By the same token, given the expansiveness of the *i*-stem pattern, traits of the *i*-stem inflections can also be expected in the masculine paradigm, where the prevailing analogical pattern was that of the *a*-stems. As the default pattern in feminine nouns is the *i*-stem inflection, the forms of ACC. SG. are not considered informative for the restructuring (cf. the paradigm of *craft*, Table 6.2). As becomes evident in the paradigms presented above, in contrast to the Ingvaeonic languages, Old Low Franconian shows no vestiges of secondary *i*-mutation in the root nouns (see also Section 7.3).

The distribution of historical and analogical inflections in the masculine and feminine root nouns is presented in Tables 6.9. Apart from the inconclusiveness of the GEN. and DAT. PL. forms, the NOM. and ACC. SG. do not provide any reliable information about the restructuring either, and are accordingly excluded from the count. Table 6.10 presents the distribution of inherited and analogical inflections with respect to number as well as the overall distribution of these forms in the analysed material.

Table 6.9 Distribution of archaic and innovative inflections in the OLF masculine and feminine root nouns

	Masculine				Feminine			
	archaic		innovative		archaic		innovative	
	SG	PL	SG	PL	SG	PL	SG	PL
NOM.	*(10)*	(4) 57%	–	(3) 43%	*(3)*	(0)	–	(1) 100%
GEN.	(0)	(6)	(1) 100%	–	(1) 17%	(0)	(5) 83%	–
DAT.	(0)	(6)	(3) 100%	–	(10) 67%	(5)	(5) 33%	–
ACC.	(1)	(2) 20%	–	(8) 80%	(8)	(1) 50%	–	(1) 50%
Total	(6) 29%		(15) 71%		(12) 50%		(12) 50%	

Table 6.10 Overall distribution of archaic and innovative inflections in the OLF root nouns

	root noun inflection	innovative inflection
singular	(11) 44%	(14) 56%
plural	(7) 35%	(13) 65%
Total	(18) 40%	(27) 60%

The above-presented data indicate that the spread of the productive inflections in root nouns affected 60 percent of forms. The cases which remained resistant to analogical pressures are the DAT. SG. in the feminine paradigm (67% of inherited inflections) and the NOM. PL. in the masculine paradigm (57%). The data testify to the expansion of two major inflectional types in the root noun paradigms: the *i*-stems and the *a*-stems, while the influence of the *n*-stem inflection is very limited (confined to a single instance of the ACC. PL. of *fōt* 'foot', *uozen*, attested in Rb). The impact of the *i*-stem pattern is evident in both the feminine and masculine paradigms, with the marker -*i* or -*e* appearing in the GEN. and DAT. SG. (*burgi* 'town', *manni* 'man', *fuoti* 'foot') as well as in the NOM./ACC. PL. (*fuoti, burge, tende*). The ending -*e* in the DAT. SG. (*manne, burge*) can be ascribed to the influence of the *a*-stem or *i*-stem inflection. Given that the restructuring was essentially guided by gender, the presence of -*e* in the masculine nouns can be attributed to the pressure of the *a*-stems, whereas in the feminine nouns, most likely, the influence from the *i*-stems was key. An unambiguous reflex of the influence of the masculine *a*-stems is the marker -*es* (-*is*) in the GEN. SG. (*mannis*). As in the other West Germanic languages, the influence of the masculine inflection in the feminine paradigm is evident in the noun *naht* 'night' (*nahtes*), which appears with the *a*-stem ending -*es* in adverbial phrases with *dages*.[293] The change of declension/gender class is triggered by the presence of the masculine *dages*, and is confined only to this specific context. The masculine inflection is attested also in a single form of the NOM. PL. *ginōtas* 'comrades' in the minor sources, namely in *Utrecht Baptismal Vow* (*Utrechtse doop-belofte*), dated to the late-eighth/early-ninth century.[294] Given that the expected analogical inflection in this form would be -*a*, from the masculine *a*-stems (*daga*), the form in -*as* can only be explained as a North Sea Germanic feature (cf. OE

---

293. E.g. ...*inde in enum* (l. *euun*, DG/Q; l. *euuin*, G) *sinro thenken sal dages inde nachtts* (l. *nachtes*, DG/G; l. *nahtes*, Q) 'in one of his thoughts shall day and night' WPs (*ONW*, s.v. *naht*).

294. *ec forsacho (...) thunaer ende uuoden* (ms.: *en deuuoden*) *ende saxnote ende allvm them unholdum the hira genotas sint.* 'I renounce (...) Thunear and Woden and Saxnot and all those demons who are their companions' Utrechtse doopbelofte CG 026,18 Utrecht, Holland, 791–800 (*ONW*, s.v. *genōt*).

-*as*, OS -*os*),[295] characteristic of this early attested text.[296] As the affiliation of this noun with the root nouns is disputed (see Griepentrog 1995: 490–491; cf. Braune/ Reiffenstein 2004: 215), it was not included in the calculation.

Apparently, the singular was slightly more affected by the restructuring than the plural, yet the difference in terms of percentages is rather inconspicuous. The pattern is unexpected in that the discrepancy between the singular and plural is much more prominent in the other declensions. Significantly, while the archaism of the feminine nouns is built predominantly on the singular, the archaism of the masculine nouns is based solely on the plural, where the historical inflection is retained in a third of forms (35%).

Although *i*-mutation was absent from the paradigm of root nouns in Old Low Franconian (as a typical feature of this declension), a root vowel alternation is attested in the paradigm of *tant* 'tooth', which consistently shows an *i*-mutated form in the NOM./ACC. PL. (*tende*, WPs). The attested forms are clearly analogical and can be attributed to the influence of the *i*-stems, where the *i*-mutated vowel (alongside the inflectional ending) was contrastive, serving to mark the distinction between the singular and the plural (*craft* – *crefte*). The details of this analogical transformation remain, however, not entirely transparent and the exact interpretation of the forms depends on the accepted chronology of analogical transitions. On the one hand, it seems feasible that the *i*-stem pattern created a template for the transformation of the paradigm, including *i*-mutation of the root vowel. The growing pressure of the *i*-stem inflection was apparently not confined to unstressed syllables, but affected also the shape of the root. Such an interpretation implies that

---

295. There are no *s*-plurals attested in WPs and LW in minor stems. Whether this inflectional marker was present in Old Dutch is a moot question. Although a number of nouns testify to the -*as* plural ending (*nestas, genotas, yrias, dadsisas, nimidas*) (Philippa 1987: 36, 44; cf. Krogh 1997: 26, 28), the interpretation of this marker poses serious difficulties. As these forms are attested in manuscripts where the Anglo-Saxon influence is evident, or in forms where the ending can arguably be ascribed to the Latin inflection, this evidence is not entirely reliable (cf. Bremmer 1989: 78–80). The emergence of the *s*-plural in Middle Dutch (South-West) is attributed to the contact situation, namely the impact of English (Anglo-Saxon) or French (Philippa 1987: 52) and it is believed that the ending spread from the south-west linguistic area (Calais). It is only in the coastal dialects of Dutch, where the earliest attestations go back to the 14th c., that this ending can be viewed as autochthonous (Marynissen 2001: 667). The question whether its origin can be sought in Old Saxon, as suggested by Philippa (1987: 35), who grounds her claim on the fact that the *s*-plural marker is more common in north-east Dutch nowadays than in the standard language, stays beyond the scope of this study (see Krogh 1996: 296–298 for a discussion of the origin of this ending).

296. In terms of the linguistic structure, this early attested text has been viewed as a hybrid, combining a number of Franconian and Ingvaeonic characteristics, evident also in the morphological layer.

the extension of the *i*-stem inflections in the root nouns must have taken place after the operation of *i*-mutation, and that the *i*-mutated vowel was adopted simply as an element of the novel pattern built on the *i*-stem paradigm. On the other hand, it could be assumed that the analogical extension of the *i*-stem inflections occurred earlier, i.e. prior to *i*-mutation (primary umlaut), and that the *i*-mutated vowel was a regular development in this class, occasioned by the presence of the new inflectional ending. Establishing the exact chronology of these processes seems fairly problematic, however.[297]

Overall, the distribution of analogical inflections and in particular the directions of interdeclensional transfers are reminiscent of the situation in Old High German (and partly Old Saxon), where the paradigm of the *i*-stems shows substantial productivity, expanding to both masculine and feminine root nouns (e.g. NOM./ACC.SG. OHG *fuozi* (m.), GEN.DAT.SG. OHG *nahti*, *burgi*; NOM.PL. OS *idisi*, NOM./ACC.PL. *buoki*; Braune/Reiffenstein 2004: 216–217; Franck 1909: 199–200; Gallée 1993: 219–220). This parallelism is a reflex of a more general, overarching trend, evident in the reshaping of the nominal inflection, whereby these Continental West Germanic languages pattern in a like manner. As regards the discrepancies between individual texts, no conspicuous patterns emerge from the attested distribution in that no significant biases were found between the data in the *Wachtendonck Psalms* and the younger and more franconised texts of *Leiden Willeram* or the *Rhyming Bible*.

6.5.5 *r*-stems

The inventory of nouns denoting kinship terms remains unchanged and all nouns belonging originally to this class are represented in the Old Low Franconian corpus. Despite the sparse attestation of this declensional type, a number of tendencies are discernible. The *r*-stem paradigms reveal the presence of *a*-stem or *i*-stem inflections, with gender being a significant determiner for the direction of analogical transfers. Accordingly, the masculine nouns tended to follow the *a*-stem inflection, whereas the feminine nouns were attracted to the *i*-stem pattern. The impact of the productive inflectional types in the *r*-stems is manifested in the following inflectional irregularities:

---

297. If primary *i*-mutation preceded apocope of short -*i* after heavy syllables in OLF (as it does in ms. S of *Heliand*), then the root vowel *e* in *tendi* would be a regular development and by the same token form a natural link to the *i*-stems; however, the inflections of OLF *mann* do not corroborate this assumption.

a. masculine nouns
   - the GEN. SG. marker -es (-is, -s) in place of the original zero ending
   - the DAT. SG. ending -e in place of the original zero ending
   - the NOM./ACC. PL. marker -a (-e) and possibly -i in place of the original zero ending
b. feminine nouns
   - the GEN. SG. ending -e or the masculine a-stem ending -es replacing the original zero ending
   - the DAT. SG. ending -e in place of the historical zero ending
   - the NOM./ACC. PL. marker -a (-e) and possibly -i in place of the original zero ending

These potential traces of analogical inflections in the (feminine) r-stem paradigm are presented in Table 6.11.

Table 6.11 The competing inflections in the OLF feminine r-stems

	archaic		innovative	
	SG	PL	SG	PL
NOM.	muoder	muoder	muoder	muodera, -i
GEN.	muoder	muodero	muodere	muodero
DAT.	muoder	muoderon	muodere	muoderon
ACC.	muoder	muoder	muoder	muodera, -i

As can be observed, the paradigm of r-stems was originally remarkably uniform, particularly in the singular, showing no distinctive inflectional markers or any internal allomorphic variation. Assuming that explicit marking of case and especially number is generally preferred over less explicit marking, it could be expected that such a paradigmatic uniformity may have served as a factor triggering the encroachment of analogical productive markers (cf. Section 1.4.4).

The results of the investigation of the historical r-stems are presented in Table 6.12, where the distribution of archaic and innovative features is shown with respect to individual categories. As the figures (i.e. token frequencies) are very low, the attestations for the masculine and feminine nouns are presented collectively, but they are treated separately in the discussion. Table 6.13 depicts the distribution of the archaic and novel inflection with respect to number, as well as the overall distribution of inflections in this class. The categories which do not provide any conclusive information about the restructuring in this class were, apart from the GEN. and DAT. PL., the NOM. and ACC. SG. Accordingly, the incidence of inherited and novel inflections could be measured only on the basis of the GEN. and DAT. SG., and the NOM. and ACC. PL.

Table 6.12 Distribution of archaic and innovative inflections in the OLF masculine and feminine *r*-stems

	archaic		innovative	
	SG	PL	SG	PL
NOM.	(*29*)	(1) 20%	–	(4) 80%
GEN.	(12) 92%	(*1*)	(1) 8%	–
DAT.	(8) 100%	(3)	(0)	–
ACC.	(*11*)	(0)	–	(2) 100%
Total	(21) 75%		(7) 25%	

Table 6.13 Overall distribution of archaic and innovative inflections in the OLF *r*-stems

	r-stem inflection	innovative inflection
singular	(22) 95%	(1) 5%
plural	(1) 14%	(6) 86%
Total	(23) 77%	(7) 23%

The paradigm of *r*-stems turned out to be archaic, with only 23 percent of forms affected by new inflectional patterns. With respect to gender, the amount of innovative inflection in masculine and feminine nouns is comparable, with 31 percent of analogical forms found in the masculine nouns and 18 percent in the feminine nouns. Significantly, traces of the productive inflection are to be found in the plural only, while the singular is hardly affected by analogical developments. There are no traces of the influence of the *a*-stems in the GEN. SG. in masculine stems, where the marker -*es* (-*is*) could be expected given its expansiveness in the other classes. The NOM./ACC. PL. testifies to the presence of the *a*- and *ō/n*-stem inflections (*fadera, sustera*), alongside the features of the *i*-stem pattern attested in LW and Rb (*bruothere, sustere*). The interpretation of the marker -*e* in these two sources is not entirely unproblematic, but its *i*-stem descent, at least in LW, can be confirmed by the fact that the contrast between final -*a* and -*e* is retained (*bruothera*, GEN. PL. vs. *brothere*, NOM. PL.). In Rb, where phonological reduction of the final vowel to *schwa* must be assumed, the origin of the marker -*e* is less transparent; the form is, however, clearly analogical, irrespective of the exact source (be it *a*-stems or *i*-stems). The singly attested GEN. SG. form *dohteron* (WPs) poses some interpretative difficulties.[298] It is classified as a DAT. SG. in the *Oudnederlands Woordenboek*, with a qualification that it may also be interpreted as a DAT. PL. (cf. Köbler 2014b,

---

298. The noun is attested in the following context: *That ih (l. ik, Q) cunde alla predigunga thina, an portun dohteron sijon.* 'That I may declare all thy praise in the gates of the daughter of Zion', WPs 72,28. ut annuntiem omnes praedicationes tuas in portis filiae Syon. (*ONW*, s.v. *dohtor*).

s.v. *dohter*). Indeed, formally the form can represent a DAT. PL., with the marker -*on* fitting more into the pattern of the DAT. PL. than the SG. The interpretation of the form as a GEN. SG., as postulated in the present study, is not uncontroversial either, yet both the Latin original (*filiae*) as well as the translation of this psalm in many other sources seem to speak in favour of a GEN. reading. The major problem with this interpretation is that if *dohteron* represents indeed a GEN. SG., it would imply the influence of the *n*-stem inflection, which, given all the available evidence, would be the only instance of the impact of this inflectional type in the *r*-stems (cf. Borgeld 1899: 77). Although the spread of the *n*-stem inflections in the *r*-stems in the other West Germanic languages is occasionally attested, it is altogether fairly limited. Most importantly, the patterns of restructuring of this declensional type in closely related Old High German do not point to an extensive spread of the *n*-stem inflection (cf. Braune/Reiffenstein 2004: 213–214).[299] Alternatively, the form could be interpreted as a GEN. PL., which does not ideally correspond to the Latin word, yet it formally matches the shape of the GEN. PL., assuming again that it is built on the *n*-stems. For reasons mentioned above, the form was interpreted as a GEN. SG. in the present study and was counted accordingly.

The pattern of restructuring in this declensional type corresponds to that found in the other investigated languages, where the *r*-stems tended to remain resistant to analogical pressures in the singular. Even a cursory look at the subsequent development of these stems in Dutch (Middle Dutch) leads to a conclusion that analogical endings appeared in these stems very late: the analogical GEN. SG. marker -*s* (*des vaders*) emerges only in the thirteenth century and the forms of the feminine nouns (*dochter, moeder, suster*) are particularly conservative, remaining endingless until the thirteenth century (van Loey 1970: 268, 1976: 25; Marynissen 1996: 340–350).

In summary, the attested distributions of archaic and novel inflections testify to an interplay of three opposing forces in the paradigm: semantics, the salience of category markers and relative frequency. The higher frequency found in the singular may have worked as a factor conserving the original inflectional pattern, while the less frequent plural forms could be more prone to analogical developments. Given the low number of attestations, such a hypothesis is not easily borne out by the data and some additional support comes rather from the material provided by the other investigated languages, where frequency turned out to be a relevant factor. Another factor, the semantic constitution of this class, may have helped preserve the old inflectional pattern (with 77% of all forms being archaic). The decisive

---

299. The weak forms appear in Old High German only sporadically, primarily in the plural, e.g. NOM./ACC. PL. *tohterun* (Notker), GEN. PL. *tohtron(o)*, but also in the ACC. SG. *fateran* (for some more details on the distribution of analogical inflections in this class in Old High German, see Adamczyk 2009).

factor, however, seems to be the salience of inflectional exponents, with the more salient analogical marker introduced to indicate the contrast between the singular and the plural. As the contrast in the category of number is more significant than of case, the fact that the analogical inflection appears to mark this contrast in the plural is not unexpected. Finally, one more fact may be important for the interpretation of the forms in the *r*-stems, namely syllable structure. The disyllabic structure displayed by all the *r*-stems may have worked as a factor inhibiting the spread of analogical inflections in the paradigm (for a theoretical discussion of this aspect, see Section 8.6.4.2).

6.5.6 *s*-stems

The evidence for this class is confined to two nouns in Old Dutch, i.e. *kalf* 'calf' and *kind* 'child', and according to the information found in the standard historical grammars, there are no traces of the archaic *s*-stem inflection in the available material. Another noun which could be affiliated with the *s*-stems is *merikalf*, found in MSS Paris, BN lat. 8670, dated to the ninth century (as a gloss to *delfin*, cf. OHG *merikalb* and OS *meriswīn*, MDu. *merkalf*) (Klein 2003: 50–51). The lack of the original inflection in the nouns affiliated with *s*-stems can essentially be ascribed to the limited set of available data, but it may also imply that the restructuring was considerably advanced in this class by the time of the first attestations of Old Dutch. In view of the later evidence from Middle Dutch, where the forms in -*ere* are well attested (e.g. *eier(e)* 'eggs', *calver(e)* 'calves', *riser(e)* 'twigs'), the limited scope of the available material seems to be a more likely explanation.[300] Also Modern Dutch, with fifteen neuter nouns showing the ending -*eren* as a regular plural marker, some of which can be unambiguously traced back to the historical *s*-stems, provides sound evidence that the plural ending -*er* must have been present in the language at an earlier stage.

Given the very scant attestation of the nouns affiliated originally with this declension, the presentation of competing inflections poses considerable difficulties, in particular when it comes to the archaic paradigm. Accordingly, the majority of

---

300. According to Franck (1883: 126), the following nouns showed features of the original *s*-stem inflection in the plural in Middle Dutch: *ey* 'egg', *been* 'leg', *blat* 'leaf', *hoen* 'hen', *jonc* 'boy', *calf* 'calf', *kint* 'child', *cleet* 'garment', *lam* 'lamb', *liet* 'song', *loof* 'leaf', *rijs* 'twig', *telch* 'offspring'. The *r*-plural is the only attested plural form for *ei* and *hoen*, and in the other nouns it remains a potential variant alongside the more regular forms. Occasionally, the different inflectional variants had the function to distinguish the meaning, e.g. *bene* 'legs' vs. *beenre* 'bones'. For a detailed and systematic dialectal analysis of analogical developments in this class in Middle Dutch, see Marynissen (1996: 356–358); cf. also Kürschner (2008) and Dammel et al. (2010).

the forms in Table 6.14, which presents the reconstructed archaic and analogical inflections in the *s*-stems, are reconstructions based on the evidence provided primarily by Old High German (cf. Braune/Reiffenstein 2004: 188–189). In line with the procedure applied in the analysis of the *s*-stems in the sister languages (and in contrast to the treatment in the other declensions), the forms of the GEN. and DAT. PL. were included in the analysis, since the presence of the *r*-formative in these categories could potentially be indicative of the historical inflection. As the class comprised neuter nouns only, inflections of the neuter *a*-stems can be expected in the paradigms, with the expansive GEN. SG. marker -*es* and the NOM./ACC. PL. zero ending. No *i*-mutation can be reconstructed in the paradigm of the *s*-stems in Old Low Franconian (Klein 2013: 179), which corresponds to the situation in the other investigated languages (partly except Old English) and Central Franconian.

Table 6.14 The competing inflections in the paradigm of the OLF *s*-stems

	archaic		innovative	
	SG	PL	SG	PL
NOM.	*kalf*	kalfar	*kalf*	kalf(a), -an
GEN.	kalfir(es)	kalfro	kalfes	kalfo, -ono
DAT.	kalfir(e)	kalfron	kalfe	kalfon
ACC.	*kalf*	kalfar	*kalf*	kalf(a), -an

The evidence for the *s*-stems is very limited (37 tokens) and except for two attestations of *kalf* (NOM. and ACC. SG.), it is confined solely to the paradigm of *kind* 'child', whose etymological status is not entirely clear (cf. *EWN*, s.v. *kind* and the discussion in Section 3.5.6.3). The analysis revealed that there are no traces of *s*-stem inflection in the paradigm of *kind*, and that the noun follows exclusively the neuter *a*-stem pattern. This parallels the situation in Old Saxon, where the noun inflects as an *a*-stem, providing thus no evidence whatsoever that *kind* had ever been affiliated with the *s*-stems. As the etymological status of the noun is fairly uncertain and as it shows no historical inflection, it seems hardly relevant to discuss the distribution of inflections in terms of a spread of innovative features. Significantly, aside from the presence of the neuter *a*-stem features, e.g. GEN. SG. *kindes* ($n = 1$), DAT. SG. *kinde* ($n = 7$), NOM./ACC. PL. *kind* ($n = 1$), there is a single DAT. SG. form *kindi* (WPs), which can be ascribed to the *i*-stem pattern, testifying to the productivity of this inflectional type in Old Low Franconian.[301]

---

301. A single endingless DAT. SG. form *kin[t]*, attested in WPs, is difficult to interpret, since the form was emended and the final shape is not entirely reliable; it was not included in the quantitative analysis.

As mentioned earlier, the attested pattern of inflection is unexpected in light of the Modern Dutch data which provides ample evidence for the presence of the *r*-formative as a plurality marker. It is present not only in the neuter nouns whose origin can be traced back to the *s*-stems (e.g. *ei-eier, hoen-hoenderen, kalf-kalveren, kind-kinderen*,[302] *lam-lammeren, rund-runderen*), but also in a number of nouns which originally had no affiliation with this class, proving that this inflectional pattern must have been productive at some stage (e.g. *been-beenderen, blad-bladeren, lied-liederen*).[303] In both subgroups a process of reanalysis of the plural pattern took place: the plural forms were reinterpreted as singular and an analogical plurality marker *-en* was added. The appearance of the new plural ending (*-en*) is dated to the thirteenth century, when it was used occasionally (Marynissen 1996: 356; 2001: 661). The development is reminiscent of the situation in the Old English *s*-stems of the type *hrīþer* 'horned cattle', where the original plural form is reinterpreted as a singular and new analogical markers are attached to it (*hrīþer-es,-e*) (cf. Section 3.5.6).[304] A further occasional expansion of the *r*-plural marker is attested also in *spaan-spaanders/spaanderen* (but *roeispaan-roeispanen* 'oar'), and *houtspaander-houtspaanders* 'wood chips'.[305] Both Modern and Middle Dutch evidence points to a development parallel to that found in High German (Old and Middle High German) in that the original inflection of the *s*-stems, as inherited from Proto-Germanic, was (to some extent) extended to stems affiliated with other declensional classes, including the *a*-stems. Accordingly, the original *s*-stem inflection, with a distinctive plural exponent, must have had some temporal productivity (which was to dwindle eventually), which is, however, not reflected in the available Old Dutch material. In conclusion, there is no positive evidence in the Old Dutch corpus that the original *s*-stem inflection was entirely non-existent.

---

302. Cf. the discussion above.

303. The possible alternations in the plural include *hoenderen~hoenders* (regionally, i.e. in the east also *hoender*), *eieren~eiers, kinderen~kinders, spaanderen~spaanders*. While Dutch has a clear preference for the *-eren*-plurals and the forms in *-ers* are essentially marked (dialectal), they are fairly common in Afrikaans (van der Toorn et al. 1997: 619; cf. the preference for the *-s*-plural after *-e[nmlr]* in Modern Dutch, e.g. *appel – appels, hamer – hamers*, etc.).

304. The synchronic interpretation of the sequence *-eren* entails the presence of stem allomorphy: it is assumed that the *-eren* nouns contain a stem allomorph (*-er-*) which is used in the plural forms (Booij 2002: 23).

305. As *hoen* and *spaan* end in /n/, they are subject to regular /d/-epenthesis before /ər/: **hoener- > hoender-, *spaaner > spaander-* (cf. Du. *minder < minn-er* 'less', *kelder < keller* 'cellar') (cf. Franck 1883: 82; *EWN*, s.v. *spaan*). It may be hypothesised that the /d/-epenthesis leads to a looser connection between the singular and the plural forms, which subsequently facilitates the reanalysis of the variant in *-ers* from, e.g., *hoen+d+er-s > hoender+s* (cf. Afrikaans: *hoender*, SG.).

At the same time, potentially some positive evidence for lack of the original *s*-stem inflection could be sought in the toponymic material, which tends to stay conservative, often fossilising the historical inflectional features (e.g. *Kalverstraat*). Accordingly, if the original *s*-stem inflection was to be preserved, it would be found most likely in the toponyms. However, no such archaic forms showing traces of the *s*-stem inflection could be identified in the available toponymic material. A piece of evidence of this nature, i.e. confirming the absence of the historical *s*-stem inflection, is found in *kalf* (*calva-*, *kalue-*, *kaues-*), e.g. in *kalfstaart* (*Calvastert*) (Guines, Northern France), as well as in *runth* (*rinth*) 'cattle', the latter attested solely in toponyms (*Hrintsalis*, *Rondeslo*).[306] The lack of the *r*-element can point to its absence from the paradigms, indicating at the same time that there may be more at stake than simply the dearth of the available data. It may imply, namely, that the *s*-stem inflection was never present in Old West Low Franconian as the nouns may have abandoned it already in prehistoric times. On the other hand, both attestations of place names come from the North Sea Germanic region and it seems feasible that they correspond to the evidence from West Saxon Old English, where the *r*-formative was absent from the singular paradigm. Representing some early western variety, these sources cannot be conclusive about the dialect of Brabant or Limburg, and as toponyms, they could be elements testifying to the North Sea Germanic substratum (where the attestation of the -*er*-plurals was limited).

The only piece of early evidence which could point to the presence of the original *r*-element in the paradigm of the *s*-stems is that provided by *lamp* 'lamb'. Although relatively well attested in Old Low Franconian material, the noun is found only in Latin contexts and therefore the interpretation of its inflectional forms is fraught with difficulties (e.g. *lampri*, *lampris*, *lampros*, *lamprorum*). As the source in which the forms are attested derives also from Flanders, it undermines the conclusion that the western provenance would disfavour the *r*-formative. Likewise, an unambiguous morphological interpretation of the forms attested in the *Salic Law* (*Lex Salica*) is problematic because of the Latin context. They were accordingly excluded from the present quantitative investigation.

To sum up, the scarcity of the data is largely responsible for the attested shape of the *s*-stem inflection and the overall picture of the reorganisation of this class. Consequently, the *s*-stems can be considered the least reliable class when it comes to providing evidence for the reorganisation of the Old Low Franconian nominal inflection.

---

306. But cf. forms such as *Honrebom* and *Ruddervoorde*, in which the -*er*- element can be traced back to the original *s*-stem inflection of the GEN. PL. Arguably, the word *Ritherlo* 'Ruurlo' could be interpreted as deriving from **rind*, but the more likely origin is in *rith* 'brook' (Quak in preparation).

6.5.7 *nd*-stems

The class of *nd*-stems is scantily attested in Old Low Franconian, comprising three nouns altogether: *friunt* 'friend', *fiund* 'enemy' and *neriand(o)* 'saviour', of which only (the first) two testify to vestiges of the historical inflection.[307] The dominant inflectional pattern most likely to be found in the paradigm of *nd*-stems is that of the masculine *a*-stems. In light of the expansiveness of the *i*-stems attested in the other declensional types, traces of this inflection can also be reckoned with. Table 6.15 presents the potentially competing inflections in the *nd*-stem paradigm.

Table 6.15 The competing inflections in the OLF *nd*-stems

	archaic		innovative	
	SG	PL	SG	PL
NOM.	*friund*	friund	*friund*	friunda, -e
GEN.	friund	*friundo*	friundes,-is	*friundo*
DAT.	friund	*friundun*	friunde	*friundun*
ACC.	*friund*	friund	*friund*	friunda, -e

Clearly, the original *nd*-stem paradigm was very uniform and undiversified, with no allomorphic variation present and the root structure identical with that of the *a*-stems. This uniformity and formal similarity with the most productive masculine declension made the paradigm prone to analogical pressures. The details of the distribution of archaic and innovative inflections in the paradigm of *nd*-stems are presented in Table 6.16.

Table 6.16 Distribution of archaic and innovative inflections in the OLF *nd*-stems

	archaic		innovative	
	SG	PL	SG	PL
NOM.	*(9)*	(2) 13%	–	(13) 87%
GEN.	*(0)*	*(1)*	(3) 100%	–
DAT.	*(0)*	(6)	(1) 100%	–
ACC.	*(0)*	*(0)*	–	(3) 100%
Total		(2) 9%		(20) 91%

The scant data testify to two major tendencies: alongside the expected impact of the *a*-stems, the features of the *n*-stem inflection, which can be interpreted as adjectival inflection, are also attested. The traces of the *a*-stem pattern are manifested

---

307. Cf. *wijgant, wigant* 'warrior' attested in the Middle Dutch sources (OHG *wigant*).

in the GEN. and DAT. SG. as well as in the NOM./ACC. PL., with the extension of the markers -*es*, -*e* and -*a* (-*e*), respectively. The weak (adjectival) inflections are found in the NOM./ACC. SG. marker -*o* (*n* = 6) and the DAT. SG. marker -*in*, attested only for *neriand(o)* (*n* = 1).[308] Although there is no doubt that the weak forms of the NOM. and ACC. SG. (*neriando*, *nereando*) are altogether analogical (irrespective of which declension they derive from), they were not included in Table 6.17. If these forms are taken into account in estimating the level of innovation, the amount of innovative inflections increases to 93 percent. As the monosyllabic *friunt* and *fiunt* are formally identical with the *a*-stems, they were inclined to follow the *a*-stem inflection and show no traces of the weak adjectival inflection. In contrast, the disyllabic *neriand* fits more into the morphological structure of participle formations based on the verb *nerian*, which followed the weak inflection of adjectives. This formal similarity must have facilitated the association with adjectival inflection of present participles.

Table 6.17 Overall distribution of archaic and innovative inflections in the OLF *nd*-stems

	nd-stem inflection	innovative inflection
singular	(0) 0%	(4) 100%
plural	(2) 11%	(16) 89%
Total	(2) 9%	(20) 91%

On a closer examination of the plural inflection in individual texts, a clear distinction emerges between the forms attested in WPs and those in the other sources, with the former showing the *a*-stem masculine marker -*a* in the NOM./ACC. PL. (*fiunda*), and the latter testifying to the presence of -*e* (*uiande*, *uiende*), which could potentially point to the impact of the *i*-stems. This source of innovation is not unlikely given that both LW and Rb tended to display more features attributed to the influence of High German inflection, where the *i*-stem pattern was productive. It is worth noting as well that the archaism of this inflectional class is built exclusively on the basis of the plural forms attested in these two texts.

Table 6.17 presents the overall distribution of historical and analogical inflections in the paradigms of the OLF *nd*-stems.

---

308. As the weak adjectival and weak nominal inflections (*n*-stems) were identical (Quak & van der Horst 2002: 42), it is hard to establish which is the actual source of the analogical forms. Given the evidence of the other examined languages, especially of Old English where the presence of adjectival inflection in the *nd*-stems is very well evinced, the adjectival influence seems more likely (cf. OHG *nerrendeo* 'saviour', *waltanto* 'warrior'; Braune/Reiffenstein 2004: 214 and Section 3.6.6).

The *nd*-stems testify to an advanced stage of inflectional reorganisation and thus hardly any synchronic alternation between the inherited and analogical forms can be observed (cf. Quak 1992: 87). The historical inflection is retained only in the plural, while all the forms attested in the singular follow the innovative pattern. This relative resistance of the plural to adopt analogical inflections continues into the Middle Dutch period, where the endingless forms of the NOM. and ACC. PL. (*viant, vrient*) are still retained alongside the dominant (analogical) *viande, vriende* (Franck 1883: 132; van Loey 1976: 25; Marynissen 1996: 377–379). Since the singular shows no traces of the historical inflection, it can be assumed that reorganisation in this declension took place early. As the token frequency is very low (four relevant forms in the singular), any such conclusion may seem too far-fetched and much caution should be exercised when interpreting the scant data. What renders the attested pattern valid, nevertheless, is the fact that it corresponds to the patterns found in the other investigated languages, where the singular tended to be much more innovative than the plural. This is especially true for the Old Frisian material, where the singular is entirely analogical, whereas the plural retains considerable archaism (cf. Section 4.5.7). This discrepancy, as could be observed there, seems to be directly related to the salience of the inflectional markers and the significance of the distinctive marking of the category of number (rather than case) (cf. Section 6.6).

6.5.8   Dental stems

Neither relics of the historical inflection nor nouns originally affiliated with the *þ*-stem declension were found in the investigated material, which could be anticipated given the size of the corpus and the attestation patterns of the dental stems in the other investigated corpora. As the vestiges of this consonantal inflection appear in Middle Dutch (endingless NOM./ACC. PL. form *maent* 'month'[309]), the lack of attested forms can be ascribed to the limited size of the corpus. The single noun originally affiliated with this declension found in the corpus is *magath* 'maid', attested as a feminine *i*-stem. The lack of ending in the DAT. SG. in LW (*magath* vs. WPs *magade*) is not a vestige of the historical consonantal inflection, but rather a reflex of a more general trend observable in this text, namely the activity of analogical levelling within the paradigm (with the template offered by the NOM./ ACC. SG. form).

---

309. Formally, the noun *maent* is classified as a feminine vocalic stem (*i-/u*-stem). The fact that it appeared frequently with numerals must have had some conserving effect, since in this context the plural could be used without any inflection, even in the vocalic classes (Franck 1883: 130; Le Roux & Le Roux 1973: 106).

6.6   Summary of the results and overview of the tendencies

The findings from the examination of individual declensional classes reveal the patterns of reorganisation of the Old Dutch nominal inflection. The major directions of interdeclensional transfers as identified in the analysis are summarised in Table 6.18 for individual declensional classes, including gender distinctions.

Table 6.18 Directions of interdeclensional transfers of minor stems in Old Low Franconian

Historical declensional class	New declensional class
u-stems (m)	=> *a*-stems, possibly *i*-stems
u-stems (f)	=> *i*-stems, *ō*-/*n*-stems
root nouns (m)	=> *a*-stems, *i*-stems
root nouns (f)	=> *i*-stems
s-stems (n)	=> (neuter) *a*-stems
r-stems (m)	=> *a*-stems
r-stems (f)	=> *ō*-/*n*-stems
nd-stems	=> *a*-stems
	=> adjectival inflection

The examined material testifies to the prevalence of the productive inflectional patterns in minor stems, with the *a*-stems and *i*-stems emerging as the dominant types. Their spread in the minor classes is gender-dependent and, accordingly, the *a*-stem inflections prevail in the masculine stems and the feminines follow largely the *i*-stems pattern. The *i*-stem inflection was particularly attractive to the feminine *u*-stems and root nouns. The non-feminine paradigms, i.e. the neuter *s*-stems, masculine *nd*-stems and *r*-stems were affected exclusively by the *a*-stem inflection. The pattern found in the masculine *u*-stems is ambiguous and difficult to interpret as there are no plural forms attested, and the analogical endings in the GEN. and DAT. SG. can be attributed to the influence of both *i*-stems or *a*-stems (cf. Section 6.5.3). Such a pattern of redistribution of nouns across classes does not comply with the situation found in the Ingvaeonic languages, where the *i*-stem inflection shows only limited traces of productivity. It is instead reminiscent of the reorganisation patterns in Old High German, where the *i*-stems show a substantial productivity and vast expansion to the minor paradigms. The influence of the *n*-stem declension is relatively limited and confined to the *u*-stems and single instances in the other classes.

Table 6.19 presents an overview of the distribution of inherited and analogical inflections in individual classes, including the overall incidence of forms in all minor stems. The fragmentary attestation of Old Dutch becomes very tangible when one considers the figures representing the number of attested lemmas in minor classes and their token frequencies. This dearth of available data calls for much caution when evaluating the material and making generalisations about the observed patterns. At the same time, the material is reliable enough to assume that the figures obtained from the quantitative study do reflect the major *tendencies* present at the early stage of the development of Dutch inflectional morphology.

Table 6.19 Summary of the distribution of archaic and innovative inflections in the OLF minor stems per class

	archaic	innovative
u-stems	(7) 10%	(63) 90%
root nouns	(18) 40%	(27) 60%
s-stems	(0) 0%	(22) 100%
r-stems	(23) 77%	(7) 23%
nd-stems	(2) 9%	(20) 91%
Total	(50) 26%	(139) 74%

As regards the distribution of innovative inflections across individual classes, it turns out that the *r*-stems remained most resistant to the analogical pressure of the productive inflections. The low percentage of innovation in the *r*-stems is to be as-cribed to a combined effect of their semantic constitution, as could be seen already in the other investigated languages, frequency of occurrence (which is, however, not directly reflected in the available material), and phonological structure (disyllabic words). The root nouns show analogical inflections in 60 percent of forms, which, in comparison with other classes, makes them relatively archaic. However, when compared to the sister languages, the class emerges as very innovative, indicating that its restructuring was more advanced in Old Dutch. A factor responsible for this divergent development may be the absence of the *i*-mutated vowel in the Old Dutch root nouns (and other consonantal stems). The lack of allomorphic varia-tion in the root nouns and thus greater paradigmatic uniformity rendered them susceptible to the impact of analogical processes and facilitated the merger with the dominant inflectional patterns, all the more so as in formal terms their paradigm was indistinguishable from the *a*-stem or *i*-stem paradigms. This assumption is corroborated especially by the Old English evidence, where the root nouns, marked by *i*-mutated vowels in the DAT. SG. and NOM./ACC. PL., remained one of the most conservative declensional classes, with residues of the original inflection retained until present-day English (cf. Section 3.5.4.2).

Some more insight into the patterns of the restructuring can be gained by comparing the figures for the singular and plural, as demonstrated in Table 6.20, which depicts the distribution of analogical inflections in individual classes with respect to number.

Table 6.20 Distribution of innovative inflections in the OLF minor stems with respect to number

	singular	plural
u-stems	87%	100%
root nouns	56%	65%
r-stems	5%	86%
s-stems	100%	100%
nd-stems	100%	89%
Total	(71) 64%	(68) 87%

The juxtaposition of the data for the singular and plural points to the fact that the plural was more susceptible to analogical pressures than the singular. The pattern runs counter to the tendencies identified in Old English, Old Saxon and Old Frisian, where the plural tended to remain more conservative. An important factor here is the salience of the inflectional exponents and the fact that across West Germanic number distinction tends to be more explicitly expressed than case distinction. With reference to Middle Dutch, this was made explicit by Marynissen (2001: 662), who states: "Die durch Analogie bedingten Veränderungen haben fast immer zur Folge, daß der Numerusunterschied formal an Erkennbarkeit gewinnt, während der Kasusunterschied hingegen oft ausgeglichen wird". The implication for the restructuring process is that the inflectional pattern that is characterised by a prominent marker in the plural will tend to win over the patterns where the plural is not marked in any distinctive way. Accordingly, the lack of distinctive plurality markers in the minor classes in Old Dutch rendered them more prone to the impact of the patterns where the plural was more prominently or explicitly marked.

Table 6.21 gives an overview of the plurality patterns found in the investigated material, juxtaposing the type of plural marker with the percentage of analogical features in individual classes (based on the NOM./ACC. PL.). The *i*-stems, representing essentially a productive declensional type in Old Low Franconian, are included in the overview for the purpose of contrasting the unproductive and productive

Table 6.21 The correlation between the salience of plural markers and the innovation level in the OLF minor stems

	plural marker(s)	% innovation in PL
i-stems	-*e*, -*i* + *i*-mutation	38%
u-stems	vocalic marker *-*iu*	100%
root nouns	Ø marker	65%
r-stems	Ø marker	86%
nd-stems	Ø marker	89%

plurality patterns. The *s*-stems could not be included in this overview on account of lack of sufficient attestations (cf. Section 6.5.6).

The validity of the above-formulated statement concerning the salience of plural markers seems to be confirmed by the patterns presented in the table. Evidently, the historical pattern of plural inflection in consonantal classes, all of which display a clear tendency towards regularisation, was characterised by a lack of both a distinctive inflectional affix and an *i*-mutated vowel. This lack of distinctive marking rendered the classes susceptible to the impact of markers from productive inflections, especially the *a*-stems, partly *ō*-/*n*-stems, but also *i*-stems. In all of these classes, the plural was marked with a relatively salient ending: *-a* in the *a*-stems, and *-a* or *-on* in the *ō*-/*n*-stems. This salience was even more prominent in the *i*-stems, where the vocalic ending was reinforced by the presence of the *i*-mutated vowel. Accordingly, the *i*-stems, although not entirely free from analogical pressures, tended to retain their original plural marking pattern, which gradually expanded to the unproductive classes. It is worth noting that this double marking of the plural turned out to be more efficient than the consonantal marker *-on*, ensuring the *i*-stems the role of the dominant feminine pattern. As can be seen in Table 6.18, the spread of the feminine *ō*-/*n*-stem inflection was relatively limited, despite the fact that the plural inflection (NOM./ACC. PL.) was marked by a consonantal suffix, which is clearly stronger with respect to phonological salience than a vocalic suffix.

This interpretation of the attested patterns does not hold for the *u*-stems, where the plural must have been originally characterised by a more salient marker, i.e. a vowel (*-iu*), and yet the restructuring is more advanced than in the other classes, which undermines the significance of salience. The irregularity could be attributed to a close relation between the *u*-stems and *i*-stems, including their largely parallel profile in Proto-Germanic and later parallel developments. Following the argumentation in Section 6.5.3.1, where the *u*-stems and *i*-stems are discussed in terms of a "super-class", with some common inherited inflectional characteristics, the plurality pattern in the *u*-stems should rather be measured with respect to the presence of the *a*- and *ō*-/*n*-stem inflections than the *i*-stem inflections. Accordingly, if the figures from Table 6.6 (reflecting the influence of the *a*- and *ō*-/*n*-stems in the *u*-stem paradigm) are taken into account, the percentage of analogical inflections in the plural paradigm drops to 54 percent. This corresponds with the patterns attested in the sister languages, confirming the assumption that a vocalic marker is more salient and thus persistent than zero marking.[310]

---

310. The salience factor seems to work somewhat differently in the neuter nouns, including the nouns which follow the pattern of the dominant neuter *a*-stems, characterised by a lack of an inflectional marker in the plural. Here factors other than salience, such as the semantic profile of the class, may have played a role. At the same time, the evidence from Middle Dutch, where

Table 6.22 presents the overall distribution of historical and analogical inflections, including the distribution for the singular and plural.

Table 6.22 Overall distribution of archaic and innovative inflections
in the OLF minor stems

	archaic	innovative
singular	(40) 34%	(78) 66%
plural	(10) 13%	(68) 87%
Total	(50) 26%	(146) 74%

Bearing in mind all the limitations of the study, it can be concluded that the investigated material testifies to an advanced stage of reorganisation of the Old Dutch
nominal inflection. With the analogical inflections present in more than 70 percent of all forms, the historical inflection can be viewed as no more than a relic of
the original pattern. When it comes to gender distinctions, no clear discrepancy
could be observed in the scale of reorganisation of the masculine, neuter and feminine paradigms in classes in which two or possibly three genders are attested, i.e.
u-stems, *r*-stems and root nouns. In terms of percentage values, the masculine
and neuter paradigms attest to the presence of analogical inflections in 78 percent
($n = 102$) and 92 percent ($n = 26$), respectively, whereas the feminine paradigm in
62 percent ($n = 68$) (in the mentioned three classes). The value of the figures for
the neuter inflection is limited as they are confined to three nouns altogether, with
innovative *kind* dominating the pattern and only the *u*-stem *fē* showing synchronic
alternation between historical and analogical inflections.

As the textual sources investigated in this study have a relatively diverse origin,
with only one of them representing a "pure" Dutch variety, and the other two showing a considerable High German influence, it can be assumed that the patterns of
restructuring differed. This potential variation was also tested in the present study
and the overall figures showing the amount of analogical inflection in individual
texts, irrespective of the declensional class and number, are depicted in Table 6.23.

Table 6.23 The percentage of innovative inflections in the minor stems
in individual OLF sources

Wachtendonck Psalms	*Leiden Willeram*	*Rhyming Bible*
(60) 83%	(26) 65%	(51) 70%

the neuter *r*-plural marker is attested in the historical *s*-stems, largely corroborates the validity
of the salience hypothesis, implying that this class of neuter nouns (original *s*-stems) retained a
distinctive (salient) plurality pattern, which is not reflected in the Old Dutch material.

The figures indicate that the restructuring trends remain essentially parallel in all three texts and the scale of reorganisation of the nominal inflection is similar, although some differences can be detected. Even if not extensive or significant, they are worth closer inspection, as they testify to the complex nature of the analysed material. The pattern found in the data indicates that the material represents a clear continuum, in which the dating of the source is correlated with the geographical place of origin. Given the dating of the three textual sources, one would expect the text of WPs, dated to the tenth century, to be the most archaic of the three. And yet, it is the other two sources, LW and Rb, that show greater conservatism in the nominal inflection, and consequently a straightforward correlation between the innovation level and the dating of the texts cannot be established. The attested state of affairs can be attributed to a few factors, the most prominent being the geographical provenance of the texts, reflected in their linguistic structure. Both LW and Rb show a clear affiliation with High German dialects, manifested primarily in phonological correspondences, and contributing to their overall linguistic heterogeneity. Many inflectional features attested especially in Rb as well as the trends observed in the analogical reshaping of inflection correspond closely to the patterns found in Old High German (Central Franconian), which tended to show more archaic inflectional characteristics. This inflectional conservatism of the High German dialects could have been a major factor enhancing the more archaic inflectional profile of these Old Dutch texts.

Another significant factor seems to be the size of the corpus and its implications for the attestation of individual classes. Due to corpus-related limitations, some of the classes tend to be underrepresented (or overrepresented) in the corpus. Such is the case with the *r*-stems, which constitute a conservative declensional class (across all Old Germanic languages). In contrast to Rb and LW, where the class is relatively well represented, the *r*-stems turn out to be scantily attested in WPs (or if attested, often found in cases which are inconclusive). The relatively high number of *r*-stems in LW and Rb has contributed to the overall conservatism of these texts. When the figures for the *r*-stems are excluded, the levels of innovation for individual texts become more consistent, with analogical inflections encompassing 82 percent for WPs, 80 percent for LW and 84 percent for Rb.

The third factor of significance for the attested pattern can account in particular for the lower percentage of innovation found in Rb, and involves the forms of the DAT. SG. Part of the inflectional archaism of this text can be ascribed to the relatively high number of archaic DAT. SG. forms in feminine root nouns. These endingless DAT. SG. forms are treated as historical on the assumption that any of the productive patterns, i.e. the *ō*-/*n*-stem or the *i*-stem inflection, could exert some influence on the root noun inflection. A closer inspection of the data, however, reveals that the predominant pattern in root nouns is that of the feminine *i*-stems, with an endless DAT. SG. rather than the marker *-e* (*craft, craft, craft, craft* instead of *craft, crefte, crefte, craft*). Given such an inflectional configuration, the endless DAT. SG. could (potentially) be treated as inconclusive. A recalculation of forms in root nouns where the DAT. SG. is considered inconclusive results in an increase in the share of analogical inflections in Rb to 92.5 percent, which renders its overall inflectional profile much less conservative.

The analysis of the Old Low Franconian morphological system leads also to some more general observations about the nature of the corpus or rather its scope. The three major texts which were analysed in this study have traditionally been considered Old Dutch, and as such they are all included in the *Oudnederlands Woordenboek* (alongside other texts having more distant affiliation with Old Dutch). The present study followed this choice of material, which seems to be based largely on phonological criteria. The major criterion distinguishing the Old Low Franconian material from Central Franconian (High German) is the absence of High German *Lautverschiebung*, and the major feature distinguishing Old Dutch from Middle Dutch is the lack of reductions in inflectional syllables. Much as these criteria are relevant for the text of WPs and largely LW, they turn out to be rather problematic in the case of the geographically more distant Rb. A closer look at the material reveals that the phonology of inflectional syllables, with frequent reductions of vowels to *schwa*, reflects the conditions commonly attested in Middle High German, which stays in contrast with the archaic conditions represented in WPs. As the absence of reduced vowels in inflectional syllables is one of the criteria for classifying texts as Old Dutch, it may be questionable whether the text of Rb can be considered "old". Equally fragile is its status as a text of Dutch provenance, which can be questioned on account of the number of forms which attest to *Lautverschiebung*. In the investigated sample (173 tokens) the share of forms unambiguously Dutch or German is almost equal, with 15 percent of forms identified as unambiguously Dutch (i.e. without *Lautverschiebung*, e.g. *uader, dohter, dure*) and 17 percent as unambiguously High German (e.g. *uoze, uater*), with the remaining portion inconclusive (e.g. *hande, naht*).

Overall, the attested patterns of restructuring correspond to the more general direction of disintegrative developments found in the nominal system across West Germanic, where the changes occur along the axis west-east, with a gradual limitation of paradigmatic allomorphy and the proneness to analogical pressures in the west, and the enhancement of the function of *i*-mutation and consequent retention of greater inflectional conservatism in the east (High German).

6.7   Taxonomic implications of the study

Even a cursory look at the earlier descriptions of the Old Low Franconian grammatical system gives the impression that the diachronic bias has hardly been part of the linguistic tradition, at least as far as nominal morphology is concerned. A strictly diachronic approach to Old Low Franconian morphology was first employed by Borgeld (1899), who provides a detailed overview of declensional classes in the *Wachtendonck Psalms*, classifying them on the basis of the stem-type criterion as inherited from Proto-Germanic. Likewise, the historical perspective is closely adhered to in van Helten's (1902) detailed treatment of the early Dutch nominal system, where the stem-type criterion is used for the classification of nouns in both "grammars", i.e. the one based on the material from the Old Low Franconian psalms and the Lipsius glosses, and the other built on the fragmentarily attested Old Southern Central Franconian psalms (*Altsüdmittelfränkische Grammatik*).

The other existing treatments of Old Dutch morphology adopt a rather synchronically-oriented approach. One of such descriptions is to be found in Cowan (1961: 34–36), who employed a three-fold grouping of declensions based on the inflectional suffix of the GEN. SG., distinguishing the following declension classes:

- class 1 with the suffix /-əs/ (comprising masculine and neuter nouns)
- class 2 with the suffix /-ə/ (feminine stems)
- class 3 with the suffix /-n/ (masculine, feminine and neuter)

From a diachronic perspective, one can recognise in the second group (class 2) a reflex of the historical feminine *i*-stems and *u*-stems, and in the third group (class 3) a reflex of the historical *n*-stems. The first group (class 1) is probably the most heterogeneous when it comes to the original declensional affiliation of nouns, covering stems originating in both vocalic and minor consonantal declensions. The classification does not treat the allomorphic variation in the paradigm (such as *i*-mutation) as an indicator of class affiliation (Cowan 1961: 34). As no meaningful vowel contrast is acknowledged for the unstressed syllables, differences such as the one between *creftin* /-ən/ and *handun* /-ən/ in the DAT. PL., corresponding to the contrast between the *i*-stem and *u*-stem from the historical perspective, remain obscure in this approach.

In his treatment of the nominal system of the *Wachtendonck Psalms*, Quak (1992) uses the category of gender as the basis for the classification, recognising at the same time the distinction between strong and weak nouns. Justifying his departure from the diachronic classification, the author states: "Auch hat es wenig Sinn, die übliche Einteilung in *a*-, *o*-, *u*-Stämme usw. ohne weiteres beizubehalten, da die 'Wachtendonckschen Psalmen' (…) offensichtlich schon ziemlich weit auf dem Weg fortgeschritten sind, der zum Mittelniederländischen führt (Quak 1992: 82). Although the postulated classification of nominal classes is essentially synchronically-oriented, references to historical declensional types are consistently made in the discussion. Such a hybrid approach has an evident advantage: on the one hand, it is an accurate reflection of the actual inflectional shape of the Old Dutch nominal system, on the other, it remains transparent from the perspective of a cross-Germanic comparison.

The distribution of inherited and analogical inflections captured in the present study indicates that the diachronic classes based on the stem-type criterion do not reflect the reality as attested in the available sources. In light of the inadequacy of the diachronic approach, an accurate description of the declensional system needs to be based on synchronic criteria, which include primarily the shape of the inflectional ending, combined with the shape of the root (i.e. the presence of allomorphic variation). In this respect, the taxonomy applied by Quak (1992) seems to come closest to a treatment which sufficiently fulfills the criteria of an adequate description of the Old Low Franconian nominal system.

6.8   Conclusions

Despite the limited size and the heterogeneous nature of the Old Low Franconian corpus, the textual material provides valuable evidence, complementing the picture of the restructuring process in the Northern West Germanic linguistic continuum. The observed trends turn out to be robust enough to allow some generalisations about the patterns of restructuring in the Old Dutch nominal system. The shape of the declensional system which emerges from the earliest Dutch sources testifies to an advanced stage of reorganisation, which at least partly (as could be seen, for instance, in the case of the *s*-stems) can be attributed to the scarcity of the available data. As in the other investigated languages, the ultimate shape of a given declensional class and the dynamics of its restructuring depend on the interplay of a number of factors which are to some extent class-specific. Despite the small corpus size, the more universal factors, such as the frequency of occurrence and the salience of inflectional exponents emerge as significant determinants in the restructuring. Of primary importance for the attested path of development is the lack of allomorphic variation in the minor paradigms (especially in consonantal stems) and the resultant greater uniformity of the paradigms, which rendered them more susceptible to analogical pressures. What is essential for the interpretation of the Old Dutch material from the perspective of the comparison with the sister languages is the chronology of *i*-mutation and consequently its varied role in the reshaping of the nominal inflection. In compliance with the developments in Old High German, the morphologisation of *i*-mutation in Old Dutch took place at a later stage. However, in contrast to High German, the effects of *i*-mutation were eliminated from the nominal inflection in the thirteenth century (Marynissen 2001: 663), and consequently they are nearly entirely absent from the present-day Dutch nominal system.[311] The morphological *i*-mutation is retained only residually in some dialects of Modern Dutch (East-Brabantian, Limburgian, Low-Rhine and IJsselland), both in inflection and derivation (e.g. *voet*: *vuut* 'feet', *boom*: *beum* 'trees') (Marynissen 2001: 663–664; de Schutter et al. 2014). This irregular development of *i*-mutation in Dutch has been viewed as an essential feature rendering Dutch distinct from the rest of West Germanic (e.g. Goossens 1980, 1988; Buccini 2010), and the germs of this difference, as could be seen, can be identified already in the earliest stage of the history of Dutch (cf. Section 7.3).[312]

A prominent feature of the restructuring in Old Low Franconian was the productivity of the *i*-stem declension, which became widespread and functioned as the default inflectional pattern for minor feminine stems. Its spread to minor masculine stems was partly inhibited by the expansive *a*-stem inflection, which turns out to have been the predominant and default pattern for masculine nouns. Although the productivity of the *i*-stem inflection was attested also in Old Saxon and Old Frisian, its extent there was much more limited and cannot be compared to the pervasiveness of this tendency in Old Low Franconian.

The declensional configuration as attested in the fragmentary material does not straightforwardly correspond to that of Modern Dutch. Due to an almost complete disintegration of the case system (excluding some residual GEN. SG. formations),[313] the correspondence to Modern Dutch can be discussed essentially only in the context of the retained plurality patterns. A feature which appears to be most striking

---

311. An exception to this general rule is the singular plural alternation of *stad/steden* 'town/towns', which derives from eastern Middle Dutch (Marynissen 2001: 663).

312. The significant role of *i*-mutation in nominal morphology, especially in the marking of the plural in the Dutch language area at a later stage was discussed by Goossens (1987: 141). According to the author, the assumed area of origin of the *Wachtendonck Psalms* shows a purely 'continental' plural morphology, staying in line with the patterns known from Modern High German, where *i*-mutation is one of the most important plurality markers (cf. the maps in Goossens 1987: 151–152, 159 and the table on p. 148). Also in this respect, the language of WPs should not be viewed as a direct ancestor of the largest share of Middle Dutch and Modern Standard Dutch where the effects of *i*-mutation are entirely eliminated.

313. The first traces of the loss of case in nominal inflection in Dutch appear in the 13th c. (Marynissen 1996: 383).

in this respect is the relatively limited productivity of the *n*-stem inflection in the earliest sources, which in present-day Dutch constitutes the main pattern of plurality marking (*-en*), found alongside the less common suffixes, i.e. *-s* and *-eren*.[314]

Despite many similarities which Old Dutch shares with Old High German, the present-day inflectional systems of the two languages show fairly different profiles. The most significant discrepancy, apart from the lack of *i*-mutation in Modern Dutch, is the absence of the ending *-er* as a productive plural marker. In present-day German, this marker, accompanied by *i*-mutation, developed as one of the major plural patterns, characteristic of monosyllabic neuter nouns (Marynissen 1996: 357; 2001: 661).

To conclude, the systematic investigation of the Old Low Franconian material allowed us to identify the predominant tendencies present in the minor paradigms, giving some insight into the directions of restructuring and its characteristics. The description of the transformation of the nominal system in Old Low Franconian completes the picture of inflectional restructuring across Northern West Germanic, testifying to its geographical gradualness. This gradualness entails the spread of innovations on the axis north-west/south-east and is reflected in two major features, namely the significance of the *i*-stem inflection (either growing or declining) and the presence of the effects of *i*-mutation as a morphological feature in nominal paradigms (either significant or insignificant) (cf. Chapter 7). Due to the limitations related to the nature of the available material, in particular the size of the corpus and, to a lesser extent, the presence of Franconian (High German) inflectional features, the findings have a restricted value; they can be given conclusive weight only within the bounds of these limitations. Finally, when it comes to making generalisations about Old Dutch as the ancestor of standard Dutch, one needs to bear in mind that the available material provides information about the eastern variety of early Dutch. Accordingly, the account of the reorganisation of the nominal inflection presented here refers essentially to this particular variety and cannot be in a straightforward way extended to other varieties for which no attestations are available.

---

314. The details of the dialectal distribution of the plural formation in present-day Dutch are to be found in Goossens (1980, 1987). An overview of the research into the plurality patterns in Dutch is offered in Philippa (1987).

CHAPTER 7

Patterns of reorganisation of the nominal system in early Northern West Germanic

A comparative overview

7.1 Introduction

This chapter presents a synopsis and comparison of the reorganisational patterns found in the nominal systems of the individual early Northern West Germanic languages. As the focus of the study was on both formal similarities (i.e. parallelisms in the shape of inflection) and distributional similarities (the distribution of patterns across individual Northern West Germanic languages), both are taken into consideration in this overview. The summary is an attempt at a typological approach to the restructuring of the nominal inflection in the Northern West Germanic language continuum. The aim of this chapter is, firstly, to summarise the findings and tendencies, both shared and divergent, found in the quantitative analyses of the nominal inflection in the examined languages. This involves examining such aspects of the restructuring as the directions of analogical transfers, the levels of archaism/innovation of individual classes and paradigms, the distribution of analogical inflections with respect to case, number, gender, syllable weight, and the correlations with factors such as frequency of occurrence or salience of inflectional marking. Secondly, the chapter attempts to account for the similarities and discrepancies in the observed patterns of inflectional restructuring. The attested patterns reflect partly the chronological disparities between the literary traditions that the investigated languages come in, but they also demonstrate some more structural cross-linguistic differences between the varieties. Examining the material from these two perspectives will make it possible to present an overarching, cross-linguistic overview of the reorganisation of the nominal inflection in Northern West Germanic languages. The discussion of the more universal factors responsible for the attested distributions and patterns, and the interactions between them, will be the focus of Chapter 8. In general, the factors conditioning the process of morphological restructuring appear to be largely non-language specific, even if the ultimate effects of their activity vary per language, being determined by the idiosyncratic characteristics of the individual languages. These different conditions render the ultimate shape of the nominal paradigms disparate across Northern West Germanic.

The process of reorganisation of the nominal inflection is unequally evinced in the investigated languages. This is a direct consequence of the discrepancies in the attestation of individual languages related to the size and nature of the available corpora. While Old English provides abundant evidence for the patterns of restructuring, Old Low Franconian can offer only a much more fragmented picture of the process. Despite this limitation, the general tendencies and patterns that could be recognised in the less abundantly attested dialects of Northern West Germanic lend themselves to a systematic cross-linguistic comparison (see Versloot & Adamczyk 2014).

The wide scope of the conducted analysis allows us to answer two major questions that were posed at the onset of this investigation with a considerable degree of accuracy. One of them was whether the attested data testify to the same or similar amount of inflectional variation (resulting from analogical developments in the nominal paradigms) across individual Northern West Germanic languages. The other question was to what extent the patterns and tendencies observed in the individual languages were parallel and to what extent language-specific.

7.2   Overview of the tendencies

The general tendencies that could be identified in the process of the reorganisation of the nominal inflection of all the examined languages, involve the following aspects of this process:

a.   the directions of analogical interdeclensional transfers
b.   the scope of the restructuring of individual classes and paradigms, i.e. the amount (percentage) of innovative inflection present in the paradigms of the minor stems
c.   the scope of the restructuring of the nominal inflection with respect to number
d.   the scope of the restructuring of the nominal inflection with respect to morpho-syntactic categories

Two further aspects, namely the scope of the restructuring with respect to the type of inflectional marker and the frequency of occurrence, are related to the mechanism of the process and will therefore be the focus of the theoretical discussion in Chapter 8. As the investigated languages, on account of the different inflectional profiles of the minor classes, show largely divergent patterns of development with respect to the type of inflectional markers and their morpho-phonological salience, this correlation will be examined also in the present chapter from a contrastive perspective.

The declensional types affected by the large-scale analogical restructuring had a common quantitative and morphological profile in all the examined languages: they were all mostly small classes (in terms of type frequency), or if larger (like the class of *i*-stems), then characterised by a relatively low token frequency, and clearly unproductive by the time of the first Germanic attestations (except for the *i*-stems in Continental Germanic). Another formal characteristic was the presence of morphophonemic alternations in the paradigms, i.e. *i*-mutation and/or consonantal stem alternation (in the *s*-stems and dental stems). These features turned out to be consequential for the subsequent development of the minor classes, which entailed extensive remodelling of their paradigms.

For the sake of transparency, the findings from the quantitative and qualitative investigation of the data from individual languages were summarised in a tabular form (Tables 7.1–7.10). One of the major tendencies observable in the data involves the directions of interdeclensional analogical shifts. An overview of these directions can be found in Table 7.1, which presents the declensional types that served as the destination classes for nouns originally affiliated with the unproductive declensions. The table includes primarily shifts that could be identified as synchronic analogical reshufflings, although most of them began definitely prior to the first written attestations of the individual varieties. This refers particularly to the dental stems, where in all languages except Old English the shift occurred predominantly at the prehistoric stage.

Table 7.1 Directions of analogical transfers in the early Northern West Germanic languages: An overview

	OE	OFris.	OS	OLF
i-stems (m)	=> *a*-stems	=> *a*-stems	=> (*j*)*a*-stems	=> *a*-stems
i-stems (n)	=> *a*-stems	=> *a*-stems	=> (*j*)*a*-stems	=> *a*-stems
i-stems (f)	=> *ō*-stems	=> *ō*-stems	=> (*j*)*ō*-stems	=> *ō*-stems
u-stems (m)	–> *a*-stems	=> *a*-stems	=> (*j*)*a*-stems, *i*-stems	=> *a*-stems, *i*-stems
u-stems (f)	=> *ō*-stems	=> *i*-stems	=> *i*-stems, *ō*-stems	=> *i*-stems, *ō*-/*n*-stems
root nouns (m)	=> *a*-stems	=> *a*-stems, *i*-stems	=> *a*-stems, *i*-stems	=> *a*-stems, *i*-stems
root nouns (f)	=> *ō*-stems	=> *ō*-stems	=> *i*-stems	=> *i*-stems
s-stems	=> *a*-stems (n, m)	=> *a*-stems (n, m)	=> *a*-stems (n)	=> *a*-stems (n)
r-stems (m)	=> *a*-stems	=> *a*-stems, *i*-stems	no innovation	=> *a*-stems
r-stems (f)	=> *ō*-stems, *a*-stems	=> *ō*-stems, *i*-stems	no innovation	=> *ō*-/*n*-stems
nd-stems (mon.)	=> *a*-stems	=> *a*-stems, *i*-stems	=> *a*-stems (n)	=> *a*-stems
nd-stems (dis.)	=> *a*-stems => adjectival infl.	=> *a*-stems => adjectival infl.	=> *a*-stems => adjectival infl.	=> *a*-stems => adjectival infl.
þ-stems (m)	=> *a*-stems	=> *a*-stems	=> *a*-stems	–
þ-stems (f)	=> *ō*-stems	=> *ō*-stems	=> *i*-stems	

The main conclusion that can be drawn from this mini-typology of interdeclensional reshufflings is that the analogical transfers of minor stems followed essentially two major directions: towards the masculine and neuter *a*-stems and the feminine *ō*-stems. This pattern is most prominent in Old English, which attests to a very strong polarisation of the minor stems towards these two declensional types. More diversification in this pattern is found in the Old Saxon and Old Low Franconian data, where the *i*-stem declension shows a noticeable amount of productivity, and traces of this productivity are occasionally visible also in Old Frisian, particularly in the *r*-stems and *nd*-stems. In other words, the Continental Old Germanic languages attest to much more diversity, with a greater range of inflectional patterns serving as destination classes for minor stems, while in Old English the polarisation towards the *a*-stems and *ō*-stems is the dominant trend. This multidirectional pattern of declensional development will become much more prominent in the later stages, where some of the originally unproductive inflectional patterns will tend to become productive in Continental Old Germanic, especially in Low and High German. In English, with the subsequent gradual loss of gender and case marking systems, the *a*-stems will emerge as the major destination class. In Frisian, the diversification of the declensional system was not sustainable, as the shift towards the etymological *i*-stem inflection was superseded by further phonological reduction processes taking place in the fifteenth century.[315]

Not all the patterns demonstrated in the material can be interpreted at face value and for some a more rigorous and critical scrutiny is required. This refers, for instance, to the Old Frisian *s*-stems, where the prevalence of the *a*-stem inflections may be a consequence of the limitations related to the nature of the corpus. Accordingly, the absence of vestiges of the original *s*-stem inflection in some lemmas in the corpus is not necessarily conclusive, since relics of the original inflection are still preserved in the plural paradigms of North and East Frisian dialects.[316]

The attraction of the minor stems to the *a*-stem inflection as attested in the Late Old English material occurs largely owing to the dissemination of the masculine NOM./ACC. PL. marker -*es* (<-*as*), which in Old English gained the status of

---

315. The contrast in the singular between endingless heavy-syllable feminine nouns, continuing the (restructured) *i*-stem inflection, and the etymological *ō*-stems in -*e* was obliterated by the general apocope of -*e* in the 15th century, which led to a merger of these two declensional patterns. The original OFris. *i*-stem plural ending -*e*, which was productive in some animate nouns affiliated with the *u*-stems, *r*-stems and root nouns, was likewise affected by the apocope, which led to the extension of other, productive plural endings in these paradigms.

316. Until ca. 1700, the historical *s*-stems in West Frisian evince the -*en* plural marker, while the original neuter *a*-stems show partly the etymological endingless plural. The original *s*-stem marker -*er*, however, has not been preserved in West Frisian (Versloot 2014: 109).

an almost hegemonic plural marker in the masculine declension. As regards the distribution and spread of this plural marker in Continental Germanic, one can observe a continuum: in Old Saxon the marker -os is only productive to a limited extent, while in Old Frisian it is non-existent as such, but the equivalent markers -ar/-an function in a similar way, showing considerable productivity; in Old Low Franconian this marker is entirely absent and the a-stems are characterised by a vocalic ending in the NOM./ACC. PL. (-a). Clearly, despite the expansiveness of the a-stem pattern, the a-stems cannot be considered the default class for the minor stems in Continental Germanic. It can be assumed that a lack of one dominant plurality marker created conditions conducive to the emergence of several competing plural exponents at a later stage of development of the Continental Germanic varieties (see the discussion in Section 7.3).

The investigated material demonstrates that the reduction of declensional diversity was essentially guided by the category of gender: the transfers of nouns towards the productive classes occurred in compliance with their original grammatical gender (see Section 8.6.4). Some deviations from this dominant trend are manifested in the occasional traces of masculine inflection in the feminine paradigms, as well as in an evident preference of the feminine stems, especially feminine root nouns and the u-stems, to follow the i-stem pattern, well attested in Continental Germanic.[317] Another pattern with regard to the gender-wise distribution of the restructuring process emerges in the Old Frisian feminine stems: the evidence provided by the feminine i-stems, u-stems and root nouns does not testify to a massive intrusion of the ō-stems, which stands in contrast to the Old English state of affairs. Instead the paradigm is characterised by considerable uniformity, showing endingless forms in the singular. In this way, a new, common pattern of inflection for the feminine nouns emerges above the level of individual classes. The undiversified shape of the singular in feminine stems is a feature encountered also in present-day Icelandic. Such a shape of the singular in Old Frisian can be interpreted as indicative of a shift of the feminine paradigm towards a word-based inflection (which occurred later in the masculine paradigm).

A noticeable feature of the presented typological summary is the absence of the n-stem declension as a potential destination class for minor stems. This may be surprising given that the n-stems in Old Germanic had the status of a productive inflectional type, fulfilling most of the criteria of morphological productivity, including the relatively high type frequency. Additionally, in the later period, this

---

317. A systematic investigation of the scale of this deviation from the original gender class affiliation stays beyond the scope of this study. The findings of a pilot study on the change of gender class alongside the declension class shift in the Old English root nouns revealed that the change involved no more than 1.6 percent of all forms (Adamczyk 2013: 22).

declensional class developed as one of the most productive (plural) patterns in Continental Germanic. In all these languages, a competition between the *n*-stem (plural) inflection and the *a*-stem plurals is very well attested in the "middle" stage, i.e. Middle English, Middle Low Saxon/German, Middle Dutch. In the investigated period of Germanic, traces of the *n*-stem productivity in the minor stem paradigms are only sporadically attested, and are confined predominantly to the class of *u*-stems. An exception here is the OE, OFris. GEN. PL. *-ena/-ana*, which can be found scattered across all the minor declensional types in all the investigated languages. The spread of the *n*-stem inflection emerges as more systematic in feminine stems in Old Low Franconian, where it interacts also with the *ō*-stem inflection, being the forerunner of the pattern to be found in the later stage of the development of Dutch (Middle Dutch and present-day Dutch) and German.

Another class showing consistent patterns which can be considered a prognostic of the later tendencies in the nominal inflection in Northern West Germanic is the small class of the *u*-stems. Old English and Old Continental Germanic languages show divergent patterns of the analogical realignments in this class, the former attesting to a unidirectional transfer of the *u*-stems to the *a*-stem declension, the latter to their relatively consistent transference to (or merger with) the *i*-stems.

Significantly, as far as parallelisms in the patterns of inflectional restructuring are concerned, it could be expected that Old English, Old Frisian and Old Saxon, all being representatives of the North Sea Germanic linguistic continuum, will tend to share many or at least some of them. As it turns out, with respect to the investigated morphological development, the Continental Germanic dialects show several common characteristics, including the weaker polarisation of minor stems towards the *a*-stems and *ō*-stems than in Old English. This refers as well to Old Frisian, which stays on the verge of the Continental continuum and is therefore somewhat isolated, which is evident in its overall linguistic profile, especially in phonology and lexicon. The investigated material testifies to a gradual emergence of the typological diversity found in the modern West Germanic languages, with Continental Germanic showing a different morphological profile than English. The divergent development of the nominal inflection in the individual languages can be ascribed to a variety of interacting factors, as could be seen in the analysis. Of primary importance here were the phonological developments, affecting individual languages at a different pace and with a different scope (see the discussion below).

The figures presented in Table 7.2 refer to the overall levels of innovation in all the minor stem paradigms in the early Northern West Germanic languages. It must be emphasised that the picture of the morphological innovations that emerges from the presented figures is largely oversimplified: the figures carry meaning only when interpreted relative to each other, and not in absolute terms. They are in a way an abstraction, being a product of an accumulation of the findings from somewhat different periods and from several declensional classes, each with their specific type and token frequencies, whose restructuring followed divergent paths. Despite this evident limitation, such a juxtaposition of the results gives some general indication as to the scope of the restructuring of the nominal system in the individual languages. Moreover, it adds to the typological dimension of the study in that it makes it possible to present a hierarchy of the investigated languages with respect to the level of morphological remodelling. Note that in the case of very small corpora, such as Old Low Franconian, the complete and exhaustive picture of the developments will never be available and conclusions can be drawn only on the basis of the limited evidence.

Table 7.2 The total amount of innovative inflection in minor stems in the investigated languages*

	OE		OFris.	OS	OLF
	EOE	LOE			
% innovation (SG. & PL.)	38% (n = 17199)		49% (n = 2334)	24% (n = 2660)	55% (n = 348)
	28%	41%			

* The figure for Old English does not include the noun *cild*, while *kind/kint* was included in the figures for the other languages. The figure for Old Frisian includes the *i*-stems *liude*, which was excluded from the Tables in Chapter 4, hence the figures do not overlap. Note also that in Old Saxon and Old Low Franconian, the GEN. PL. and DAT. PL. forms were included in the figures for the *i*-stems, as in this class the alternation between the inherited and archaic inflections is occasionally visible.

The figure for Old English does not include the highly frequent nouns *sunu* and *man(n)*, and the results for the *i*-stems come from the analysis of the representative sample of the *i*-stems, not the entire class, as it was the case in the other languages. Based on the information about the overall proportion of the *i*-stems in the corpora of the other languages (where the analysis of the *i*-stems was exhaustive and where the *i*-stems constituted approximately 45% of all tokens in the minor stems), an extrapolation could be made for the Old English *i*-stems.[318] If the number of the *i*-stems is extrapolated, the level of innovation in the Old English material increases to 40 percent, which constitutes only a minor increase when compared to the sample used in the analysis. *N* refers here (and in the consecutive tables) to the

---

318. The extrapolation was considered useful not because the sample was not representative enough, but rather because in Old English the process of restructuring affected the *i*-stems already at the prehistoric stage and consequently only very few paradigms showed synchronic alternation between archaic and innovative inflections that could be captured in the analysis.

overall number of tokens, both archaic and innovative (excluding the inconclusive (neutral) forms).

Bearing in mind all the limitations entailed in such a general presentation, a clear pattern can be identified: the dialects form a continuum with respect to the restructuring of nominal inflections in that the levels of innovation correlate approximately with the average attestation dates of the individual languages. Old Saxon emerges as the most archaic variety of early Northern West Germanic, while Old Low Franconian, with its mixed textual sources, turns out be the most innovative. The evident outlier is Old Frisian – commonly recognised as one of the most morphologically innovative languages in the Germanic group – which turns out to be more archaic than could be expected based on its relatively late date of attestation (ca. 1300–1400). It must be emphasised, however, that the present study was based on the material classified as 'classical' Old Frisian, which means that the texts dated later than 1400 were not incorporated in the study. The analysis of the data indicates that the level of innovation in the Old Frisian nominal paradigms is not as substantial as has been claimed. Given that all the sister languages were by that time already in the 'middle' stage of their development, this relative inflectional archaism may be considered indicative of the fact that Old Frisian was, around 1300, one of the most conservative West Germanic dialects.

The figure for the Old English data refers to the entire Old English material, which spans several centuries. As the analysis in Chapter 3 revealed, this wide time span is reflected in the different distributions of archaic and innovative forms in Early and Late Old English. The level of innovation in Early Old English, with traces of analogical inflection attested in 28 percent of all forms, corresponds to the amount of innovation found in Old Saxon, while the percentage of analogical forms in Late Old English (41%) parallels approximately the innovation level found in Old Frisian.

Admittedly, the attestation dates of the extant material from individual dialects can largely account for the distributions; however, the cross-linguistic disparities found in the examined material are to be ascribed also to other factors, including language-specific developments and their chronology, all of which need to be considered when trying to explain the attested patterns. The distribution presented in Table 7.2 can be illustrated graphically as in Figure 3, where the investigated languages are put on a scale presenting their level of innovation/archaism, estimated on the basis of the changes in the minor paradigms.[319]

---

319. One of the lesser known classifications of Germanic languages was established based on the frequency and productivity of the *nd*-stems (Kärre 1915: 214). While the *nd*-stems are fairly well attested in Coastal Germanic, Old Low Franconian, complying with the pattern of attestation found in Old High German, shows very scant attestations of this class, with the inherited

archaic   innovative

⟶

| Old Saxon | Old English | Old Frisian | Old Low Franconian |

Figure 3. The level of archaism/innovation in the minor stems in the early NWGmc. languages

More insight into the restructuring process can be gained by examining the figures in Table 7.3, which refer to the levels of innovation (i.e. the percentage of analogical forms in the paradigm) in individual declensional classes, and which are thus more transparent and more easily interpretable. The class of dental stems was not included in the summary, as the data is very limited in all the examined languages, except in Old English. Note that the analysis of the Old English *i*-stems was confined (a) to a sample of this large class of nouns, and (b) to those paradigms which showed a synchronic alternation between inherited and innovative features. Since a large part of the restructuring process occurred in this class already in the prehistoric period, and these paradigms could not be taken into account in the analysis (because they show no synchronic alternation), the class emerges as more archaic than could be expected. As the investigation was conducted on a sample of the *i*-stems, again an extrapolation of the results was made to the entire class based on the proportions of the various subtypes found in the other examined languages. Accordingly, the figure marked with an asterisk refers to the extrapolation (41%), while the figure of 28 percent refers to the results obtained from the analysis of the sample.

Table 7.3 Overall percentage of innovation in the minor stems in the investigated languages

	OE	OFris.	OS	OLF
i-stems	28% ($n = 2002$)/ 41%*	51% ($n = 958$)	21% ($n = 1433$)	32% ($n = 158$)
u-stems	45% ($n = 3565$)	28% ($n = 624$)	21% ($n = 221$)	90% ($n = 71$)
root nouns	21% ($n = 4514$)	60% ($n = 413$)	24% ($n = 604$)	60% ($n = 45$)
r-stems	36% ($n = 3241$)	54% ($n = 147$)	0% ($n = 49$)	23% ($n = 30$)
s-stems	68% ($n = 443$)	84% ($n = 126$)	59% ($n = 37$)	100% ($n = 22$)
nd-stems	53% ($n = 2582$)	52% ($n = 46$)	38% ($n = 308$)	91% ($n = 22$)

---

inflection limited to two nouns only (*friund* and *fiunt*, cf. Braune/Reiffenstein 2004: 214). Kärre (1915: 214) suggested the following arrangement of the Old Germanic languages with respect to the frequency and productivity of the *nd*-stems: OHG – OS – Gothic – ON – OE, where OHG is the dialect with the lowest and Old English with the highest scores.

The distribution of analogical features across declensional classes and languages shows some evidently parallel patterns. The r-stems, despite attesting to a remarkably uniform paradigm, with few distinctive inflectional features, emerge as the most conservative and stable class in Old Saxon and Old Low Franconian. A low level of innovation is found also in the i-stems in these two languages, which in view of the subsequent development of this class as a productive pattern, is not surprising. In Old English and Old Frisian, the i-stems show a parallel pattern as well, both being increasingly susceptible to the analogical pressure from the productive declensions. At the other extreme of the scale is the class of s-stems, which turned out to be the most innovative declension in all the examined languages (not to count the dental stems whose restructuring occurred predominantly in the prehistoric period). The other classes do not show entirely parallel levels of innovation across individual languages, and more parallelisms can be identified when analysing some further details of the distribution. The individual classes did not subdue to the restructuring process in the same way and to the same extent, which may be attributed to a range of interacting factors which include: the date of attestation, which differs per language, the size of the declension classes, the phonological shape of the paradigms, the frequency of occurrence and percentage of neutral forms in the paradigm. The importance of the first of these factors was already mentioned. In most general terms, the date of attestation correlates with the advancement of the restructuring process, but its impact is limited by the relative archaism of Old Frisian, which seems to render the absolute dating of the available material somewhat less relevant. The significance of the size of the declensional class was alluded to by Prokosch (1939: 257), who with reference to Germanic root nouns, argued that analogical forms may be expected primarily in small classes. However, what turned out to be significant in this study was not so much the size of the class as expressed by type frequency, but rather by the summed token frequency of all lemmas in a given class. Accordingly, the class which emerges as the most prone to analogical pressures in all the investigated languages is the class of s-stems, where the summed token frequency of the nouns in each of the analysed languages is relatively low.[320] As regards the impact of the neutral forms in the paradigms, their percentage turns out to be a direct incentive for the appearance of analogical pressure in the paradigm. The correlations with other factors will be discussed in more detail below, as well as in Chapter 8.

---

320. This factor strongly correlates with type frequency ($r > 0.9$), but in a direct competition with the summed token frequency, type frequency seems to be overruled by the former. The summed token frequency expresses the same principle as type frequency, but it implies that the impact depends on the cognitive generalisation over the individual exemplars (tokens) rather than over the abstract lemmas. This can be illustrated by the distribution in the r-stems, which constitute the smallest class in terms of type frequency, yet the token frequency renders them much more resistant to analogy (see Section 8.6.1).

Further insights into the patterns of restructuring can be gained by examining the distribution of archaic and innovative inflections with respect to the category of number and case. Table 7.4 depicts the overall distribution irrespective of the declensional class. As is mostly the case with such cumulated figures, they conceal the subtler distinctions and patterns of distribution. In order to capture these details of the distribution and to account for them, the figures in Table 7.5 present the incidence of analogical forms with respect to number in the individual classes.

Table 7.4 Distribution of innovative forms in the minor stems with respect to number

	OE*	OFris.	OS	OLF
% innov. SG.	35% ($n = 11750$)	45% ($n = 1700$)	22% ($n = 1605$)	46% ($n = 246$)
% innov. PL.	43% ($n = 5449$)	58% ($n = 634$)	26% ($n = 1055$)	75% ($n = 102$)

* The figures for Old English include the results from the analysis of the *i*-stem sample.

Table 7.5 Distribution of innovative forms across individual classes with respect to number

	% innov.	OE	OFris.	OS	OLF
i-stems	SG.	13%	44%	9%	31%
	PL.	80%	93%	3%	38%
u-stems	SG.	40%	26%	21%	87%
	PL.	71%	69%	23%	55%
root nouns	SG.	28%	75%	61%	56%
	PL.	6%	19%	70%	65%
r-stems	SG.	9%	42%	0%	4%
	PL.	82%	85%	0%	100%
s-stems	SG.	90%	100%	100%	–
	PL.	36%	51%	6%	–
nd-stems	SG.	88%	100%	36%	100%
mon.	PL.	9%	21%	27%	89%
dis.	PL.	100%			

The most straightforward conclusion that can be drawn from the figures in Table 7.4 is that the plural tends to be in general more prone to analogical pressures. This observation is, however, a consequence of accumulating the findings from a range of classes which actually show divergent patterns of restructuring with respect to the category of number. The factor that emerges as potentially significant is the frequency of occurrence: the paradigm of the singular tends to be in all the investigated languages more frequent than the plural. In order to assess whether this general correlation holds, a closer look at the details of this distribution across classes is needed (Table 7.5).

The most striking feature of the distribution with respect to number is the discrepancy between the vocalic and consonantal stems. In the former, in all languages except Old Saxon (where the differences are minimal), the singular turns out to be more conservative than the plural. The correlation is particularly visible in Old English and Old Frisian, and can be accounted for by the pattern of inflection found in the light-syllable stems, where the final vowel in the NOM./ACC. SG. was retained and was fairly resistant to analogical influence. In the consonantal stems, the pattern is – with two exceptions – exactly the opposite, namely, the singular paradigm turned out to be more prone to analogical processes, while the plural remains much more conservative. The first exception is the class of *r*-stems, which demonstrated considerable sensitivity to the frequency profiles of individual nouns. The other outlier is the class of root nouns in Old Saxon and Old Low Franconian, which will be discussed below. Some further patterns related to the salience of the inflectional marker are observable in the Old English *nd*-stems, where the level of innovation is different in the monosyllabic and disyllabic stems (cf. the discussion below). In general, the salience of the inflectional exponent emerges as a factor that can largely account for the attested patterns of distribution. The correlations with the type of stems as well as the frequency are not very conspicuous in Old Saxon, which attests to its remarkable conservatism and stability, manifested in the resistance to analogical pressures. The correlation of the attested distribution with the type of stem is demonstrated in Table 7.6, where the accumulated results for vocalic and consonantal stems are juxtaposed.

Table 7.6 Distribution of innovative forms with respect to number in vocalic and consonantal stems

	% innov.	OE	OFris.	OS	OLF
vocalic classes	SG.	30%	35%	11%	47%
	PL.	75%	90%	4%	63%
consonantal classes	SG.	35%	70%	43%	42%
	PL.	33%	48%	36%	82%

A close examination of the distribution of forms with respect to the category of case and number allows us to find some further correlations in the data. Accordingly, Tables 7.7 and 7.8 present the percentages of innovative inflection in individual cases in the singular and plural paradigms, respectively.[321]

---

321. In both tables, the figures for the *u*-stems in Old Saxon and Old Low Franconian refer to the findings from the standard interpretation. Likewise, the figure for the root nouns in Old Saxon reflects the traditional approach where the *i*-ending is interpreted as innovative.

Table 7.7 Distribution of innovative features in the singular paradigm across individual classes

SG	% innov.	OE	OFris.	OS	OLF
i-stems[*]	NOM. SG.	6%	27%	2%	31%
	GEN. SG.	–	100%	74%	29%
	DAT. SG.	–	100%	16%	34%
	ACC. SG.	15%	41%	0%	25%
u-stems	NOM. SG.	16%	3%	7%	94%
	GEN. SG.	87%	70%	100%	100%
	DAT. SG.	43%	33%	96%	100%
	ACC. SG.	7%	22%	3%	63%
root nouns	NOM. SG.	87%	–	–	–
	GEN. SG.	83%	98%	100%	86%
	DAT. SG.	25%	77%	46%	44%
	ACC. SG.	3%	0%	–	–
r-stems	NOM. SG.	–	–	–	–
	GEN. SG.	17%	62%	0%	8%
	DAT. SG.	2%	46%	0%	0%
	ACC. SG.	–	3%	–	0%
s-stems	NOM. SG.	–	–	–	–
	GEN. SG.	96%	100%	100%	–
	DAT. SG.	81%	100%	100%	–
	ACC. SG.	–	–	–	–
nd-stems	NOM. SG.	–	–	12%	–
	GEN. SG.	99%	100%	100%	100%
	DAT. SG.	76%	100%	82%	100%
	ACC. SG.	–	–	3%	–

[*] The figures for the Old English *i*-stems in the singular are based on the data from the light-syllable stems (masc. and neut.) and in the ACC. SG. they include also the forms of the heavy-syllable stems.

Table 7.8 Distribution of innovative features in the plural paradigm across individual classes

PL	% innov.	OE	OFris.	OS	OLF
i-stems	NOM. PL.	78%	90%	1%	50%
	ACC. PL.	80%	96%	4%	20%
u-stems	NOM. PL.	74%	63%	11%	100%
	ACC. PL.	69%	76%	29%	100%
root nouns	NOM. PL.	5%	13%	94%	50%
	ACC. PL.	6%	30%	52%	75%
r-stems	NOM. PL.	81%	86%	0%	80%
	ACC. PL.	83%	75%	0%	100%
s-stems	NOM. PL.	33%	67%	–	100%
	ACC. PL.	39%	44%	–	100%
nd-stems	NOM. PL.	15%	5%	31%	87%
	ACC. PL.	15%	71%	24%	100%

In most classes the categories of the NOM./ACC. SG. were not informative about the reorganisation of inflections. The *i*-stems and *u*-stems are exceptions here as the alternation in the light-syllable stems is relevant, reflecting competition between the inherited vocalic ending and analogical zero marker (or geminated consonant). The alternation found in the Old English root nouns in the NOM. SG. relies only on one subclass, the light-syllable feminine nouns (of the type *hnutu*), in which the interpretation of forms posed some methodological problems. The figure for the ACC. SG. is based primarily on the feminine heavy-syllable stems (cf. Section 3.5.4.2).

Overall the paradigms of the singular show considerable levels of innovation. In the classes where the alternation can be captured in all cases, namely in the *i*-stems and *u*-stems, it can be observed that the GEN. and DAT. SG. tend to be more easily influenced by analogical inflections, while the NOM. and ACC. SG. tend to remain more resistant. A parallel pattern is found in the Old Saxon *nd*-stems, where the alternation in the NOM./ACC. SG. reflects the presence of the adjectival inflection, which was relatively well attested in this language (in contrast to the other languages where, if attested at all, it is found in other categories). Although this general tendency holds for almost all classes, there are clear deviations from this pattern. This refers in particular to the considerably lower level of innovation in the GEN. and DAT. SG. in the *r*-stems in all languages except Old Frisian, as well as in the DAT. SG. in the Old English root nouns. These asymmetries in the distribution can be explained by recourse to two major factors involved in the restructuring process: namely, for the GEN. SG., the (relative) frequency of occurrence, and for the DAT. SG., the salience of the inflectional marker (i.e. the *i*-mutated vowel).

Table 7.8 presents the distribution of forms in the plural paradigm across classes, taking into account the NOM. and ACC. PL. only, i.e. those categories where the alternation between the historical and innovative forms could be captured in the analysis. This means that the results from the GEN. and DAT. PL., which were also relevant in the *s*-stems in all languages and in the *i*-stems in Old Saxon, were not included in this summary (cf. the respective chapters for discussions).

The Old English and Old Frisian material shows comparable levels of innovation in the NOM./ACC. PL. The most unexpected feature of the distribution is found in the Old Saxon root nouns (in particular in the NOM. PL.), which show a very high level of innovation when compared to the other investigated languages, where this class is very conservative. A potential explanation for this irregularity may involve a revision of the origin of the NOM./ACC. PL. marker *-i* in this class; namely, the marker could arguably be interpreted as inherited rather than analogical (from the *i*-stems), assuming that its distribution (involving *i*-apocope) was guided by (token) frequency (of individual lemmas) (see Section 5.6.4). The similarly high innovation level in the root nouns in Old Low Franconian, can be accounted for by the overall innovative profile of this language. It must be observed that the level of innovation found in the Old Low Franconian *s*-stems is based solely on *kind* and does not match the linguistic reality in any later Low Franconian variety, where the plural is marked by -*r*-. It rather reflects the fact that the noun *kind* was a newcomer to the class of the historical *s*-stems, and apparently had not yet adopted the *s*-stem inflection. A parallel pattern was found in Old Saxon, where *kint* consistently follows the *a*-stem inflection.

The susceptibility of individual cases and categories to analogical developments strongly correlates with their frequency of use. The correlations can be better captured in Old English and Old Frisian than in Old Saxon, which in general remains very archaic, or Old Low Franconian, which stays at the other end of the continuum, showing a high innovation level in the plural inflection. The categories of the nominative and accusative tended to be more frequent than the genitive and dative, and as the data demonstrate, the level of innovation in the latter two categories is higher than in the former. This correlation is not always straightforward and, admittedly, some deviations from this general tendency could be found in the analysed material. They can be a result of certain less common frequency patterns found in certain categories, but they clearly support the claim that frequency of use is a crucial factor determining the pathways and the dynamics of the restructuring process. For instance, the *u*-stems in Old English and Old Frisian are due to their semantic profiles (often denoting topographical features, e.g. *forest, field*) very well attested in the DAT. SG. As can be seen in Table 7.7, this category shows a relatively moderate level of innovation when compared to the other classes, which can be ascribed to its high frequency of occurrence in the *u*-stems, working as a conserving factor. In the majority of classes, the nominative remains unmodified by analogical developments, constituting the "important" category (Lahiri & Dresher 1984), which in practice means the most frequent case in the paradigm.

A number of factors emerge as relevant for the attested distribution of analogical forms across classes in all the investigated languages. Apart from the aforementioned frequency of occurrence, visible on various levels, including the frequencies of individual grammatical categories, they include also the salience of the inflectional exponents, and the semantic constitution of the classes (e.g. *r*-stems). In this chapter the significance of these correlations will be discussed only in the context of differences between individual languages, while their more theoretical aspects are taken up in Chapter 8. In particular, two major correlations become evident in this comparative overview, namely the effects of salience of inflectional exponents and the frequency of occurrence. The interplay of these factors turns out to have had a major bearing on the ultimate shape of the paradigms.

The most transparent correlation found in the material is that between the level of innovation and the salience of the inflectional markers. A salient marker, such as the *i*-mutated vowel or the *r*-element, can be viewed as a stable type of marker and will tend to be more resistant to analogical restructuring. In contrast, a less salient marker will be more easily replaced by a distinctive marker from other declensional classes. The correlation becomes most conspicuous in the paradigm of the plural, where a variety of markers can be found, ranging from zero marking, through several vocalic markers, to consonantal and vowel stem alternation. In the singular, the situation is more straightforward as the inflectional markers can be divided into two groups, i.e. the salient GEN. SG. marker *-es* (*-as*) and the less salient vocalic or zero markers. The only category consistently marked by the *i*-mutated vowel is the DAT. SG. in the OE root nouns, *r*-stems and monosyllabic *nd*-stems, and, as can be seen in Table 7.7, it remains very conservative there. The consonantal modulation of the stem, found originally in the GEN. and DAT. SG. in the OE *s*-stems, is eliminated very early and its correlation with the level of innovation is not directly observable (in contrast to the plural paradigm).

The correlation between the type of inflectional marker and the percentage of innovative inflections in the NOM./ACC. PL. is presented in Table 7.9. The type of plural marker is juxtaposed with the percentage of analogical inflections in the plural paradigms in individual classes. In terms of the type of plural marking, Old English and Old Frisian can be grouped together as they show almost identical types of inflectional markers (and the relevant discrepancies will be discussed below). Likewise, Old Saxon and Old Low Franconian display largely parallel features with respect to the type of inflectional marking and are thus arranged together. The figures refer essentially to the forms of the NOM. and ACC. PL., except in the

Table 7.9 The correlation between the percentage of innovation in the plural paradigms and the salience of inflectional markers

plural (NOM./ACC.PL.)	OE/OFris. PL. marker	OE % innov.	OFris. % innov.	OS/OLF PL. marker	OS % innov.	OLF % innov.
i-stems	vocalic	80%	93%	*-i* + *i*-mutation	3%	38%
u-stems*	vocalic	71%	69%	*-i* + *i*-mutation	23%	55%
root nouns	*i*-mutation	6%	19%	Ø	70%	65%
r-stems	Ø	82%	85%	Ø	0%	86%
s-stems	*-er*	36%	51%	*-er*	6%	(100%)
nd-stems (mon.)	*i*-mutation	9%	21%	Ø	27%	89%
nd-stems (dis.)	Ø	100%				

* The figures for the OS and OLF *u*-stems and root nouns refer to the 'traditional' counting, not the alternative interpretation. Accordingly, in Old Saxon the ending *-i* is considered to be the inherited marker in the *u*-stems and innovative in the root nouns; in Old Low Franconian it is interpreted as innovative in both classes. See Sections 5.6.3 and 6.5.3 for the discussion of the alternative interpretations.

s-stems in Old Saxon and Old Low Franconian, where the GEN. and DAT. forms were included.[322]

The level of innovative inflection in the individual classes strongly correlates with the salience of plural exponents. The less distinctive (salient) the inflectional marker is, the more widespread the presence of analogical inflections in the paradigm. The correlation is evident in Old English and Old Frisian, to some extent also in Old Low Franconian, while Old Saxon shows a remarkably conservative inflectional profile, with no clear correlation. In Old English and Old Frisian, the highest levels of innovation are found in classes where there is no explicit plural marker, especially in the *r*-stems and in disyllabic *nd*-stems (in Old English), and in the vocalic classes, *i*-stems and *u*-stems, where the plural is marked by a vowel. The low salience of these two markers, i.e. the vocalic and zero marker, renders the paradigms susceptible to analogical pressure from the productive classes. An exception here are the Old Frisian *nd*-stems which, despite the zero marker in the NOM./ACC.PL., display a very low level of innovation. This deviation from the general pattern can be accounted for by the frequency profile of this class (cf. Section 4.5.7). In contrast, the presence of *i*-mutation as a distinctive case-and-number exponent (though essentially a receding feature) turns out to have been a major factor that inhibited the activity of analogical processes in the paradigms. This is confirmed by the root nouns, as well as monosyllabic *nd*-stems in Old English, where the contrast between the level of innovation in the nouns where the plural was marked by an *i*-mutated vowel and those without *i*-mutation is very prominent. In languages where this morphophonemic alternation was reduced through intraparadigmatic analogical levelling (e.g. in Old Frisian), or where *i*-mutation did not exist as a distinctive feature (e.g. in Old Saxon or Old Low Franconian), the paradigms of root nouns and *nd*-stems became much more prone to analogical pressures. In other words, the reduction of morphophonemic alternation (or its absence) engendered a decrease in the formal variation, as a result of which the paradigms became more uniform and less distinctive. In Old Low Franconian the correlation with *i*-mutation can be found in the *i*-stems and *u*-stems, where it is not an independent marker, yet seems to have some effect on the inflectional pattern. The patterns of restructuring found in these stems give some insight into the complex issue of the

---

322. The figure for the *s*-stems in Old Low Franconian is based only on the attestations to *kind*, which is etymologically ambiguous, and therefore it cannot be viewed as representative of the class. The figure for the OS *s*-stems includes also the GEN. and DAT. PL. as the attestations to the NOM. ACC. PL. are confined to two tokens only, and are thus unreliable. The figures for the *s*-stems in Old English and Old Frisian are based only on the NOM. and ACC. PL. If the GEN. and DAT. PL. forms were included, the level of innovation would increase to 42% and 76% in Old English and Old Frisian, respectively.

dating and status of secondary *i*-mutation in Old Low Franconian. Although a discussion of this long-debated issue is beyond the scope of this study (see e.g. Salmons 2012: 120–127), it is worth observing that the classes with potential *i*-mutation in the plural are typologically in line (i.e. show parallel levels of innovation) with the other classes where *i*-mutation was part of the plural marking pattern, rather than with the classes where the plural was marked only with a vowel. This may imply that by the time of the first Old Low Franconian attestations, secondary *i*-mutation had already been implemented (Braune/Reiffenstein 2004: 55–56 suggests a datum ante quem for secondary *i*-mutation in Old High German of ca. 1000, while Gütter 2011 dates it to the ninth century). In contrast, in the root nouns, where *i*-mutation was not the marker of the NOM./ACC. PL., the level of innovation is very high.[323]

Another salient marker of plurality in Old English and Old Frisian is the *r*-formative present in the *s*-stems, which turned out to have a conserving effect as well. The high percentage of analogical forms in the *s*-stems in Old Low Franconian is to be ascribed to the fact that all the attestations in this class belong to one lemma, *kind*, whose status as an original *s*-stem is ambiguous. Its remarkable resistance to analogical pressure attested in Old Saxon can be viewed as a forerunner of the tendencies to be found in the later stages of the development of (Low) German, where the *r*-formative became one of the more widespread inflectional exponents of plurality.

The high levels of innovation attested in the other classes in Old Low Franconian where the NOM./ACC. PL. were expressed by the zero marker, i.e. *r*-stems and *nd*-stems, correspond to the patterns found in Old Frisian and Old English. As mentioned earlier, hardly any of these correlations were identified in Old Saxon. This fact must be ascribed to the conservatism of Old Saxon and the absence of analogical pressures in the minor stem paradigms. The least expected feature of the distribution of analogical forms in Old Saxon is the high level of innovation attested in the root nouns (70%). A potential explanation of this abnormality has already been addressed in Chapter 5, where it was indicated that in view of the overall archaic profile of Old Saxon nominal morphology emerging from this study, the endings in -*i* should rather be interpreted as historical than as analogical (see Section 5.6.4). This explanation could potentially be extended to the Old Low Franconian root nouns, where the level of innovation is high, when compared to Old English and Old Frisian.

It must be observed that the correlation with the salience of the inflectional exponent, although very strong in Old English and Old Frisian, did not guarantee long-term stability of the inflectional patterns. The phonological and analogical developments affecting the paradigms led to further restructurings in the subsequent

---

323. The percentage of innovation in the root nouns is based on the traditional approach, where forms in -*i* were counted as innovative.

stages of development of the individual Northern West Germanic languages, rendering markers such as the *i*-mutated vowel, though remarkably resistant to analogy at the early stage, a relic pattern of the original plural inflection. The stability of this exponent is, however, reflected in the later development of nominal morphology of Continental Germanic, which will be discussed in Section 7.3. The other salient exponent, the *r*-element, was altogether not very widespread and clearly not productive in the investigated period of Germanic. Its secondary productivity developed only later in Continental West Germanic, especially in Middle and Early New High German, where the *-ir-* (*-er-*) element emerged as a new, expansive plural marker, disseminating to masculine nouns affiliated originally with other inflectional classes (for details, see e.g. Wurzel 1989, 1992; Kastovsky 1995; Harnisch 2001; Klein 2013).[324]

A final aspect of the distribution is related to the presence of forms classified as *neutral* in the present analysis, i.e. the forms which were not informative about the process of restructuring and therefore were excluded from the calculation. The neutral forms are inflectional forms that overlap with the forms of the productive declensions, either as an effect of phonological processes that rendered them identical (e.g. the endingless NOM./ACC. SG. of consonantal stems), or as a result of an early, prehistoric extension of the productive inflections (e.g. in the GEN. and DAT. PL.). In other words, the percentage of the neutral forms present in the paradigms can be interpreted as a measure of the paradigm overlap with the productive declensions. The number of these forms is considerable, as can be seen in the tables presenting the distributions for individual classes in the respective chapters, and it varies depending on the class and paradigm (i.e. the type of stem). In the context of the present quantitative analysis, the existence of such ambiguous forms is an unfortunate circumstance, especially for the scantily attested languages, such as Old Low Franconian. At the same time, a closer scrutiny of the distribution of these neutral forms across declensional classes turned out to be revealing for the present study. The number of neutral forms corresponds in a rather straightforward way to the innovation levels attested in the minor paradigms. Table 7.10 presents the correlation between the percentage of neutral forms and the innovation level in the minor paradigms in Old English, Old Frisian and Old Saxon. As the number of attestations for Old Low Franconian was very low, they were not included in this summary.[325] A distinction is made between the light- and heavy-syllable stems, since they show divergent percentages of the neutral forms present in the paradigms.

---

324. The marker *-er* became particularly productive in the 16th c. as a reaction to *schwa*-apocope (Salmons 2012: 246–247).

325. The correlation was present in *Wachtendonck Psalms*, but it was based on very few attestations and thus not entirely reliable; it was absent from RB and LW.

Table 7.10 The correlation between the percentage of neutral forms and the level of innovation in the minor stems in Old English, Old Frisian and Old Saxon

	OE		OFris.		OS	
	% innov.	% neut.	% innov.	% neut.	% innov.	% neut.
i-stems L	15%	48%	33%	43%	12%	2%
i-stems H	55%	69%	55%	53%	24%	20%
u-stems L	30%	28%	19%	18%	13%	6%
u-stems H	51%	51%	53%	40%	71%	79%
root nouns	21%	38%	60%	63%	24%	34%
r-stems	36%	59%	54%	53%	0%	61%
s-stems	68%	52%	84%	43%	59%	35%
nd-stems (mon.)	23%	54%	52%	59%	38%	16%
nd-stems (dis.)	88%	74%				

The correlation between the percentage of neutral forms in the paradigm and the level of innovation (in the non-neutral categories) is robust, although not ideal, as this is obviously not the only factor at play. The strength of the correlation differs per class, but the interdependence of these two variables is clearly visible: the higher the number of neutral forms in the paradigm, the higher the level of innovation in the non-overlapping forms. Altogether, for the three languages depicted in the table, the correlation between the percentage of neutral forms and the percentage of innovative inflection is 0.49 ($p = 0.014$). This correlation becomes most prominent in the heavy-syllable *u*-stems in all languages, in light-syllable *u*-stems in Old English and Old Frisian, in root nouns and *r*-stems in Old Frisian, and in heavy-syllable *i*-stems in Old Frisian and Old Saxon. This factor turns out to be of primary importance for explaining the patterns of restructuring found in Old Saxon, where the attested distribution cannot be accounted for by the salience of inflectional markers, but it shows a clear correlation with the percentage of neutral forms in the paradigms (the only outlier here is the class of *r*-stems). Importantly, as the percentage of neutral forms reflects essentially the scale of overlap with the productive inflections, it can be interpreted as a gauge of the analogical attraction of minor stems by the productive paradigms (see also Versloot & Hoekstra 2016). The paradigms with a large number of inflections overlapping with those of the productive classes will tend to be less stable and more prone to analogical adjustments. It has to be emphasised at the same time that the proportion of neutral forms in the paradigms is only one of the determinants of inflectional restructuring, and other factors, such as the (average) date of attestation of the languages, salience of inflectional markers, type frequency (per class) and token frequency, each contribute significantly to the level of innovation within paradigms.

7.3   Explaining the divergent development of the nominal inflection across Northern West Germanic

Despite their close genetic affiliation, the investigated varieties of early Northern West Germanic followed partly divergent paths of development with respect to the reorganisation of their declensional systems. Although the overall diachronic tendency towards a simplification of the declensional configuration, understood as a reduction in the declensional diversity inherited from Proto-Germanic, is discernible in all the investigated languages, the final outcome of the process varies across individual languages. The attested discrepancies in the restructuring patterns can be summarised in the following way. In Old English, especially in the later period, the original declensional configuration was largely disturbed by analogical developments and the declensional diversity was gradually eliminated. The nominal system of Continental Germanic, as illustrated here by Old Saxon and Old Low Franconian, was characterised by greater declensional diversity, which in the long run turned out to be a stable and salient feature of nominal morphology of Continental Germanic. Significantly, Old Saxon retained considerable variation and conservatism in inflectional marking, in contrast to Old Low Franconian, which although inflectionally diversified, shows a much less conservative inflectional profile. These different profiles of the two Continental sister languages with respect to the level of innovation are to be ascribed to the discrepancy in the dates of their attestation. Old Frisian occupies clearly an intermediate position, with two prominent characteristics: (a) its relatively high level of archaism (given its late date of attestation), and (b) the presence of various inflectional parallelisms shared with the Continental dialects rather than Old English despite their fundamental similarities.

The disparate restructuring patterns recognised in the course of the investigation, in Old English and Old Frisian on the one hand, and Old Saxon and Old Low Franconian on the other, can be largely attributed to the divergent phonological developments in these languages.[326] Two major phonological processes and the dynamics of interactions between them played a decisive role in the unfolding of the restructuring process in the examined languages:

1. the operation of *i*-mutation, with its different scope and chronology across West Germanic
2. the operation of apocope and weakening (reduction) of final vowels, in particular /i/ > /e/ (in Old English and Old Frisian).

---

326. Admittedly, the rate of change in the individual languages was determined also by language-external factors. This refers in particular to the developments in English, where language contact had a considerable bearing on its linguistic structure.

The significance of apocope is not as explicit as that of *i*-mutation in that the process does not directly lead to the divergent restructuring patterns in the nominal inflection, but it rather determines the phonological shape of the minor stem paradigms, contributing to the distinctive profiles of light- and heavy-syllable stems. This is best manifested in the paradigms of the *i*-stems, *u*-stems and root nouns. In the light-syllable stems, the final vowels (-*i*, -*u*) are retained in the NOM./ACC. SG., while in the heavy-syllable stems, they are eliminated at the prehistoric stage, which generates the overlap with the forms from the productive classes. The subsequent differing susceptibility of these two stem types to analogical pressures from the productive declensions is a consequence of this early phonological development. While the light-syllable stems remained fairly resistant to analogical pressure, the heavy-syllable stems, where the interface with the productive paradigms is established already at the prehistoric stage, turned out to be more susceptible to it.

Apocope interacted with *i*-mutation and depending on the relative chronology of these two processes, this interaction had diverse consequences for the morphological system. In Old English and Old Frisian, where *i*-mutation preceded apocope of the final */i/ (after a heavy syllable), the process of *i*-mutation was morphologised relatively early. A reverse order occurred in the Continental languages, Old Saxon and Old Low Franconian, where apocope eliminated the environment conducive for the operation of *i*-mutation in various morpho-syntactic categories. In English and Frisian the unaccented vowels that were not affected by apocope underwent a subsequent weakening, whereby /i/ was reduced to /e/ (Campbell 1977: 153–154). The absence of a parallel vowel quality reduction in Continental Germanic, where the final /i/ remained unreduced longer, rendered the operation of *i*-mutation possible at a later stage.[327]

The major determinant for the restructuring discrepancies in the investigated languages was, therefore, the operation of *i*-mutation, which had a different scope and chronology across Germanic. The process occurred early in North Sea Germanic, but relatively late on the Continent, i.e. in the High German and Franconian dialects. Accordingly, *i*-mutation was phonologised early in Old English and Old Frisian, while in Continental Germanic, especially in early Old High German and in Old Low Franconian, the process is believed to have been phonetic, not yet phonological (for an overview of a range of interpretations, see Braune/ Reiffenstein 2004: 56–57). The distribution of the process across the West Germanic

---

327. In Old High German, apocope (*i*-apocope) was more widespread on account of its interaction with the High German consonant shift, whereby new heavy-syllable stems arose from etymologically light-syllable ones, e.g. *baki (OS beki, biki) > *bahhi, which was apocopated to *bahh > OHG bah (Boutkan 1996: 242–243; cf. Braune/Reiffenstein 2004: 60–64). The chronology of these two developments seems to be crucial for this interpretation, and accordingly *i*-apocope is believed to have occurred after the consonant shift.

continuum with respect to absolute chronology has been summarised, among others, by Buccini (2003): " …at the time when the process of *i*-umlaut had almost without doubt been completed in Old English and probably generally in North Sea Germanic, to wit, roughly around 650–700 A.D., the South Germanic dialects were in the period of transition between the two types of umlaut, that is, they were in the stage of primary *i*-umlaut." (Buccini 2003: 194, cf. Buccini 1995: 24ff.; Prokosch 1939: 107–112; Salmons 2012: 124–127). The consequence of this different chronology was the later morphologisation of *i*-mutation in the Continental varieties and its lexicalisation in North Sea Germanic. The dissemination of *i*-mutation in the nominal inflection across West Germanic has been described in the following way:

> Across West Germanic, umlaut morphologized as a plural marker even where there was no historical phonetic motivation for the process (…). [T]his pattern spread across many or even most nominal classes in the apocopating modern German dialects, even to the far larger *a*-stem classes, apparently in order to maintain plural forms distinct from the singular (…). [I]ndependent phonological developments promoted the spread of umlaut qua apophonic plural marker in dialects where umlaut had reached a full flowering. By contrast, in Dutch and English, where umlaut matured to a much lesser extent, the process tended to recede over time, leaving only a few marginal traces in the plural systems ….
>
> (Iverson & Salmons 2004: 84)

The morphologisation of *i*-mutation, whereby this originally phonological alternation became morphologically conditioned, is significant in the context of the present study in that it involved the development of the *i*-mutated vowel as the primary exponent of plurality. In Old English and Old Frisian, the *i*-mutated vowel served as a plural marker only in a few declensional classes (root nouns and only in OE *nd*-stems), and was at this stage not yet an independent marker of number, but expressed the fused categories of case and number (NOM./ACC. PL. and in Old English also the DAT. SG. and occasionally the GEN. SG.). In Old Saxon or Old Low Franconian, the *i*-mutated vowel was not present as a category exponent at this early stage, but the relative stability of the vocalic classes (*i*-stems and *u*-stems) in Old Low Franconian may be indicative of the actual phonologization of *i*-mutation by the year 1000.

The divergent chronology of the operation of *i*-mutation across West Germanic is reflected in the most direct way in the development of the *i*-stems. In this class, the relatively late operation of *i*-mutation in Continental Germanic admitted of its subsequent functionalization as a plurality exponent in these languages. In consequence, the inflection of the *i*-stems, where the contrast between the singular and plural was expressed by the *i*-mutated vowel, was later to become one the most productive inflectional patterns (cf. Modern Low and High German), competing with the *a*-stem and *ō*-stem patterns. In contrast, the lack of functionalization of *i*-mutation in English in the *i*-stems, where *i*-mutation occurred at an early stage and could not serve any distinctive function in this class, led to a gradual and fairly early submission of the *i*-stems to the inflectional patterns of the *a*- and *ō*-stems (e.g. OS *gast* – *gesti* vs. OE *giest* – *giestas*).

Concluding, the absolute and relative chronology of *i*-mutation in West Germanic languages, and especially the discrepancy with respect to this chronology between North Sea Germanic and Continental West Germanic (i.e. the High German, Franconian and Saxon dialects) was of a profound significance to the reorganisation of the nominal inflection. In particular, the morphologisation of *i*-mutation in Low (and High) German can be viewed as the basis for the subsequent divergent development of English and German (e.g. Klein 2013: 184). Both the chronology of *i*-mutation, operating later on the Continent (except in Frisian), and its limited scope there at the early stage, were essential determinants of the dynamics of the restructuring process in the "Old" period.

As in most West Germanic languages the case marking system has been lost or at least considerably reduced, any systematic comparison of the declensional systems from a present-day perspective must be confined to the plurality marking patterns. The gradual decline of the case marking system, most consistently carried out in English, reduced the inflectional variation, leading to the emergence of number as the major exponent of declensional class (except German where case has remained a relevant criterion in the declensional classification). The stage of the development of Germanic languages examined in this study still testifies to the relevance of case as a correlate, allowing a cross-linguistic comparison that involves the patterns of restructuring with respect to the category of case as well.

Another prominent inflectional feature that distinguishes English and Frisian from the Continental sister languages when seen from the present-day perspective is the development of the *s*-stems. While in the Continental languages (Low and High German) the original *-ir*-formative developed a secondary productivity and functions as a plural exponent, disseminating to many nouns originally not affiliated with the *s*-stems, both the spread and the functionalization of the *-(e)r*-formative as a plural marker is entirely absent in English (save for the single noun *children*). Modern Dutch and modern dialects of Frisian, especially East and Northern Frisian, preserve some relics of the original *s*-stem inflection. The analysed Old Germanic material does not explicitly admit of detecting this divergent trend in the development of the *s*-stem pattern, later to be found in the sister languages. The reason for the absence of features that could be the forerunners of the subsequent tendencies is that the functionalization of this inflectional exponent was a later development, occurring in the Middle period of the respective languages, whereas in the Old Germanic period this marker was still occasionally present in the paradigm of the singular (e.g. in Old English). The elimination of the

-(e)r-formative from the singular in the historical *s*-stems (in Old English from the *lamb*-type, where the *r*-element marked the plural) was the factor that furthered its functionalization as a number (plural) exponent.[328] Additionally, the reinterpretation of the *-(e)r-* as a plural marker is believed to have been facilitated by the elimination of the *i*-mutated forms from the singular. The ensuing dissemination of *i*-mutation in the plural in Continental Germanic is considered to have enhanced the *-(e)r*-element as a plural marker in that the overall salience of this exponent increased (Klein 2013: 184). According to Kastovsky (1995: 231), the presence of the *i*-mutated vowel in the paradigm created "enough critical mass" for the reanalysis of the *r*-formative as a plural marker. The emergence of the *r*-element as an independent exponent of plurality was rendered possible owing to a typological shift, namely, the (gradual) dissociation of case and number, whereby these two categories were no longer expressed by one formal marker.

In Old English, the restructuring of the *s*-stem paradigms followed an entirely different path, largely because the *hrīþer*-type was more common than the *lamb*-type (not necessarily in terms of token frequency, but clearly in terms of type frequency). In this subtype, the *r*-formative was in many nouns restored from the GEN. and DAT. SG. to the NOM./ACC. SG., and consequently the *s*-stems were indistinguishable from the *a*-stems ending in *-er* (e.g. *wæter*).[329] As a result, most of these nouns followed eventually the *a*-stem pattern and the *s*-stem inflection never emerged as a potentially competing type in English or in Frisian.[330]

The divergent development of the nominal inflection in the Northern West Germanic languages is summarised in Figure 4. The figure illustrates the potential expansion of the *a*-stem inflection and the significance of *i*-mutation in the restructuring and in the divergent development of the declensional systems in the two West Germanic subgroups. The minor classes included in this overview are those where *i*-mutation had an impact on the inflectional profile of the paradigms, and thus they turned out to be relevant for the reorganisation of the declensional system.

---

328. This inflectional exponent develops from a purely derivational suffix. Its development as a plural marker entailed an interaction of phonology, analogical levelling and reanalysis (exaptation) (Fertig 2013: 38).

329. This development is reminiscent of the situation in North Germanic, where the *s*-stems as such are non-existent because the *r*-formative (sometimes even the pre-rhotacism *s*-formative, as in the Modern Danish *høns* 'poultry') is consistently retained throughout the entire paradigm, and accordingly, these nouns follow the *a*-stem inflection (e.g. Boutkan 1996: 264–265).

330. According to Kastovsky (1995: 236), three factors contributed to the fact that the *s*-stem inflection did not survive and did not disseminate in English. They include: (a) the early phonemicization of *i*-mutation, (b) the development of a monoparadigmatic noun morphology, i.e. the prevalence of the *a*-stem inflection, and (c) the early generalisation of word-based inflectional morphology.

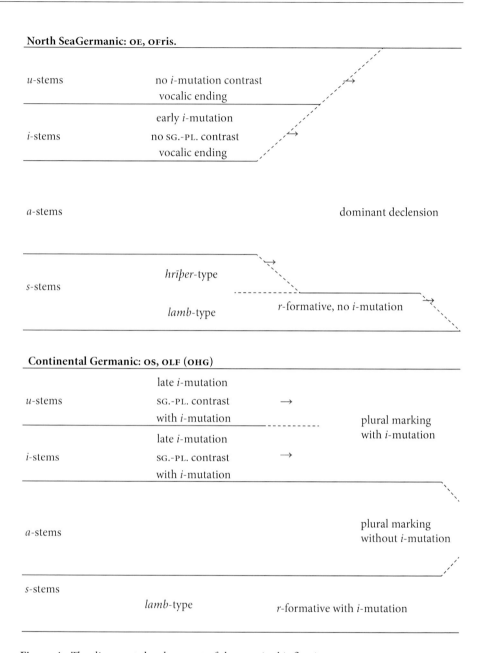

Figure 4. The divergent development of the nominal inflection in the NWGmc. languages

The dividing line across the West Germanic languages, established on the basis of phonological and morphological characteristics, runs between the Continental varieties of High and Low German on the one hand, and the North Sea Germanic languages, English and Frisian, on the other. Modern Dutch, with its notorious absence of morphological *i*-mutation, occupies a special position in this respect. One of the main criteria for this division is the aforementioned chronology of *i*-mutation, which occurred early in North Sea Germanic, but relatively late on the Continent, i.e. in the High German and Franconian dialects (Buccini 1995, 2003; see also Section 7.2 for the dating of secondary *i*-mutation in Old Low Franconian). In the context of the present study, one may ask what picture of the mutual relations between the examined languages emerges when the nominal inflectional morphology is taken as the primary and only criterion for the comparison. The present investigation into the changes in the nominal inflection allows one to make a refinement of the above-presented demarcation within West Germanic, especially by revising the status of Old Saxon, and to some extent Old Frisian.

The close affinity between Anglo-Saxon and Old Frisian seems to be largely substantiated by the data. These two closely related sister languages demonstrate parallel inflectional tendencies in all minor classes, including the consistent, parallel correlations between the levels of innovation and the types of inflectional exponents, which were nearly identical in Old English and Old Frisian. Old Frisian attests overall to a more advanced level of innovation, which could be expected in view of its relatively late date of attestation. At the same time, it evinces some more diversity in the types of inflection that served as the destination classes for minor stems (especially the spread of the *e*-plural inflection), which places it closer to its Continental sister languages.[331]

Old Frisian occupies a middle ground position between Old English on the one hand, and Old Saxon and Old Low Franconian on the other, with respect to the retention of the inherited Proto-Germanic nominal morphology. What stands out in the attested patterns of restructuring across Northern West Germanic is the position of Old Saxon. As it turns out, the patterns of morphological innovation found in the Old Saxon material allow one to place it much closer to its Continental sister languages than to any of the other North Sea Germanic dialects. Evidently, Old Saxon shows patterns of restructuring largely parallel to those found in Old Low Franconian (and implicitly Old High German) rather than Old English and Old Frisian. This is manifested especially in the development of the *i*-stems, which attest to some productivity in Old Saxon, as well as in the overall inflectional

---

331. A close affinity of Old Frisian with Old Saxon rather than with Old English is visible in the developments of the *ō*-stems, where many parallel intraparadigmatic reshufflings can be found (for details see Versloot 2016b).

profiles of the root nouns and *nd*-stems, which in contrast to Old English (and to some extent Old Frisian), lack *i*-mutation. Old Saxon emerges also as the most conservative of the investigated languages, with a level of innovation lower than Early Old English. This conservatism can be partly accounted for by the early date of attestation of Old Saxon; however, given that Modern Low German is morphologically more conservative than English, Frisian and Dutch, the higher level of archaism in the Old Saxon inflectional morphology should rather be viewed as a typological indicator.

This observation leads us to the last aspect of the restructuring process to be discussed in this chapter. The range of languages investigated and compared in this study allows for certain generalisations of a typological nature. Admittedly, a study like the present one should be treated primarily as a contribution to contrastive linguistics, and as such it cannot make true typological claims.[332] Bearing this limitation in mind, a few observations of a typological nature can nevertheless be attempted. The analogical changes in the declensional systems in the Old Germanic period can to a large extent be considered the beginning of a more significant typological shift which occurred in the subsequent developmental stages of individual Germanic languages. The typological shift was a large-scale development, affecting the entire structure of the language, including inflectional morphology, and was most conspicuously visible in the evolution of English, having far-reaching consequences there (e.g. Croft 2003; Bertacca 2009; Hawkins 2015). With regard to inflectional morphology, it involved a gradual transition in the typological status of inflection from root-based to stem-based inflection, which was a characteristic of the Proto-Germanic nominal system, and a subsequent shift to word-based inflection. The stem-based type of inflection was lost earliest in the productive classes (*a*-stems and *ō*-stems), while the minor classes tended to retain it for a longer time. The shift to word-based inflection was identifiable already in Old English, and it is estimated to have taken place in pre-Old English (Kastovsky 1995: 228), while the Continental Germanic languages tended to preserve the stem-based type of inflection longer (e.g. Werner 1987; Kastovsky 1985, 1995; Harnisch 2001).

---

332. This has been made explicit by van der Auwera (2012) who states: "There may indeed be areas of grammar where even a pilot study of just three languages – and even related ones – provides a decent initial typology. But three-way contrastive linguistics must remain pilot typology, for true typology is about all of the world's languages through the prism of a well argued and ideally large sample." (van der Auwera 2012: 10). And: "[e]ven though contrastive linguistics can count as pilot typology, the demands and falsifiability of contrastive linguistics and typology are different. More specifically: an explanation may well be valid for a difference between two or three languages, without having universal validity." (van der Auwera 2012: 16).

The type of inflection is closely related to another tendency of a typological nature easily observable in the material, namely the emergence of a contrast between the polyparadigmatic noun morphology, where more than one declensional type can be productive, and the monoparadigmatic noun morphology, with one dominant declensional pattern serving as a template for nouns of various origin (Kastovsky 1995: 236). Old English and Old Saxon occupy here the opposite poles of the continuum, the former showing a strong gravitation towards one dominant inflectional pattern (*a*-stems), the latter, retaining considerable inflectional diversity and admitting of the simultaneous existence of more than one inflectional type (i.e. the plural inflection of the original *n*-stems, *i*-stems and *s*-stems). Just like in Old High German, the stem inflection remained the dominant type in Old Saxon and the typological reorientation took place only later (Harnisch 2001: 63, 289; Wurzel 1989: 91, 103). In fact, the *Stamm-Prinzip*, i.e. stem-based inflection/ derivation is considered to have remained, to a lesser or greater extent, a significant feature of German nominal morphology (Harnisch 2001: 300).

Significantly, there was no explicit candidate for a default plural suffix in Proto-Germanic, and many of the inflectional endings served at the same time to mark the singular. A potential candidate for a default marker could be the final -*s*, which was originally frequent in the plural, e.g. NOM. PL. *-*ōs*, ACC. PL. *-*ons*, DAT./ INSTR. PL. *-*mis*. However, this potential general case-independent marker was at an early stage undermined by the *Auslautgesetze* and by the presence of the PGmc. *-*s* (> *-*z*) ending in the NOM. SG. Consequently, the markers which in present-day Germanic emerge as default markers are the result of later, largely language-specific developments.

The reasons for the enormous productivity of the *a*-stems in Old English were discussed already in Chapter 3. By way of summary, it can be stated that the productivity of this declensional pattern was secured by three main features: (a) the number of nouns affiliated with this type, i.e. its remarkably high type frequency (the class comprised 60 percent of Old English lexical stock), (b) the lack of morphophonemic alternation in the paradigm, which rendered the paradigm transparent, as well as (c) the presence of two salient inflectional exponents in the paradigm, the GEN. SG. marker -*es* and the NOM./ACC. PL. marker -*as*. Both managed to survive the large-scale reorganisation and eventual decline of the inflectional system in English. The role of the latter marker was particularly significant in that it helped retain a functional contrast between the singular and plural. The lack of such a functional distinction in the other classes, e.g. in the light-syllable *i*-stems, where the ending -*e* served as an inflectional marker for the NOM., ACC. and DAT. SG., as well as the NOM./ACC. PL., or in the *u*-stems, where the ending -*a* served as an inflectional marker for the GEN. and DAT. SG., as well as the NOM./ACC. PL., was one of the important features that rendered these paradigms susceptible to the analogical influence of the productive plural markers. Another factor contributing to the stability of the *a*-stem inflection was the typological status of the *a*-stems, which represented word-based inflection rather than stem-based inflection (but for a few exceptions), and as such was morphosemantically and morphotactically more transparent (Kastovsky 1997: 67). The typological shift, whereby the inherited stem-based inflection lost its ground in favour of word-based inflection, could be one of the factors which contributed to the large-scale dissemination of the *a*-stem inflections in Late Old English.

The question which remains to be answered is why the *a*-stems did not become equally productive in the other Northern West Germanic languages. The most significant factors that contributed to the attested divergent paths of inflectional development are phonological in nature. Firstly, the Continental West Germanic varieties were phonologically more conservative, which was manifested especially in the domain of unstressed syllables, where the reduction processes occurred later than in English or Frisian. The other phonological factor that emerges as crucial is the chronology of *i*-mutation, as discussed earlier in this chapter. The fact that *i*-mutation occurred later in Continental Germanic, led to the emergence of the *i*-mutated vowel as a distinctive inflectional exponent, which helped retain the contrast between the singular and plural, and whose significance increased with time. Another factor is related to the salience of inflectional exponents and their distribution in the paradigms. The NOM./ACC. PL. *a*-stem marker -*os* in Old Saxon, although equivalent in terms of salience to the Old English marker -*as*, was not the only maker in this category, but was competing with the ending -*a*, enhanced by the influence of the Franconian dialects. In Old Low Franconian, the NOM. and ACC. PL. were marked by a vowel -*a*, which was not a very salient type of inflectional exponent.[333] In Old Frisian, the ending -*ar*, though fairly salient, was competing with a vocalic marker, which again undermined the strength of the former. The existence of two competitive markers in these categories worked against the productivity of a marker that could potentially develop as dominant. Consequently, the number of lemmas showing the markers -*os* and -*ar* in Old Saxon and Old Frisian respectively was much lower than those showing the ending -*as* in Old English. A further important reason for the retention of the declensional diversity in Continental Germanic is related to gender. A gender distinction was maintained in Continental Germanic and additionally the subsequent merger of the feminine *ō*-stems and

---

333. The spread of the marker -*s* in Modern Dutch began primarily in nomina agentis in -*ere* (historical *ja*-stems) in the 13th c. and was confined to the western region, i.e. Flanders and Holland (Marynissen 2001: 666). Further dissemination of this marker from the west is reflected in present-day Limburgian, where -*s* is common in this class (i.e. disyllabic words with an unstressed second syllable).

n-stems, attested in Old Low Franconian, resulted in a strong inflectional pattern for the feminine nouns, which became productive. Another factor relevant for the explanation of the declensional configuration across West Germanic is related to the transparency of the type of inflection, mentioned above. As demonstrated in the data from the most conservative of the investigated languages, stem-type inflection was to a large extent a characteristic of the Old Saxon nominal system. The coexistence of these two types of inflection, stem- and word-based, rendered the system free from the bias that came with the prevalence of the morphotactically and morphosemantically transparent word-based type.

The interaction of all these factors led to a situation where a number of inflectional patterns could develop a secondary productivity. This refers not only to *i*-mutation, but also to the inflection of the original *s*-stems, which in Continental Germanic, especially in Low (and High) German emerged as one of the most widespread inflectional patterns. One of the classes where the productivity of the *i*-mutation pattern and the disparate development in English and Low German is evident is the class of *r*-stems as attested in the later period: while Modern English preserves no characteristics of the original paradigm, having generalised the uniform masculine plural marker -*as* (> -*es*), Modern German (since the extensive spread of *i*-mutation in the Middle High German period) has favoured *i*-mutation over an inflectional ending, adopting it consistently as a marker of plurality in all the *r*-stems except in *Schwester*, which cannot be mutated and therefore takes a weak inflectional ending in the plural (hence the *i*-mutated plurals *Väter*, *Mütter*, *Brüder* and *Töchter* vs. *Schwestern*).

The last aspect to be discussed in this context is the development of the *n*-stems, which already in Proto-Germanic constituted a productive declensional type. In the later period, the *n*-stems show quite a divergent development in the individual West Germanic languages. The extension of the *n*-stem pattern is clearly a feature better attested in Continental Germanic than Old English. The suffix -*en* emerges as the most common plurality suffix in present-day Dutch and is viewed as "more continental" (Booij 2002: 23).[334] It coexists with the other productive marker, -*s*, and their distribution is prosodically defined, with a preference for a trochaic foot (e.g. Booij 2002: 24).[335] Likewise, in Modern German (Low and High), the ending -*en* is the most common plural marker, considered to be the default (prototypical) plural

---

334. This does not apply to the present-day Limburgian dialect, which is the more direct successor of the *Wachtendonck Psalms* idiom and has a more Franconian-oriented profile (Goossens 1987).

335. Accordingly, the marker -*en* appears in nouns with final syllable stress, and -*s* is attached to nouns with penultimate syllable stress.

marker (Köpcke 1988; Kürschner & Nübling 2011: 366; cf. Wegener 2002, 2004).[336] Its spread, however, was not yet very conspicuous in the Old Low Franconian or Old Saxon material, although the Old Low Franconian feminine nouns showed a clear preference for the *n*-stem inflection, which eventually resulted in the merger with the *ō*-stems. In Frisian, the development of this pattern is even more complex, as the plural marker -*n*, common in modern dialects of Frisian, is not a continuation of the original *n*-stem marker but rather an ending borrowed from Dutch in the thirteenth century (Bremmer 2009: 6; Section 4.3). In contrast to the other Germanic languages, the development of the *n*-stem inflection followed a different path in English. Traces of the instability of this declensional type can be found already in the Old English period, where this declension is in fact still productive. The Middle English period witnessed a revival of the *n*-stem inflectional pattern, and given the substantial number of nouns declining according to the weak pattern at that time, especially in the dialects of the south, the declension may be perceived as stable (Wełna 1996: 88–90). The later competition between the *n*-stem and *a*-stem patterns was towards the end of the Middle English period (with the details depending on the dialect) won by the latter on account of the formal characteristics of the *a*-stems. Consequently, the role of the *n*-stem inflection was considerably marginalised. The relics of the original inflection retained in present-day English, including forms such as *oxen*, *brethren*, *children*, or the poetic *eyen*, bear witness to the earlier productivity of this pattern.

Finally, a typological development that all the investigated languages shared was the gradual shift from synthetic to agglutinative noun morphology (e.g. Wurzel 1992; Kastovsky 1995). This was manifested in the gradual dissociation of the category of case and number that were originally (in Proto-Germanic) fused, i.e. expressed jointly. In consequence, certain inflectional markers, such as the *r*-element in Continental Germanic, could be reinterpreted as independent exponents of plurality.

To conclude, the restructuring of the nominal inflection was a gradual phenomenon, which continued into the later stages of development of the individual Northern West Germanic languages. The retention of the archaic features in the examined material portends the tendencies to appear in the development of English, Frisian and German. Both the gravitation of nouns towards one declensional type

---

336. On a theoretical plane, the opinions as to which plural marker is the default marker in Modern German seems to vary. E.g. Marcus et al. (1995) and Clahsen (1999) regard the *s*-plural as the only productive marker in German, viewing all the other plural markers as lexicalised. Given that the *s*-plural has a limited scope (typically foreign words, short words, and proper names), such an interpretation is questionable. Much as the pattern is productive, it is a minority pattern and thus it is hard to view it as a default pattern (cf. Köpcke 1988, 1993, 1998).

and the tendency towards diversification of the declensional system are easily detectable at this early stage in the respective nominal systems. The only language where the observed tendencies cannot be viewed as directly indicative of the subsequent development is Old Low Franconian. This is due to the fact that present-day Dutch is not a direct continuation of Old Low Franconian, and the inflectional diversity found in Modern Dutch originated at a later stage, i.e. in Middle Dutch. Finally, it can be concluded that the extensive spread of *i*-mutation as a marker of plurality in (Low) German is a major feature which rendered the declensional system of German different from that of English, Frisian and Dutch. A typological corollary of the changes in the nominal system that occurred in the earliest period is the different level of morphological complexity found across present-day West Germanic, which entails the contrast between the rich and conservative nominal morphology of present-day Low (and High) German, manifested in the relatively well-retained plural marking system, and the inflectionally much less elaborate nominal systems of Dutch, Frisian and especially English.[337]

---

337. An even higher level of morphological complexity, with a more archaic inflectional system, is attested in the Swiss dialects of German, e.g. Wallis (Baechler 2015).

CHAPTER 8

Mechanisms and dynamics of the restructuring process in West Germanic

8.1 Introduction

As the aim of any investigation into language change phenomena is essentially towards identifying patterns and tendencies of a more universal nature, and formulating, as far as possible, universal principles underlying the mechanisms of change, the present chapter explores the theoretical aspects of the inflectional restructuring as attested in the early Northern West Germanic languages. The focus of this chapter is on the description of the actual linguistic mechanisms entailed in the process of reorganisation of the nominal inflection. The discussion of the theoretical implications draws upon the findings from the investigated material presented in the individual chapters, as well as the more general observations summarised in Chapter 7. By examining the tendencies observed in the analysed material in the individual languages, both parallel and divergent, an attempt is made at establishing and formulating the principles which underpinned the reorganisation of the nominal inflection.

Given that the attested inflectional variation in the nominal paradigms was patterned rather than random, it was one of the objectives of this study to identify the determinants of these patterns. The new, unetymological shape of the minor paradigms owes its emergence to a number of interacting forces, some of them working towards retaining the inherited inflectional patterns, others triggering numerous analogical reshufflings across paradigms and declension classes. The systematic comparative analysis conducted in the present study made it possible to capture various factors involved in the restructuring of the nominal inflection, and to estimate their contribution to the process. The investigated languages, despite their common point of departure, followed largely divergent paths of morphological development, which indicates that some of the factors involved in the conditioning were language-specific (see Chapter 7). This chapter concentrates on the factors of a more universal nature, adducing the idiosyncratic features only occasionally, where they are considered relevant for the discussion.

8.2   The course of restructuring: The prehistoric stage

The findings of the comparative study revealed that the restructuring of the nominal inflection began at the prehistoric stage (cf. the tables in Chapter 2). A more precise relative chronology of this development can be established by examining the earliest configuration of the nominal inflections across Old Germanic. Namely, the generalisation of the GEN. PL. ending -ōn (of whatever origin) was a common development in Northwest Germanic, but not in Gothic. In turn, the extension of the DAT. PL. ending -um was clearly an areal feature, encompassing North and North Sea Germanic, including Old Low Franconian, but leaving parts of Old Saxon and Old High German (where the marker -im is still attested in the i-stems) out of its scope. These two analogical shifts demonstrate that the restructuring process began relatively late, i.e. after the split of Gothic, which complies with the fact that relatively few morphological developments were common-Germanic.[338] Significantly, these early analogical extensions (in the GEN. PL. and DAT. PL.) were not directly related to the application of the *Auslautgesetze* in that they did not have an effect of restoring the inflections that would have otherwise disappeared. In this sense, the early interdeclensional shifts such as the replacement of the DAT. PL. i-stem marker -im by -um were of a different nature than, for instance, the substitution of the endingless GEN. SG. form in the root nouns by the analogical a-stem ending -es, -as at a later stage. A direct consequence of the latter was an evident increase in the transparency of the paradigms (cf. the discussion in Section 8.5 below).

The activity of the *Auslautgesetze* induced the fusion of stem elements with inflectional endings, and the apocope of many inflections, resulting in the emergence and widespread presence of zero markers in the paradigms. These developments served as a trigger for the process of gradual analogical remodelling of the paradigms, with some inflections being restored, while others replaced by new markers from the productive classes. This remodelling of paradigms involved two developments, namely (1) the "counter"-phonological preservation of inflections, and (2) the replacement of (potential) ambiguous zero markers by explicit inflectional markers from the productive classes. Already at this early stage, the dynamics of these analogical realignments seem to have been controlled by two factors: (a) the frequency of the paradigm form, and (b) the salience of inflectional exponents. More specifically, the low frequency paradigm categories, such as the GEN. SG. or GEN. and DAT. PL., were hardly ever common enough to retain their inherited, synchronically 'irregular' inflection, while moderately or highly frequent paradigm

---

338. According to Nielsen (2000: 289), the first North Germanic/North Sea Germanic isoglosses involving morphological features can be dated no earlier than ca. AD 200.

categories, such as the NOM./ACC. PL. and DAT. SG. were more likely to conserve the original inflection. The salience of the inflectional exponents (e.g. containing *i*-mutated vowels in the NOM./ACC. PL) could enhance this conserving effect in high frequency forms. This can be observed in the paradigms of root nouns in North Sea Germanic and North Germanic. As the close interaction between the shape of the paradigms and the frequency of occurrence seems to have been the major determinant of the restructuring of the nominal inflection in the investigated historical period, it will be discussed in detail in Section 8.6.1.

Another significant aspect of these early analogical developments is related to gender. In Proto Germanic no straightforward correlation existed between gender class and declension class: the original inflectional endings were largely independent of gender, and gender information was encoded in the stem. However, some gender biases in the distribution of lemmas across classes were present, even in the paradigms which had a parallel morphological structure. As a result of the fusion of stem formatives with inflectional endings, the new inflectional suffixes received a more direct association with a specific gender in Old Germanic languages. In other words, the association of gender with a specific declensional pattern became more consistent, and the declensional class affiliation allowed a relatively unambiguous assignment of gender (Schwink 2004: 17). Given that paradigm/class affiliation, just as gender, is a feature of the lemma, these two became associated with each other. Accordingly, the *a*-stems were typically masculine and neuter, the *ō*-stems feminine, the *n*-stems predominantly feminine, and the *u*-stems predominantly masculine. The *i*-stems, as the Gothic material indicates (Thöny 2013: 59), had competing masculine and feminine inflections. In North Germanic, this competition was won by the feminine inflection, which fused with the inflection of the *ō*-stems in the singular, retaining the *i*-stem pattern in the plural. In North Sea Germanic, the masculine *i*-stems merged with the *a*-stems with few vestiges of the original inflectional pattern, while in Continental Germanic, the *i*-stems coalesced with the masculine *a*-stems to become the dominant pattern in the plural. Once this association between gender and declension class was well established, gender specific endings, such as the masculine GEN. SG. marker *-es* (*-as*), could start disseminating across paradigms.

The consequence of these early developments is the situation found in the earliest attested sources (7th c./8th c.) onwards: a wide majority of forms regularised into a few type-frequent, partly gender-specific classes (*a*-stems, *ō*-stems, *n*-stems), and a periphery of mostly token-frequent lemmas with distinctly 'irregular' paradigms (such as root nouns, dental stems or *s*-stems), where the distinctive forms appeared only in the more frequent morphosyntactic categories (i.e. NOM./ACC. PL., DAT. SG.). The further development in Germanic is largely dialect- and language-specific. While West Germanic languages attest to many endingless and often syncretic paradigm forms, North Germanic (Old Icelandic) retained a fairly archaic shape of paradigms, largely phonologically-defined, and a relatively large lemma inventory also for the minor classes, such as the *u*-stems and root nouns. The retention of the word-final *r*-element and the operation of a range of mutations (*i*-, *a*- and *u*-mutation), which resulted in the higher salience of many paradigm forms, are considered the major factors responsible for the remarkably conservative inflectional profile of North Germanic. Early fourteenth-century Old Frisian shows a relatively late, but still, for its time, archaic pattern, which is similar to that found in Modern High German in that the paradigmatic irregularities are largely confined to the NOM./ACC. PL. forms.

Given the dialect-specific details of the vowel reduction processes in unstressed syllables (*Auslautgesetze*), with many areal features shared by several dialects, the reorganisation of the nominal inflection can be dated no earlier than the fourth century, and possibly even later. By the seventh century, i.e. by the time of the earliest attestations of West Germanic (Old English), the declensional systems of the individual languages must have been already considerably remodelled when compared to the system of their Proto-Germanic ancestor.

The analogical reshufflings of nouns occurring at the prehistoric stage had a wider range in terms of the number of destination classes and thus the directions of transfers. Accordingly, some of the root nouns tended to shift to the *u*-stems (e.g. *duru, nosu*, by reinterpretation of their original dual inflections), many of the original *s*-stems transferred to both the *a*-stems and *i*-stems, with an accompanying change in gender (to masculine), and many of the original *u*-stems moved to the *i*-stems (especially in Continental Germanic) or *a*-stems (in Anglo-Frisian). Although the direction of these analogical shifts was essentially from the minor unproductive classes to the productive ones, occasionally a transfer in the opposite direction can be observed. An example of such a shift is the Go. *skadus* 'shadow', which is considered to be an etymological *wa*-stem, but shows the *u*-stem inflection in Gothic. Likewise, the OS *segg* 'man' originated in the *ja*-stems, but follows the *i*-stem pattern, and arguably, the OS *i*-stem *meni* (*halsmeni*) 'necklace' can be traced back to the *ja*-stems (< **manja-*) (Dal 1934: 246; cf. Boutkan 1996: 210). In all these examples, the shift was facilitated by the largely parallel structure of the stems, i.e. the *i*- and *ja*-stems, and the *u*- and *wa*-stems. In the later period the interaction between the *i*-stems and *ja*-stems results in the analogical shifts to the *ja*-stem pattern, which are well attested in Old Saxon and Old English.

8.3 The historical stage of restructuring: Emerging patterns

As discussed in the previous section, a range of phonological developments that occurred at the prehistoric stage led to a diversification of the Proto-Germanic nominal system, i.e. an increase in the number of declensional classes. This increase in declensional class diversity was brought about largely by the fusion of stem formatives and inflectional endings, whereby the morphological structure of the nouns was reanalysed. At a later stage, i.e. in the historical period, an opposite tendency prevails, namely, the inflectional class diversity is gradually reduced, primarily as a result of newly emerging case syncretisms across paradigms. These syncretisms were occasioned by both phonological and analogical processes, and consequently a relatively transparent Proto-Germanic declensional system became largely opaque in the Old Germanic languages.

As in the prehistoric stage, the restructuring of the nominal inflection in the historical period entailed analogical developments both within and across paradigms. As regards the former, the restructuring process involved especially the levelling of morphophonemic alternations. This involved the elimination of the *i*-mutated vowels from the paradigms of the root nouns, *nd*-stems (OE, OFris.), and the *s*-stems (OE), as well as the elimination of consonantal alternations from the *s*-stems (OE, OFris.). As the analysis demonstrated, the consonantal alternations in the dental stems were eliminated largely at the prehistoric stage, except in Old English, where the synchronic alternation (-*þ*- ~ ø) is still detectable. The elimination of these morphophonemic alternations from the nominal paradigms rendered them more uniform and more similar to the productive paradigms, which were not characterised by internal stem/root modulation. Such inflectional uniformity worked to the disadvantage of the historical paradigms, rendering them susceptible to analogical pressures from the productive declensions (cf. the discussion below). As demonstrated in Chapter 7, the scope of these morphophonemic alternations differed in the individual languages, being eventually one of the major factors responsible for the divergent shape of the nominal systems across (Northern) West Germanic.

As far as the interparadigmatic changes are concerned, the inflectional patterns of the *a*-stems and *ō*-stems served unquestionably as a template for the analogical restructuring of the minor stem paradigms across early Northern West Germanic languages. At the same time, an evident preference for the *i*-stem inflection can be observed in Continental West Germanic, where the *i*-stems provide an inflectional pattern for the masculine nouns. The influence of the *n*-stems on the minor paradigms, although discernible in the material, is rather limited at this early stage, even in Old Saxon and Old Low Franconian, where in the later period the *n*-stem inflection emerges as the default pattern for the feminine nouns (in the plural).

It must be emphasised that most of the nouns affiliated with the minor classes did not consistently adhere to their historical inflectional pattern, and hence the question of class affiliation turns out to be very problematic. Stability of minor paradigms with respect to class affiliation was essentially a privilege of the most frequent nouns, which were the last to be affected by the analogical pressure.

The synchronic irregularities in the minor paradigms could have two sources, analogical or phonological in nature. The phonologically regular (expected) forms could directly be affected by analogy, which introduced phonologically 'irregular' forms into the paradigms. In the paradigms where analogy operated very early, the synchronic variation in inflection is not attested. An example of such a development is the Old English masculine heavy-syllable *i*-stem paradigm, which adopted the *a*-stem inflections at a prehistoric stage (cf. Section 3.5.2). Another source of paradigmatic variation was the resistance of certain forms to phonological reduction processes, pertinent especially to low frequency forms, such as the retention of the *r*-formative throughout the paradigm in most of the *s*-stems in Old English (including the NOM./ACC. SG. forms). The majority of the lemmas in this declensional class probably never developed the phonologically regular *s*-stem inflection, with a zero marker in the NOM./ACC. SG. and the *r*-element in the rest of the paradigm. This pattern was characteristic only of a few high frequency nouns that were able to develop and preserve a (synchronically) irregular, purely phonologically-defined paradigm (e.g. OE *cealf* 'calf' or *lamb* 'lamb').[339]

Another characteristic of the restructuring process is related to its multilayered nature, i.e. the fact that the change of class affiliation entailed sometimes more than one layer of transition. Some of the nouns from the minor *consonantal* classes tended to be attracted to the minor *vocalic* types (especially the *i*-stems) and only later did they transfer to the productive *a*- or *ō*-stems. Such a double shift is reconstructable for some Old English and Old Frisian *s*-stems, which were attracted to the *i*-stems prior to eventually following the *a*-stems and *ō*-stem patterns (cf. *sige* < PGmc. NOM./ACC. SG. **sigiz*). Likewise, the Old Frisian *r*-stems and root nouns, showing traces of the *i*-stem inflection in the NOM./ACC. PL. (-*e*), shifted in the later (post-classical) period to the *a*-stem declension. In many cases, the exact paths of such multiple transitions cannot be uncovered on account of the lack of sufficient evidence.

Occasionally, the existence of inflectionally mixed paradigms (i.e. showing inflectional inconsistencies) cannot be attributed purely to a change in class affiliation, but rather to some incongruities they exhibit with respect to gender class affiliation. A number of nouns, known as multiple gender nouns (e.g. OE *ǣrist* 'resurrection' m.f.n., OE *lyft* 'air' m.n.f., OE *flōd* 'flood m.n.), attest to more than one inflectional

---

339. The presence/absence of the marker -*i* in the NOM./ACC. PL. of the Old Saxon and Old Low Franconian root nouns can be interpreted in the same way, assuming that this ending is etymological and not analogical (see Section 5.6.4).

paradigm. The origin of such paradigms has been variously interpreted and attributed to different factors. Such fluctuations testify to a close interaction between gender and declension class affiliation. At the same time, they are a manifestation of an increasing confusion of case-and-number exponents and gender markers, which in the long run undermined the stability of the declensional system.[340]

The examination of the available material has revealed that individual categories, classes and lemmas succumbed to analogical pressures to various extents. As the scope and the dynamics of the process were discussed from a comparative perspective in Chapter 7, the present discussion will focus predominantly on the mechanisms of the restructuring process as attested at the earliest stage of Northern West Germanic, including the factors that conditioned it.

8.4   Framing the mechanisms of the process

The mechanisms involved in the process of restructuring of the nominal inflection can be framed in a number of systematic principles and tendencies. They are related to the motivations of the changes, the factors triggering the changes (8.5), the dynamics of the changes, as well as the factors conditioning the process (8.6).[341] One of the essential forces in the mechanism of inflectional reorganisation, which can be considered the impulse for the changes, was the need to retain (or restore) the functionality of the system. This refers in particular to the functionality of the morphosyntactic categories as expressed by the distinctive inflectional exponents. The functionality of the nominal system was considerably disrupted by the earlier phonological and analogical developments which affected the paradigms. The most direct source of this disruption was the emergence of syncretisms and the dissemination of zero markers across the paradigms, whereby case and number distinctions were no longer explicitly and/or unambiguously coded (see Section 8.5).

---

340. A notable example of cross-Germanic instability of gender is the paradigm of *book*, which attests to different affiliations in the individual Germanic languages. In Old Frisian and Old Saxon the noun *bôk* vacillates between neuter and feminine, while in Old High German *buoh* is attested as neuter and occasionally declines as feminine and masculine. The noun derives from PGmc. feminine **bōks* and the neuter gender was initially introduced into the plural most likely by analogy to monosyllabic neuter nouns, and subsequently extended to the singular (cf. OHG light-syllable masculine *ja*-stems, which tended to shift to the neuter declension: *heri* 'army', *wekki* 'wedge', *meri* 'lake'; Bammesberger 1990: 197–198; Lahiri & Dresher 1984: 143, 160).

341. It has to be emphasised that such a categorisation of factors is an abstraction given the dynamic and adaptive nature of linguistic systems, with many negative and positive feedback loops. Some of the mentioned processes and factors could just as well be subsumed under another label than that used here.

The underlying mechanism of the gradual transference of nouns from minor to major declensional types involved the process of analogy, aimed at levelling irregularities within and across paradigms. The theoretical aspects of this process were discussed in Chapter 1 (Section 1.4.2) and in what follows the application of the process will be sketched, based on the patterns observed in the examined material. Clearly, the scope of the activity of analogy in the nominal system depended on several factors of a qualitative and quantitative nature, including the degree of the similarity of forms and paradigms (formal overlap), and the frequencies of the categories affected by analogy. The trigger for the analogical developments in the minor classes was the presence of syncretic forms in the paradigms, which tended not to be well tolerated by the system.

The analysed data reveals that the scope and intensity of analogical pressures in the minor paradigms was largely dependent on the percentage of neutral inflections in the paradigms, i.e. forms which overlapped with those from the productive declensions. In other words, the percentage of neutral forms in the paradigm correlates closely with the level of innovation, being an indicator of how powerful the analogical processes were in a given paradigm. The paradigms in which the percentage of neutral forms was high were more easily affected by analogy, showing a high level of innovation (cf. Table 7.10, Section 7.2). This complies with the claim that the analogical attraction between linguistic items (here paradigms) is proportional to the formal similarity between them (here the formal overlap between forms/paradigms) (Versloot & Hoekstra 2016). The process of analogical remodelling of the minor paradigms was triggered by the presence of overlapping forms, which created a direct interface between the unproductive and productive patterns of inflection. Of particular significance was the formal overlap in the "important" category across different classes, namely the NOM. SG., which opened the way for the restructuring in the other morphosyntactic categories, eventually leading to the generalisation of declensional shifts. Already the prehistoric interdeclensional shifts were conditioned by the phonological similarity of the NOM. SG. across classes. For instance, the large-scale transition of the OE heavy-syllable *i*-stems to the *a*-stem declension was triggered primarily by the overlap of forms in the NOM. SG. The formal overlap was a result of a regular phonological development, whereby the final vowels were lost in heavy-syllable stems in the NOM. SG. A parallel mechanism is visible in the development of the historical neuter *s*-stems, which at the prehistoric stage shifted predominantly to the *i*-stems, and this transition was facilitated by the presence of the *i*-mutated vowel in the NOM./ACC. SG. (e.g. neut. OE *flǽsc* 'flesh', OE *flīes, flēos* 'fleece', light-syll. OE *sige* < PGmc. **sigiz* 'victory').[342]

---

342. The transition involved a morphological reanalysis, whereby the morphological structure of the *s*-stem **sigiz*: sig_{root}-$i_{thematic\ vowel}$-$z_{stem\ formative}$ was replaced by the *i*-stem structure: sig_{root}-$i_{stem\ formative}$-$z_{case\ ending}$.

Occasionally, the overlap of forms may have had another effect on the paradigms. Namely, it may have led to an enhancement of the inherited infections in the contexts where they matched (overlapped with) other, more frequent endings from the productive classes. Such an effect is recognisable in the OFris. GEN. DAT. SG. in the *u*-stems, which tended to overlap with the *n*-stem endings. This formal overlap did not result directly in a disintegration of the *u*-stem paradigm, but rather rendered the paradigm, especially the singular, more resistant to the analogical pressure from the *a*-stems.

The most important observation that can be made on the basis of the examined material regarding the mechanism of the analogical developments is that the analogical restructuring of inflection operated predominantly along morpho-syntactic categories and not along entire declensional classes or paradigms. In all the observed analogical realignments between paradigms we are dealing rather with an extension of individual case-and-number endings from the productive declensional classes than an extension of the entire patterns of inflections (paradigms). This means that a shift in class affiliation (declensional shift) involved a change on the level of the paradigm cell,[343] i.e. paradigm cell-by-paradigm cell, rather than on the declension class level, i.e. class-by-class. Accordingly, the change of class affiliation occurred gradually and entailed a steady dissemination of analogical inflections in the paradigm, rather than their wholesale transfer to all the cells in the paradigm. The evidence for the claim that the process went along the morphosyntactic category comes, for instance, from the pattern of the spread of the GEN. PL. *n*-stem marker *-ena*, which was found in many nouns in Old English (and to some extent) Old Frisian, even though the *n*-stem inflection as such was not very widespread. Likewise, the dissemination of the *a*-stem GEN. SG. marker *-es* in Old English and *-as* in Old Saxon cannot be viewed as an extension of the entire *a*-stem inflectional pattern to the minor paradigms. Since not all the paradigm forms of a given lemma were affected by analogy to the same extent, mixed paradigms emerged, which showed characteristics of the inherited inflection and new analogical features. The order of categories to be affected by analogy was regulated largely by their frequency of occurrence. Analogy tended to affect the less frequent paradigm forms earlier (e.g. GEN. SG., GEN. PL. and DAT. PL.), and the more frequent categories later (e.g. NOM./ACC. SG. and PL.) (see Section 8.6.1). Another implication of this tendency is that the intraparadigmatic regularity was apparently less desirable than the cross-paradigmatic uniformity, which again proves that the process of restructuring (and analogy) was sensitive to individual categories, not paradigms. This is evident, for instance, in the development of the DAT. PL. in Old English and Old Frisian, where the uniform DAT. PL. ending *-um* replaced the original distinct

---

343. The 'cell' refers to "each individual property or property combination" within a paradigm (Carstairs-McCarthy 1998: 322).

endings (*-*am*, *-*im*) across all paradigms. This analogical development was one of the earliest interedeclensional shifts, occurring in the prehistoric period.

Yet a different tendency in the reorganisation patterns can be found in a few individual instances, which give some further insight into the mechanisms of the restructuring process. One of them is the plural paradigm of the original *u*-stem *magu* 'boy', where the distribution of the *n*-stem and *a*-stem forms turns out to be nearly complementary, with the singular dominated by the former (*maga*) and the plural by the latter inflections (*-as*). Although the *n*-stem forms attested in the corpus are traditionally classified as belonging to a different lemma, the *n*-stem *maga*, if all the attestations, i.e. weak and strong, are taken together, it can be concluded that *maga* and *magu* formed one paradigm, with the *n*-stem and *a*-stem inflections present in different paradigmatic categories. A parallel pattern is found in the OE light-syllable *i*-stem *mete*, where the geminated form *mett-*, emerging under the *ja*-stem influence, is found consistently in the plural. The consistency in the appearance of the analogical forms in one number paradigm (plural) can be interpreted as indicative of the fact that if analogical shifts did not advance along the morphosyntactic categories, then apparently along the category of number, rather than along the entire paradigm.

This reveals another characteristic of the restructuring process and analogical change as part of its mechanism, namely the gradualness of its application. This gradual nature of the process is not always easy to capture, primarily due to the corpus-related limitations, i.e. the low number of attestations to many lemmas, and the fact that some nouns were attested only with either the archaic or innovative inflections. The gradualness of the process can be to some extent captured in Old English, where the corpus was divided into two sub-corpora representing two diachronic stages. There, in the paradigms of some nouns a steady increase in the level of innovation is noticeable. In the other languages, however, this characteristic of the process is hardly determinable.

It has been argued that the dissemination of analogical changes appears to be to some extent "tied to particular lexical items; thus, unlike sound change (...), morphological change, especially analogical change, is sporadic in its propagation" (Joseph 2001: 366). Consequently, the spread of analogical changes may often entail lexically-specific developments, and therefore some of the inflectional irregularities found in the paradigms can be explained by taking such an individual, lexeme-based approach. For instance, the paradigm of OE *neaht* showed a clear preference for the masculine inflection in the GEN. SG. (*neahtes*). As this tendency was not very common in the other root nouns, it has to be ascribed to a close semantic relation between *neaht* and *dæg*, which are often found in the collocation *dæges and neahtes*.

8.5 Functionality of the system

The loss of functionality of the nominal system in Germanic languages is considered to have been a consequence of two major developments: (1) the syncretisms of various case forms across declensional classes, especially of the nominative and accusative, known as formal syncretism, and (2) the reduction in the number of cases, i.e. functional syncretism. In the longer perspective, the former could be compensated by a stricter word order, while the latter was eventually compensated by the increase in the use of prepositions (in English). When seen from the present-day perspective, all the investigated languages show the effects of the process of gradual deflection. In the Old Germanic period the actual deflection is not visible: all the examined languages stick to the four-case system, and the loss of case marking comes only later.[344] An exception here is the Late Old English period, where first traces of the demise of the case system can be detected. The Old Germanic stage attests primarily to the presence of numerous formal syncretisms in the nominal system, while the merger of cases was a characteristic of the prehistoric stage and of the later post-Old Germanic stage, with chronological details depending on the language. Although traces of the loss of the functionality can be found already in the (reconstructed) Proto-Germanic nominal system, the growing lack of functionality is rather a feature of the nominal systems in the earliest attested stages of the individual Germanic languages.[345]

The indirect trigger for the reduction of functionality were the developments in the phonological system, as argued, among others, by Wurzel (1989: 190–191):

> Phonological changes – which proceed in a direction that improves the adaptation of forms to the conditions of articulation and perception – have a disturbing and destructive effect on morphology. (…) They eliminate functional distinctions and create non-functional distinctions between forms.

---

344. Admittedly, the four-case system was an effect of a reduction of cases, entailing the loss of the vocative (still present in Gothic) and instrumental (vestiges still present in the Old West Germanic languages).

345. Another feature of a morphological system which has been interpreted as a symptom of a gradual loss of its functionality is the existence of stable or superstable markers, which are expansive category exponents, disseminating to the less stable declensional types. The presence of such markers can be dated already to the prehistoric stage, when the GEN. PL. and DAT. PL. markers (*-ō, *-um) tended to spread to many declensional classes. An example of a stable marker in the attested stage of Germanic is the GEN. SG. -es (-as). The presence of such exponents has been considered to be indicative of the weakening of the category of case and ultimately of deflection (Dammel & Nübling 2006: 104; Wurzel 1989). The divergent development of the GEN. SG. marker across Germanic substantiates the claim: the expansion of this inflectional marker was most successful in languages characterised by a considerable degree of deflection (as English or Swedish), while much less so in more inflectionally stable languages (as in German where the marker -s has a more limited range).

The development of the nominal systems in early West Germanic languages instantiates this mechanism. As a result of the activity of extensive reduction processes (*Auslautgesetze*) in the prehistoric period of Germanic, the nominal systems of Old Germanic languages emerged as fairly deficient. The number of formal exponents by which grammatical categories were expressed (i.e. case, number, and gender) was considerably reduced when compared to the system reconstructed for Proto-Germanic. For instance, in the OE *u*-stems, the ending *-a* came to serve as an inflectional exponent of four different morphosyntactic categories: GEN., DAT. SG. and NOM./ACC. PL. Such a homonymy and consequently multifunctionality of nominal inflections resulted in a growing lack of transparency of the paradigms, rendering them less stable. Given that transparency is a feature of paradigms which contributes to their learnability, its absence was clearly a factor undermining the original functionality of the system.

The rearrangement of inflectional exponents and consequently the shifts of nouns across different declensional classes, evident at the earliest attested stage of Northern West Germanic, was a reaction to the phonological developments. Accordingly, the restructuring of the nominal inflection can be interpreted as an attempt at bringing back the earlier transparency and functionality of the system. In this sense, the reorganisation of the elaborate system of nominal inflections, including their considerable reduction, can be perceived as "a sign of streamlining and sophistication" (Aitchison 2001: 7). Such an interpretation complies with the views of Jespersen (1922), who claimed that in the course of constant development, inherent in the nature of language, language evolves towards a more efficient shape. With particular reference to changes in inflectional morphology, Jespersen (1922) argued: "In the evolution of languages the discarding of old flections goes hand in hand with the development of simpler and more regular expedients that are rather less liable than the old ones to produce misunderstanding" (Jespersen 1922: 263). It implies that simplicity and regularity are the two qualities essential for a morphological pattern, construction or form to remain efficient and thus functional (cf. Dahl 2004).

Importantly, in light of the above, the analogical changes in the nominal system should not be interpreted as indicative of a *disintegration* of the system, but rather as a *restoration* of the paradigmatic distinctions, which were largely lost in the aftermath of the extensive operation of *Auslautgesetze*. This is well evinced in the Northern West Germanic languages, where the operation of the vowel reduction processes deprived many paradigm forms of inflectional endings, rendering the paradigms vulnerable to analogy. The effect of this development was not – as could be expected – a complete decline of the nominal paradigms, but an enhancement of the contrasts by the extension of inflections from the productive classes to non- or less-functional paradigm forms. The interparadigmatic analogical changes worked towards restoring the transparency and functionality of the paradigms by introducing distinctive markers into the increasingly undiversified paradigms. Since analogy favoured the spread of more transparent exponents, i.e. those serving unambiguously one function, markers such as the OE GEN. SG. *-es* or the NOM./ACC.PL. *-as* were very successful in expanding to the unproductive paradigms and replacing the less transparent or homonymous markers, such as vocalic or zero endings.

Additionally, the elimination of morphophonemic alternations, which can be observed in the earliest attested stages of the individual Old Germanic languages, whereby many opaque ablaut and *i*-mutation allomorphs were lost, contributed to an increase in the uniformity of the paradigms. As non-diversified paradigms, i.e. those containing few distinctive markers, were generally less stable, in such paradigms stability tended to be resumed by the introduction of distinctive markers from other classes. In other words, the developments in the declensional system can be interpreted in a way that the phonological erosion of the inflectional endings was compensated by the extension of the more common, more explicit and less ambiguous markers. The result of these developments was a system of nominal inflection that, although not as functional as that of its ancestors (PIE, PGmc.), managed to survive for many centuries in all Germanic languages, and in some, e.g. in Icelandic and Modern High German, until present-day.

One of the factors which played a role in the process of restructuring and had a bearing on the system functionality is the semantic transparency of grammatical categories, including the category of case and number. It is commonly recognised that "if nouns and other nominal words inflect for both Case and Number, Case, a surface syntactic category, is less important than Number, a referential semantic category, hence will more readily admit non-distinctions." (Plank 1991: 23). In other words, the 'superiority' of the category of number comes from the fact that being a referential semantic category, it is an inherent property of the noun, in contrast to case, which is syntactically determined (e.g. Kastovsky 1995: 234; Booij 1996).[346] Consequently, the category of number tends to be more stable and more resistant to syncretisms, while the category of case remains more exposed to reduction. In the context of the present study, this means that the inflectional markers that encode referential categories, such as number (but also tense or aspect), i.e. categories that are semantically transparent, will tend to be less easily affected by analogical developments than markers that encode formal categories, such as declension class or grammatical gender. From the point of view of the functionality of the system, the lack of a contrast in number is dispreferred and avoided, and tends to be repaired by a recovery of the inflectional distinctions in the paradigm. The extension of a

---

346. Booij (1996) considers number to be a part of *inherent* inflection, whereas case a part of *contextual* inflection.

new analogical ending to restore the contrast between the singular and plural could be seen in many paradigms. The stability of the opposition between the singular and plural was undermined in the first place by the appearance of the formal syncretisms of the NOM./ACC. SG. and NOM./ACC. PL., induced by vowel reductions in inflectional syllables. This is illustrated by the developments in the OE light-syllable *i*-stems, where the etymological NOM./ACC. PL. marker *-e* overlapped with the NOM./ACC. SG. form (e.g. *wine* 'friend', PL. *wine*). The introduction of the *a*-stem marker *-as* in the NOM./ACC. PL. enabled restoring the singular/plural contrast in the paradigm. Another example is provided by the *r*-stems where the NOM./ACC. SG. – NOM./ACC. PL. distinction was lost in the etymological paradigm. Except for Old Saxon, where the *r*-stem paradigm is entirely archaic (100%), all other languages attest to a widespread innovation in the NOM./ACC. PL., with analogical endings extended from the *a*-stems (masc.) (in Old Frisian also *i*-stems) and *ō*-stems (fem.). In all these instances, the change is triggered by the need to keep such crucial oppositions as that of number (NOM. SG. vs. NOM. PL.) in the declensional system.

The significance of the category of number in the morphological system is confirmed in the subsequent development of the Germanic nominal system. Especially the changes in the case and number marking system in Continental Germanic have been explained by recourse to the concept of category profiling (or strengthening) and reduction, where 'profiling' refers to an increase in the salience of grammatical markers that express a category. This refers to both an increase in the phonological salience as well as in the number of allomorphs. Accordingly, in German, the category of number has been profiled to the disadvantage of the category of case, which has been reduced (Nübling 2008; Kürschner 2008; Kürschner & Nübling 2011: 362). The developments have commonly been referred to as *Numerusprofilierung* and *Kasusnivellierung* – the terms used first by Wegera (1985: 1314–1316; cf. Wurzel 1989). This evident exponence of the number category is considered to be the dominant feature of the present-day German nominal inflection.

Another tendency revealed in the analysed material is related to the hierarchical structure of morphological categories. The analogical changes in the minor paradigms tended to adhere to a hierarchy of morphological categories (known also as markedness hierarchies; Hawkins 2015: 218). This hierarchy, as discussed in Section 1.4.3, is very tightly dependent on the frequency of occurrence. It can be concluded that certain forms in the morphological paradigm (here the nominal paradigm) are more important than others in language change, and their importance seems to be reflected in their frequency of occurrence. The lower positions in the case/number marking hierarchy will be characterised by more syncretisms and consequently greater vulnerability to analogy. The relevance of the hierarchy of categories is evident, for instance, in the development of the GEN. SG., which being lower on the markedness hierarchy scale, was affected by analogy very early. The salient marker -*es* (-*is*) was extended to many nouns affiliated with the minor stems, which were marked by a zero ending (after the operation of phonological reductions). In contrast, the markers of the NOM. SG. in the OE and OFris. light-syllable *i*-stems and *u*-stems remained resistant to analogical pressure relatively long. The relevance of the hierarchy of morphosyntactic categories in the restructuring process is reflected in the pattern of retention of *i*-mutation in the Old English and Old Frisian root nouns and *nd*-stems. While the *i*-mutated vowel was retained (and subsequently specialised) in the NOM./ACC. PL. as a marker of plurality, it was eliminated relatively early from the DAT. SG. This retention of *i*-mutation as a marker of plurality (and its loss as a case marker) complies also with the assumption that the categories which are more relevant, such as the referential category of number, tend to have "a greater morphophonemic effect on the stem than the less relevant categories" (Bybee 1985: 25). In other words, the inflectional exponents involving stem (or root) modulation are more likely to mark the more important categories.

Further evidence for the claim that many of the changes in the nominal system had a functional motivation comes from the paradigmatic developments which involved the acquisition of a new function. The process whereby morphological elements acquire a new function has been referred to as *exaptation* (cf. Lass 1990, 1997a). The development of originally derivational suffixes as exponents of morphosyntactic categories, such as the *r*-formative from the **-es*/-*os* suffix of the *s*-stems and the *n*-formative in the *n*-stems, can be considered as instances of exaptation. The originally derivational suffix of the *s*-stems, used in Proto-Indo-European to form action nouns, acquired a new function in Germanic, being reanalysed as an inflectional marker. More specifically, the 'surface' material that secured the original derivative function of this element was reused for a new purpose (cf. Lass 1997a: 317). Another process which could be interpreted in the same way is the morphologisation of *i*-mutation in Continental Germanic, where its original purely phonological nature was reinterpreted on the morphological level, whereby the *i*-mutated vowel came to serve as a new plurality exponent. The most advanced stage of these developments is found in present-day German, where both the -*er*-element and the *i*-mutated vowel became productive plural markers, the former characterising neuter and masculine nouns, the latter predominantly masculine nouns.[347]

Both the presence of *i*-mutation and consonantal alternations in the paradigms at the early stage, where they did not have a distinctive function (yet), have been considered "a formal complication without functional gain, violating the principle of one function: one form" (Wurzel 1986: 76). Once the alternations were eliminated

---

347. The expansion of the *i*-mutated vowel and the -*er*-element as exponents of plurality in Low and High German was triggered by apocope of word-final *schwa*, beginning in the late Middle Ages (Salmons 2012: 247).

from the singular, especially in root nouns, *nd*-stems and *s*-stems in Old English and Old Frisian, the *i*-mutated vowel and the *r*-formative could serve the exclusive function of marking the plural. In other words, the emergence of an independent marker of plurality was a development that clearly increased the functionality of the paradigms. Such a rearrangement of grammatical functions in the system involved an interplay of phonological changes, reanalysis and analogical processes (Fertig 2013: 38). The emergence of these new functions was possible because language is not an entirely coherent system (Lass 1997a: 317); it is dynamic and, as such, able to adapt and readapt to the changing conditioning, to the effect that certain synchronically unmotivated irregularities tend to be reanalysed to become functional.

A closer examination of the restructuring developments reveals the complexity of the restructuring process and its dependence on functionality. For instance, in Old English, the consonantal alternation in the *s*-stems (and in the dental stems) was less functional than the vocalic alternation in the root nouns. With the extension of the *r*-formative to the entire *s*-stem paradigm in many nouns, the *r*-formative lost its distinctive function as a potential plural marker. In contrast, with the elimination of the *i*-mutated vowel from the singular of the root nouns, the vowel could emerge as a distinctive exponent of the NOM./ACC. PL., as it was the case in Continental West Germanic (Low and High German) (see Klein 2013). Although at first glance the functionality of these two inflectional exponents happens to correspond to their salience, no such straightforward correlation can be made. In fact, *i*-mutation was originally present in the OE *s*-stems as well (in the NOM./ACC. SG., e.g. Angl. *cælf* vs. DAT. SG. *calfur*), but serving no specific function in the paradigm, it was eliminated relatively early. Even though a vocalic alternation is ranked higher on the salience scale than a consonantal one (cf. Section 1.4.6.2), as long as it serves no specific purpose in the paradigm, it will tend to be eliminated. In other words, the persistence of a given inflectional feature is determined to a large extent by its functionality, while the salience of the exponent seems to play a secondary role, and its significance is relative, depending on whether it is functional.

8.6   Factors conditioning the restructuring process

It was one of the main objectives of the present study to investigate the role of the factors which conditioned the restructuring of the nominal inflection, and to uncover the relationship between them and possibly their hierarchy. The factors come from various domains and can be divided into two main groups, namely (a) factors of a more universal nature (i.e. non-language-specific) and (b) language-specific factors, the latter being the source of the discrepancies in the development of the nominal inflection in the examined languages. The latter group encompasses also factors of extralinguistic nature, such as the attestation dates of the extant sources, the geographical conditions (e.g. the vicinity of the West Germanic dialects on the Continent) and socio-political circumstances (e.g. the socio-cultural impact of Franconian on the surrounding dialects). Language-specific factors have been discussed already in Chapter 7 and therefore the discussion in the ensuing sections of this chapter will focus only on the factors of a universal nature. The present study demonstrates that the attested inflectional variation in the minor paradigms can be ascribed to an interaction of three major factors: (1) the frequency of occurrence, (2) the salience of inflectional exponents and (3) semantics. The order of presentation of these factors reflects largely the hierarchy of their significance in the reorganisation of the nominal paradigms. The final outcome of this restructuring was a cumulative effect of interactions between these factors and several other determinants that had a bearing on the final shape of the paradigms, including the syllable structure and gender (cf. Section 8.6.4).

8.6.1 Frequency of occurrence

As discussed in Chapter 1, the presence of morphological irregularity in the paradigms correlates with the frequency of occurrence of forms. The lexical items and paradigms which are characterised by high frequency of occurrence tend to resist analogical change longer than the lower frequency items. The examined material illustrates very well the effects of the working of frequency in all the investigated languages, manifested on the level of phonology and morphology. Particularly visible in the paradigms of minor stems is the conserving effect of token frequency, which can account for many of the patterns found in the analysed material. The interaction of frequency of occurrence and morphological structure involved a few distinct planes, and accordingly four manifestations of frequency can be identified:

a. frequency of the paradigm form (i.e. morphosyntactic category) (e.g. NOM./ ACC. SG. VS. GEN./DAT. SG.)
b. lemma frequency (token frequency)
c. frequency of the paradigm/scheme (patterns) (type frequency)
d. relative frequency (e.g. the singular/plural proportion)

The frequency of case-and-number form (paradigm form) turns out to be the most significant factor in the restructuring process. The frequency of a given paradigmatic category is defined by extra-linguistic factors, i.e. real-world factors in combination with how the linguistic system functions. The high (token) frequency of certain paradigmatic forms functioned as a conserving factor, rendering them more resistant to analogical pressures. Accordingly, the NOM. SG., which is the most frequent category, tends to remain mostly unaffected by analogical influence from other declensional types, while low frequency categories such as the GEN. and DAT. PL. tend to show considerable susceptibility to the impact of analogical pressures. This correlation has a clear implication for the relative chronology of the changes in the paradigms, in that analogy tends to affect first the categories that are less frequent. Consequently, categories such as the GEN. SG., GEN. PL. and DAT. PL. tend to be affected very early. The spread of the marker -es in the low frequent GEN. SG. to various declensional classes, which occurred partly in the prehistoric period, is one of the expressions of this correlation; another one is, for instance, the archaic shape of the NOM. SG. of the OE and OFris. light-syllable i-stems and u-stems (cf. the tables in Chapter 7). The correlation with frequency can be observed already in the earliest developments in the inflectional configuration in Proto-Germanic. The i-mutated vowel is preserved in the NOM./ACC. PL. (in OE, OFris. root nouns and nd-stems), which are more frequent categories than the GEN./DAT. SG., where it tended to be eliminated already at the prehistoric stage (in OFris.). In the historical stage, for instance, the u-stems show a clear bias resulting from different frequencies of individual paradigmatic categories. The class comprised many nouns denoting natural environment and describing certain topographical features. On account of their semantics they do not tend to function as agents in the sentence, but rather appear in prepositional phrases, usually in the dative, i.e. in a category that is otherwise not characterised by high frequency. The frequent attestation of these nouns in the DAT. SG. in this class led to a conservation of the archaic inflection in this category, not found in any other minor declension. In contrast, the r-stems, denoting kinship terms (referring to people, i.e. agents) may be expected to be attested (and used) more often in the nominative than in the other cases. The emergence of such biases is eventually conditioned by semantic factors, and involves the concept of relevance. In other words, the semantic constitution of the entire class may determine the frequency patterns. The significance of semantics and its interaction with the other factors will be given more attention is Section 8.6.3.

The attested pattern of distribution of analogical inflections in the minor paradigms indicates also the impact of the reducing effects of (token) frequency, apparent on the phonological level. The phonological erosion, which affects the most frequent categories, items or paradigms, leads to a situation where the most frequent morphosyntactic categories are characterised by the simplest morphological exponents (often zero markers). Therefore, high frequency categories, such as the NOM./ACC. SG. tend to be endless in many classes, while low frequency categories, such as the GEN. and DAT. PL. will tend to be explicitly marked. The changes in the nominal inflection illustrate very well the close interaction between the phonological and morphological effects of frequency of occurrence in the linguistic system.

As far as the lexical level of the operation of frequency is concerned, inflectional irregularity correlates with frequent lexical entries. The effects of the frequency on the lemma level involve token rather than type frequency. The distribution of the analogical inflections in the paradigms of very high frequent lemmas, such as 'man', 'son', 'father', 'town (borough)' turns out to be different from the patterns found in the paradigms of other lexemes from the respective classes. In general, the high frequency lemmas show much more conservative inflectional profiles. A closer scrutiny of their paradigms, however, leads to the observation that the levels of conservatism depend again on the individual morphosyntactic categories rather than on the absolute frequency of a lemma. This is evident, for instance, in the masculine root nouns, which show very archaic NOM. and ACC. PL. in contrast to a fairly innovative GEN. and DAT. SG. (OE and OFris.). Here again the semantic aspect comes into play as their occurrence in a given paradigm form is determined by their semantics. Accordingly, *feet* and *teeth*, which most often come in pairs or multiple sets, are more frequent in the plural than in the singular, and hence the retention of irregular patterns in their plural paradigm is possible.

The examination of the reorganisation of the nominal paradigms revealed the relevance of both type and token frequency in the process, with the effects of the latter being more prominent. Significantly, type and token frequency had quite different effects in the restructuring process, resulting in opposite directions of morphological change. As has commonly been recognised, type frequency is one of the major determinants of the productivity of morphological patterns, including the productivity of declensions. The major assumption made by Bybee (1985: 133) with reference to the interaction of frequency and productivity of morphological patterns is that the patterns "found in a few very high-frequency items will not spread to other items as readily as those patterns that are found in a larger number of medium- and low-frequency items". The process of reorganisation of the inflectional systems in early Northern West Germanic languages consistently revealed this tendency. The major declensional classes, i.e. the *a*-stems, *ō*-stems and *n*-stems (and to some extent also *i*-stems), were characterised by high type frequency and comprised the majority of the lemmas, which were mostly of low-frequency. The minor classes contained fewer lexical items, which were very often high-frequent (e.g. nouns of relationship, *sunu* 'son', *man(n)* 'man'). Accordingly, the high level of productivity could develop in the former classes characterised by low token and high type frequency, but not in the latter, characterised, in contrast, by high token but low type frequency. As the data indicate, for the developments in the minor declensional classes, it is the token frequency that turns out to be the decisive factor, manifested primarily on the level of lemma and morphosyntactic category. This high token frequency allowed them to survive as relics of inflectional patterns that were once, i.e. at the prehistoric stage (PIE), productive, or that emerged as the result of phonological changes, such as *i*-mutation.

The productivity of inflectional patterns is closely related to the concept of lexical strength. The low frequency items tend to form much stronger lexical connections to other items within a declensional class, thus creating patterns. Accordingly, morphological (inflectional) patterns tend to be reinforced in the classes which contain many low-frequency nouns, such as the *a*-stems or *ō*-stems in Old Germanic. An opposite tendency is found in the paradigms of high-frequency nouns, often affiliated with minor declensions. Having more lexical strength and being thus more autonomous, i.e. not dependent on the common pattern, highly frequent nouns tend to have weaker lexical connections to other items from the same class (see Section 1.4.5). This lexical strength impedes a potential spread of an inflectional pattern to other paradigms, i.e. inhibits its productivity. In other words, the impossibility of high (token) frequency items to become productive can be ascribed to their lexical strength (Bybee 1995: 434).

The examined material demonstrated also the relevance of relative frequency, which was most prominent in the Old Frisian and Old English data, where the plural proportion turned out to be decisive in accounting for the patterns of distribution of archaic and analogical inflections. The resistance of the plural paradigm of the OFris. *nd*-stems to analogical levelling, which cannot be accounted for by the salience of the inflectional exponent, can be explained by the high frequency of the plural forms in certain *nd*-stems. In other words, the low salience of the plural marker in the *nd*-stems was compensated by their relatively high frequency of occurrence in the plural, and consequently, the dissemination of analogical endings in the plural paradigm was inhibited by the high token frequency of the plural forms. In the longer diachronic perspective, the relative frequency turns out to be the strongest statistical index of morphological archaisms both in English and Frisian (Versloot & Adamczyk forth.).

The most extreme effects of frequency are to be found in morphological patterns that involve suppletion and lexicalization of high frequency forms. The former is typically one of the patterns of inflectional abundance, which can be a feature of high frequent items, as observed by Plank (1991): "blatant disregard for economy by providing two or more entirely dissimilar stems per word to be inflected is supposedly something only particularly frequent words (…) will be able to afford." (Plank 1991: 26). The investigated material does not offer such instances in the early Northern West Germanic paradigms, but the pattern is attested, for instance, in the later stages of Frisian, with the plural form *bäiste* 'animals' reinterpreted as the suppletive plural of *ku* 'cow' (animals → cows) (Saterland East Frisian), replacing an earlier irregular plural **käi* (cf. for English *OED*, s.v. *beast*, 3a). In turn, an example of lexicalization of individual paradigm forms is the development of the

Modern German form *Stätte* 'place' (LG *Stê(e)* vs. *Stadt* 'city'). The form goes back to an original DAT. SG., marked by *i*-mutation and an inflectional ending *-e*. The high frequency of this noun in this morphosyntactic category led to a conservation of the historical inflection, and a reinterpretation of the DAT. SG. form as a NOM. SG., whereby a new lexeme with a new meaning was created (also *Duden*, s.v. *Statt*: "*spätmhd.* stete, entstanden aus den flektierten Formen von *mhd.* stat"; cf. Kluge 2011, who attributes it to the original plural form).[348] Another instance of lexicalization is found in the paradigm of West Frisian *lid* (SG.) 'member, limb', where a new singular lemma *lea*, meaning 'body', developed from the OFris. plural form *litha* 'limbs'.[349]

Admittedly, a limitation in investigating the significance of the frequency factor in the restructuring process is the fact that the actual frequency of lemmas is not always reflected in the frequency in the texts (e.g. Haspelmath 2006: 45–46). This fact has some evident methodological implications for the analysis. Namely, certain lexemes used in the more elevated register will tend to be more frequently attested in the textual material, while the nouns denoting lower register concepts and items, for example, animals or parts of body, although probably frequent in everyday language, will not appear frequently in the texts. This limitation has a more general nature, and is inherent in any historical study of a language which can be accessed only through a limited textual material.

8.6.2 Salience of inflectional markers

Another factor which turned out to be crucial for the restructuring process is the salience of inflectional exponents. The criteria relevant for defining the salience of inflectional markers were discussed in Section 1.4.6.2. They involved two

---

348. In the Old Saxon corpus, the form *stedi* is attested in 31 tokens. The most numerous morphosyntactic category is the DAT. SG. with 11 tokens, followed by the ACC. SG. and NOM. PL. with 7 tokens each. In Old Frisian the proportion is: 10 DAT. SG. forms and 11 ACC. SG. forms, out of 29 tokens.

349. Certain developments in the dental stems could be interpreted also as an instance of lexicalization, or arguably of 'semantic' exaptation. The dental element -*þ*-, present originally in the oblique singular cases and in the plural of the Proto-Germanic dental stems, was employed to create a new meaning. More specifically, the OE *mona* 'moon' is a secondary formation based on the NOM. SG. of the PGmc. **mēnōþ-* < PIE **meh₁-not-*, while in OE *mōnaþ* 'month' the dental element from the oblique cases and the plural was used as the base form of the paradigm, with the dental element -*þ*- preserved throughout the entire paradigm (e.g. *EWN*, s.v. *maand*). Although this development does not involve the emergence of a new grammatical function, the redistribution of the morphological element, which originally functioned as a stem formative, resulted in two separate paradigms for lemmas with two different meanings.

parameters, namely, the phonological salience (perceptual salience) and morpho-logical complexity (complexity of formal marking). The prediction made on the basis of the salience scale was that salient markers will tend to be less susceptible to the analogical pressure from the productive inflections than the less salient ones, and that overt marking will be preferred over zero marking. The analysed material confirms the validity of these assumptions. Although occasionally viewed as an epiphenomenon of frequency, salience emerges as an independent factor in the reorganisation of the nominal inflection, which admittedly tightly interacts with frequency and other factors conditioning the process. Its relevance is reliant also on the function of the expressed categories in that the salient exponents are expected to be found in marked (infrequent) categories, while the low-salience exponents appear in the unmarked ones, i.e. frequent categories (in compliance with the prin-ciple of minimal effort).

The significance of salience as a factor conditioning the restructuring process is best attested in Old English and Old Frisian. The zero marker, which occupies the lowest rank on the salience scale, turned out to be the least preferred marker, i.e. one which will tend to be easily eliminated, especially when serving as an exponent of plurality. This can be best observed in the masculine *r*-stems, which in most ex-amined languages showed a clear preference to transfer to the *a*-stems, where the plural was marked by a salient and transparent ending, and thereby the zero plural marking could be avoided. This correlation did not apply to the NOM. SG., where the zero marking is a result of high frequency of this morpho-syntactic category, complying with the principle of least effort (i.e. the reducing effect of frequency). The *i*-mutated vowel, i.e. vocalic stem modulation, occupying the other end of the salience scale, turned out to be the most resistant inflectional exponent (see Section 1.4.6.2). The correlation is best evinced in the paradigms of Old English and Old Frisian root nouns, and in Old English monosyllabic *nd*-stems, where *i*-mutation gradually came to serve the function of distinguishing the singular from the plural. Likewise, the presence of the consonantal alternation in the paradigm could have a conserving effect on inflection, as demonstrated by the development of the *s*-stems, especially in Continental Germanic. A clear correlation between salience and the level of innovation, irrespective of the declension class, is reflected in the dissemination of the masculine GEN. SG. marker -*es* (-*as*), which was one of the markers earliest extended from the productive pattern, partly already at the pre-historic stage. Its early extension is confirmed by the fact that in many unproductive inflectional types no synchronic alternation between the archaic and innovative variants is attested in the GEN. SG. Its high ranking on the salience scale is secured by the presence of the perceptually robust /s/, and its long-term resistance to analogy is corroborated by its retention until present-day English (see Section 1.4.6.2). A comparable rank on the sonority scale is occupied by another expansive marker in

Old English, i.e. the NOM./ACC. PL. -as, which shows a strong tendency to expand (in the absence of other salient markers). The marker -an/-en, which is another relatively salient exponent, shows hardly any traces of productivity at this early stage, either in Anglo-Frisian or in Continental Germanic.[350] Its subsequent development in Continental Germanic, including Frisian, Dutch and German – and regionally in Middle English – indicates that it had a potential to develop into a productive marker. An exception here is the spread of the GEN. PL. marker -ena, which is well attested in the material, especially in Old English and Old Frisian, competing with the prevalent ending -a. As the GEN. PL. was a weak morphosyntactic category, i.e. infrequent and low on the salience scale, a more prominent marker than a vowel was apparently desirable to encode it.

The material demonstrates clearly that the paradigms which showed no morphophonemic alternation tended to be more susceptible to interparadigmatic analogical pressures. Although the vocalic alternation as such was placed very high on the salience scale, its success, measured as resistance to analogy, was not entirely independent of other factors, such as the frequency of occurrence. Accordingly, it is not only the salience of the marker containing the *i*-mutated vowel that renders the category it marks resistant, but rather the interaction of salience with how frequent a given category is and how relevant, i.e. what function it serves. Accordingly, the fact that root nouns retain the historical inflection in the plural is to be ascribed to both their high frequency in a specific paradigm form (i.e. in the plural) as well as to their salience. This is corroborated especially by the divergent fate of the *i*-mutated vowel in the singular and plural (e.g. in the root nouns), which was eliminated from the DAT. SG., but retained in the plural, where it served an important function of marking the opposition in number (see Section 8.5).

That salience on its own cannot account for all the patterns found in the investigated material is well demonstrated by the dental stems. Their paradigms were originally characterised by the presence of a consonantal alternation in the GEN., DAT., ACC. SG. and in the NOM./ACC. PL., which ranks high on the salience scale. Yet, this class turned out to be one of the first classes to have undergone extensive inflectional restructuring, and one where a salient inflectional exponent was abandoned. The reason for it must be the fact that the class of dental stems comprised only four nouns in the Old Germanic period, and their low frequency of occurrence (both type and token frequency) was not enough to secure the preservation of the historical pattern.

It is assumed that regularity (here inflectional) and lack of complexity of morphological markers are essential properties that guarantee a high level of

---

350. An exception is Old West Frisian, where -an replaced the earlier ending -ar and disseminated to nearly all masculine NOM./ACC. PL. forms (Versloot 2014).

functionality of a linguistic system (Jespersen 1922). The tendency to eliminate allomorphic alternations from paradigms, attested especially in Old English and Old Frisian, seems to comply with this assumption. Also from the point of view of language acquisition, stem/root vowel or consonant alternations are not the easiest inflectional markers, as the one-to-one relationship between form and meaning that generally facilitates the acquisition is obscured (Goldschneider & DeKeyser 2001: 36). Additionally, *i*-mutation is only applicable in a limited phonological context, i.e. when the root vowel is an open or back vowel, which limits its default application. In other words, although *i*-mutation is a salient inflectional exponent, it may be too complex to become a productive inflectional pattern and tends to be eliminated from the paradigms. However, the evidence of Continental Germanic morphology invalidates this assumption, as allomorphic alternations there serve as productive patterns of marking case/number distinctions. The functionality of the system, including the distinction between the singular and plural, is safeguarded by the presence of morphological complexity in the paradigm, i.e. a salient/complex marker, such as the *i*-mutated vowel. *I*-mutation serves effectively, alongside suffixation, as a productive way of forming the plural in German, exemplifying the interaction between salience and functionality. In fact, German nominal morphology shows not only the preservation but also an increase in allomorphy, which is a tendency running counter to what can be found in English or Frisian.[351] In the languages where this rich allomorphy was reduced through intraparadigmatic analogical levelling (e.g. in Old Frisian root nouns and *nd*-stems), the paradigms became more susceptible to external analogical pressure. The main reason for it was that the reduction of paradigmatic allomorphy induced a decrease in the formal variation in the paradigms, rendering them more uniform.

As mentioned earlier, the salience of inflectional exponents did not guarantee the survival of the historical inflectional pattern over time. Even the forms which showed *i*-mutation at the earliest attested stage were at a later stage largely eliminated from the paradigms (at least in English, Frisian and Dutch), and the paradigms tended to regularise on the template of the productive types (e.g. OE *neaht*, *bōc*). This complies with the observation that suffixation as a mechanism of expressing plurality or case/number relations tends to be preferred to internal stem alternation (Dressler 1985b). Even if such a generalisation is not universal (e.g. Bybee & Newman 1995), it seems to apply to the history of Germanic languages.

---

351. The variation in the allomorphy across West Germanic, visible in the plural marking pattern, is due to phonological developments and the redistribution of the variants in the respective morphological systems. The lack of morphologisation of stem-allomorphy (*i*-mutation) in languages other than High German, most of Low German and Limburgian was of particular significance for the subsequent development of their respective declensional systems, as discussed in Chapter 7.

Accordingly, the *i*-mutated forms in the DAT. SG. or NOM./ACC. PL. of, for example, monosyllabic *nd*-stems, in the long run, stood little chance of remaining unaffected by the analogical pressure of the inflectional suffixes from the *a*-stem declension.

In view of the fact that suffixation is the dominant mechanism of marking grammatical relations in Germanic languages, the most salient and complex markers, i.e. vowel and consonant stem alternations, can be considered to be irregular markers. Such irregular markers can be preserved in the long run only in forms or items that are highly frequent, as these irregular forms stand a chance to be well entrenched in the mental lexicon. In other words, morphological (here inflectional) irregularity is tolerated only in high frequency forms, testifying to the conserving effect of frequency. This pattern is one of the underlying principles of the interaction between frequency and salience of inflectional exponents.

Another inflectional characteristic related to salience is the development of double markers, whereby the salience of the inflectional exponent increases. The early Northern West Germanic languages do not provide much evidence for this morphological development; several isolated instances include: OE GEN. SG. *sylan*, NOM. SG. *sulh*, with the *i*-mutated vowel and the *n*-stem ending *-an*; OFris. ACC. PL. *clathera* with the *s*-stem plural marker *-r* and the *a*-stem ending *-a*. Double marking is more frequently found in present-day Germanic, especially in nouns originally affiliated with the minor declensions, where the development of the double marker reinforces the number exponence (e.g. *Männer*; *children, kine, brethren*; Du. *kinderen*).[352] It involves mostly the presence of the *i*-mutated vowel or the *(e)r*-element, which accompany the regular suffixation pattern. The mechanism of double marking has been interpreted as an instance of non-proportional analogy, or alternatively, as reanalysis followed by proportional analogy (Becker 1990: 24). This morphological development cannot be considered functional and clearly does not comply with the economy principle. A plausible explanation of such forms is that the speakers faced with a lack of an explicit or "recognizable formal clues" as to the basic form interpret the plural forms as singular and then form the plural in line with the regular pattern (Fertig 2013: 65).[353]

---

352. Note that Modern West Frisian (and various Dutch dialects) have plurals in *-ens* (= *en* + *-s*), as in *learzens* 'boots' (SG. *lears*). The ending subsequently undergoes a phonological reduction: [əns] > [ɔs] > [əs], which eliminates the actual double marking (Tiersma 1999: 51).

353. A similar reanalysis of the archaic plural form as singular is found also in Du. *spaander* 'wood chip' (used alongside *spaan*) and colloquial *hoender* 'hen, chicken' (used alongside *hoen*).

8.6.3 Semantics

Semantics is yet another factor that turned out to be relevant for the reorganisation of the nominal inflection, being manifested on a few different levels. One of the assumptions made at the beginning of this investigation was that the semantic profile of declensional classes may influence the pattern of restructuring. As some of the classes have a transparent semantic core, it could be expected that semantically coherent groups will tend to display a distinct pattern of restructuring. This refers in particular to the *r*-stems, denoting kinship terms, and *s*-stems, designating mostly animals. Given the retention of the historical inflection in certain semantically coherent groups of nouns, such as the PDE heavy-syllable neuter *a*-stems denoting game animals (e.g. *deer* – *deer*), which show no marking in the plural, it can be expected that such classes will tend to remain more archaic. Much as the data from the examined languages indicate that semantic similarity was an important organisational factor in the extension of inflectional patterns, the class-semantics was not a decisive factor. Admittedly, the *r*-stems tended to retain the historical inflection to some extent (which is best evinced in Old Saxon), but it was not the class pressure that enhanced the historical pattern, but rather the relatively high token frequency of these nouns. Likewise, in the *s*-stems it was not the semantics of the class that determined the preservation of the *r*-formative as a plurality exponent (in Continental Germanic), but rather the salience of this inflectional marker, combined with the need to retain a functional contrast between the singular and plural, as well as the high proportion of plural tokens in many of these lemmas. Two instances where the appearance of the inflectional marker can be ascribed purely to semantics are (a) the retention of the plural marker -*e* in the masculine *i*-stems denoting tribal names in Old English (not included in the quantitative analysis in this study), and (b) the local productivity of the NOM./ACC.PL. ending -*e* in nouns denoting humans in Old Frisian (irrespective of the original declensional class, i.e. *friund, fiand, man, brother*) (see Versloot & Adamczyk 2013).[354]

---

354. More examples of semantically-motivated analogy are found in the later varieties of Germanic, e.g. PDE plural forms of animals, such as *antilope, fish, moose* (SG. = PL.), which emerged by analogy to *deer, sheep*; Modern Dutch terms of measurement based on endingless plurals of neuter nouns: *twee jaar, twee pond* vs. *twee dagen* 'two years, pounds, days', and by analogy *twee kilo, twee euro* (both common gender), optionally *twee maand(en)* vs. *twee weken* 'two months, weeks'. Another set of examples comes from the 19th-century East Frisian Wangerooge dialect, which exhibits plurals in -*er* in a number of nouns, including historical *s*-stems (e.g. *kalwer* 'calves', *laumer* 'lambs'). The plurals *kiier* 'cows' and *schaiper* 'sheep' and potentially the masculine *hingster* 'horses' (an original *a*-stem with the OFris. ending -*ar*) can be considered a result of semantic association with the historical *s*-stems. Other nouns denoting human beings

The implication that these observations have is that semantics does not directly regulate the restructuring process, but plays an essential role indirectly, being expressed through other factors, especially through frequency. The interaction of semantics and frequency is essential for the mechanism of the process, as the frequencies of lemmas or of morphosyntactic categories are determined by the extralinguistic (real world) conditions, i.e. semantics. The effect of semantics is particularly visible in the frequencies of individual morphosyntactic categories and consequently in the patterns of remodelling of inflection in them. On account of their semantic properties, certain nouns tend to be used more often in certain morphosyntactic categories (see also the discussion in 8.6.1). For instance, the nouns denoting body parts, such as *feet*, *teeth*, *hands*, tended to be more frequent in the plural than in the singular, and they consistently show a greater resistance to analogical pressures in the plural. In nouns of relationship, the nouns *mother* and *father* were found more often in the singular, while the terms *sisters*, *brothers*, tended to be more frequent in the plural. The innovation level in these lemmas directly correlates with frequency, which is ultimately determined by semantics. Another example of this type of interaction comes from the root nouns, many of which denote small animals and thus tend to be used more often in the plural. The high token frequency in the plural allowed forms such as *louse* and *mouse* (in contrast to *goats*) to preserve their historical plural inflection until present-day English (see Krygier 1997).[355] Finally, nouns affiliated with the historical *u*-stems, which often denoted locations (e.g. *eard* 'earth', *wudu* 'wood'), are frequently attested in the DAT. SG., whereas *nd*-stems, denoting agents, are more frequently attested in the nominative. The susceptibility of these stems to analogical pressure is conditioned by their frequencies in individual categories, and indirectly by their semantics inasmuch as it determines their frequencies. In other words, it can be concluded that individual paradigms had different semantically, i.e. "extramorphologically based frequency profiles" (Karlsson 1986: 23), and the dynamics of the analogical changes in these paradigms were largely conditioned by them.

Another field where semantics functions as an independent factor in determining the restructuring pattern is the level of phrase, involving specific collocations. An example is the extension of the GEN. SG. marker to the feminine root noun *neaht* in Old English and Old Frisian by analogy to the inflection of the *a*-stem *dæg* (cf.

---

belonging to the household seem to have joined this *Hühnerhof* class: *beener* 'children', *fauner* 'girls', *fenter* 'boys', *knechter* 'servants', *sjeeler* 'men', *wüüfer* 'wives'. This list leaves a lot of lemmas with -*er* in the Wangerooge dialect unexplained (Versloot 2017b: 452–453; cf. Philippa 1989: 14).

355. The frequencies from the British National Corpus for *lice* and *mice* fit the observed pattern, which is largely determined by relative frequency (of the plural) (Versloot & Adamczyk forth.).

OE *dæges and neahtes*). A similar pattern can be found in the *u*-stems, where the noun *summer*, not affiliated originally with this declensional class, by analogy to the related noun *winter*, followed the masculine *u*-stem inflection in all West Germanic languages. It is clearly the semantic association of these two nouns that facilitated such a shift in the inflectional pattern, which additionally entailed a change in gender (cf. the PGmc. neuter **sumara-*, ON n. *sumar*; Kroonen 2013, s.v. **sumara-*). The relevance of semantics in the restructuring process as evinced in collocations involves also the contexts where two nouns follow the same innovative inflectional pattern, as in the Old Frisian expression: *tha fiunde alsa friunde* 'the enemies and friends', where both lemmas show the analogical *i*-stem marker *-e*.

8.6.4 Other controlling factors

8.6.4.1 *Gender*
Gender in Old Germanic languages had no overt exponents and thus needed to "select" exponents of other, overtly marked morphological categories (case and number), determining thus "the realisation of the categories of case and number within the noun itself, which result[ed] in a number of inflectional paradigms ..." (Kastovsky 2000: 710). Accordingly, it was signalled by the forms of the attributes (in agreement with the noun) and served as a means (not the primary one though) of ascribing nouns to a specific declensional class. This rule does not hold for a few classes, where the link with gender was more explicit, namely, the *s*-stems, which contained only neuter nouns, the *ō*-stems, consisting solely of feminine nouns, and the *nd*-stems, which essentially comprised only masculine nouns. The shape of the NOM. SG. could occasionally indicate gender, as, for instance, in Old English where the marker *-a* was characteristic of masculine *n*-stems, the ending *-u* of the feminine nouns (*ō*-stems), and where certain derivational suffixes were gender-specific (e.g. OE feminine *-nes(s)*, masculine *-dōm*, or neuter *-et*). These, however, cannot be viewed as entirely reliable criteria for gender assignment.[356] In the later stages of the development of Germanic, especially of Continental Germanic (Low and High German), gender emerges as the primary criterion for the organisation of declensional classes. This refers in particular to the plurality marking patterns, where it becomes functionalised as a "Pluralzuweisungsprinzip" (Dammel et al. 2010: 636; Ramat 1981). The process whereby gender emerges as a criterion for the distribution of inflectional allomorphs, ensuring an opposition between the masculine and neuter gender on the one hand, and feminine, on the other, is commonly known as *Genusprofilierung* (Wegera 1985; cf. Duke 2005: 43).

---

356. The class of *r*-stems was the only declensional type in which gender was assigned purely on a semantic basis.

Gender turns out to be an important factor in the mechanism of the inflectional reorganisation, although it did not directly affect the dynamics of the process. Instead, it served as a force consistently guiding the directions of interdeclensional analogical shifts. The attested patterns of restructuring comply with the principle of gender conservation (Keyser & O'Neil 1985) in that the extension of analogical inflections proceeds in line with the original gender. The analogical declension shifts go along gender classes in all the examined languages, including Old English, where the spread of the masculine inflection of the *a*-stems was extensive, but largely confined to masculine nouns. While the material does show some traces of unhistorical gender assignment, appearing alongside declensional realignments, the scantily attested irregularities are far from reflecting a systematic gender class change. Some tendencies observable in the material include:

a. the presence of the masculine marker -*es* (-*is*) in the feminine paradigms, especially in the root nouns in Old English
b. the consistent extension of the masculine marker -*is* (-*as*) in the feminine root nouns in Old Saxon
c. the extension of the NOM./ACC. masculine marker -*as* in the neuter *s*-stems in Old English
d. the fluctuation of gender in certain nouns between feminine and masculine inflection (e.g. OFris. *kere* 'statute'), and feminine and neuter inflection (e.g. *book* in all examined languages).

The attested pattern of preservation of the etymological gender testifies also to the fact that the gender system did not suffer any major distortion alongside the declensional class shift.[357]

Gender can also be considered the factor responsible for the divergent pattern of spread of the *s*-plural marker across West Germanic. The discrepancy is evident in the comparison between Old English and Old Saxon: while in Old English this ending emerges as the most productive (plural) inflectional exponent, in Old Saxon (and later Low German) the productivity of the marker -*os* was fairly limited. The reason for such a state of affairs is the chronology of changes in the gender system, and in particular the fact that the disintegration of the gender system occurred earlier in English than in Low German. The findings from the present study indicate that as long as a gender distinction was preserved, interdeclensional transitions occurred within gender classes, i.e. gender was guiding the directions

---

357. Importantly, the analysed changes in the nominal inflection were not triggered by or related to the dissolution of the grammatical gender system. In most of the investigated languages this process occurred later: in English (no gender), West Frisian and Dutch (3 > 2 genders) in the Middle period; Low and High German as well as some dialects of Frisian still retain a three-way contrast in gender.

of interparadigmatic transfers. Towards the end of the Old English stage, when the first traces of dissolution of the gender system can be observed (e.g. Curzan 2009), this consistency of transfers within gender class declined. Accordingly, the expansive salient NOM./ACC. PL. marker -as tended to be attached more and more often to the feminine and neuter nouns, undermining the general rule of declension class shift in compliance with gender. In contrast, in Old Saxon, gender was a very stable feature, retained well into the Middle Low German period and later, and as such it remained the factor controlling the directions of interdeclensional shifts for much longer. Therefore, the expansion of masculine markers, such as -os, to feminine or neuter stems was in Old Saxon not attested at all (cf. Kürchner 2008; Versloot 2017a).[358] Consequently, the chance for sub-patterns, such as r-plurals, or n-plurals to persist in (Low) German was higher inasmuch as the competition between inflectional patterns involved also medium-size patterns, i.e. moderately prevalent inflectional (plural) patterns, rather than one predominant type, like the a-stems in Old (and Middle) English, whose stability was additionally enhanced by the disintegrating gender system.

Occasionally, the shift of nouns to productive declensions has been interpreted as a reaction to the confusion in the gender assignment rule, which aimed at bringing back transparency in the gender assignment system (Schwink 2004: 68). This statement seems to be too far-fetched in light of the findings from the present study: the role of gender in the transformation of the nominal system was confined to guiding the directions of interdeclensional shifts rather than being the ultimate motivation for the restructuring. If there was any teleological ingredient in the repatterning of the nominal inflections, it was to make the system functional, i.e. to restore or retain the contrast in case, and especially that in number.

8.6.4.2 *Prosodic structure: stem weight*

The syllable structure is yet another factor which influenced restructuring of the nominal inflection. The phonological developments, operating at the prehistoric stage, affected the light- and heavy-syllable stems in different ways, and in this sense the weight of the stem determined the divergent inflectional shapes of these paradigms. This refers in particular to the apocope of vowels in unstressed syllables in West Germanic, whereby the short vowels were lost after a heavy syllable, and the long ones (some from PGmc. diphthongs) were shortened after both light and heavy syllables (Boutkan 1995: 39–42). This observation is relevant to the pattern

---

358. In fact, Old Saxon shows a tendency towards reducing the scope of the ending -os/as-. It was gradually replaced by the less salient marker -a, most likely under the Franconian influence (Quak 1991a). In Middle Low German, this new a-stem ending -a and the i-stem ending -i merged into a *schwa* (-e), and i-mutation came to serve as a marker of plurality (just as in High German).

of restructuring in the *i*-stems, *u*-stems and root nouns, where the reorganisation in the light-syllable and heavy-syllable stems had different dynamics. The original vocalic markers were retained in the NOM./ACC. SG. in the light-syllable *i*-stems, *u*-stems and root nouns, which rendered them distinct from the heavy-syllable nouns, consistently ending in a consonant (i.e. with a zero marker). In most cases, the heavy-syllable stems turned out to be subject to remodelling more easily and earlier, often at the prehistoric stage (e.g. OE *i*-stems and *u*-stems). This tendency, however, cannot be ascribed to a special propensity of heavy-syllable stems to analogical pressure, but rather to the effect of the activity of the phonological developments, which rendered the shape of the NOM. SG. in minor heavy-syllable stems identical with that of the productive *a*- or *ō*-stems (see the discussion about the formal overlap as a measure of analogical attraction in Section 8.4).

As the findings demonstrate, the heavy-syllable nouns clearly disfavoured the attachment of analogical endings (e.g. endingless DAT. SG. of OFris. root noun *bōk* or OE, OFris. *u*-stem *hand*). In contrast, the light-syllable stems tended to aim at reaching a balance in the metrical structure (i.e. the trochaic foot), as demonstrated in the NOM. SG. of light-syllable feminine root nouns, where the ending -*u* was added against the historical pattern, whereby it was rendered disyllabic (e.g. OE **hnit > hnitu*, **hnut > hnutu*).

Another, less explicit (from a synchronic perspective) effect of the interaction of stem-weight-defined apocope and analogical levelling is found in the *s*-stems. After the elimination of the word-final -*r*-element (< **-z-*) from the NOM./ACC. SG., the remaining inflectional vowel was subject to reduction after a heavy syllable (as in OE *cælf* 'calf' < PGmc. **kalfiz*). This development facilitated the association of these stems with the neuter *a*-stems, and induced their transfer to the *a*-stems. In contrast, the final vowel was retained in light-syllable stems (*sige* 'victory' < early-OE **sigi* < PGmc. **sigiz*, or *sele* 'hall' < early-OE **sæli* < PGmc. **saliz*). This retention of the vowel rendered the structure of the original light-syllable *s*-stems identical with that of the light syllable *i*-stems, and triggered an early (prehistoric) shift of these stems to the *i*-stem declension.

One more class where the role of the syllable structure may have been relevant is the group of *r*-stems. The noun *father* (OE *fæder*) is the only noun in this class which is composed of two light syllables (with the structure L L), while the other nouns contain a heavy syllable followed by a light one (H L) (e.g. *mōdor*). The investigated material indicates that *father*, despite its high token frequency, shows the most innovative paradigm of all the nouns in this class, with no traces of historical inflection attested in the NOM./ACC. PL. The tendency to adopt an analogical pattern of inflection could be partly ascribed to the fact that in order to comply with the trochaic metrical structure (Germanic foot structure), the sequence of two light syllables was more prone to add a new light-syllable element (-*as*, i.e. L L L = H L) than a sequence of a heavy syllable followed by a light one (H L L) (cf. Lahiri & Dresher 1991; Flikkert et al. 2009: 127; cf. Section 3.5.5.2). In this sense, the weight of the first syllable in *father* may be considered a factor encouraging the activity of analogical developments in its paradigm. Given that this correlation is recognisable only in the Old English material and is not sufficiently substantiated by the other languages, the validity of such an interpretation is debatable. It must be emphasised, at the same time, that syllable weight is only one of the factors involved in the mechanism of the restructuring of the *r*-stems, and it interacts with frequency and salience of inflectional exponents (cf. Table 3.28).

8.6.5 Interactions between conditioning factors

As observed already in the previous sections, the factors conditioning the process of reorganisation of the nominal inflection in early Northern West Germanic languages did not function independently, but closely interacted with each other. These interactions could have essentially enhancing or neutralising effects. In most cases the conditioning factors operated in a synergetic way, reinforcing each other, but they could also interact in such a way that their effects were complementary. An example of an interaction between factors where their effects are corresponding is the development of the GEN. SG. and NOM. SG. In both categories frequency of occurrence and salience interact in a way that low salience corresponds to high frequency and high salience corresponds to low frequency. Accordingly, the GEN. SG., which is a relatively infrequent morphosyntactic category, is marked by a salient ending (-*es*, -*is*), while the NOM. SG., being a frequent category, appears predominantly with no marker (i.e. zero marker, which occupies the lowest position on the salience scale).

Another example of an interaction between frequency and salience, where their effects are complementary, is the development of the GEN. PL. The GEN. PL., being one of the low frequency categories, was prone to analogical pressure already at the prehistoric stage, where the ending *-ōn* (OE, OFris. -*a*, OS, OLF -*o*) disseminated to many declensions. In the later stage, as the data indicate, the *n*-stem form -*ena*, -*ana* tended to disseminate to many declensional classes, despite the fact that in other paradigmatic categories the spread of the *n*-stem inflections was very limited. Clearly, it was the salience of this inflectional marker that rendered it competitive and contributed to its extension across paradigms. But frequency of occurrence also had a share in this development in that the GEN. PL. was one of the rarest morphosyntactic categories. Accordingly, the spread of this new inflectional marker was successful, since less frequent categories need to be encoded by stronger, more explicit markers. In contrast, categories such as the NOM. SG. are mostly endingless as their high frequency renders the presence of an explicit marker redundant.

A third example of an interplay between salience and frequency is offered by the Old English root nouns, where the NOM./ACC. PL. demonstrate the reinforcing effect of these two factors. These forms are both relatively frequent in many lemmas (e.g. OE *tēþ* 'teeth', *gēs* 'geese', *mȳs* 'mice', etc.), and the plural marker is highly salient (the *i*-mutated vowel). The overlapping effect of these two factors is responsible for the resistance of these nouns to analogical plural formation until present-day English. The same synergetic effect cannot be observed, for instance, in Old Frisian, where the absence of *i*-mutation in various nouns in this class was not compensated by their (moderate) frequency. At the same time, the Old Frisian nouns that showed *i*-mutation turned out to be as resistant to analogical change as the root nouns in Old English.

The share of each of these two factors is in general not easy to estimate, but some individual instances can give some more insight into the nature of this interaction. As root nouns belong to the more frequent part of the lexicon, one may expect that frequency is the major factor responsible for conserving the historical inflection in the paradigms. A closer examination of the distribution of forms in the OE root nouns *fōt* 'foot' and *meolc* 'milk' indicates that in the absence of a difference in frequency it was the salience of inflectional exponents that determined the patterns of restructuring in these lemmas. Although similarly frequent in the DAT. SG. (both in absolute and relative terms), these two lemmas show different levels of innovation in the DAT. SG., as illustrated in Table 8.1.

Table 8.1 Distribution of innovative forms in the DAT. SG. of OE *fōt* and *meolc*

OE root nouns	Total SG (n)	DAT SG	% innov.
fōt – fēt	293	52 (18%)	14%
meolc – meolc(e)	196	59 (30%)	95%

The presence of the *i*-mutated vowel in the DAT. SG. of *fōt* rendered it much more resistant to analogy. An opposite effect is found in *meolc*, where the absence of *i*-mutation in the DAT. SG. made it highly susceptible to analogical pressure.[359]

An example of an interaction between syllable structure and gender is found in the masculine light-syllable *i*-stems in Old Frisian. On account of their syllable structure, the forms of the NOM. and ACC. SG., both feminine and masculine,

---

359. The word *meolc* is the only lemma in Old English with a vowel that cannot be mutated, and of all root nouns it has the most innovative DAT. SG. (followed by *neaht* where the innovation level reaches 51%).

are expected to retain their final vowel, e.g. *breke* (masc.) 'breach', *stede* (fem.) 'city, place'. As the competing forms of the masculine *a*-stems are endless, the masculine light-syllable *i*-stems can be expected to lose the final vowel. Formally, however, the masculine forms in *-e* overlap with the feminine *ō*-stems (in *-e*). This mismatch between their formal shape and gender leads to two possible outcomes: (1) the more expected situation, i.e. the loss of final vowel under the analogical pressure of the *a*-stems (attested in 15% of forms in the NOM./ACC. SG.), and (2) the rarer situation, i.e. the change of the original gender to feminine (as observed, for instance, in the noun *kere* 'statute').

Finally, the Old Saxon class of *r*-stems illustrates a situation where the expected effect of salience (or any other factor for that matter) is *not* found. Low salience of inflectional exponents in general promotes a strong inclination towards innovation in the paradigms. Given the undiversified paradigm of the *r*-stems, which lacked any salient markers, the effects of analogical pressure can be expected to be widespread in the paradigm (despite the overall archaic profile of Old Saxon). The absence of analogical forms in the analysed Old Saxon material is remarkable, especially in view of the evidence from the sister languages. The potential explanation for this unexpected profile of the *r*-stem declension may involve a combination of semantics (kinship terms) and a uniform phonological structure of these stems (σ-*ar*) which – at least at this early stage that Old Saxon represents – may have prevented any analogical intrusion of analogical inflections in this class.

As all these factors are not independent of each other, it is difficult to estimate their precise share in the restructuring process. The findings indicate that the relevance of salience and semantics as conditioning factors seems to be outranked by frequency of occurrence (both absolute and relative), which is, however, itself largely defined by semantics (see also Versloot & Adamczyk forth.).

8.7   Implications for the taxonomy of nouns in early Northern West Germanic

Although the present study did not aim at revising the traditional approach to classifying the nominal declensions, the analysed material demonstrates that such a revision would be necessary if one wants to approach the nominal morphology from a synchronic perspective. The idea of classifying nouns on the basis of synchronic criteria, such as the inflectional endings, is not novel and has evolved mostly with reference to the Old English nominal system. The approach was most notably employed in the publication of Hogg & Fulk (2011), where separate sections are devoted to the discussion of the diachronic and synchronic classifications of Old English nouns. The present quantitative investigation reveals that the traditional classification, with the foundation in the Proto-Germanic nominal system, does not ideally reflect the linguistic reality as it is attested in the available Old Germanic sources. At the same time, the necessity for revising the taxonomy of nouns differs, depending on the language. Clearly, the findings from the present study have certain implications for the classification of nouns in Old English, where the range of declensional classes originally based on the etymological criterion can be reduced. A purely synchronic approach to the Old English nominal inflection necessitates merging some of the classes and subsuming them under the productive declensions (cf. Section 3.7). In view of the results of the quantitative analysis, two of the minor classes in Old English could be relatively easily subsumed under the productive inflectional paradigms of the a-stems and $\bar{o}$-stems. One of them is the class of the i-stems, where traces of the historical inflection (the etymological marker -e in the NOM./ACC. PL. in masculine stems and the endingless ACC. SG. in feminine heavy-syllable stems) are so rare that they should be interpreted merely as vestiges of the original i-stem pattern. In turn, the s-stems, where the singular is almost entirely dominated by the a-stem inflection (except for early Anglian sources), could be viewed as a subtype of the neuter a-stems, with several lexicalised relic plurals showing the r-formative (cf. Braune/Reiffenstein 2004: 188). A similar status can be assigned to the dental stems, where a number of petrified forms were preserved only in the plural.

As far as the other investigated languages are concerned, an alternative classification seems hardly expedient. Most of the accounts and classifications of Old Frisian nominal paradigms allowed for the residual condition of some of the minor paradigms, adhering essentially to a twofold division into strong and weak declensions (most recently Bremmer 2009). The reason for not following the etymologically-based taxonomy in the tradition of Old Frisian studies may be partly due to the nature of the extant Old Frisian material, characterised by relatively scant attestations to minor stems, whose inflectional patterns have not so far been given much attention. The analysis of the Old Frisian material attested prior to 1400 indicates that especially the inflections of minor vocalic classes, i.e. the i-stems and u-stems, turn out to be fairly well retained, even when compared to the state of affairs in Old English. As regards Old Saxon, the findings of the study indicate that the nominal system remained remarkably conservative, so applying the etymological criterion to the classification of nouns is entirely justified (cf. Rauch 1992a). The historical paradigms, although exhibiting some influence from the productive inflections, are still well preserved. Of the four investigated languages, Old Low Franconian turns out to be the most innovative with respect to the shape of the nominal inflection. This fact has been acknowledged in earlier studies, where typically an opposition is made between weak (n-stems) and strong (vocalic stems) declensional types, with a recognition of some vestiges of specific historical declensions (e.g. Quak 1992). These accounts accordingly correspond to the findings from the present quantitative investigation of the Old Low Franconian nominal system.

8.8 Concluding remarks

The gradual reorganisation of the declensional system in early Northern West Germanic languages was a consequence of partly universal, partly language-specific interactions between linguistic subsystems, including phonology, morphology and semantics. The catalyst of the break-down of the declensional system inherited from Proto-Germanic were the phonological developments, whose range and chronology varied depending on the language. The changes in the nominal system involving analogical realignments and interdeclensional shifts can be considered a reaction to the phonological innovations. In other words, the shape of the nominal inflection adapted to the new conditions brought about by the changes in the phonological system. In this way, the process of reorganisation of the nominal inflection testifies to an interdependence and complex interaction between morphology and phonology.

The patterns of inflectional reorganisation reflect the underlying tendency in language towards regularisation, and its largely frequency-driven foundation. This stays in line with the claim that "(…) there is a tendency in languages to treat the members of a lexeme class alike, even if this makes the system less efficient from a processing point of view. With lexemes of very high frequency, languages sometimes tolerate radical irregularity, but the great majority of lexemes in most languages inflect according to some general pattern." (Haspelmath 2014: 204). All the minor declensions, and in particular the consonantal ones, when seen from a synchronic perspective, were classes characterised by a range of inflectional irregularities, and their survival until the early stages of the attestation of Germanic indicates that they must have been once productive classes, comprising of high frequency nouns. Additionally, all the discussed phenomena point to a clear morphological tendency present in Old Germanic towards a reduction of inflectional class diversity, which can be viewed as another expression of the regularisation tendency.

The remodelling of the nominal inflection emerges as a multifaceted development, which involved analogical forces operating within and across the nominal paradigms. The dynamics of the restructuring process were controlled by a range of interacting factors, the most important of them being the frequency of occurrence, the salience of inflectional exponents and semantics. The explanation for most of the inflectional patterns found in the examined material comes from the frequency of occurrence, operating at different levels, which itself is defined extramorphologically, i.e. by semantics. Significantly, neither frequency nor salience can be considered epiphenomena in the process under study, but both are independent factors regulating the dynamics of the developments in the nominal system (cf. Becker 1990).

Finally, the process of restructuring of the nominal inflection in Northern West Germanic languages can be framed in terms of the rule "the survival of the fittest", where the fittest is equivalent to functional. The fittest forms do not seem to be universal, but they are largely language-specific. This rule seems to be most relevant for the developments in the English nominal inflection, where the number of forms which turned out to be fit enough to survive over the centuries is considerably limited. In the other examined languages and their later stages, in particular (Low) German, a range of inflectional patterns still qualify as 'fit' and are able to successfully compete until the present-day.

Conclusions

The general aim of this study was to investigate and characterise the process of morphological reorganisation of the nominal inflection in early Northern West Germanic languages. The principal research question underlying the study referred to the mechanisms involved in the restructuring process, its dynamics, the conditioning factors, and the scope in the individual languages. From the micro-perspective, the study presented a systematic account of the restructuring tendencies leading to a gradual transformation of the nominal paradigms in the individual languages. The investigation focused on the inflectional variation attested in the paradigms of nouns originally affiliated with the unproductive declensional classes, and featured its detailed characterisation and interpretation. The corpus-based quantitative analysis allowed the identification of patterns behind the dissemination of the productive inflectional endings in the minor stem paradigms. By examining these patterns some insight into the mechanisms of the process of analogical restructuring could be gained, including its advancement and reliance on a number of interacting factors, both structural and extramorphological. From the macro-perspective, the study examined some general theoretical implications of the changes in the nominal system for the theory of morphological change. Attention was given to facets such as how the process of analogical remodelling of the paradigms unfolded and by which factors it was determined. Two more peripheral questions addressed referred to the taxonomy of the nominal paradigms, i.e. the evaluation of the validity of the traditional, diachronically-biased classification of nouns, and the interpretation of the identified patterns and tendencies in the context of the affinities between the dialects in the West Germanic linguistic continuum.

The quantitative investigation involved a systematic comparison of the declensional systems of the individual Northern West Germanic languages at their earliest attested stages. The abundance of the examined material made it possible to determine the scope and dynamics of the process of inflectional reconfiguration, revealing its complexity. Despite the limitations related to the nature of the analysed corpora – unbalanced in terms of size and genre composition – the extant material from each of the investigated languages contributed to identifying the patterns and making generalisations about the operation of the process. Quite expectedly, the advancement of these developments could be best observed in the better attested dialects, especially in Old English, where the relatively wide time span of the available sources afforded a diachronic perspective. At the same time, the inclusion of the material from the more scantily attested languages, especially Old Low Franconian, rendered the picture of the nominal inflectional morphology of early Northern West Germanic more thorough and complete.

The findings of the present study indicate that the declensional systems of the early Northern West Germanic languages were exposed to extensive analogical pressures, which rendered them different from a system that could be expected to emerge from regular phonological processes. The process of restructuring involved a gradual analogy-based permeation of the productive inflections (from the *a*- and *ō*-stems and partly *i*-stems and *n*-stems) into the paradigms of the unproductive types. The resulting fluctuation between the inherited and analogical inflections in the minor stem paradigms led to interparadigmatic (interdeclensional) analogical reshufflings, and consequently to the eventual demise of the etymologically-based declensional distinctions. In the longer diachronic perspective, these (and related) developments resulted in the neutralisation of case opposition (best attested in the Late Old English period), and the differentiation of number paradigms.

One of the major diachronic tendencies that emerged in the cross-linguistic comparison is a reduction in declensional diversity, which was a direct consequence of interparadigmatic reshufflings. Despite the growing tendency towards simplifying the declensional system, the restructuring process did not lead to a complete elimination of declensional classes, and with a notable exception of English, present-day Germanic languages retain considerable diversity in their nominal inflections. This refers in particular to the nominal paradigms of the North Germanic dialects, i.e. Modern Icelandic, Faroese and Elfdalian, which, despite certain modifications, still stay closer to the historical paradigms. The extent to which such changes affect individual languages depends on a number of factors, both language internal and external, including language contact and sociolinguistic variation.

The examination of the material and the comparison of the findings from the individual languages gave some insight into the mechanisms of the restructuring process. The gradual reshaping of the declensional system of early Germanic can be described as an effect of language-specific interactions between linguistic subsystems, including phonology, morphology and semantics. The incentive of the transformation of the declensional system were the phonological processes, which had wide-ranging morphological consequences, with different scope and chronologies in the individual languages. The system of the nominal inflection was exposed to substantial pressures, operating on two different levels, namely the regular phonological innovations, which destabilised the earlier transparency and coherence of the inflectional system, and the (largely ensuing) analogical readjustments, which aimed at re-establishing the transparency. These analogical developments were gender-sensitive in that the interdeclensional shifts of nouns were congruous with their gender class affiliations.

The analysed material demonstrated that the dynamics of the changes in the nominal system worked towards retaining or enhancing the functionality of the nominal system. The major feature securing the functionality of the system was the existence of the contrasts between different grammatical categories, such as the contrast in number. The opposition could be maintained by the distinct inflectional exponents, preferably the salient ones. Accordingly, the phonological erosion of inflections was compensated for by the levelling of more common, explicit and less ambiguous endings. This compensation mechanism seems to have been the pivot of the restructuring process.

In order to explore the mechanisms of the process, the study focused also on identifying the factors controlling the processes and the interactions between them. The two key factors which turned out to have most profoundly influenced the restructuring patterns are frequency of occurrence, with token frequency as a factor conserving morphological patterns, and the morpho-phonological salience of inflectional exponents. A third factor which emerged as crucial for the mechanism of the interdeclensional shifts was semantics. All these factors conspired or conflicted with each other in the competition between the morphological variants, defining the final shape of the nominal paradigms. Much as the explanatory power of frequency (operating on various levels) and salience in the transformation of Old Germanic morphology has been acknowledged in earlier studies, it has not been sufficiently substantiated with corpus data analysis – a gap which this study has tried to respond to.

The findings of the investigation indicate that of these three contributing factors, frequency of occurrence is the most powerful determinant of the inflectional patterns, which can account for the majority of inflectional variation found in the examined paradigms and classes. This complies with the observation that frequency, being an important determinant of shaping language, can explain many asymmetries in language structure (Haspelmath 2006: 33), and that patterns of change depend largely on the frequency with which words are used in discourse. The explanatory power of this factor in the process of restructuring and language change is related to the fact that it can be taken as a manifestation of the way linguistic knowledge is entrenched and processed in the cognitive system (cf. Köpcke 1993). In other words, frequency of use is correlated with entrenchment and processing of linguistic constructions or expressions in the mental grammar. The frequency of linguistic expressions and structures has an effect on the "representation and activation of linguistic knowledge", reinforcing their mental representation (Diessel 2004: 23). The interparadigmatic (interdeclensional) transfers were guided largely by frequency of occurrence, operating on the level of the morphosyntactic category and lemma. The data indicates that morphological irregularities (irregular inflectional patterns) tended to be retained in forms of high frequency of occurrence. This conserving effect is exerted by high token frequency, while type frequency ensures rather the productivity of the paradigms, which is well evinced in classes such as the *a*-stems, *ō*-stems or *n*-stems.

As frequency is determined itself by extramorphological factors, i.e. semantics, the role of semantics in the process cannot be underestimated. This factor had primarily an indirect effect on the patterns of restructuring, being expressed through the frequency of morphosyntactic categories, lemmas and classes. An immediate impact of semantics on the restructuring patterns, in terms of an association between meaning and morphological shape, is rarely found, but appears incidentally.

As regards the role of morpho-phonological salience, a clear correlation was found between the level of innovation in the paradigms and the salience of inflectional markers. The presence of morphophonemic alternations in the paradigm, such as the *i*-mutated vowel, or the *r*-formative, rendered the paradigms more resistant to analogical pressures, and thus more likely to retain the inherited inflection. In contrast, the least salient zero marker tended to be assigned to the most frequent categories, such as the NOM./ACC. SG., which were affected by analogical developments only sporadically. All the other morphosyntactic categories which were low frequency and not encoded by a salient marker were much more susceptible to analogical levelling, following consequently the regular (majority or default) inflectional patterns. In other words, the irregularities, understood as relics of the original inflection, could be preserved in paradigm forms which were either very frequent or very salient (e.g. root nouns in NSGmc. and North Gmc.), or matched other, more frequent endings (e.g. the GEN./DAT. SG. in the OFris. *u*-stems, resembling the *n*-stems).

The picture emerging from the examination of the nominal systems in the early Northern West Germanic languages is one of dynamic and evolving systems. The inflection of nouns affiliated with the historical minor classes was in a state of constant fluctuation. In view of the dynamic, constantly changing nature of language, motivated either externally (e.g. by language contact) or by internal drift, such a state of flux is in no way surprising. The developments investigated in the present study, entailing analogical shifts between nominal paradigms, substantiate the claim that language is a complex adaptive system (Beckner et al. 2009). They reflect the *perpetual dynamics* of language – one of its major characteristics – which is an immediate consequence of the fact that a linguistic system (understood as a product of speakers' activity) constantly adapts and readapts to the new conditions. The changing phonological conditions, especially in the wake of the *Auslautgesetze*, invoked the reaction in the morphological system, which was manifested in the numerous analogical developments, resulting in a reconfiguration of the paradigms. The emergent patterns and their complexity are determined by a range of factors and interactions between them (*adaptation through competing factors*). In this dynamical model of language and grammar, frequency of occurrence plays an essential role, being, alongside cognitive and psychological ingredients (i.e. analogy), the major factor contributing to the emergence of linguistic structure (Diessel 2007: 124). The findings from the present investigation fully corroborate the importance of this factor in the reconfiguration of the nominal system.

Another theoretical aspect which has been addressed refers to the question of complexity vs. simplicity of morphological (nominal) systems. One is inclined to conceive of the changes that occurred at the early stage of development of the nominal systems in Northern West Germanic languages as an instantiation of a large-scale structural simplification (of the system), or reduction in the amount of structural complexity. This inclination is part of a broader tendency, recognised, among others, by Dahl (2004), who states: "There is a pervasive tendency in modern linguistics to think of language change primarily in terms of simplification, even if nobody would seriously claim that all changes make languages simpler." (Dahl 2004: 269). Admittedly, some aspects of the restructuring process can be viewed as a reflex of simplification. Such a generalisation can be made, for instance, with reference to the reduction of the declensional class diversity, which is well attested in all the examined languages. Another morphological field where the term simplification seems relevant is the reduction in the formal distinction of cases. As a result of the activity of analogical processes, leading to a gradual decay of the inflectional contrasts, the formal distinctions of cases tended to be gradually eliminated, although the loss of the four-case system took place in most Germanic languages only in the course or towards the end of the "middle" stage.

However, the other tendencies observed in the investigated material attest to a transformation of the nominal system rather than its *simplification*, which involved repatterning and redistribution of inflections across paradigms, guided by functional objectives. In fact, an opposite tendency towards *complication* (*complexification*), i.e. an increase in complexity in certain areas of nominal morphology, can be observed. It is manifested primarily in the marking of grammatical categories in Continental Germanic, where *i*-mutation and the *r*-formative (as well as the *n*-formative in the *n*-stems which are beyond the scope of this study) were morphologised, and developed as sole exponents of the category of number. The increase in the amount of complexity can also be a "side-effect" of regularisation, which involves a limitation in the number of markers to express a given grammatical category. Such a superficial regularity can lead in fact to an increase in the amount of complexity of a given system, since grammatical changes always leave some residual areas where irregularity emerges (cf. Dahl 2004: 289), as shown by the plurality patterns of present-day English.

The nominal inflection of the minor declensional classes was clearly one of the areas of considerable instability in Northern West Germanic languages. But can this instability be considered an outstanding attribute of the nominal system at this early stage? Inasmuch as language is a dynamic system, it is hardly possible to conceive of any stage of the morphological development as an equilibrium, where the system is balanced and no changes occur. Admittedly, in the wake of the large-scale phonological reductions, the Old Germanic stage may have been more extensively affected by the developments of analogical nature, which constituted a counterbalance to the asymmetries brought about by phonology. But evidently, the reorganisation of the nominal paradigms has been a continuous development, rather than one taking place only at discrete points in the history of Germanic. As indicated by the interdeclensional shifts occurring at the prehistoric stage, the process must have begun already in Proto-Germanic, but its intensity and scope clearly increased in the Old Germanic period.

A further related implication of this study is that the declensional systems and the nominal paradigms as presented in the standard grammars of the Old Northern West Germanic languages are an idealisation of the linguistic reality. The analysed material points to a wide inflectional variation present in the minor stem paradigms, testifying to their internal dynamics. This stays in contrast with the traditional treatments of nominal morphology, where paradigms are often depicted as static constructs (with some discussions of the paradigmatic variation relegated to footnotes). This aspect invokes the question of the taxonomic classification of the nominal paradigms, which although peripheral to the research question of this study, was given some attention in the respective chapters. It can be concluded that the most accurate classification of the declensional classes, as it turns out, requires an intermediate approach which mediates between the reality of the still existing inherited inflection as well as the reality of the novel patterns, introduced through extensive analogical reshufflings. Such an intermediate approach would also need to take into account the advancement of the restructuring process with respect to the individual morpho-syntactic categories, as the unfolding of the process was clearly dependent on this factor. A revision or at least a refinement of the existing taxonomic classification of the nominal paradigms turned out to be most requisite for Old English, where especially the Late period attests to a more advanced stage of remodelling of minor paradigms, especially of the *i*-stems or the *u*-stems.

Another facet of the restructuring process is related to the idiosyncrasies of the process across Northern West Germanic. Accordingly, the study examined also the factors responsible for the divergent development of the declensional systems in the investigated languages. The advancement of the restructuring process in the individual Germanic languages varied, as was demonstrated and discussed in

Chapter 7. It turns out that these divergent effects of the process across (Northern) West Germanic depended on the chronology, dating and scope of the operation of certain phonological processes. This refers in particular to the relative chronology of apocope and *i*-mutation. A clear boundary emerges between Old English and Old Frisian on the one hand, where the process of *i*-mutation operated and was phonologised earlier, and Old Saxon and Old Low Franconian on the other, which at this early stage did not attest to the operation of (secondary) *i*-mutation. In Old Saxon (just as in Old High German), *i*-mutation occurred later and had an allophonic status for a longer period. This late dating and restricted scope of *i*-mutation led to its morphologisation only at a later stage. Consequently, the activity of *i*-mutation in Low (and High) German extends far beyond the "middle" stage, in marked contrast to Old Dutch, Old Frisian or Old English, where the paradigmatic analogical levelling resulted in its nearly complete elimination from the nominal inflection (except for some relic forms). The analysed material demonstrated that the presence of the *i*-mutated vowels in the paradigms had an important impact on the dynamics of the changes, working in general towards the retention of the archaic patterns. Additionally, in Continental West Germanic (especially in Late OHG) the operation of *i*-mutation coincided with morphological simplification, whereas in Old English these two developments were chronologically distant, which can also have been a factor contributing to the divergent system dynamics across West Germanic. Another characteristic which is a consequence of the different pace of phonological developments in the paradigms, is the widespread expansion of the *a*-stem pattern in Old English, unparalleled in any other attested Germanic language. In Old English, the *a*-stem inflection, with its stable markers (GEN. SG. *-es* and the NOM./ACC. PL. *-as*), disseminated widely to the minor paradigms, resulting in a general gravitation of nouns towards this pattern. A parallel development was prevented in Old Low Franconian and later in Old Saxon, where the NOM./ACC. PL. of the *a*-stems were marked by the ending *-a*, which was much less salient and distinctive, and hence much less expansive.

As regards the chronology of the process, some refinement of the views expressed in the standard historical grammars can be made based on the findings of this investigation. The large-scale transformation of the nominal system has traditionally been placed in the "middle" periods (especially in the publications on the restructuring of the English nominal morphology). The findings of the present study indicate that the process can be dated earlier than hitherto claimed. Much as the transformation of the case and gender system, and the large-scale deflection can be dated to this late stage, the process of restructuring involving analogical interdeclensional shifts must be dated earlier. The beginning of the process can easily be dated to the prehistoric stage, while the Old Germanic period abounds in the evidence testifying to the fact that the nominal system was in a stage of gradual transformation.[360] The process becomes even more dynamic in the later stages of the individual West Germanic languages, where it interacts with the developments which involve the abovementioned transformation of the case and gender system, having immediate wide-ranging implications for the structure of Germanic. The subsequent changes in the nominal system in Northern West Germanic lead to the emergence of typological differences and consequently divergent typological profiles of the individual languages.

Given the inflectional shape of present-day Germanic languages, it must be concluded that the process of restructuring was an ongoing, continuous development, with a varying progression across (Northern) West Germanic. As a result of the reconfiguration of the nominal systems, entailing wide-ranging reductions in the case marking system, the original declensional classes hardly exist in present-day West Germanic, being confined to different plurality marking patterns, with a distinct number of plural allomorphs in the individual languages. The data demonstrate that the seeds of the divergent paths of the later morphological and consequently typological development of the Germanic languages are to be found in the earliest attested stages of the individual languages. This complies with the observation that "[i]n a long-term perspective, the history of the Germanic languages has always been one of diversification on different structural levels, but on the morphological and syntactic level the diversification process has clearly gained momentum since the Late Middle Ages." (Askedal 2006: 188). This increased momentum is most conspicuous in English, where additionally intense language contact influenced the pace of development considerably. The examined material indicates that the inflectional systems of the individual sister languages in their earliest attested stages witnessed the emergence of typological diversity as found in the modern Germanic languages.

A number of theoretical inferences and generalisations could be made based on the restructuring patterns found in the investigated data. Some of these generalisations have a general validity for the theory of morphological change. The most significant tendency identified in the examined material refers to the unfolding of the restructuring process and in particular the fact that the process operated along morphosyntactic categories and not along declensional classes or paradigms. Accordingly, individual morphosyntactic categories are affected by analogical pressure to various extents and at different paces. This observation can be generalised to the mechanism of the operation of morphological change, i.e. analogy, which is one

---

360. Cf. Late Old English attests to 41% of innovative forms in the minor paradigms (see Table 7.2), and the plural is predominantly innovative in the majority of the examined classes in at least three of the investigated languages (see Table 7.5)

of the most pervasive factors in language change. The analogical extension of forms occurs gradually, affecting individual items (paradigm cells) rather than entire patterns of inflection. Analogical shifts of nouns begin with "local" extensions of novel paradigm forms, and only in its most advanced stage do they involve the entire paradigm. The factor triggering the activity of analogical processes in paradigms is the formal similarity between paradigms, manifested in the spontaneous overlap of forms (i.e. forms considered neutral in this study). In the restructuring process this formal overlap had certain class effects, in that the declensional classes which were most exposed to analogical pressures were those in which the percentage of the overlapping forms was very high. The analysed data indicate as well that the process of morphological change turns out to be frequency-sensitive: analogy more easily affects items (forms) which are characterised by lower (token) frequency than high frequency forms, which tend to remain resistant.

The comparative nature of the study allows a refinement of the traditional account of the interdialectal relations within the West Germanic language continuum, and in particular the re-evaluation of the position of Old Saxon and (partly) Old Frisian. The traditional grouping of Old English, Old Frisian and Old Saxon under the label of North Sea Germanic is based predominantly on phonological criteria. However, as the findings of the present investigation indicate, the morphological profile of Old Saxon clearly stands out, showing many characteristics in common with Old Low Franconian. Consequently, if it is only the morphological criteria (i.e. nominal morphology) that are taken as the basis for the grouping of West Germanic languages, Old Saxon should rather be placed among its Inland Germanic sister languages than in the North Sea Germanic continuum. Fundamental contrasts include the morphological impact of *i*-mutation, its consequences for the shape of the paradigms of the *i*-stems, *u*-stems and root nouns, as well as the "high reflex" developments in the *u*-stems, leading to the presence of the marker -*i* in the DAT. SG. and NOM./ACC. PL., where both Old English and Old Frisian show -*a*. All of these features are shared with Old Low Franconian. The other incongruity involves the Old Frisian morphological profile, which likewise attests to certain patterns which show its inclination towards Continental Germanic. Firstly, Old Frisian turned out to be less consistent in the application of *i*-mutation in the declensional classes which are typically characterised by it in Old English, i.e. the root nouns and *nd*-stems, staying thus in line with the Continental languages. Secondly, the spread of the historical *i*-stem plural marker -*e* in Old Frisian, although limited, is clearly reminiscent of the Continental tendencies rather than those of Old English, where this pattern is not found at all.

A final remark must be made about the dialectal aspect of this study, which due to the size and the nature of the examined corpora, could be explored in a systematic way only for Old English. The data revealed certain local diatopic trends which emerged not only in the rich corpus of Old English, but also in the much more limited corpus of Old Frisian and even Old Low Franconian. However, the systematic dialectal investigation of the Old English data did not reveal striking discrepancies in the patterns of inflectional restructuring between dialects, and the observed tendencies were largely parallel. Where attested, the differences reflect mostly a different stage of the process rather than some idiosyncratic traits of a dialect. This evident lack of a dialectal diversification at the early stage finds its confirmation in the evidence from the present-day Germanic languages. For instance, the plurality patterns in Modern Scots do not differ fundamentally from those of Standard English. Likewise, the variation found in present-day Low German is predominantly the result of more recent developments, including the *schwa*-apocope and a different lexical distribution of plural allomorphs over various declensional classes. In turn, the striking differences between the Modern Frisian varieties involve in particular the deviating development of the *a*-stem inflection, and not so much the discrepancies in the patterns of restructuring of the minor stems. The dialectal contrast which can be considered a continuation of the original distinction is found in the *s*-stems in Old Frisian, which are entirely absent in West Frisian, while present in the East and some present-day Northern varieties.

The present book was intended as a contribution to the study of Germanic historical morphology, offering a more systematic and detailed picture of the numerous and complex analogical developments which affected the nominal systems of the Northern West Germanic languages. It certainly does not exhaust the topic, and some further research questions could be formulated. One of the aspects deserving attention could be the relevance of the mechanisms and factors which were found essential for the changes in the nominal inflection for the other inflectional systems, such as the verbal and adjectival systems. Furthermore, the present cross-linguistic perspective could be extended to the remaining early Germanic languages – Old Scandinavian, Old High German and Gothic – with a view to investigating the restructuring patterns in these languages. Finally, the present study demonstrates that a cross-linguistic, here cross-Germanic, perspective on linguistic phenomena constitutes a worthwhile and promising path of research, lending more general validity to the observations and insights gained from the investigation. Combined with a corpus-based, quantitative approach to the extant material, it can constitute an efficient modus operandi for the study of the historical stages of Germanic, rendering it more detailed, nuanced and comprehensive.

Appendix

The following list is an inventory of nouns affiliated with the minor classes in Northern West Germanic languages, which were included in the investigation. The list is divided into two subsets: (1) *Early transfers*, comprising nouns which transferred to other declensions prior to the first attestations of the individual languages, and retained thus no traces of the historical inflection, and (2) *Historical transfers*, comprising nouns which (potentially) vacillated between the inherited and innovative inflections in any of the investigated languages. The latter subgroup refers to the nouns which constituted the core of the quantitative analysis, and the distribution of archaic and innovative features in their paradigms is presented in the individual chapters. The list of *i*-stems in Old English is not exhaustive and contains only those nouns that were included in the sample (see Chapter 3, Section 3.5.2 for details). The *Early transfers* are based primarily on the Old English forms, as they are most robustly attested. Where possible, information from the other Northern West Germanic languages was added. In most cases, it is the Gothic evidence that provides information about the original class affiliation and that is why the Gothic forms were occasionally included. In cases where Gothic does not provide any direct evidence for the original declensional class, the affiliation of nouns is confirmed by recourse to extra-Germanic material. Not all the lemmas included in the Appendix were actually attested in the investigated material. Relevant additional information is provided in the footnotes. The asterisk indicates that the nouns were not attested in the corpus in the NOM. SG., but were found in other categories.

As the *i*-stems constituted a numerous class and in the prehistoric period (as well as in Continental Germanic) were productive, a systematic study of these early transfers of the *i*-stems stayed beyond the scope of the investigation (cf. Thöny 2013). Likewise, the transfers of the disyllabic *nd*-stems, which were relatively recent, and of the *r*-stems, which constituted a closed class, must be dated rather to the historical stage. Accordingly, the examples of the early transfers are presented only for the *u*-stems, root nouns and *s*-stems.

Early transfers

U-STEMS

a. MASCULINE STEMS

OE *ār*, OS *ēr* (*eri*) (*i*-stem) 'messenger' (Go. *airus*) (*a*-stem), OE *bend* 'band', OE *bōh*, OS *bōg* 'bough, arm' (Skt. *bāhú-*), OE *cwiþ(a)* 'womb' (Go. *qiþus*), OE *dēað*, OFris. *dād, dāth*, OS *dōð*, OLF *dōt* 'death' (Go. *dauþus*), OE *feorh*, OFris. *ferch* (*fereh*) (n.), OS *ferh* (*ferah*) 'life, soul' (Go. *faírhwus*) (also n.), OE *flōd* (also n.), OS *flōd*, OLF *fluot* 'flood, wave'[361]

---

361. The noun transferred to the *a*-stems; in Old Saxon its inflection is ambiguous: it shows both the *a*-stem and *i*-stem features. The noun testifies to considerable gender variation across West Germanic, vacillating between masculine and neuter in Old English, showing neuter gender in Old Frisian, masculine in Old Low Franconian, and three genders in Old Saxon.

(Go. *flōdus*), OE *fri(o)þ* 'peace' (also n.), OE *-gār* (*ǣtgar*), OFris. *etkēr*, OS *gēr* 'spear'[362], OE, OFris. *grund*, OS *grund* (*i*-stem), OLF *grunt* 'ground, foundation' (Go. **grundus, grunduwaddjus*), OE *hād*, OS *hēd* 'person' (compounds in -*hēd: frevelhēd, cristinhēd jug-uthhēd, lēfhēd, magadhēd, wilthēd, wārhēd*), OE *hungor*, OFris., OLF *hunger*, OS *hungar* 'hunger' (Go. *hūhrus*)[363], OE *liþ* 'limb' (Go. *liþus*) (also n.), OE, OFris. *lust* 'desire, pleasure' (Go. *lustus*)[364], OE *sēaþ*, OFris. *sāth* 'stream', OE *scield* (*sceld*), OFris. *skeld*, OS *scild, skilt* 'shield' (*i*-stem) (Go. *skildus*), OE *ðorn*, OFris. (*hage*)*dorn*, OS *thorn* (*a*-stem, *i*-stem), OLF *thorn* 'thorn' (*haginthorn*) (Go. *þaúrnus*), OE *þurst*, OS *thurst*, OLF *thurst* 'thirst' (*i*-stems) (OIr. *tart*), OE *wāg*, OFris. *wāch* 'wall' (also f.) (Go. *-waddjus*), OS *werd* (*a*-stem), OFris. *hūs-werda* 'landlord' (Go. *waírdus*), OE *weþer*, OFris. *wethar*, OS *wethar*, OLF *uuither* 'ram, wether' (Go. *wiþrus*)

b. FEMININE STEMS

OS *armōdi* 'poverty' (*ja*-stem, n.), OS *ēnōdi* 'desert' (*ja*-stem, n.), OE *cyn(n), cin*, OFris. *kin(-)*, OS *kin* (*kinni*) 'chin' (*i*-stem or *ja*-stem, n.)[365] (Go. *kinnus*), OE *fri(o)þu* 'peace' (Go. *friþus*), OE *leoþu* (*lioþu*) 'limb' (Go. *liþus*), OE *lust* (*lest*) 'desire' (m. f.), OE *sceadu*, OS *skadu* (*scado*) (*wa*-stem, m.)[366], OLF *skado* (*scada*) 'shadow'[367] (Go. *skadus*)[368]

c. NEUTER STEMS

OE *cwidu* 'cud, quid' (Skt. *játu*), OE *fala* 'plank' (Lat. 'tabula')[369], OE *feoh* 'cattle, money, property' (Go. *faíhu*)

d. DEVERBAL NOMINAL FORMATIONS in -*(n)oð*, -*(n)að* (Go. -*ōdus*), e.g. OE *drugað* 'dryness' (f.), OE *faroð* 'stream' (m. n.), OE *fiskoð* 'fishing' (m.), OE *folgað* 'pursuit, retinue' (m.), OE *hæftnoð* 'confinement' (m.), OE *hleonað* 'shelter' (m.), OE *huntoð* 'hunting' (m.), OE *innoð* 'inside, womb' (m. f.), OE *langoð* 'longing' (m.), etc.

---

362. The form *ǣtgaru* is considered to be an *u*-stem plural form by Brunner (1965). Hogg & Fulk (2011: 35), following Dahl (1938), interpret it as a NOM. SG., i.e. as a regular phonological continuation of the PGmc. *jō*-stem **atgairijō*. Given that the form is attested only in glossaries, its interpretation is ambiguous.

363. Cf. OHG DAT. SG. (INSTR. SG.) *hungiru* (< *hungiriu*), with traces of the *u*-stem inflection (in the heavy-syllable stems) (Braune/Reiffenstein 2004: 205).

364. The etymology of OE *lust* is not entirely transparent and its identity as an original *u*-stem can be questioned (Bammesberger 1990: 157–158; cf. van Helten 1890: 481, 484; Kroonen 2013, s.v. *lust*).

365. Cf. Gallée (1993) where it is classified among the *u*-stems.

366. Gallée (1993) includes *skado* 'shadow' in the inventory of the OS *u*-stems. On account of the evidence from the sister languages, it was classified as a *wa*-stem and thus not included in the present investigation.

367. The inflection of this noun in OLF is ambiguous. Van Helten (1891: 481–482) suggests a possible reflex of the original *u*-stem in the DAT. SG. *scado*, alongside the more probable (from a comparative Germanic perspective) *wa*-stem origin.

368. The Go. *skadus* is considered to be an original *wa*-stem, which at some point followed the paradigm of the *u*-stems (e.g. DAT. SG. *skadau*) (Bammesberger 1990: 85; cf. Hogg & Fulk 2011: 36).

369. The etymology of this noun and its affiliation with the *u*-stems is not entirely clear. A PGmc. root **fahan-* (m.) was postulated by Kroonen (2013, s.v. **falan-*(m.)), who assumes also a connection to a Slavic form.

ROOT NOUNS

OLF *al(rūda)* '(destruction of a) temple', OE *duru*, OFris. *dore* 'door', OE *nosu*, OFris. *nose* 'nose', OE *spyrd* 'racetrack' (Go. *spaúrds)

S-STEMS

light-syllable:
OE *bere* 'barley' (Go. *baris, barizeins*), OE *ege* 'terror' (Go. *agis*), OE *hete*, OS *heti* 'hatred' (Go. *hatis*), OE *mene* 'necklace', OE *ofdele* (*ofdæle*) 'descent', OE *oferslege* 'lintel', OE *orlege* 'war', OS *halsmeni*, OE *sele*, OS *seli* 'hall', OE *sife* 'sieve', OE *sige*, OS *sigi* 'victory' (Go. *sigis*), OE *spere*, OFris. *spiri, spere* 'spear'

heavy-syllable:
OE *flǣsc* 'flesh', OE *flīes* (*flēos*) 'fleece', OE *gǣst* 'spirit, OE *geban(n)* 'summons', OE *gedyre* 'door-post' (Go. *daúr*), OE *gefōg* 'joint', OE *geheald* (*gehield*) 'keeping, guard', OE *gehlȳd* 'noise', *gehnāst* 'conflict, clash', *geswinc* 'toil, effort', *gewēd* 'rage, madness', OE *gewealc* 'rolling', OE *gehield* 'guard', OE *hǣl* 'health', OE *hilt* (*helt*) 'handle', OE *hlǣw* 'mound', OE *hrǣw* 'body', OE *lǣn* 'loan, grant', *sweng* 'blow'

Historical transfers

Old English

I-STEMS (selection)

    a. MASCULINE STEMS
        light-syllable: *bere* 'barley', *bite* 'bite', *byre*[370] 'youth, son', *gryre* 'terror', *hete* 'hate', *hyse* 'youth', *mere* 'lake', *mete* 'food', *wine* 'friend', *wlite* 'countenance'
        heavy-syllable: *dæl* 'part'
    b. FEMININE STEMS (heavy-syllable)
        brȳde 'bride', *cwēn* 'woman', *dǣd* 'deed', *dryht* 'army', *hȳf* 'hive', *tīd* 'time'
    c. NEUTER STEMS (light-syllable)
        clyne 'mass, lump', *gdyre* 'door post', *ofdæle* 'downward slope'

U-STEMS

    a. MASCULINE STEMS
        light-syllable: *bregu* (*breogo*) 'prince', *heoru* 'sword', *lagu* 'lake', *magu* 'youth, boy'[371], *me(o)du* 'mead' (also neut.), *sidu* 'custom', *spitu* 'spit'[372], *sunu* 'son', *wudu, wi(o)du*

---

370. Bammesberger (1990: 132) points to at least three other meanings of OE *byre* (Go. *baúr* 'son'), namely (a) 'time, occasion', (b) 'hill, mound', (c) 'gale', and attributes this multiplicity of meanings to the polysemic development of the PGmc. *bur-i*.

371. The frequently attested plural forms *magas* and *mæcgas* (Bosworth & Toller 1898, s.v. *mæcg*, *mecg* 'man', NOM. SG.) are closely related, the latter being affiliated with the *ja*-stems. The forms *magas*, in contrast to *mæcgas*, were included in the quantitative analysis.

372. Cf. Bosworth & Toller (1898) and Clark Hall & Merritt (1960) where the noun is classified as feminine in contrast to Campbell (1977) and Hogg & Fulk (2011). The attested inflections are ambiguous.

'wood'; heavy-syllable: *æppel* 'apple', *eard* 'country', *færeld* 'journey'[373], *feld* 'field', *ford* 'ford', *hearg* 'shrine', *sumor* 'summer'[374], *weald* (Ang. *wald*) (*ut-*, *wudu-*) 'wood, forest', *winter* 'winter'

   b. FEMININE STEMS

      cweorn 'hand-mill', *duru* 'door', *flōr* 'floor' (f. m.), *hond* 'hand', *nosu* 'nose'

   c. NEUTER STEMS

      feolu, fe(o)la 'much'

ROOT NOUNS

   a. MASCULINE STEMS

      ealh 'residence'[375], *fōt* 'foot', *man(n)* 'man', *ōs* 'immortal being'[376], *tōþ* 'tooth'

   b. FEMININE STEMS

      light-syllable: *hnitu* 'nit', *hnutu* 'nut', *studu* (*stuðu*) 'pillar'

      heavy-syllable: *āc* 'oak'[377], *bōc* 'book', *brōc* 'trousers', *burg* 'borough', *cū* 'cow', *dung 'prison'[378], *ēa* 'river'[379], *furh* 'furrow, ditch', *furh* 'fir', *gāt* 'goat', *gōs* 'goose', *grūt* 'groats'[380], *lūs* 'louse'[381], *meolc* 'milk', *mūs* 'mouse', *neaht* (*niht*) 'night', *sulh* 'plough', *turf* 'turf', *þrūh* 'trough', *wlōh* 'fringe'

---

373. The only cognate form is ON *farald* 'travelling', based on the suffix -*alda* (Krahe & Meid 1967: 188).

374. The noun is commonly included in the *u*-stem inventory in Germanic languages, but it is not an original *u*-stem. It followed the inflection of the semantically related masc. *u*-stem *winter*. According to Kroonen (2013), the PGmc. form was a neuter **sumara-*. The West Germanic languages attest to the masculine gender of this nouns, and Old Norse to the neuter gender (ON *sumar*) (Kroonen 2013, s.v. **sumara-*).

375. The available evidence does not unambiguously testify to its origin in the root nouns, but rather indicates that the noun followed the *a*-stem inflection. According to Griepentrog (1995: 41), if the noun were a continuation of a root noun, it should show feminine rather than masculine inflection.

376. The noun is attested only in two categories in the Old English material: the NOM. SG. *ōs*, denoting a rune name, and the GEN. PL. *ēsa*.

377. The form *æc*, when denoting the runic letter, is classified as a masc. *a*-stem (PL. *æcas: Acas twegen* (Riddles 42)), and it was not included in the quantitative analysis. For details of the attestations of *æc* in the Old English material, see Moffat (1987).

378. The noun is attested only once as the *i*-mutated DAT. SG. *ding: ða com hæleða þreat to ðære dimman ding* 'the troop of heroes came to the dark dungeon' (And).

379. The interpretation of the forms belonging to this lemma posed some difficulties. The singular is almost consistently attested as *ēa*, allowing hardly any conclusive statements about inflectional changes, and the plural forms are likewise largely ambiguous (except when influenced by the *n*-stem or masculine *a*-stem inflection); accordingly, the noun was not included in the calculation.

380. The form is attested alongside the fem. *n*-stem *grytte* 'grit', PL. *grytta(n)*.

381. The early departure from the original paradigm is evinced in Old Saxon and Old High German, where the noun follows the pattern of the feminine *i*-stems (MLG *lūs*, OHG *lûs*, PL. *liusi*).

c.   NEUTER STEMS

bū 'dwelling', *scrūd* 'garment, clothing'

R-STEMS

brōþor (-er, -ur) 'brother', *gebrōþor* (PL.) 'siblings', *dohtor* 'daughter', *fæder* 'father', *mōdor* 'mother', *sweostor* 'sister', *gesweostor* (PL.) 'siblings'

S-STEMS

a.   *cealf (cælf)* 'calf', *cild* 'child', *dōēg (dōgor)* 'day', *æg* 'egg', *hrēð (hrōþor)* 'glory', *lomb* 'lamb'

b.   *alor (alr)* 'alder-tree', *ægor/ēgur* 'sea', *ēar (eher, æhher)* 'ear of grain', *gycer* 'acre'[382], *halor* 'salvation', *hōcor* 'mockery', *hrīðer, hrȳðer* 'horned cattle', (m.) *nicor* 'water-monster'[383], *sigor (cf. sige)* 'victory'[384], *salor (cf. sele)* 'hall', *wildor* 'wild animal'

ND-STEMS

æfterfylgend 'successor', *ælædend* 'legislator', *ælærend* 'teacher of law', *ælewealdend* 'all-ruler, almighty', *āgend* 'owner', *agyltend* 'sinner', *ālȳsend* 'liberator', *anbūend* 'settler', *anfond* 'supporter', *āstīgend* 'rider', *bædend* 'inciter', *bannend* 'summoner', *bebēodend* 'master', *bēcnend (bīcn(ig) end)* 'one who indicates', *begetend* 'one who gets', *begimend* 'ruler', *beswīcend* 'deceiver', *bētend* 'restorer', *bīsmeriend* 'mocker', *bodiend* 'preacher', *borgiend* 'lender', *borhhend (borhgiend)* 'usurer', *būend (fold-)*'builder', *būgend* 'dweller', *bycniend* 'one who indicates', *byrgend* 'grave-digger', *cost(n)igend* 'tempter', *(-)dēmend* 'judge', *dihtend* 'leader', *eardiend* 'dweller', *edgyldend* 'remunerator', *edleaniend* 'one who rewards', *edniwigend* 'restorer', *edstaþeligend* 'restorer', *efenlæcend* 'imitator', *eorðbend* 'dweller', *fēond* 'enemy' *(ealdfēond)*, *fordemend* 'accuser', *forescēawigend* 'spectator', *foreseond* 'provider', *foresingend* 'precentor', *foresprecend* 'defender', *(fore)stihtend* 'ruler', *forhicgend* 'despiser', *forhogiend* 'despiser', *foresingend* 'precentor', *forlicgend* 'fornicator', *forsawend* 'one who despises', *forscrencend* 'supplanter', *forspennend* 'procurer', *forspillend* 'destroyer', *forestæppend* 'antecessor', *forswelgend* 'devourer', *frēfrend* 'comforter', *frēond* 'friend' *fultum(i)end* 'helper', *galdergalend* 'magician', *geedleanend* 'rewarder', *geedstaþeliend* 'one who repairs', *gefiend* 'enemy', *gēocend* 'saviour', *gescildend* 'protector', *gōddōnd/gōddēnd* 'benefactor', *gōdfremmend* 'doer of good', *grīpend* 'seizer', *gyltend* 'sinner, debtor', *gymend* 'governor', *hælend* 'saviour', *hālsi(g)end* 'soothsayer', *healdend* 'guardian', *helpend* 'helper', *hergiend* 'plunderer', *hettend* 'enemy' *(eald-)*, *hliniend/hlingend* 'one who reclines', *hlystend* 'listener', *lænend* 'lender',

---

382. The noun is singly attested in the OE material (*Leiden Glossary*: iugeres *gycer*), presumably in the singular (cf. Sauer 1917). Bammesberger (1965: 418), following Noreen's (1894) and Streitberg's (1920) interpretation of the related Go. *jukuzi* (f.), rejects the *s*-stem origin and interprets the OE form as an original active perfect participle. A consequence of such an interpretation is the reassignment of gender to feminine.

383. The OHG *nichus (nihhus)* 'crocodile' seems problematic since it constitutes counterevidence to the origin of the OE *nicor* as an *s*-stem (cf. ON *nykr*). See Classen (1915: 85–6) for an alternative explanation of the OE *nicor*.

384. The OE *sigor* is attested as a masc. noun, which can be attributed to the influence of the related masculine *i*-stem *sige* 'victory'.

læstend 'performer', *læwend* 'traitor', *līþend* (*ea*-)'sailor', *lufiend* 'lover', *metend* 'measurer', *neah-būend* 'neighbour', *nerg(i)end* 'saviour', *onfōnd* 'supporter', *ongalend/āgalend* 'enchanter', *on-hyrg(i)end* 'emulator', *rǣdend* 'ruler', *reccend* 'ruler', *rīdend* 'horseman', *rihtend* 'ruler', *rōwend/rōrend* 'sailor', *scēawigend* 'spectator', *sceotend* 'warrior', *sc(i)eppend* 'creator', *sceððend* 'adversary', *scyldend* 'protector', *secgend* 'narrator', *semend* 'umpire', *sellend* 'giver', *seðend* 'affirmer', *settend* 'ordainer', *speli(g)end* 'representative', *spyri(g)end* 'inquirer', *stihtend* 'disposer', *swefni(g)end* 'dreamer', *swelgend* 'drunkard', *swelgend* (f.) 'whirlpool', *syllend* 'giver', *tǣlend* 'reprover', *tēond* 'accuser', *þeccend* 'protector', *þreagend* 'one who reproves', *timbr(i)end* 'builder', *tyd(d)riend* 'propagator', *wealdend (waldend)* (*eall*-) 'ruler', *wemmend* 'fornicator', *weriend* 'grudger', *weriend (werigend)* 'defender', *wið(er)feohtend* 'adversary', *wīgend* 'warrior', *winnend* 'fighter', *wīssi(g)end* 'governor', *wrecend* 'avenger', *wrēhtend* 'instigator'

DENTAL STEMS

ealu 'ale' (n.), *hæle* 'hero (m.), *mæg(e)ð* 'maiden' (f.), *mōnað* 'month' (m.)

Old Frisian

I-STEMS

    a.   MASCULINE
        light-syllable:
        bite 'bite', *breke/bretse* 'breach', punishment', *hei* 'thought', *hrene* 'smell', *keme* 'arrival', *kere* 'choice' (also f.), *mete* 'food', *rene* 'flow', *sige* 'victory', *skete* 'shot', *slei-* 'blow, hit'[385], (*aft*-, *thing*-) *slit(e)* 'disruption', *steke* 'stitch', *stepe* 'step', *wine* 'friend', *wlite* 'face'

        heavy-syllable:
        abēl 'scar', *benk/bank* 'bench'(also f., n.), *breid* (*-breid*) 'pulling', *-breng* (*boldbreng* 'dowry'), *dēl* 'part' (also n.), *fecht (facht)* 'fruit', *fang* 'grasp', (-)*fell* 'hide', *iest* 'guest'[386], (*biār*)*hlem* 'hit', (*bek*)*hlēp* 'leap', *kerf* 'cut', *liude* 'folk', *rend* 'tearing, injury', *skeft* 'spear'[387], *slēk* (*-slēk*) 'hit', (*spēdel*)*spreng* 'flow', *stēt* 'blow', *sweng* 'swing', *tins* 'tax, profit', *wend* 'return', *werp* (*-werp*) 'throw'[388]

    b.   FEMININE
        light-syllable:
        stede 'place', (*lith*)*wei (lithwege)* 'contortion' (m.)

---

385. Attested only in compounds.

386. Not attested in the examined material.

387. Not attested in the examined material.

388. Another noun which could be added to the masculine *i*-stems is *walubera* (*-bora*) (R_1), *walebera* (H_2, E_1, F), which is attested only as the first element of compounds, and therefore it was not included in the analysis. Beyond the scope of the investigation is also the form *haet* (E_3) (OE *hete*, Go. *hatis*), in which the absence of *i*-mutation may point to its *u*-stem origin (van Helten 1890: 148).

heavy-syllable:

acht 'jury', *arn* 'harvest'[389], *bend* 'band' (also m.), *berde* 'birth', *breid* 'bride', *dēd(e)* 'deed', *drecht (twī- ēn-)* 'crowd', *ē(n)st* 'favour'[390], *evēst* 'disfavour, jealousy', *ferd* 'journey', *fēst* 'fist', *flecht* 'escape' (*of-, on-, tō-*), *frist* 'deadline'[391], *frucht* 'fruit', *glēde* 'glow', *grēde* 'meadow', *greft* 'ditch', *hēd* 'skin', *heft* 'imprisonment', *hēte* 'heat', *jecht* 'gout', *jecht* 'confession'[392], *kenst(e)* 'knowledge', *kest* 'choice, statute', *kleft* 'court district', *kost* 'cost', *kreft* 'power', *list* 'knowledge', *mecht/macht* 'power', *nēd* 'need', *nifte* 'niece, ondwerd 'presence', *plicht* 'plight, obligation', *secht* 'disease', *sēle* 'pillar', *sēkene* 'fine, seeking', *siune* 'sight', *skelde* 'guilt', *skrift(e)* 'script' (m. n.), *tīd* 'time', *(nēd)threft* 'need'[393], *unhlest* 'inquietness'[394], *(ūr-)wald* 'power', *warld* 'world', *werd* 'fate', *werne* 'pledge', *wicht* 'weight', *wīk* 'quarter', *(hond-, fōt-)wirst* 'wrist'

c. NEUTER
    light-syllable: *spere* 'spear'; heavy-syllable: *(on-)tiūch* 'testimony'

U-STEMS

a. MASCULINE
    light-syllable: *frethe (fretho)* 'peace', *mage (mach)* 'boy, child', *mede* 'mead', *side* 'custom', *sunu* 'son', *widu-*[395]

    heavy-syllable: *appel* 'apple'[396], *erd* 'country, soil', *feld* 'field' (also n.), *ford(a)* 'ford' (f.?)[397], *ongest* 'fear', *sumer* 'summer', *wald* 'forest', *winter* 'winter'

b. FEMININE
    dure 'door', *flēr/flōr* 'floor'[398], *hond* 'hand', *nose* 'nose', *quern* 'mill'

c. NEUTER
    fiā 'cattle, property', *felo (fele, fel)* 'a lot, many', *lith* 'member'

---

389. Not attested in the examined material.

390. Not attested in the examined material.

391. The noun is characterised by shifting gender; it is not attested in the analysed material.

392. Not attested in the examined material (in either meaning).

393. Not attested in the examined material.

394. Unclear gender (van Helten 1890: 145).

395. Attested only as the first element of the compounds *widubill* 'hatchet', *widuhoppa* 'hoopoe'.

396. Not attested in the analysed corpus; appears only in the post-classical material (U-LwB).

397. Although the noun is attested primarily in place names, it was included in the counting as it appears in the running text and the context allowed us to identify the grammatical forms relatively easily.

398. Attested only in post-classical Old Frisian.

ROOT NOUNS

    a.   MASCULINE

        (hals)dōc 'cloth'[399] (n.), *fōt* 'foot', *mon* 'man', *tōth* 'tooth', *turf* 'turf' (cf. OE fem. *turf*), *tusk* 'tusk'[400]

    b.   FEMININE

        bōc 'book', *brēc* 'breech'[401], *burch* 'town', *ēk* 'oak'[402], *furch* 'furrow, ditch', *kū* 'cow', **melok* 'milk', *nacht* 'night'

    c.   NEUTER

        bē 'possession, property'[403], *skrēd* 'cut'

R-STEMS

brōther 'brother', *dochter* 'daughter', *feder* 'father', *aldafeder* 'grandfather', *stiapfeder*, *mōder* 'mother', *stiapmōder, suster (swester)* 'sister', *sinsuster*

S-STEMS

ār 'ear of corn', *hrīther* 'rind', *kind* 'child', *klāth (klēth)* 'a piece of clothing'

ND-STEMS

berand 'guarantor', *fīand* 'enemy', *friōnd* 'friend', *werand* 'guardian', *wīgand* 'warrior'

DENTAL STEMS

*megith 'maid'[404] (f.), *mōnath* 'month' (m.)

---

399. Its affiliation with the root nouns is confirmed by the presence of the *i*-mutated NOM./ACC. SG. forms *dēk*, which emerged under the influence of the *i*-mutated GEN. and DAT. SG., and NOM./ACC. PL. (< **dōk-iz*) (van Helten 1890: 157).

400. The noun was included in the analysis on account of the *i*-mutated form of the NOM. PL. *tesch*, attested in manuscript E$_2$.

401. The noun is attested only in the plural form, and is an instance of *pluralia tantum*, or arguably a singular form with an unetymological root vowel (van Helten 1890: 158). It is not found in classical Old Frisian.

402. The noun transferred to the fem. *i*-stems (van Helten 1890: 158). Since it is attested as the DAT. SG. *êke* in the corpus (*mit eerda ende mit <u>eke</u>* 'with soil and with oak' (Jus); *is under <u>eke</u> and under eerthe bislaghen* 'is under oak and under soil buried' (E$_1$)), its assignment to any class is difficult.

403. The gender of this noun is unclear; the evidence of some other Germanic languages points to its neuter origin (OE *bū* n., ON *bū* n., but cf. OHG *bū* m.). The noun was not attested in the analysed sample.

404. The noun was attested only in the plural form *megitha, -etha (megitha* (R$_1$ 23,32)).

Old Saxon

I-STEMS

    a. MASCULINE STEMS[405]

light-syllable: *biti* 'bite' (*muthbite*), *bruki* 'breach', *cumi* 'coming, approach', *flugi* 'flight', *fluti* 'flow', *gruri* 'terror', *hardburi* 'authority', *heti* 'hatred', *hugi* 'mind' (*nîthhugi* 'hate' *morthhugi* 'thought of murder', *strîdhugi* 'fighting spirit'), *meri* 'sea', *meti* 'food', *missiburi* 'misfortune', *quidi* 'speech' (*gelpquidi* 'mockery', *firinquidi* 'wicked speech', *harmquidi* 'abuse', *wordquidi* 'speech'), *seli* 'hall, room' (*gastseli* 'hall, hostel', *hornseli* 'gabled house', *wînseli*, (*uuînseli*) 'tavern'), **segi* 'victory'[406], *selfkuri* 'discretion', *slegi, ôrslegi* 'blow, beat', *stiki* 'stitch', *thili* 'orator, narrator', *wini* 'friend', *wliti* 'countenance, beauty'
heavy-syllable:
balg 'husk', *bendi/band* 'band', *hēmbrung* 'return', *bisprāki* 'calumny', *eldi* 'people', *first* 'roof ridge', *fruht* 'fruit', *gast* 'guest', *giwunst* 'profit', *liudi* 'people', *pāl* 'peg', *rōk* 'smoke', *slēk* 'killing', *strīd* 'quarrel', *stunk* 'stink', *tharm* 'guts', *tīns* 'tax', *trahan* 'tear', *wīk* 'village', *wurm* 'worm'

    b. FEMININE STEMS

light-syllable: *ewi* 'ewe', *stedi* 'place'
heavy-syllable: *ābulht* 'rage', *abunst* 'envy', *ambusn* 'order', *anst* 'grace', *arbēd* 'labour', *bank* 'bench', *brūd* 'bride', *brust* 'breast', **burd* (*ēthiligiburd, athaligiburd* 'noble birth', *kuniburd* 'descent', *mundburd* 'protection, *rādburd* 'reign'), *giburd* 'birth', *dād* 'deed', **drān* 'drone' (NOM.PL.), *ēht* 'property', (-)*fard* 'journey', *farnumft* 'understanding', *fust* 'fist', *bigraft* 'grave', *hanocrād* 'cockcrowing', (*ge)hugd* 'mind', *hlust* 'hearing, ear', *hūd* 'hide', *hurth* 'hurdle', *iuguth* 'youth', *craft* 'might', *cunst* 'wisdom', *cust* 'choice, preference'[407], *list* 'cleverness', *brūdlōht* 'wedding celebration', *māht* 'might', *gimāht* 'genitalia', *ginist* 'redemption', *nōd* 'need', *quān* 'noblewoman', *gisiht* 'sight', (*gi)siun* 'sight', *giscaft* 'destination', *giscrift* 'scripture', *gispanst* 'enticement', *sculd* 'guilt' (*hofsculd* 'tribute', *kōg-skuld* 'poldertribute', *landskuld* 'profit, rent'), *slaht* 'ethnic group', *snarh* 'string', *spōd* 'success', (-)*suht* 'illness' (*balusuht* 'bad disease', *fætsuht* 'gout', *gelasuht* 'jaundice', *kelasuht* 'throat inflammation'), *sūl* 'pillar', *tīd* 'time' (*gitīd* 'time of prayer', *hōhgitīd* 'high feast', *morgantīd* 'morning', *untīd* 'wrong time'), *githāht* 'thought', *thionost* 'service'[408], *githuld* 'patience', *thrum* 'force', *thurft* 'need' (*nōdthurft*), (-)*tuht* 'discipline' (*āthom-tu-h-t**), *unkust* 'craft', *urslaht* 'rush', *ūst* 'tempest', *giwald* 'power', *werold* 'world', *wurd* 'fate', (-)*wurht* 'sin', (-)*wurt* 'root', *wurth* 'mound'

---

405. The nouns in -*scepi* were not included in the analysis. They are essentially classified as masculine, although a few of them were neuter (Gallée 1993: 209). Their gender tended to correspond to the gender of the first element of the compound, e.g. *folcscepi* (n.), *landscepi* (n.), cf. *folc* (n.), *land* (n.) vs. *ambahtscepi* (m.), *friundscepi* (m.), cf. *ambaht* (m.), *friund* (m.) (Schwink 2004: 54).

406. Attested only in the compound *sigi-drohtin* 'God'.

407. Cf. Holthausen (1921: 242) where the form is classified as a *u*-stem.

408. Classified as a neut. *a*-stem in Köbler (2014a).

c.   NEUTER STEMS

aldarlagu 'age', *dēl* 'part', *halsmeni* 'necklace'[409], *sif* 'sieve', *urlagi* 'war', *wiht* 'thing, creature' (m. 'ghost') [410]

U-STEMS

a.   MASCULINE STEMS

light-syllable: *friðu (freðu)* 'peace', *heru(-)* 'sword'[411], *lagu* 'lake', *lith* 'limb', *magu* 'son', *medo* 'mead'[412], *sidu* 'custom' (*aldsidu, landsido*), *sunu* 'son', *widu-* 'wood'[413]
heavy-syllable: *appul(-)* 'apple'[414], *ard* 'soil', *sumar* 'summer', *wald* 'forest', *sinwald (sinweldi)* 'woodland'[415], *wintar* 'winter'

b.   FEMININE STEMS

duru 'door', *hand* 'hand', *lust* 'lust'[416], *nase(-)* 'nose', *quirn* 'mill'[417]

c.   NEUTER STEMS

fehu (fihu) 'cattle, property', *feld* 'field', *filo, filu* 'much'

---

409. According to Dal (1934: 246), the noun is not an *i*-stem, but an early transfer from the *ja*-stems (< **manja-*) (cf. Boutkan 1996: 210).

410. The nouns **wrisi* 'giant' and **muni* 'love' were excluded from the quantitative analysis as they appear only in compounds in the function of adjectives: *wrisi-lik* and *muni-lik* (Holthausen 1921: 101). The noun *halsmeni*, declining as masculine in Old English, is neuter in Old Saxon.

411. The noun *heru* 'sword' is attested only in compound formations as the first element, e.g. *herubendi* 'fetters', *herugrim* 'fierce' (Holthausen 1921: 105).

412. The form is attested in the Latin context, primarily with Latin inflections. The forms of the NOM. SG., attested twice in glosses (UrbWerdC and UrbWerdE), can be interpreted as Old Saxon (Tiefenbach 2010, s.v. *medo*).

413. It is used only as the first element in compounds, e.g. in *widohoppa, widomānōth, widowinda*, where the original *u*-stem element is retained as *-o*; cf. Holthausen (1921: 105) who views it as a neuter stem. The Germanic cognates testify to its masculine gender: OE masculine *wudu*, ON *viþr*, OHG *witu* (Prokosch 1939: 248).

414. The noun is attested only in compounds (e.g. *appeldranc*); as a simplex it appears in glosses, or in fragments of glossaries which are classified as Old High German rather than Old Saxon (*afful-ephili*, GlSpet; Tiefenbach 2010).

415. The form is classified as a *ja*-stem in Tiefenbach (2010, s.v. *sinweldi* 'vast wilderness').

416. The related *farlust* and possibly *gilust* are *ti*-stem derivations and are classified as fem. *i*-stems (Kroonen, s.v. **lusti-*). The paradigm of *lust* shows traces of the original inflection.

417. The form *quernon* (RegFrek, DAT. PL.) is believed to belong to a parallel feminine *ō*-stem *querna* (Tiefenbach 2010: 227; cf. Gallée 1993: 212). It was included in the present study on account of the evidence form the sister languages.

ROOT NOUNS

a. MASCULINE STEMS

alah 'temple', *fōt* 'foot', *man(n)* 'man', *-man*, *tand* 'tooth' (*tan-stuthlia* 'pectine dentium'), *turf* 'turf'[418]

b. FEMININE STEMS

acus 'ax', *aha* 'river', *bōk* 'book', *brōg* (*brōc*) (*brōk*) 'breech'[419], *burg* 'city', *ēc* 'oak'[420], *ērwit* 'pea', *gās/gōs* 'goose'[421], *gēt* 'goat', *idis* 'woman', *kō* 'cow', *merikō* 'sea-cow', *middilgard* 'earth', *miluk* 'milk'[422], *mūs* 'mouse', *naht* 'night'[423], *thrūh* 'fetter', *wlōh* 'piece of wool'[424,425]

---

418. The attestation to this noun points to its masculine rather than feminine gender (DAT. SG. *turua*); cf. the evidence from Old Frisian, where the noun is also formally classified as masculine.

419. The phonological shape of one of the two attested forms (*broah*) is to be attributed to the impact of Alemannic and the presence of a parallel text in the St. Gall manuscript (Griepentrog 1995: 82).

420. The exact class affiliation of *ēc* 'oak' is difficult to establish as it is attested only in the NOM. SG. in Vergil glosses. The evidence of Middle Low German implies that the noun may have belonged to the ō-stems (Griepentrog 1995: 22).

421. The noun is attested twice in the NOM. SG.: in the runic alphabet as *gâs* and as *gôs* in Glossarium Werthinense (Griepentrog 1995: 215). The later Low German evidence suggests that it eventually followed the *i*-stem pattern (cf. OHG *gensi*). The form is not found in Tiefenbach (2010), cf. Holthausen (1967), s.v. *gās* and *gōs*.

422. On account of its semantics, the formally plural form of *meloc* 'milk', *melokon* < *melukum*, attested in R_1 (I, 44–5), is believed to represent a singular meaning (*thet lond thet flāt fon melokon and fon hunige...*) (Boutkan 1999: 421; cf. OE *meolcum* in a similar context: *Is þæt ealond welig on meolcum & on hunige* (Bede 1)). See Boutkan (1999: 421–6) for a discussion on the possibility of adding another Old Frisian noun to the eleven confirmed forms of the DAT. PL. with a singular meaning, attested in the Old Germanic languages.

423. Cf. a derived *ja*-stem formation *sinnahti* 'eternal night'.

424. The singly attested form *uuuloo* (Lat. *floccus*), a cognate of OE *wlōh*, is formally classified as an *i*-stem (e.g. Köbler 2014a, s.v. *wlōh*). According to Wadstein (1899), the form represents the NOM. SG., whereas Griepentrog (1995: 435) interprets it as a NOM. PL.; Tiefenbach (2010: 474) classifies it as an ACC. PL. As its attestation is limited in the Old Saxon material, it is problematic to state conclusively whether the form represents a continuation of the original Proto-Germanic form, or whether it should rather be viewed as a borrowing from Old English (the form is attested in Oxford Vergil glossary) (for details see Griepentrog 1995: 434–435). As the present investigation follows essentially Tiefenbach's (2010) interpretations, the form was included in the present study as an ACC. SG.

425. The PGmc. noun *furhχ* 'furrow' is attested only in the compound *furlang(-as, -um)* and accordingly provides no information about the restructuring of inflection.

R-STEMS

brōthar 'brother' (*gibrōthar* 'siblings', *spunnibrōthar* 'foster-brother'[426]), *dohtar* 'daughter', *fadar* 'father' (*aldfadar* 'progenitor', *godfadar* 'godfather', *himilfadar* 'heavenly father', *gisunfadar* 'son and father'), *mōdar* 'mother' (*fostarmōder*), *swestar* 'sister', *giswestar* 'siblings'[427]

S-STEMS

ehir (< *ēr*) 'ear (of corn)', **ei* 'egg', *hōn* 'hen'[428], **hrīs* 'twig', **hrīth* 'cattle', **kalf* 'calf' (*rēhkalf*, *merikalf* 'dolphin'[429]), *kind* 'child' (*wasunkind*), *lamb* 'lamb'

ND-STEMS

-berand (*helm-*, *wāpanberand* 'warrior') 'bearer', **costond* (*costondero*) 'tempter', **erðbūand* (*erdbuandiun*) 'terrestrian', *fiond* (*fīund*) 'enemy', *gērfiund* 'deadly enemy', *friund* 'friend', *hēland* 'saviour', *hēmsittiand* 'prince', *hettiand* (*hettend*) 'persecutor', *lēriand* 'teacher'[430], *-liðand* (*lagu-*, *sēo-*, *wāg-*) 'traveller, sailor'[431], *neriand* 'saviour', *rādand* 'emperor', *waldand* (*alowaldan*) 'ruler', *sakwaldand* 'opponent', *wīgand* 'warrior'

DENTAL STEMS

helith 'hero'[432], *mānuth* 'month', *magað* 'girl, maid'

---

426. The noun *spunnibrōther* (related to OHG *spunnibruoder*) is attested as the NOM. SG. *spunnebrother* in an abbreviated form in GLMarf III, 715,47 (Tiefenbach 2010: 367; cf. Köbler 2014a: 1039).

427. The forms *stiiffader* 'stepfather', *stefmōder* 'stepmother', *stefdohter* 'stepdaughter' are attested in glosses which are classified as Old High German and were not included in the analysis of the Old Saxon material (for details of these attestations, see Tiefenbach 2010: 375).

428. Some other related compound formations are unattested in the Old Saxon material, e.g. *erdhōn* 'partridge', *hasalhōn* 'hazelhen', *rebahōn* 'partridge', *berkhōn* 'quail', *feldhōn* 'partridge', *watarhōn* 'coot'. They are found in Tiefenbach's *Dictionary* (2010), but they come from sources belonging to Old High German.

429. Attested in Old High German glosses only.

430. The two attested instances of the NOM. PL. *leron, lereon* (1736 M, C und 1834 M, C) are believed to belong to this lemma according to Sehrt (1966) and Tiefenbach (2010: 237); cf. Köbler (2014a: 729) who assigned them to a masculine *n*-stem **lērio* (*lereo*) 'teacher'.

431. The nouns *sēulīthand* 'sailor' and *lagulīthand* (as well *hēmsittiand*) are treated as participles which follow the *ja*-stem inflection, with *sēulīthandio, lagulīthandio, hēmsittiandi* as the basic forms (Tiefenbach 2010). The basis for such a classification are the forms in which they are attested, which point clearly to the impact of the *ja*-stems (e.g. *seolithandiun, lagolithandia, hemsittendion*). These forms were interpreted as analogical, i.e. resulting from the pressure of the *ja*-stems or potentially *i*-stems.

432. The OS *helith* 'hero' follows consistently the *a*-stem inflection (cf. Gallée 1993: 219).

Old Low Franconian

I-STEMS

a. MASCULINE

    appel 'apple', *balg* 'husk', *bant* 'band', *beke* 'brook', *dēl* 'part', *disk* 'table', *drank* 'drink', *liut* 'people', *rōk (rouc)* 'smoke', *skaft* 'spear', *slag (slege)* 'stroke', *sprunk* 'jump', *stōt* 'thrust', *thurst* 'thirst', *trān* 'tear', *tūn* 'fence', *wān* 'hope', *wine* 'friend', *wurm* 'worm'

b. FEMININE

    ald 'people', *beki* 'brook', *craft* 'might', *dāt* 'deed', *dugath* 'virtue', *farth* 'journey', *fluht* 'refuge', *frist* 'deadline', *fruht* 'fruit', *githult* 'patience', *giwalt* 'power', *nōt* 'need', *skrift* 'script', *skult* 'guilt', *stat/stedi* 'place', *sūl* 'pillar', *tīt* 'time', *tuhti* 'discipline', *werilt* 'world'

U-STEMS

a. MASCULINE

    furda (uorda) 'ford'[433], *fritho* 'peace', *sido (sidin)* 'custom', **harug* 'shrine'[434], *lit (lid)* 'member'[435], *(drūt)sun(u)* 'son', *uuald* 'forest', *widu* 'wood', *wintar* 'winter'

b. FEMININE

    dura 'door', *fluor(-)* 'floor'[436], *hant* 'hand', **spitta* 'spit'[437]

c. NEUTER STEMS[438]

    fē 'cattle, property', *felt* 'field', *vilo* 'much'

ROOT NOUNS

a. MASCULINE

    ambachtman 'servant', *fuot* 'foot', *blāofuot* 'blue foot', *forafuot* 'forefoot'[439], *ginōt* 'companion', *hūsginōt* 'house companion'[440], *man* 'man', *tant* 'tooth'

---

433. The word is attested only in toponyms, once in the Latin context as a simplex, and otherwise as the first or the second part of compound toponyms. These forms were not included in the analysis.

434. Cf. OHG *harug* 'grove', *harughūs (haraho)*. The form is attested in the Latin context and in toponyms only; the DAT. PL. form seems the most reliable. It was not included in the analysis.

435. The word is attested only in the Latin context.

436. Attested only in toponyms as the first element.

437. The form *spitta* is reconstructed on the basis of the singly attested DAT. SG. form *spizzon*, found in LW, which testifies to the *n*-stem inflection. Its origin in the *u*-stems is confirmed by the Old English material, where *spitu* is attested (cf. OHG *spiz*, declined as an *a*-stem or *i*-stem; cf. MDu. *spit, spet*, MLG *spit (spyt)*, WFris. *spit*).

438. The original neuter form *vilo* 'much', originating in this declensional type, is attested only as an adverb.

439. Both forms *blāofuot* and *forafuot* are attested in the corpus only in the Latin context and therefore they were not included in the analysis.

440. The noun is attested singly in the Latin context and thus it was not included in the analysis.

b.   FEMININE

buok 'book', *burg* 'city', *weriltburg* 'earthly city', *godesburg* 'the city of God', *kuo* 'cow', *naht* 'night'[441]

R-STEMS

bruother 'brother', *spunnibrōthar* 'foster-brother', *dohter* 'daughter', *fadar* 'father', *aldarfadar* 'grandfather', *muoder* 'mother', *suster* 'sister'

S-STEMS

kalf 'calf', *kint* 'child', *drūtkind* 'beloved child', *lamp* 'lamb'

ND-STEMS

fiunt 'fiend', *friunt* 'friend', *neriando* 'saviour'

---

441. According to Franck (1883: 133), the original consonantal inflection can be sought also in *cnecht* 'boy', which still in Middle Dutch shows endingless plural forms; however, its origin in root nouns is not confirmed by any external evidence.

References

Adamczyk, E. 2007. On the (In)Stability of the Old English Weak Declension. In M. Krygier & L. Sikorska (eds.), *The Propur Langage of Englische Men*, Medieval English Mirror 4, 9–28. Frankfurt am Main: Peter Lang.

Adamczyk, E. 2008. Disintegration of the Nominal Inflection in Anglian: The Case of *i*-stems. *Studia Anglica Posnaniensia* 44. 101–120.

Adamczyk, E. 2009. Evolution of Germanic Nominal Inflection: The Case of West Germanic Kinship Terms. *Sprachwissenschaft* 34. 398–433.

Adamczyk, E. 2010. Morphological Reanalysis and the Old English *u*-declension. *Anglia. Zeitschrift für englische Philologie* 128(3). 365–390.

Adamczyk, E. 2011. Towards a Diatopic Approach to the Old English *s*-stem Declension. *Neuphilologische Mitteilungen* 112(4). 387–416.

Adamczyk, E. 2012. On Morphological Realignments in Old English Root Nouns. *Transactions of the Philological Society* 110. 1–27.

Adamczyk, E. 2013. *Þǽre nihte* or *þæs nihtes*? Some Remarks on the Relationship between Gender Shift and Declension Shift in Old English. In M. Krygier (ed.), *Of fair speche, and of fair answere*, Medieval English Mirror 8, 7–36. Frankfurt am Main: Peter Lang.

Adamczyk, E. 2014. Patterns of Reorganisation of the Early English Nominal Inflection: The Case of Old English Consonantal Stems. In H. F. Nielsen & P. V. Stiles (eds.), *Unity and Diversity in West-Germanic*. Volume III, NOWELE 67, 51–76. Odense: Odense University Press.

Aitchison, J. 2001. *Language Change: Progress or Decay?* 3rd edn. Cambridge: Cambridge University Press.

Alegre, M. & Gordon, P. 1999. Frequency Effects and the Representational Status of Regular Inflections. *Journal of Memory and Language* 40. 41–61. doi:10.1006/jmla.1998.2607

Allen, C. L. 1995. *Case Marking and Reanalysis: Grammatical Relations from Old to Early Modern English*. Oxford: Clarendon Press.

Antilla, R. 1977. *Analogy*. Berlin: Mouton de Gruyter. doi:10.1075/lisl.1

Antilla, R. 2003. Analogy: The Warp and Woof of Cognition. In B. D. Joseph & R. D. Janda (eds.), *The Handbook of Historical Linguistics*, 425–440. Oxford: Blackwell. doi:10.1002/9780470756393.ch10

Antonsen, E. H. 1975. *A Concise Grammar of the Older the Runic Inscriptions*. Tübingen: Niemeyer. doi:10.1515/9783111411583

Aronoff, M. 1994. *Morphology by Itself*. Cambridge: MIT Press.

Århammar, N. R. 1967. *Die Syltringer Sprache. Die Syltringer Literatur. Sonderdruck aus "Sylt - Geschichte und Gestalt einer Insel"*. Itzehoe-Voßkate: Hansen & Hansen.

Århammar, N. R. 1969. *Die Amringer Sprache: die Amringer Literatur: mit einem Anhang über die Amringer Pflanzen- und Vogelnamen*. 2nd edn. Itzehoe-Münsterdorf: Hansen & Hansen.

Århammar, N. 1990. Friesisch und Sächsisch. Zur Problematik ihrer gegenseitigen Abgrenzung im Früh- und Hochmittelalter. In R. H. Bremmer Jr., G.van der Meer & O. Vries (eds.), *Aspects of Old Frisian Philology, Amsterdamer Beiträge zur älteren Germanistik* 31/32, 1–25. Amsterdam & Atlanta: Rodopi.

Århammar, N. 1995. Zur Vor- und Frühgeschichte der Nordfriesen und des Nordfriesischen. In V. F. Faltings, A. G. H. Walker and O. Wilts (eds.), *Friesische Studien* II (NOWELE 12, 63–96). Odense: Odense University Press.

Askedal, J. O. 2006. Some Typological Differences between the Modern Germanic Languages in a Historical and Geographical Perspective. *Tidsskrift for Sprogforskning* 4. 187–207. doi:10.7146/tfs.v4i1.317

van der Auwera, J. 2012. From Contrastive Linguistics to Linguistic Typology. *Languages in Contrast* 12. 69–86. doi:10.1075/lic.12.1.05auw

Baayen, R. H. 1992. Quantitative Aspects of Morphological Productivity. In G. E. Booij & J. van Marle (eds.), *Yearbook of Morphology 1991*, 109–149. Dordrecht: Kluwer Academic Publishers. doi:10.1007/978-94-011-2516-1_8

Baayen, R. H. 2009. Corpus Linguistics in Morphology: Morphological Productivity. In A. Lüdeling & M. Kyto (eds.), *Corpus Linguistics. An International Handbook*, 900–919. Berlin: Mouton De Gruyter. doi:10.1515/9783110213881.2.899

Baechler, R. 2015. Inflectional Complexity of Nouns, Adjectives and Articles in Closely Related (Non-)Isolated Varieties. In R. Baechler & G. Seiler (eds.), *Complexity, Isolation and Variation*, 15–46. Berlin: Mouton de Gruyter.

Baerman, M., D. Brown & G. G. Corbett. 2005. *The Syntax-Morphology Interface: A Study of Syncretism*. Cambridge: Cambridge University Press. doi:10.1017/CBO9780511486234

Ball, C. J. 1970. The Language of the Vespasian Psalter Gloss: Two Caveats. *Review of English Studies* 21(84). 462–465. doi:10.1093/res/XXI.84.462

Bammesberger, A. 1965. Old English *gycer* and Gothic *jukuzi*. *Language* 41(3). 416–419. doi:10.2307/411784

Bammesberger, A. 1984. *A Sketch of Diachronic English Morphology*. Regensburg: Pustet.

Bammesberger, A. 1985. Die Endung für Nom. Akk. Pl. bei altenglischen *u*-Stämmen. *Anglia* 103. 365–370.

Bammesberger, A. 1989. The Weak Forms in the Germanic *r*-Stem Paradigm. *Journal of Indo-European Studies* 11. 105–116.

Bammesberger, A. 1990. *Morphologie des Urgermanischen Nomens*. Heidelberg: Winter.

Bammesberger, A. 2001. *um* (> *-on*) as Marker of the Instrumental Singular in Old English and Old Frisian. *Neophilologus* 85(2). 287–290. doi:10.1023/A:1004816411356

Bammesberger, A. 2009. Altenglisch *scepen* in Cædmons Hymnus. *Anglia* 127. 106–114. doi:10.1515/angl.2009.007

Bauer, L. 2004. *Morphological Productivity*. Cambridge: Cambridge University Press.

Becker, Th. 1990. *Analogie und morphologische Theorie*. München: Fink.

Beckner, C., R. Blythe, J. Bybee, M. H. Christiansen, W. Croft, N. C. Ellis, J. Holland, J. Ke, D. Larsen-Freeman & T. Schoenemann. 2009. Language Is a Complex Adaptive System: Position Paper. *Language Learning* 59(2). 1–26.

Beekes, R. S. P. 1995. *Comparative Indo-European Linguistics*. Amsterdam: John Benjamins. doi:10.1075/z.72

Behaghel, O. & B. Taeger. 1984. *Heliand und Gensesis*. Tübingen: Niemeyer.

Bennett, W.H. 1972. Prosodic Features in Proto-Germanic. In F. van Coetsem & H. Kufner (eds.), *Toward a Grammar of Proto-Germanic*, 99–116. Tübingen: Niemeyer. doi:10.1515/9783111549040.99

Berr, S. 1971. *An Etymological Glossary to the Old Saxon Heliand*. Bern & Frankfurt am Main: Herbert Lang.

Bertacca, A. 2001. Naturalness, Markedness and the Productivity of the Old English *a*-Declension. *Studia Anglica Posnaniensia* 36. 73–93.

Bertacca, A. 2009. *Natural Morphology and the Loss of Nominal Inflections in English*. Pisa: Plus-Piza University Press.

Bischoff, B. 1956–1957. Rezension von William Foerste, *Niederdeutsche Mundarten*. *Anzeiger für deutsches Altertum* 69. 122–131.

Bjorvand, H. 1995. *Nominale Stammbildung des Germanischen: maskuline Verbalnomina: a-Stämme oder i-Stämme?* NOWELE Supplement Volume 13, 1–69. Odense: Odense University Press.

Blech, U. 1977. *Germanistische Glossenstudien zu Handschriften aus französischen Bibliotheken*. Heidelberg: Winter.

Blevins, J. P. 2004. Inflection Classes and Economy. In G. Müller, L. Gunkel & G. Zifonun, (eds.), *Explorations in Nominal Inflection*, 41–85. Berlin: Mouton de Gruyter. doi:10.1515/9783110197501.51

Blevins, J. P. & J. Blevins. 2009. Introduction: Analogy in Grammar. In J. P. Blevins & J. Blevins (eds.), *Analogy in Grammar: Form and Acquisition*, 1–12. Oxford: Oxford University Press. doi:10.1093/acprof:oso/9780199547548.003.0001

Bliss, A. J. 1967. *The Metre of Beowulf*. Oxford: Blackwell.

Boer, R. C. 1924. *Oergermaansch handboek*. Haarlem: H.D. Tjeenk Willink & Zoon.

Booij, G. 1996. Inherent versus Contextual Inflection and the Split Morphology Hypothesis. In G. Booij & J. van Marle (eds.), *Yearbook of Morphology 1995*, 1–16. Dordrecht: Kluwer Academic Publishers. doi:10.1007/978-94-017-3716-6_1

Booij, G. 2002. *The Morphology of Dutch*. Oxford: Oxford University Press.

Borgeld, A. 1899. *De oudoostnederfrankische Psalmen. Klank- en Vormleer*. Groningen: J.B. Wolters.

Bosworth, J. (ed.) 1898. *An Anglo-Saxon Dictionary*, Supplement by T. Northcote Toller, Oxford, 1921; Addenda and Corrigenda by A. Campbell, Oxford, 1972. Oxford: Clarendon Press. https://www.ling.upenn.edu/~kurisuto/germanic/oe_boswothtoller_about.html

Boutkan, D. 1992. Old English *-ur/-or* in the *r*-stems and *s*-stems. *NOWELE* 20. 3–26. doi:10.1075/nowele.20.01bou

Boutkan, D. 1995. *The Germanic 'Auslautgesetze'*. Amsterdam & Atlanta: Rodopi.

Boutkan D. 1996. *A Concise Grammar of the Old Frisian Dialect of the First Riustring Manuscript*, NOWELE Supplement 16. Odense: Odense University Press. doi:10.1075/nss.16

Boutkan D. 1999. Another Old Frisian 'Instrumental Singular' in *-um*? *Neophilologus* 83(3). 421–426. doi:10.1023/A:1004577917823

Boutkan, D. 2001. Morphology of Old Frisian. In H. H Munske (ed.), *Handbuch des Friesischen/ Handbook of Frisian Studies*, 620–626. Tübingen: Niemeyer.

Boutkan, D. 2003. On Gothic *magaþ* ~ Old Frisian *megith* and the Form of Some North European Substratum Words in Germanic. *Amsterdamer Beiträge zur älteren Germanistik* 58. 11–27. doi:10.1163/18756719-058001003

Boutkan, D. & S. Siebinga. 2005. *Old Frisian Etymological Dictionary*, Leiden Indo-European Dictionary Series, Volume I. Leiden: E. J. Brill.

Braune, W. & F. Heidermanns. 2004. *Gotische Grammatik*. Tübingen: Niemeyer. doi:10.1515/9783110945089

Braune, W. & I. Reiffenstein. 2004. *Althochdeutsche Grammatik I*. 15th edn. Tübingen: Niemeyer. doi:10.1515/9783110930887

van Bree, C. 1987. *Historische Grammatica van het Nederlands*. Dordrecht: Foris.

Bremmer, R. H., Jr. 1989. Is de Nederlandse meervouds *-s* van Engelse komaf? *Amsterdamer Beiträge zur älteren Germanistik* 28. 77–91.

Bremmer, R. H., Jr. 2007. Language and Contents of the Old Frisian Manuscripts from Rüstringen (c.1300): *A Veritable Mixtum Compositum*. In R. H. Bremmer Jr, S. Laker & O. Vries (eds.), *Advances in Old Frisian Philology, Amsterdamer Beiträge zur älteren Germanistik* 64, 29–64. Amsterdam: John Benjamins.

Bremmer, R. H., Jr. 2008. North-Sea Germanic at the Cross-roads: The Emergence of Frisian and Hollandish. *NOWELE* 54/55. 279–308. doi:10.1075/nowele.54-55.09bre

Bremmer, R. H., Jr. 2009. *An Introduction to Old Frisian: History, Grammar, Reader, Glossary*. Amsterdam: John Benjamins. doi:10.1075/z.147

Brown, T. J. 1982. The Irish Element in the Insular System of Scripts to Circa A.D. 850. In H. Löwe (ed.), *Die Iren und Europa im früheren Mittelalter*, 101–119. Stuttgart: Klett-Cota.

Brunner, K. 1965. *Altenglische Grammatik (nach der angelsächsischen Grammatik von Eduard Sievers neubearbeitet)*. 3rd edn. Tübingen: Niemeyer. doi:10.1515/9783110930894

Buccini, A. F. 1995. Ontstaan en vroegste ontwikkeling van het Nederlandse taallandschap. *Taal en Tongval* 8. 8–66.

Buccini, A. F. 2003. "Ab errore liberato": The Northern Expansion of Frankish Power in the Merovingian Period and the Genesis of the Dutch Language. *Amsterdamer Beiträge zur älteren Germanistik* 57. 183–220.

Buccini, A. F. 2010. Between Pre-German and Pre-English: The Origin of Dutch. *Journal of Germanic Linguistics* 22. 301–314. doi:10.1017/S1470542710000073

Bybee, J. 1985. *Morphology: A Study of the Relation between Meaning and Form*. Amsterdam: John Benjamins. doi:10.1075/tsl.9

Bybee, J. 1995. Regular Morphology and the Lexicon. *Language and Cognitive Processes* 10(5). 425–455. doi:10.1080/01690969508407111

Bybee, J. 2003. Mechanisms of Change in Grammaticization: The Role of Frequency. In B. D. Joseph & J. Janda (eds.), *The Handbook of Historical Linguistics*, 602–623. Oxford: Blackwell. doi:10.1002/9780470756393.ch19

Bybee, J. 2007. *Frequency of Use and the Organisation of Language*. Oxford: Oxford University Press. doi:10.1093/acprof:oso/9780195301571.001.0001

Bybee, J. 2010. *Language, Usage and Cognition*. Cambridge: Cambridge University Press. doi:10.1017/CBO9780511750526

Bybee, J. 2013. Usage-Based Theory and Exemplar Representation. In Th. Hoffman & G. Trousdale (eds.), *The Oxford Handbook of Construction Grammar*, 49–69. Oxford: Oxford University Press.

Bybee, J. & J. E. Newman. 1995. Are Stem Changes as Natural as Affixes? *Linguistics* 33. 633–654. doi:10.1515/ling.1995.33.4.633

Bybee, J. & P. Hopper. 2001. Introduction to Frequency and the Emergence of Linguistic Structure. In J. Bybee & P. Hopper (eds.), *Frequency and the Emergence of Linguistic Structure*, 1–26. Amsterdam: John Benjamins. doi:10.1075/tsl.45.01byb

Cadovius-Müller, J. & L Kükelhan. 1875. *Memoriale linguae Frisicae (verfaszt von Johann Cadovius-Müller)*. Leer: W. J. Leendertz.

Cameron, A. 1973. A List of Old English Texts. In R. Frank & A. Cameron (eds.), *A Plan for the Dictionary of Old English*, 25–306. Toronto: University of Toronto Press.

Campbell, A. 1952. *Thet Freske Riim. Tractatus Alvini*. The Hague: Nijhoff. doi:10.1007/978-94-015-7156-2

Campbell, A. 1977. *Old English Grammar*. Oxford: Clarendon Press.

Campbell, L. 2004. *Historical Linguistics: An Introduction*. 2nd ed. Cambridge: MIT Press.

Carroll, R., R. Svare & J. C. Salmons. 2012. Quantifying the Evolutionary Dynamics of German Verbs. *Journal of Historical Linguistics* 2(2). 153–172. doi:10.1075/jhl.2.2.01car

Carstairs, A. 1987. *Allomorphy in Inflection*. London: Croom Helm.

Carstairs-McCarthy, A. 1991. Inflection Classes: Two Questions with One Answer. In F. Plank (ed.), *Paradigms*, 213–253. Berlin: Mouton de Gruyter. doi:10.1515/9783110889109.213

Carstairs-McCarthy, A. 1994. Inflection Classes, Gender and the Principle of Contrast. *Language* 70. 737–788. doi:10.2307/416326

Carstairs-McCarthy, A. 1998. Paradigmatic Structure: Inflectional Paradigms and Morphological Classes. In Spencer, A. & A. Zwicky (eds.), *The Handbook of Morphology*, 322–334. Oxford: Blackwell.

Carstairs-McCarthy, A. 2000. Inflection Classes. In G. Booij, Ch. Lehmann, & J. Mugdan (eds.), *Morphology: A Handbook on Inflection and Word Formation*, 630–637. Berlin: Mouton de Gruyter.

Casaretto, A. 2000. Korpussprachen und Produktivität. Einige Überlegungen zu den Gotischen *s*-Stämmen. *Historische Sprachforschung* 112. 210–238.

Cathey, J. E. 2000. *Old Saxon*. München: Lincom Europa.

Cathey, J. E. 2010. The Historical Setting of the Heliand, the Poem, and the Manuscripts. In V. A. Pakis (ed.), *Perspectives on the Old Saxon Heliand*, 3–31. Morgantown: West Virginia University Press.

Chase, C. (ed.) 1997. *The Dating of Beowulf*. Toronto: University of Toronto Press.

Clackson, J. 2007. *Indo-European Linguistics: An Introduction*. Cambridge: Cambridge University Press. doi:10.1017/CBO9780511808616

Clahsen, H. 1999. Lexical Entries and Rules of Language: A Multidisciplinary Study of German Inflection. *Behavioral and Brain Sciences* 22. 991–1060. doi:10.1017/S0140525X99002228

Clark Hall, J. R. & H. D. Merritt. 1960. *A Concise Anglo-Saxon Dictionary*. 4th edn. Cambridge: Cambridge University Press.

Clark, C. 1992. Onomastics. In R. M. Hogg (ed.), *The Cambridge History of the English Language*, Volume I, 452–487. Cambridge: Cambridge University Press. doi:10.1017/CHOL9780521264747.008

Classen, E. 1915. O.E. 'Nicras' ('Beowulf', 422, 575, 845, 1427). *Modern Language Review* 10. 85–86. doi:10.2307/3712950

van Coetsem, F. 1988. *Loan Phonology and the Two Transfer Types in Language Contact*. Dordrecht: Foris.

van Coetsem, F. 1994. *The Vocalism of the Germanic Parent Language: Systemic Evolution and Sociohistorical Context*. Heidelberg: Winter.

van Coetsem, F. 2000. *A General and Unified Theory of the Transmission Process in Language Contact*. Heidelberg: Winter.

Coleman, R. 1991. The Assessment of Paradigm Stability: Some Indo-European Case Studies. In F. Plank (ed.), *Paradigms: The Economy of Inflection*, 197–212. Berlin: Mouton de Gruyter. doi:10.1515/9783110889109.197

Collinge, N. E. 1985. *The Laws of Indo-European*. Amsterdam: John Benjamins. doi:10.1075/cilt.35

Colman, F. 2004. Kentish Old English <b>/<B>: Orthographic 'Archaism' or Evidence of Kentish Phonology? *English Language und Linguistics* 8. 171–205. doi:10.1017/S1360674304001364

Corbett, G., A. Hippisley, D. Brown & P. Marriott. 2001. Frequency, Regularity and the Paradigm: A Perspective from Russian on a Complex Relation. In J. Bybee & P. Hopper (eds.), *Frequency and the Emergence of Linguistic Structure*, 201–226. Amsterdam: John Benjamins. doi:10.1075/tsl.45.11cor

Corbett, G. & N. Fraser. 1993. Network Morphology: A DATR account of Russian nominal inflection. *Journal of Linguistics* 29(1). 113–142. doi:10.1017/S0022226700000074

Cordes, G. 1956. Zur Frage der altsächsischen Mundarten. *Zeitschrift für Mundartforschung 24*. 1–51;65–78.

Cordes, G. 1973. *Altniederdeutsches Elementarbuch Wort- und Lautlehre* (*mit einem Kapitel „Syntaktisches" v. F. Holthausen*). Heidelberg: Winter.

Cosijn, P. J. 1896. De Oudnederfrankische Psalmen. *Tijdschrift voor Nederlandse Taal- en Letterkunde 15*. 316–323.

Cowan, H. K. J. 1957. *De oudnederlandse (oudnederfrankische) psalmenfragmenten, met inleiding en frankischlatijnse woordenlijst opnieuw uitg. door H. K. J. Cowan.* Leiden: E. J. Brill.

Cowan, H. K. J. 1959. De lokalisering van het Oudnederfrankisch der psalmfragmenten. *Leuvense Bijdragen 48*. 1–47.

Cowan, H. K. J. 1961. Esquisse d'une grammaire fonctionelle du vieux-néerlandais (vieux-bas-françique). *Leuvense Bijdragen 50*. 2–54.

Croft, W. 2000. *Explaining Language Change: An Evolutionary Approach*. 2nd edn. Harlow & Essex: Longman.

Croft, W. 2003. *Typology and Universals*. 2nd. edn., Cambridge Textbooks in Linguistics. Cambridge: Cambridge University Press.

Crowley, J. P. 1986. The Study of Old English Dialects. *English Studies 67*. 97–112. doi:10.1080/00138388608598430

Cummins, A. H. 1887. *A Grammar of the Old Friesic Language*. Strassburg: Trübner.

Curzan, A. 2009. *Gender Shifts in the History of English*. Cambridge: Cambridge University Press.

D'Alquen, R. 1988. *Germanic Accent, Grammatical Change and the Laws of Unaccented Syllables.* Frankfurt am Main: Peter Lang.

Dahl, I. 1938. *Substantival Inflexion in Early Old English*. Lund: C.W.K. Gleerup.

Dahl, Ö. 2004. The Growth and Maintenance of Linguistic Complexity. Amsterdam: John Benjamins. doi:10.1075/slcs.71

Dahl, Ö. & M. Koptjevskaja-Tamm. 2006. The Resilient Dative and Other Remarkable Cases in Scandinavian Vernaculars. *Sprachtypologie und Universalienforschung 59*(1). 56–75.

Dal, I. 1934. Zur Geschichte der *-ia* Stamme im Westgermanischen. *Norsk Tidsskrift for Sprokvidenskap 7*. 243–252.

Dal, I. 1954. Zur Stellung des Altsächsischen und der Heliandsprache. *Norsk Tidsskrift for Sprogvidenskap 17*. 410–424. Reprinted in I. Dal, 1971. *Untersuchungen zur germanischen und deutschen Sprachgeschichte*, 74–85. Oslo: Universitetsforlaget.

Dal, I. 1983. Altniederdeutsch und seine Vorstufen. In G. Cordes & D. Möhn (eds.), *Handbuch zur niederdeutschen Sprach- und Literaturwissenschaft*, 69–97. Berlin: E. Schmidt.

Dammel, A. & D. Nübling. 2006. The Superstable Marker as an Indicator of Categorial Weakness? *Folia Linguistica 40*. 97–113. doi:10.1515/flin.40.1part2.97

Dammel, A. & S. Kürschner 2008. Complexity in Nominal Plural Allomorphy: A Contrastive Survey of ten Germanic Languages. In M. Miestamo, K. Sinnemäki & F. Karlsson (eds.), *Language Complexity: Typology, Contact, Change, Studies in Language Companion Series 94*, 243–262. Amsterdam: John Benjamins. doi:10.1075/slcs.94.15dam

Dammel, A., S. Kürschner & D. Nübling. 2010. Pluralallomorphie in zehn germanischen Sprachen. Konvergenzen und Divergenzen in Ausdrucksverfahren und Konditionierung. In A. Dammel, S. Kürschner & D. Nübling (eds.), *Kontrastive germanistische Linguistik*, 587–642. Hildesheim: Olms.

Diessel, H. 2004. *The Acquisition of Complex Sentences, Cambridge Studies in Linguistics 105.* Cambridge: Cambridge University Press. doi:10.1017/CBO9780511486531

Diessel, H. 2007. Frequency Effects in Language Acquisition, Language Use, and Diachronic Change. *New Ideas in Psychology* 25(2). 104–123. doi:10.1016/j.newideapsych.2007.02.002

Diessel, H. 2016. Frequency and Lexical Specificity: A Critical Review. In H. Behrens & S. Pfänder (eds.), *Experience Counts: Frequency Effects in Language*, 209–237. Berlin: Mouton de Gruyter.

DOEEC: Healey, A. de Paolo, J. Holland, D. McDougall, I. McDougall & X. Xiang (eds.) 2009. *The Dictionary of Old English Corpus in Electronic Form*. Toronto: University of Toronto Press.

Dressler, W.U. 1985a. *Morphonology: The Dynamics of Derivation*. Ann Arbor: Karoma Press.

Dressler, W.U. 1985b. On the Predictiveness of Natural Morphology. *Journal of Linguistics* 21. 321–337. doi:10.1017/S002222670001029X

Dressler, W. U. 2003. Degrees of Grammatical Productivity in Inflectional Morphology. *Rivista di Linguistica* 15(1). 31–62.

Duden: Grebe, P. (ed.) 1963. *Der Grosse Duden. Etymologie. Herkunftswörterbuch der deutschen Sprache*. Mannheim: Dudenverlag.

Duke, J. 2005. Gender Systems and Grammaticalization: Evidence from Germanic. In T. Leuschner, T. Mortelmans, S. de Groodt (eds.), *Grammatikalisierung im Deutschen*, 31–57. Berlin: Mouton de Gruyter. doi:10.1515/9783110925364.31

Ehrentraut, H. G.[1849] 1968. *Friesisches Archiv. Eine Zeitschrift für friesische Geschichte und Sprache*. Volume I. Oldenburg:Rudolf Schwarz.

Eichner, H. 1974. *Untersuchungen zur hethitischen Deklination*. Bamberg: Difo Druck.

Enger, H.-O. 2004. On the Relation between Gender and Declension: A Diachronic Perspective from Norwegian. *Studies in Language* 28. 51–82. doi:10.1075/sl.28.1.03eng

Enger, H.-O. 2010. How Do Words Change Inflection Class? Diachronic Evidence from Norwegian. *Language Sciences* 32. 366–379. doi:10.1016/j.langsci.2009.07.005

EWN: Philippa, M. A. I. (eds.). 2003–2009. *Etymologisch woordenboek van het nederlands*. Amsterdam: Amsterdam University Press. http://www.etymologiebank.nl

Fertig, D. 2013. *Analogy and Morphological Change*. Edinburgh: Edinburgh University Press.

Findell, M. 2009. *Vocalism in the Continental Runic Inscriptions*. Nottingham: University of Nottingham.

Fisiak, J. 1994. Linguistic Reality of Middle English. In F. Fernández, M. Fuster & J. J. Calvo (eds.), *English Historical Linguistics 1992, Papers from the Seventh International Conference on English Historical Linguistics (ICEHL-7)*, 47–61. Amsterdam: John Benjamins.

Flikkert, P., B. E. Dresher & A. Lahiri. 2009. Prosodic Preferences: From Old English to Early Modern English. In A. van Kemenade & B. Los (eds.), *The Handbook of the History of English*, 125–150. Chichester: Wiley-Blackwell.

Foerste, W. 1950. *Untersuchungen zur westfälischen Sprache des 9. Jhs.* Marburg: Münstersche Forschungen.

Fortson, B. W. 2010. *Indo-European Language and Culture: An Introduction*. Chichester: Wiley-Blackwell.

Franck, J. 1883. *Mittelniederländische Grammatik: mit Lesestücken und Glossar*. Leipzig: T.O. Weigel.

Franck, J. 1909. *Altfränkische Grammatik. Laut und Flexionslehre*. Göttingen: Vandenhoeck & Ruprecht.

Fulk, R. D. 1988. PIE *e* in Germanic Unstressed Syllables. In A. Bammesberger (ed.), *Die Laryngaltheorie und die Rekonstruktion des indogermanischen Laut- und Formensystems*, 153–177. Heidelberg: Winter.

Fulk, R. D. 1992. *A History of Old English Meter*. Philadelphia: University of Pennsylvania Press.

Fulk, R. D. 1998. The Chronology of Anglo-Frisian Sound Changes. *Amsterdamer Beiträge zur älteren Germanistik* 49. 139–154.

Gallée, J. H. 1894. *Altsächsische Sprachdenkmäler*. Leiden: E. J. Brill.

Gallée, J. H. 1903. *Vorstudien zu einem altniederdeutschen Wörterbuch*. Leiden: E. J. Brill.

Gallée J. H. [1910] 1993. *Altsächsische Grammatik*. 3rd edn. Tübingen: Niemeyer.

Gardani, F. 2013. *Dynamics of Morphological Productivity. The Evolution of Noun Classes from Latin to Italian*. Leiden: E. J. Brill. doi:10.1163/9789004244658

Gildemacher, K. F. 1993. *Waternamen in Friesland*. Leeuwarden: Fryske Akademy.

Goldschneider, J. & R. DeKeyser. 2001. Explaining the 'Natural Order of L2 Morpheme Acquisition' in English: A Meta-Analysis of Multiple Determinants. *Language Learning* 51. 1–50. doi:10.1111/1467-9922.00147

Goossens, J. 1980. *Middelnederlandse vocaalsystemen (Verslagen en Mededelingen van de Koninklijke Academie voor Taal- en Letterkunde 1980)*. 2nd edn. Gent: Koninklijke Academie voor Nederlandse Taal- en Letterkunde.

Goossens, J. 1987. Schets van de meervoudsvorming der substantieven in de Nederlandse dialecten. *Taal en Tongvaal* 39. 141–173.

Goossens, J. 1988. Het Nederlandse taalgebied. In *Gedenkboek van de eeuwfeestviering van de Koninklijke Academie voor Taal- en Letterkunde (1886–1986)*, 65–88. Gent: Koninklijke Academie voor Nederlandse Taal- en Letterkunde.

Gordon, E. V. & A. R. Taylor. 1981. *An Introduction to Old Norse*. 2nd edn. Oxford: Clarendon Press.

de Grauwe, L., 2004. Zijn olla vogala Vlaams, of zit de Nederlandse filologie met een koekoeksei in (haar) nest(en)? *Tijdschrift voor Nederlandse Taal- en Letterkunde* 120. 44–56.

Greenberg, J. H. 1960. A Quantitative Approach to the Morphological Typology of Language. *International Journal of American Linguistics* 26(3). 178–194. doi:10.1086/464575

Greenberg, J. 1966. *Language Universals*. Berlin: Mouton de Gruyter.

Griepentrog, W. 1995. *Die Wurzelnomina des Germanischen und ihre Vorgeschichte*. Innsbruck: Innsbrucker Beiträge zur Sprachwissenschaft.

Gütter, A. 2011. Frühe Belege für den Umlaut von ahd. /u/, /ō/ und /ū/. *Beiträge zur Geschichte der deutschen Sprache und Literatur (PBB)*, 133(1). 1–13. doi:10.1515/bgsl.2011.002

Gysseling, M. 1964. Proeve van een oudnederlandse grammatica (2^e deel). *Studia Germanica Gandensia* 6. 9–43.

de Haan, G. J. 2001. Why Old Frisian Is Really Middle Frisian. *Folia Linguistica Historica* 22. 179–206.

Haiman, J. 1983. Iconic and Economic Motivation. *Language* 59. 781–819. doi:10.2307/413373

Haiman, J. 1994. Iconicity. In R.E. Asher (ed.), *The Encyclopedia of Language and Linguistics*, 1629–1633. Oxford: Pergamon Press.

Harbert, W. 2007. *The Germanic languages*. Cambridge: Cambridge University Press.

Harnisch, R. 2001. *Grundform- und Stamm-Prinzip in der Substantivmorphologie des Deutschen*. Heidelberg: Winter.

Haspelmath, M. 2006. Against Markedness (and What to Replace It with). *Journal of Linguistics* 42(1). 25–70. doi:10.1017/S0022226705003683

Haspelmath, M. 2008. Frequency vs. Iconicity in Explaining Grammatical Asymmetries. *Cognitive Linguistics*. 19(1). 1–33. doi:10.1515/COG.2008.001

Haspelmath, M. 2014. On System Pressure Competing with Economic Motivation. In B. MacWhinney, A. L. Malchukov, & E. A. Moravcsik (eds.), *Competing Motivations*, 197–208. Oxford: Oxford University Press.

Haspelmath, M. & A. Sims. 2010. *Understanding Morphology*. London: Routledge.

Hawkins, J. A. 2004. *Efficiency and Complexity in Grammars*. Oxford: Oxford University Press. doi:10.1093/acprof:oso/9780199252695.001.0001

Hawkins, J. A. 2015. Typological Variation and Efficient Processing. In B. McWhinney & W. O'Grady (eds.), *The Handbook of Language Emergence*, 215–236. Chichester: Wiley-Blackwell.

Heeroma, K. 1951. *Oostnederlandse taalproblemen*, Mededelingen der Koninklijke Nederlandse Akademie van Wetenschappen. Afd. Letterkunde. Nieuwe reeks, deel 14.8. Amsterdam: North Holland.

Heeroma, K. 1965. Wat is Ingweoons? *Tijdschrift voor Nederlandse Taal- en Letterkunde* 81. 1–15.

Heeroma, K. 1972. Zur Raumgeschichte des Ingwäonischen. *Zeitschrift für Dialektologie und Linguistik* 39(3). 267–283.

van Helten, W. L. 1890. *Altostfriesische Grammatik*. Leeuwarden: A. Meijer.

van Helten, W. L. 1891. Grammatisches [I–XII]. *Beiträge zur Geschichte der deutschen Sprache und Literatur* 15. 455–488.

van Helten, W. L. 1902. *Die altostniederfränkischen Psalmenfragmente, die Lipsius'schen Glossen, und die altsüdmittelfränkischen Psalmenfragmente, mit Einleitung, Noten, Indices und Grammatiken*. Groningen: J. B. Wolters.

van Helten, W. L. 1906. Zum altfriesischen Vokalismus. *Indogermanische Forschungen* 19. 171–201.

van Helten, W. L. 1911. Grammatisches. *Beiträge zur Geschichte der deutschen Sprache und Literatur* 36. 435–515.

Heuser, W. 1903. *Altfriesisches Lesebuch mit Grammatik und Glossar*. Heidelberg: Winter.

Heusler, A. [1913] 1977. *Altisländisches Elementarbuch*. Heidelberg: Winter.

Heyne, M. 1867. *Kleinere altniederdeutsche Denkmäler, mit ausführlichen Glossar*. Paderborn: F. Schöningh.

Heyne, M. 1873. *Kleine altsächsische und altniederfränkische Grammatik*. Paderborn: F. Schöningh.

Hirt, H. 1931. *Handbuch des Urgermanischen I. Laut- und Akzentlehre*. Heidelberg: Winter.

Hirt, H. 1932. *Handbuch des Urgermanischen II. Stammbildungs- und Flexionslehre*. Heidelberg: Winter.

Hock, H. H. 1986. *Principles of Historical Linguistics*. Berlin: Mouton de Gruyter.

Hock, H. H. 2003. Analogical Change. In B. D. Joseph & R. D. Janda (eds.), *The Handbook of Historical Linguistics*, 441–460. Oxford: Blackwell. doi:10.1002/9780470756393.ch11

Hoekstra, J. 2001. Comparative Aspects of Frisian Morphology and Syntax. In H. H. Munske (ed.), *Handbuch Des Friesischen/Handbook of Frisian Studies*, 775–786. Tübingen: Niemeyer. doi:10.1515/9783110946925.775

Hofmann, D. 1982. Zur Syntax der Zehnerzahlen mit Substantiv in den Altgermanischen Sprachen insbesondere im Altfriesischen. *Us Wurk* 31. 85–104.

Hofmann, D. & A. T. Popkema. 2008. *Altfriesisches Handwörterbuch*. Heidelberg: Winter.

Hofstra, T. 2003. Altniederländisch und Altfriesisch. *Amsterdamer Beiträge zur älteren Germanistik* 57. 77–92.

Hogg, R. M. 1980. Analogy as a Source of Morphological Complexity. *Folia Linguistica Historica* 1(2). 277–284.

Hogg, R. M. 1988. On the Impossibility of Old English Dialectology. In D. Kastovsky & G. Bauer (eds.), *Luick Revisited: Papers Read at the Luick-Symposium at Schloß Liechtenstein, 15–18 September 1985*, 183–203. Tübingen: Narr.

Hogg, R.M. 1992a. *A Grammar of Old English. Volume I: Phonology*. Oxford: Blackwell.

Hogg, R. M. 1992b. Phonology and Morphology. In Hogg, R. M. (ed.), *The Cambridge History of the English Language. The Beginnings to 1066*, 67–167. Cambridge: Cambridge University Press.

Hogg, R. M. 1997a. Some Remarks on Case Marking in Old English. *Transactions of the Philological Society* 95. 95–109. doi:10.1111/1467-968X.00014

Hogg, R. M. 1997b. The Morphology and Dialect of Old English Disyllabic Nouns. In R. Hickey & S. Puppel (eds.), *Language History and Linguistic Modelling*, 113–126. Berlin: Mouton de Gruyter. doi:10.1515/9783110820751.113

Hogg, R. M. 1998. On the Ideological Boundaries of Old English Dialects. In J. Fisiak & M. Krygier (eds.), *Advances in English Historical Linguistics*, 107–118. Berlin: Mouton de Gruyter.

Hogg, R. M. & R. D. Fulk. 2011. *A Grammar of Old English. Volume II: Morphology*. Chichester: Wiley-Blackwell.

Holthausen, F. 1921. *Altsächsisches Elementarbuch*. 2nd edn. Heidelberg: Winter.

Holthausen F. 1967. *Altsächsisches Wörterbuch*. 2nd edn. Köln: Böhlau.

Holthausen, F. & D. Hofmann. 1985. *Altfriesisches Wörterbuch*. 2nd edn. Heidelberg: Winter.

Hooper, J. B. 1976. Word Frequency in Lexical Diffusion and the Source of Morphophonological Change. In W. M. Christie (ed.), *Current Progress in Historical Linguistics*, 96–105. Amsterdam: North Holland.

Huisman, J.A. 1986. Die Straubinger Heliandfragmente als altwestfriesische Übersetzung. In H. L. Cox, V.F. Vanacker and E. Verhofstadt (eds.), *Wortes anst - verbi gratia - donum natalicium Gilbert A.R. de Smet*, 227–235. Leuven & Amersfoort: Acco.

Igartua, I. 2005. Structural Analogy and the Inflectional Fate of the Slavic *a*-Stems. *Indogermanische Forschungen* 110. 282–307.

Itkonen, E. 2005. *Analogy as Structure and Process: Approaches in Linguistics, Cognitive Psychology and Philosophy of Science*. Amsterdam: John Benjamins. doi:10.1075/hcp.14

Iverson, G. K. & J.C. Salmons. 2004. The Conundrum of Old Norse Umlaut: Sound Change versus Crisis Analogy. *Journal of Germanic Linguistics* 16(1). 77–110. doi:10.1017/S1470542704000364

Jespersen, O. 1922. *Language its Nature, Development and Origin*. London: George Allen & Unwin Ltd.

Johnston, Th. S.B. 2001. The Old Frisian Law Manuscripts and Law Texts. In H. Munske (ed.), *Handbook of Frisian Studies*, 571–587. Tübingen: Niemeyer. doi:10.1515/9783110946925.571

Jones, Ch. 1967. The Functional Motivation of Linguistic Change. *English Studies* 48. 97–111. doi:10.1080/00138386708597271

Jones, Ch. 1988. *Grammatical Gender in English: 950-1250*. London: Croom Helm.

Jörgensen, T. V. 1978. *Spräkeliir foon dåt Mooringer Frasch*. Bräist: Nordfriisk Instituut.

Joseph, B. D. 2001. Diachronic Morphology. In A. Spencer & A. M. Zwicky (eds.), *The Handbook of Morphology*, 351–373. Oxford: Blackwell.

Kastovsky, D. 1985. Typological Changes in the Nominal Inflectional System of English and German. *Studia Gramatyczne* 7. 97–117.

Kastovsky, D. 1990. Whatever Happened to the Ablaut Nouns in English and Why did it not Happen in German? In H. Andersen & E.F.K. Koerner (eds.), *Historical Linguistics 1987. Papers from the 8th International Conference on Historical Linguistics, Lille, August 30-September 4, 1987, Current Issues in Linguistic Theory 66*, 253–264. Amsterdam: John Benjamins.

Kastovsky, D. 1994. Typological Differences between English and German Morphology. In T. Swan, E. Mørck & O. Jansen Westvik (eds.), *Language Change and Language Structure: Older Germanic Languages in a Comparative Perspective*, 135–157. Berlin: Mouton de Gruyter. doi:10.1515/9783110886573.135

Kastovsky, D. 1995. Morphological Reanalysis and Typology: The Case of the German *r*-Plural and Why English did not Develop it. In H. Andersen (ed.), *Historical Linguistics: Selected Papers from the Eleventh International Conference on Historical Linguistics, Los Angeles, 16–20 August 1993, Current Issues in Linguistic Theory 124*, 227–238. Amsterdam: John Benjamins.

Kastovsky, D. 1997. Morphological Classification in English Historical Linguistics: The Interplay of Diachrony, Synchrony and Morphological Theory. In T. Nevalainen & L. Kahlas-Tarkka (eds.), *To Explain the Present: Studies in the Changing English Language in Honour of Matti Rissanen, Mémoires de la Société Néophilologique de Helsinki 52*, 63–75. Helsinki: Société Néophilologique.

Kastovsky, D. 2000. Inflectional Classes, Morphological Restructuring, and the Dissolution of Old English Grammatical Gender. In B. Unterbeck & M. Rissanen (eds.), *Gender in Grammar and Cognition. Approaches to Gender, Manifestations of Gender, Trends in Linguistics. Studies and Monographs*, 709–728. Berlin: Mouton de Gruyter.

Kärre K. 1915. *Nomina Agentis in Old English. Part 1. Introduction*. Uppsala: Uppsala University Press.

Keyser, S. J. & W. O'Neil. 1985. The Simplification of the Old English Strong Nominal Paradigms. In R. Eaton, O. Fischer, W. F. Koopman, F. van der Leek (eds.). *Papers from the 4th International Conference on English Historical Linguistics, Amsterdam, April 10–13, 1985, Current Issues in Linguistic Theory 41*, 85–107. Amsterdam: John Benjamins.

Kitson, P. 1995. The Nature of Old English Dialect Distributions, Mainly as Exhibited in Charter Boundaries. In J. Fisiak (ed.), *Medieval Dialectology*, 43–135. Berlin: Mouton de Gruyter. doi:10.1515/9783110892000.43

Kitson, P. 2004. On Margins of Error in Placing Old English Literary Dialects. In M. Dossena & R. Lass (eds.), *Methods and Data in English Historical Dialectology*, 219–241. Frankfurt am Main: Peter Lang.

Klein, E. 1971. *A Comprehensive Etymological Dictionary of the English Language*. Amsterdam: Elsevier Scientific Publishing Co.

Klein, Th. 1977. *Studien zur Wechselbeziehung zwischen altsächsischem und althochdeutschem Schreibwesen und ihrer Sprach- und kulturgeschichtlichen Bedeutung*. Göppingen: Kümmerle.

Klein, Th. 1979. Zum altniederländischen 'Leidener Willeram' und zu einigen westgermanischen Pronominalformen. *Zeitschrift für deutsche Philologie* 98. 425–447.

Klein, Th. 1987. Zur althochdeutschen Flexionsmorphologie in synchroner Sicht. In R. Bergmann, H. Tiefenbach, L. Voetz (eds.), *Althochdeutsch. I. Grammatik. Glossen und Texte*, 147–168. Heidelberg: Winter.

Klein, Th. 1990. Die Straubinger Heliand-Fragemente: Altfriesisch oder Altsächsisch? In R. H. Bremmer, O. Vries & G. van der Meer (eds.), *Aspects of Old Frisian Philology, Amsterdamer Beiträge zur älteren Germanistik* 31/32, 197–225. Groningen/ Amsterdam & Atlanta: Rodopi.

Klein, Th. 2000a. Phonetik und Phonologie, Graphetik und Graphemik des Altniederdeutschen (Altsächsischen). In W. Besch, A. Betten, O. Reichmann & S. Sonderegger (eds.), *Sprachgeschichte. Ein Handbuch zur Geschichte der deutschen Sprache und ihrer Erforschung. Volume II*, 1248–1252. Berlin: Mouton de Gruyter.

Klein, Th. 2000b. Zur Stellung des Altsächsischen. *Niederdeutsches Jahrbuch* 123. 7–32.

Klein, Th. 2001. Merowingerzeit. § 1. Sprachliches. In H. Beck & D. Geuenich & H. Steuer (eds.), *Reallexikon der Germanischen Altertumskunde*. 2nd edn. 579–587. Berlin: Mouton de Gruyter.

Klein, Th. 2003. Althochdeutsch und Altniederländisch. *Amsterdamer Beiträge zur älteren Germanistik* 57. 19–60.

Klein, Th. 2004a. Wann entstand das Altsächsische? *Niederdeutsches Jahrbuch* 127. 7–22.

Klein, Th. 2004b. Im Vorfeld des Altsächsischen und Althochdeutschen. In A. Greule, E. Meineke & Ch. Thim-Mabrey (eds.), *Entstehung des Deutschen: Festschrift für Heinrich Tiefenbach*, 241–270. Heidelberg: Winter.

Klein, Th. 2013. Zum *r*-Plural im Westgermanischen. *NOWELE* 66(2). 169–196. doi:10.1075/nowele.66.2.03kle

Kluge, F. 1885. Zur Geschichte der Zeichensprache. Angelsächsische *Indicia Monasterialia*. *Internationale Zeitschrift für allgemeine Sprachwissenschaft* 2. 117–140.

Kluge, F. 1913. *Urgermanisch. Vorgeschichte der altgermanischen Dialekte*. Strassburg: Trübner.

Kluge, F. 1926. *Nominale Stammbildungslehre der altgermanischen Dialekte*. Tübingen: Niemeyer.

Kluge, F. 2011. *Etymologisches Wörterbuch der deutschen Sprache. 25. durchgesehene und erweiterte Auflage von Elmar Seebold*. Berlin: Mouton de Gruyter.

Kortlandt, F. 1978. On the History of the Genitive Plural in Slavic, Baltic, Germanic, and Indo-European. *Lingua* 45. 281–300. doi:10.1016/0024-3841(78)90027-X

Köbler, G. 1987. *Sammlung aller Glossen des Altsächsischen, Arbeiten zur Rechts- und Sprachwissenschaft, Bd. 32*. Gießen: Arbeiten Zur Rechts- und Sprachwissenschaft Verlag.

Köbler, G. 2014a. *Altsächsisches Wörterbuch*. 5th edn. http://www.koeblergerhard.de/aswbhinw.html

Köbler, G. 2014b. *Altniederfränkisches Wörterbuch*. 5th edn. http://www.koeblergerhard.de/anfrkwbhinw.html

König, W. 2001. *Dtv-Atlas Deutsche Sprache*. München: Deutscher Taschenbuch Verlag.

Köpcke, K. M. 1988. Schemas in German Plural Formation. *Lingua* 74(88). 303–335. doi:10.1016/0024-3841(88)90064-2

Köpcke, K. M. 1993. *Schemata bei der Pluralbildung im Deutschen: Versuch einer kognitiven Morphologie*. Tübingen: Narr.

Köpcke, K. M. 1998. The Acquisition of Plural Marking in English and German Revisited: Schemata Versus Rules. *Journal of Child Language* 25(2). 293–319. doi:10.1017/S0305000998003407

Krahe, H. & W. Meid. 1967. *Germanische Sprachwissenschaft III. Wortbildungslehre*. Berlin: Walter de Gruyter.

Krahe, H. & W. Meid. 1969. *Germanische Sprachwissenschaft II. Formenlehre*. Berlin: Walter de Gruyter.

Krause, W. 1953. *Handbuch des Gotischen*. München: C. H. Beck'sche Verlagsbuchhandlung.

Krogh, S. 1995. Zur Sprache des Sächsischen Taufgelöbnisses. *Zeitschrift für deutsches Altertum und deutsche Literatur* 124(2). 143–150.

Krogh, S. 1996. *Die Stellung des Altsächsischen im Rahmen der germanischen Sprachen*. Göttingen: Vandenhoeck & Ruprecht.

Krogh, S. 1997. Zur Entstehung des Niederländischen. In E. Glaser, M. Schlaefer & L. Rübekeil (eds.), *Grammatica ianua artium. Festschrift für Rolf Bergmann zum 60. Geburtstag*, 21–31. Heidelberg: Winter.

Krogh, S. 2002. Noch einmal zur Stellung des Altsächsischen. Eine Antwort auf Thomas Klein. *Niederdeutsches Jahrbuch* 125. 7–25.

Krogh, S. 2013. Die Anfänge des Altsächsischen. *NOWELE* 66(2). 140–168.
    doi:10.1075/nowele.66.2.02kro

Krogmann, W. 1969. Altfriesisch. In L. E. Schmitt (ed.), *Kurzer Grundriß der germanischen Philologie bis 1500*. Volume I: Sprachgeschichte, 190–210. Berlin: Walter de Gruyter.

Krogmann W. 1970. Altsächsisch und Mittelniederdeutsch. In L.E. Schmitt (ed.), *Kurzer Grundriß der germanischen Philologie bis 1500*. Volume I: Sprachgeschichte, 211–252. Berlin: Walter de Gruyter.

Krogmann, W. 1973. Die Praefatio in librum antiquum lingua Saxonica conscriptum. *Niederdeutsches Jahrbuch* 69/70, 1948, 141–163 (Wiederabdruck in J. Eichhoff & I. Rauch (eds.), *Der Heliand*, 20–53. Darmstadt: Wissenschaftliche Buchgesellschaft).

Kroonen, G. 2011. *The Proto-Germanic n-Stems: A Study in Diachronic Morphophonology*. Amsterdam & Atlanta: Rodopi.

Kroonen, G. 2013. *Etymological Dictionary of Proto-Germanic*. Leiden: E. J. Brill.

Krug, M. 2003. Frequency as a Determinant in Grammatical Variation and Change. In G. Rohdenburg & B. Mondorf (eds.), *Determinants of Grammatical Variation in English*, 7–68. Berlin: Mouton de Gruyter. doi:10.1515/9783110900019.7

Krygier, M. 1996. Plural Markers of the Old English Nouns of Relationship in the Two Manuscripts of Layamon's *Brut*. In J. Fisiak (ed.), *Middle English Miscellany. From Vocabulary to Linguistic Variation*, 47–68. Poznań: Motivex.

Krygier, M. 1997. *From Regularity to Anomaly: The Lexicalisation of Inflectional i-Umlaut in Middle English*. Frankfurt am Main: Peter Lang.

Krygier, M. 1998. On a Synchronic Approach to Old English Morphology. *Folia Linguistica Historica* 19. 119–128.

Krygier, M. 2002. A Re-Classification of Old English Nouns. *Studia Anglica Posnaniensia* 38. 311–319.

Krygier, M. 2004. Heargas þēoda: In Search of the *u. In R. Dylewski & P. Cap (eds.), *History and Present-day Pragmatics of the English Language*, 7–13. Łódź: Wyższa Szkoła Humanistyczno-Ekonomiczna w Łodzi.

Kufner, H. L. 1972. The Grouping and Separation of the Germanic Languages. In F. van Coetsem & H. L. Kufner (eds.), *Toward a Grammar of Proto-Germanic*, 71–97. Tübingen: Niemeyer. doi:10.1515/9783111549040.71

Kuhn, H. 1955. Zur Gliederung der germanischen Sprachen. *Zeitschrift für deutsches Altertum und deutsches Literatur* 86. 1–47.

Kuhn, S. M. 1959. The Vespasian Psalter Gloss: Original or Copy? *PLMA* 74. 161–177.

Kürschner, S. 2008. *Deklinationsklassen-Wandel eine diachron-kontrastive Studie zur Entwicklung der Pluralallomorphie im Deutschen, Niederländischen, Schwedischen und Dänischen*. Berlin: Mouton de Gruyter. doi:10.1515/9783110210842

Kürschner, S. & D. Nübling. 2011. The Interaction of Gender and Declension in Germanic Languages. *Folia Linguistica* 45(2). 355–388. doi:10.1515/flin.2011.014

Kyes, R. L. 1967. The Evidence for *i*-Umlaut in Old Low Franconian. *Language* 43. 666–673. doi:10.2307/411809

Kyes, R. L. 1969. *The Old Low Franconian Psalms and Glosses*. Ann Arbor: University of Michigan Press.

LAE: Orton, H., S. Sanderson, J. Widdowson. 1998. *The Linguistic Atlas of England*. London: Routledge.

Lahiri, A. & B. E. Dresher 1984. Diachronic and Synchronic Implications of Declension Shifts. *The Linguistic Review* 3. 141–163.

Lahiri, A. & B. E. Dresher. 1991. The Germanic Foot: Metrical Coherence in Old English. *Linguistic Inquiry* 22. 251–286.

Langacker, R. W. 1987. *Foundations of Cognitive Grammar. Volume I: Theoretical prerequisites.* Stanford, CA: Stanford University Press.

Langacker, R. W. 1988. A Usage-Based Model. In B. Rudzka-Ostyn (ed.), *Topics in Cognitive Linguistics*, Current Issues in Linguistic Theory 50, 127–161. Amsterdam: John Benjamins.

Langacker, R. W. 1999. *Grammar and Conceptualization.* Berlin: Mouton de Gruyter. doi:10.1515/9783110800524

Lane, G. S. 1951. The Genesis of the Stem Vowel *u(o)* in the Germanic *r*-stems. *Journal of English and Germanic Philology* 50. 522–528.

Lasch, A.[1914] 1974. *Mittelniederdeutsche Grammatik.* Tübingen: Niemeyer.

Lass, R. 1980. On Some Possible Weaknesses of 'Strong Naturalism'. In T. Thrane, V. Winge, L. Mackenzie, U. Ganger & N. Ege (eds.), *Typology and Genetics of Language*, 93–102. Copenhagen: TCLC.

Lass, R. 1986. Words without Etyma: Germanic 'Tooth'. In D. Kastovsky & A. Szwedek (eds.), *Linguistics across Historical and Geographical Boundaries: In Honour of Jacek Fisiak on the Occasion of his Fiftieth Birthday*, Trends in Linguistics 32, 473–482. Berlin: Mouton de Gruyter. doi:10.1515/9783110856132.473

Lass, R. 1990. How to Do Things with Junk: Exaptation in Language Evolution. *Journal of Linguistics* 26. 79–102. doi:10.1017/S0022226700014432

Lass, R. 1992. Phonology and Morphology. In N. Blake (ed.), *The Cambridge History of the English Language*. Volume 2. 1066–1476, 23–155. Cambridge. Cambridge University Press. doi:10.1017/CHOL9780521264754.003

Lass, R. 1997a. *Historical Linguistics and Language Change.* Cambridge: Cambridge University Press. doi:10.1017/CBO9780511620928

Lass, R. 1997b. Why *House* is an Old English 'Masculine a-Stem'? In T. Nevalainen & L. Kahlas-Tarkka (eds.), *To Explain the Present: Studies in the Changing English Language in Honour of Matti Rissanen*, Mémoires de la Société Néophilologique de Helsinki 52, 101–109. Helsinki: Société Néophilologique.

Lass, R. 2000. Language Periodisation and the Concept of 'Middle'. In I. Taavitsainen, T. Nevalainen, P. Pahta & M. Rissanen (eds.), *Placing Middle English in Context*, 7–41. Berlin: Mouton de Gruyter. doi:10.1515/9783110869514.7

Laver, J. 1994. *Principles of Phonetics.* Cambridge: Cambridge University Press. doi:10.1017/CBO9781139166621

Lehmann, W. P. 2005–2007. *A Grammar of Proto-Germanic.* University of Texas at Austin. http://www.utexas.edu/cola/centers/lrc/books/pgmc00.html

Liberman, A. 2001. Apocope in Germanic, or an Ax(e) to Grind. In I. Rauch, & G. F. Carr (eds.), *New Insights in Germanic Linguistics II*, 81–93. Frankfurt am Main: Peter Lang.

Lieberman, E., J.-B. Michel, J. Jackson, T. Tang & M. A. Nowak. 2007. Quantifying the Evolutionary Dynamics of Language. *Nature* 449 (7163). 713–716. doi:10.1038/nature06137

van Loey, A. 1970. Altniederländisch und Mittelniederländisch. In L. E. Schmitt (ed.), *Kurzer Grundriß der germanischen Philologie bis 1500*. Volume I: Sprachgeschichte, 253–287. Berlin: Walter de Gruyter.

van Loey, A. 1976. *Middelnederlandse spraakkunst. Deel I. Vormleer.* Groningen: H.D.Tjeenk Willink.

Looijenga, T. & E. Knol. 1990. A Tau Staff with Runic Inscriptions from Bernsterburen (Friesland). In O. Vries, R. H. Bremmer Jr. & G. van der Meer (eds.), *Aspects of Old Frisian Philology, Amsterdamer Beiträge zur älteren Germanistik* 31/32, 226–241. Amsterdam & Atlanta: Rodopi.

Looijenga, T. 2003. *Texts and Contexts of the Oldest Runic Inscriptions*. Leiden: E. J. Brill.

van Loon, J. 2005. *Principles of Historical Morphology*. Heidelberg: Winter.

Lowe, K. A. 2001. On the Plausibility of Old English Dialectology: The Ninth Century Kentish Charter Material. *Folia Linguistica Historica* 22. 67–100.

Lühr, R. 1982. *Studien zur Sprache des Hildebrandliedes*. Frankfurt am Main: Peter Lang.

Luick, K.[1921] 1964. *Historische Grammatik der englischen Sprache*. Oxford: Blackwell.

Luraghi, S. 1987. Patterns of Case Syncretism in Indo-European Languages. In A. Giacalone Ramat . (eds.), *Papers from the 7th International Conference on Historical Linguistics*, 355–371. Amsterdam: John Benjamins. doi:10.1075/cilt.48.28lur

Lutz, A. 2002. When Did English Begin? In T. Fanego, B. Méndez-Naya & E. Seoane (eds.) *Sounds, Word, Texts and Change: Selected Papers from 11 ICEHL*, 145–172. Amsterdam: John Benjamins. doi:10.1075/cilt.224.11lut

Mańczak, W. 1970. *Z zagadnień językoznawstwa ogólnego*. Wrocław & Warszawa & Kraków: Ossolineum.

Mańczak, W. 1980. Frequenz und Sprachwandel. In H. Lüdtke (ed.), *Kommunikationstheoretische Grundlagen des Sprachwandels*, 37–79. Berlin: Mouton de Gruyter.

Marcus, G. F., Brinkmann, U., Clahsen, H., Wiese, R., & Pinker, S. 1995. German Inflection: The Exception that Proves the Rule. *Cognitive Psychology* 29. 186–256. doi:10.1006/cogp.1995.1015

Markey, Th. L. 1976. *Germanic Dialect Grouping and the Position of Ingvaeonic*, Innsbrucker Beiträge zur Sprachwissenschaft 15. Innsbruck: Institut für Sprachwissenschaft der Universität Innsbruck.

Markey, Th. L. 1981. *Frisian*. Berlin: Mouton de Gruyter. doi:10.1515/9783110815719

van Marle, J. 1985. *On the Paradigmatic Dimension of Morphological Creativity*. Dordrecht: Foris.

Marynissen, A. 1996. *De flexie van het substantief in het 13de-eeuwse ambtelijke Middelnederlands. Een taalgeografische studie*. Leuven: Peeters.

Marynissen A. 2001. Die Flexion des Substantivs in der mittelniederländischen Amtssprache des 13. Jahrhunderts. In K. Gärtner, G. Holtus, A. Rapp & H. Völker (eds.), *Skripta, Schreiblandschaften und Standardisierungstendenzen: Urkundensprachen im Grenzbereich von Germania und Romania im 13. und 14. Jahrhundert*, 659–672. Trier: Kliomedia.

Mayerthaler, W. 1980. *Morphologische Natürlichkeit*. Wiesbaden: Athenaeum.

McKitterick, R. 2008. *Charlemagne: The Formation of a European Identity*. Cambridge: Cambridge University Press. doi:10.1017/CBO9780511803314

McMahon, A. M. S. 1994. *Understanding Language Change*. Cambridge: Cambridge University Press. doi:10.1017/CBO9781139166591

Meier-Brügger, M. 2010. *Indogermanische Sprachwissenschaft*. Berlin: Mouton de Gruyter.

Meijering H. D. 1985. *'Chindh uuirdit uns chiboran': Over het woord 'kind' in het oudere Duits*. Amsterdam: VU.

Meijering, H. D. 1989. Het oudfriese *ar*-meervoud. Feiten en interpretaties. *Amsterdamer Beiträge zur älteren Germanistik* 28. 21–41.

Meillet, A. 1917. *Caractères généraux des langues germaniques*. Paris: Hachette.

Meillet, A. 1970. *General Characteristics of the Germanic Languages*. 2nd edn. Translated by William P. Dismukes. Tuscaloosa: University of Alabama Press.

Miestamo, M. 2008. Grammatical Complexity in a Cross-Linguistic Perspective. In M. Miestamo, K. Sinnemäki & F. Karlsson (eds.), *Language Complexity: Typology, Contact, Change.* Amsterdam: John Benjamins. doi:10.1075/slcs.94.04mie

Miller, T. 1890–1898. (ed.) *The Old English Version of Bede's Ecclesiastical History of the English People.* London: Early English Text Society.

Mills, A. D. 2011. *A Dictionary of British Place Names.* Oxford: Oxford University Press.

Moffat, D. 1987. The Occurrences of *āc* in Old English: A List. *Mediaeval Studies* 49. 534–540. doi:10.1484/J.MS.2.306898

Moore, S. 1928. Earliest Morphological Changes in Middle English. *Language* 4. 238–266. doi:10.2307/409140

Mottausch, K. H. 2011. *Der Nominalakzent im Frühurgermanischen. Konstanten und Neuerungen, PHILOLOGIA,* Sprachwissenschaftliche Forschungsergebnisse 159. Hamburg: Verlag Dr. Kovač.

Möllencamp, R. 1968. *Die friesischen Sprachdenkmale des Landes Wursten.* Bremerhaven: Heimatbund der Männer vom Morgenstern.

Nerbonne, J. 2010. Measuring the Diffusion of Linguistic Change. *Philosophical Transactions of the Royal Society of London. Series B, Biological Sciences* 365. 3821–3828. doi:10.1098/rstb.2010.0048

Nielsen, H.F. 1985. *Old English and the Continental Germanic Languages: A Survey of Morphological and Phonological Interrelations,* IBS 33, Innsbruck: Institut für Sprachwissenschaft der Universität Innsbruck.

Nielsen, H.F. 1989. *The Germanic Languages: Origins and Early Dialectal Interrelations.* Tuscaloosa: University of Alabama Press.

Nielsen, H.F. 1990. W.L. van Helten's *Altostfriesische Grammatik* Viewed from a Comparative Angle. In R. H. Bremmer Jr., G. van der Meer & O. Vries (eds.), *Aspects of Old Frisian Philology, Amsterdamer Beiträge zur älteren Germanistik* 31/32, 349–356 In Amsterdam & Atlanta: Rodopi.

Nielsen, H. F. 1991. The Undley Bracteate, 'Continental Anglian' and the Early Germanic of Schleswig-Holstein. In Askedal, J. O., H. Bjorvand & E. F. Halvorsen (eds.), *Festskrift til Ottar Grønvik på 75-årsdagen den 21. oktober 1991,* 33–52. Oslo: Universitetsforlaget.

Nielsen, H. F. 1994. Ingerid Dal's Views on Old Saxon in the Light of New Evidence. In T. Swan, E. Mørck & O. Jansen (eds.), *Language Change and Language Structure,* 195–212. Berlin: Mouton de Gruyter. doi:10.1515/9783110886573.195

Nielsen, H. F. 2000. *The Early Runic Language of Scandinavia: Studies in Germanic Dialect Geography.* Heidelberg: Winter.

Nielsen, H. F. 2001. Frisian and the Grouping of the Older Germanic Languages. In H. H. Munske (ed.), *Handbook of Frisian Studies,* 512–523. Tübingen: Niemeyer. doi:10.1515/9783110946925.512

Noreen, A. 1894. Etymologisches. *Indogermanische Forschungen* 4. 320–326.

Nübling, D. 2000. *Prinzipien der Irregularisierung. Eine kontrastive Analyse von zehn Verben in zehn germanischen Sprachen.* Tübingen: Niemeyer. doi:10.1515/9783110915082

Nübling, D. 2008. Was tun mit Flexionsklassen? Deklinationsklassen und ihr Wandel im Deutschen und seinen Dialekten. *Zeitschrift für Dialektologie und Linguistik* 75(3). 282–330.

OED: Simpson, J. A. & E. S. C. Weiner (eds.). 2004. *Oxford English Dictionary.* http://www.oed.com/

OFO: Sipma, P. (ed.) 1927, 1933, 1941. *Oudfriesche Oorkonden, I-III.* OTR 1–3. The Hague: Nijhoff; Vries, O. (ed.) 1977. *Oudfriese Oorkonden IV.* OTR 14. The Hague: Nijhoff.

ONW: Pijnenburg W. J. J. (eds.). *Oudnederlands Woordenboek.* http://www.inl.nl/onderzoek-a-onderwijs/lexicologie-a-lexicografie/onw

Page, R. I. 2001. Frisian Runic Inscriptions. In Munske (ed.), *Handbuch des Friesischen/ Handbook of Frisian Studies*, 523–530. Tübingen: Niemeyer. doi:10.1515/9783110946925.523

Paul, H. 1920. *Prinzipien der Sprachgeschichte.* 5th edn. Tübingen: Niemeyer.

Philippa, M. A. I. 1987. *Noord-Zee-Germaanse ontwikkelingen.* Alblasserdam: Offsetdrukkerij Kanters B. V.

Philippa, M. A. I. 1989. Het meervoud op -ar in het Oudfries. Stand van zaken. *Amsterdamer Beiträge zur älteren Germanistik* 28. 5–20.

Pijnenburg, W. J. J. 2003. Das Altniederländische Wörterbuch. *Amsterdamer Beiträge zur älteren Germanistik* 57. 5–18.

Piper, E. 1897. *Die Altsächsische Bibeldichtung (Heliand und Genesis).* Stuttgart: Cotta.

Pieper, P. 1989. *Die Weser-Runenknochen. Neue Untersuchungen zur Problematik: Original oder Fälschung.* Oldenburg: Isensee

Plank, F. 1987. Number Neutralization in Old English: Failure of Functionalism? In W. Koopman, F. van der Leek, O. Fischer. & R. Eaton (eds.), *Explanation and Linguistic Change*, 177–238. Amsterdam: John Benjamins.

Plank, F. 1991. Of Abundance and Scantiness in Inflection. In F. Plank (ed.), *Paradigms: The Economy of Inflection*, 1–39. Berlin: Mouton de Gruyter. doi:10.1515/9783110889109.1

Pokorny, J. 1959. *Indogermanisches etymologisches Wörterbuch.* Bern: Francke.

Primer, S. 1881. On the Consonant Declension in Old Norse. II. *The American Journal of Philology* 2(6). 181–203. doi:10.2307/287457

Prokosch, E. 1939. *A Comparative Germanic Grammar.* Baltimore: Linguistic Society of America.

Quak, A. 1973a. *Studien zu den altmittel- und altniederfränkischen Psalmen und Glossen.* Amsterdam& Atlanta: Rodopi.

Quak, A. 1973b. Das Leeuwardener Fragment der sogenannten Wachtendonckschen Psalmen. *Amsterdamer Beiträge zur älteren Germanistik* 5. 33–62.

Quak, A. 1975. *Wortkonkordanz zu den altmittel- und altniederfränkischen Psalmen und Glossen.* Amsterdam & Atlanta: Rodopi.

Quak, A. 1981. *Die altmittel- und altniederfränkischen Psalmen und Glossen.* Amsterdam & Atlana: Rodopi.

Quak, A. 1989. Meervoudsvorming in Oudsaksisch en Middelnederduits. *Amsterdamer Beiträge zur älteren Germanistik* 28. 43–54.

Quak, A. 1991a. Altfriesische und altenglische Runen. In A. Bammesberger (ed.), *Old English Runes and their Continental Background*, 287–298. Heidelberg: Winter.

Quak, A. 1991b. Zur Runeninschrift von Bernsterburen. *Amsterdamer Beiträge zur älteren Germanistik* 34. 19–21.

Quak, A. 1992. Versuch einer Formenlehre des altniederländischen auf der Basis der Wachtendonckschen Psalmen. In R. H. Bremmer & A. Quak (eds.), *Zur Phonologie und Morphologie des Altniederländischen*, 81–123. Odense: Odense University Press. doi:10.1075/nss.7.04qua

Quak, A. & J. M. van der Horst. 2002. *Inleiding Oudnederlands, Ancorae*, Steunpunten voor studie en onderwijs 16. Leuven: Universitaire Pers Leuven.

Quak, A. 2003. Altfriesisches in Altniederländischen Ortsnamen. *Amsterdamer Beiträge zur älteren Germanistik* 57. 281–310.

Quak, A. (in preparation). Pluralformen bei Substantiven in altniederländischen Ortsnamen.

Ramat, P. 1981. *Einführung in das Germanische*. Tübingen: Niemeyer. doi:10.1515/9783111346113

Rauch, I. 1970. *Heliand* i-Umlaut Evidence for the Original Dialect Position of Old Saxon. *Lingua* 24(4). 365–373. doi:10.1016/0024-3841(70)90088-4

Rauch, I. 1992a. *The Old Saxon Language: Grammar, Epic Narrative, Linguistic Interference*. Frankfurt am Main: Peter Lang.

Rauch, I. 1992b. Old Saxon Barred Vowel. In I. Rauch & C. Kyes (eds.), *On Germanic Linguistics: Issues and Methods*, Trends in Linguistics 68, 245–252. Berlin: Mouton de Gruyter. doi:10.1515/9783110856446.245

Ringe, D. 2006. *A Linguistic History of English. Volume II: From Proto-Indo-European to Proto-Germanic*. Oxford: Oxford University Press. doi:10.1093/acprof:oso/9780199284139.001.0001

Ringe, D. & A. Taylor. 2014. *A Linguistic History of English. Volume II: The Development of Old English*. Oxford: Oxford University Press.

Roediger, M. 1893. *Paradigmata zur altsächsischen Grammatik*. Berlin: Weidmann.

Roedler, E. 1916. Die Ausbreitung des *s*-Plurals im Englischen. *Anglia* 28. 420–502.

Rooth, E. 1932. Die Sprachform der Merseburger Quellen. In *Niederdeutsche Studien. Festschrift zum sechzigsten Geburtstag für Professor Conrad Borchling*, 24–54. Neumünster: Wachholtz.

Rooth, E. 1949. *Saxonica. Beiträge zur niedersächsischen Sprachgeschichte*. Lund: C.W.K. Gleerup.

Rooth, E. 1956. *Über die Heliandsprache. Fragen und Forschungen im Bereich und Umkreis der germanischen Philologie. Festgabe für Theodor Frings zum 70. Geburtstag; 23. Juli 1956*. Berlin: Akademie-Verlag.

Ross, A. S. C. 1937. *Studies in the Accidence of the Lindisfarne Gospels*. Leeds: Kendal.

Ross, A. S. C. 1954. Contribution to the Study of *u*-Flexion. *Transactions of the Philological Society* 53. 85–128. doi:10.1111/j.1467-968X.1954.tb00280.x

Rösel, L. 1962. *Die Gliederung der germanischen Sprachen nach dem Zeugnis ihrer Flexionsformen*, Erlanger Beiträge zur Sprach- und Kunstwissenschaft 11. Nürnberg: Carl.

Rowley, Sh. M. 2011. *The Old English Version of Bede's "Historia ecclesiastica"*, Anglo-Saxon Studies 16. Cambridge: D. S. Brewer.

Le Roux, T.H. & J. J. Le Roux. 1973. *Middelnederlandse Grammatika: Van Stamverwante Bodem*. Pretoria: Van Schaik.

Salmons, J. 2012. *A History of German: What the Past Reveals about Today's Language*. Oxford: Oxford University Press.

Sanders, W. 1968. Zu den Altniederfränkischen Psalmen. *Zeitschrift für deutsches Altertum* 97. 81–106.

Sanders, W. 1970. Der altniederländische Leidener Willeram. In D. Hofmann & W. Sanders (eds.), *Gedenkschrift für William Foerste*, 412–423. Köln: Böhlau.

Sanders, W. 1974. *Der Leidener Willeram. Untersuchungen zu Handschrift, Text und Sprachform*. München: Fink.

Sanders, W. 1982. *Sachsensprache, Hansesprache, Plattdeutsch. Sprachgeschichtliche Grundzüge des Niederdeutschen*. Göttingen: Vandenhoeck & Ruprecht.

Sanders, W. 1983. Altsächsische Sprache. In J. Goossens (ed.), *Niederdeutsch. Sprache und Literatur. Eine Einführung. Volume I: Sprache*. 2nd edn. 28–65. Neumünster: Wachholtz.

Sanders, W. 2000a. Lexikologie und Lexikographie des Altniederdeutschen (Altsächsischen). In W. Besch, A. Betten, O. Reichmann, S. Sonderegger (eds.), *Sprachgeschichte. Ein Handbuch zur Geschichte der deutschen Sprache und ihrer Erforschung*. Volume II, 1257–1263. Berlin: Mouton de Gruyter.

Sanders, W. 2000b. Die Textsorten des Altniederdeutschen (Altsächsischen). In W. Besch, A. Betten, O. Reichmann & S. Sonderegger (eds.), *Sprachgeschichte. Ein Handbuch zur Geschichte der deutschen Sprache und ihrer Erforschung*. Volume II, 1276–1283. Berlin: Mouton de Gruyter.

Sanders, W. 2000c. Reflexe gesprochener Sprache im Altniederdeutschen (Altsächsischen). In W. Besch, A. Betten, O. Reichmann & S. Sonderegger (eds.), *Sprachgeschichte. Ein Handbuch zur Geschichte der deutschen Sprache und ihrer Erforschung*. Volume II, 1288–1293. Berlin: Mouton de Gruyter.

Sauer, R. 1917. *Zur Sprache des Leidener Glossars. Cod. voss. lat. 4° 69*. Augsburg: Ph. J. Pfeiffer.

Schaffner, S. 2001. *Das Vernersche Gesetz und der innerparadigmatische grammatische Wechsel des urgermanischen im Nominalbereich*. Innsbruck: Institut für Sprachwissenschaft der Universität Innsbruck.

Schenker, W. 1971. *es/-os*-Flexion und *-es/-os-* Stämme im Germanischen. *Beiträge zur Geschichte der deutschen Sprache und Literatur* 93. 46–59.

Schlerath, B. 1995. Bemerkungen zur Geschichte der *-es-* Stämme im Westgermanischen. In H. Hettrich (ed.), *Verba et Structurae. Festschrift für Klaus Strunk zum 65. Geburtstag*. 249–264. Innsbruck: Institut für Sprachwissenschaft der Universität Innsbruck.

Scheuermann, U. 2000. Die Diagliederung des Altniederdeutschen (Altsächsischen). In W. Besch, A. Betten, O. Reichmann & S. Sonderegger (eds.), *Sprachgeschichte. Ein Handbuch zur Geschichte der deutschen Sprache und ihrer Erforschung*. Volume II, 1283–1288. Berlin: Mouton de Gruyter.

Schlüter, W. 1892. *Untersuchungen zur Geschichte der altsächsischen Sprache*. Göttingen: R. Peppmüller.

Schmid, H. U. 2006. Ein neues 'Heliand'-Fragment aus der Universitätsbibliothek Leipzig. *ZfdA* 135. 309–323.

Schmid, H. U. 2007. Nochmals zum Leipziger 'Heliand'-Fragment. *ZdfA* 136. 376–378.

Schoonheim, T. H., K. Louwen, M. A. Mooijaart, W. J. J. Pijnenburg & A. Quak (eds.) 2009. *Oudnederlands woordenboek*. Leiden: Instituut voor Nederlandse Lexicologie.

Schutter, G. de, B. van den Berg, T. Goeman, Th. de Jong (eds.). 2014. *Morphological Atlas of the Dutch Dialects I (MAND)*. Amsterdam: Amsterdam University Press.

Schwink, F. W. 2004. *The Third Gender: Studies in the Origin and History of Germanic Grammatical Gender*. Heidelberg: Winter.

Seebold, E. 2013. Die Aufgliederung der germanischen Sprachen. In H. F. Nielsen & P. V. Stiles (eds.), *Unity and Diversity in West-Germanic*. Volume I, NOWELE 66, 55–77. Odense: Odense University Press. doi:10.1075/nowele.66.1.04see

Sehrt, E. H. 1966. *Vollständiges Wörterbuch zum Heliand und zur altsächsischen Genesis*, 2nd edn. Göttingen: Vandenhoeck & Ruprecht.

Siebs, T. 1901. Geschichte der friesischen Sprache. In H. Paul (ed.), *Grundriß der germanischen Philologie*. Volume I, Germanische Sprachen und Literaturen: Sonstiges, 2nd edn., 1152–1464. Strassburg: Trübner.

Sievers, E. (ed.) 1878. *Hêliand*. Halle: Verlag der Buchhandlung des Waisenhauses.

Sjölin, B. 1966. Zur Gliederung des Altfriesischen. *Us Wurk* 15. 25–38.

Sjölin, B. 1969. *Einführung in das Friesische*. Stuttgart: J. B. Metzlerische Verlagsbuchhandlung.

Sjölin, B. 1970. *Die "Fivelgoer" Handschrift*. Den Haag: Martinus Nijhoff. doi:10.1007/978-94-015-3393-5

Sjölin, B. 1984. Die Gliederung des Altfriesischen – ein Rückblick. In N. Århammar (eds.), *Miscellanea Frisica: in nije bonddel Fryske stúdzjes (= een nieuwe bundel Friese studies/ a new collection of Frisian studies)*, 55–66. Assen: Van Gorcum.

Skousen, R. 1989. *Analogical Modeling of Language*. Dordrecht: Kluwer Academic Publishers.

Skousen, R. 1992. *Analogy and Structure*. Dordrecht: Kluwer Academic Publishers. doi:10.1007/978-94-015-8098-4

Smith, J. 1976. Mittel- und niederfränkisches in den Wachtendonckschen Psalmen. *Niederdeutsches Wort* 16. 63–74.

Smith, A. 2001. The Role of Frequency in the Specialization of the English Anterior. In J. Bybee & P. Hopper (eds.), *Frequency and the Emergence of Linguistic Structure*, 361–382. Amsterdam: John Benjamins. doi:10.1075/tsl.45.18smi

Steins, C. 1998. Against Arbitrary Features in Inflection: Old English Declension Classes. In W. Kehrein & R. Wiese (eds.), *Phonology and Morphology of the Germanic Languages*, 241–265. Tübingen: Niemeyer. doi:10.1515/9783110919769.241

Steller, W. 1928. *Abriss der altfriesischen Grammatik, mit Berücksichtigung der westgermanischen Dialecte des altenglischen, altsächsischen und althochdeutschen*. Tübingen: Niemeyer.

Stemberger, J. P. & B. MacWhinney. 1986. Frequency and the Lexical Storage of Regularly Inflected Forms. *Memory and Cognition* 14(1). 17–26. doi:10.3758/BF03209225

Stiles, P. V. 1984. On the Interpretation of Older Runic *swestar* on the Opedal Stone. *NOWELE* 3. 3–48. doi:10.1075/nowele.3.01sti

Stiles, P. V. 1988. Gothic Nominative Singular *brōþar* 'brother' and the Reflexes of Indo-European Long Vowels in the Final Syllables of Germanic Polysyllables. *Transactions of the Philological Society* 86. 115–143. doi:10.1111/j.1467-968X.1988.tb00396.x

Stiles, P. V. 1995. Remarks on the 'Anglo-Frisian' Thesis. In V. F Faltings, A. G. H. Walker & O. Wilts (eds.), *Friesische Studien II: Beiträge des Föhrer Symposiums zur Friesischen Philologie vom 7.–8. April 1994*, 177–220. Odense: Odense University Press. doi:10.1075/nss.12.11sti

Streitberg, W.[1896] 1963. *Urgermanische Grammatik*. Heidelberg: Winter.

Streitberg, W.[1897] 1920 . *Gotisches Elementarbuch*. 6th edn. Heidelberg: Winter.

Sturtevant, E. 1947. *An Introduction to Linguistic Science*. New Haven: Yale University Press.

Suzuki, S. 1996. Preference Conditions for Resolution in the Meter of 'Beowulf': Kaluza's Law Reconsidered. *Modern Philology* 93(3). 281–306. doi:10.1086/392320

Sytsema, J. 2012. *Diplomatic Edition Codex Unia*. http://tdb.fryske-akademy.eu/tdb/index-unia-en.html

Szemerényi, O. 1977. Studies in the Kinship Terminology of Indo-European Languages. *Acta Iranica* 7. 1–238.

Szemerényi, O. 1999. *Introduction to Indo-European Linguistics* (Translation of *Einführung in die vergleichende Sprachwissenschaft*, 4th edn.). Oxford: Oxford University Press.

Taeger, B. 1979–1984. Das Straubinger >Heliand<-Fragment. Philologische Untersuchungen. *PBB* 101. 181–228, *PBB* 103 (1981) 402–424, *PBB* 104 (1982), 10–43; 106 (1984) 364–389.

Taeger, B. 1983. *Heliand, VL III*. 958–971.

Thöny, L. 2013. *Flexionsklassenübertritte. Zum morphologischen Wandel in der altgermanischen Substantivflexion*. Innsbruck: Institut für Sprachwissenschaft der Universität Innsbruck.

Tiefenbach, H. 2000. Morphologie des Altniederdeutchen (Altsächsischen). In W. Besch, A. Betten, O. Reichmann & S. Sonderegger (eds.), *Sprachgeschichte. Ein Handbuch zur Geschichte der deutschen Sprache und ihrer Erforschung*. Volume II, 1252–1257. Berlin: Mouton de Gruyter.

Tiefenbach, H. 2010. *Altsächsisches Handwörterbuch/A Concise Old Saxon Dictionary*. Berlin: Mouton de Gruyter. doi:10.1515/9783110232349

Tiersma, P. 1982. Local and General Markedness. *Language* 59. 832–849. doi:10.2307/413959

Tiersma, P. 1999. *Frisian Reference Grammar*. Leeuwarden: Fryske Akademy.

Toon, T. E. 1987. Old English Dialects: What's to Explain: What's an Explanation? In W. Koopman, F. van der Leek, O. Fischer. & R. Eaton (eds.), *Explanation and Linguistic Change*, 275–293. Amsterdam: John Benjamins.

Toon, T. E. 1992. Old English Dialects. In R. Hogg (ed.), *Cambridge History of the English Language*, 409–451. Cambridge: Cambridge University Press. doi:10.1017/CHOL9780521264747.007

van den Toorn, M. C., W. Pijnenburg, J. A. van Leuvensteijn & J. M. van der Horst (eds.). 1997. *Geschiedenis van de Nederlandse taal*. Amsterdam: Amsterdam University Press. doi:10.5117/9789053562345

Trask, R. L. 1993. *Dictionary of Grammatical Terms in Linguistics*. London: Routledge.

von Unwerth, W. 1910. Zur Geschichte der Indogermanischen *es/os*-Stämme in den Altgermanischen Dialekten. *Beiträge zur Geschichte der deutschen Sprache und Literatur* 36. 1–42. doi:10.1515/bgsl.1910.1910.36.1

de Vaan, M. A. C. 2010. Another Frisianism in Coastal Dutch: *Traam, Treem, Triem* 'Crossbeam'. *Journal of Germanic Linguistics* 22(4). 315–335. doi:10.1017/S1470542710000085

de Vaan, M. A. C. 2017. The Dawn of Dutch. *Language Contact in the Western Low Countries before 1200*. John Benjamins.

van Veen, P. A. F. & N. van der Sijs. 1997. Etymologisch woordenboek. *De herkomst van onze woorden*. Utrecht & Antwerpen: Van Dale Lexicografie.

Versloot, A. P. 2004. Why Old Frisian is Still Quite Old. *Folia Linguistica Historica* 25. 253–304.

Versloot, A. P. 2008. *Mechanisms of Language Change*. Utrecht: LOT.

Versloot, A.P. 2014. Die *-ar*-Plurale im Altwestfriesischen mit einem Exkurs über die sächlichen Plurale im Westfriesischen. *Us Wurk* 63. 93–114.

Versloot, A. P. 2016a. Unstressed Vowels in Runic Frisian. The History of Frisian and the Germanic 'Auslautgesetze'. *Us Wurk* 65. 1–39.

Versloot, A. P. 2016b. The Development of Old Frisian Unstressed *-u* in the Ns of Feminine ō-stems. In A. Bannink & W. Honselaar (eds.), *From Variation to Iconicity (Festschrift for Olga Fischer)*. 377–392. Amsterdam: Pegasus.

Versloot, A. P. 2017a. Die Endungen *-os/-as* und *-a* des Nominativ/Accusativ Plurals der *a*-Stämme im Altsächsischen. *Amsterdamer Beiträge zur älteren Germanistik* 76. 464–477.

Versloot, A. P. 2017b. The Riustring Old Frisian *-ar* Plurals: Borrowed or Inherited? *Amsterdamer Beiträge zur älteren Germanistik* 77. 442–458.

Versloot, A. P. 2017c. *Mith frethe to wasane* 'to be in peace': Remnants of the instrumental case in 13th and 14th century Old Frisian. *Filologia Germanica–Germanic Philology* 9. 201–230.

Versloot, A. P. & E. Adamczyk. 2013. The Old Frisian *e*-Plurals. In H. Brand (ed.), *De tienduizend dingen. Feestbundel voor Reinier Salverda*, 419–434. Leeuwarden: Fryske Akademy & Afûk.

Versloot, A. P. & E. Adamczyk. 2014. Corpus Size and Composition: Evidence from the Inflectional Morphology of Nouns in Old English and Old Frisian. In R. H. Bremmer Jr., S. Laker & O. Vries (eds.), *Directions for Old Frisian Philology, Amsterdamer Beiträge zur älteren Germanistik* 73. 539–569.

Versloot, A. P. & E. Adamczyk. 2017. Geography and Dialects of Old Saxon. River Basin Communication Networks and the Distributional Patterns of North Sea Germanic Features in Old Saxon. In J. Hines & N. IJssennagger (eds.), *Across the North Sea*, 125–148. Woodbridge: Boydell and Brewer.

Versloot, A. P. & E. Adamczyk. forth. A Multivariate Analysis of Morphological Variation in Plural Inflection in North Sea Germanic Languages. In A. Dammel, M. Eitelmann & M. Schmuck (eds.), *Reorganising Grammatical Variation: Diachronic Studies in the Retention, Redistribution and Refunctionalisation of Linguistic Variants*. Amsterdam: John Benjamins.

Versloot, A. P. & E. Hoekstra. 2016. Attraction between Words as a Function of Frequency and Representational Distance: Words in the Bilingual Brain. *Linguistics*. 1223–1240.

Voyles, J. B. 1992. *Early Germanic Grammar: Pre-, Proto-, and Post-Germanic languages*. San Diego: Academic Press.

Wadstein, E. (ed.) 1899. *Kleinere altsächsische Sprachdenkmäler. Mit Anmerkungen und Glossar*. Norden-Leipzig: Soltau.

Walker, A. G. H. 1990. Frisian. In Ch. Russ (ed.), *The Dialects of Modern German*, 1–30. London: Routledge.

Waxenberger, G. 1996. *Die Zuordnung der altenglischen Substantive zu den Flexionstypen untersucht am Buchstaben*. Frankfurt am Main: Peter Lang.

Wegener, H. 2002. Aufbau von markierten Pluralklassen im Deutschen: eine Herausforderung für die Markiertheitstheorie. *Folia Linguistica* 36. 261–295. doi:10.1515/flin.2002.36.3-4.261

Wegener, H. 2004. Pizzas und Pizzen, die Pluralformen (un)assimilierter Fremdwörter im Deutschen. *Zeitschrift für Sprachwissenschaft* 23. 47–112. doi:10.1515/zfsw.23.1.47

Wegera, K.-P. 1985. Morphologie des Frühneuhochdeutschen. In W. Besch, O. Reichmann & S. Sonderegger (eds.), *Sprachgeschichte. Ein Handbuch zur Geschichte der deutschen Sprache und ihrer Erforschung*, 1313–1322. Berlin: Walter de Gruyter.

Wegera, K.-P. 1987. Flexion der Substantive. In H. Moser, H. Stopp, W. Besch (eds.), *Grammatik des Frühneuhochdeutschen. Beiträge zur Laut- und Formenlehre*. Heidelberg: Winter.

van Weringh, J. J. 1984. De oorsprong van een vroeg-middeleeuwse gospelstory. In K. Sierksma (ed.), *Liudger - Bemlef - Heliand. Het Drie-Koningenvemaal in de Lage Landen taal van het jaar*. 815, 2–22 In Muiderberg: Stichting Comité Oud Muiderberg.

Wełna, J. 1996. *English Historical Morphology*. Warszawa: Wydawnictwo Uniwersytetu Warszawskiego.

Werner, O. 1987. The Aim of Morphological Change is a Good Mixture – Not a Uniform Language Type. In A. Giacalone Ramat . (eds.), *Papers from the 7th International Conference on Historical Linguistics*, 591–616. Amsterdam: John Benjamins. doi:10.1075/cilt.48.43wer

Weyhe, H. 1906. Beiträge zur Westgermanischen Grammatik. *Beiträge zur Geschichte der Deutsche Sprache und Literatur* 31. 43–90.

Willemyns, R. 2013. *Dutch: A Biography of a Language*. Oxford: Oxford University Press.

Winter, W. 1971. Formal Frequency and Linguistic Change: Some Preliminary Comments. *Folia Linguistica* 5. 55–61. doi:10.1515/flin.1969.5.1-2.55

Wolff, L. 1934. Die Stellung des altsächsischen. *Zeitschrift für deutsches Altertum und deutsche Literatur* 71. 129–154.

Wrede, F. 1924. Ingwäonisch und Westgermanisch. *Zeitschrift für deutsche Mundarten* 19. 270–283.

Wright, J. & E. Wright [1908] 1982. *Old English Grammar*. 3rd edn. Oxford: Oxford University Press.

Wright, J. 1957. *Grammar of the Gothic Language*. Oxford: Clarendon Press.

Wurzel, W. U. 1986. Die wiederholte Klassifikation von Substantiven: Zur Entstehung von Deklinationsklassen. *Zeitschrift für Phonetik, Sprachwissenschaft und Kommunikationsforschung (ZPSK)* 39(1). 76–96.

Wurzel, W. U. 1987. System-Dependent Morphological Naturalness in Inflection. In W. Dressler (eds.), *Leitmotifs in Natural Morphology*, 59–96. Amsterdam: John Benjamins. doi:10.1075/slcs.10.22wur

Wurzel, W. U. 1989. *Inflectional Morphology and Naturalness*. Berlin: Akademie-Verlag.

Wurzel, W. U. 1990. Morphologisierung – Komplexität – Natürlichkeit. Ein Beitrag zur Begriffsklärung. In N. Boretzky, W. Enninger & Th. (eds.), *Spielarten der Natürlichkeit – Spielarten der Ökonomie. Beiträge zum 5. Essener Kolloquium über 'Grammatikalisierung: Natürlichkeit und Systemökonomie' vom 6.10.-8.10. 1988 an der Universität Essen*, 129–153. Bochum: N. Brockmeyer.

Wurzel, W. U. 1992. Morphologische Reanalysen in der Geschichte der deutschen Substantivflexion. *Folia Linguistica Historica* 13. 297–307.

Wurzel, W. U. 2001. *Flexionsmorphologie und Natürlichkeit*. 2nd. edn. Berlin: Akademie-Verlag.

Zipf, G. K. 1929. Relative Frequency as a Determinant of Phonetic Change. *Harvard Studies in Classical Philology* 40. 1–95. doi:10.2307/310585

Zipf, G. K. 1936. *The Psychobiology of Language*. London: Routledge

Zwicky, A. M. 1986. The General Case: Basic Form versus Default Form. *Berkeley Linguistics Society* 12. 305–315. doi:10.3765/bls.v12i0.1875

Index